EMERGENCY TELEPHONE NUMBERS

DOCTOR _____

HOSPITAL _____

POISON CONTROL CENTER _____

FIRE DEPARTMENT _____

POLICE DEPARTMENT _____

THE PARENTS' ENCYCLOPEDIA
of Infancy, Childhood, and Adolescence

THE PARENTS' ENCYCLOPEDIA

of Infancy, Childhood, and Adolescence

MILTON I. LEVINE, M.D.,
and JEAN H. SELIGMANN

Foreword by Lee Salk, Ph.D.

THOMAS Y. CROWELL COMPANY
NEW YORK   ESTABLISHED 1834

DESIGNED BY VISUALITY

MANUFACTURED IN THE UNITED STATES OF AMERICA

LIBRARY OF CONGRESS CATALOGING IN PUBLICATION DATA

Levine, Milton Isra, 1902-
    The parents' encyclopedia of infancy, childhood, and
adolescence.

    Bibliography: p.
    1. Infants—Care and hygiene.   2. Children—Care
and hygiene.   3. Children—Diseases.   I. Seligmann,
Jean Hortense, joint author.   II. Title.
[DNLM: 1. Adolescent psychology—Encyclopedia—
Popular works.   2. Child guidance—Encyclopedia—
Popular works.   3. Parent-child relations—Encyclo-
pedia—Popular works.   4. Pediatrics—Encyclopedia—
Popular works.   WS 13 L665p   1973]
RJ61.L552   649'.1'03   72-83769
ISBN 0-690-60969-8
 2 3 4 5 6 7 8 9 10

Dedicated to
Carol and Ann
and
Franz, Denise, Sara, and Eva
and
all your children
and
grandchildren
today and tomorrow

Acknowledgments

We are deeply indebted to the following persons for their generous help and cooperation in the preparation of this book.

Dr. Charles H. Bauer, Clinical Associate Professor of Pediatrics, New York Hospital-Cornell Medical Center; Director, Newborn Service, Roosevelt Hospital, New York City.

Dr. Myron Buchman, Clinical Associate Professor of Obstetrics and Gynecology, New York Hospital-Cornell Medical Center.

Mr. Thomas Burke, Safety Consultant, Metropolitan Life Insurance Company.

Dr. Lester L. Coleman, Attending Surgeon, Otolaryngology, Manhattan Eye, Ear and Throat Hospital, New York City.

Dr. M. Joel Freedman, Clinical Associate Professor of Pedodontics, New York University College of Dentistry.

Dr. Margaret W. Hilgartner, Medical Director, Metropolitan Chapter, National Hemophilia Fund; Assistant Attending Pediatrician, New York Hospital-Cornell Medical Center.

Dr. David Kligler, Associate Clinical Professor of Pediatrics and Pediatric Neurologist, Speech and Hearing Clinic, Albert Einstein College of Medicine, New York City.

Dr. Deborah S. Kligler, Associate Director, Sound View-Throg's Neck Community Mental Health Center, Albert Einstein College of Medicine, New York City.

Dr. Bernard Kronenberg, Clinical Professor of Ophthalmology, New York Medical College; Attending Ophthalmologist, New York Eye and Ear Infirmary.

Dr. Donald N. Louria, Professor of Preventive Medicine and Community Health, New Jersey Medical School, Newark, N.J.

Dr. Virginia Lubkin, Attending Ophthalmologist, New York Eye and Ear Infirmary; Assistant Clinical Professor of Ophthalmology, Mt. Sinai School of Medicine, New York City.

Dr. Henry T. Lynch, Professor and Chairman, Department of Preventive Medicine and Public Health, Creighton University, Omaha, Neb.

Dr. Wallace W. McCrory, Professor of Pediatrics and Chairman, Department of Pediatrics, New York Hospital-Cornell Medical Center.

Ann L. Parker, M.Ed., former teacher, Pilot School for Blind Children, Washington, D.C.

Carol L. Paasche, M.Ed., Teaching Master of Early Childhood Education and Psychology, Seneca College of Applied Arts and Technology, Toronto, Canada.

Dr. John C. Ribble, Director, Division of Infectious Diseases, Department of Pediatrics, New York Hospital-Cornell Medical Center.

Dr. Lee Salk, Director, Division of Pediatric Psychology, New York Hospital-Cornell Medical Center.

Dr. Marvin Snider, Family Therapist, North Shore Family Institute, Danvers, Mass.

None of the above, of course, are in any way responsible for the facts or opinions set forth in this book, which are the full responsibility of the authors.

We also wish to express our appreciation to the American Academy of Pediatrics, the National Society for Crippled Children and Adults, and the National Foundation for permission to reprint material from their publications.

Special thanks must be given to Margaret Miner, our editor, whose wide interest in the field of child care and development made her advice invaluable in the preparation of this book.

Preface

So much has changed during the past few years in science and technology, social attitudes, education,—virtually all aspects of life—that practically a new world exists for the child of today. It is in many respects a happier and safer world but in some respects a world that is much more difficult to face and in which to maintain balance.

Medical science, with amazing advances, has certainly assured children a healthier life. And new knowledge of child development and insights into child behavior have given us a greater understanding of the needs of children and the factors that affect their behavior. There are also great and new opportunities for the prevention and treatment of emotional problems during childhood.

Recent medical gains have been very exciting and almost too numerous to count. A list of these would include such major advances as the development of the measles vaccine, which has literally wiped out this potentially dangerous disease in those localities where the vaccine has been administered competently; the rubella (German measles) vaccine, which should eventually eliminate birth defects caused when mothers contract this disease in early pregnancy; the mumps vaccine, especially important to adolescents and adults, who may suffer dangerous complications from mumps; treatment to prevent birth defects in babies born to Rh-negative mothers; the amazing open-heart operations for congenital cardiac defects; the kidney and other organ transplants; the techniques to test for defects in a fetus caused by chromosome abnormalities; and the new and successful treatment of jaundice of the newborn.

In addition, in the area of behavior and learning it has been discovered that often hyperactivity and perceptual difficulties are related to a mild dysfunction of a tiny part of the brain; in numerous cases medication and special tutoring techniques have helped children who previously had grave difficulties in school to work and play to full capacity.

On the other hand, as our adolescent children are often the first to remind us, we should not be complacent about all of the progress made in science and technology. Along with improvements in our standard of living have come a host of new problems ranging from air pollution to the greatly increased number of dangerous household products that all too often cause poisoning in young children. Indeed, almost daily some new hazard is brought to our attention. In writing this book we have tried to discuss fully the problems of this type that concern parents most.

In family life today it is parenthood—rather than motherhood or fatherhood—that is stressed. And our understanding of the very great importance of both parents' giving a child love and interest throughout childhood is far more acute than in the past. We now know that a newborn infant begins to react to his environment immediately after birth, and that his responses throughout infancy to light, sound, touch, and motion are far more sensitive than previously believed. A baby needs not only security and basic care, but for emotional and intellectual growth needs much handling and fondling, and interesting sights and sounds around him. We also are much more aware of the deep emotional hurt that can be caused by any prolonged or frightening separation of a child from his parents. Throughout the book we try to remind parents of the many ways they can stimulate their child and the numerous safeguards they should observe against building feelings of rejection, insecurity, and panic.

Another important influence in contemporary family life is the new strength of the feminist movement. Its effect is just beginning to be felt, but assuredly in many respects it should improve the future opportunities and recognition of the girls of today. It is to be hoped that parents will become ever more aware of the ways in which their daughters can be encouraged to resist the social pressures that have caused so many girls and women to feel inadequate and restricted. (Incidentally, we should mention at this point that the terms "he," "his," or "him" used so often in this book when referring to a child of either sex are employed as a convenience according to an accepted convention. They refer equally to "she," "hers," or "her." We hesitate to call a youngster "it.")

Another advance associated with the increasing opportunities for women in business and professional life is that many young parents today desire to avoid some of the difficulties associated with the traditional family pattern, in which the father is a distant figure always out at work (or play) and the

mother's whole world is homemaking. The attitude we have brought to this book is that any change that brings more happiness and satisfaction into family life is for the good. Presently more women are working than ever before, and many need or wish to continue working after becoming wives and mothers. This is very probably the trend of the future, and day-care centers will undoubtedly become a more important factor in child raising. We warn, however, that it is essential that the child's need for love and assurance, particularly in the crucial early years, not be neglected.

Regarding guidance and discipline, about which parents have so many questions, we have tried to offer both specific guidelines and general principles. Discipline is a definite requirement for the normal and full development of each child. This does not mean a return to the rigid, heartless discipline that characterized child raising for so many years. It does mean that there should be reasonable limits on a child's behavior—he must not, for example, be allowed to hurt other children. In numerous articles we have tried to give advice and examples that will help parents to judge whether a rule is reasonable, how much flexibility is appropriate, whether a child's objections are reasonable. We try to show ways of helping the child to develop self-discipline and responsibility and ways of guiding without punishing.

Parents today are especially worried about the problem of discipline during the adolescent years. Our children are maturing more rapidly physically, sexually, and perhaps intellectually. Certainly teen-agers today seem to be better informed and more sophisticated than in the recent past. Many are, in their own way, affected by the social and economic problems that concern adults. During their teen years a great many boys and girls feel pressured, anxious, and disillusioned with adult standards and ideas. Many are resentful of the "credibility gap" between professed values and behavior in the adult world. The rebelliousness that is natural to adolescents of all generations may take the form of an extreme activism and opposition to the "establishment," or it may result in attempts to escape from pressures by retreating into religious cults or the use of drugs.

The experimentation with drugs and drug addiction has created at the present moment a serious problem that is almost out of hand. It will require the combined efforts of parents, schools, communities, states, and even nations before the dangerous inroads can be contained and finally eliminated.

In general, however, the great majority of teen-age boys and girls who get into serious trouble are from homes where there has been a lack of concerned interest, a lack of close feeling, a lack of involved understanding and communication between child and parents. We have attempted to give practical advice on understanding adolescents and coping with some of the crises that arise during this period. But parents should take reassurance from the fact that a happy and responsible child is usually well prepared to meet the problems of adolescence.

There are no perfect parents. No mother or father, and no physician or book, can have all the answers to the multitude of problems and questions faced by all parents. Birth, infancy, childhood, and adolescence—each brings with it changes with which parents must constantly cope. Each child is an individual, and no two children, except possibly identical twins, live in the same environment. Happily, though, in most families parents and children learn from each other, and mistakes, imperfections, and misunderstandings turn out to be not so significant. Good books on child care and development can help by giving parents guidance and information. In this volume we have attempted to present the most modern concepts of child development, child rearing, approaches to discipline and education, and present-day knowledge of child health and safety.

If there is one primary message we would bring to all parents it is to enjoy your children fully and instill in them the conviction that they are very much loved and very much wanted. This is basic for the happiness of all children, and when they are fully assured of this kind of commitment and love from their parents, many serious problems are sure to be avoided.

—Milton I. Levine, M.D., and
Jean H. Seligmann

Foreword

A confident parent is by far the best parent when it comes to the health and welfare of children. The parent who lacks self-confidence in rearing children is more apt to make poor decisions in dealing with the many crises, both large and small, that occur in the everyday care of a child. And parents who lack self-confidence in many subtle ways convey their feelings of insecurity to their children.

While there may be many reasons for a parent's lack of confidence, I feel very strongly that one of the most important ways to help parents is to be sure that they are informed about matters concerning the health and development of their children. We have not adequately met this need of parents for a sound basic understanding of how children grow and develop. Young parents turn to relatives and well-meaning friends for information about children, and much of what they learn is confusing and not relevant to their own situation.

The more fortunate parents have an experienced, warm, and understanding pediatrician available to help them with their problems and to reinforce a sense of confidence. Among those fortunate people have been Dr. Milton I. Levine's patients. Through the years their trust in him has been conveyed to me over and over again. The interest and care with which he approaches each problem, whether serious or slight, have given thousands of people a feeling that the only thing that matters to Dr. Levine is that particular patient at that particular moment.

In *The Parents' Encyclopedia of Infancy, Childhood, and Adolescence* readers will find for themselves the benefits of Dr. Levine's warmth, patience, experience, and great knowledge of pediatric medicine. With his dedicated wife and coauthor, Jean H. Seligmann, Dr. Levine has written a comprehensive and informative book. *The Parents' Encyclopedia* is a reference book, but I am sure that you will find, as I did, that it entices you to keep reading from entry to entry for discussions of matters you have wondered about but that were never explained as completely and clearly as here in this book. On questions of health and development, Dr. Levine has drawn from both the most recent discoveries and the wisdom of experience. His explanations are free of professional jargon, frank, informative, and extremely helpful.

Every parent has been exposed to a well-meaning doctor who in a matter-of-fact way used big words or professional jargon in explaining something. These expressions were probably somewhat overwhelming, but as a parent you may have been too embarrassed to ask what those words meant. You were therefore left with an incomplete explanation of something of great importance to you. You will undoubtedly find most of these unexplained areas, problems, conditions, or procedures explained in this book.

As a pediatric psychologist deeply concerned about the kind of information parents have and about their feelings of self-confidence, I am delighted that this book is now available to take away the anxiety and uncertainty that many parents have. You will no longer have to survey your friends and relatives to find out what the answers are. You will no longer have to feel embarrassed about not understanding certain medical terminology. Those of you who are hesitant about calling your busy pediatrician to ask questions about matters of varying importance will find this encyclopedia exactly what is needed.

In my opinion, *The Parents' Encyclopedia* is one of the most valuable contributions to the field of child care and human development.

—Lee Salk, Ph.D.
Clinical Professor and Director,
Division of Pediatric Psychology,
The New York Hospital–
Cornell Medical Center

THE PARENTS' ENCYCLOPEDIA
of Infancy, Childhood, and Adolescence

A

Abdomen
The belly. The portion of the body below the chest extending to between the hips. The belly contains the stomach, intestines, liver, spleen, kidneys, pancreas, and adrenal glands as well as arteries and veins. In infancy the abdomen often appears very large, especially after nursing or bottle feeding. The abdomen also appears large when a baby starts to stand and during the following two or three years. This is not abnormal; it occurs because the abdominal muscles have not yet developed enough tone (strength) to hold back the abdominal contents.

Abdominal distention
Bloating and swelling of the abdomen. The frequent distention of the abdomen in infancy after the baby is fed is perfectly normal. In general, if the child shows no signs of diarrhea or pain (is not crying or pulling up his legs), then all is well. In older children bloating is usually caused by an excess of gas in the intestines, most frequently the result of indigestion, constipation, or infection.

An infant or child with chronic distention should be examined by a doctor to rule out colic, celiac disease, fluid in the abdomen, or an abdominal tumor.

See also **Colic; Celiac disease.**

Abdominal pain
Many conditions may cause abdominal pain in children. In infancy, the most common disorder is distention of the stomach and intestines by gas (see **Colic**), usually caused by an inability to properly digest the formula, an allergy to cow's milk, a sensitivity to vitamins or a particular kind of food, or constipation.

In older children abdominal pain may be related to emotional causes, which create tension and spasm of the intestinal muscles. But physical causes are also common and can be as various as gastrointestinal virus, acute appendicitis, bladder infection or obstruction, intussusception, pneumonia, allergies to certain foods, infections of the throat, and the early stages of some contagious diseases, such as chicken pox, mumps, and measles. Stomach ulcers, although comparatively rare, must also be considered when a child has chronic abdominal pain.

Diagnosis of the cause of abdominal pain must always be made by a doctor; treatment should not be attempted by parents.

Abrasions   see **Scrapes.**

Abscess
A localized collection of pus in any part of the body, formed by a disintegration of tissues and usually surrounded by an area of inflammation (redness). Most abscesses are caused by bacterial infection. Abscesses of the skin and the tissue beneath the skin are commonly called boils. Abscesses in other parts of the

body are rarer but may be more serious, and should be under a doctor's care.

An abscess starts as a small red, swollen, painful area which enlarges, forming a hard and tender lump. Within a few days, in most cases, pus forms in the abscess and the center of the hard lump softens. At this stage the abscess opens spontaneously on the surface of the skin and discharges the pus. In many instances a doctor will lance the soft abscess to release the pus. The lesion usually heals faster and leaves less scarring if it is opened and drained by a doctor at the appropriate time than if it is left to open and heal by itself. Local pain subsides almost immediately once the abscess opens.

The soft texture of the skin of infants and young children makes it susceptible to the formation of abscesses. In infancy multiple abscesses of the scalp frequently occur, because the bacteria from one sore get on the sheet under the baby's head and are rubbed into other hair openings in the scalp. To prevent this spreading, wash the baby's scalp twice a day with soap and water. Apply an antibiotic ointment such as Neosporin, Neo-polycin, or Garamycin (gentamicin). Then cover the head with a light bonnet so that bacteria cannot be rubbed onto the sheet or diaper under the head. Do not use Band-Aids or any adhesives on the scalp to cover the lesions, since removing the adhesive may abrade the skin or pull out hair, leaving additional openings for bacteria to invade. In severe cases, a doctor may advise antibiotic treatment by mouth or by injection.

Treatment of a single abscess in a child of any age usually involves an effort to bring the abscess to a head rapidly so that it will drain itself or can be successfully lanced. Local wet dressings using water at room temperature or, better still, using a solution made by boiling a cupful of water and a tablespoonful of Epsom salts or magnesium sulfate will aid in rapidly bringing the abscess to a head. Wet dressings are best made of gauze pads held in place by gauze bandages wound around the affected part of the body. They should be kept wet by adding more solution, using an eyedropper, every few hours. During the night the dressings should be covered with a thin, transparent plastic covering (such as Saran Wrap) to hold the moisture in and to prevent the bed from becoming damp. Antiseptic or antibiotic ointments are of very little help in treating an abscess, although they may prevent the spreading of the pus to surrounding areas.

If more than one abscess forms, further lesions can usually be prevented by washing the body every day with soap and washing the clothes in contact with the abscesses. The doctor may take a culture of the pus to identify the bacteria and prescribe an antibiotic by mouth or by injection that will kill the particular bacteria causing the infection.

Children who have frequent skin infections should have their urine examined to rule out diabetes, since the sugar in the blood of diabetics makes it an excellent culture medium for bacteria.

See also **Earaches; Gum boil; Wet dressings.**

Abuse, child   see **Child abuse.**

Accidents

Young children are especially prone to accidents because of their poor coordination, their lack of experience, and their tendency to explore and to put things in their mouths. Most accidents can be avoided by watching small children closely and by eliminating household hazards. Accidents occur most frequently in the home, but as children get older, more and more accidents occur in the outside world. See **Accident prevention, indoors; Accident prevention, outdoors.**

Accident prevention, indoors

The greatest number of accidents to children occur in the home. Almost all of them can be prevented if some general safety rules are observed and if parents remain constantly alert to the need for safety.

Infants *Never leave an infant or a small child alone in the house, even for a few moments.*

When an infant is in his crib, be sure that the sides of the crib are up and fastened to prevent the baby from falling out. Once the baby is able to climb out, attach extensions to the crib sides that are high enough to make climbing out impossible. Be sure that the bars of the crib are close enough together so that the baby cannot force his head or chest through the openings. The space between the slats should be no more than 3½ inches. Avoid cribs with hinged covers designed to prevent children from climbing out. If the cover is loose or not securely locked it is easy for a standing baby to force his head between the crib and the cover and choke.

Babies should be held securely when in a Bathinette.

Be sure sleeping garments and blankets cannot twist about the child's neck and smother him. Tuck in the covers. Do not leave loose pillows in the cribs of young infants.

Place the baby's high chair or crib at least 3 feet away from the stove or kitchen working counters.

Never leave an infant or small child by himself in the bath. He may turn on the hot water or slide under the water and drown.

Be certain that open safety pins, knives, scissors, razor blades, and other sharp objects are out of the child's reach. Forks, small spoons, or any sharp or small objects should not be given to very young children, who put everything in their mouths, and often swallow objects or injure the palate or throat.

Be sure that clothing and bedding are made of flame-retardant fabrics. (See **Flammable clothing and bedding.**)

Creepers, toddlers, and young children Tape or plug unused light sockets. Be sure that the cords of all lamps and appliances are well insulated. (See **Electric shock.**)

Be sure the floor is free of exposed nails or splinters.

Fasten a gate at the top of the stairs. Always keep the stairs well lighted. In addition, stairs should be fitted with carpets or treads and should have handrails.

Keep all medicines locked up, not in an ordinary medicine cabinet but in a locked closet or cabinet. Lock up cleaning fluids and other cleaning preparations, lye, camphor balls, and hair spray. Check the contents of all household preparations and keep under lock any that contain substances that can poison a child. This is very important. A small amount of many common liquid and powder detergents, for example, can seriously burn a child if put into the mouth or swallowed. Keep syrup of ipecac on hand; administer it to induce vomiting in poisoning cases except when the child has swallowed petroleum distillates, such as gasoline, kerosene, benzine, cigarette-lighter fluid, naphtha, or lye, acid, or other corrosives. In case of poisoning, call a doctor or the poison-control center in your locality for advice. (See **Poisons: first-aid treatment.**)

The following substances should either *not* be in homes with young children or be locked away out of the child's reach:

Household products

Ammonia
Antifreeze solution
Benzene
Benzine
Bleaches
Camphor
Carbon tetrachloride
Cigarettes and cigars
Clorox
DDT
Deodorizers
Disinfectant
Drain cleaners
Fire-extinguisher fluid
Furniture polish
Gasoline
Hair sprays, dyes, and setting lotions
Ink eradicator
Kerosene
Leather polish and dyes
Lighter fluid
Liquor and beer
Lye
Matches
Mole killers
Mouse and rat poisons
Mothballs, moth flakes, and
deodorant cakes
Nail polish and remover
Oven cleaner
Paint thinner
Roach and ant poison
Rust remover
Spot remover
Toilet cleaners

Turpentine
Varnish
Washing soda

Medicines and drugs

Amphetamines
Antihistamines
Aspirin
Atropine
Barbiturates
Belladonna
Boric acid
Codeine
Cough medicine
Decongestants
Digitalis
Depilatories
Iodine
Laxatives
LSD
Morphine
Reducing pills
Sedatives
Sleeping pills
Suntan lotion
Tranquilizers
Wintergreen

Keep matches and cigarette lighters out of the reach of small children. (See **Fires.**)

Cover or insulate hot radiators and hot pipes. Install guards around floor heating-registers, furnace grates, and space heaters.

Place pots on the stove with the handles facing the rear of the stove.

Install window guards on all the windows.

Do not allow children to get near clothes wringers in operation. Thousands of injuries, mostly to children under 5, are caused by such appliances yearly in the United States.

Do not bring into the house or immediately destroy plastic covers or bags for the protection of clothes unless they have holes punctured throughout.

Be sure all toys are splinter free and have no sharp edges. Toys for young children should not be so small that they can be swallowed, or have small parts that break off easily. Also be sure that no parts of toy animals or dolls—such as the eyes—are attached on pins that a child can remove. (See **Toys and safety**.)

Fasten rugs to the floor or attach non-skid backings to them.

Keep small children out of the kitchen unless an adult is present, so that a child cannot turn on the gas or play with any electrical appliances. Take the same precautions with any woodworking tools in the home workshop.

Guns and other firearms should not be kept in the home. But if they are, they should be locked securely out of reach. Ammunition should be stored in another location, also securely locked.

Accident prevention, outdoors

Walking A young child should never cross a street by himself until he has learned to observe traffic rules and is fully dependable. It is important to actually spend years in preparing a youngster to cross by himself without supervision. A very young child must hold tightly to an adult's hand when crossing the street. He should be strongly scolded if he tries to cross by himself. As he grows older, teach him about the dangers of being hit and hurt by cars, trucks, and other vehicles. Later, he can be shown that green means "go" and red means "stop," but not until he is at least 5 should he be permitted to cross

by himself, and then only under the supervision of an adult. In most cases children should not be allowed to cross streets alone without supervision until they are about 7. For some weeks before this, you should observe your child, first by walking on the opposite side of the street and later by walking a block behind him, to be sure that he looks to the left and the right, observes the traffic rules, and takes no chances.

If your child has several streets to cross on his way to school, it is best if he can walk with other children, at least at first.

Older children who walk on darkened streets or roads at night should attach a piece of reflective material to their coats or jackets in front and behind so that they will be seen by autos in the dark.

Outdoor equipment Do not allow your child to approach power lawn mowers, buzz saws, and so forth while the equipment is in operation. Sharp garden tools should be safely stowed away. All refrigerators that have been discarded as junk or are not in use should have their doors removed so that children cannot climb inside, close the door, and suffocate.

Bicycle riding Children must learn to follow all safety and traffic rules (see **Bicycles**), and parents should check from time to time to be sure these rules are being observed. Generally, riding after dark should not be allowed, but if this must be done, headlights and reflectors are essential. Parents should avoid high-rise bikes, which are less stable than ordinary bikes. Some special features, such as stick gearshifts, can also increase chances of injury.

Automobile riding The following auto

safety measures should be strictly enforced: keep all the doors locked; use safe car seats (dated after April 1971) for infants and toddlers and safety belts for older children at all times—not merely when going on a long ride; do not allow children to stand up in a car or put their heads, arms, or hands out of the windows; lock automatic windows; be alert to the possibility of a door slamming on a child's finger; and never leave a child alone in a car with the key in the ignition or where he can release the brakes. (See **Automobile travel with children.**)

Swimming and water All swimming pools should be completely fenced off when children are young. All water barrels, cisterns, wells, troughs, and garden pools should be carefully covered or fenced off. Young children should be under constant supervision when in the water, even if the water is only 12 inches deep; older children should *never* swim alone and should be taught to check that water is deep enough before diving. (See **Swimming.**)

Children should never be allowed to go out in any kind of boat alone, unless they are adolescents who have received special training in boating and life-saving techniques. Children should always wear life jackets in boats, and a boat should never be crowded or overloaded. A child should not attempt to water-ski until he is an excellent swimmer. Even then he should always wear a life jacket, and the adult running the boat should be experienced in this sport and have knowledge of life-saving techniques. (See **Mouth-to-mouth resuscitation.**)

Ice Ice skating or playing on ice should not begin until the ice is 4 inches thick. If possible, children should skate only on ice over shallow water and never on ice over swift-flowing water or on salt-water ice. Always have safety equipment at hand: a rope, a ladder, a pole or a long stick, a plank, and a ring life buoy connected to a rope. Teach your child that if he falls through the ice, he should extend his arms over the unbroken ice and kick his legs behind him as vigorously as possible to propel his body forward over the unbroken ice. Once on solid ice, he should roll to safety. (See **Ice skating.**)

See also **Fireworks; Halloween safety; Mushroom poisoning; Plants, poisonous; Snakes and snakebite.**

Accident-prone children

Children who are repeatedly involved in accidents. Numerous studies have been made of these children since Freud first suggested in 1914 that many accidents that seemed to happen by chance were purposeful and caused by some subconscious need. Some controlled studies have demonstrated that a great many accident-prone children are emotionally upset. Typically, these children are in need of sympathy and affection and look on their parents as punitive and unloving. Accidents may be an attempt to gain sympathy or to punish the parents. Other studies have shown that some children who are prone to accidents are hyperactive rather than upset. Bad coordination and mental or physical handicaps also tend to promote accident proneness.

The treatment of accident-prone children usually requires the help of a doctor, a child guidance expert, or a child psychologist to determine the cause. If emotional causes are suspected, professional guidance should be sought, for parents are often unable to view clearly the emotional relationships between themselves and their children.

Acetylsalicylic acid   see **Aspirin.**

Achievement   see **Aggressiveness; Competitiveness.**

Achievement tests   see **Tests.**

Achilles' tendon
The thick tendon at the rear of the heel extending upward and connecting to the calf muscles. It was named after the Greek hero whose mother, according to mythology, held him by the heel and immersed him in the river Styx, thus protecting the child from injury except for the heel, which remained vulnerable.

When the Achilles' tendon is too short the child walks on tiptoe and sometimes experiences pain in the calf muscles. These tight tendons often stretch spontaneously, although it may take years. Building up the heel of the shoe, either inside or outside, will bring relief from muscle pain. In severe cases surgical lengthening of the tendon is necessary.

Acid (LSD)   see **Drug abuse.**

Acne
An inflammatory condition of the oil glands of the face, the upper back, and occasionally the chest; usually occurs during adolescence. When boys and girls enter adolescence the oil glands in the skin start a rapid secretion of oil. The ducts opening to the skin are too narrow to accommodate the additional oil and, consequently, the glands underneath swell, causing pimples. As the oily material at the opening of the ducts dries, contact with the air turns it black, causing blackheads. The bacteria normally found on the skin often infect the material in the duct and sac below and a pussy pimple or small abscess develops. No way to prevent acne is known.

To treat acne locally, wash the area three or four times a day, using ordinary soap, a nonallergenic soap, such as Nutrogena, or a special drying soap such as Fostex or Resulin. This treatment should remove much of the surface oil and prevent the formation of infected lesions or areas. Drying lotions may also be applied. Wash the hair twice a week.

The greatest single advance in many years in the treatment of acne has been through the use of the antibiotic tetracycline, given orally. Studies from 1956 on have shown that it is not only very effective but safe for young people when used under the direction of a doctor. Tetracycline remains in the skin, so its effect can be obtained with comparatively small doses. The beneficial effects of tetracycline treatment become evident usually after two to three weeks. As a rule, treatment with small doses of the antibiotic is continued for several months, but for some teen-agers a tiny daily dosage is necessary as long as they have the tendency to develop acne. (For possible antibiotic reactions, see **Tetracycline.**)

Dietary restrictions, used in the past in the treatment of acne, have been found to be ineffective. A well-balanced diet should be advised.

Ultraviolet therapy or simple exposure to the sun often aids by causing peeling of the skin.

In stubborn or severe cases a dermatologist should be consulted to prevent deep scars and pitting where possible. Teen-agers should be warned not to pick or pinch pimples, since this can spread the underlying infection and cause a larger area of inflammation and possibly permanent scars.

See also **Blackhead.**

Acrophobia see **Phobias.**

ACTH

Adrenocorticotropic hormone; a hormone produced by the pituitary gland, which stimulates the adrenal gland to produce cortisone. ACTH is given by injection for severe allergies that have not responded to antihistamines or cortisone.

Active immunization see **Immunity.**

Adam's apple

A protuberance of cartilage in front of the throat, which normally develops in the adolescent male and remains throughout his life.

Addis count see **Nephritis.**

Addison's disease see **Adrenal glands.**

Adenoidectomy

Surgical removal of the adenoids. Although a fairly simple operative procedure, an adenoidectomy, nevertheless, requires anesthesia. As a rule, the child stays overnight in the hospital. Recovery is usually complete in five days.

See also **Hospitalization.**

Adenoids

A mass of tissue in the nasopharynx, the upper throat above the soft palate and behind the nose. If enlarged, adenoids may block breathing or block the eustachian tubes, the small tubes connecting the throat with the ear, which may cause a partial, temporary deafness or even an inflammation of the inner ear. (See **Eustachian tubes.**)

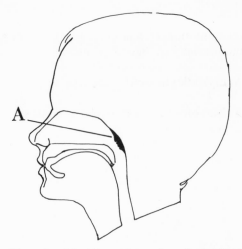

The adenoids (A) are located at the back of the pharynx, at the base of the nasal passages.

Adenoids are often removed surgically if the child has frequent ear infections or his breathing is badly obstructed by a large mass of adenoid tissue.

Adhesions, labial see **Labial adhesions.**

Adolescence

The growing period between puberty and adulthood, approximately 12 to 18 in girls and 13 to 21 in boys. During this period secondary sexual characteristics develop. These include the growth of hair under the arms and on the lower abdomen in boys and girls, and on the face and chest in boys. In boys there is an increase in the size of the genitals, a deepening of the voice, and a development of the muscles. In girls the breasts develop and menstruation begins. In both boys and girls heterosexual interests, desires, and urges normally develop during this period.

See also **Puberty.**

Adolescence, problems of

Adolescence is by far the most difficult

stage for the growing child because he usually has to contend with many physical and emotional problems arising in a relatively short span of time.

The first real problems are often caused not so much by the body changes themselves but by the young person's comparison of himself with his friends. Almost all adolescents wish to grow up, but they also want to be like their companions. Developing early, which is accompanied by a spurt in height, is usually most difficult for girls. Developing late, although a problem for both sexes, is much more difficult for boys. The rate of development seems to be largely familial. It is quite normal for one girl to start developing at 10 or 10½ or even a year or two younger, while another, just as normal, may not develop until 15 or 16.

Slow development is usually particularly upsetting for boys because adolescence is an age when muscular powers and athletics mean so much. And since sex interests and urges usually accompany body development, the underdeveloped boys and girls are behind socially as well as physically.

Adolescents are also often upset by the almost sudden rush of sex interests, desires, and urges. They should be given an understanding of these changes and, in addition, the assurance that although this rush of new interest must be curbed to some degree, the desires and urges are normal and natural and occur in all normal human beings.

Finally, the adolescent is frequently faced with apparently critical decisions regarding his schooling and future and often feels insecure regarding his ability to find a satisfactory role in the adult world.

See also **Adolescent panic; Adolescents, understanding; Sex curiosity and interests; Sex education in the schools; Sexual behavior in adolescence.**

Adolescent, helping to be more attractive

The importance of aiding an adolescent to be accepted by his peers cannot be overestimated. Parents should do everything possible to overcome physical conditions that might detract from a teen-ager's appearance and tend to make him less popular.

Teeth Protruding or malpositioned teeth should be corrected by orthodontics. If braces are necessary, they should be applied when the child is 11, at the latest, so that they can be discarded when the teen-ager is trying to be attractive to the opposite sex.

Skin Acne should be treated so that permanent as well as temporary skin defects are minimized. Besides medical treatment, a skin-colored cream or powder may be used to completely cover the lesions. Among such are Acnomel Cake and Acne-Dome Cake. (See **Acne.**)

Weight If a youngster is overweight, he should be advised as to the proper diet and it should be prepared for him. Weight Watchers, an organization that has been highly successful in reducing weight, has many branches for teen-agers. (See **Obesity.**)

Ears Protruding ears, which are especially disturbing to boys, can be easily corrected by plastic surgery.

Eyes If glasses must be worn, provide attractive frames. Even better, if possible, get contact lenses, prescribed by a qualified physician, for social use. (See **Eyeglasses.**)

Nose Plastic surgery for straightening the contour of the nose should be deferred until the nose is fully developed, which is usually not until 17. (See **Nose, plastic surgery on.**)

Clothing and hair Parents should try to be sensitive to an adolescent's wishes with regard to clothing and hair styles. Teen-agers very much need to appear attractive according to the standards of their group. (This need is also felt by younger children; many adults can remember the discomfort of being forced by their parents to wear clothing or a hair style that was unfashionable among their classmates.) Adolescents benefit from the cooperation of their parents in achieving the appearance they desire. And parents who spend a little extra time helping a youngster find the right style of jeans or jacket will probably be listened to more respectfully when, for example, they suggest that an old army shirt isn't appropriate attire when guests are coming to dinner. Many girls enjoy sewing, especially when they realize they can have more good-looking clothes for the same money. Some teen-age girls may be encouraged to make simple items of clothing; others dislike sewing and shouldn't be required to do it.

Adolescent, retarded see **Mental retardation.**

Adolescent dating see **Dating.**

Adolescent panic
A condition in which an adolescent boy or girl becomes depressed and develops an inability to concentrate or study.

Good students may suddenly find themselves in scholastic difficulty. Some refuse to attend school. Many become morose, upset (often antisocial), and panicky—hence the term adolescent panic.

The cause is entirely emotional. The adolescent is weighed down by many problems, which he usually keeps to himself. Among these are his concerns about the many changes occurring in his body, his new urges and desires relating to the opposite sex, arguments with his parents that are part of an attempt to gain more freedom, and his feeling of being misunderstood and unloved.

Almost all adolescents undergoing this kind of panic need a temporary period of psychotherapy. Discussions with a person skilled in guidance can usually unearth the difficulties and clear up the provoking problems. Most teenagers with adolescent panic crave this help and improve rapidly in treatment. The condition should never be ignored, for some adolescents become suicidal.

Adolescent sex education see **Sex education in the schools.**

Adolescent sexuality see **Sexual behavior in adolescence.**

Adolescents, understanding
Among the most difficult problems facing parents are those that occur when their children reach and pass through the adolescent years. These problems are largely the result of the growing child's conscious and subconscious efforts to gain independence. This desire for independence is normal and very important in the development of the child. He is gradually becoming an adult who must be on his own, and he has an inner drive to sever the cord that

binds him to parental authority; consequently, he resists, resents, and argues. He is secretive and seclusive, shutting the door when he talks on the phone to a friend. For the time being he prefers his friends to his family. He demands his own key to the house and attempts to set the hours of his homecoming at night. He is quick to argue with his parents over almost anything.

Parents should realize the meaning of their adolescent child's resistance during this period. As few demands as possible should be made and rigid codes of discipline should be relaxed. This does not mean, however, that discipline must be discontinued, for all adolescents still need a degree of reasonable discipline and intelligent guidance. They are not by any means ready to run their own lives. Underneath all the resistance and bravado every teen-ager still expects and wants the guidance of his parents.

Parents should also realize the adolescent's great need to be accepted by his peers. In meeting this need adolescents want to do what their companions are doing and to dress and generally look like their friends. Parents should help their youngsters to fulfill these needs. This does not mean that parents should permit harmful habits such as the use of drugs. Parents can and must still exert some authority.

Adoption

More than 150,000 children are legally adopted each year in the United States, of whom about 60,000 are adopted by relatives. The children adopted by non-relatives are obtained through adoption agencies or from private doctors.

There is as a rule a great difference in the approach of recognized adoption agencies and private doctors in placing children for adoption. The adoption agency concentrates on assuring that the child will have a happy and stable home with the knowledge, as far as can be determined, that the parents will be with the child at least through his childhood and adolescence. The private doctor, on the other hand, is more likely to be interested in satisfying the needs and desires of people who are seeking a child to adopt.

The adoption agency not only aims at assuring the child a good home but also at protecting the adoptive parents. In the first place, the agency obtains, if at all possible, a careful history of the biological mother and father of the child to learn various details of the family background, such as the existence of familial diseases. In most instances, the pregnant mother is interviewed before and after the infant's birth to be sure that she really wishes to give up her baby and will not change her mind once the baby is turned over to the adoption agency.

And once an infant or child has been assigned to the agency, the biological mother becomes anonymous. Every effort is made to be certain that she can never learn who has adopted her child and that the adoptive parents can never learn the names of the child's parents (although the agency will usually give them some details as to the child's background). Of equal importance is the fact that the adopted child can never find his original parents—an attempt sometimes made by adopted children when they are teen-agers.

Adoption agencies can also arrange for the adoption of children of interracial background and children of different nationalities and cultures such as American Indians, Koreans, and Vietnamese.

The adoption agencies, in trying to assure a potentially happy and stable home for the child, carefully investigate the physical and emotional condition of the prospective parents. Both the husband and wife receive complete physical examinations to rule out chronic disabling diseases such as chronic heart disease, chronic kidney disease, or cancer. Agencies also attempt to ensure that both parents are emotionally stable and emotionally prepared to be devoted parents. They question both potential parents carefully to determine that they really want a child and will love it. (In too many instances people unable to have children of their own and who are having marital difficulties feel that if they only had a child their problems would dissipate. This is not true. In other instances, people view an adopted child as a possession or want a child because all their friends have children. At other times, only one parent is desirous of adopting a child.)

Most adoption agencies limit applications for children to parents under 40 years of age. This is based not only on statistical probability that people over 40 years will not live as long as people in their 20's or 30's, but on the fact that men and women over the age of 40 are usually not as resilient as younger parents and are likely to be more established and rigid in their way of life.

Contrary to the opinion held by many, the financial status of the applying couple has little if anything to do with their acceptance as parents as long as they are financially secure. The owner of a small grocery store who has a small but stable income has just as good a chance of being accepted for child adoption as a well-paid executive who lives on an estate. And it is not necessary to give a donation to the agency, although there may be some fee.

Since there are seven or more families applying for each child to be adopted through adoption agencies, it is obvious that not all of them will be successful in getting a baby. The birth-control pills and the ease of obtaining legal abortions in many parts of the United States has limited the number of available babies greatly.

As a consequence, a great many of the people rejected by the agencies for one reason or another will turn to doctors in their efforts to obtain a child to adopt. A good many of these people may be able to adopt children from this source, but, with few exceptions, these adoptions are not as secure for either the adoptive parents or the children. In the first place, the doctor may have only a slight knowledge of the infant's natural parents. He may know who they are but rarely delves into their family history. And he rarely determines if the couple seeking the child are healthy emotionally and physically. Then, too, the anonymity of the natural and adoptive parents is extremely difficult to maintain. In many states, by law, in private adoptions the natural mother of the baby must personally hand the baby to the adoptive parents. Only too often, remorseful over having given up their babies, the natural mothers of babies who were adopted sit in the park watching their children grow up. At other times, the natural mother changes her mind and demands her child back before the legal adoption has taken place. Also, in private adoptions there is always the chance that in later years a child will seek out and even find his natural mother or father. The results of such a search, whether successful or not, are almost always disastrous.

In most adoption agencies it usually takes about nine months to a year from the time of the potential parents' application to the time they receive a baby. This may seem a long time, but it is not much longer than the usual pregnancy.

It is much to be preferred that the child be under 6 months of age when taken into the adoptive home. For after this time children begin to relate to one or two people for their security, comfort, and stimulation—a most important, almost vital, need for stable emotional health. Older children placed for adoption will, as a rule, be more emotionally secure and adjusted if they have lived with their parents or in a secure and happy foster home during the period prior to adoption. Children of a year or older who have lived in an institution or have been shifted from one foster home to another are usually emotionally upset, and it is very difficult for them to form a close relationship with the adoptive parents.

Of course, it is a wonderful thing if parents can take an older child into their home, but they should be prepared for some problematic times. They should certainly not act on impulse. There are great emotional rewards in giving such a child a good home. But the prospective parents must carefully and honestly evaluate their strengths and commitment to helping an older child.

Telling a child of adoption   Ideally, it would be best if children never knew that they were adopted, but complete secrecy can almost never be achieved. Someone always knows, and for a child to learn (especially when he is a teenager or older) that he was adopted is always painfully upsetting.

Most authorities feel that a child should be told that he is adopted as early as 3 or 4 years of age. He should be told that his original father and mother could not take care of him—for what must have been very important reasons—and they looked for people who would also love him very much and care for him always. And his adoptive parents, whom he calls mother and father and who are now his real mother and father, saw him and immediately fell in love with him and wanted him very much to be their own. And so they adopted him and he was their very own. They might read the child the book *The Family That Grew* (within a two-volume set for adults, *The Adopted Family*, by Florence Rondell and Ruth Michaels: see **Bibliography**).

Adoptive parents should use the words "adopted" and "chosen" as very special affectionate terms in speaking to a young child. But they should always look upon the child and feel toward him as their own child. A child should be introduced as "our son" or "our daughter," and not "our adopted son (or daughter)."

Many adoptive parents feel that the job of raising an adopted child is more difficult than if the child had been born to them. They often tend to be too permissive or indulgent in an effort to assure the child's affection. At times they are apt to blame a child's temper or his misdeeds on his natural parents. Often overemphasis is placed on problems which would be passed over in the ordinary family relationship.

An adopted child, especially an adolescent, who has been scolded by his or her parents may cry out, "You wouldn't treat me this way if I were your real child!" The child is hitting the parents where he knows it hurts most. The child may really feel that this is so, but essentially he is acting like a normal rebellious teen-ager, and his taunt should not unduly upset the parents. All teen-agers argue with and resist their parents, and if they have a special dart that they can throw at their parents, they will throw it.

But if throughout childhood and adolescence the adopted child, in spite of normal arguments and necessary discipline, always knows that he is very much loved, wanted, and admired by his parents, then no special problems should arise.

Adrenal glands

Two endocrine glands, also called suprarenal glands, one at the top of each kidney. These glands are among the most important in the body.

The adrenals produce cortisone and hydrocortisone, which aid in metabolism. These glands also secrete substances that stimulate the development of pubic and axillary hair in both boys and girls at puberty. In the pubertal boy, the adrenal secretion—in combination with testosterone from the testes—produces hair on the face, chest, and extremities, and a deepening of the voice. The same secretion is also partly responsible for adolescent acne in both boys and girls.

In addition, these glands produce epinephrine (adrenalin), which affects the heart rate, blood pressure, sweating, sugar digestion, and nervous activity. Adrenal insufficiency may cause low blood pressure, a weak pulse, vomiting, and diarrhea. Chronic deficiencies, such as Addison's disease (from which President John F. Kennedy suffered), may produce weakness, loss of appetite and weight, vomiting, abdominal pain, and even convulsions. A child with this deficiency may have an intense craving for salt, and his skin is usually pigmented brown. Usually the condition is treated successfully by daily doses of cortisone or hydrocortisone.

Oversecretion of the adrenals is usually caused by tumors or excessive growth of the glands. It may result in masculinization in girls, producing an enlarged clitoris and increased body hair; in boys an oversecretion may cause markedly excessive growth of the genitals, increased body hair, and deepening of the voice. This condition is more difficult to treat; usually surgery is necessary.

Affection   see Love

Afterbirth

The placenta, the sac that encloses the baby, and the umbilical cord, which are expelled from the mother's body after the baby's birth.

See also Placenta.

Agammaglobulinemia   see Gamma globulin.

Age   see Chronological age; Developmental age; Mental age.

Age-height-weight tables   see Body measurements.

Aggressiveness

Aggressiveness is found in varying degrees in every normal child. It is an integral and essential part of a child's personality. The overly aggressive child will often be disliked socially, but the passive child, although perhaps more socially acceptable, has at least equal difficulty in coping with the world. (See Passivity.)

Being aggressive in the good sense of the word is to push forward and succeed in some desire or effort in spite of obstacles and difficulties without hurting or upsetting other people.

Being aggressive in the bad sense of the word involves destructively overriding the rights and feelings of others in order to get what one wants.

Aggressiveness itself is instinctive, but the acceptable limits of aggressiveness must be learned. What is considered acceptable varies from culture to culture and person to person. And most people have ambivalent feelings about aggressiveness, which children become aware of very quickly. A mother may tell her child not to grab things, fight, and so forth. But when the child brings his mother a series of complaints, such as "Jimmy took my shovel" and "Larry pinched me," he may be told to take the shovel away from Jimmy, pinch Larry back, and stop being such a crybaby.

Children need guidance from their parents to learn how best to express their aggressive energies in different social situations. At 2 a child should be taught that he must not bite or kick other children because he wants to play with their toys or wants an adult's undivided attention. (See **Biting, kicking, hitting, pushing.**) But, at the same time, a child needs the support and encouragement of his parents in finding constructive outlets for his aggressiveness and in trying to reach his goals. A school-age child may approach a project with lots of energy and immediately be discouraged by a small setback. His parents should reassure him that difficulties and occasional failures are inevitable but can be overcome with persistence, and that they have faith in his abilities. He should not, however, be pushed to try for goals that are beyond his abilities. Repeated failures can turn an outgoing, healthily aggressive child into a withdrawn, discouraged child. Children, and especially young adolescents, who are full of aggressive energy often benefit by taking part in competitive sports, where aggressiveness brings rewards rather than criticism.

Most children, given intelligent and relatively consistent guidance, learn how to express aggressiveness in acceptable and constructive ways. Some, however, develop self-defeating patterns of behavior. The persistent bullying of other children is usually a sign of insecurity. The bully is an unhappy child who needs special attention. (See **Bullying.**) Some children consistently give up much too easily or will not even begin to compete. They may be frightened that if they once begin to express anger they will be overwhelmed by their own hostility. Or they may feel that bad experiences, for example constant failures in school, have shown them that they haven't got a chance and might as well not try. These children, too, need special attention. In both types of cases professional counseling or psychotherapy may be indicated.

See also **Anger; Temper and temper tantrums.**

Agoraphobia   see **Phobias.**

Air, moisture in   see **Moisture in air.**

Air pollution

The problem of air pollution is an outgrowth of modern technological development. To supply man's needs for power and electricity, fuel is burned, and as it burns, it gives off pollutants. As more and more automobiles crowd the highways, their exhaust fumes add more pollutants to the air. The garbage burning in city dumps releases yet more pollution—and these are by no means the only causes.

Studies have shown the harmful

effects of the various air pollutants. They irritate the sinuses, bronchial tubes, and lungs of children, as well as adults.

Part of the function of the bronchial tubes is to remove bacteria and other irritating foreign substances that may have been inhaled. Polluted air interferes with this function and slows the removal not only of bacteria but of other foreign substances as well.

A great deal of evidence has been accumulated to demonstrate that severe and chronic bronchitis and sinusitis in childhood may be caused by inhalants. Several studies have also demonstrated the relationship of polluted air to asthma. One study in Yokohama, Japan, indicated that polluted air might precipitate asthmatic attacks. Another report from New Orleans suggested that a change of winds that brought in material from the burning in city dumps caused asthmatic attacks.

It is most important that efforts be made to remove pollutants from the air before their continued irritation of the bronchial tubes and lungs produces serious and permanent damage.

Parents can do their share to reduce air pollution by cooperating with anti-pollution legislation and recommendations regarding automobiles, by not burning leaves in the fall, and by working in their communities to eliminate the pollutant smoke production of all buildings and manufacturing plants.

Air sickness   see **Motion sickness.**

Alcohol poisoning see **Poisons: first-aid treatment.**

Alcohol rub
Hand rubbing with alcohol, used to reduce fever, usually when the tempera-

ture is 104 degrees or more. The evaporation of the alcohol cools the surface of the skin, reducing the fever.

If you are advised to give a child an alcohol rub, this is the procedure to follow. Mix equal parts of rubbing alcohol and lukewarm water. Cover the child. Expose a leg and rub gently but vigorously with the alcohol solution until it is dry. Cover the leg. Rub the other leg, then the arms, then the neck, covering each area when dry. Go on to 6-inch squares of the chest and abdomen, and then the back. Repeat every four hours if necessary. If the process upsets the child, don't continue.

Alimentary canal
The gastrointestinal tract, comprising the esophagus, stomach, small intestine,

Alimentary canal: 1. Esophagus. 2. Stomach. 3. Duodenum, which leads to the small intestine. 4. Jejunum, first part of the small intestine. 5. Ileum, which leads to the large intestine. 6. Ascending colon, first part of the large intestine. 7. Transverse colon, middle part of the large intestine. 8. Descending colon, which leads to rectum. 9. Rectum.

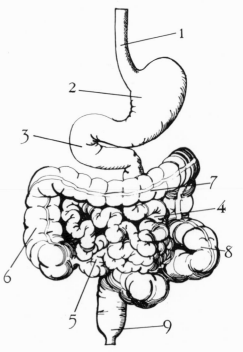

in which food is digested, and large intestine. (See illustration.)

See also **Choking; Intestines.**

Allergen

A substance capable of stimulating an allergy. For example, the protein of the ragweed pollen is an allergen capable of causing the irritation of the mucous membranes of the nose and eyes that characterizes hay fever.

Allergy

High sensitivity to specific substances inhaled, eaten, touched, or injected by an insect bite or hypodermic. Among the allergic reactions are hay fever, asthma, hives, eczema, diarrhea, and angioneurotic edema (a swelling of a body part).

Allergies can usually be diagnosed by skin tests, patch tests, or a systematic withdrawal of substances suspected of causing reactions. They can often be successfully treated by avoiding the offensive agents; by using antihistamines or other preparations that counteract the action of the allergic material; or by injecting solutions of the allergic material, starting with very weak dilutions and increasing gradually to build up a person's toleration of the irritating substance.

A dangerously acute allergic reaction is called anaphylaxis.

See also **Anaphylaxis; Angioneurotic edema; Asthma; Bee stings; Colic; Diet, elimination; Eczema; Hay fever; Hives; Insect and spider bites; Penicillin allergy.**

Allergy, milk   see **Milk allergy.**

Allergy tests   see **Skin tests for allergies.**

Allowances

A regular allowance teaches a child the value of money, how to handle money himself, and how to make decisions. It also gives him an opportunity to learn how to save up for something he really desires.

Allowances should usually be started at about 6, although some children may be ready as early as 4. To prepare a child to use an allowance wisely it is advisable to take him shopping, show him objects, and teach him how much they cost in coins. Let him hand some of the money to the cashier.

An allowance is generally understood to be the money given to a child to spend as he wishes, although some parents include money for some necessities—bus fares, school lunches, church offerings. There is no standard amount for any specific age, but at adolescence, if a family can afford it, the allowance might include enough for a movie, an occasional snack, or special social occasions.

Allowances should not be withdrawn because of a child's behavior or poor marks at school. An allowance should be looked upon as something that is given to the child without any strings attached and on which he can depend.

See also **Savings accounts.**

Alopecia areata   see **Baldness.**

Amaurotic idiocy   see **Tay-Sachs disease.**

Amblyopia   see **Eye defects.**

Amebic dysentery

Chronic diarrhea, often bloody, caused by intestinal infection by the ameba *Entamoeba histolytica*. It is contracted from water or food contaminated by fecal matter containing the living ameba. It can be diagnosed by microscopic examination of the feces and effectively treated by drugs prescribed by a doctor. Occasionally a complication of liver abscess arises.

Amebic dysentery is not common throughout the United States, being largely restricted to the South Central states. It is frequently contracted when traveling abroad. When traveling with children in an area where dysentery is a hazard, it is important to drink bottled water only, to avoid uncooked fruits and vegetables, and not to swim in polluted waters.

Amenorrhea see **Menstruation.**

American Youth Hostels see **Recreational organizations.**

Ammonia poisoning see **Poisons: first-aid treatment.**

Ammoniacal dermatitis see **Diaper rash.**

Amnesia

Loss of memory. Rare in childhood, amnesia does occasionally occur in adolescence. The child forgets who he is and what he has been doing for a certain period of time. This temporary amnesia results from emotional distress and must be treated by psychotherapy.

Amniocentesis

A technique for diagnosing certain disorders that may be present in a fetus. Some of the amniotic fluid surrounding the fetus is withdrawn by inserting a needle through the mother's lower abdomen into the uterus and the amniotic sac. This may be done when the fetus is 8 to 12 weeks old. The fetal cells obtained in the fluid are studied to deter-

mine if the unborn child has any of a group of seriously debilitating or disabling diseases, including Mongolism or reactions resulting from an Rh factor incompatibility in the infant. In the case of the latter, transfusions may be given the fetus through the uterus wall to prevent injury to the fetus.

See also **Genetic counseling; Rh Factor blood incompatibility.**

Amniotic sac

The membranous sac that surrounds the unborn baby while it is still within the uterus. It contains fluid (amniotic fluid) in which the baby floats.

Amphetamine see **Brain dysfunction, mild; Drug abuse.**

Amphetamine poisoning see **Poisons: first-aid treatment.**

Amusements

The type of amusement suitable for a child varies, of course, with the age and maturity of the child. There are numerous toys and other playthings available for the indoor amusement of children at all age levels. These range from infants' toys, such as crib mobiles, squeeze toys, and rattles, through numerous games and activity toys for older children, to microscopes, chemistry sets, and planetariums for quite mature children. (See **Toys and play materials.**)

There is no special need for planning an "exciting adventure" outdoors for a toddler, because to a young child a simple walk on the street or in the park or a trip to the zoo is as exciting and as memorable as anything else that can be offered. Looking at a crane, different automobiles, store windows, the passing animals, all are interesting experiences and true amusements for the infant and growing child.

As children grow older, they desire and need more varied amusements, different from their ordinary routine. Whenever possible, they should be encouraged and helped to attend events of interest—good movies, theater, concerts, and ballet. And such perennial favorites as the circus and ice shows, which are intended especially for children, can be great fun for the whole family. Sports events, such as baseball, basketball, hockey games, tennis matches, and track meets, are enjoyed by many school-age children and adolescents. Outdoor excursions such as hiking, camping, and skiing offer a wealth of experience. And the more a parent is interested in and is able to share the child's enthusiasm for an event, the more meaningful and more memorable these occasions become for the child.

See also **Art; Music in the home.**

Anal fissure

A crack in the mucous membrane of the anus. This causes such great pain during a bowel movement that children with this condition often withhold their feces—eventually, if untreated, developing chronic constipation. Since the fissure may bleed when stretched during a bowel movement, bright red blood may appear on the outside of the feces or a drop of blood may fall into the toilet bowl following evacuation; blood is usually seen on the toilet tissue as well.

Treatment, which may take several months, should be prescribed by a doctor. It consists of keeping the bowel movement very soft—through the daily oral administration of mineral oil, or a mild laxative such as Syrup of Figs, Castoria, or Malt-Supex—and of applying healing ointment to the fissure in the anus.

Anaphylaxis

A severe allergic reaction to a particular substance. The reaction may be sudden, dangerous, even fatal. For example, an anaphylactic reaction to penicillin may cause a swelling of the lining of the throat and larynx that leads to choking and severe difficulty in breathing. The most common causes of such reactions are the bites or stings of insects, especially bees and wasps.

Acute attacks of anaphylaxis are treated by injections of Adrenalin (epinephrine) followed by the administration of oral antihistamines. The substance that causes anaphylaxis should be identified and avoided if at all possible. If the substance cannot be avoided, as wasp and bee stings cannot, the child should be desensitized, if possible. (See **Bee stings.**) Children who are prone to severe reactions should carry a Medic Alert emblem. (See **Medic Alert.**)

If you suspect that your child is suffering an unusually strong reaction to an insect bite, jellyfish sting, penicillin injection, or the like, contact a doctor immediately or take the child to the nearest clinic.

Anemia

A condition in which the blood is deficient either in the amount of hemoglobin (the red coloring matter of the blood that carries oxygen through the body) or in the number of red blood cells.

Anemia occurs frequently in children; the symptoms include paleness, lack of energy, and poor appetite. Its causes include a deficiency in iron (needed for the production of red blood cells), acute or chronic infections, and any of several blood diseases. Certain kinds of anemia occur in infants, premature ones especially, at or before birth. A rare type of anemia in early infancy is the result of an incompatibility of the mother's and the infant's blood, such as in Rh incompatibility. (See **Rh factor blood incompatibility.**) Some anemias are hereditary, such as Mediterranean anemia, found among children of Italian background, and sickle-cell anemia, found among Negroes. (See **Mediterranean anemia; Sickle-cell anemia.**)

The most common anemia in early childhood is iron-deficiency anemia, which occurs especially during the first few months of infancy. The normal newborn baby has stored up iron from his mother's blood while in the uterus. He does not start forming his own iron supply until he is about 3 months old. Therefore, babies born of anemic mothers may be anemic. Premature infants may also be anemic because they have not had adequate time to store up a full supply of iron; twins are often anemic because they have shared the mother's supply of iron. Also, in infancy, babies whose diet consists almost entirely of milk become anemic, for milk, in spite of its excellent food value, contains practically no iron. All of these children must have iron added to their diet, both through iron drops or tablets and solid foods rich in iron.

After the first year of life the greatest cause of childhood anemia is infection, for the toxins of streptococcus, staphylococcus, and other infections break down the red blood cells.

Recent studies have shown that many infants and toddlers are somewhat anemic (usually because of iron deficiency) even though they are eating a fair amount of solid food. For this reason, in December 1970 the American Academy of Pediatrics urged that all infants receive either iron-fortified milk until they are at least 12 months old or extra iron in drops or some other form. Iron has, therefore, been added to prepared infant formulas and to evaporated milk. It cannot be added to whole milk because it hastens the development of rancidity.

Anger

A basic human emotion aroused by frustration or a feeling of wrong or injury. Anger is a normal reaction, experienced by all human beings from time to time, whether it is displayed outwardly or not.

Infants show anger at least as early as 5 or 6 months when frustrated, for example, if something they are holding and enjoying is taken away from them. During their first year, when they are beginning to creep around, exploring and discovering, children easily become angry if they are restrained in their movements or denied in any way. This continues throughout the second year of life—the toddler stage—when the youngster is still eagerly investigating the world around him.

The typical means of expressing anger is enraged crying. From about 18 months to 3 years, breath-holding may follow crying. At approximately 2, when children become more aggressive, they may express anger by physical attacks. And between 2 and 4 many children have temper tantrums. (See **Biting, kicking, pushing, hitting; Breath-holding; Temper and temper tantrums.**)

Throughout childhood many situations arouse anger, including the usual frequent flare-ups among children in the same family or among children and their friends, often accompanied by yelling, punching, and pushing. The violence is generally of short duration and the children start playing together again in a few minutes. At times parents must intervene if the fighting lasts too long or is too violent. (See **Quarrels.**)

A deeper anger is often stimulated by a child's feeling that the parents are showing too much attention to or are favoring another child. Anger as a response to rejection is also common when parents go away on extended trips or vacations. When they return, their children may be sullen and refuse to speak to them.

Certain parental attitudes may lay the foundation for excessive anger in children. Overpermissive and overindulgent parents who immediately satisfy every whim or desire of their child make him vulnerable to frequent frustrations as he gets older. Parents who exert too little authority or are inconsistent in their discipline will usually bring forth anger in their children, who do not know what to depend on or what to expect. If parents themselves indulge in frequent displays of temper, their children are likely to imitate them. And, above all, parents who do not give their children the security of being loved, promote a deep anger and bitterness in these children.

In our culture the open display of anger is generally frowned upon. A person is supposed to keep his feelings to himself, at least outside the home. Nevertheless, an outward expression of anger, by which a child can release his emotions, is far preferable to the holding in of his resentment, which causes inner seething and often depression and silent frustration. A child must be taught that he cannot hurt others physically in his anger, but he should not be made to feel that it is wrong to get angry. This can only add guilt and fear to the feelings of anger.

Parents should not worry if a child becomes furious now and again. However, if a child's anger is constant and overwhelming, to the point that it interferes with normal activities or is danger-ous to others, it must be realized that the child may be deeply upset. He may need professional counseling or psychotherapy to help him resolve his frustrations and resentment.

See also **Aggressiveness; Arguments between parents.**

Angiogram   see **Heart murmur.**

Angioneurotic edema
An allergic reaction, resulting in a severe swelling of one or more parts of the body, especially of the face, hands, or genitals. It is generally caused by a food the child has eaten, but it may be caused by a drug or bacterial allergy. As a rule it may be treated successfully by oral antihistamines or, when severe, by the injection of Adrenalin (epinephrine).

Animal bites   see **Rabies; Rat-bite fever; Snakes and snakebite.**

Animals   see **Fears; Pets.**

Anorexia nervosa
A condition usually occurring after puberty in which various emotional problems prompt a young person—almost invariably a girl—to starve herself.

Although most of these girls rationalize that they are only trying to get or stay thin, the real reason usually is a fear of growing up. These girls are afraid of becoming women, afraid of becoming mothers, of having babies, of sexual relationships. The condition can be so severe that the young person may literally starve herself to death. In severe cases hospitalization is required and food is given by stomach tube. Psychotherapy must be initiated and continued until the condition has completely subsided.

Anthelmintic

An agent that destroys or rids the body of worms. The specific anthelmintic to be used depends upon the particular worm infecting the body of the child. (See **Worms.**)

Antibiotics

Chemical substances produced by living organisms, usually microscopic, which in dilute solutions inhibit the growth of or destroy bacteria or other microorganisms. Penicillin, streptomycin, and tetracycline are examples of these substances.

Antibiotics, one of the greatest advances in medicine, have largely eliminated such conditions as lobar pneumonia, mastoiditis, septicemia, empyema, and quinsy sore throats and have minimized the dangers of many other serious infections.

But antibiotics should be used judiciously and not simply administered at the slightest sign of an infection. The human body must be given an opportunity to build up its own antibodies to fight off infection. These antibodies serve as a protection against future infections by the same organisms.

The use of antibiotics should be left to the discretion of the doctor, who will usually prescribe them if he feels the type or severity of the infection warrants it.

Antibiotics are not effective in preventing the growth of or in destroying viruses and therefore are not used in the treatment of virus infections unless a bacterial infection is also present.

See also **Bacterial infections.**

Antibodies

Substances produced by the body to counteract an infecting or allergenic substance. For instance, a child who has had chicken pox cannot contract the disease a second time because the body has built up antibodies against it. In hay fever the body has built up antibodies against the ragweed pollen, and the reaction to exposure to the pollen produces a nasal discharge and sneezing in an effort to rid the body of the irritating substance.

In rare instances antibodies are not built up or are poorly developed by the body, as when there is a lack of gamma globulin. (See **Gamma globulin**.)

Anticoagulant

Any substance that prevents the clotting (coagulation) of blood. Those most commonly used for treatment to prevent clotting are heparin and the warfarin preparations, such as Coumadin, Dicumarol, and Tromexan.

Pregnant women or nursing mothers who are taking anticoagulant drugs must be given special attention. Heparin is considered safe for maternal use, because it does not pass from the mother into fetal blood nor does it enter breast milk in a nursing mother. The warfarin preparations, which may cause fetal deaths, should not be used by pregnant women or by nursing mothers, since they can also pass into breast milk and cause bleeding in babies.

Antidote

A remedy used to counteract a poison that has entered the body. Syrup of ipecac, the best general antidote, should be kept in all homes. It induces vomiting. For correct use, see **Poisons: first-aid treatment.**

Antigen

A substance taken or injected into the body that causes the formation of antibodies. For instance, diphtheria toxoid, an antigen injected beneath the skin, causes antibodies to be formed against diphtheria. Oral poliomyelitis vaccine is an antigen that causes antibody formation against poliomyelitis.

Antihistamine poisoning see Poisons: first-aid treatment.

Antihistamines

Drugs used to counteract the histamines, which are irritating substances formed in the tissues in allergic reactions.

In hay fever, for example, when certain pollens floating in the air reach the mucous membranes of the nose and eyes of people sensitive to these pollens, there is an irritating histamine response of the mucous membranes—sneezing, running nose, and red eyes. Oral antihistamines counteract those histamines in the irritated areas and relieve the symptoms in most cases. Some antihistamines, including Benadryl (diphenhydramine hydrochloride), may cause drowsiness, and users should be warned against driving a car after taking these preparations. Antihistamines that do not produce drowsiness should be substituted. Treatment should be prescribed by a doctor.

Antiseptic

A substance that inhibits the growth of bacteria or destroys them. Among such substances are alcohol, creosote, phenol, and chlorine. However, the best antiseptic for general use is plain soap and water, which washes away bacteria. Soap and water (a mild solution) may be used to wash a cut or scrape. In addition, iodine or Betadine (providone-iodine), which does not sting, may be used to keep the wound clean. (See **Cuts.**)

Antisocial behavior see **Juvenile delinquency.**

Antitoxin

A type of antibody that counteracts a specific toxin (poison) produced by bacteria. For instance, to make diphtheria antitoxin, horses or rabbits are injected with some of the toxins of the diphtheria bacteria. Their blood builds up substances that counteract these toxins. These substances are the antitoxins. If a child develops diphtheria he receives an injection of the horse or rabbit serum containing these antitoxins and they counteract the diphtheria bacteria.

Antitoxins are also used to prevent the development of a disease in people exposed to but not previously immunized against the disease.

Antivenom serum

Serum containing an antitoxin that counteracts the poison of poisonous snakes or poisonous spiders. (See **Insect and spider bites; Snakes and snakebite.**)

Anxiety

A fear reaction to an intangible or imaginary danger rather than a real one, or a fear response that is far out of proportion to the actual danger.

The age at which anxiety appears in children is a controversial question, partly because it is difficult to define what sort of fear or worry in a very young child or infant should be considered unrealistic; the infant does not have sufficient experience to separate imagination from reality. An infant who cries for his feeding might be said by some to have anxiety, an unrealistic fear that he will not be fed. An infant who cries when his mother leaves the room might be said to have anxiety, an unrealistic fear of being alone or fear that she will not return. Between ages 2 and 5, however, many children appear clearly to suffer from anxieties. These may be apparent in recurring nightmares or bizarre fears that cannot be easily dispelled, such as a persistent fear that a lion is hiding in the closet. Usually such periods of anxiety will pass in a few weeks if the child is given extra reassurance by the parents. And, of course, parents should be careful not to stimulate a child's worries by threats of the bogeyman type.

The deeper anxieties of preschool and school-age children involve primarily the fear of loss of love or fear of separation. These fears are often precipitated by the birth of a new baby, hospitalization, temporary separation from the parents, or the death of a parent, friend, or neighbor.

In psychoanalytic theory, anxiety is associated with feelings of guilt, and one of the chief causes of anxiety in young children is held to be guilt feelings involved in the Oedipus complex. (See **Oedipus complex.**) Guilt feelings over masturbation are also a common cause of anxiety.

As in adults, it is frequently difficult to discover the cause of anxiety, which may be experienced as a generalized feeling of tension and worry. (Acute anxiety resembles feelings of panic.) A child is even less able than an adult to explain just what he is feeling or to understand all that is bothering him. There are, however, numerous symptoms of anxiety in a child, the most common of which are tics, stammering, stuttering, bed-wetting, nightmares and night terrors, sleepwalking, soiling, nail-biting, finger-sucking, and excessive masturbation. Extreme patterns of aggressiveness or passivity are also signs of anxiety.

The anxieties of some children are focused on school. It is natural for a child to go through periods of unhappiness regarding school and separation from his mother, but at times this may become so serious that the youngster cannot function in the school situation. (See **School phobia.**)

During adolescence anxieties are common, for this is a period of great uncertainty and concern. Many teenagers worry deeply about whether they are developing normally, about their appearance, about being accepted by the opposite sex, about their ability to succeed in school, college, and later life. Many are fearful of growing into adulthood and all that usually goes with it—sex relations, marriage, and children. These fears may lead to a sense of panic and depression in which the youngster questions the value of life and becomes extremely depressed. (See **Adolescent panic.**)

Unfortunately, it is impossible to protect a child from all anxiety, but most children learn to overcome or control their anxieties successfully. This can be accomplished much more readily when the child is sure of the love and support of his parents, and when parents make intelligent efforts to discover and alleviate their child's difficulties. However, when anxieties or the signs of anxiety are persistent, parents should not hold to the hope that a child's unhappiness will clear up in time. In many instances, such youngsters need the additional help of psychotherapy.

See also **Fears; Guilt; Phobias.**

Aorta

The large main artery leading from the heart, carrying blood to all portions of the body through its branches.

The upper portion of the aorta supplies blood to the head, neck, arms, and the heart muscle. The lower portion descends behind the chest and abdomen next to the backbone. It supplies blood to the chest muscles, stomach, intestines, kidneys, liver, pancreas, spleen, genital organs, and lower extremities.

See also **Heart.**

Apgar rating

A score reflecting the physical condition of a newborn child, given sixty seconds after birth and again at five minutes. It includes heart rate, breathing effort, color, muscle tone, and the reflex response of a sneeze or cough to the insertion of a small rubber tube in a nostril. The infant is graded from 0 to 10, 10 indicating excellent condition.

Aphasia

In the past this term referred to all conditions in which a person was unable to express himself by speaking, whether the cause was brain damage or brain disorder, autism, schizophrenia, mental retardation, or even a disorder of the muscles used in speaking. Today the word "aphasia" is more or less limited to the inability to speak that is caused by brain damage, brain disorder, or a congenital brain defect.

Aphasia may be manifested by an inability to understand the spoken word (word deafness) or the inability to remember the words for what one sees (word blindness). Children with aphasia may have normal or even high intelligence, but because of their inability to speak, or at times even to understand, they may appear to be retarded.

Children who do not learn to speak by 2½ years should be examined by a doctor to determine if aphasia is the cause. Deafness, mental retardation, and autism must be ruled out.

Treatment of aphasia should be under the direction of an experienced speech therapist. Parents with an understanding of the problem can also aid greatly in training the child to speak. An excellent book that will direct parents of aphasic children in such training is *Speech and Language Delay* by R. Ray Battin and C. Olaf Haug. (See **Bibliography**.) The authors are both speech pathologists with more than thirty years' experience in the field. This book contains specific lesson plans for language and speech building.

See also **Speech delay.**

Appendix

A worm-shaped sac extending from the first part of the large intestine. It is located in the right lower portion of the abdomen. It serves no known purpose in the body of modern man but may in prehistoric days have served as a storage space for food, as it does in certain mammals today.

Appendectomy

Surgical removal of the appendix. This is a simple operation if the appendix has not ruptured. The hospital stay is usually five or six days. In the case of a ruptured appendix, the child may have to stay in the hospital several weeks.

See also **Hospitalization.**

Appendicitis

Inflammation of the appendix, causing abdominal pain, usually in the right lower abdomen. As a rule, but not always, the child vomits and has a moderate rise in temperature.

There is no way a parent can be sure that a child has appendicitis. If the condition is suspected a doctor should always be called to examine the child immediately, since there are other conditions that may cause pain in the same location. The doctor examines the child by feeling the child's abdomen in an attempt to localize the pain and to detect a rigidity of the muscles over the area of inflammation. A blood count and urine analysis will also be ordered. If acute appendicitis is diagnosed an appendectomy is indicated.

If the appendix ruptures, the child's condition becomes serious and may even become critical, for pus usually forms in the abdomen, causing peritonitis—a severe inflammation within the abdomen. The pus must be drained out by tubes inserted through the incision. Otherwise, abscesses may form within the abdomen and these plus the peritonitis may result in paralysis of the intestines. With the use of modern antibiotic therapy, the dangers associated with a ruptured appendix have been greatly reduced.

Apperception test   see Tests.

Appetite

The degree of appetite is normally variable. It is dependent on the child's age, physical condition, individual capacity, diet (including minerals and vitamins), and emotional condition. Appetite usually increases during periods of rapid growth, especially in the first year of life and in early adolescence.

A good appetite is usually a healthy sign, but many unhappy, anxious children overeat, gaining pleasure from eating to compensate for their unhappiness.

See also **Obesity.**

Appetite, poor

Poor appetite can have both physical and emotional causes. Physical causes include teething, which sometimes occasions a temporary loss of appetite; fatigue; anemia; acute or chronic infec-

tions; digestive disturbances, such as a poor digestion of starches and fats; and diseases, such as hepatitis.

Approximately 75 percent of all problems of poor appetite in children are emotional in origin and can be corrected. Suggestions for the effective treatment of poor appetite in healthy children are:

1. Never force a child to eat.
2. Give only the foods that a child likes, even if they are very limited and seem boring to you. Small children are creatures of habit and can take the same foods every day for months at a time. If a child refuses vegetables he can be given plenty of fruit to compensate. If a child refuses cereal he can be given bread, crackers, even cookies. New foods should be added to the diet gradually.
3. Give very small portions, so that the child has no difficulty finishing what has been given him and must ask for more if he desires it.
4. Frequently, when a child goes too long without eating, he loses his appetite. Therefore, for the preschool child a glass of orange juice in midmorning and a midafternoon snack of fruit juice or milk and cookies are advisable as long as they are given at least one and a half to two hours before a meal.
5. Let the child choose his own diet as much as possible, and encourage him to help in preparing the meal.
6. Forget table manners for the time being.
7. Invite one or two playmates to eat with the child occasionally.
8. Remove the anxious worried look from your face. Children react very quickly to the tenseness and anxiety of parents.
9. Let the child eat with you as often as possible.

Poor appetite is not to be confused with a young person's refusing to eat to the point of starvation. (See **Anorexia nervosa; Dieting.**)

Aptitude tests   see **Tests.**

Arguments between parents
Arguments between parents are quite normal and occur in a majority of families. However, all loud and violent arguments bother children greatly, because the atmosphere of the home becomes tense and the authority of one or both parents is weakened in the eyes of the child.

When highly excited and hysterical arguments are accompanied by threatened or actual violence, the child is frightened and deeply disturbed, fearing that one parent will hurt the other. In the heat of arguments parents at times yell such phrases as "I wish you were dead," "I'm going to jump out of the window and end it all," "Get out of the house and stay out," "I wish I'd never married you." Children learn to accept minor arguments without getting too upset, but arguments that are this violent should never be held in the presence of children—although many parents with quick tempers may find it difficult to contain themselves.

Further harm to the child occurs when one or both of the parents attempt to bring the child into the argument, asking him to take sides—for example, "Didn't Daddy say he was coming home early tonight?" Here the child, who very much wants to be loyal to both parents, is being forced to take sides, against his will. Usually this makes him feel very guilty and upset—at times close to a traitor. Using the child as an unwilling ally occurs very frequently in separations and divorces.

See also **Divorce.**

Arguments children give
Arguments in which a child expresses his disagreement with his parents or some other person's statements, suggestions, or demands are frequent and normal during childhood and—especially—adolescence.

In early childhood, arguments are usually unsophisticated attempts by the child to avoid something or to get what he wants when he wants it: "Why must I wear a coat?" "Why must I go to bed so soon?" But arguments may also represent the testing of a parent's authority rather than the child's strong desire for anything in particular. As children grow older their arguments become more logical, although their logic may not be acceptable. For example: "John's mother lets him watch TV at 10 P.M. Why can't I?"

Unless a child's arguments are entirely unreasonable they should be listened to seriously, because arguing is an expression of opinion and should be encouraged rather than suppressed. But once the parent has listened and then explained his own reasons, certain laws can be regarded as beyond argument—for example, "When it's cold we wear coats"; "When it's raining we wear rubbers."

Many arguments can be expected during adolescence. This is the period in which a child begins to break the bonds that hold him so tightly to the direction of his parents. He is seeking independence and will differ with many and perhaps with most of his parents' suggestions. He may even argue against the values his parents regard highly. Arguments must be understood as part of the growing-up process—an indication that the child is on his way to becoming an adult, with his own ideas, desires, and way of life.

See also **Excuses; Quarrels.**

Armpit temperatures   See **Temperature taking.**

Arson

Setting fire deliberately to destroy property. When children commit arson the act usually represents extreme rebellion against parents or the authority of school or some other institution. The child vents his antagonism by attempting to burn down, disfigure, ruin, or destroy the property of adults. Much less common are those children who set fires for excitement or to become "heroes" to their peers.

Children who set fires need a great deal of psychiatric help. Arson is often associated with other acts of delinquency—truancy, stealing, vandalism, running away. Any procrastination in getting the child into treatment is dangerous.

Art

Art is an extremely important form of self-expression for children and a wonderful creative outlet.

All children, if given the opportunity, enjoy art. Young children, even toddlers, love to scribble with a pencil or crayons. At first they simply play around, scrawling and experimenting. Eventually they discover how to control lines to represent objects and produce patterns. These may not always look meaningful to adult eyes, but they are very significant to the child.

The young child or the preschool child most often draws those things that are most important to him, primarily the people and animals in his life. In drawing a person the preschool youngster often draws only a large circle, usually with big eyes, a nose, and a mouth. This represents the total person. But as he grows older, he attaches lines to the side of the head for arms, and lines coming down from the head for the legs. Still later, another circle is placed below the head to represent the body, and later still, clothes are added and even hair and hats. At about this time, too, he draws the sun, moon, clouds, houses, and so on.

The use of pencils and crayons produces essentially line drawings. During the preschool years the child will also enjoy the use of paints for more colorful, fuller, and more varied expression.

Painting should be encouraged at all ages, and materials and a place to work should be available.

Paint can be applied by young children in various ways:

1. With a paintbrush. Here a broad bristled, firm brush is better than a camel's hair brush. A ½-inch bristle brush is a good starting brush for a young child.
2. With fingers or hands. Finger painting and hand painting are very satisfying to children.
3. With a small 4-inch roller and a large vegetable or fruit can for the paint. Very interesting results may be obtained.
4. With a sponge.

Watercolors, tempera, or poster paints, which can be obtained in either liquid form or as a powder to be mixed with water, are usually the most useful for both the young child and those under high-school age. Paint-box paints, while excellent for older children, are very difficult for young children to use. The older child, more organized and capable, may successfully use and enjoy acrylic and oil paints, employing the appropriate brushes.

A child should have an area in the house where he can paint without concern about the messiness that might result. A plastic tablecloth or a painter's

1. Drawing of a person by a 3-year-old. 2. Drawing of a person by a 4-year-old. Note, the 4-year-old has not yet begun to draw the body, but he includes feet and does very well with the hands and fingers, hair, ears, and face.

drop sheet will serve very well to protect the floors. The kitchen table may be used or the bathroom floor. Children of 4 years and older can use an easel with a shelf attachment containing holes for the various jars of paint. Muffin tins make good containers for different colored paints—or custard cups containing the paints may be set in muffin tins to accommodate drips. A separate brush for each color should be provided, or a jar of water to wash the brush in between colors.

A word must be said about coloring books and painting-by-number books. Although most children enjoy these books, filled-in predrawn pictures are by no means a substitute for the child's own creative drawings or paintings. The results may be pleasing, but they do not express anything of the child.

Finger painting is fine for the preschooler as well as older children. The paints can be bought, but they can also be made at home. Mix 1 cup of white sugar, 1 cup of flour, and a few scraps of soap. Add 2 quarts of water and cook until thick. Add ¼ can (2 teaspoons) of powdered alum and beat well with a rotary beater. Store in covered jar in cool place. Add liquid or powdered poster paint as needed. Colors should be clear and strong. Glazed shelf paper or brown paper is fine for painting on. This finger paint does not curl paper and dries to a hard gloss. If it is used in sufficient thickness, it can be broken up for collage when it dries.

For the child's first experience with finger paints, use a white plastic table cover firmly tied to a table. Let the child have generous globs of finger paint. Start with strong, clear colors, then give him the uncolored material and shakers with powdered tempera paint to mix his own colors. Encourage the child to use his whole hand, palm, nails, side of hand, both hands (sometimes two children like to work together). A child needs plenty of time and encouragement to experiment and to stand back to see what he is producing. As he begins to consciously "make pictures," you can use them when dry to cover books or containers, or you can frame them with mats.

Other popular art activities include making collage constructions and modeling with clay. Collages are made by pasting assorted materials and objects on a background material. Give a youngster a piece of cardboard or construction paper as a background, various materials and objects with which to make designs, and a bottle of white glue, such as Elmer's Glue-All. All he needs to know is that he can spread the glue in designs of his choosing on the paper or cardboard, and then place his materials on the glue. The materials that may be used are innumerable, including sand, rice, corn, dried peas and beans, bottle caps, pieces of colored paper, buttons, feathers, paper clips, toothpicks, leaves, and cotton. Let the child look around the house and out-of-doors for suitable articles.

The making of mobiles is a similar activity. Using a wire coat hanger or even a twig, various objects are attached to it with thread or string. Again, the choice of objects is almost endless—pieces of Styrofoam cut from containers, pieces of brightly colored sponge, feathers, colored paper, cupcake baking cups, straws, toothpicks, pieces of colored cardboard, bottle caps, and so on.

Clay, Play-Doh, and modeling clay (oil-base clay, Plasticine) give a child the opportunity to experiment in a three-dimensional form. Clay may be bought in powdered form to which water is added to make it pliable. It can also be obtained already prepared in five-pound tins (this clay must be stored in the container and covered with a moist cloth to keep it from hardening).

Play-Doh may be purchased, or it can be made at home in various ways. One method: mix well 4 cups of pastry flour (hard wheat flour has gluten that changes the texture) with 2 cups of fine salt. Add vegetable coloring to about a cup of water and stir into flour-salt mixture gradually until it forms small balls (using water only as needed), then knead to a smooth consistency, like bread dough. One teaspoon of vegetable oil or lard may be added. This material keeps well if wrapped in plastic and kept in a covered container. A plastic ice-cream container placed on a table, with balls the size of a large orange, allows each child in a group to choose his dough and mold, squeeze, roll, or pinch it. It is best used like clay. After the children have enjoyed playing freely with the dough alone, supply cookie cutters, rollers, and other accessories for manipulating the dough. Clay and Play-Doh will harden when dry and may be painted.

Modeling clay will not harden. Although it seems fairly stiff, the warmth of the hands softens it. Modeling dough, however, does harden, and it can be made at home. One method: mix 2 cups of fine salt and ⅔ cup of water in a saucepan, stir well, and heat three or four minutes. Remove from heat and add 1 cup of cornstarch which has been mixed with ½ cup of cold water. Stir quickly to mix. This makes a stiff dough for modeling. It hardens at room temperature in thirty-six hours and can be painted with poster paint. Keep wrapped in foil in the refrigerator.

Children from about 18 months up will enjoy handling these modeling materials and producing their own creations. The young child will roll and knead and pat and pummel the clay, usually without too much thought of a finished product. These early experimentations often result in something that the youngster recognizes and identifies as "a snake," "a ball," "a snowman." He may flatten out a ball of clay and poke a nose, a mouth and eyes in it.

As he gets into the nursery-school age, he will usually start modeling animals, figures, and objects such as dishes and ashtrays. Parents should realize that these early attempts are generally fairly crude, not too well put together, and that they frequently fall apart. However, a child who retains a liking for art through the elementary-school years and into adolescence will gain in sophistication and may be working at a professional level in high school.

Parents can do a great deal to encourage a child's interest and enjoyment in art. They should show an appreciation of his efforts and accomplishments, praising when something is well done. Youngsters love to see their artwork displayed in the home, and this type of informal exhibit can serve as further stimulus.

The child should never be ridiculed or compared with other children; his art is an expression of his own feelings and interpretation. Parents should not attempt to force a child to see things or represent them as they see them, nor should their standards of perfection be too high. Technique and exactness should not be imposed by parents unless the child specifically requests advice; this kind of pressure can interfere with the child's spontaneity.

Many elementary and high schools have art instructors to stimulate interest in art and teach techniques, but here again care should be taken that the teaching does not destroy the child's own personal creative sense.

There are several tests available that presumably determine artistic aptitude. Probably the best known is the Meier Art Judgment Test. In this a child is shown a series of pictures, each consisting of a pair of art masterpieces, one of which is distorted in some way. The child is asked to choose the better picture and tell why the pictures differ. In another test, the Horn Art Aptitude Test, the child is presented with patterns of lines and dots and asked to produce a sketch from these.

As with music aptitude tests, the results of art aptitude tests cannot be considered as final. The opinion of experts in the field of art is of much greater importance in assessing a child's artistic ability or potential.

Arthritis

Inflammation of a joint. The joint affected is not only painful but is usually swollen, reddened, and warm to the touch. Children may have rheumatoid arthritis, or they may have arthritis in association with such conditions as rheumatic fever, streptococcus sore throat, mumps, German measles, gonorrhea, and occasionally gout.

The pain of arthritis can usually be relieved by aspirin. Diagnosis and treatment of the underlying condition should be in the hands of a doctor.

See also **Rheumatic fever; Rheumatoid arthritis.**

Artificial respiration see **Mouth-to-mouth resuscitation.**

Ascorbic acid see **Nutrition.**

Aspirin

Acetylsalicylic acid, the most commonly used agent for the relief of pain or the reduction of fever. It is also the commonest cause of poisoning in children, not only because aspirin preparations for children have been made to look and taste like candy but also because parents often leave the bottle exposed for small children to find.

Aspirin is supplied in many forms for children—tablets, chewing gum, and liquids in many colors and flavors, and as suppositories. The maximum dosage of aspirin for children, to be given only every four hours, is as follows:

Under 1 year	Use only under the doctor's directions
1–2	$\frac{1}{4}$ adult or 1 children's aspirin
2–3	$\frac{1}{2}$ adult or 2 children's aspirin
3–4	$\frac{3}{4}$ adult or 3 children's aspirin
Over 4	1 adult or 4 children's aspirin

Aspirin poisoning
An overdose of aspirin can be extremely dangerous. If untreated it may be followed by breathing difficulty, vomiting, coma and convulsions, even death.

Immediate treatment is to induce vomiting (see **Poisons: first-aid treatment**). Call your doctor or local poison control center. If vomiting still does not occur, the child's stomach should be washed out by a doctor. The doctor will also take blood specimens to see how much of the aspirin has been absorbed. He will then determine if hospitalization and intensive medical care is necessary.

Asthma
An allergic condition characterized by rapid, difficult breathing, wheezing, and coughing, often accompanied by a constricted sensation in the chest. In children it is most frequently caused by an allergy to bacteria and occurs when a child develops a respiratory infection. It can also be caused by the inhalation of pollens, animal dander, dust, or molds floating in the air, or by other substances to which a child is allergic, including certain foods—a rare cause. Asthma is not an emotional condition, but the allergic condition can be stimulated or exaggerated by emotional upsets. Many children outgrow asthma as they get older, especially if they have received adequate treatment.

During an asthmatic attack the irritated breathing tubes go into spasm and become narrower, so that the child has to breathe faster to get the necessary amount of air into and out of the lungs. To add to this difficulty, the mucous membrane lining the breathing tubes becomes irritated and secretes mucus, thus further obstructing the already narrowed tubes. The narrowing of the tubes causes rapid breathing; the mucus causes the wheezing and coughing.

Diagnosis   To determine the cause of sensitivity, a tiny drop of an extract of the possible cause—pollen, horse hair, dog hair, molds, a specific food—is injected under the surface of the child's skin. If the child is sensitive to the substance a ragged welt develops around the site of the injection.

Treatment   The treatment of asthma is twofold: prevention of further attacks and treatment of acute attacks as they occur.

The prevention of further attacks depends on the substance that causes the asthmatic reaction. If the agent is bacteria, the child is protected against infections either by a bacterial vaccine or by injections of gamma globulin, which contain concentrated antibodies against infection. Some asthmatic agents can simply be removed—a dog, a cat, tobacco, insect repellent. When the sensitivity is to a horse-hair mattress or feather pillows, an allergy-proof plastic covering or the substitution of a foam rubber mattress and pillows should prevent attacks. When it is impossible to remove the substance that causes the allergy, as in the case of dust or molds in the air, the bedroom is stripped of carpets and curtains and an air filtering machine can be placed in the room. Injections against dust and molds are also advised.

Attacks of asthma can be treated in various ways. Aminophylline-ephedrine preparations, in liquid or tablet form, relax the spasm of the bronchial tubes so that the child can breathe more easily. Aminophylline can also be given very successfully by suppository.

Special atomizers, inhalation nebulizers, which spray Adrenalin (epinephrine) or Adrenalin-like preparations in very tiny droplets into the mouth to be inhaled are also available. As a rule, nebulizers relieve the symptoms within a few minutes. They should not be used more than once or twice an hour. Overuse must be avoided, as it can be dangerous, and the doctor should be informed if the child is using the nebulizer more often than prescribed.

If none of these methods is effective Adrenalin (epinephrine) given by injection usually works to markedly lessen the symptoms in a few minutes.

In very resistant cases treatment by oral cortisone preparations for a few days or weeks may be very helpful in securing relief, but this treatment should be closely supervised by a doctor.

Astigmatism   see Eye defects.

Athlete's foot
Ringworm of the foot. A chronic superficial fungus infection of the skin above and between the toes, causing marked itching and burning irritations and cracks. It is contagious and is usually contracted by walking barefooted on damp surfaces recently walked on by a person suffering from the condition. The floors of a shower room or a swimming pool are often sources of the infection. This condition may be largely prevented by having footbaths of dilute chlorinated lime in public shower rooms and swimming pools.

Treatment of athlete's foot is usually successful. Specific ointments, which are rubbed into the infected area, are available, as are specific powders that are dusted inside the socks.

Attention span, short
Inability to concentrate on an activity or thought for a normal length of time. Most parents are aware that a short attention span is frequently associated with some physical or emotional disorder. It may be a symptom of mild brain dysfunction, mental retardation, or emotional disturbance. But it should be remembered that many children have a short attention span by adult standards and that preschool children normally have a much shorter attention span than those of school age. There is no cause for worry with a young child unless he persistently turns from one activity to another in a matter of moments. School-age children often seem to do their work in fits and starts. But if there is any real problem with the attention span this will be apparent when the child falls behind in his classwork.

See also **Brain dysfunction, mild; Hyperactivity; Mental retardation.**

Audiogram
A chart illustrating the acuteness of hearing of an individual. Following testing with an audiometer, an audiogram is prepared that identifies the degree of deafness or the pitches (wave lengths)

for which hearing is impaired, as in nerve deafness.

See also **Deafness.**

Autism

A psychosis of infancy and childhood in which the children seem to be living in a world of their own. It usually has its onset in early infancy. Children with this condition rarely smile, pay very little attention to those around them, have only tenuous relationships with other people, and tend to be unresponsive to sound. They also tend to have a retardation of speech, and when they do speak they usually exhibit echolalia (repetition of the same words and phrases over and over again). Many of these children have repetitive mannerisms such as rhythmically shaking the head, or flipping the ears constantly with a finger, or running around and around in circles—and while engaged in these activities they cannot be distracted. They have a short attention span, are often compulsive and ritualistic, and resist any attempt to interfere. They also have a tendency to self-injury.

The cause of autism has not as yet been determined. There are no reliable data to show that it is hereditary; in fact, one study reports that in a group of 55 autistic children there was no history of schizophrenia or other psychoses in the families with the exception of the aunt of one child. So far no chromosomal changes have been found in the cells of these children.

Some investigators believe that autism represents some prenatal disorganization or damage of the brain, since there is a high incidence of convulsions in children with this condition and a great many of them have abnormal electroencephalograms. If this is so, the part of the brain affected seems to be associated with language ability, for many of these children are quite adept with music, feats of memory, and sometimes numerical calculation. Also they may understand pictures better than words.

Some authorities believe that autism, if present at birth, cannot be prevented from developing: they point to the fact that autistic youngsters often seem withdrawn and unresponsive from their earliest days. Others feel that autism may exist as a tendency, which can possibly be averted if the baby is given a great deal of mothering, cuddling, fondling, caressing, and warm attention during his early months. The treatment for autism has not, on the whole, been very successful. Only a very few of these children appear to have recovered by adolescence or early adulthood. Although psychotherapy has been attempted in many cases, there is no evidence that it has been effective. The response to drug therapy, which seemed at one time to offer some promise, has been generally disappointing. Dr. Bruno Bettelheim has been able to achieve improvement in some autistic children by removing them from their homes and providing them with intensive personal care for long periods of time. It is hoped that some of the newer educational methods will aid children with this condition, but so far this has not been adequately studied. In general, when improvement is spoken of, what is meant is that the child may learn to understand very simple concepts and language and to control his behavior better, and that he may begin to relate better to the people he knows very well. Follow-up studies of autistic children seem to show that improvement tends to be greater when the early language disability is less severe. The children who have learned to respond to voices and to speak in their early years seem to have a better prognosis, and among the much improved children a few have even been able to attend schools and hold jobs.

It is a great shock for parents to learn that their child is autistic, and difficult decisions and adjustments inevitably lie ahead. It is important for these parents to learn as much as possible about autistic children and the latest methods of handling and educating them, and to be in communication with other parents who have faced the same difficulties. For information regarding local treatment facilities, parents may write the National Association for Mental Health, Inc., 10 Columbus Circle, New York, N.Y. 10019, or get in touch with their local mental health center. (See **Appendix D.**)

See also **Schizophrenia.**

Automobile travel with children

Automobile trips can be made safer, more comfortable, and more relaxing for both children and parents in a variety of ways.

Safety rules   Use safety belts for older children and all adults. The lap belt should not ride up across the child's abdomen.

Do not hold an infant or child on your lap, or use an adult seat belt to restrain both yourself and a child on your lap.

Fasten infants or toddlers in a safe harness or car seat. Be sure the safety seat is stamped no earlier than April 1971, the date of enforcement for new standards.

Safe harnesses and seat belts for infants and young children are a special problem, since ordinary seat belts are ineffective and even unsafe for children under 4 and those who weigh less than about forty pounds. In 1971 the Physicians for Automotive Safety listed the following manufacturers' harnesses as effective: Sears Roebuck, J. C. Penney, American Safety Equipment Corp., Rose Manufacturing Co., Hankscraft Co., Irvin Industries, and Market Forge Co. All harnesses can be bought with confidence if labeled as meeting Federal Motor Vehicle Safety Standard No. 209, Type 3.

Effective car seats and carriers include the following products; weight specifications should be observed:

Tot-Guard, Ford Motor Co. (accommodates 25–50 pounds)
Infant Carrier, General Motors Corp. (for infants unable to sit up)
Protecta-Tot, Hamill Manufacturing Co. (20–35 pounds; make sure car's seat back meets manufacturer's recommendations for height of child)
The Guardian, Pride Products Co. (15–50 pounds)
Auto-Safe, Strolee of California (17–37 pounds)
Bobby-Mac, Bobby Mac Co. (7–35 pounds)

All car seats can be bought with confidence if they are labeled as meeting Federal Motor Vehicle Safety Standard No. 213.

Additional safety rules are:

Do not allow children to stand up.
Do not allow children to put their heads, arms, or hands out the window or throw trash out of windows.
Keep the doors locked at all times when driving.
Have behavior rules in the car. Many accidents result when the driver is distracted by boisterous children.
On long trips stop frequently, at least

every hour or two, to let the children run for a few minutes.

Don't plan to travel too great a distance in one day; 300 to 350 miles is best.

Try to stop driving before dusk, which is the most dangerous period of the day for car accidents.

Infants A safe carrier or car seat is useful for infants, but it is advisable to let the baby try it out a bit before the trip so he'll be accustomed to it. Disposable diapers are most essential. A dry-milk-powder formula, which is prepared with water, can be used. A bottle warmer that can be plugged into the cigarette lighter is also available. And, of course, some of the baby's favorite toys should be brought along to keep him occupied when he is awake.

Older children Older children are likely to get restless and must be kept occupied. Games such as who will see the first dog, or naming everything seen along the road starting with a certain letter in the alphabet, are popular. Picture books and coloring books can be brought along. Singing together or listening to the radio are helpful—if they don't irritate the driver beyond reason.

See also **Motion sickness.**

Automobiles and adolescents

The same qualities that make teen-agers excellent in sports—the desire to achieve speed and to compete—may also make them dangerous drivers. In addition, the adolescent is an enthusiast with a limited sense of physical vulnerability. He often cannot believe that he can be injured or killed.

In many high schools in the United States courses in automobile driving and mechanics are being offered to teen-agers. In many localities boys and girls can get driver's licenses at 16. Proportionally, more than three times as many accidents occur among drivers who are 16 and 17 than among those over 20. Insurance rates, consequently, are also much higher for adolescents than for adults, reflecting the frequency of accidents in this group.

Although many parents question the licensing of adolescent drivers, many teen-agers of 16 and 17 have their hearts set on driving a car, and most parents will feel forced to consent if they can afford the extra expense of teen-age auto insurance. The car has become a status symbol, and most adolescents want all the things their friends have. However, until the parent is assured that his teen-ager has good judgment and follows the laws of good driving, he should not permit the adolescent to drive without supervision.

Many boys and girls save their money to buy a secondhand car. This is commendable, but it is vital that the parents are assured before the car is bought that it is in good working condition, that it is mechanically safe, and that the tires and other equipment are safe. A competent mechanic should check the car thoroughly before it is purchased.

It should be understood by all auto drivers between 16 and 18 that the privilege of driving will be withdrawn if traffic laws are not observed.

Driving courses offered in school are excellent and should be continued. Perhaps, however, it would be safer to license drivers at 18 years or, if licensed earlier, limit their speed to 40 miles an hour with the provision that the license will be revoked if that limit is not observed. A parent should not hesitate to forbid driving privileges if he has good evidence that the youngster has been driving recklessly.

Awkwardness

The causes of awkwardness may be physical or emotional. Normally many boys and girls approaching adolescence, when they are having sudden spurts in growth, go through a period of clumsiness and are temporarily gawky. Following this period, when the bone and muscle structures are once again balanced, the teen-ager usually becomes well coordinated. Awkwardness may also be caused by flat feet, toeing in or out, knock-knee, or obesity, which results in waddling. Occasionally, mild brain damage may cause a slight lack of coordination. A child who is extremely awkward should receive a neurological examination.

At times children who are emotionally upset or very shy are poorly coordinated, but once these children are stimulated by pleasurable activity, this can change rapidly. One can easily observe the change in certain poorly coordinated children of nursery-school and early-grade-school age who suddenly become beautifully graceful when encouraged to dance to music and rhythms.

B

Baby, first see **Parents, expectant.**

Baby, newborn see **Newborn, characteristics of.**

Baby, older child and new see **Sibling rivalry and jealousy.**

Baby carriage see **Carriage.**

Baby oil
Although not essential in infant care, baby oil is of particular value if an infant's skin is very dry or as a lubricant for the diaper area, applied in an effort to prevent diaper rash. Mineral oil may be used, or the doctor may recommend a commercial baby oil.

Baby-sitters
Every parent needs to know one or more baby-sitters with whom a child may be safely left. Sitters can usually be obtained from colleges, nursing homes, or hospitals, and such organizations generally evaluate the personalities of the sitters they recommend. Never employ a sitter without carefully looking into the sitter's references or the reputation of the recommending organization. It is advisable to use the same sitter continuously once a good relationship has been established. Responsible teenagers who like children and who are acquainted with the family are often excellent sitters, for the job may be quite special to them and their attention may be a treat for the child.

The first time you hire a sitter, ask her (or him) to arrive at least half an hour early, so that you and your child can get to know her and to allow time to explain the child's habits and needs. Always leave a telephone number where you can be reached and the number of your child's doctor. If you find the sitter unpleasant or apparently incompetent at this first meeting, it may be best to cut short your evening or even cancel it.

When you return, always ask the sitter how the evening went. This is not just for politeness; the answers will often indicate whether the sitter took good care of the child. Children generally enjoy the time spent with a sitter, and if a child really complains about a sitter, you should consider the possibility that the sitter is not right for the child or that you are leaving the child too often.

In many areas mothers baby-sit for one another, either in their own homes or in their friend's homes. Grandparents are usually ideal baby-sitters, because they know the children well and the children feel secure with them. But grandparents should not be forced to be baby-sitters—or be made to feel guilty if they cannot or refuse to baby-sit.

Baby teeth see **Teeth.**

"Babyish" behavior see **Regression.**

Bacteria
Any of the numerous one-celled microorganisms occurring as rods, spheres, or spirals. Many of these are the caus-

ative agents of inflammation and disease in the human body.

Bacterial infections
Infections caused by bacteria rather than viruses include acute tonsillitis, boils and abscesses, scarlet fever, diphtheria, pneumonia, and meningitis. Practically all bacterial infections can be eradicated with modern antibiotics. (Virus infections do not respond to antibiotics.)

For scientific treatment of an infection, a culture is made—from a throat smear, ear discharge, or pus from an abscess, for example—and the specific bacteria causing the infection are isolated. These bacteria are then tested with a variety of antibiotics to learn which are best suited for eradicating them.

For convenience and speed many doctors without facilities for culturing bacteria use broad-spectrum antibiotics—antibiotics which are known to prevent or inhibit the growth of many different infectious organisms.

See also **Staphylococcus infections; Streptococcus infections.**

Bad breath
Comparatively rare in young children, bad breath becomes more common during later childhood and adolescence. It may be caused by decayed teeth, poor mouth hygiene (as when particles of food collect in crevices between teeth), postnasal discharge from infected adenoids or sinuses, or maldigestion of food in the stomach.

Mouth washes and chewing gums and tablets designed to counteract bad breath, or baking soda mixed with water, may be of temporary help. Chronic bad breath should be investigated by the dentist and the doctor.

Bad language   see **Swear words.**

Baldness
Partial or complete loss of hair on the scalp. Baldness sometimes occurs in childhood, most commonly as a bald spot. The various types of baldness include:

Spot baldness (alopecia areata) Localized baldness—single or multiple patches of baldness on the scalp, usually localized there but at times involving the eyebrows and eyelashes. The patches appear rather suddenly and may increase in size from that of a dime to a half dollar. They may last from several weeks to several months. There is no medical treatment, but a gradual regrowth of hair occurs until the denuded areas are once again covered.

A high incidence of alopecia areata occurs in children with severe emotional problems, suggesting the possibility that it is a psychosomatic disturbance. It may appear at almost any age.

Ringworm of the scalp An infection of the hair follicles by a fungus that causes patches of baldness. The condition is usually contracted from other children or pets. The baldness starts as a small spot and spreads outward in a circular manner, which is why it is called ringworm.

It is very successfully treated by a drug, griseofulvin, given orally until the infection has disappeared.

Ringworm of the scalp differs from spot baldness in that with ringworm the hair shafts are broken off and can be seen through a magnifying glass, while in alopecia areata the hair has completely disappeared from an area. A dermatologist can quickly differentiate between the two by shining a special fluorescent lamp, a "Wood's light," on the area. The area with ringworm will glow under this light.

Hair-pulling baldness see **Hair, pulling out.**

Congenital baldness A very rare condition in which a defect in the development of hair follicles prevents the growth of hair. This congenital condition is usually associated with other difficulties such as defective, usually decaying teeth and a defective secretion of sweat. Congenital baldness is usually a permanent condition, although in rare instances there is a growth of hair during adolescence. Wigs or hairpieces may be used to cover the affected areas.

Toxic baldness A rare condition that follows severe infections usually accompanied by high fever. This baldness may be permanent.

Burn-induced baldness A result of deep burns caused by intense heat, X ray, acids, or chemicals. Such baldness is usually permanent.

Bank accounts see **Savings accounts.**

Barbiturate poisoning
Poisoning with barbiturates, which are widely used as sedatives, is not uncommon among children, who are apt to swallow brightly colored capsules and tablets left within reach by parents. To prevent accidents with barbiturates, adults should be sure that all pills are safely locked up. If a child does swallow barbiturates, induce vomiting immediately to prevent respiratory failure and even death. Then call your doctor or local poison control center. If the child is unconscious or if vomiting cannot be induced, hospitalization is indicated for stomach washing and further observation and treatment.

For methods of inducing vomiting see **Poisons: first-aid treatment.**

See also **Drug abuse.**

Barbiturates see **Drug abuse.**

Baseball finger
An injury sustained when an extended finger is hit forcibly by a ball, forcing it back and tearing the ligaments at the first or second joint. It occurs most frequently in baseball, but it may occur in basketball, football, or similar games.

The finger joint affected is swollen and painful. A doctor should examine the injury; a splint or taping may be advisable to immobilize the joint temporarily. Healing usually takes three or four weeks or longer.

Basic foods see **Foods, basic.**

Bassinet
Essentially a basket padded on the sides and with a mattress on the bottom, used as the baby's first bed. Bassinets can be bought already fitted out, but they can easily be made out of a wash basket, a bureau drawer, or even a sturdy box. The sides should be at least 12 inches deep so that the baby cannot fall or roll out. The mattress should be firm (see **Mattress**), although a folded blanket or a folded pad will serve adequately for the short period it will be used. The baby can use the bassinet for about two months and then should be moved to a crib. (See **Crib.**)

Bath see **Bathing the infant; Bed bath; Sponge bath for the newborn.**

Bath, bed see **Bed bath.**

Bathing the infant
Newborn infants should be sponge-bathed until the umbilical cord has fallen off and the navel is dry. Also, baby boys who have been circumcised should not be bathed in the bathinette or tub until the circumcision has healed. (See **Sponge bath for the newborn.**)

The bath is most conveniently given in a Bathinette or a plastic baby-size bathtub. A sink or a dishpan can also be used if necessary.

The bath may be given either in the morning at about 9 A.M. or in the afternoon at about 5 P.M., depending largely upon the convenience to the mother. However, in colder weather it is preferable to bathe the baby in the afternoon, since it is not advisable to take a child with wet hair outdoors in the cold.

While bathing a baby, hold him at all times and be sure his head cannot slip under the water.

The temperature of the water should be approximately that of the body. A bath thermometer is not a necessity, for most mothers can tell if the temperature is comfortably warm by placing their elbow or the back of their wrist in the water. (100 degrees Fahrenheit on the thermometer is about the correct temperature.) Castile soap or one of the many mild soaps such as Ivory may be used.

During the bath itself, the baby should be held firmly with your left arm behind his head and neck, always holding the baby's head out of the water. First gently clean the baby's face with a soft washcloth using only water—no soap. Then carefully lather the scalp so that none of the soap gets in the baby's eyes. Rinse off the soap and pat the scalp dry. Do not fear to wash or even pat the soft spot—there is no danger.

Next, continuing to hold the baby's head above water, soap and wash his body gently, using the soft washcloth. After rinsing, lift the baby out of the tub, wrap a bath towel around him, and pat him dry.

Certain parts of a baby's body should receive special care. In girls the external genitals (vulva) should be separated and washed gently from front to back with soft cotton moistened with water or baby oil, using each piece of cotton only once. In baby boys who are not circumcised, the foreskin should be pulled back and the crown of the penis cleaned, using water or baby oil.

After the bath the baby should be powdered or gently rubbed with a powder or lotion, which has been recommended by your doctor. Whatever powder you use, do not shower it on the baby in a cloud. Even the "safest" powders may harm the baby when inhaled. Rub in the powder a little at a time.

At times, an older infant might start resisting the bath for some reason or other—possibly he has been splashed or his head has momentarily slid under the water. In such cases it may help to bathe the child in the sink. If this is still unsuccessful, the baby should be taken into the bath with the mother—this almost always relieves the fear in a very short time.

See also **Hair washing.**

Baths

Once a child is approximately a year old he may be bathed in the family bathtub. There are certain precautions, however, that should be taken. The parent should never leave the room; the water should be no more than waist-high; the child should not stand up until it is time to be lifted from the tub, since the bottom may be slippery; a rubber mat on the bottom will keep a young child from slipping around.

Children should continue to be bathed by a parent until they are approximately 4 years old, although they can "help" wash themselves before that. However, when children are even as young as 2 years, they must be taught never to touch the faucet lest they turn on water that is too hot. They may play with bath toys for periods before and after the actual bathing, but a parent should always remain in the room when a young child is in the tub.

Most children will learn to bathe themselves—and will enjoy it—between the ages of 4 and 5 years. Once a parent is sure that a youngster can safely be left alone, continous supervision can be stopped, although the parent should be nearby.

Two children may take baths together until they are about 7 years old or even a little older, providing the tub is large enough. This refers to brothers and sisters as well as children of the same sex.

There should be a routine time for baths when children are younger. When they approach the teen years, however, bathing may be left to the boys and girls themselves—although a minimum of several baths a week should be the rule.

Battered child   see **Child abuse.**

BCG vaccination

A vaccine—Calmette-Guerin bacillus—used in the prevention of tuberculosis, and named after its originators, Dr. Albert Calmette and Dr. Alphonse Guerin of France. It is composed of living but permanently weakened tuberculosis bacteria from cows, gives a fairly strong immunity against the human type of tuberculosis, and lasts approximately ten years.

Although rarely used in the United States, BCG vaccine is used extensively in countries where facilities to detect, treat, and follow up persons with the disease are inadequate.

Bed   see **Bassinet; Crib; Junior bed.**

Bed bath

Bed baths are necessary when children are ill or when they are temporarily confined to bed by an injury, such as a broken leg.

To prepare for a bed bath, close the windows and doors and check that the room temperature is 70–75 degrees Fahrenheit. Gather together the following equipment:

1. A rubber sheet to place under the child.
2. A large bath towel or blanket to cover the child.
3. A bath towel, a face towel, and a washcloth.

4. A mild soap.
5. Two basins of warm water.
6. Talcum powder.

Put the rubber sheet over the regular sheet. Remove the clothing from the child and cover him with the bath towel.

Wash the child's body part by part, being careful not to expose too much of the body at one time. Wash the face without soap and pat dry. Then soap the washcloth and wash the neck and ears. Rinse the washcloth, use to wash the soap off, and dry the child carefully. Expose the chest and arms. Wash them. Dry them and powder them and do the same with the back. Then let the child put on a pajama top or nightgown. Next, expose one leg and wash it, then wash the other leg. Wash the abdomen and genitals last. Finally, finish powdering all washed areas.

Bed, junior see **Junior bed; Mattress.**

Bedridden child

When a child is bedridden the prime concerns of the parents are following the doctor's orders and keeping a normally active child occupied, happy, and free of boredom.

Organizing a routine for the day is very important, but the parent must first ascertain how much leeway the doctor will permit the "bedridden" child. May he walk to and from the bathroom? May he spend his day on a couch in another room? May he sit at the dinner table? May he get dressed during the day? Most children with acute illnesses—sore throats, influenza, contagious diseases, pneumonia—do not have to remain in bed, but may relax on a couch in another room if they so desire, even if they have fairly high temperatures.

A child who feels sick, whether he has a sore throat, earache, nausea, vomiting, abdominal cramps, general achiness, or other discomfort, needs and wants a great deal of attention from his parents. In order to get it, he may often revert to much younger, infantile behavior. Of course parents should temporarily do all they can to make the child as comfortable and happy as possible, but they should not allow indulgence to become a way of life after the child is completely well.

The child's routine should be as close as possible to that of the rest of the family. He should not be left alone for too long—when you are busy, perhaps an occasional call or a knocking on the wall or a peek in the room from time to time is all that is necessary to make the bedridden child realize that he is not forgotten.

Try to take the child's mind off his illness by talking about the future plans you are making for him. Encourage the child by remarking how quickly he is improving, and reassure him of how strong he will be once the illness is over. Do not appear anxious or depressed around the child—he will usually be quick to note this and react accordingly.

Television, although loved by most children and valuable in relieving tedium, should not be overdone. The child should be given many opportunities to keep himself occupied; when he feels well enough, supply him with a table or a bagful of toys next to the bed, books, a radio, a record player, and especially constructive activities, such as crayons, puzzles, dot-to-dot pictures. Ask to see each project when it is finished. Read to him when you have the time and encourage him to read or look at books.

The bedridden child should also be

given chores and other things to do to make him feel that he is an important member of the family. The jobs can be as simple as sticking trading stamps in the stamp book, polishing silverware, or matching socks after they have been washed. Even placing stamps on outgoing mail and if the child is old enough, sewing on an occasional button makes the child feel a necessary part of the family.

A child who is bedridden should be permitted to shout, sing, even use a loud musical instrument. He needs an opportunity to release as much of his pent up energy and frustrations as possible. This doesn't mean that loud noisemaking should continue throughout the day—it should be limited to an hour or so.

Tell the child what his friends are doing and encourage him to call or write them, or, if he is not contagious, invite them to visit. The continuance of friendships during an illness is most important.

If old enough, a bedridden child should have a telephone next to his bed so he can talk to his friends. If they come to visit, he should have social games at hand—checkers, Monopoly, dominoes, and card games.

If a child is to be bedridden for any period of time it is important for him to keep up with his schoolwork so that when he gets back to school he will be on the same level as his classmates. The parents should get the child's school books and homework and help him with his work if the stay at home is less than a week or so. For a child confined at home for an extended period, many communities have special teachers who visit in the home to help the child keep up with his work.

Parents should do everything possible to make convalescence an active and interesting period, free of boredom, so that it passes as happily and as quickly as possible.

Bedrooms, sharing

Many questions often arise about sharing bedrooms. Should children ever sleep with their parents or in their parent's room? How long should brothers and sisters sleep in the same room?

Under ordinary circumstances children should not sleep in the parents' bedroom and especially not in their bed. It is a bad habit to form and one that is very difficult to break. After a child is approximately 15 months he should not sleep in the parents' bedroom, except on rare occasions when the child is ill or temporarily upset.

Brothers and sisters can share the same room when they are young children and can continue to share it until they are about 9. Usually they should have their own rooms when the girl starts to develop or when the boy starts to enter puberty, when increased sex interests and urges appear. If separate rooms are not available, a partition of beaver board or plywood can be built to give each child his own section of the room and privacy.

Bedtime hour

For the infant there is no specific bedtime. The newborn or very young child sleeps most of the time between feedings, sometimes as much as twenty to twenty-two hours a day. But after the first month or so he is awake considerably more, the sleeping hours varying with the individual child. The very active (hypertonic) baby will usually sleep less than the child who is more complacent.

The bedtime hour varies greatly as a child grows older. Toward the end of the first year most infants take two naps during the day and start their bedtime hour at about 6 or 7 P.M., although this can be flexible, according to family routine.

From approximately one year of age to 5 years most children take a nap or rest period during the day and have a bedtime hour of about 7 or 7:30 P.M. Usually children of this age need twelve hours sleep at night but this, too, can vary with the individual. If a child is healthy and happy and shows no sign of fatigue he is most likely getting the needed amount of sleep.

Between 6 and 9 years the bedtime hour may be set at about 8 P.M., and from 9 to 12 years the hour might be set at 8:30 or even 9 P.M., depending on the time needed for study.

From 12 to 16—years of increased social interests and educational needs—the hour for bed may be set at 10 P.M. at the latest on school nights, and later on other nights—possibly to midnight.

These bedtime hours may be adjusted according to the particular needs of the family and the child, always bearing in mind that the child needs a good night's sleep and most children benefit from a routine as long as it isn't too unreasonable or inflexible. If the child has difficulty falling asleep, it is often wise to allow him a quiet half hour with the lights on—reading or listening to the radio.

See also **Naps; Sleep; Sleep problems.**

Bed-wetting

Bed-wetting (enuresis) in a child over 6 can have either physical or emotional causes. A child whose bladder is too small or who has some defect in the urinary system may continue bed-wetting. In very rare instances diabetes may be the cause. Most frequently, however,

bed-wetting is caused by tensions and anxieties, and these may have to be relieved before the condition is cured. Scolding, spanking, teasing, making a child change his wet bed, and other punishments are of little help and make the child feel more unhappy and guilty. Encouragement is most important, and, in consultation with a pediatrician, the following measures may be tried.

1. Ask the child to hold in his urine as long as possible during the day. This is to stretch the bladder. Studies have shown that a great many bed wetters have small bladders, and stretching the bladder makes it capable of retaining more urine before it is released.

2. Make the evening hours as relaxed as possible, without excitement or turmoil. Exciting television programs should be avoided.

3. Limit fluids after 4 P.M.

4. Give the child a salty pretzel or a salt tablet before bed. High salt in the bloodstream slows down the amount of fluid entering the kidneys.

5. The doctor may recommend that chewable tablets of Enuretrol (ephedrine and atropine) be taken before going to bed. They relax the bladder muscles so that the bladder holds more urine, and cause a slight muscle contraction at the end of the bladder so that urine is not easily passed during sleep.

6. Many doctors suggest a mild tranquilizer, Tofranil (imipramine hydrochloride), to relieve the child of tensions and relax the bladder. Considerable success has been reported with it.

7. A bed-wetting apparatus to condition the child against wetting has also been successful. A pad attached by wire to a small box containing a buzzer and a light is placed under the sheet. As soon as the pad gets the least bit wet, the buzzer sounds, awakening the child, and

the light turns on. The child jumps out of bed and goes to the bathroom. In most cases bed-wetting ceases after several weeks—the child is thus conditioned to wake automatically when he is about to urinate. This method should not be used if it upsets the child, but in careful tests it has not been found to be psychologically harmful, and the results were good. (Note: It is usually less expensive to buy rather than rent such devices. Check the price at a reputable establishment such as Sears Roebuck or Dryomatic Co., Annchester Rd., Detroit, Mich. 17668. Beware of hucksters who operate door to door or via media advertising.)

If the child does not respond to any of these methods, he should have a urological examination to be sure no abnormalities of the kidneys, bladder, or tubes are responsible for the bed-wetting. If no abnormalities are revealed, then emotional factors must be sought.

Most children of 6 and over are eager to overcome the bed-wetting habit and are delighted when it has been conquered.

See also **Toilet training.**

Bee stings

The stings of bees, hornets, wasps, and yellow jackets usually cause severe pain and swelling at the site of the sting. Since the stinger of a bee is hooked at the end it often remains in the skin and appears as a little black spot. It should be removed like a splinter. Wasps, hornets, and yellow jackets do not leave their stingers in the skin.

To relieve the immediate discomfort of the sting, cover the area with a paste of baking soda (sodium bicarbonate) and water or apply a compress wet with weak ammonia water (household ammonia diluted with an equal amount of water).

Some children are extremely allergic to these insect stings and may react with severe hives, swelling up of various parts of the body, and even with difficulty in breathing. This reaction, known as anaphylaxis (see **Anaphylaxis**), may be so severe that unless treated quickly, death may result. These children should receive oral antihistamines immediately and Adrenalin (adrenaline or epinephrine) injections to avoid the serious effects.

Allergic children may be desensitized against insect stings by inoculation. If not inoculated, it is advisable to have an insect-sting kit on hand at all times when an insect sting is a possibility. Center Laboratories, Inc., 35 Channel Drive, Port Washington, N. Y., sells an insect sting first-aid kit. This contains the medication needed to avoid severe reactions and instruction for use, as well as instructions on how to avoid wasps and bees.

Children with insect-sting sensitivity should also carry a Medic Alert emblem on a bracelet or as a pendant. (See **Medic Alert.**)

Behavior, causes of

Numerous factors determine the behavior of children, factors that together influence the way growing boys and girls act and think. They can be grouped most generally as hereditary, developmental, environmental, and physical.

Hereditary factors   Although a great controversy still exists regarding the extent to which heredity influences behavior, there is nevertheless no doubt that heredity does play a role, perhaps as a tendency toward certain behavior patterns. For example, the general degree of activity an infant shows at birth is apt to remain with him throughout life. Some infants are very active and awake a good deal of the time (hypertonic babies), while others are calm and relaxed and during early infancy sleep a great deal. Active infants will usually grow into active adults and calm infants will be more relaxed and deliberate.

Developmental factors   Generally in the course of a child's development, he will exhibit various normal patterns of behavior that are determined by developmental factors. These patterns of behavior include, for example, the tendency of the one-year-old to cling to his mother, the 2-year-old's aggressiveness, the need of the school-age child to be accepted by his peers, and the negativism of the adolescent. (See **Development in the first five years.**)

Environmental factors   These factors include the stability of the home, the child's relationship with his parents, the place of the child in the family—whether he is an only child, a middle child, and so forth—his relationship to his peers and companions, and his adjustment at school. Environmental factors are crucial in forming the personality of the child and interact with physical factors to the extent that it is often in practice impossible to separate them.

Physical factors   A child's state of health influences his behavior, sometimes markedly. For example, a child who is undernourished, or malnourished, subject to chronic infection, or anemic may appear listless and dull. His behavior can change dramatically if the condition is cleared up. Children suffering from mild brain dysfunction may be hyperactive and distractible, and appear to be willfully fidgety and obstreperous. Medical treatment under the care of a doctor has helped many of these children to settle down and become calmer.

See also **Mental retardation.**

Belching
The expulsion of gas from the stomach through the mouth. This is a normal occurrence in infancy after the child has nursed or taken part or all of a formula. A certain amount of air is sucked in with the milk and forms a bubble in the stomach. This air is belched (burped) up during or after the feeding. (See **Bubbling [burping] the baby.**)

Belching in older children is rare and is usually caused by the formation of gas in the process of digestion in the stomach or may accompany a mild stomach upset.

Bellybands
Cotton or flannel strips of cloth for winding around a newborn's abdomen over the umbilical cord until it dries up and drops off; also used to bind a protruding navel (umbilical hernia). Bellybands are seldom used today. Hernias are either strapped in by adhesive tape or, if not too large, left alone.

Benadryl   see **Antihistamines.**

Benzine and benzene poisoning   see **Poisons: first-aid treatment.**

Bicycles
Bicycle riding is a healthy pastime for the whole family, and almost all children look forward to getting their own bike. But many serious accidents involving bicyclers occur each year, and parents should be sure that their children

follow basic safety rules, especially if they are riding in traffic. The following rules for youngsters have been formulated by the Bicycle Institute of America and by the Accident Prevention Committee of the American Academy of Pediatrics.

1. Learn and observe all local laws affecting bicycles. If you move to a new town, ask the police for the rules on bicycles.
2. Observe all traffic rules—red and green lights, one-way streets, stop signs. Use arm and hand signals to show when you intend to turn or stop. Ride with the flow of traffic, on the right side of the street, not against it.
3. Do not ride bicycles on streets with heavy automobile traffic. If you have to cross or turn at a heavy traffic intersection, dismount and walk the bike across at the pedestrian crossing. If riding on sidewalks is legal, do not speed when there is a chance of hitting someone.
4. Watch carefully for cars pulling out and into traffic, and keep a sharp lookout for the sudden opening of the doors of parked automobiles. Drivers often do not see bicycles approaching.
5. Ride in single file. Keep a safe distance behind all vehicles. Do not pass or ride too close to other vehicles.
6. Do not carry packages that obstruct vision or prevent the proper control of the bike.
7. Slow down at street intersections and look in both directions before crossing.
8. Ride in a straight line and do not weave in and out of traffic or swerve from side to side.
9. Do not ride double on one bike. It makes balancing difficult and prevents a clear view of the road.
10. Never hitch on to other vehicles, stunt-ride, or race in traffic on the street. If you want to try riding with no hands, standing on the seat, or racing, do it in a field or yard.
11. Do not ride your bike on streets after dark. If it becomes necessary to occasionally ride after dark, be sure to have a bell or a horn, a headlight, and a red reflector on the rear, and wear light-colored clothing for visibility.
12. Keep your bicycle in good condition. Check your tire pressure; oil and grease the bicycle when necessary. See that the bell or horn is always working.
13. Do not ride too far too fast. When you are tired, you are not a safe bike rider.
14. When selecting a bicycle think twice—high-rise bicycles are not as safe as standard bikes.

Big Brothers; Big Sisters

Big Brothers is an organization of men who interest themselves in boys who have no fathers or meaningful and worthwhile father substitutes in their lives. Each man devotes himself to a particular boy, often one who has been brought before the Children's Court for some antisocial act, misdemeanor, truancy, or other difficulty.

The Big Brothers become close friends of the boys, taking them to sporting events and on excursions—the primary purpose being to let the boys realize that someone cares very much for them, and also to give to each boy a devoted father substitute of high moral character whom he can use as a model of masculinity.

Big Sisters groups have also been organized for girls who need a mother-like person in their lives. There are branches of Big Brothers and Big Sisters in most large cities of the United States and Canada.

Bigotry see **Intolerance and prejudice.**

Bile

The golden-yellow digestive juice secreted by the liver. It enters into the intestine through the bile duct and plays an important part in the digestion of fats. It also furnishes the coloring matter that gives feces their brown or yellow color.

See also **Jaundice.**

Bilingual families

Young children have an amazing ability to learn two languages at the same time and to separate these two languages when speaking. But learning two or more languages at once does present some difficulties. Children in bilingual homes begin speaking as early as other children, but several studies have shown that they have a smaller vocabulary in each language and a smaller total vocabulary in both languages than single-language children. How long this deficiency lasts has not been fully determined.

Learning a second language is best begun at 3 to 6 years, when children learn languages quickly and enjoyably.

Birth

Few if any events in the life of a human being are more critical than that of being born. The sudden change from the almost complete security within the womb, where a child has no need to eat or breathe and where he is kept warm and comfortable, to the outside world necessitates drastic bodily adjustments. Suddenly the infant must breathe by himself, bringing oxygen to the blood for the first time. He must maintain his own temperature in spite of varying surrounding temperatures, and his body for the first time will take food through the mouth and digest it in his gastrointestinal tract.

The birth process begins, as a rule, when the baby has been within the uterus for a little over nine months—280 days, or 40 weeks, from the onset of the last menstrual period. At birth the muscles of the uterus start contracting and pressing down upon the whole amniotic sac containing the baby. The contractions, which cause cramplike pains, start at intervals of about thirty minutes and gradually occur more and more closely together. The muscles of the uterus push down with greater and greater force un-

Baby at birth with umbilical cord still uncut.

til the opening at the end of the uterus, through the cervix, is widened enough to permit passage of the baby's head and body. Then the amniotic sac bursts, the baby passes out of the uterus into the birth canal (vagina) and out of the mother's body. The umbilical cord connecting the baby to the placenta is then cut and tied, and the infant is on his own to make important adjustments to an outside world under the attention of those who care for him.

Although the birth process may involve dangerous complications, in the modern world of today it is much easier and safer for both mother and child. The best way to be sure that all goes well in this critical stage is to have good obstetrical care and to follow your doctor's recommendations regarding the care of your health during pregnancy.

See also **Natural childbirth; Newborn, characteristics of.**

Birth canal   see **Vagina.**

Birth certificate
A document certifying the date and place of birth, the sex of the child, and the parents' names. Legally, a birth certificate must be filed for every child born in the United States. This document is much more important than most parents realize, and the copy sent to the parents should be kept in a safe place. It is legally required as evidence of the date of birth in many situations—public school registration, registering for voting, and so on.

Parents should try to name the newborn child in time to submit the name with the birth certificate form while the mother and infant are still in the hospital. If no name is submitted, the certificate reads "Baby Boy" or "Baby Girl" with the last name. A name selected

after the mother and infant have left the hospital should be sent to the municipal Bureau of Vital Statistics so that a second certificate can be issued that includes the name of the child. If the birth certificate has not been received by the time a baby is 2 months old, the parents should write to the Bureau and request one.

Birth defects
Birth defects are abnormalities resulting from defective development of the embryo and fetus; chromosome defects and heredity; diseases contracted in the uterus; blood differences between the mother and her baby; and injury or lack of oxygen during the process of birth.

Serious birth defects are still not too uncommon but the effort to reduce birth defects and to treat existing defects is advancing. Potential parents can do their part by using genetic counseling and by carefully following the instructions of the obstetrician regarding care during pregnancy.

See also **Birth injuries; Genetic counseling; Parents, expectant.**

Birth injuries
Injuries occurring to the infant during labor or birth. The incidence of birth injuries has been greatly reduced in recent years, and many of them can be treated with complete success. Among the most common birth injuries are:

Fracture of the clavicle (collarbone) The clavicle is particularly vulnerable in difficult deliveries of the shoulders. A fracture is usually detected early because the baby fails to move the arm on the affected side. It is easily treated and heals perfectly.

Fracture of the arm or leg long bone An arm or leg fracture may occur in difficult deliveries of an extremity. It is either detected at birth or shortly afterward, when the infant fails to move the arm or leg. Treatment involves setting the bone and applying a cast, and the result is usually perfect—no disability.

External hemorrhage The most common external hemorrhage is a collection of blood from bleeding beneath the scalp (cephalohematoma). It is indicated by a swelling on one side of the head beneath the scalp. At first it is a soft mass, but as it subsides it hardens around the edges, unnecessairly worrying many parents who think it is an opening of the skull into the brain. The mass may take some months to subside but it does disappear completely and without aftereffects.

Internal hemorrhage A serious consequence of a difficult labor, internal hemorrhage may occur when the infant's head is too large for the pelvic opening, when labor is prolonged, when forceps are improperly used, when oxygen is insufficient, or when the infant has a disease that weakens the capillaries. The hemorrhage is often within the skull or even in the brain substance and is always serious. The infant needs intensive medical care and in some cases surgery.

Paralysis of an arm Arm paralysis may occur in difficult deliveries when an obstetrician pulls too forcibly on a baby's head without freeing the shoulder. This tears or stretches the nerves going to the arm. If the nerve is only stretched, motion of the arm will return in a few months. If the nerve is completely severed, the arm will remain paralyzed and will not grow to full length. (Full paralysis, however, is rare.)

Birth weights

A baby's weight at birth is a fairly good indication of the development of the baby's body before birth. In the United States the normal range is five to nine pounds, the average being approximately seven pounds.

The weight of a baby, however, is not as important as the length of the pregnancy. A four-pound full-term baby is much more healthy and capable of survival than a four-pound baby born one month or six weeks early—though many full-term babies of low weight have, for one reason or another, been poorly nourished while in the uterus and so are not usually as strong as the infant of normal weight.

Those babies born late who weigh nine or ten pounds or more are not usually as healthy as full-term babies. Adequate nutrition from the mother's blood apparently is not available to the infant who overstays his time in the uterus. Consequently, when birth does finally occur, these babies are somewhat malnourished, with insufficient fatty tissue beneath the skin.

See also **Premature baby; Postmature baby.**

Birthdays

From the child's own viewpoint his birthday—his own very special day—is often the most important day in the year. It is a day when everyone says "Happy birthday" to him and to him alone, when he receives birthday presents, when he may have a birthday party in his honor with his closest friends and family around him.

In many nursery schools and kindergartens teachers make a special announcement of the "birthday child." Occasionally a birthday party is held in the classroom at the end of the school day. When parents supply the food and other party necessities, which they may be asked to do, they should remember that teachers usually are careful to keep the party relatively simple, so that no parent can outdo the other.

Birthday cards are always enjoyed and immensely appreciated by the child, and parents should notify all interested relatives of the coming event so the cards will be received in time to be displayed or carried around by the honored child.

Give the child some special recognition at a family meal on his birthday to mark this particular day as very special—whether a birthday party is scheduled or not. A "happy birthday" card at his place at the table, his favorite foods, and possibly a special dessert in his honor add to the child's joy. It is most important that both parents be with the child on his birthday. His parents should also attend the birthday party if one is held. Some parents hold the birthday party on the weekend so it will not interfere with school. Some of the unhappiest birthday children are those whose parents are away on vacation when the child has his prearranged birthday party.

See also **Parties.**

Birthmarks

Very common in infancy, many birthmarks disappear before the child is one year old. Most babies are born with red mottled markings on the backs of their heads and extending down to the upper neck. Red flushes on the upper eyelids and above the nose between the eyes are also common. All of these gradually disappear within twelve months.

Brown birthmarks (moles), caused by pigment in the skin, and dark purple marks (port-wine stains), which are created by widely dilated capillaries, do not disappear.

Dark red birthmarks (strawberry marks) may be flat, raised, or deep in the tissues. Called hemangiomas, these marks are caused by dilated blood vessels in the upper layers of the skin. Many strawberry marks start as a small red spot and increase in size for five or six months. Then they start fading, often becoming hardly noticeable at about a year or a year and a half. Small marks that do not disappear can be treated by a doctor with dry ice. The ice freezes the area and a scab forms; when the scab drops off, the skin is left in a normal condition. Deeper hemangiomas may require surgery.

Another treatment method is to inject the birthmark with substances that shrink the blood vessels—substances similar to those used on adults to shrink varicose veins.

Birthmarks can also be covered with a cosmetic preparation, Covermark, that comes in different shades to match various skin tones. Applied as a cream, it completely obliterates the birthmark, is waterproof and kissproof, and is easily removed with cold cream.

Bites see **Bee stings; Insect and spider bites; Rabies; Rat-bite fever; Snakes and snakebites.**

Biting, kicking, pushing, hitting

Many, if not most, children between the ages of about 18 months and 3 years go through an aggressive period. They do not understand the right of possession and they resent being thwarted. In an attempt to gain their own way, many youngsters resort to biting, kicking, pushing, or hitting other children.

Since children cannot be permitted to hurt other children, this potentially harmful behavior must be stopped. It will do little or no good to spank the child or bite him to show how it hurts. It is much more effective to take the child away from the other children immediately and have him sit down next to his mother. Tell him firmly, "We do not hurt other children. You cannot play with other children if you hurt them. You sit here with me for a while." And the child should be forced to sit next to his mother for fifteen or twenty minutes even if he resists. This separation from their companions has been most successful in teaching young children that if they want to play with other children, certain rules have to be followed.

Older children (those over 4) also often behave aggressively and hit out against other children. By then the child should know better, and if a child persists in dangerously aggressive behavior, the parents must begin to consider the possibility that he is emotionally distressed. The child who is much too rough—who, for example, pushes other children on a flight of steps or hits out with a heavy object—is not only a danger to others (and unpopular), but is often frightened by his own feelings of being out of control. He may need professional help.

Isolated instances of hitting or kicking are not cause for parental worry, although the child should be disciplined. And quite rough play in safe surroundings, such as on the lawn in the backyard, is perfectly normal.

See also **Anger; Temper and temper tantrums.**

Biting the nails   see **Nails, biting.**

Black eye

A black eye is essentially a bruise. Because the tissue beneath the eye is spongelike, a blow around the eye, the upper nose area, and even the lower forehead will often cause a black eye, which is the result of blood seeping from the area of broken capillaries into the area below the eyes. A black eye may last a week or longer before disappearing.

Usually no treatment is indicated, but various enzymes, which hasten its disappearance, can be prescribed by a doctor. Among such enzyme preparations, which are given orally or by injection, are Varidase, Chymolase, Ananase, and Chymoral. The time-honored beefsteak remedy is probably of help only because it is in effect a cold compress applied to the bruised area. The application of cold compresses, however, is not really very effective, and many children hate it.

Blackhead

Also called a comedo. A small mass of hardened oily matter with a black top that plugs up the duct of an oil gland in the skin, usually on the face or upper back, and often occurring in acne.

Very frequently in the course of adolescence the oil glands in the skin become more active. A thick secretion of oily matter comes up the duct from the

Blackhead (comedo) remover.

gland to the surface of the skin. When this thick, oily material is exposed to the air the top dries and contact with the oxygen in the air turns it black.

Blackheads should not be picked at or squeezed, for this can cause infection, scarring, or enlarged pores. They can, however, often be successfully removed by softening the area around the spot with warm water and pressing down around it with a comedo remover, a small flat piece of metal with a hole at one or both ends. The hole is placed over the blackhead and the instrument is pressed down. The blackhead is forced out of the duct, appearing as a tiny wormlike substance.

See also **Acne.**

Bladder control   see **Bed-wetting; Toilet training.**

Blanket, security   see **Security object.**

Blanket sucking   see **Sucking, blanket.**

Bleaches, poisoning   see **Poisons: first-aid treatment.**

Bleeding   see **Cuts; Nosebleed.**

Bleeding, nose   see **Nosebleed.**

Bleeding time
The length of time bleeding continues from a small puncture. Bleeding time is an indication of how long it takes blood to clot. Clotting depends on the number of platelets (tiny discs of protoplasm in the blood, smaller than red blood corpuscles). These platelets can be seen and counted on microscopic examination. Doctors use various methods of testing bleeding time, such as puncturing the lobe of a child's ear with a very small lancet. The bleeding should cease within three minutes. In conditions such as hemophilia and purpura the bleeding will continue as a rule for much longer.

Blepharitis   See **Eyelids, granulated.**

Blindness
The definition of blindness has a wide range. It includes children and adults who are totally blind, those who have only light perception; those who are only able to distinguish hand movements; and those with a marked vision defect. This latter group refers to people who, even with the best corrective glasses, can only see at 20 feet what normal eyes can see at 200 feet (spoken of by physicians as $20/200$ vision).

Causes   Within the past twenty years two of the major causes of blindness in children—retrolental fibroplasia and maternal rubella, or German measles—have been overcome.

Retrolental fibroplasia—in which a white membrane forms behind the lens of the eye—was a major cause of blindness in premature babies until about 1954. At that time it was discovered that an excess of oxygen in the incubator caused the condition. Once the oxygen level was reduced, there were almost no further cases of blindness from this condition. There are still, however, in the United States today approximately 10,000 blind late adolescents and young adults, the result of this man-made condition.

German measles of the pregnant mother, another cause of blindness at birth, has largely been overcome by the use of rubella vaccine and the testing of exposed pregnant mothers to determine if they are susceptible to the disease.

Ophthalmia neonatorum, an infection

of the eyes usually caused by gonorrhea, was responsible for 30 percent of all cases of blindness during the early part of the century. This cause was almost completely removed by antiseptic drops routinely placed in the eyes of all newborn infants.

Among other rare congenital causes of blindness are congenital glaucoma (a hardening of the eyeball caused by increased pressure of the fluid within); congenital cataracts; and congenital defects of the retina. The glaucoma and cataracts can usually be treated successfully if diagnosed early, and blindness will be averted.

Unfortunately, injuries to the eyes still remain as a cause of blindness. These have been decreased with the use of unbreakable lenses and the banning of fireworks. However, prevention of eye injuries must be stressed at all times.

In 1966 almost half of all the children in residential schools for the blind in the United States were totally blind or had only light perception. The other half could only see hand movements or had sight of less than $20/200$ with the best corrective glasses.

Care and education of blind children Sight is the most important sense of an infant. He looks at objects—their color, size, and shape. He watches his parents. He thrills with excitement when his food approaches, and after a few months he recognizes his parents and gives them a special smile. He hears a sound and looks to see what causes it. The blind child has none of these exciting experiences. He is shut in by darkness.

It is a devastating experience for parents to learn that their child will never see. They often feel an unwarranted sense of guilt. But the situation becomes much more difficult for the child if the parents hold to their depression, thus depriving the infant of the full amount of attention he so desperately needs. Some parents may need guidance, help, and specific direction before they can give their blind infant the best care in their power.

First and foremost it must never be forgotten that a blind child is a child like any other, with the same needs and desires. But of necessity he is more dependent on his parents and has to be helped a great deal to develop and achieve a sense of independence. Above all, the blind infant needs more handling and love and cuddling and talking to than the sighted infant.

He begins to discover his world in the early weeks of life from sounds and from being fed and changed and talked to. At about 3 months he can be given rattles to hold. From this time on it is essential to continue giving a wide variety of objects to hold and feel. There should be things hanging above the crib to reach and find and objects hanging on the wall by the crib to be felt.

A blind child, like all children, has a great desire and need to explore and discover. When he starts to creep, usually at 9 to 11 months, he should be permitted to wander about—protected from danger but not overprotected. The child should be permitted to bump into various things and discover what he has bumped into—to gradually learn about the world around him. He soon gets to know the feel of different objects, the sounds of his world—and he tries to locate these sounds and respond to them.

Toys for blind children should be essentially the same toys used by sighted children, but with special emphasis on those that can be felt and understood, and especially those that make sounds. Large balls, rattles, and toys that make sounds by being squeezed or blown into are examples. Paper to crumple and cellophane and aluminum foil to crackle are also much enjoyed.

When a blind child reaches school age he should receive much the same education as sighted children. Formerly it was felt that schools for the blind were best, but more recently the feeling has been that blind children gain a great deal more from being in classes with sighted children. However, in most large communities there are specially trained teachers that visit the school and spend about one hour daily with each blind child, giving him specific learning instruction. In communities that do not have these facilities it may be better, if possible, to send a child away for his education.

Vocational range   During the last two years of high school, preparation should be made for the child's future life and occupation. Those who are intellectually capable should go on to college. Most legally blind children and adults have some degree of vision and they must learn to use it fully. But a great many occupations are also available to those who are totally blind. In fact, the vast majority of professional, mechanical, and business opportunities are now open to the blind person. According to the American Foundation for the Blind, of the 31,000 occupations listed in the *Dictionary of Occupational Titles*, the blind can successfully participate in 28,000. Many blind persons are successfully working as teachers, lawyers, and researchers. Electronics has opened up a large new field for the blind, many of whom have been trained as programmers. Special auditory tools have been devised for blind auto and airplane mechanics. The vocational possibilities for the blind are wide enough to suit all individual capacities.

Organizations for parents   Both parents and children benefit greatly when parents join organizations of parents with similarly handicapped children. By working together and sharing experiences they can accomplish a great deal for all blind persons, and can get and give invaluable practical and emotional support. Parents of blind children should contact the American Foundation for the Blind, 15 West 16th Street, New York, N.Y. 10011 for information.

Blindness, color   see **Color blindness.**

Blindness, night   see **Night blindness.**

Blinking   see **Tics.**

Blister
A localized collection of fluid under the skin, which is an attempt of the body to soothe an irritated area. For example, in the case of burns, the fluid is an aid in protecting the burned, sore portion of the body. Blisters should not be opened except under sterile conditions and on the advice of a doctor. If the blister is apt to get dirty or rubbed (as on the foot), keep it bandaged. If left alone and not further irritated, most blisters will dry up and open spontaneously. In the meantime a new growth of skin under the blister has taken place.

Blocked tear duct   see **Tear ducts.**

Blocks
Blocks are perhaps the most valuable and important of all children's toys.

Many kinds of blocks are used and enjoyed by children, starting from the time infants first sit up and continuing through the early school years. At each age level, blocks satisfy a different need and give great enjoyment to the child.

The sitting-up baby loves to handle and bang small blocks and is especially interested if they rattle, are colorful, or have pictures of animals and other objects on them.

The toddler enjoys carrying blocks with him from place to place and possibly piling one on another, or throwing a block to see what happens to it. At the throwing stage, sponge rubber or plastic blocks would be suitable.

Between 2 and 3, the child needs blocks of many sizes. Boys and girls begin to turn to the constructive use of blocks, attempting to build towers, houses, forts—and their constructions will become more ambitious and imaginative in the years that follow. For the older child, blocks of various shapes and sizes will give him many added opportunities to use his imagination in the development of more complicated and varied structures.

Blocks also add greatly to the enjoyment of other toys. Children make corrals for their toy animals, forts for their knights or soldiers, houses for their dolls, garages for their trucks and autos—the uses are innumerable. Few other toys can be used in so many ways in the early years.

Blood count

The determination and differentiation of the number of red and white cells in a specific volume of blood. This is undoubtedly the most frequent, if not the most important, diagnostic procedure performed on children.

The complete count can be made from a drop of blood obtained from a prick of the heel in infants and from the finger in older children. This drop of blood is placed in a special chamber where the number and type of cells in one cubic millimeter of blood can be counted. Some of the blood is also thinly smeared on a glass slide and stained so that the blood cells can be closely examined and differentiated under a microscope. A complete blood count includes measurement of the amount of coloring matter (hemoglobin) in the blood, which indicates whether a child is anemic.

The count and differentiation of the white blood cells are used in many ways. These procedures can often determine if an infection is caused by bacteria or a virus. They can rule out leukemia, infectious mononucleosis, and agranulocytosis (a lack of white blood cells). They can often indicate whether a child has an allergic reaction or a worm infection rather than a bacterial infection.

The count and examination of the red blood cells give the number of cells—a low count denoting anemia—and the shape and color of the cells. In severe anemia the shape of the cell may be distorted; in sickle-cell anemia many of the red blood cells are crescent-shaped or sickle-shaped. (See **Sickle-cell anemia.**)

The blood count also gives the number of platelets, the small particles in the blood that are responsible for clotting. If the number of platelets is inadequate, the child bleeds too easily.

The approximate normal values of a complete blood count during childhood are as follows:

Hemoglobin, 12 to 14 grams per 100 cubic centimeters of blood (sometimes referred to as 80 percent to 100 percent hemoglobin).

Red blood cells, 4,500,000 to 5,500,000 per cubic millimeter
White blood cells, 6,000 to 11,000 per cubic millimeter
Platelets, approximately 200,000 per cubic millimeter

Blood in urine   see **Urine and urinary difficulties.**

Blood types

Of the various blood-type classifications in use, the A, B, AB, and O classification is of major importance. Blood types are inherited and are not related to sex or race, although certain geographic areas and ethnic groups have statistically higher frequencies of one or another blood type. Generally, therefore, a child's blood type depends on the combination of blood types of his parents. The following combinations are some of those that are possible:

One Parent	Other Parent	Baby
A	A	A
A	O	A
B	B	B
B	O	B
A	B	AB
O	O	O

The matching of blood types for transfusions is essential; improper matching may cause clotting of the blood and death (accurate typing is relatively simple). The following table shows which types may supply blood (donors) and which may receive it (recipients):

Types	May Give Blood To	May Receive Blood From
A	A or AB	A or O
B	B or AB	B or O
AB (universal recipient)	AB only	A, B, AB or O
O (universal donor)	All	O only

Another classification of blood, Rh positive or Rh negative, is not related to blood type but is always recorded with it, as, for instance, O+ or AB− (see **Rh factor blood incompatibility.**)

Blowing the nose

A child should not be told to blow his nose until he learns how to do it properly. Instruct him to close one nostril and blow moderately. If both nostrils are held closed and the blowing is vigorous, infected material is likely to be blown into the eustachian tubes leading to the ears, and this may result in ear infections and accompanying earaches. Most children cannot learn to blow their noses properly and safely until they are 6 or 7.

Blue baby

An infant who from birth or shortly after birth has a dusky or bluish body tint, which is caused by a lack of oxygen in the blood. This lack of oxygen causes the child to be weak and to gain weight poorly, but in most cases the disorder can be corrected by modern surgery, usually performed at about age 5.

The cause of the baby's difficulty may be any one of a number of congenital defects resulting in either an inadequate amount of blood reaching the lungs to obtain oxygen or in a mixing of blue blood and red blood. (See **Heart.**)

The most common defect causing blueness is one in which there is a large opening in the thick membrane that separates the two sides of the heart, one containing blue blood returned from the body, the other containing red blood returned with oxygen from the lungs. This defect is commonly combined with a narrowing of the valve through which blood passes to the lungs.

The blueness caused by congenital cardiac defects is not to be confused with the temporary blueness sometimes occurring at or shortly after birth, which is caused by a plug of mucus in the back of the infant's throat. This can be easily removed by suction.

Blues, maternity see **Maternity blues.**

Boarding schools

Although teen-agers may benefit from the experience of boarding school, the child of elementary school age should be separated from his home environment only in exceptional circumstances. Boarding school for the younger child, who is still in great need of his parents and a home environment, should be considered only when the home is so disturbed and destructive that boarding school may offer the child a more relaxed and stable world for a period of time.

If a young child is to be sent to boarding school, a small school with warm and interested teachers should be sought. Before enrolling a child, the school should be visited and carefully investigated. It should also be close enough to home so that the child may visit every weekend if this is desired.

Attending boarding school at the high school level may be scholastically advantageous, for many boarding schools are extremely helpful in aiding a student to gain admission to a college of high rating. If parents cannot afford boarding school, however, or if it is more desirable for the youngster to remain at home, there is no reason to worry. The high academic standing of many local public schools and the new college entrance policies that make admission much easier now often provide the same opportunities for the graduates of both public and boarding school.

Boarding school, however, may have advantages other than scholastic for some youngsters. It can, for example, be a maturing experience, for going away to school gives the youngster a chance to live with those of his own age and to gain a greater degree of independence. This can be especially important for the child who lacks the companionship of others his own age at home.

The selection of a boarding school should be undertaken with careful consideration of what type of school is best suited to the individual child: small or large, coeducational or single-sex, strict or relaxed, emphasis or deemphasis on sports. The school's scholastic standing, its physical plant, and the caliber and maturity of the teachers must also be investigated thoroughly.

Many cities have private school advisory services, and some elementary and junior high schools have guidance experts who can advise on the boarding schools best suited to the individual child. *Handbook of Private Schools* (See **Bibliography**) can be helpful in making a selection.

When a boarding school is being considered the child should—if at all possible—visit it, meet some of the children attending it, and come to his own conclusions about it. Very unfortunate consequences can result if a child is sent to a boarding school that he dislikes.

Boasting

Occasional boasting is normal, and no cause for worry. But chronic boasters are generally insecure children who attempt to build themselves up in the eyes of their friends. Usually their boasts are unfounded—"My father's the strongest man in the country" or "We own three Cadillacs and have two big boats at our home in Florida." These children, striving desperately to be accepted and looked up to by their peers, exaggerate or make false boasts to gain this acceptance. Chronic boasting usually occurs during the school-age period, when the greatest desire and need of a child is to be accepted by his peers.

Boasting of this kind is usually a symptom of a child's unhappiness and every effort must be made to unearth his problems and relieve them. In this, par-

ents, teachers, and if necessary a psychotherapist should work together. The child needs additional love and reassurance.

During adolescence boasting is fairly common, not only to cover up inadequacies but to impress the opposite sex. It usually subsides as the teen-ager matures.

Body, structural changes

Many structural changes take place as a child grows from infancy through adolescence. First, there are remarkable changes in body proportions. At birth the baby's head is one-quarter the length of his body, at 2 years it is one-fifth the length, at 6 years it is one-sixth; and finally, at 15 it is one-seventh, the proportion that is stable for life.

Physical development of the female body. 1. Age ten months. 2. Age four. 3. Age seven. 4. Age eleven. 5. Age thirteen. 6. Age seventeen.

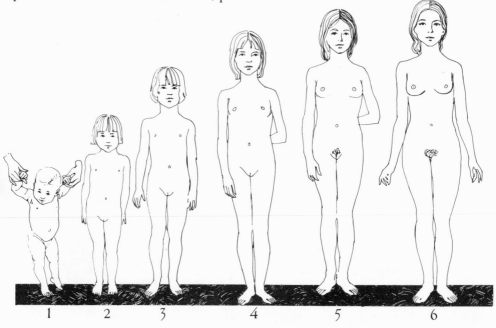

1   2   3   4   5   6

The face changes greatly in the course of a child's growth. At birth and during infancy the forehead is high and much wider than the chin, the lower jaw is small and usually receding, the nose is small and often upturned, and the eyes appear to be wide apart, for the bridge of the nose has not yet developed. As the child grows, the jaw widens and becomes more prominent; the bridge of the nose develops and during adolescence assumes its adult size and shape.

Muscle development is also significant. During infancy the muscles constitute only about a fourth of the child's weight; by about age 9 or 10, muscles constitute approximately a half of the body weight, a proportion that continues into adult life.

In both boys and girls the greatest change in body structure occurs during puberty and adolescence. Boys experience a widening of the shoulders, considerable development of the muscles, and a marked increase in the size of the penis and scrotum. The adult female contour develops with the growth of a layer of fatty tissue under the skin, the maturing of the breasts, and a widening of the hips. Both boys and girls develop hair in the pubic region and in the armpits. Boys, in addition, develop hair on the face and chest during this period.

Body measurements

Body measurements usually include height, weight, and circumference of the head and the chest.

Although each child grows at his own rate, the average measurements are as follows:

Age	Sex	Weight (lbs.)	Height (in.)	Head Circumference (in.)	Chest Circumference (in.)
Birth	Boy	7.5	19.9	14.0	13.1
	Girl	7.4	19.8	13.9	13.0
1 month	Boy	9.7	21.2	15.4	14.2
	Girl	9.0	20.7	14.7	14.1
3 months	Boy	12.6	23.8	16.1	16.0
	Girl	12.4	23.4	15.7	15.7
6 months	Boy	16.7	26.1	17.0	17.2
	Girl	16.0	25.7	16.7	16.9
9 months	Boy	20.0	28.0	18.1	18.1
	Girl	19.2	27.6	17.6	18.0
12 months	Boy	22.2	29.6	18.6	18.7
	Girl	21.5	29.2	18.1	18.5

Age	Sex	Weight (lbs.)	Height (in.)	Head Circumference (in.)	Chest Circumference (in.)
18 months	Boy	25.2	32.2	19.4	19.5
	Girl	24.5	31.8	18.5	19.2
2 years	Boy	27.7	34.4	19.7	20.0
	Girl	27.1	34.1	18.9	19.7
3 years	Boy	32.2	37.9	19.8	20.6
	Girl	31.8	37.7	19.4	20.4
4 years	Boy	36.4	40.7	20.4	21.1
	Girl	36.2	40.6	19.9	20.9
5 years	Boy	40.5	42.8	20.5	21.7
	Girl	40.5	42.9	20.3	21.4
6 years	Boy	48.3	46.3	20.6	22.1
	Girl	46.5	45.6	20.4	21.3
7 years	Boy	54.1	48.9	20.7	22.8
	Girl	52.2	48.1	20.5	22.1
8 years	Boy	60.1	51.2	20.8	23.6
	Girl	58.1	50.4	20.5	22.5
9 years	Boy	66.0	53.3	20.9	24.3
	Girl	63.8	52.3	20.6	23.5
10 years	Boy	71.9	55.2	21.0	25.1
	Girl	70.3	54.6	20.8	24.2
11 years	Boy	77.6	56.8	21.2	25.9
	Girl	78.8	57.0	20.9	25.2
12 years	Boy	84.4	58.9	21.2	26.6
	Girl	87.6	59.8	21.0	26.2
13 years	Boy	93.0	61.0	21.7	27.7
	Girl	99.1	61.8	21.6	27.0

14 years	Boy	107.6	64.0	22.2	29.4
	Girl	108.4	62.8	22.0	27.5
15 years	Boy	120.1	66.1	22.5	30.7
	Girl	113.5	63.4	22.2	27.9

Body types

Many different body types occur—tall, short, slender, broad, light-boned, heavy-boned, narrow-muscled, and broad-muscled—as well as various combinations of body types, depending largely on heredity.

It is obvious, then, that the "weight-for-age" and "height-for-age" measurements can only be an average. A normal broad-muscled, heavy-boned child of a specific age will usually weigh considerably more than a normal narrow-muscled, light-boned child of the same age. Often two perfectly healthy children of entirely different body types are found in the same family, having inherited their body structure from different forebears.

If a child is healthy in every way, no detrimental comparisons should be made. Any decision as to whether a child is too thin, too heavy, or growing too quickly or too slowly should be made by your doctor.

Body weight   see Weight.

Boils   see Abscess.

Bones, fractures   see Fractures; Fractures, first-aid treatment.

Books

Of great value and importance in the education and development of a child, books extend his world through a wealth of new information, they stimulate his imagination, teach him to understand and feel for other people, give him heroes, heroines, and ideals on which to fashion his life, and influence his character and personality.

Books suited to children of all ages are available, from the baby just sitting up to the adolescent in high school. Books for the youngest child should be made of cloth or untearable or unbreakable cardboard.

In selecting picture books for a young child, parents should look for pictures that are large, realistic, brightly and appropriately colored, and uncluttered. The story line for the young child under age 3 should be simple, with the words placed on the same page as the picture or the facing page.

The child between 1 and 2 enjoys simple stories, for reading aloud, about people with whom he's familiar (such as mommies and daddies, policemen, mailmen), animals and familiar objects, and common events in his life (such as going to the zoo, going to the doctor's office, or taking a walk). And, of course, nursery rhymes and illustrated songs are always great favorites.

The function of books for the child below nursery school age is not to provide new information but to present to him familiar objects and experiences in the world he knows, thus strengthening his understanding of that world.

Reading aloud to a child has a special

meaning for him, for it is a time of closeness to the parent and of mutual interest and discussion. It is also an excellent stimulus for learning to read. But even when children have learned to read for themselves, they still greatly enjoy having stories and books read to them by their parents.

A book should be read to the child slowly, with expression. Each picture and experience should be discussed with him, and questions should be asked relating to the pictures. As the child becomes older and the story becomes more important, too many questions and discussions may become an intrusion and unnecessary.

As children mature, their interests differ—some become avid readers, some read very few books; some love adventure stories, some love biographies and stories about heroic persons; some like books on animals, insects, birds, trees, and flowers. There are good books to satisfy all these interests.

Comic books are enjoyed by most children, but they should not and cannot take the place of good literature (see **Comic books**).

A book is always a potentially excellent gift for a child—a gift that may endure a lifetime. And no family need be limited to the books it owns. Public libraries have excellent books for children, and it is a good learning experience for the child to become familiar with using the library. Most libraries list books for children of all ages. *Children's Books of the Year*, compiled annually by the Child Study Association (see **Bibliography**), also is helpful in selecting good books.

See also **Fairy tales; Learning difficulties; Nursery rhymes; Reading readiness.**

Booster inoculations   see **Immunization schedule and tests.**

Boric acid poisoning

Boric acid solution was formerly used to clean nursing bottles, to clean the mother's breasts before nursing, and to wash the infant's eyes. Actually, boric acid has practically no value as an antiseptic and has no place in the home where there are children. When swallowed by infants or children, boric acid solution, which is colorless and looks like water, can be extremely dangerous and may even cause death. Mothers, mistaking the solution for water, have given it to their infants, and small children have made the same mistake and poisoned themselves.

Boric acid poisoning causes severe stomach upsets and if not treated, much more intense symptoms—shock, convulsions, coma—and even death.

When a child has swallowed boric acid he should be forced to vomit immediately. See **Poisons: first-aid treatment** for methods of inducing vomiting. Also call your doctor or local poison control center or take the child to a hospital for further treatment.

Bottle feeding

Although many of today's mothers feel guilty if they prefer bottle feeding to breast feeding their babies, their guilt is unwarranted. If the bottle baby's needs for affection and sucking are fulfilled, he will usually be just as healthy and happy as his breast-fed contemporary.

Bottle feeding provides more emotional satisfaction if the baby is held in a semi-upright position in the mother's arms. In this position he can be cuddled, feel the comfort of being held, and enjoy looking at the person who is giving him this pleasure. A baby left lying in a crib with a bottle propped on a pillow loses a great part of the satisfaction gained during a feeding. Moreover, when lying down, any air that is sucked in is likely to go into the intestines at the end of the stomach, often causing colic pain.

Since the baby's need for sucking will not be fulfilled by the relatively brief periods of bottle feeding, he should be allowed to suck on a pacifier.

While feeding the baby, the bottle should always be held so that the nipple is filled with formula, to avoid the baby's taking in the air in the bottle. There are various other means of minimizing the amount of air sucked in. Test the nipple to see if it has the right number of holes by turning the filled bottle upside down. The formula should slowly and steadily drip out; if it runs out too fast, the holes are too large or there are too many holes, and if it does not drip steadily, the holes are too few or too small. This can be corrected by making one or two new holes in the nipples by perforating them quickly with a red-hot needle (making new holes is much easier than enlarging the holes already there). Bottles made of collapsible plastic (Playtex, for example) prevent air from entering as the baby sucks. Nevertheless, almost all babies—whether on breast or bottle—swallow a certain amount of air during a feeding. When a baby is held during a feeding, the air forms a bubble that remains at the top of the stomach; it can usually be burped up with ease.

For equipment and sterilization of bottles, see **Formulas.**

Weaning from the bottle The ease or difficulty of weaning varies with the individual child. Many infants enjoy the sucking activity immensely, and no effort should be made to wean them until they are 18 months to 2 years old. Evidently sucking satisfaction is a physiological need, and the readiness for weaning differs with different children.

After 18 months the need gradually subsides, and usually by 2 years sucking is largely a habit rather than a need. It is then time to wean to a cup.

There are two rules to keep in mind. First, wean gradually. It may take several weeks to several months. And second, do not attempt to wean and toilet-train at the same time.

Start by giving the baby orange juice or water in a cup. Most children will take these from a cup much more readily than they will take milk. It is also advisable to use a cup that is colorful and unbreakable—one that the child will want to have as his own.

When milk is first offered, put a small amount in the cup for a single daytime feeding, gradually increasing the amount each day until the child takes at least 2 or 3 ounces. Then that one bottle can be eliminated. Some children who resist drinking from a cup will readily suck milk through a straw.

Then repeat the process for each of the other daytime feedings. The bedtime bottle is the last to be withdrawn. Once all of the bottle feedings have been discontinued they should not be started again, even though the child may be unhappy for several days.

Don't worry too much about insufficient quantities of milk being taken by the baby during the weaning period. Powdered skim milk may be added to the child's solid food, and Junket, puddings, cheese, ice cream, and milk toast can make up for the lack of milk.

See also **Breast feeding; Bubbling (burping) the baby; Feeding, self-demand; Feeding schedules.**

Bowel movements

Bowel movements normally vary in color, consistency, and frequency, depending largely on the child's age and diet. One or two loose movements a day is not diarrhea. However, when the frequency increases, and especially when large amounts of fluid are lost with each movement, your doctor should be notified. On the other hand, if the movements are constantly hard and difficult for the child to pass, the doctor may want to regulate his diet or give him a mild laxative temporarily.

During the first few days of life the bowel movement consists of a sticky dark green substance (meconium) composed primarily of mucus and bile from the liver. Once the newborn baby starts receiving milk from the breast or a formula, the color of the movement changes to brown or yellowish, with a consistency varying from slightly loose or curdy to well formed. The number of movements daily varies largely with the diet; those babies fed on the breast usually have more frequent movements (approximately four or five daily) than those receiving formulas (approximately two or three daily).

There is no need to worry if the stool is curdy and slightly loose one day and fairly firm the next day. It is of no consequence if an infant on the breast has six or seven loose stools a day as long as he seems well and relaxed and is gaining weight normally.

If there is mucus or blood in the stool your doctor should be notified. Mucus is usually a sign that the intestines are irritated by some virus or bacteria, or by a food to which the child is sensitive or allergic.

Blood in a bowel movement may have a number of causes, including severe irritation, ulceration of the mucous membrane of the stomach or intestines, an intestinal allergy, a tear in the mucous membrane of the rectum or anus, or an anal crack (anal fissure). Bright red blood in the stool usually comes from a lesion in or near the anus, such as a crack, tear, or polyp (a growth with a bleeding point). Blood from the stomach or small intestines usually colors the stool black. Bowel movements that contain blood and mucus (cranberry stools) and are accompanied by severe, intermittent abdominal pain may be caused by a serious intestinal blockage (intussusception) and should receive the immediate attention of a doctor.

Movements may also be colored red by harmless agents, by beets or red Jell-O, for example, while oral iron supplements usually color the stool black.

See also **Anal fissure; Constipation; Diarrhea; Intussusception; Soiling, chronic; Toilet training.**

Bowel training   see **Toilet training.**

Bowels   see **Intestines.**

Bowlegs
Legs that curve out from the knees. Practically every newborn baby has bowed legs, a result of the fetal position of the infant in which the legs are crossed over one another. As the bones grow and develop during the first year, practically every child's legs straighten out perfectly, and no treatment is necessary.

Bowlegs caused by a softening of the bones resulting from inadequate vitamin D—rickets—was once common but is now rare.

Some toddlers—18 months and older—who walk with their knees spread apart appear to be bowlegged. These "bowlegs" are usually a result of thick diapers that cause the thighs to be held widely apart. The child should be dressed in less bulky diapers or in training pants and plastic protective pants.

Boy Scouts see **Recreational organizations.**

Braces, dental see **Dental braces.**

Bragging see **Boasting.**

Brain, inflammation of see **Encephalitis.**

Brain, water on see **Hydrocephalus.**

Brain damage
Brain damage can have a number of causes:

Injury Examples include skull fracture and any birth injury causing bleeding within the brain or bleeding that produces pressure beneath the skull on the brain. In most instances prompt diagnosis and treatment will prevent any aftereffects, and the child will be completely normal in every way.

Lack of oxygen If the brain receives inadequate oxygen before birth or at any time thereafter, this may cause permanent damage such as cerebral palsy or mental retardation. In many cases the damage is slight—as for example, mild difficulties in perception, and with help the child can learn to overcome the problem.

Infection This includes infection of the mother during the early months of pregnancy, for example by German measles. Infections suffered by the child (for example, measles and sleeping sickness) sometimes cause inflammation of the brain (encephalitis) and permanent brain damage. Mumps encephalitis and chicken pox encephalitis are not dangerous. The virus of the smallpox vaccination may—but only very rarely—cause brain damage.

Fever Fevers over 106 or 107 degrees may be followed by brain damage, but it is not known whether the cause is the fever itself or the virus associated with the fever.

Malnutrition A protein-deficient diet in the early months and years of life can limit brain development, causing permanent damage.

Jaundice of the newborn In this condition, which is usually caused by a blood incompatibility between mother and infant (see **Rh factor blood incompatibility**), there is excess bile pigment (bilirubin) in the blood. There must be close supervision to prevent an excessive rise of bilirubin, which may be absorbed into the brain, causing damage. The danger exists only for newborn infants, who have not yet developed a barrier to the absorption of bilirubin. With treatment, this danger can usually be averted.

Toxic substances Certain toxic substances can cause brain damage. The most common problem of this type is lead poisoning. (See **Lead poisoning.**)

A diagnosis of brain damage does not necessarily mean, however, that a child will have severe aftereffects which will prevent him from having an active and productive life and becoming self-sufficient. The prognosis varies according to the degree of brain injury and the location of the injury. For example, many children having mild brain injury with signs of cerebral dysfunction outgrow the condition during adolescence. Other children with cerebral palsy may have brilliant minds, go through college, and enter professions. Still others may have mild mental retardation but are capable of being educated and trained for worthwhile positions that will make them self-supporting.

See also **Mental retardation.**

Brain dysfunction, mild

Also called minimal brain dysfunction, minimal brain damage, mild brain damage, mild cerebral dysfunction. In recent years these very general terms have come to be used with a fairly specific reference to a pattern of symptoms believed to be caused or partially caused by a relatively slight disorder in brain function or structure. The cluster of symptoms occurs fairly commonly in childhood and includes one or more of the following:

1. Hyperactive and disordered behavior; restless activity without clear direction; shifting from one activity to another every few moments.
2. Short attention span; inability to concentrate; difficulty in finishing any task.
3. Rapid changes in moods and emotions; sudden outbursts of rage, grief, or aggressiveness.
4. Impulsiveness and often destructiveness; lack of self-restraint or control.
5. Poor muscular development and/or poor coordination.
6. Poor social development; difficulties getting along with other children.
7. Dyslexia: perceptual difficulties (may see letters or numbers reversed or have difficulty recognizing letters and words or numbers); impaired visual memory (difficulty in remembering material that is read); impaired auditory memory (difficulty in remembering what is heard); poor handwriting, including a tendency toward mirror writing.

These symptoms need not all be present; for example, perceptual problems may be predominant or hyperactivity may be marked while perception is normal. The child may have a low intelligence, but usually intelligence is normal or high.

The diagnosis may be difficult. It depends upon neurological testing and also testing to rule out other possible causes of the child's difficulty, such as emotional disturbance or some other physical disorder. The signs of brain dysfunction, such as a variation from normal in electroencephalographic tracings, may be absent or so minimal that details of the patient's history (whether there were difficulties during birth, for example) are needed to support the diagnosis. In many cases, perceptual difficulties may indicate brain dysfunction even though the electroencephalogram readings are normal.

The case history may reveal the probable cause of the disorder. Often it appears that the cause is a temporary lack of oxygen supplied to the child's brain either before, during, or just after birth. In some cases perceptual difficulties appear to run in families, and there may be some slight hereditary change in brain function.

Treatment is of the symptoms only. Among markedly hyperactive and easily distractible children drug therapy (which is entirely safe and not habit-forming), perhaps in conjunction with psychotherapy and special tutoring, may be indicated. Drug therapy reduces the hyperactivity, decreases distractibility, and increases the attention span. (See **Hyperactivity.**) When perceptual difficulties are marked, special training may be needed to help the child work with symbols and words. (See **Dyslexia.**) The drug therapy should be closely supervised by a doctor. There is still much to be learned regarding brain function and diagnosis of neurological disorders, and the best guard against mistakes in any individual case is to follow the child closely to be sure that he is actually being helped by the treatment and that no undesirable side effects occur.

With treatment the outlook is good. Thousands of children who have been previously written off as too disturbed or too unintelligent to succeed in school have rapidly improved and done as well as, or much better than, average. Most children outgrow the condition in early adolescence.

Breast development

Breast development, which starts normally between age 9 and 15, usually begins with a slightly tender nodule forming beneath the nipple, with the breast gradually increasing in size for the next year or two. Often one breast develops for some months before the other begins to develop. This is quite normal. Where there is considerable enlargement of the breasts, red streaks appear on the side of the breasts, resulting from the stretching of the skin and the underlying tissue. In time the redness fades and becomes silvery and the streaks become hardly noticeable.

Many boys in early adolescence also develop nodules under their nipples. These may be somewhat sore for a while, and the boy may think he was bruised while playing. The nodules are perfectly normal and no cause for concern, and they disappear in a few months.

Breast feeding

Most modern pediatricians feel strongly that if a mother can nurse her baby and wants to nurse him, she should definitely do it. For although artificial formulas today are almost the equal of breast milk in caloric value and in the

A two-piece suit worn with a sweater or blouse is convenient for nursing the baby.

proportion of nutrients and minerals, there are deep emotional values in breast feeding, for mothers who enjoy it, which cannot be duplicated by bottle feeding.

There is a very warm relationship between a mother and her nursing infant—a closeness and relaxation—and a great satisfaction for the mother in knowing that she is responsible for her baby's development and well-being. No mother who wishes to nurse should ever be discouraged from doing so by doctors, nurses, or even her husband. Mothers who do not know if they want to nurse or not should always be encouraged to try. In most instances they will enjoy the experience.

However, breast feeding is of real advantage over bottle feeding only if the nursing is mutually satisfying to both mother and baby. A mother who reacts strongly against nursing or who does not enjoy nursing should not do it. There are a few mothers whose permanently inverted nipples make it impossible or almost impossible for the infant to nurse without great difficulty. In such rare instances it is better to feed the baby by bottle. The same is true if the mother's nipples become cracked or the breasts become abscessed, causing her severe pain. Also, there are many working mothers whose jobs make it impossible for them to nurse more than the first few weeks. Women who wish to nurse but cannot for various reasons should realize that their infants will do very well on the bottle if the time spent with their mothers is enjoyable and satisfying and the relationship loving and close.

Preparation of the breasts for nursing Breasts should be prepared for nursing from approximately the fourth month of pregnancy until the birth of the baby.

The primary effort should be to assure that the nipples will be sufficiently elongated so that the infant will have no difficulty sucking on them. This is of particular importance when nipples are small or retracted. Every day the mother-to-be should pull out each nipple and roll it between her thumb and forefinger about ten or twelve times. She should not become discouraged if she thinks her nipples are too small, since the nursing itself tends to elongate them considerably.

The next effort is to prepare the nipples so that they will be able to withstand the nursing process without pain and without the suffering of cracked nipples. For cracked nipples cause severe pain on nursing and are the most frequent cause of mothers discontinuing breast feeding.

Toughening the nipples should begin when the mother is approximately six months pregnant. One of the methods used is to rub each nipple daily with a wet terry-cloth washcloth, starting with ten rubs daily and increasing every few days until the breasts are rubbed fifty times daily. Then the breasts are rubbed instead with a dry bath towel, again starting with ten rubs each and increasing up to fifty times daily. After each rubbing, a light oil or white cocoa butter should be applied to the nipples to keep them soft. Oil or cold cream applied to the area around the nipple will also aid in keeping the skin soft and pliable.

Care of the breasts during the nursing period A nursing brassiere—one that supports the breasts from the bottom and sides, and does not compress the nipples—should be used during the nursing period. These brassieres can be opened for nursing and usually have a pocket in which a cotton pad may be inserted to absorb any dripping milk.

Breasts should be washed daily with a soft, wet cloth from the nipple to the outside of the surrounding pigmented area. Very little, if any, soap should be used, since most soaps are drying and may cause cracking of the nipples. Masse cream or some preparation recommended by the doctor should be applied after each nursing to keep the nipple soft and to prevent cracking.

Position of the baby while nursing Holding the baby semi-upright is advisable, for if the baby is fed lying down, the air sucked in while nursing will pass through the end of the stomach and into the intestines, often causing colic pains. When the infant is held upright, the air bubble is at the top of the stomach above the milk that has been swallowed and, as a rule, is easily bubbled or "burped" up and out. (See **Bubbling [burping] the baby.**)

Nursing the baby   During the first three days after birth, when colostrum is being secreted (see **Colostrum**), the infant should be placed on the breasts for five minutes each side at each feeding time. After the third or fourth day, when the milk has come in, the baby may be placed fifteen minutes on the first breast and about twenty-five minutes on the second breast, alternating the side of the first breast at each nursing. It is rarely necessary to nurse more than forty-five minutes at any feeding.

During the first week of life, the baby should be fed on a self-demand or modified self-demand schedule. (See **Feeding schedules; Feeding, self-demand**.) Often a newborn will nurse ten to twelve times daily during the first week, cutting down gradually until, at the end of the second week, the average baby feeds only six or seven times daily—eventually working into approximately a four-hour schedule.

A nursing mother should be aware that the more a baby is nursed and the more stimulation the breasts receive through nursing, the more milk will the breasts secrete. For this reason it is best for nursing mothers not to bottle-feed at all during the first few weeks so that the breasts will be fully stimulated to supply an adequate amount of milk. Thereafter, bottle feeding may be done as convenient; and it is advisable for the baby to have some experience in using the bottle (a "relief bottle"), in case breast feeding should become impossible for any reason, even temporarily.

The relief bottle can be of mother's milk or formula. Given only once or twice a week, a relief bottle will not interfere with the flow of breast milk or with the infant's desire to take the breast. Unless a baby is accustomed to an occasional bottle, he may strongly resist any sudden break in breast feeding.

The relief bottle can be one of the commercially prepared formulas, already sterilized and bottled; it can be a commercially prepared powdered formula, or a simple formula of 4 ounces of whole milk, 2 ounces of water, and 2 teaspoons of sugar. If the formula is made ahead of time, the bottle and nipple should be sterilized. (See **Formulas**.)

One excellent method of assuring an adequate production of milk is by an old process, "stripping the breasts"— emptying the breasts by manual expression, which for some reason or other is rarely used today. The mother washes her hands and places her thumb just above the areola (the brown area surrounding the nipple) and her forefinger beneath the breast. Then the fingers are gently pressed toward one another and down toward the end of the nipple. The mother continues to express the milk in this way until only a drop appears with each expression, with a limit of fifteen minutes each time. This is only performed with the first breast used, after each feeding. After three weeks there is usually no further need to express the remaining milk following a feeding, for the baby is, as a rule, strong enough at that time to empty the breast himself. The expressed milk may be used for the relief bottles. It should be kept in the refrigerator in a sterile bottle. Remember that it must go directly into a sterile container. (For methods of sterilization see **Formulas**.)

Is the baby gaining adequately?   When a baby is being breast-fed, the mother usually has no idea how much milk the baby takes at each feeding. And so she often wonders if the baby is receiving enough and if he is gaining adequately.

Some mothers have infant scales at home and weigh the baby every day or every other day.

This frequent weighing is a mistake, for only too often, if an infant's gain is inadequate from the mother's point of view, the mother feels incapable of supplying enough milk. Since breast feeding is so largely dependent upon the mother's state of mind, the milk supply is usually reduced when a mother worries that she cannot provide sufficient milk for her infant. At the most, infants should be weighed once a week or, better still, once a month at the doctor's office. The average gain in weight of a breast-fed baby is five to seven ounces a week.

At times the child's doctor may wish to determine just how much milk a child is obtaining from the breasts. To make this determination he has the mother weigh the infant before and after each breast feeding (without changing the diapers between weighings) for at least five feedings. This number of determinations is necessary, for the amount taken by the baby varies. At one feeding an infant may take three ounces of breast milk, while at the next he may take six ounces. The doctor determines the average amount received and will advise the mother if steps are needed to increase her supply of milk.

The mother's diet during the breast-feeding period A nursing mother can, as a rule, follow a full, well-balanced diet. Although milk is an excellent food for a lactating mother, it is not essential. A mother taking six to eight glasses of water daily with a good general diet will produce an adequate supply of nutritious breast milk for her infant. The mother should also take multivitamins and iron.

Fruits should be limited if they tend to make the milk laxative. The same should be said for laxative drugs such as cascara or milk of magnesia. Cigarette smoking should also be limited to half a pack a day at the most.

If there is a high degree of allergy in the family, many pediatricians advise that commonly allergenic foods, such as oranges, eggs, and tomatoes, be limited if not eliminated from a mother's diet until the infant is at least 6 months old.

How many months of breast feeding? This depends largely on the mother's own desire—within limitations. Some mothers say that they wish to nurse until a baby takes milk happily from the cup. However, this plan is subject to the needs of the individual baby. Some infants have a sucking need that is a drive for only seven months, while others desire to suck rather than drink for almost two years. The sucking needs of babies vary greatly from one child to another.

Most mothers want to nurse their infants for seven or eight months, but some mothers say they want to nurse until the child rejects the breast. Experience has proven that this is not feasible, for some children on this plan have demanded breast feeding until approximately age 4. The baby should be taken off the breast at the latest at age 2, for at this time the sucking need has disappeared in practically all infants. Further breast feeding would only be indulgence and would tend to keep the child infantile. The breast can be taken away gradually, leaving the night feeding as the last to be removed.

The 2-year-old child, withdrawn from the breast, may be upset for several days but adjusts very quickly.

Discontinuing breast feedings The switch from breast feeding to bottle feeding must be done gradually, not only for the sake of the baby but for the sake of the mother as well. Removing the breast feedings too abruptly may cause severe pain to the mother, whose breasts will become distended with milk.

A typical plan of switching from breast to bottle for a young infant, with three-day intervals between changes, is shown at the bottom of the page.

When the breast feedings are discontinued, the mother should wear a tight brassiere and cut down on her intake of fluids for two days. Usually by this method weaning is easily accomplished without causing her pain.

Mothers who wish to know more about breast feeding should write for literature to the La Leche League, an organization dedicated to the encouragement of breast feeding. Its headquarters are in Franklin Park, Ill., and it has branches in most large cities.

Breath see **Bad breath.**

Breath-holding
This is a result of anger or fright, and it is fairly common among infants and young children up to age 4 or 5. Typically, the child is crying angrily, and then holds his breath. Or he may be startled by the sudden appearance of someone or something, or by a fall, a bump on the head, or the like—and hold his breath.

Breath-holding does no harm, although the child may hold his breath long enough to turn blue or (in rare cases) briefly lose consciousness or convulse. (See **Convulsions.**)

The only way to prevent or shorten an attack of breath-holding would be to protect the child from loud sounds and anything painful or frightening, thus eliminating his need to cry, which is, of course, impossible. The effort, which would involve excessive coddling, would be upsetting to the child and undermine the parents' authority. If parents attempt to treat breath-holding in this manner, they will soon observe that their child has learned very quickly that

Weaning Schedule:

Feeding hours:	6 A.M.	10 A.M.	2 P.M.	6 P.M.	10 P.M.
At start	Breast	Breast	Breast	Breast	Breast
First step	Breast	Breast	Breast	Bottle	Breast
Second step	Breast	Bottle	Breast	Bottle	Breast
Third step	Bottle	Bottle	Breast	Bottle	Breast
Fourth step	Bottle	Bottle	Bottle	Bottle	Breast
Fifth step	Bottle	Bottle	Bottle	Bottle	Bottle

by starting to cry and holding his breath he can have his own way.

Breathing see **Bronchial tree; Diaphragm; Lungs; Respiratory tract.**

Breathing difficulties see **Asthma; Breath-holding; Bronchiolitis; Croup; Hyaline membrane disease; Pneumonia.**

Breathing in foreign objects see **Foreign objects, inhalation of.**

Breathing through the mouth

Air passing through the nose is moistened, warmed, and somewhat filtered of dirt and dust. Air breathed through the mouth, especially during the winter months, is likely to be dry and often cold. The drying of the mucous membranes of the throat and breathing tubes, and probably the cold air as well, makes them more susceptible to infections.

Most children breathe through their mouths temporarily when the mucous membrane of the nose is swollen and the nasal passages are filled with mucus as a result of a cold or an allergy. When mouth breathing is chronic, it is almost always caused by large adenoids that obstruct the normal air passages behind the nose, a chronic allergy that swells up the mucous membrane folds of the nose, or a protruding upper jaw that keeps the mouth constantly open.

Mouth breathing can be cured by attacking the cause—removal of the adenoids, allergic treatment, or orthodontics.

Breech delivery

The birth of a baby with the buttocks, rather than the head, coming out of the mother's body first. It occurs in a little over 4 percent of all births.

One potential difficulty of a breech birth is that the opening at the bottom of the uterus is not dilated as perfectly as when the round top of the head is pushed through. There is a greater chance of a tear of the vagina and a greater chance of over-pulling on the infant's neck in an attempt to bring out the head, which may stretch or tear some of the nerves going to the arms. With good obstetrical care, however, serious difficulties are now much rarer.

Bribes and rewards

Giving a child a gift or money or making promises in order to get him to do something or behave well is rarely of permanent disciplinary value. Children who are frequently bribed soon learn to take advantage and exact bribes at every opportunity. At times, however, a bribe may help a child overcome some specific and not too strong fear or anxiety, such as a fear of sitting on the toilet.

Rewards are somewhat different. They are given without strings attached for something well done. An occasional reward can do no harm if the child doesn't come to expect to be rewarded for every accomplishment.

Neither bribes nor rewards should be given in connection with routine activities. For example, a child should be responsible for a share of the household chores without being bribed or rewarded for doing his jobs. But special consideration may be given if the child makes a special effort—for example, if he volunteers to help clean out the attic.

When a child's prime motivation for achievement is to get some material reward, he is not learning to take satisfaction from the value of his accomplishment and he is not developing a sense of personal responsibility. Problems usually lie ahead.

For most children the most meaningful reward is parental interest in and approval of their behavior and activities.

Bright child see **Intelligence, exceptional.**

Broken bone see **Fractures; Fractures, first-aid treatment.**

Broken home see **Divorce.**

Bronchial tree
The branched structure leading from the main breathing tube (the trachea) into the air sacs (alveoli) of the lungs. From each side of the trachea a large bron-

Bronchial tree: 1. Trachea (main breathing tube). 2. Bronchi. 3. Bronchioles. 4. Lung. Detail in circle shows the bronchioles branching into the alveoli (5), or air cells of the lungs.

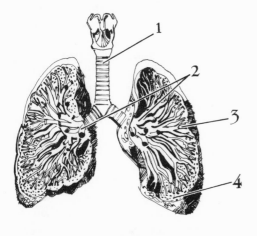

chus leads toward the lungs. These tubes subdivide into smaller bronchi, which subdivide into the tiny bronchioles going into the air sacs.

Bronchiectasis
A dilation of the smaller tubes of the bronchial tree, caused by a chronic infection in the tubes that penetrates the walls and destroys the muscles and elastic tissue surrounding the tubes. With the constricting elastic tissue badly weakened or destroyed, the tube dilates permanently and becomes a receptacle for infected mucus and pus. This condition can only be completely diagnosed by a bronchogram, an X-ray of the affected tube taken after an opaque liquid is instilled into it.

Bronchiectasis is much less common today than it was thirty or forty years ago, probably as a result of the almost complete eradication of whooping cough and measles. It still occurs as a complication of tuberculosis, asthma, and chronic bronchitis.

Treatment includes antibiotic therapy, postural draining (the child leans over the side of the bed so that the mucus drains by gravity), and pounding on the chest during postural draining. The surgical removal of the affected portion of the lung is necessary for a complete cure.

Bronchiole see **Bronchial tree.**

Bronchiolitis
An acute inflammation of the smaller branches of the bronchial tree occurring primarily during the first year of life. Usually the result of virus, the infection causes a swelling of the inner lining of the tubes and produces mucus as well. Since an infant's tubes are so small, they are easily blocked, and extremely rapid

respiration results. Those infants most severely affected have a bluish color.

The doctor may prescribe antibiotics or may recommend that the infant be moved to a hospital in order to receive extra oxygen and humidified air. The severe difficulty in breathing usually lasts only a day or two, subsiding rapidly, and recovery is almost always complete within seven to ten days.

Bronchitis
An inflammation of the bronchial tubes, usually following an infection of the nose and throat. It may be caused by bacteria, viruses, or the inhalation of irritating substances (such as smoke, acid fumes, smog) or allergenic substances; it may be acute or chronic. One form of bronchitis very frequent in children is allergic bronchitis, an asthmatic reaction to bacteria or a substance (usually inhaled or eaten) to which the child is sensitive.

Bronchitis produces a persistent cough, dry and irritative at first but usually loosening with the production of sputum.

Treatment depends entirely upon the cause of the condition and should be under the supervision of a doctor.

See also **Colds; Coughs.**

Bronchopneumonia   see **Pneumonia.**

Bronchus   see **Bronchial tree.**

Brownies   see **Recreational organizations.**

Bruises
Injuries caused by the breaking of tiny blood vessels (capillaries) just below the surface of the skin. The broken vessels ooze blood into the surrounding tissue, producing the bluish discoloration known as a bruise.

Some children, especially those who are very active, have a greater tendency to get bruises than others. If bruises occur only on the arms and legs they are usually of little significance, since these areas are naturally and frequently bruised in the normal course of play. However, if bruises appear over the body as well, the child's blood, coagulation time, and capillary strength should be investigated immediately by a doctor.

Bubbling (burping) the baby
Patting the baby's back to bring up a bubble of gas from the stomach. Most infants swallow a certain amount of air while sucking on the breast or the bottle. This air is taken into the stomach with the milk. If it remains in the stomach it may later cause the baby to regurgitate a great deal of milk as the air bubble forces it way up and out of the baby's body; or it may pass down into the intestines, causing colic pains.

Most infants need to be bubbled at least once in the course of feeding and again when the feeding has been completed. The most usual method is to hold the baby upright against your shoulder, which should be covered with a diaper for protection. Pat the baby firmly on the back (faint taps or rubbing are not as effective). Some babies bubble better if placed face down over the knee and patted. Some bubble better if held up in a sitting position and patted.

Some babies do not burp as much as others—they suck in less air when nursing.

See also **Bottle feeding.**

Three positions for bubbling the baby.

Bugs see **Bee stings; Insect and spider bites.**

Bullying

Among children of all ages, there are some who regularly pressure, browbeat, and even hurt other children. The bully may be male or female, and often the bullying seems to be done for no clear gain—except to establish that the bully is boss.

Strangely enough, the bully is almost always an insecure, anxious child unable to make his place among other children in a normal way. He doesn't know how to get along with other children. He feels unsure and inadequate and attempts to overcome this feeling by his bossiness. He is afraid that if he loses control the other children will boss him and overpower him.

Treatment of this asocial condition is primarily the parents' responsibility, although the cooperation of the child's teacher can be extremely helpful.

First, the parents should explain to the child that such aggressiveness is resented by others—and that they, his parents, do not like it either.

Second, and perhaps most important, they should give their youngster a great deal of love and genuine affection. They must reassure him of his worth by doing everything they can to make him feel that he is somebody.

Third, they should do everything in their power to help him to be accepted by other children by encouraging friendships and attempting to nip in the bud any excessive bossiness during play. It is best to invite only one companion over at a time so that the child can learn to form a friendship in a normal way.

Putting such a child in a group of older children often helps to curb bullying tendencies, but by itself this tactic will not overcome the child's anxieties or teach him how to establish normal relationships. He will still need the help of his parents, teachers, and possibly even the aid of a guidance counselor.

See also **Aggressiveness; Sadism.**

Burn

An injury produced by fire, heat, or a chemical on the surface of the skin or deeper. Burns are usually classified by their seriousness. First-degree burns make the skin reddened and sore, as in a typical sunburn, and leave no scars. Second-degree burns cause blisters to form, and usually leave no scars. Third-degree burns involve deep tissue beneath the skin, usually destroy the tissue above, and result in scar formation.

It is often difficult to estimate the seriousness of a burn or to judge how deep it is. The doctor should be advised of any burn that is at all extensive or causes persistent pain.

If burns cover more than one-tenth of the child's body he should be hospitalized. Hospitalization is also advised if the burn is deep and may cause scarring. Deep burns at the elbows and behind the knees should be under the care of a doctor, for scar tissue may form, contract, and cause a permanent bend of the arm or leg joint.

Treatment   The first treatment of burns is to apply cold water—ice is even better—to the child's skin. This often prevents blistering if the burn is not too severe. It also greatly relieves the pain. Then apply a nonoily burn ointment, such as Furacin (nitrofurazone). Keep the burn covered at least three or four days before changing the dressing to prevent infection, for every time the burn is exposed it may become infected from bacteria in the air. A blister over a burn should not be touched. It will usually rupture by itself in a few days, but until that time the fluid in it serves as a cushion and protection for the denuded skin underneath. Once the blister breaks, the dead skin will dry and come off by itself when the burn is healed.

Burping see **Belching; Bubbling (burping) the baby.**

C

Calcium see **Nutrition.**

Calorie
An energy unit of food capable of raising the temperature of one gram of water one degree centigrade. Some foods, of course, have more calories, or potential energy, than others. Cake, for example, is high in calories, whereas melons are low in calories. If the calories from food are not used up, they are stored in the fat cells of the body. Dieting for the reduction of weight in children depends in large part on a reduction in calorie intake, and efforts to increase a child's weight are usually directed at increasing the calorie intake. (See **Dieting; Obesity; Appendix B: Calorie Chart.**)

Normally active boys and girls of different age levels require different amounts of calories daily for the maintenance of good nutrition. The Food and Nutrition Board of the National Research Council has listed the following as the necessary caloric requirements for the various age groups:

    4 to 6 years—1,700 calories
    7 to 9 years—2,100 calories
    10 to 12 years—2,500 calories
    13 to 15 years—3,100 calories (boys)
                         2,600 calories (girls)

However, caloric needs also vary according to how active a child is, whether he has a heavy or light build, and other factors. So any change in diet to lose or gain weight should be undertaken only after consultation with the child's doctor about his or her particular needs.

Camp Fire Girls see **Recreational organizations.**

Camphor poisoning see **Poisons: first-aid treatment.**

Camps
Each year many parents give considerable thought toward planning a worthwhile summer for their children. They may consider a farm, the seashore, traveling, or a summer camp. In the selection a great deal depends on the child's age. Either a day camp or a farm experience is wonderful for a young child, and traveling provides an ideal summer for boys and girls of 15 and older. But for most boys and girls of approximately 8 to 14 a good summer sleep-away camp probably offers the richest and most rewarding experience. The summer camp is essentially a child's world with many companions of the same age and interests. The activities offer children numerous outlets for their interests and energy, and typically include team games, arts and crafts, swimming, boating, dancing, dramatics, nature studies, canoe trips, and mountain climbing.

Among the less expensive camps, where children usually spend only part of the summer, are the Scout camps and organization camps such as those run by the YMCA, settlement houses, and religious and charitable groups.

There are specialized camps concentrating on boating and sailing, fishing, tennis, music, nature, dramatics, dancing, and horseback riding. There are also camps for overweight children and children with learning problems. (See **Camps for the handicapped.**)

For children in the early teens, approximately 13 to 16, there are good work camps where boys and girls take part in constructive programs of building, farming, caring for farm animals, playing in orchestras, photography, painting, dramatics, ceramics, dancing, and other activities of special interest to their age level.

Some children, especially older children, may have their own ideas about where they want to go to camp. They may want to be with a particular friend or to attend one of the specialized camps. This certainly makes it easier for the parent, since all he need do is investigate the one camp under consideration. Younger children, especially those who have not been to camp before, will usually not have such a strong preference and may be somewhat fearful of the idea. In addition to looking for a responsible camp that the child will enjoy, the parent should consider the advantage of having the child go with friends he knows and who are enthusiastic about going to camp. Often siblings can be sent to the same camp. Familiar company often eases the transition.

A summer camp for a child should be selected not on the basis of a beautiful brochure with attractive pictures, but by the character, background, and experience of the camp director and the maturity of his counsellors. Adequate facilities for the child's health, such as an infirmary with a full-time nurse and a doctor readily available, are also of primary importance. The area in which the camp is located is a factor if a child is allergic to pollens of grasses, weeds, or trees.

The day camp has become more and more popular in recent years, especially for children between the ages of 4 and 8. The youngsters are picked up at their homes and transported by car or bus to the camp, where there are facilities for swimming, sports, arts and crafts, and nature study. The children receive their lunch, followed by a rest period. After a day of varied activities the children are returned home in the late afternoon.

Such day camps, if well organized and well staffed, are ideal for children who are as yet too young to leave their parents and go to sleep-away camps. Before choosing a day camp for a child, however, the father or mother should visit the camp to observe its facilities, should meet the camp director and the child's potential counselor, and should see that the camp is not too far away—a ride no more than thirty to forty minutes—since a long ride is often quite fatiguing for young children.

See also **Farm camps and farm vacations; Homesickness.**

Camps for the handicapped

There are many camps throughout the United States organized specifically for the handicapped child. Among these are camps for children with arthritis, rheumatism, asthma, blindness, brain damage, cardiac disorders, cerebral palsy, diabetes, emotional disturbances, epilepsy, mental retardation, physical disability, speech or hearing defects, and visual impairments.

The *Directory of Camps for the Handicapped* may be obtained by writing to the American Camping Association, 342 Madison Avenue, New York, N.Y. 10017. The cost is $1.00.

Cancer

Any malignant overgrowth of tissue or cells which tends to spread through the body. Cancer is comparatively rare in children with the exception of leukemia, Hodgkin's disease, and tumors of the kidney.

See also **Hodgkin's disease; Leukemia; Neuroblastoma; Wilms' tumor.**

Candy and chewing gum

Candy and chewing gum and other sweets are loved by almost all children. This desire is natural and should be satisfied, but with special care, because sugar tends to cause decay and cavities in teeth. Sugar may also spoil the appetite, so sweets should not be taken too soon before a meal.

It is much better to give a child fruit instead of candy. Fruits that are particularly liked by children are raisins, grapes, figs, dates, apples, pears, bananas, and cherries.

If candy is necessary—and occasionally it is because other children get it— then it is best given at the end of a meal or on special occasions. Also, there are numerous sweets that do not contain either sugar or cyclamates. Examples are Estee's Lollipops and Trident Chewing Gum.

An occasional piece of candy or chewing gum will do no harm. It is the frequent use that is damaging to teeth. Try not to keep chewing gum or candy around the home—it's too tempting.

Canker sores

Very painful white ulcers of the mucous membrane of the mouth. They appear as white patches on the inside of the lips and cheeks, or on the gums and tongue, and they are usually caused by a reaction to a virus or a food allergy. Canker sores are sometimes referred to as a type of herpes simplex.

The condition is best treated by the application of Glyoxide, a carbamide peroxide preparation. It should be applied on a cotton swab to the affected areas four times a day, or applied directly from the squeeze bottle. Small amounts may be swallowed without ill effects. This preparation relieves the pain, cleans the affected area, and also prevents the growth there of bacteria and fungi.

The sucking of numbing lozenges, often used for relieving the pain of sore throats, will also temporarily relieve the pain of canker sores.

Car see **Automobiles and adolescents; Automobile travel with children.**

Car seats see **Automobile travel with children.**

Car sickness see **Motion sickness.**

Carbohydrates see **Nutrition.**

Carbon monoxide poisoning

A very serious poisoning caused by the inhalation of carbon monoxide—a colorless, odorless, poisonous gas. This type of poisoning most usually results from a child's breathing in gas from an unlit but open tap on a stove or heater, or from inhaling the exhaust fumes of an auto.

The first symptoms are generally not recognized, for they consist of drowsiness and a headache, usually accompanied by dizziness and a faint feeling. If one continues to breathe in the carbon monoxide, lethargy increases and is followed by stupor, coma, convulsion, and death.

Carbon monoxide is dangerous because when inhaled it is taken up by the red corpuscles in the blood in the place of the oxygen they normally carry. Carbon monoxide clings to the red blood corpuscles, and the more it saturates the blood, the less oxygen is carried to the brain and other parts of the body.

Treatment

1. Move the child immediately from exposure to carbon monoxide.
2. If child is in coma, try to get emergency aid immediately, for he should be treated with a respirator as soon as possible. If there are two persons present, one should begin mouth-to-mouth resuscitation immediately and the other should call the police emergency number (usually 911) or the local poison-control center for help. Give name, location, and make it clear that the child is suffering from carbon monoxide poisoning. If you are alone, and the child is not breathing, begin artificial respiration at once.
3. When the child is in the care of a doctor, he will be placed in a respirator. Blood-replacement transfusions will be given as soon as possible to remove the damaged red blood cells and replace them with normal red blood cells capable of taking up and circulating oxygen.

See also **Mouth-to-mouth resuscitation.**

Carbon tetrachloride (Carbona) poisoning   see **Poisons: first-aid treatment.**

Cardiac disease   see **Heart disease.**

Cardiac defects   see **Blue baby; Heart murmur.**

Career, guiding children toward

Many parents have ambitious futures planned for their children. Often these parents wish to satisfy an unfulfilled desire they themselves had when young—sometimes for reasons of personal pride, sometimes in an attempt to better the family socially or economically.

In many instances this pressure on a child can be very upsetting, and at times it can be disastrous. But there are ways by which parents can aim children in the direction of certain careers or other attainments without hurting them. This can be attempted, often with some degree of success, by subtly encouraging a child's interests in a particular field.

If a child develops and shows a special interest or quality suiting him for a particular worthwhile profession or activity, he should receive the support, praise, and interest of his parents, but no real pressure. Pressure can produce a negative reaction and blunt or destroy an interest. It is often helpful, to arrange for special lessons or courses or to buy special equipment, but parents must constantly make sure that these are truly welcomed by the child. A child's direction toward a profession should satisfy his own interests primarily, rather than those of his parents. And a parent should take care that in his effort to develop a child's ability, he is not keeping him from normal and adequate relationships with other children, and the normal interests of the growing child.

See also **Intelligence, exceptional; Talent, exceptional.**

Caries, dental   see **Tooth decay.**

Carriage

A baby carriage is not a necessity, but it is a great convenience for the mother in caring for her infant in the first year or so. Carriages are particularly helpful for the city mother who wants her baby to have plenty of outdoor sunshine and (hopefully) fresh air, and who herself enjoys outings to the park where there are other mothers with infants and children.

In recent years many mothers have made use of back or side slings to carry their babies from place to place on shopping tours and other excursions. These are very handy, especially for short trips, but do not take the place of a carriage or stroller and may be fatiguing to a mother when the child begins to double and triple its weight. It may be easier for the father to carry the heavier child in the sling.

During outings in the carriage, the baby will at first sleep most of the time, but within a few months he will begin to enjoy the carriage trips for the new experiences they bring him. Once the child is sitting up he can have a full view of the world around him: other children, autos, dogs and cats, trees and flowers, store windows, and people dressed in different clothing and different colors. The outdoor walk with the child sitting in the carriage brings him a wealth of stimulation.

It is important to strap the baby in the carriage once he is able to sit up—and especially once he is able to pull himself up and stand.

For safety, a carriage must be sturdy enough not to topple if a baby climbs or moves around in it. The wheels should be large enough so that going up and down curbs can be managed easily. The carriage should come with a harness or be equipped for attaching one. It should have a good safety brake. It should be roomy enough that the baby will be able to lie down comfortably throughout the first year. It should be high enough from the ground to protect the baby from being spattered by passing cars or getting covered with dust from the street.

See also **Stroller.**

CAT   see **Tests.**

Cat scratch disease
A virus disease caused by the scratch or bite of a cat. The cats that transmit the disease are entirely well and show no evidence of any illness. A person affected with cat scratch diesase is not contagious.

The signs and symptoms appear between ten and thirty days after a child is scratched by a cat. There is general malaise, headache, a low-grade fever, and usually a large swelling of the lymph nodes near the area of the scratch. At the height of the signs and symptoms a red pimple appears at the site of the scratch and persists for several days. The child, as a rule, does not feel very ill and the signs and symptoms subside in a few days, except for the enlarged lymph nodes, which may remain enlarged for several months.

Although some cat lovers deny the existence of cat scratch disease, it has been proven to be a specific entity not only by skin tests made from gland material which are positive only in those who have had the condition, but also by the fact that extracts of the glands injected into men and monkeys cause the disease.

This disease is not sufficiently serious or common to warrant denying a child the pleasure of having a kitten or cat in the home as a pet.

Cataract
A clouding of the lens of the eye causing blindness unless the lens is removed sur-

gically. Cataracts are rare during childhood, but may be present at birth or may develop during the course of a child's development.

The most common cause of cataracts in the newborn is German measles contracted by the mother during the first three months of her pregnancy. In the older child cataracts may be caused by a number of disorders of which the most common is diabetes. They may also result from penetrating wounds of the eyeball or even from a severe blow to the eye without any evidence of damage.

Once the cataract is removed the child will have to use strong eyeglasses or contact lenses permanently, but will be able to lead a completely normal life.

Cathartic   see **Laxatives.**

Celiac disease
A disorder characterized by chronic diarrhea and a failure to gain adequately in weight or height. The disease may occur at a few months of age or later and is generally outgrown by age 5. The symptoms usually include poor appetite, wasting of the body, and distension of the abdomen. As a rule the child is very irritable and unhappy.

Celiac disease is caused by an intolerance to wheat or rye. The smallest amount will upset the whole digestive system, causing severe, foul-smelling diarrhea.

It can be cured, although the treatment may take several years. If it is not treated properly, the child's growth will be retarded and he will never grow to full height.

Treatment   All wheat and rye is eliminated from the child's diet, usually for several years. Many substitutes can be used to make bread, cake, and other desserts—cornmeal, rice flour, potato flour, banana flour. An excellent recipe book for the mothers of celiac children is *Cooking for Your Celiac Child* by C. B. Sheedy and Norman Kaifitz (see **Bibliography**).

Cephalohematoma   see **Birth injuries.**

Cereals
Cereals are one of the first solid foods offered to babies, and are usually given when the baby is 4 to 6 weeks old. At first only 1 to 2 teaspoons of cereal are given. As the baby adjusts to taking solids, the amount is rapidly increased to 2 tablespoons or even more.

There are many excellent precooked cereals on the market providing a variety of different grains such as rice, barley, oatmeal, and wheat. Most of these cereals contain added amounts of iron and vitamin B complex. They are readily prepared by adding milk, formula, or water.

See also **Solid foods, introducing.**

Cerebral damage   see **Brain damage.**

Cerebral palsy
A lack of muscular control, resulting from brain damage. The condition may be mild, moderate, or severe.

There are a number of distinct types of cerebral palsy, although mixed types are common.

1. The spastic type, in which the involved muscles remain tense and contracted.
2. The athetoid type, in which there is constant uncontrolled movement of the hands, face, neck, and at times also the legs.
3. The rigid type, in which the muscles

resist movement, causing the children to move slowly.

4. The ataxic (lack of balance) type, which causes the child to lose balance and fall frequently.

5. The tremor type, in which the hands and feet shake and are difficult to control.

The physical symptoms of cerebral palsy may be associated with mental retardation, but many affected children possess normal or high intelligence.

There are a number of conditions before, during, and after birth that can damage the brain so as to give rise to cerebral palsy. Among these are the following:

1. A lack of adequate oxygen going to the baby's brain. This may be caused by a pregnant mother's being severely anemic and lacking sufficient oxygen herself; premature separation of the placenta; or any condition that prevents oxygen from entering the baby's bloodstream or his brain before, during, or after birth. Much of this can be prevented by good obstetrical care.

2. Infections of the mother, especially German measles contracted during her first three months of pregnancy. This disease may be prevented by inoculating all susceptible mothers with the rubella (German measles) vaccine at least a few months before pregnancy.

3. Infections that severely damage a child's brain such as poliomyelitis or measles encephalitis or severe meningitis. Poliomyelitis and measles can now be eliminated by vaccination, and some of the most serious forms of meningitis (such as those caused by the tuberculosis bacteria or the meningococcus organism) can be prevented by modern antibiotics once the diagnosis of the disease is made.

4. Rh blood incompatibility, in which the mother's blood forms substances (antibodies) which go through the placenta and destroy the baby's red blood cells. The destruction of the red cells causes jaundice—and deep jaundice damages the brain of the infant. This danger can also be completely eliminated by giving the mother an injection of a special Rh-immune globulin following the birth of her first baby and after each baby subsequently. (See **Rh Factor blood incompatibility.**)

5. Toxic substances, usually swallowed. The most important substance here is lead, which many children absorb after chewing off lead paint on repainted cribs, chairs, toys, wall plaster, and the like. The lead in the child's bloodstream may cause encephalitis, damaging the youngster's brain permanently. This danger can be completely eliminated by determinedly using only lead-free paints on all cribs, playpens, high chairs, toys, etc., and by preventing children from biting on other painted objects around the house. (See **Lead poisoning.**)

Treatment Cerebral palsy cannot be cured, for the nerve cells of the brain have been permanently damaged. But many children with this condition can be greatly helped by orthopedic and neurological care, including physical therapy. Many communities have special schools and psychological units devoted to helping these children. In high school they are given vocational guidance.

Information on the local organizations devoted to cerebral palsy, as well as on the care of children with the condition, may be obtained from the United Cerebral Palsy Association, 141 East 40th Street, New York, N.Y. 10016, and the National Society for Crippled Children and Adults.

See also **Crippled child, helping the.**

Cesarian birth

The delivery of a baby through a surgical incision from the mother's abdomen into the uterus; also called Cesarian section. Cesarian section is not a dangerous operation, and most mothers leave the hospital in seven to nine days. If they decide to breast-feed, they may do so. A full-term baby delivered by Cesarian section is just as healthy as any baby delivered normally. A baby delivered prematurely is given the same care and has the same excellent prognosis as most premature babies.

The most common reasons for performing a Cesarian section are:

1. The space between the mother's pelvic bones through which the baby must pass is too narrow. This can be determined ahead of time by the obstetrician.
2. The placenta covers the opening at the end of the uterus (placenta praevia). When the opening starts to dilate during the process of birth, the placenta tears and bleeding is profuse. A Cesarian delivery is urgently necessary to save the life of both the mother and the infant.
3. The heart sounds of the baby, heard through the mother's abdomen, indicate that the child is in great distress from a lack of oxygen.
4. The infant's head is unusually large and will be unable to pass through the opening between the mother's pelvic bones, even if the opening is of normal size.
5. The mother has had a previous Cesarian delivery. Many obstetricians feel that since scar tissue does not stretch, the scar in the wall of the uterus from the previous Cesarian operation might rupture during the pressures of labor.
6. The mother's kidneys are unable to function for both mother and child during the later stages of pregnancy, and are failing.
7. The mother habitually aborts late in pregnancy—that is, during the seventh or eighth month. In this situation a Cesarian is performed just before the usual time of aborting.
8. The mother has diabetes, the baby is growing rapidly within the uterus, and efforts to induce labor have failed.

Chafing

An irritation usually caused by the rubbing of skin in the folds and creases of the body. Chafing is especially likely when the skin is moist and usually occurs in the creases of the buttocks and thighs and the folds of the neck.

Chafing bothers many infants and toddlers because of the plumpness and tenderness of their skin. It is aggravated when the weather is hot and the child is dressed too warmly, because of the extra perspiration that is produced.

It can be prevented or treated by the use of a good baby powder, or cornstarch (although this tends to cake). The powder not only absorbs any moisture, but smoothes the surface of the skin, preventing friction rub. In applying the powder, sprinkle it on and rub it in; do not shake it all around the baby so that he breathes it in.

Chalazion   see **Stye and chalazion.**

Chancre   see **Syphilis.**

Change of voice   see **Voice.**

Chapped Lips   see **Lips, chapped or cracked.**

Chapped skin

Redness, roughness, or cracking of the skin caused by a combination of cold and moisture. It is especially likely to occur when skins are sensitive.

Many of the baby oils and ointments commonly used to prevent diaper rash also prevent chapping if rubbed in well before exposure to moist cold.

Once the chapping has occurred it will usually respond very readily to any soothing lotion, cream, or ointment.

Chapping see Lips, chapped or cracked.

Cheating

Most adults have cheated at some time or other during their childhood, and cheating, unfortunately, is not uncommon in later years. Today's children, like their parents and grandparents before them, live in a competitive society where achievement receives high priority. The child is given games of chance—Parchesi, for example—and learns many games of skill in which the object is to win. When he does win, he is highly praised and feels great satisfaction and a sense of superiority.

In spite of the intense desire of almost every child to win—whether in sports, in school subjects, or in some other field—he must learn that everyone cannot win, or excel, all the time. Games should be played, studies pursued, pictures painted, instruments practiced for the pleasure of the activity itself. A reasonable and relaxed attitude by parents toward competitive situations is the best preventive measure against cheating. (See **Competitiveness.**)

When a child cheats repeatedly, it is probable that he is unhappy, and insecure, and the cheating is an attempt to feel important, to gain the approval of his parents and the admiration of his peers.

He may feel insecure because his parents or teachers set high standards for accomplishment which he finds extremely difficult to meet. He cheats to gain their approval.

He may be insecure because he feels unable to compete physically with his peers and companions, and desperately seeks their admiration and acceptance.

He may feel inferior to other children because of his family's financial position, a broken home, lack of parental love, or any factor that makes him feel less completely accepted than other children.

He may be insecure because he feels that his brothers and sisters get much more love and attention from his parents than he does. At times this sibling rivalry is so intense that it carries over to the youngster's relationship with his peers. He always needs to feel superior and so he cheats as often as he can in an effort to be the winner.

In all cases of habitual cheating, the causes should be unearthed and studied, and every effort made to correct them. Children who cheat need building up, not punishment, to increase their self-confidence. Parents and teachers should also make sure that standards of achievement are not set too high, that there is not too much emphasis on good grades or winning, and that the child is not in a class where he cannot compete successfully. Whenever possible he should be praised for his accomplishments, and his failures or lack of success should be treated lightly. If the combined efforts of home and school have not been of help, professional aid should be sought.

Chest

The upper part of the torso, enclosed by the ribs, breastbone, and spine. The chest contains the heart and the vital blood vessels going to and from it; the lungs; the trachea and the bronchial tree (the breathing tubes); the esophagus (gullet), which extends from the throat to the stomach; and the nerves which control the heart and the diaphragm—the large, flat muscle separating the chest from the abdomen that is used in breathing.

The breastbone, the ribs, the muscles between the ribs, and the backbone form the protective cage that contains and protects the heart and lungs. The ribs and the muscles between them are also of help in breathing.

See also **Bronchial tree; Diaphragm; Heart.**

Chewing

Chewing is the first step in the process of digestion. While food is being chewed it is mixed with saliva, which not only enhances taste but also aids in the digestion of starches.

The infant's food should be pureed or cut into small pieces until he is about 14 months, when the first chewing teeth—molars—appear. Once the child is old enough to chew properly, every effort should be made to protect and preserve the teeth. Decayed teeth should be treated immediately, for if a child is unable to chew well, he will sooner or later develop digestive disturbances as a result of swallowing large particles of food.

Food should be chewed thoroughly, but unless a child is gulping his food without chewing at all, it is usually not worthwhile to nag about it.

See also **Candy and chewing gum; Solid foods, introducing; Teeth.**

Chicken pox

One of the most contagious of the infectious diseases, caused by a virus (probably the same virus that causes shingles in the adult). Chicken pox is characterized by an itchy rash which appears first as small, pink pimples on any part of the body and then spreads to all areas including the scalp. Within twelve hours most of these pimples develop small, soft blisters which resemble little drops of water when viewed closely in a strong light. Within a day or two the blisters break and scabs form. The scabs usually drop off in seven or eight days, in most cases leaving no scars. There is no immunization for chicken pox. With very rare exceptions it is not a dangerous disease, but you should certainly call the doctor to verify the diagnosis.

Mode of transmission Chicken pox is spread through nose and throat secretions by direct contact with an infected person. It cannot be carried by someone who does not have the disease and it cannot be transmitted via objects—books, letters, or clothing.

Period of contagion A person with chicken pox is contagious from one day before the onset of the rash until seven days after its appearance (or when all the scabs are dry). After that time, although there may be many dry scabs on the body, the person is not contagious.

Incubation period A susceptible person exposed to chicken pox will usually develop the disease between twelve and nineteen days after the date of exposure—the most likely days being the thirteenth and the fourteenth. No special care is prescribed for exposed persons.

Signs and symptoms Usually there is a fever and headache at the onset, followed within twenty-four hours by the appearance of the rash. The rash takes two or three days to come out fully, during which time the fever continues. The rash usually causes considerable itching. On about the fourth day, when the rash is out fully, the temperature drops, and within twenty-four hours the itching subsides.

Treatment There is no specific treatment. The primary effort is to relieve the itching and prevent scratching, for scratching can cause scars and infection of the lesions. Fingernails should be closely cut. Lotions that both dry the blisters and relieve the itching may be applied liberally. Calamine lotion (zinc carbonate) with one percent phenol, or Caladryl lotion (calamine, plus a little camphor, Benadryl—diphenhydramine hydrochloride—and rubbing alcohol) are usually effective. However, if further relief is needed, a doctor may prescribe antihistamines to reduce the itching. Very effective treatment for the relief of itching is Aveeno Colloidal Oatmeal bath or Soyalid colloidal bath. With Aveeno use 1 cup to a bathtub of water or ½ cup to a Bathinette or infant tub of water. With Soyalid use 1 envelope to a bathtub of water or ½ envelope for an infant's bath.

Chiggers

Tiny red mites that are common in the southern and central states, but are found in other parts of the country as well.

The mites live most of their lives in the ground, but during a short stage in their development they need the blood of warmblooded animals. The mites appear on the surface of the ground or on low branches of trees, shrubs, and other vegetation. If a person or any warm-blooded animal touches them, they scramble onto the body.

On a human being, the mite runs up on the skin rapidly until it meets an obstruction such as a belt, and it attaches itself to the skin at this point. It does not burrow into the skin, but remains on top piercing the skin and sucking the blood. After two to four days the mite drops off, having obtained all the blood juices it needs.

Signs and symptoms The earliest sign of a chigger bite is a small red spot on the skin which does not itch. Using a magnifying glass one can easily see in the center of this spot the small, dark-red mite. Within three to twenty-four hours the area becomes a raised hive that itches intensely. On the abdomen, legs, or genitals the lesions become purplish. Usually, because of the itching, the lesions are scratched and may become secondarily infected.

Although the chigger drops off in a few days, the lesions last for several weeks, during which time they itch.

Treatment Since the bite which causes the itching has already occurred and the mite drops off the body almost before any anti-mite treatment can be given, treatment is usually focused on relieving the itching.

Caladryl lotion (zinc carbonate, plus a little camphor, Benadryl—diphenhydramine hydrochloride—and rubbing alcohol) may be applied locally, and Tacaryl (methdilazine) or Temaril (trimeprazine tartrate) syrup or tablets may be taken by mouth—½ teaspoon or ½ tablet three times a day for children under 3 years; 1 teaspoon or 1 tablet every four hours for children over 3 years.

If itching is still intense, baths may be given containing Aveeno Colloidal Oatmeal—1 cup to a bathtub of water; ½ cup to a Bathinette or infant tub of water. Or use Soyalid colloidal bath—1 envelope to a bathtub of water or ½ envelope to a Bathinette or infant tub of water. Or Linit or Argo (prepared starches) may be added to lukewarm water—½ to 1 pound with a full bathtub of water for older children; ¼ pound or a little more to a Bathinette or infant tub of water.

Prevention Because the itching from chigger bites is so intense, prevention, if possible, is most important.

1. In locations where chiggers are present, avoid areas of heavy vegetation.
2. If this is impossible, clothing should fit tightly at wrist, ankles, and collars.
3. The insect repellent Off (Diethyltoluamide) may be sprayed on exposed skin and may even be lightly applied to shoes, socks, collars, or other articles of clothing. In applying the repellent, follow the directions for use, being careful that it is not breathed in and does not get in the eyes.
4. When camping out in chigger-infested areas, always use cots to avoid contact with the ground.

Child, oldest   see Oldest child.

Child abuse
Serious neglect or frequent and severe beating of a child by his parents—the "battered child" syndrome. This is much more frequent than most people realize. There is evidence that in 1966 between 10,000 and 15,000 children in the United States were severely injured by their parents. Of these 5 percent were killed and 25 percent permanently injured.

The parents responsible for neglecting or beating their children are almost always emotionally ill, come from all social and economic levels, and are not confined to any racial group or geographic area. Very often such parents were themselves severely abused in their childhood, and they may feel hopelessly out of control in their relationship with their child. Psychological help is essential.

Prevention of child abuse depends at least in part on suspected cases being reported to the police by neighbors, doctors, nurses, or social workers. Neighbors can reasonably suspect that children are being dangerously beaten if they hear them screaming frequently and often see them with bruises on the face and arms, black eyes, or unexplained cuts over the body. The anonymity of a person reporting a suspected case of child abuse is protected by law.

Doctors today are so aware of child abuse that the diagnosis is considered in almost every case of injury to a small child. If a child is brought in to a doctor, clinic, or hospital with an injury to the head or an abdominal injury, X rays are taken of all the bones of the body. This is because in many cases of child abuse, signs of previously broken bones are found.

The doctor who suspects child abuse sends the child into the hospital for observation without openly accusing the parents. Once in the hospital, the social workers take over, and if the diagnosis of child abuse is made, the case is reported to the police. In cases of severe child abuse the child should be removed temporarily from the home while the parents responsible for the neglect or beatings receive psychotherapy.

All fifty states have passed laws requiring doctors, hospitals, social workers, and other medical and paramedical personnel to report such cases to the police or to child-protection agencies.

Prevention of child abuse can also be very effectively pursued by the establishment of organizations for abusive parents who recognize that they need help. A few such organizations have recently come into being. They are modeled after the principles of Alcoholics Anonymous and Gamblers Anonymous. In Los Angeles Mothers Anonymous was started by a group of mothers seeking mutual support for their common problem—abuse of their children. In New York City Parents Anonymous also offers such troubled parents an opportunity to meet together and help each other. Parents who get in touch with these organizations for information or advice can be assured of receiving understanding and help. The New York organization is located at 1841 Broadway, and there is a 24-hour telephone service: the numbers are 765-2336 and 765-2378. Those who call are not required to give their names.

Childbirth see **Birth.**

Children's apperception test see **Tests.**

Clorox poisoning see **Poisons: first-aid treatment.**

Chlorpromazine (Thorazine) poisoning see **Poisons: first-aid treatment.**

Choking

Choking is caused by anything in the throat or large windpipe (trachea) that obstructs or blocks the passage so as to interfere with air reaching the lungs. A child may accidentally breathe in a piece of meat, a hard candy, or a coin, or a toy he has put in his mouth.

If the choking is due to something the child has swallowed, do not panic—in

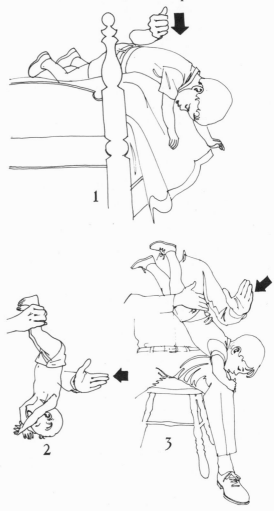

To remove a foreign object choking a child, place the child stomach down on a bed with his head hanging over the edge, and hit him sharply between the shoulder blades. The child may also be held in the air or held over one's knee.

panic one may do exactly the wrong thing. First determine whether the child is getting enough air to breathe. The fact that he is choking and coughing does not mean that the breathing passage is completely obstructed. If the child is able to breathe, rush him to a doctor or a hospital for the removal of the object. Too often parents in their hurried anxiety push a partially obstructing object down the throat and completely block the breathing tube.

But if the child is unable to breathe, he should be held upside-down or be placed on his abdomen over the side of a bed with head and shoulders hanging over the edge. While in such a position he should be slapped sharply on the back between the shoulders. This is to dislodge the object so that it will either be coughed out or at least allow some passage of air.

If a child has breathed in a piece of food or other foreign object but does not seem to be in distress, he should still be taken to the doctor. Serious complications can result if the object remains in the breathing tubes.

See also **Foreign objects, inhalation of.**

Chorea   see **Saint Vitus's dance.**

Chores

Those jobs around the home which a child does routinely as his share in the day-to-day activities of the family. Chores are not paid for—unlike special jobs which a child may perform from time to time—and they have nothing to do with his allowance.

These unpaid-for chores are important in the life of a boy or girl, for they teach cooperation, dependability, and responsibility—valuable qualities for any human being.

Chores may be given to youngsters as young as 3, although without undue pressure. Most little children love their simple jobs and proudly perform them. Among such chores might be the placing of napkins in each place on the dinner table, emptying the wastepaper baskets, watering the plants, helping with the dusting, feeding the family pet.

When children get older, chores may be more complex—washing or drying the dishes, mowing the lawn, taking out the garbage, sweeping the floor.

Of course, during adolescence, when a child has many involvements and interests, he may balk at some of the chores that are his responsibility. An adolescent should not be allowed to avoid his chores, but parents must be flexible and understanding. They should see to it that the chores are not too confining and do not compete with the important activities in the young person's life or with his studies. Furthermore, parents should be sure they are not exploiting their children in order to avoid doing their own share of the work.

Chromosomes

Threadlike particles within the cells of all human beings (and animals and plants) that carry the genes inherited from parents and ancestors. A disarrangement of the chromosomes is responsible for many congenital abnormalities. But today it is possible to examine the chromosomes of the parents' cells and the chromosomes of the fetus, and there is an excellent chance that with this newer knowledge we may be able to prevent the birth of children with certain serious congenital defects.

See also **Genetic counseling; Heredity.**

Chronological age

The actual age of a person in months and years, measured from birth. This technical term is often used with reference to IQ, which is determined by dividing the mental age (as measured in an intelligence test) by the chronological age and multiplying by 100. Chronological age is also contrasted with developmental age.

See also **Developmental age; IQ.**

Cigarettes

An impressive amount of accumulated evidence has demonstrated the dangerous effects of cigarette smoking. The damage is gradual and insidious, and in a great many instances leads to cancer and to lung or heart disease. It has also been demonstrated that cigarette smoking by pregnant women affects the infant before birth. All studies have indicated that more low-birthweight babies are born to smoking mothers than to nonsmokers. Anything that retards the normal weight gain of the child before birth cannot be good for the child.

Combined efforts should be made by parents, doctors, schools, and all health agencies to discourage and, if possible, to prevent our children from developing the habit of cigarette smoking. But very little headway can be made unless adults themselves stop smoking. Almost all adolescents want to be like adults, and if smoking is a sign of being grown up, youngsters will want to smoke.

It is almost impossible to frighten teen-age boys and girls with stories of lung cancer and heart disease because they rarely worry about the future. And they are especially unimpressed if they see their parents and other adults, who should have even more reason to worry, continuing to smoke cigarettes. Teenagers are also easily swayed by advertising which associates social acceptance, success, and glamor with smoking.

Efforts are being made by the Ameri-can Medical Association, the American Academy of Pediatrics, the American Cancer Society, and the American College of Chest Physicians to deter children from smoking cigarettes through TV advertisements, pamphlets, posters, and school education. But it must be emphatically reiterated that the parents themselves, as models for their children, have by far the greatest influence on their children's smoking habits.

As long as cigarette manufacturers blatantly portray the smoking of cigarettes as an adult and accepted way of life, parents must do their utmost to counteract this propaganda.

Circulation of blood see **Aorta; Heart.**

Circumcision

The surgical removal of the loose fold of skin (foreskin) covering the head of the penis.

This operation has been part of the religious rites of Jews, Moslems, and other groups for many centuries. It has also been, and still is, advised by many doctors as a hygienic measure to prevent irritating material from collecting under the foreskin.

Basically there is no need for circumcision if the foreskin is easily retracted over the head of the penis. But if the foreskin is tight and cannot be retracted, or if the foreskin is very elongated, circumcision is advisable.

If a child is to be circumcised, it should be done, if possible, during the first ten days of life, when the nerves are still disorganized and the infant suffers only momentary pain. It is not uncommon to see a week-old infant sucking quietly on a pacifier or a bottle only moments after circumcision.

Circumcisions performed when infants are older may be much more painful, despite anesthesia; and in later infancy, childhood, and adolescence they may also be of great harm psychologically.

In past years many boys were circumcised as a treatment for masturbation. This was entirely ineffective and greatly added to the child's emotional problems.

City home   see **Home, location of.**

Claustrophobia   see **Phobias.**

Clavicle   see **Collarbone, fracture of.**

Cleaning fluid poisoning   see **Poisons: First-aid treatment.**

Cleanliness
"Cleanliness is next to godliness" is certainly not meant for children, for in the course of their wholehearted, unrestricted play they cannot help getting their clothes and themselves dirty. A youngster who comes home from play with clothing clean and unruffled and hands and face clean is usually an unhappy child who has been badly restricted.

Children can easily learn, however, that although there are few if any restrictions about getting dirty during play, there are times when they should be clean—when they visit relatives or friends and when they go to parties, church or synagogue, theater, the ballet, concerts, and the like.

Although there is no reason to be concerned that germs in the dirt on hands and face are dangerous to a child, it is important to encourage children to wash their hands after going to the bathroom and before eating. This is not only a matter of esthetic cleanliness but at times may aid in preventing such conditions as pinworms and other intestinal parasites.

As boys and girls approach puberty they often resist baths, washing, and generally keeping clean. They resent being nagged and are usually negativistic at this stage. But as soon as they begin to take an interest in the opposite sex, they usually make an effort to be clean and attractive. Despite appearances, even youngsters who follow the sloppier fashions are usually clean. A young person who is offensively dirty and unwashed most of the time is rare—and probably suffers from more serious problems.

See also **Washing the hands.**

Cleft lip   see **Harelip.**

Cleft palate
An opening in the midline of the palate present at birth and due to a failure of the two sides of the palate to come together and fuse during embryonic development. It is often accompanied by a cleft lip (see **Harelip**). Cleft palate or harelip occurs about once in every 1,000 births.

The cause of this condition is not fully known. In some cases it is probably due to some temporary interference such as an infection or a drug taken by the mother with the development of the embryo in the sixth to seventh week of pregnancy when the lip and palate should normally close. There is evidence also that occasionally the condition is hereditary, for it has occurred in successive generations and in brothers and sisters.

The cleft must be closed surgically, usually by a plastic surgeon. The results are generally excellent, but the operation should not be attempted until there is sufficient growth and development of the upper jaw and palate. Typically it is performed when the child is between 12 and 18 months. If the cleft is left open too long, the nasal quality of speech will remain, and complete correction is almost impossible.

Until the cleft is completely closed, care must be taken in feeding the child. Large or special nipples must be used to prevent milk or food from entering the child's nose and being inhaled. Some children with a cleft palate are fed by dropper.

Every child who has a cleft palate should be under the care of a speech therapist from the time he first starts to speak.

Climbing

Most infants start climbing at about 10 to 11 months, when they are able to creep and pull themselves up to a standing position. Often they will climb onto low chairs or even up stairs. When they are about 15 to 18 months, they often develop the ability to pull themselves up and climb over the side of the crib. This potential danger can be avoided by attaching extension bars on the side of the crib, making it too high for the child to climb out. (See **Crib.**)

If there are stairs in the house, a young child from about 1 to 2 years will enjoy climbing them and should be permitted to do so under close supervision. (At other times the stairs should be guarded by a safety gate.) As a matter of fact, a child of this age will attempt to climb on and off almost anything—sofas, chairs, beds, park benches, rocks. This is all an important part of developing physical coordination, self-confidence, and muscular strength. Although certain pieces of furniture can be designated as off limits, the youngster should

be allowed sufficient scope for climbing activity.

There are also climbing toys that youngsters enjoy when they are old enough. There are climbing stairs—several steps to climb up, a platform in between, and more steps to climb down. This can be enjoyed as early as 2½ years of age. Small ladders and jungle gyms may be enjoyed safely usually from age 3 and for many years thereafter. All of these give children self-confidence and a sense of accomplishment and prepare them with safety for the days when they will be climbing trees and large ladders.

Although the young child needs close supervision, especially when he starts to hang upside down with his legs bent over the bars of a jungle gym, the adult should let him make his experiments as a youthful acrobat. Youngsters usually know how much they can safely attempt, and if permitted to climb will become more and more proficient. At times the less adventuresome child may even need encouragement until he or she feels confident and secure.

Clinging child

All young children look to their parents for safety and protection, and often run to them and cling if insecure or frightened.

A great many children at approximately one year or a few months later start clinging to their mothers whenever a stranger is nearby. Just why this shyness occurs, even to youngsters who have up until then been outgoing and friendly to everyone, is not fully understood. Perhaps it is because they are beginning to realize how greatly dependent they are on their mothers. Children at this age are starting to explore their world more fully, and it is usually their mothers who are constantly warning them and protecting them from potential hazards.

Mothers are faced with the problem of whether to withdraw their children when they are fearful or to make them meet the situation. There is nothing to be gained by trying to keep a youngster away from strangers, or from friends or relatives who come to visit. Sooner or later he will have to learn to accept them. But a mother should be casual, and should tell outsiders to be casual and not to pressure the child. Eventually he will get used to these "strangers" and realize that they will do no harm. Relatives should be told not to be hurt if a child temporarily "dislikes" them and runs to his mother for protection. If handled calmly and intelligently, this type of clinging will last only a month or so.

For the next year or two, most children, although generally bolder, will still cling to their parents or want them nearby when facing and adjusting to new situations. When children enter nursery school for the first time many of them will cling to their mothers until they make an adjustment and are willing to accept the teachers as a mother substitute.

The overprotected child will often continue clinging, frequently refusing to go to parties unless his mother stays around, and refusing to play at other children's homes, although he enjoys playing with other children at his home. And the shy child may also be a clinging child until he gains more self-assurance.

See also **Nursery school; Overprotective parent; Shyness.**

Clinics

Divisions of a hospital or a health center for the treatment of nonresident patients.

Most hospitals have general pediatric clinics for children from families unable to pay the expense of a private doctor. Here there is continuing treatment—children are followed routinely throughout childhood, given their standard inoculations, and diagnosed and treated when ill.

In many of the larger hospitals and medical centers there are clinics conducted by doctors specializing in specific medical fields. These specialty clinics not only treat children referred to them from the general clinic, but are often used by private doctors as an aid in diagnosing and advising on certain of their patients. Such clinics often have access to sophisticated equipment and laboratory facilities which are almost impossible for the private doctor to maintain in his office.

These clinics study and treat a wide range of physical problems, including allergies, diabetes and glandular difficulties, blood diseases, gastrointestinal disturbances, lung diseases, kidney disorders, cardiac disorders, and nerve diseases. In addition there are psychiatric clinics for the study and treatment of emotionally disturbed children and genetic clinics for the study and followup of children with known or suspected chromosome disorders and for the counseling of parents and would-be parents.

See also **Genetic counseling; Mental health centers.**

Clitoris

The small female genital organ comparable to the penis of the male, and situated in the midline at the upper end of the vulva.

In the newborn girl the clitoris may be much enlarged, having been affected by female sex hormones from the mother. This enlargement usually subsides within two weeks.

The clitoris is the most sensitive sexual organ in the female child as well as in older girls and women. It is common for infants under the age of one year to have found that it is pleasurable to touch the clitoris, and by the time most girls are between 3 and 5 years old they have found that they can get great pleasure by stimulation of this organ. Such activity is completely harmless.

See also **Masturbation.**

Clothing

When buying clothes for an infant, remember that a baby grows approximately seven inches in the first year: the average birth height is twenty-one inches, and at a year it is approximately twenty-eight inches. Therefore, a baby's clothes should almost always be bought large enough for the child to grow into—at least a 6-month size for the newborn baby and least a year-size for the 6-month-old. Also an infant's clothes should be loose-fitting, giving the child a great deal of freedom to kick and move around. This is important exercise. The clothing that touches the baby's skin should preferably be cotton, silk, or synthetic material rather than wool, since wool often irritates sensitive skin. (See **Layette.**)

Toddlers, preschoolers, and young schoolchildren should have tough, durable clothing for school and play. They should not feel restricted by having to keep their clothes clean and fresh. For practical reasons clothes should be easily washable and if possible drip-dry. Dressing up is for special occasions.

When buying clothes (or bedding) for people of all ages, but especially for young children, it is extremely important that the fabric be flame-resistant or flame-retardant. (See **Flammable clothing and bedding.**)

Up to about 6 or 7, children usually accept the clothes parents buy for them and wear them without resistance. But once they start school, they want very much to wear what their classmates and companions are wearing. This is well worth a parent's concern. The child should be encouraged to make suggestions about the type of clothes he wants, and, if at all reasonable, and practical, these suggestions should be met.

During adolescence it is most important that both boys and girls have the opportunity to select or help select their clothes. This is essential, for adolescents have a great need not only to be accepted by their companions, but also to feel a real degree of self-reliance and independence. Sometimes the style of teen-age dress may be very informal or even sloppy by adult standards, but parents should realize the importance to their children of being in style and accepted by their peers.

Clubfoot see **Feet.**

Cocaine see **Drug abuse.**

Cod-liver oil

Oil from the liver of the codfish containing fairly high quantities of the necessary vitamins A and D. Formerly it was used regularly to prevent rickets—it was the first vitamin supplement given to babies and was used exclusively until about 1930, when more concentrated forms of vitamin supplements were prepared.

Cod-liver oil had to be given in a dosage of one tablespoon daily. It has a strong fishy odor, would stain the infants' clothes if spilled, and if the baby inhaled it while swallowing or spitting up, the oil could irritate the lungs.

The concentrated vitamin drops given to babies today not only contain vitamins A and D in greater amounts than in a tablespoon of cod-liver oil, but contain vitamins B and C as well.

Coeducation

The values of coeducation in elementary school, high school, and college are now widely recognized. The former separation of schools and colleges for males and females was an outgrowth of the belief that boys and men, preparing for business and the professions, should be fully educated, but that girls had no need for higher academic education unless they were to become teachers of young children or other girls. This attitude was also fostered by an old idea that girls should be educated in a manner appropriate for girls, and boys in a manner appropriate for boys, this manner presumably reflecting differences in character and personality between the sexes. And it was further agreed that adolescents would be unable to keep their minds on their work if members of the opposite sex were present.

Such theories, of course, are under attack today, and it is generally felt by educators and child-development experts that boys and girls profit greatly from attending coeducational schools where they can get to know, understand, and work with one another. Furthermore, girls and women are preparing for and entering almost all the careers formerly restricted to men.

In view of these changes in attitude and actuality, most high schools, colleges, and universities have become coeducational.

Cold Sores

A common virus condition (herpes simplex) usually associated with or following a cold. It is characterized by a group of tiny blisters at the border of the lip where the mucous membrane joins the skin. These blisters break and form a scablike lesion. This may itch, feel irritated, or burn slightly.

The condition usually clears and disappears in 7 to 10 days. No ointments or lotions are effective as treatment, although the application of spirits of camphor is recommended by many doctors.

Colds

Mild respiratory infections caused by bacteria or viruses. The signs and symptoms of a cold depend on the location of the infection: an infection localized in the throat causes a sore throat; in the larynx (laryngitis), hoarseness and at times a croupy cough; in the trachea (tracheitis) and the bronchial tubes (bronchitis), a hard and frequent cough; in the sinuses (sinusitis), a runny nose and usually a cough as well.

Susceptibility to colds is not fully understood, but among the conditions that can make a person vulnerable are poor nutrition, chronic focuses of infection in the body (such as diseased tonsils and adenoids), and lack of adequate gamma globulin in the blood. (See **Gamma globulin.**)

Young infants are particularly susceptible to colds, since they have not had an opportunity to build up their own antibodies. The idea, which many mothers hold, that newborns and young infants are resistant to colds, is entirely untrue, although they do retain—for about six months—immunity against contagious diseases the mother has had.

In early infancy nostrils clogged with mucus become a difficult problem, for a baby cannot suck and breathe at the same time. The doctor may advise such mild nose drops as Otrivin pediatric nose drops (xylometazoline hydrochloride) or Neo-synephrine (phenylephrine) ¼ percent nose drops—two drops in each nostril five minutes before a feeding. Occasionally, if the nostrils are too clogged with mucus, a nasal aspirator may be used to suction off the mucus very gently. The aspirator is a rounded glass or plastic nozzle that fits into the nostril, attached to a bulb. When the bulb is compressed, it expands, sucking out the mucus. It must be used slowly and gently so that suction does not dilate the blood vessels in the nose, further clogging it. The nose drops may be inserted in the nostrils after as much of the mucus has been suctioned off as possible.

The majority of colds in infants and children are comparatively mild— mostly head colds with stuffy or runny noses and occasionally coughs and mild sore throats. A stuffy nose is rarely a problem for older children.

The treatment of colds depends entirely on the severity of the infection and the part of the respiratory tract involved. Nose drops should only be used on a doctor's advice (they are rarely prescribed) because they usually give only temporary relief and the condition often returns with even greater severity than before the drops were used. Antihistamines and decongestants given by mouth will often help dry up head colds in children past infancy.

There are many mild cough medicines for simple coughs, but stronger cough medicines may be needed for the more persistent and intense coughs. These should be prescribed by the child's doctor.

Antibiotics should not be used unless the doctor prescribes them. Antibiotics, which are of value in severe colds of bacterial origin, are of no value in the treatment of colds caused by viruses.

No treatment is necessary for a simple cold, but if the child runs a fever, the doctor should be called.

See also **Moisture in the air; Steam treatment.**

Colic

Severe and repeated attacks of abdominal pain, typically occurring in infants aged 1 to 3 months. As a rule these attacks occur after a baby has been fed, and the pain is due to distension of the stomach and intestines by gas. During these attacks the baby usually draws up his legs toward his stomach to relieve the pain.

Colic is frequently traceable to sensitivity to cow's milk, although at times it may be due to sensitivity to multivitamin drops or to the swallowing of air during feeding. Another quite common cause is tension.

If the colic seems to be caused by cow's milk, the infant may be shifted to a formula made of soybeans or to a meat-base formula in which the

Typical signs of colic include distended abdomen, legs drawn up to relieve pain, angry crying.

amounts of sugar, fat, and protein are the same as in breast milk. One of these formulas will usually relieve colic in a very short time. Occasionally the use of goat's milk is successful.

If multivitamin drops are suspected as the cause, they can be omitted for a few days to ascertain if they are responsible. Should they appear to be the cause, various other vitamin drops may be used.

When swallowing air is suspected as the reason for colic, try a change of nipple—the nipple may not be suited to the baby's mouth. Also check if the hole in the nipple is too small, or if the bottle is tilted up high enough when the baby is fed. Usually, however, if a child is bubbled regularly, any air swallowed will be burped up. (See **Bottle feeding; Bubbling [burping] the baby.**)

Many babies develop colic as a result of tenseness. Often an infant needs more sucking satisfaction than he is deriving from the bottle or breast. This frustration makes him tense, and his intestinal muscles tense up as well. Such colic can be quickly relieved by giving the infant a pacifier.

At times a baby becomes tense from being handled by a tense, nervous person. If this is the mother or father, she or he should make every effort to eliminate the tenseness.

Colic may also be relieved by medicine containing atropine and a small amount of phenobarbital, which relaxes the muscles of the stomach and intestines. But it is much better to remove the cause of colic than to treat the symptoms.

See also **Milk allergy.**

Colitis, ulcerative

A chronic inflammatory disease of the large intestines characterized by a tendency to produce ulcers in the inner mucous lining. It may appear at any time from early infancy through adolescence. The most usual period of onset is between ages 5 and 16. The cause is unknown and various possible explanations have been suggested—including allergy, bacterial infections, deficiency of vitamins and minerals—but none of these has been adequately verified. Considerable evidence points to emotional factors as important in the onset, persistence, and reoccurrence or relapses of colitis.

Treatment is both medical and psychological, and usually considerable relief can be expected. In certain persistent, difficult cases surgical removal of the ulcerative portion of the colon (large intestine) is indicated. This usually brings great relief.

Collage   see **Art.**

Collarbone, fracture of

The collarbone (clavicle) is the bone most frequently broken during birth. This fracture occurs especially in difficult births when the obstetrician has problems in delivering the shoulders of the child. It may, however, occur from time to time in normal, uncomplicated births.

It is usually detected quickly, for the infant fails to move, or to move freely, the arm on the affected side. He cries if the arm is moved forcibly.

Treatment is orthopedic. It consists in pulling the shoulder back and using bandages to hold it in this position without motion for a few weeks. The fracture usually heals in a few weeks, and after several months the broken collarbone generally appears as normal as the unbroken one on the other side.

Collarbone fracture may occur throughout childhood and adolescence from accidents, but it is not serious and heals readily when held in position.

Collections   see **Hobbies.**

College, preparation for
Much publicity has been given to the need for a college education if one is to succeed in the modern world. This does not mean that every child is college material, or that a young person should be forced to attend college if he doesn't want to. However, all boys and girls should be given the opportunity of a college education—if not in a regular liberal arts college, then in a community or two-year college.

The desire in children to continue their education into and through college is stimulated primarily by parents and teachers. It is almost a rule that when parents plan for and expect their children to enter college, the children grow up planning to enter college. Such parents also tend to take an active interest in their children's daily activities and progress at school. This attitude encourages the school staff to take greater interest in a youngster. Some schools attempt to prepare virtually all their students for college. But others are, for various reasons, less college-oriented; and in these schools children will usually benefit if their parents show their concern for their children's progress, the aims of the teachers, the curriculum, and school problems in general.

A child who is not a particularly good student in high school may still be a good college student. There are certain youngsters who are "late bloomers"— children who suddenly seem to find interest and excitement in their studies. There are others whose achievements have not lived up to their potential because of some emotional situation, but

who overcome their former difficulties in college.

Community colleges and two-year colleges are especially valuable for those boys and girls who have not done well in high school. Many students prove themselves in these institutions and later transfer to regular four-year liberal arts colleges.

Colon, enlargement of
A dilatation (widening) of the lower portion of the large intestine. Possible causes are an improper function of the nerves controlling this segment of the bowel (Hirschsprung's disease); an obstruction lower down, such as a narrowing of the anus; or emotional factors, causing the child to withhold bowel movements either for fear of pain during evacuation or when resisting the pressures of toilet training.

Hirschsprung's disease can be treated with drugs, although occasionally surgical correction is necessary. Enlargement of the colon due to a tight or narrow anus is treated medically by dilating the anus and is not a difficult procedure. Enlargement due to a child's resistance to bowel movements can be corrected by eliminating the cause. If the child is suffering pain, this is commonly the result of an anal fissure and can be treated. If the child is reacting negatively to toilet training, a change of approach is needed—it may even be best to give up efforts at training for the time being.

See also **Anal fissure; Toilet training.**

Color blindness
A hereditary inability or difficulty in differentiating between certain colors, most usually red and green. Partial color blindness is sex-linked, occurring far more frequently among males than fe-

males. Approximately 800 out of 10,000 white American men have some degree of color blindness, whereas only 44 out of 10,000 women are affected. Partial color blindness occurs less frequently among Negroes and American Indians.

The condition is present at birth and continues throughout life. In children under 6 it is rarely suspected or looked for, although sometimes it becomes obvious that the child has difficulty in differentiating between certain colors, especially green and red traffic lights.

As a rule, color blindness is no more than a relatively minor annoyance, and in certain jobs requiring discrimination of forms it is an advantage. However, tests for color blindness are included in many physical examinations, such as those required by most colleges, since in some jobs (commercial artist, for example) a good sense of color differentiation is important.

Color of eyes   see **Eyes, color of.**

Colostrum
A thin, yellow fluid secreted by the breast of the mother for the first two or three days after the birth of a baby. Colostrum is thought to be mildly laxative, clearing out the baby's digestive tract before it receives breast milk. Although popular opinion has held that it contains large amounts of antibodies against disease, this is not true. Colostrum contains only minute amounts of antibodies; the basic antibody protection against disease in an infant comes through the placenta before the birth of the child. Colostrum is, however, rich in protein, and an excellent food for the newborn.

Coma
A state of complete loss of consciousness from which a person cannot be aroused even by the strongest stimulation. Coma may be due to many causes, and treatment depends on the cause. For instance, diabetic coma can be quickly and completely relieved by insulin. (See **Diabetes mellitus.**) Coma from certain types of meningitis, such as that caused by the bacteria of tuberculosis or by meningococcus, can usually be treated successfully by the proper antibiotics. (See **Meningitis.**) Among other causes of coma in children the most common are an overdose of drugs, as when a child swallows a large number of sleeping capsules (see **Barbiturate poisoning**); an inflammation of the brain (see **Encephalitis**); and an injury to the brain due to fractures of the skull (see **Fractures**).

Comedo   see **Blackhead.**

Comedo remover   see **Blackhead.**

Comic books
Almost all children love the so-called "comic books" from the time they are first able to read—and sometimes even before that. It has been estimated that 98 percent of all children between the ages of 8 and 18 read these magazines.

In subject matter, style, and level of sophistication there is great variety among comic books. Some are indeed comic; some are devoted to tales of mystery, fantasy and adventure; some recount biblical stories, events of history, or the plots of famous books; some emphasize crime or horror; some are based on romance.

During the past thirty years there have been many discussions concerning the values or dangers of comic books. The arguments against them have ranged from claims that they discourage the reading of good literature to claims that they present the child with pictures and stories of violence and even sadism that cause him to develop tensions, fears, and undesirable, antisocial behavior.

Before a parent denounces comic books, however, or attempts to prevent his child from reading them, he should consider certain factors. Why is the reading and enjoyment of these magazines almost universal among children? Some special needs must be satisfied.

Of course, comic books are colorful, cheap, and widely displayed. Most children can buy them out of their own allowances. It is also a social advantage to have such magazines to trade with other boys and girls.

But other factors also influence children. Young children who cannot yet read easily can understand and enjoy comic books, for the story is usually developed in cartoons. For the beginning reader, this may be an aid in learning new words, for very often a child can figure out the meaning of the word from the context; but there is no pressure on him to do so, and he does not become discouraged if he cannot understand the word the first few times he sees it. Comic books are also read by youngsters when they want to relax rather than read material that requires concentration. In this sense comics are similar to the light detective stories that the intellectual adult reads for relaxation.

Moreover, in recent years publishers of comic books have been subject to increasing legal and social pressures to improve the quality of their magazines, and a number of more psychologically sophisticated approaches have been developed: superheroes now frequently express self-doubt, and many characters are a mixture of good and bad rather than pure hero or pure villain. These new approaches have proved extremely popular with youngsters.

It should be stressed that comic books need not and certainly should not take the place of worthwhile books. Parents should be sure that plenty of good, interesting, and well-illustrated books are available, and children should be encouraged—not forced—to read them. Reading to children from good books will usually stimulate their desire to read them themselves. Having a child join a lending library is an added incentive to the reading of books. And children should not be permitted to spend most of their free time reading comic books any more than they should spend all of their free time watching television.

There is, however, no evidence to show that comic books have harmed children who are basically stable, or that they have prevented these children from making progress in reading or enjoying good literature.

Those children who seek out comic books dealing with crime, violence, and even cruelty, and who seem to be inspired by these books to commit antisocial acts, are basically emotionally upset children. Their problems will not be solved by forbidding them to read comic books. This may, in fact, create increased conflict between parent and child. These children need professional guidance and usually psychotherapy.

Because of the many types of comic books available—some of real value, some entertaining, some innocuous, and a few still concentrating on crime and sadism—it is advisable for parents to exercise guidance in the selection of these books, as far as possible.

Companions

Before age 2 or so, a child has very little need for playmates or companions. His parents satisfy his day-to-day desires for play and activity. But children between 2 and 3 begin to show a desire to be near other children, playing side by side rather than actually with them, and doing what the other children are doing. Companionship with other children of about the same age becomes more meaningful at about 3 and thereafter becomes increasingly important.

It is through companionship with other children that a child learns sharing, respect for others' property and opinions, and cooperation. He also gains the joy of communicating with people of his own age with similar interests and mutual understanding. Many young children without companions of their own age invent imaginary companions with whom they talk, walk, eat, and even play. (See **Imaginary companions.**)

During the elementary-school years boys and girls typically go about in groups—usually boys with boys and girls with girls—and it becomes a primary concern for them to be members of a group and to be looked up to by other members in the group. Youngsters gain a feeling of self-assurance, pride, and poise through their companions.

This need for group activity and acceptance remains strong in puberty and adolescence, when previously secure youngsters may become unsure of their roles in the world and how they should relate to others. In particular, their new interest in the opposite sex raises problems for many young people. They need to talk about this with others of their own age and to have the assurance of being liked by their companions.

It is because companions are so important in the development of a child that parents are invariably advised to do what they can to be sure that their children have sufficient companionship. If a child is isolated from other children, the parents should consider a nursery school or play-group for a young child, and membership in youth organizations such as the Boy Scouts or an athletics group for an older child. If a child lacks companions because of unpopularity, parents should attempt to discover and alleviate the causes of this.

See also **Friends, close; Unpopularity.**

Comparing children

Most parents have a tendency to compare a child with his brothers or sisters or with other children. They compare birth weights, degree of activity, time of sitting up, standing up, walking, talking—each stage of development and progress. Usually these comparisons are expressions of interest, and at times of pride. But sometimes comparisons are upsetting, to the parent as well as to the child, if another youngster weighs more, is more active, develops more rapidly, has rosier cheeks.

All children are individuals with different backgrounds and growth patterns. There are normally great differences in all phases of development. A doctor will be the first to tell the parents if the child is below par physically or mentally and to prescribe treatment if necessary.

In all cases parents should guard against comparing a youngster unfavorably or expressing disappointment concerning some factor over which the child has no control. Children should always be made to feel that they are loved and wanted, not that they are a source of unhappiness to their parents.

Even if the parent feels that the child does or should have some control over the matter in question, negative comparisons are an ineffective means of correction. A child's most probable reaction to a remark such as "I guess John's the athlete in the family" or "Mary always has her homework done on time" will be a feeling of dislike for John or Mary, rather than a feeling that he can or wants to improve.

The standards for each child must be different, and they should be reasonable. Each child has different strengths and problems that should be dealt with on an individual basis.

See also **Sibling rivalry and jealousy.**

Competitiveness

All societies encourage a competitive spirit to some degree in their children, and our society is especially concerned with competing successfully. When our children are still very young they see who can find the most Easter eggs, who can run the fastest, who can jump the highest. They play simple games to see who wins: racing toy autos down inclines, throwing rings on stakes. Later they learn more complex games of competition: checkers, chess, card games, board games.

In almost all school situations children compete for good marks and other signs of achievement. They engage in competitive sports and cheer for their chosen teams. Children, like many adults, are thrilled when their team wins and subdued when it loses. And during these learning years they are more and more exposed to the rewards of winning in the adult world of business and politics. They live in a world of competition where the winner gains praise and adulation.

But children must learn that one need not be the winner in every game and in every effort. Pleasure should be gained by playing a game or pursuing an activity for enjoyment, for fulfillment. And improvement almost always will come

with practice. If the child is to learn to enjoy work and play for their own sake, and not to be so concerned with winning and losing, parents and teachers must help. The emphasis should be on the work done rather than the mark received. Parents should praise children for their efforts rather than their standing on a competitive scale.

Since every child needs to be admired, parents should do their utmost to find some area in which their child can reach some degree of recognition. The best way to do this is to encourage the child in his individual interests and abilities. A short boy can become a first-rate swimmer. A girl with poor vision can be an excellent guitar player. Whatever the child's leaning—painting, dancing, science, public speaking, hobby collections, dramatics, writing, crafts—it should be encouraged and the results praised when warranted.

The aim is for the child to grow up with self-confidence and the feeling that he can succeed on his own terms and is able to hold his own with others.

Compulsions

Very strong impulses, conscious or subconscious, to do a certain thing over and over again. Compulsive behavior is fairly common in a minor way during early childhood. Some children *must not* step on the cracks in the sidewalk, or *must* run up and down the front steps of each home they pass. Children as young as two develop certain temporary compulsions: before they will sleep, a glass of water must be in a special place on the table next to the bed, the Teddy bear must be sitting in a certain chair, and the slippers must be placed under the table. Usually such minor compulsions are of very little significance and disappear as the child gets older.

In some children, however, compulsions persist to the point that they interfere with normal activities—for example, the child who must stop to say his prayers three times an hour, the child who always clears his throat twice before reciting. Compulsions can take numerous forms, each of which is related to some deep-seated psychological fear, usually associated with feelings of guilt or anxiety. In certain instances, severe and deep compulsions may be a symptom of autism or schizophrenia.

Some compulsions may arise from fears that a parent has communicated to a child—for example, repeated hand-washing from an irrational fear of dirt or germs. But very many are formed subconsciously in the child's own mind as a means of warding off punishment or avoiding impulses that he believes are evil. The child who compulsively prays may feel that he is warding off God's punishment for evil thoughts or acts relating to masturbation. A child who cannot speak without clearing his throat may be full of hostile feelings toward a sibling and fearful that these will pour forth if he speaks spontaneously. In psychoanalytic theory compulsions are often explained in terms of the sexual feeling a child may have toward the parent of the opposite sex and his hostile feelings toward the parent of the same sex. (See **Oedipus complex.**)

Strong and persistent compulsions almost always require treatment by a child therapist. Parents are too closely involved with the child and his feelings to treat the child themselves.

Youngsters with compulsions should not be criticized, ridiculed, or humiliated because of them. The child will usually improve with the help of a professionally trained adult with whom he feels entirely free to discuss his feelings toward his family, thereby relieving himself of feelings of guilt or helplessness.

Concussion   see **Head injuries.**

Congenital defects
Physical defects of the child that are not hereditary but that develop in the course of the pregnancy when the child is still within the uterus.

See also **Birth defects; Genetic counseling; Prenatal care.**

Conjunctivitis
An inflammation of the conjunctiva, the delicate mucous membrane that lines the inner eyelids and covers the outer surfaces of the eyeball. There are numerous causes of conjunctivitis. Among the most common are the bacterial, allergic, and chemical types.

Bacterial infections   These may result from bacteria being rubbed into the eyes; from infections of the nose traveling up the tear ducts to the eyes; or from contact with the eye secretions of other persons suffering from a contagious type of conjunctivitis, especially the type called pink-eye. Bacterial forms of conjunctivitis usually produce a yellowish pussy discharge, often causing the eyelids to be stuck together in the morning after sleep. All forms of bacterial conjunctivitis can be treated and cured with specific antibiotics in the form of eyedrops or ointments. In severe cases antibiotics are given by mouth as well.

Allergic conjunctivitis   This type of inflammation is most usually caused by an allergy to tree and plant pollen. It can usually be treated successfully with antihistamines and special eyedrops, but if known to occur severely, preventive antiallergic inoculations may be given. (See **Hay fever.**)

Chemical conjunctivitis This is due to irritations caused by various chemicals. The most common types of irritation are caused by air pollution, chlorine in swimming pools, and the antibacterial drops placed in the eyes of newborn infants.

Conscience see **Guilt.**

Constipation
Difficult or infrequent evacuation of the bowels. Many parents are greatly disturbed because their infants or young children are subject to constipation. But unless the constipation is caused by a congenital abnormality of the bowels (which would be diagnosed shortly after birth), it is not really dangerous, even when it is severe.

In the young infant constipation is almost always caused by diet, although occasionally the muscles of the anus are tight for a few weeks, causing a child to strain before having a movement. For constipation caused by diet, a doctor will usually advise giving the baby prune juice or adding a mildly laxative malt-sugar preparation to the baby's diet.

Constipation in a child of 15 months or older may be due to an anal fissure (a tear in the mucous membrane of the anus). The child will cry with pain every time he has a movement, and may start withholding his movements. Treatment consists of keeping the stools very soft, even loose, with mineral oil or laxatives daily, and applying a healing ointment (such as a cod-liver oil ointment) to the anus. This treatment usually takes 2 to 3

months before the tear in the anal mucous membrane is healed. (See **Anal fissure.**)

Another type of constipation occurs when the child starts resisting the pressures of toilet training. This type will clear up if the parents change their attitude and approach and are more casual while attempting toilet training. (See **Toilet training.**) The doctor may also prescribe large doses of mineral oil daily for several weeks so that the child finds it difficult or impossible to withhold his movements. This breaks the pattern, and if the child's colon has become distended from withholding masses of feces, it will return to its normal size.

Although severe and chronic constipation may temporarily require the use of laxatives, suppositories, and even an occasional enema, none of these should be used routinely in the treatment of mild constipation or in its prevention unless ordered by the doctor. Suppositories and enemas should be avoided as much as possible, for they produce an abnormal anal sensation and may be upsetting emotionally.

It is much better to regulate the bowels with laxative fruits and vegetables and plenty of fruit juices and other liquids.

See also **Bowel movements; Enemas; Laxatives.**

Contact lenses see **Eyeglasses.**

Contrariness see **Negativism.**

Convalescence see **Bedridden child.**

Convulsions
Seizures typically characterized by twitchings or stiffness of the muscles of the arms, legs, and face, and usually loss of consciousness. The vast majority of

convulsions in children are brief and not at all dangerous. Under the age of 5 the most frequent cause of convulsions is high fever (febrile convulsions). These occur only in certain children whose nervous systems are sensitive to high fever. Usually these children become jumpy and shaky when the fever rises and then suddenly lose consciousness— eyes rolling up, face dusky, and body stiffening or twitching. The child may stop breathing for a second or so, or the breathing may become heavy and snorting. The seizure lasts only about a minute. These convulsions are not dangerous.

When a child has had a fever convulsion, it is often recommended that he be given a little phenobarbital (usually one teaspoonful of phenobarbital elixir) along with aspirin as a preventive measure during fever episodes. The tendency to have convulsions associated with high fever almost always disappears by the time a child reaches five.

There are other and much rarer causes of convulsions in children. An inadequate amount of calcium or sugar in the blood may cause convulsions in the newborn baby. This situation, if due to low calcium, can easily be corrected by giving the baby calcium solution by mouth for a few days, and no side effects remain. A lack of sufficient sugar can be corrected by temporarily giving the infant glucose by mouth and by injection as well. In rare cases brain damage or brain inflammation also causes convulsions in the newborn. Epilepsy, encephalitis, breath-holding that reduces the oxygen in the brain, and acute lead poisoning also may lead to a seizure. Convulsions caused by hysteria occasionally occur in children with a highly neurotic makeup. These can be easily differentiated by the doctor from other types of convulsive seizures.

See also **Breath-holding; Epilepsy; Encephalitis.**

Cookouts   see **Picnics and cookouts.**

Corporal punishment see **Punishment.**

Cortisone and hydrocortisone

Two of the potent and very important hormones secreted by the adrenal glands. They have, besides other qualities, the ability to reduce inflammation and to suppress allergic reactions. It is for these effects that they are primarily used in the treatment of children.

Numerous synthetic cortisone preparations are made. These are available in tablet and liquid form to be taken orally; in creams, ointments, and aerosol sprays for local application to the skin; and in an injectible form, rarely used in infancy and childhood.

In children, cortisone preparations are given by mouth for such conditions as asthma, rheumatic fever, rheumatoid arthritis, nephrosis, ulcerative colitis, chronic leukemia, and Hodgkin's disease. They are also given by mouth in the treatment of severe hay fever, poison ivy, and drug and serum reactions.

When used in the treatment of asthma or hay fever, the cortisone preparations given by mouth should only be used to control acute symptoms when other usual methods have failed. Only rarely should they be used over long periods of time.

Given by mouth, these potent drugs must be carefully controlled by the doctor, for they may be very harmful if improperly used. When taken orally over long periods of time, these preparations may slow down a child's rate of growth, may cause stomach ulcers or a puffiness of body tissues, may light up a quiescent tuberculosis lesion, or may cause chicken pox, generally a mild infection, to become virulent and possibly fatal.

During childhood the greatest use of cortisone preparations is for application on the skin in the form of creams, ointments, and aerosol sprays. As such they give great relief in eczema and other allergic skin conditions, and in cases of itching and skin inflammation. However, although these local applications relieve and temporarily cause the disappearance of the lesion, they do not cure. The cause should always be sought and treated or removed if possible.

Cosmetics see **Makeup.**

Coughs

There are numerous causes of coughs in children. Probably the most common of these is a virus infection which usually also causes a runny or stuffy nose and at times a sore throat as well.

There are coughs caused by postnasal dripping from infected adenoids and occasionally from infected sinuses. These are most usually the result of bacterial infections.

There are the croupy coughs caused by infections or irritation of the larynx (the voice box). These coughs have a hollow sound like the bark of a seal. They may be due to either viruses or bacteria.

Then there are the coughs caused by viral or bacterial infections of the breathing tubes (tracheitis, bronchitis, bronchiolitis) and the lungs (pneumonia). These coughs are usually hard and dry at the outset of the infection but gradually become looser.

A further common cause of coughing is allergy—an irritative response of the breathing tubes to some substance to which the body is sensitive. The allergic cough may vary from a hard, dry cough to one associated with rapid breathing and a wheezing sound on expiration.

There are also certain coughs in which the mucus in the breathing tubes is very difficult to cough up. The child coughs and coughs and coughs, at times almost losing his breath. Whooping cough is typical of this type of infection. It is very rarely seen today in communities where the routine vaccination against this disease has been given in infancy.

Treatment It is obvious that no single treatment or medicine will suffice for all coughs. Therefore parents should consult the doctor so as to obtain the correct medication and treatment for a particular type of cough.

The average cough due to a mild irritation of the throat and trachea will usually respond to a simple, soothing cough medicine that liquefies and loosens the mucus. The deeper and more severe coughs may require some sedative as well as liquefying action, so that the coughing is not too fatiguing but is just sufficient to bring up the mucous secretions.

The allergic coughs are usually either treated with antihistamine cough medicines or, in the case of asthmatic coughs, by a cough medicine that will relax the spasm of the breathing tubes as well as loosen the secretion.

At times, steaming is indicated in the treatment of coughs; at times, antibiotics.

A croupy cough or a persistent cough should always be under the care of a doctor.

See also **Asthma; Bronchitis; Bronchiolitis; Croup; Expectorants; Foreign objects, inhalation of; Laryngitis; Postnasal drip; Steam treatment; Tuberculosis; Whooping cough.**

Counseling, educational and guidance

Most of the better schools and school systems in the United States and Canada have special counselors who advise in situations when children are having academic or emotional problems.

Such counselors observe and study those children who are having difficulties. On the basis of their findings they advise the teacher on the handling of the child, discuss with the parents their attitudes and relationships toward the child at home, and often counsel the child as well.

A counselor may or may not be a certified school psychologist. If she (or he) is, then she herself usually does the diagnostic intellectual and psychological testing of the children referred to her to determine their mental ability and to unearth any emotional factors that might be upsetting them.

The school may have a separate school psychologist, who does the testing. The guidance counselor receives her report of the testing along with her recommendations. In some school systems a school psychologist travels from school to school, and the guidance counselors at the individual schools are responsible to the psychologist.

On the basis of diagnostic testing, a counselor can usually determine if a child's problems are related to his intelligence level, or if he is emotionally upset, or both.

Then the counselor works closely with the teacher, suggesting methods of educating the child and dealing with his individual problems. She may also give the child some counseling or advise that he receive psychotherapy. In some schools the counselor may also do remedial work with the child.

Further, the counselor often investigates the child's home environment and his relations with other boys and girls. Finally, she meets with the child's parents and discusses with them how best they can help their child in his school adjustment.

In some schools guidance counselors are called upon to give the courses in family living and sex education. (See **Sex education in the schools.**)

In the high schools the educational and guidance counselors are usually also called upon to advise students on college selection, choice of occupation, vocational or other training, or alternative future plans. (See **Vocational guidance.**)

Counting

Most children, if they have had the attention of an interested parent, start to count between 2 and 3 years of age. They may start by counting the fingers on their hands or stones or sticks they have collected, often counting no more than five and sometimes mixing up the order of the numbers. By the time they enter kindergarten most youngsters can count to twenty or higher.

There are many toys and books that will aid children in learning to count, including beads, blocks, marbles, toy clocks, and counting books.

Although a child who learns to count early is usually bright and observant, the child who does not count so early is not necessarily less intelligent. He may not have had the attention and stimulation given the early counter.

Country home see **Home, location of.**

Cow's milk see **Milk, cow's.**

Cracked lips see **Lips, chapped or cracked.**

Cradle cap
A thick scaling or greasy crusting that often develops on the scalps of young infants. It may cover certain patchy areas or the whole scalp. It is due to an excessive secretion of the oil glands in the skin and occurs even in those infants whose scalps have been kept clean.

This scaling or crusting can usually be effectively removed by oiling the scalp with Vaseline, mineral oil, or baby oil and gently combing the hair through with a fine-toothed comb.

If this method of removal is not successful, a doctor can prescribe a specific ointment to dissolve the scales and oily crusts.

Cramps, abdominal see **Abdominal pain; Appendicitis; Colic; Intussusception.**

Cramps, menstrual
Pain associated with menstruation, usually occurring the first day or two of the menstrual period; also called dysmenorrhea. The cause is not completely understood, although it is believed to be a combination of two things: the congestion of blood in the uterus at the beginning of the period and a spasm of the opening of the uterus into the vagina.

This pain can usually be relieved by aspirin or some other analgesic such as Midol (aspirin, cinnamedrine hydro-chloride, and caffeine) and by the application of a heating pad over the lower abdomen. If the pain is too severe, a doctor should be consulted.

However, the pain is rarely so severe that a girl is forced to abstain from normal activities. She should not feel that she is an invalid during the days when she has menstrual cramps.

The pain may be accentuated by a girl's attitude toward menstruation, often gained from her mother or other girls who refer to the condition as "the curse" or "getting unwell." It should be made clear to the girl that menstruation is a normal function in a healthy woman, and is in no way an illness. Some girls are not ready to accept adult sexuality and responsibility; they may resent menstruation, and this, too, can exaggerate the pain.

If a prescription drug is given for the pain, parents should be aware that some of these medications may contain habit-forming drugs such as codeine and amphetamine. Both parent and child should be alert to the dangers of taking the medicine too freely.

See also **Menstruation.**

Cramps, muscle see **Muscle pains.**

Cranberry stools see **Bowel movements.**

Crankiness
Crankiness in infancy and childhood may be due to numerous causes. In the infant it may be caused by teething, wet or soiled diapers, an upset stomach with colic or diarrhea, diaper rash or other skin irritations, a need for sucking satisfaction, sleepiness, hunger, fatigue, or a respiratory or other infection.

In later years crankiness may be due to many emotional causes as well as physical ones. A child may be depressed, anxious, or fearful. He may feel rejected by parents or companions. He may feel jealous or insecure. He may be having problems in school.

On the other hand, the child may be anemic and feel under par; he may be fatigued or suffering from lack of sleep; he may have a low-grade infection or may be coming down with a cold or other infection. He may have a stomachache or a headache. And occasionally in adolescent girls crankiness may be related to the tensions of menstruation.

In other words, crankiness is a symptom of something, and if physical causes are ruled out, then emotional causes should be investigated.

See also **Crying; Fatigue.**

Creeping

Crawling—one of the stages in a child's efforts to move from place to place, usually starting between 7 and 12 months. There are many different methods of learning to creep. Some infants propel themselves with their arms alone, dragging their legs after them. Some start by creeping backward; others use an awkward sidewise motion. However, after practice most babies adopt the usual alternation method: right arm and left leg, then left arm and right leg. A few babies do not creep at all but go directly from sitting to walking. There is no scientific evidence for the idea that a child who does not creep will be handicapped later by stammering, stuttering, or difficulty in learning to read.

Cretinism

Complete or almost complete inactivity of the thyroid gland.

The condition is rarely recognized until the child is at least 3 or 4 weeks old,

since his body contains thyroid secretion produced by his mother and transmitted through the placenta. But after this is used up, the baby becomes slow and inactive and his face develops a characteristic appearance—a heavy, droopy expression, wrinkled forehead, abnormally flat nose, and a large protruding tongue. The abdomen is very large because of poor muscle tone, and the navel almost always protrudes.

Children with this condition develop slowly physically and mentally, and if not treated early will be mentally retarded for life. If treated early, they have an excellent chance of being perfectly normal mentally.

The condition can be diagnosed very easily by blood tests.

Treatment consists in giving the child either thyroid secretion (thyroxine) in tablet form or tablets of dried thyroid gland. This must be continued throughout life. With adequate treatment the child's physical development is normal. The degree of mental development largely depends on when the deficiency commences, its duration before treatment, its degree, and the adequacy of thyroid given in treatment.

See also **Thyroid gland.**

Crib

A crib is probably the baby's most important piece of furniture. As such, it must be comfortable, durable, and safe. In selecting a crib there are certain features of special importance:

1. All new cribs, by law, must be painted with lead-free paint. This is important because many babies, when they cut teeth and stand up, gnaw on the sides of the crib and absorb the paint products into their systems. Lead, which is found in most paints, is ex-

tremely dangerous if taken into the system. (See **Lead poisoning.**) This fact should be remembered when buying a second hand crib—it should not be used if there is any possibility the paint contains lead.

2. The bars should be close enough together—no more than three and a half inches apart—so that no baby could force his head or even his torso between them.

3. Do not use a hinged cover over the top of the crib. Too often it is possible for the baby to push his head between the side of the crib and the top, and in this way he may strangle.

4. The sides of the crib should be movable to at least two heights. One height should be high enough so that the baby cannot climb out. (This may have to be increased by an extension in the case of very active and well-coordinated children.) The second, lower, height should permit a child to climb out when parents feel he is old enough. It should also be possible to lower the side when the child is being diapered or otherwise cared for.

5. The height of the mattress should also be adjustable to save mothers the effort and discomfort of bending over too often when caring for the child.

6. The crib should be large enough so that the baby will have plenty of freedom in which to move, creep, walk around, and even play as he gets older.

7. The crib mattress should be firm and not likely to sink in permanently from the weight of the youngster. All mattresses should be covered with a waterproof or water-resistant cover.

See also **Mattress.**

Crib bumpers

Cushioning—bought or made—to prevent an infant from striking his head on the wooden bars, the head, or the bottom of the crib as he rolls from side to side. Later, when children sit up in their cribs or get on their hands and knees, a certain number bang their heads rather violently and rhythmically on the top or bottom of the crib. The bumpers cushion the blows—although these blows are not dangerous.

Bumpers may be fashioned out of blankets or quilts fastened securely by cords around the sides, the head, and the bottom of the crib.

See also **Crib rocking.**

Crib death

A type of sudden, unexpected death (Sudden Infant Death Syndrome) that occurs occasionally among basically healthy babies, usually between 1 month and 5 months old.

The great majority of these deaths take place at night—therefore the term "crib deaths." The infant is apparently in good condition when put to bed and is found dead in the course of the night or in the morning.

Suffocating was once blamed for these unexplained and sudden deaths, but studies by pathologists proved that this was not the cause. The actual cause is not as yet known.

Many doctors believe it is due to a virus infection causing a sudden spasm of the larynx so that the child cannot breathe, for the condition occurs primarily during the winter months when infections are most common. There is no evidence that it is due to any congenital malformation of the heart or other organs, and there is no evidence that it runs in families.

Several facts should be of interest to parents concerned about this condition:

1. It rarely occurs during the first month of life.

2. Ninety percent of the cases occur at the age of 1 to 5 months. After this there is virtually no danger.

3. No person is responsible for a crib death, and no guilt should be felt if it occurs. Nevertheless the grief of losing a child is often made even more painful and damaging by accusations and feelings of guilt. The marriage may break up or one or both of the parents may be afraid to have another child. In such cases parents should consider special counseling or talk with other parents who have suffered the same experience. The National Foundation for Sudden Infant Death was founded to help parents who have lost a child through crib death. The address is 1501 Broadway, New York, N.Y. 10036.

Crib rocking

When babies are able to get up on their hands and knees, at about 9 months, many of them rock back and forth before going to sleep, or when they have just awakened. Sometimes they will add to this activity by banging their heads on the crib each time they rock forward. This banging causes no injury. Some babies sit up and sway forward and backward, hitting their heads on the backward swing.

The cause of this rocking and head banging is not entirely understood. Some child-behavior experts feel that the child enjoys the rhythmic sensation of the rocking; some, that the child enjoys the visual movement; others, that it is a release for certain inner tensions; while still others feel it is a masturbatory activity.

But, whatever the cause, it is of no real importance, except perhaps to the child, who does get satisfaction from the activity. The only problem is the repetitive and perhaps loud and annoying sound of the rocking as the crib moves on the floor or the child's head bangs against the crib. The noise can be reduced by placing rubber cups under the legs of the crib, tightening the crib's screws, and padding the top and bottom with crib bumpers, pillows, or thick blankets.

Many parents worry that the head banging may damage the child's brain, but this is not so. In spite of the fact that some children bang their heads so forcibly that a bump develops on the skull, it never harms them in any way. The bump disappears when the head banging ceases, usually at about 18 months to 2½ years.

Crippled child, helping the

The crippled child, whether his disability is the result of cerebral palsy, poliomyelitis, congenital abnormality, injury, or some other cause, has the same basic emotional needs as every child. He needs the love of his parents, the deep knowledge that he is wanted and enjoyed. He needs and seeks approval. And like other children he needs discipline and understanding.

In the early years, at least, the crippled child will need extra attention from his parents, who do what they can to make him happy and as normal as possible. But there is a potential danger that the parents' love and sympathy, plus possible guilt feelings, may cause them to do too much for the child, spoiling him and retarding his efforts toward self-dependence and self-reliance. Like other children the crippled child has a need for independence and will seek it if not restricted or indulged.

It is important that he be given opportunities for self-help as soon as possible. Of course, he must learn what he can or cannot do. Perhaps he can't run fast or play some of the games other children do, but usually he can acquire other skills. He can usually be taught to feed and dress himself and take care of his personal needs. But the ability to do things will vary with his specific disability, with his use and control of his affected limbs. In cerebral palsy, for instance, there may be poor coordination caused by spasms of muscles and uncontrolled motions. But a crippled child should gradually learn to increase his skills in line with his mental and physical abilities.

All normal children learn to control their arms and legs gradually—first the arms and legs and later the fingers and toes. The crippled child follows the same sequence unless there is a paralysis of the muscles. Motor development will often be much slower, and the child may need the help of adults to aid him in moving his head, arms, and legs. The child may even need help in directing his head so that his eyes can see what his hands are doing or touching.

In encouraging a crippled child toward self-dependence, there are three important steps:

1. Teaching him to dress himself.
2. Teaching him to take care of his personal appearance.
3. Teaching him to take care of his own toilet needs.

These are usually hard enough tasks for any youngster to learn to accomplish, and the problems are necessarily multiplied for the child who is crippled. They are multiplied not only because he is crippled, but, as was mentioned before, because parents tend to form the habit of doing almost everything for the child—a necessity in the very early years but an unfortunate habit later on.

Teaching a crippled child to dress himself   For the child who is mildly or moderately crippled, the following suggestions may be of help, as formulated by the National Society for Crippled Children and Adults:

1. Start first with undressing and work up to dressing.
2. Give the child "just a little" help, such as pulling the shoe or sock partly off, and let him do the rest.
3. Place his clothes within his reach and in the correct position and order to make it easier for him to get into them. A mark to indicate front or back of clothing may be helpful.
4. Let the child practice one movement at a time and, if necessary, on one garment at a time. When this phase is mastered, he can gradually do more.
5. In learning to push his arm through a sleeve, have the child make a fist so that his fingers will not get caught. It may be necessary for the adult to assist at first by reaching through the cuff of the sleeve to help pull the child's arm through. Gradually the child can learn to do it by himself.
6. Put the more handicapped arm into the sleeve first and in undressing take it out last. It may be necessary to assist the child in bringing the garment around his shoulder, after which he may insert his least handicapped arm without assistance.
7. Try to use the same routine for the procedures of undressing and dressing. Verbalizing each step of the action may help him remember the proper order for taking off and putting on his clothes.
8. Let the child do the easier tasks while you do the more difficult ones. When he is ready, have him try the harder tasks.
9. Dressing should be done in the child's most normal position for the activity,

either while lying down, sitting, or standing. Try to establish normal motion without tension in the child as he attempts dressing or undressing.

10. Make a realistic list of the things the child can do, those things he thinks he can learn within a short time, and then have him start with the things he is interested in learning.

11. When a child has learned to do something well, he should be given honest praise.

12. The child should realize that he is being given help, but that as he gains in skill he will not need, nor should he accept, as much help. Say often to the child, "I will help you a little and by and by you will be able to do it by yourself."

Most children who are mildly or moderately handicapped may be taught to dress themselves. Children who are severely crippled may need the aid of an occupational therapist to finally get the necessary use of finger, hand, and arm muscles to dress.

In learning to dress and undress it is most important that these children should have suitable clothing. The clothes should be durable and should give plenty of freedom for activity. They should be as near as possible in appearance to the clothes of other children in the child's age group. They should also be easy to button and unbutton and easy to get on and take off. Many of the modern clothes for the crippled child fasten together with Velcro, a fabric that adheres to another similar strip of fabric. When buttons are used, they should be down the front of the clothing and should be large, with big, loose buttonholes. If zippers are used, a large ring or bead should be attached to the pull end. Another type of suitable clothing is that which has a large neck opening that can be pulled over the head without difficulty. Long tipped shoelaces and large eyelets in the shoes make it much easier for a child to learn to tie his shoes. There are also elastic shoelaces for oxfords that once tied stay tied.

Clothes should also be selected that will not cause difficulty when a child has to go to the bathroom. Pants and trousers should have a fairly wide, loose elastic band around the waist so that they can be slipped down with ease. Boys' trousers that are zippered should have a large ring or pull-bead attached to the zipper for quick and easy usage.

For girls it is also desirable to have clothes that will zip or button down the front. Coats should be loose and have large armholes. They can be fastened in front with Velcro, or with large buttons, or with a single button or fastener with a loop at the top.

Caring for personal appearance This includes washing the face and hands, taking a bath, getting dried off, combing and brushing the hair, and brushing the teeth. Most of these steps are learned gradually, with the parent giving the child as much independence as possible. For tub bathing it may be necessary to use special fixtures and equipment, such as a railing attached to the wall nearby and on the side of the tub which can be used when getting into or out of the bath.

Brushing the teeth is of particular importance, especially in children with cerebral palsy, since their teeth have a tendency to decay. At first most children can learn to clean their teeth by using a cloth wrapped around the forefinger. Later a toothbrush with a widened handle should be used.

Brushing and combing the hair may

be started when the child is young. The hair style should be simple but becoming, and should not require too much manipulation. Here again, the style of the hairdo and the ability of the child to brush and comb it depends on the child's physical capability.

Learning to handle toilet needs When a child is unable to sit, stand, or walk without great difficulty, he will usually be slow in gaining bladder and bowel control. The speed of learning will also be influenced by the condition which has handicapped the child and by how much control he has over his muscles of evacuation.

Most crippled children eventually learn to make their toilet needs known to their parents and most of those of normal mentality will have good control during the daytime at least by the time they are 5 years old. As soon as a child shows signs of training readiness, diapers should be discarded and training pants used.

As soon as a child understands what it is for, he should be given a potty chair which is specially built so that it slopes down at the back, preventing the child from sliding off in front. The chair should have sides to give added support. The child's feet should be firmly on the floor or on a firm footrest. In many cases it is also advisable to have a wide band that can be fastened loosely around a child's chest to help him sit in an upright position or lean slightly forward if he so desires.

As in almost all other situations, the crippled child must be gradually helped to independence in fulfilling his toilet needs. As mentioned, pants that are easy to pull up or down should be used. Trousers should be closed either by Vel-cro or by a zipper to which a large ring or bead is attached.

Hand bars or parallel bars on either side of the toilet will help a child in sitting down and rising. They are also of great advantage for a boy to grasp while standing and urinating. Older boys who cannot walk can be taught to use a urinal. The child should be taught the use of toilet paper and how to flush the toilet.

There are many valuable equipment aids to help crippled children. These can be purchased, but many can also be made by parents. A list of companies making such appliances and blueprint diagrams for constructing them at home may be obtained by writing to the National Society for Crippled Children and Adults, 2023 West Ogden Avenue, Chicago, Illinois.

A good many very helpful pamphlets concerning the crippled child may also be obtained from the National Society for Crippled Children and Adults.

It is also of the greatest help for parents of crippled children to join a group of parents with similar problems. They can learn a great deal and be of mutual aid to one another in discussing their experiences. There are parents' organizations in almost all the larger communities. A list of such local organizations may also be obtained from the National Society for Crippled Children and Adults.

Cross-eyes see **Eye defects.**

Crossing streets see **Accident prevention, outdoors.**

Croup
A condition caused by a spasm or inflammation of the larynx (voice box)

and characterized by a frequent, dry, brassy cough that sounds like the barking of a seal. It may occur in infants or young children up to the age of 5.

There are really two different kinds of croup. The first, spasmodic croup, is frightening but usually of no danger. In this type the child usually goes to bed perfectly well but suddenly awakens in the middle of the night with great difficulty in breathing, with rapid, wheezing respirations, and with a frequent, barking cough. The child is frightened and in great distress. There is rarely any fever. The difficulty is caused by a sudden spasm of the larynx, and can usually be quickly relieved by taking the child to the bathroom, and turning on the hot water so that the whole room is steamed up. Inhalation of this warm steam relaxes the laryngeal spasm. A warm-steam vaporizer will serve the same purpose if the child inhales the steam directly with an open mouth. (Always be careful that the youngster does not topple the vaporizer and burn himself.) If the difficulty in breathing is very severe, you can give the child a tablespoon of syrup of ipecac in a glass of water. This will cause vomiting, and the force of the vomiting usually relieves the spasm.

If a child has a tendency toward croup, it is advisable to keep an air humidifier in his room.

The second type of croup is extremely dangerous; it requires the close attention of a doctor, and hospitalization is often necessary. This type of croup almost always develops out of a respiratory infection. The child starts breathing with some difficulty and develops a croupy cough and fever. He looks ill and is ill. The doctor should be notified immediately, for the difficulty in breathing may increase rapidly and the child may suddenly die. If the doctor cannot be reached, take the child to the hospital. This croup is not only due to a spasm, but to an inflammation caused by viruses or bacteria. This inflammation swells the inner lining of the breathing tubes, narrowing the passages, and also causes the formation of a very thick mucus which may collect in the tubes and literally drown the child.

If the respirations become too rapid and the child is having great distress breathing, the doctor will rush him to a hospital. There he will be given oxygen mixed with fine droplets of water containing a substance to thin the mucus. At times, as a life-saving measure, a tracheotomy (surgically cutting an opening into the trachea through the front of the lower neck) is performed. This permits the introduction of oxygen and moisture below the swollen larynx and also permits suctioning off the obstructing mucus. This treatment is usually completely successful.

Cruelty   see **Bullying; Sadism.**

Crushes
Intense emotional attachments which some preadolescent or early adolescent girls develop for another girl (usually older), a woman teacher, or some other woman outside the home whom they admire greatly. This is almost like an adolescent love interest. The girl wants to be near her idol as much as possible. She gets up early to meet the object of her affection and walks her to school. She takes money out of her bank or uses her allowance to buy presents for her—often elaborate and valuable ones. She thinks almost constantly of the one she admires and talks about her whenever she gets a chance.

Crushes occur most frequently at girls' schools and girls' camps where there are no boys and few men on whom to focus burgeoning sex urges and desires. Usually the girls who get crushes are normal girls with normal desires for boys—but either there are no boys available or the girls are temporarily shy or afraid of them, or perhaps not yet ready for them.

These crushes almost always disappear when boy-girl relationships are established. Although they often cause parents considerable concern because of the homosexual overtones, there is usually no need for worry. The best thing the parents can do is let the child live through this phase without upsetting her further with teasing or criticism. If guidance seems necessary (for example, if it appears that the older girl or woman is not a person of good character, or if there are repeated crushes and no interest in the opposite sex), then it should be undertaken as gently and tactfully as possible.

Crying

It used to be believed that crying during early infancy was beneficial. "It helps to expand the baby's lungs," many mothers were informed by their doctors. But this theory was abandoned when scientific studies proved that the lungs of the newborn baby completely expand within several hours.

Crying in all human beings of all ages is a sign of discomfort, pain, fear, anger, or other unhappiness. In infancy it may be a sign of any one or all of these various sensations. The infant, unable to talk, cries to let his needs and feelings be known. He may cry because he is hungry or uncomfortable; he may want to be held and cuddled; he may desire more sucking satisfaction and will cease crying when given a pacifier.

It is not necessary to let a baby cry

for fear of spoiling him. An infant cannot be spoiled before he is 10 to 12 months old, and a parent should not be afraid to pick him up when he cries. This does not mean that a baby must be picked up the minute he cries; if a parent has important things to do, a baby can be allowed to cry for five or even ten minutes, but should be picked up as soon as possible. The infant who has had his needs responded to promptly, and who feels basically secure, will usually be better able to accept some frustration later on.

Crying is frequently a sign of pain. The most common cause is colic; other causes include teething, constipation, a crack in the mucous membrane of the anus (see **Anal fissure**), sore throat, and earache.

Usually parents can diagnose the cause of the infant's discomfort or pain, but if an infant cries incessantly and cannot be quieted, he should be seen by a doctor.

Once a child is past the period of infancy and certainly when he is able to understand a certain number of words, the causes of crying are usually quite easily detected, and parents should not give in to the crying as readily as when the child was younger. As an example, the year-old child who cries when put to bed may be left to cry for a while without fear of harming him. (See **Sleep problems.**)

From approximately the first birthday on, parents should not feel that they have to accede to the crying child if his demands are not reasonable. The youngster who cries because he wants a candy before dinner or because he would rather see TV than go outdoors can be permitted to cry. The child with temper tantrums must not feel he can control parents or break down their authority by this means. (See **Temper and temper tantrums.**) Only if the child is subject to frequent and inexplicable fits of crying need one look to deeper physical or emotional causes.

Crying in older children is most often caused by unhappiness, disappointment, and anger. Your reaction to this show of emotion depends entirely upon the circumstances that cause the upset. At times the child needs love, comforting, and understanding; at other times, the firmness of authority. Again, frequent episodes of crying should be taken seriously, for the child may be chronically unhappy or unwell.

Cub Scouts   see **Recreational organizations.**

Cup, drinking from   see **Bottle feeding.**

Curiosity

Children manifest curiosity almost from the moment of birth. An infant a few days old looks at colored mobiles and lights. Infants 1 and 2 months old follow larger objects with their eyes and love to be carried from place to place observing changing scenes, the wallpaper, the pictures, the different people.

At 3 months curiosity starts to become more active. The baby becomes more aware of his surroundings and begins to grasp objects in his hands. From that time on his curiosity becomes more and more intense, and as the months pass he begins to interpret sounds and to recognize differences of hardness and softness, weight, size, shape, and color. He not only feels with his hands and fingers but with his lips and mouth as well, placing almost all objects he can grasp up to his lips or into his mouth.

Once the child is able to crawl or

walk by himself, he becomes an explorer and discoverer and must be watched closely, both for his own safety and to prevent unnecessary damage in the household. But he should be given as much freedom as possible to satisfy his curiosity—during the first three years of life the child learns more than he will learn all through his school and college years; he is finding a whole world of which he knows absolutely nothing.

The preschool child asks his parents many questions. At first the questions are directed at the names of things: "Mommy, what is that?" Later, especially between 3 and 5, the questions turn to "how" and "why": "How does the wind blow?" "Why does it blow?" "Why does smoke go up?" "Why is the sky blue?" "Why does the dog bark?" "Why do you cut off the fingernails that God put there?" And usually also between 3 and 5, children start asking questions about their own origins: "Where did I come from?" and questions on birth and reproduction. (See **Sex education in the home.**)

All questions should be answered seriously. If the question is a difficult one or one that you can't answer, you can simply say, "Really, I don't know the answer, but I'll look it up and tell you." You should do your research as soon as possible and give the answer to the child. The child should feel that he can always turn to his parents with his questions and expect truthful answers.

By stimulating and satisfying a child's natural curiosity, parents can make it possible for him to develop his mental and emotional capabilities to the fullest. See also **Stimulating the child.**

Cuts

Cuts and other wounds should be treated at once to avoid infection and to promote the quickest and best possible healing.

The first bleeding of a cut is of value, for it may wash away bacteria that would otherwise infect the area; after most cuts the blood will coagulate normally, and bleeding will normally cease within three minutes.

If a cut is bleeding profusely, apply firm direct pressure on the cut itself, preferably using a gauze pad. This will control the bleeding from the small blood vessels in the skin (capillaries) and even from veins within a few minutes. Bleeding from an artery will continue to spurt profusely and must be treated by a doctor. The bleeding of a scalp wound is almost always very abundant but will stop with pressure in about three minutes.

Even in cases of arterial bleeding tourniquets should not be attempted unless there is imminent danger of death from loss of blood (a tourniquet should

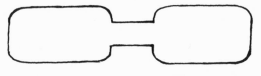

Butterfly Band-Aid. The wide parts of the Band-Aid should go on either side of the cut, with the narrow part crossing the lips of the cut. This Band-Aid should act as a suture, holding the cut closed.

never be made of a narrow material such as a cord, but rather of a wide piece of cloth). If bleeding from a cut is severe, continue direct pressure and elevate the wound if possible. In cases of severe bleeding from a cut on the arm or leg that does not respond to direct pressure, you may also (without ceasing direct pressure) attempt to check bleeding by pressure on the inside of the upper arm or at the groin midway on the line from the crotch to the hip bone.

Once the bleeding has ceased, the wound should be cleansed with soap and water to remove any dirt that may have entered. Then an antiseptic solution should be applied—such as iodine or Betadine (povidone-iodine, which does not burn the skin). A dirty wound is more apt to form a scar, and if a wound is so deep that it is difficult to clean out, the child should be taken to a doctor. He will wash the wound thoroughly. The temporary discomfort is unavoidable.

A small cut can then be covered with a Band-Aid. In the case of a gaping cut, the edges of the wound should be put together and held there by sterile adhesive tape or better, if possible, by butterfly Band-Aids. If too wide and gaping or too irregular, the cut may require stitching by a doctor to guarantee a minimum of scarring.

Any serious cut should then be cov-

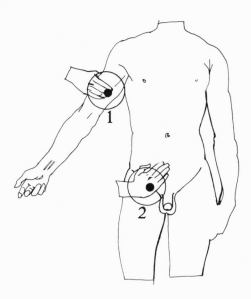

Position of pressure points for checking bleeding in the arm (1) and the leg (2).

ered with one or more gauze pads that have been lubricated with an antiseptic ointment or Vaseline to prevent sticking. These should be held down by adhesive tape.

The stitches, butterfly Band-Aids, or adhesive tape holding the edges of a cut together should be removed in approximately six days, by which time the wound should have grown together. In removing adhesive tape, pull from the ends on both sides toward the center to avoid tearing open the healing wound.

Any cut on the face that might cause disfiguring scarring should be seen by a doctor, who may recommend that it be treated by a plastic surgeon.

Cutting teeth   see Teeth; Teething.

Cyst, pilonidal   see Pilonidal cyst.

Cystic fibrosis
A hereditary disease, in which the secretions of the mucous membrane of the bronchial tubes (the smaller breathing tubes) become abnormally thick, causing clogging of the tubes. This leads to pneumonia and eventually to bronchiectasis, in which there is destruction of the lung tissue. There is also a thickening of the secretions of the pancreas, which clogs up the ducts that normally secrete pancreatic juice—the most important digestive juice—into the intestine. This latter difficulty causes imperfect digestion, often leading to diarrhea and gas formation. The portion of the pancreas that secretes pancreatic digestive juice deteriorates and shrinks. The portion of the pancreas that secretes insulin remains normal.

Signs and symptoms of cystic fibrosis usually appear within the first few weeks of life. In 5 to 10 percent of the children with this condition, a symptom of this disease is present a few hours after birth: a blockage of the intestines caused by a thick, sticky plug of meconium which cannot be passed. Surgery for removal of the plug is necessary.

In children with cystic fibrosis there is also a marked increase in the amount of salt in their sweat. This increase in salt is present from birth and remains high throughout the life of the child. This increase in sweat salt provides the primary diagnostic test for the disease.

In most children with this condition the diagnosis of cystic fibrosis is suspected when an infant develops bronchitis or pneumonia during the early months of its life.

Treatment   At present there is no cure for cystic fibrosis, but treatment continued throughout the child's life has been very successful. Many children with cystic fibrosis who have been treated with the following modern methods are now attending high school and college.

1. The child should sleep in a plastic tent each night, in which he breathes in minute droplets of water in the air he inhales. This loosens the mucus in the breathing tubes.
2. The child is given pancreatic digestive substances by mouth to substitute for the pancreatic juice that normally reaches the intestines.
3. Antibiotics are given at the first sign of a respiratory infection in an attempt to prevent pneumonia.
4. The child should stay cool during the summer months and take extra salt in his diet, plus a great deal of fluid. This is necessary because of the extra salt in the child's perspiration; the loss of salt during hot weather tends to cause heat prostration.

Cystitis

An inflammation of the urinary bladder. It is usually caused by bacteria entering the bladder from below through the urethra (the tube through which urine flows from the bladder out of the body).

Cystitis occurs quite frequently in girls but very rarely in boys. This is because the female urethra is short and leads directly out of the body, whereas in boys the urethra must pass through the length of the penis.

The bacteria that cause cystitis are usually the colon bacilli, bacteria normally found in the feces. Normally the colon bacilli are not irritating in the intestines or on the surface of the unbroken skin, but are very irritating to the inner lining of the urinary bladder. This is why girls should always be taught to wipe themselves from front to back after a bowel movement.

The symptoms of cystitis are usually low abdominal pain and pain or burning on urination. There is often fever. In severe cases, the urine may be bloody. Cystitis in girls is so common that urine should always be examined when there is a fever of unknown origin or chronic abdominal pain with or without fever.

The diagnosis of cystitis is easily made by a microscopic examination of the urine.

Treatment consists in taking antibiotics by mouth until the condition is cleared up. Repeated attacks of cystitis require further investigation by the doctor or by a urologist.

D

Dance see **Rhythms and dance.**

Dandruff

A condition of the scalp characterized by the formation of fine, white, slightly greasy scales.

It is rarely seen during childhood but not infrequently arises during adolescence. Its cause is unknown, although it may run in families. Some doctors have reported finding bacteria and fungi in the scales of dandruff. However, most dermatologists feel that these bacteria and fungi are not the cause of dandruff but find the oily condition of the scalp a favorable place in which to grow.

There is no known cure at the present time, but the condition can be controlled by shampooing the scalp once or twice a week.

Certain medicated shampoos are especially advised for their effectiveness. Among the most recommended are Selsun Blue (selenium sulfide detergent) and Zincon Dandruff Shampoo (pyrithione zinc 1%).

Dark, fear of the see **Fears.**

Dating

At the present time many boys and girls as young as 13 or 14 are already dating. Most dates are in the afternoon but some are in the evening. Many parents feel that this age is too young for dating and that their children have not as yet developed adequate responsibility.

Since 13- and 14-year-olds are experiencing their first surge of adult sex interests, desires, and urges, some checking is advisable until a gradual adjustment has been attained. Nevertheless, these young teen-agers should be permitted to date, for it is now the accepted rule.

Wanting to have unchaperoned parties, many young teen-agers ask their parents to go out on the evening of the party; if the parents object, their teen-ager violently protests that "all the other parents do it." True or not, parents should not submit to such demands. Generally, if a resistant parent contacts other parents he will find that their children have told them the same story. Regardless of their children's protests, parents should remain at home during these parties. It is not necessary to "oversee" every minute of the party, however. An occasional appearance in the party area from time to time, bringing drinks and snacks, in a pleasant and friendly manner, will suffice.

When young people are 16 and older, it becomes less necessary for parents to chaperone all get-togethers and parties. In some communities this may be possible, but in many communities teenagers do frequently have parties alone. Parents must remember that these youngsters will very soon be on their own in the world, and must be able to regulate their own behavior. At this age parents must rely more upon the sense of responsibility they have helped a teen-ager to develop and less upon direct supervision.

The dating patterns of these older teen-agers also may cause parents concern. Today dating is often "steady." A boy and girl date no one else; at dances, they usually dance with no one else. This is probably different from the parents' own dating patterns when they were young, although steady dating has been in favor with young people for quite a while and perhaps some parents followed this fashion.

Parents complain that steady dating limits a teen-ager's opportunities to meet and get to know other boys and girls of their own age. This is undoubtedly true, but steady dating is nevertheless the code among young people today and must be accepted. And although it does have disadvantages, it also has certain advantages for adolescents. They gain great pride in knowing that someone cares for them enough to want to go steady and a good deal of satisfaction in knowing that a fixed date is scheduled for Friday and Saturday evenings.

Parents should not feel that just because two teen-agers are going steady, they will be married when they are older. This may of course happen, but it is usually not the case. Parents of today, however, do have important and real concerns about their children's dating. Drug addition among teen-agers, promiscuity, the "pill," the free life of the hippies, drinking, and speed driving are, of course, real causes of concern.

Teen-agers still need guidance and still need limits. Proper guidance and self-imposed limits must come from discussions at home as well as in school. Adolescents are likely to resist their parents or call them old-fashioned, but if they know that their parents have a real interest in them, and an understanding of their problems, they are more likely to act with responsibility. Parents must

do everything they can to establish a relationship with their teen-agers that encompasses mutual trust and confidence when the adolescent is dating.

Even when parents have confidence in a teen-ager, and are happy that he or she is going out on dates, they often still ask whether dates should be limited to weekends and how late a young person should be permitted to stay out. There are three factors to consider here: the teen-ager needs about eight hours of sleep, needs time to do homework, and doesn't want to be obliged to get home a great deal earlier than the other boys and girls in his or her group. In general, evening dates should be limited to Friday and Saturday nights. Children younger than 16 should be home between 10 and 11 P.M. and older teen-agers should be home about midnight. The exact time should depend on what sort of evening is planned and should be worked out with the youngster. The parents should always know where their child is and with whom, and the youngster should be responsible for telephoning if there is a change in plans or he is coming home later than planned. Girls should be told not to try to get home alone at night if, for whatever reason, they are not being escorted home. They should telephone their parents so that arrangements can be made to get home safely.

See also **Drinking, adolescent; Drug abuse; Sexual behavior in adolescence.**

Dawdling
Wasting time by trifling or idling. Although dawdling is a common experience among adults as well as children, a chronic dawdler nevertheless provokes concern in parents.

Parents interested in the development of their child want to determine why he dawdles. The primary reason for dawdling is a simple one: the child, or adult, dawdles when he doesn't like what he's doing. The task may be distasteful to him; or he's bored with it; or he doesn't like to do it because you were the one who told him to do it (many children who resent doing errands for their parents are quick to do errands for a teacher). Or a child may dawdle in the hope that he will not have to do whatever he is supposed to be doing.

To counteract the dawdling tendency, a wise parent should show interest in and appreciation for what the child is doing. At times, helping him may be the answer. Sometimes changing a chore helps, if the chore has been boring. If a child dawdles excessively in getting ready for school or in doing his homework, try to find out if anything serious is bothering him about his school life. Sometimes, however, it is better to permit dawdling rather than nag and create further resentment.

Day care centers

Facilities set up for the care of groups of infants or young children by a community, church, business, or other organization, either private or public. The day care center is for the benefit of the children of working mothers or of mothers who for whatever reason are unable to care for their children during the day.

In most communities, day care centers must be licensed by the city or state and supervised by a person trained in child care.

A good day care center not only provides for the children's basic physical needs but must often also serve as a parent substitute, since so many of the children are in the center for most of their waking hours. Because of this, day care centers must be capable of meeting the emotional and intellectual needs of the growing child. A good center must have adequate space, a variety of indoor and outdoor equipment, and—most important of all—adequate staffing by warm and devoted people.

Because the children are so young, the day care center plays an important role in the development of language, social values, physical skills, and healthy habits. Before placing a child in a center, parents should carefully investigate its staff, facilities, and program. Just because the children in a center seem quiet, well-behaved, and reasonably content does not mean that the center is doing all that should be done for them. Children also need stimulation and activity and should not be passive and "institutionalized."

The cost of care in a center varies considerably. Where the centers are publicly assisted, cost varies according to family finances and size. In many centers run by churches, welfare organizations, or cooperative parent groups, care is free to people in low economic brackets but may be quite costly for people with higher incomes.

Daydreaming

The daydreamer sits looking into the distance, withdrawn from the world about him, completely absorbed in his own imaginings and thoughts. Daydreaming is common among school-age children, and especially among adolescents. It has been the object of considerable theorizing as to its significance. Some theories explain that, like night dreams, daydreams provide a valuable release of emotions and help a youngster to solve some of his problems. The daydreamer vividly imagines what he would like to do or what he might do. He may also imagine situations in which problems arise, and then he imagines different ways of resolving them.

Although a certain amount of daydreaming is normal and expected, an excessive of amount of daydreaming is a sign of emotional disturbance. A deeply disturbed boy or girl will often spend a great deal of time daydreaming because his daydreams transport him from his unhappy world to happier places. A disturbed daydreamer is often unaware and almost unresponsive at school and at home during long periods of daydreaming. The home and the school environment should be studied for the causes of the child's unhappiness, and whatever steps necessary to improve the situation must be taken.

See also **Fantasy.**

DDT poisoning   see **Poisons: first-aid treatment.**

Deafness

Most parents of children who are deaf or partially deaf do not realize that their infant has a hearing handicap until the baby is 3 months of age or older. One exception is when an infant is born to a mother who contracted German measles during the first three months of her pregnancy. In such a case deafness may be suspected at birth.

However, parents usually become suspicious only when their apparently alert and interested infant fails to respond to sound. It is most important that a diagnosis be made at this time so that, if necessary, treatment may be started at once. Not only does an infant with impaired hearing miss a great deal of stimulation from the sounds of the world around him, but his relationship with his mother is impaired as well. The sound of a mother's voice means a great

deal to all infants, and the sounds of her movements are often an additional reassurance to the infant that she is nearby.

Of course, the deaf child, being unable to hear, is unable to mimic sounds and so is unable to learn speech spontaneously.

In the course of his development the child who is deaf or markedly hard of hearing is further handicapped, for he can neither hear the reassuring, approving voice of his parents, nor can discipline be explained to him except by physical means.

The parents' job is often quite difficult, for they, as well as the child, often feel frustrated. And, as with other handicapped children, parents at times feel guilt as well as resentment. To minimize these problems, it is most important that the child be given a hearing aid and taught to lip-read at the earliest possible time.

Causes   A 1968 study reported the frequency of the causes of childhood deafness to be: heredity, 18 percent; prematurity, 14 percent; German measles (rubella), 9 percent; meningitis, 8 percent; Rh factor, 3.5 percent; and cause unknown, 30 percent.

Deafness from German measles during a mother's pregnancy should be almost completely eliminated through the immunization of all children and susceptible women with the new rubella vaccine. And with the new serum given to Rh negative mothers immediately following each birth, deafness from that difficulty should be prevented (see **Rh factor blood incompatibility**). Prematurity has been reduced by better obstetrical care. With the immunization of children against measles, that most dangerous type of meningitis, measles meningitis, can be avoided. Hereditary deafness may be reduced in the foreseeable future by new genetic knowledge.

Diagnosis   Whether an infant is deaf or has a hearing defect can occasionally be determined by making a loud clap under a table or bathinette on which the baby is lying. The noise will cause the hearing infant to blink or at least pause in his movements.

If deafness is suspected, more accurate tests may be made by skilled investigators or ear specialists. One method is by the use of the electroencephalogram, which graphically records brain waves. Noises, if heard, cause changes in these tracings. Another method is the measurement of the amount of perspiration of the skin, which increases with loud noises.

When a child is older than 3 years, tests are easily made with an audiometer, an instrument that produces various sounds from low-pitched to high-pitched in varying degrees of loudness. This method determines not only how much a child hears but also if he has a nerve deafness that allows him to hear only sounds of certain pitches. For instance, a child with nerve deafness might be able to hear a deep boat whistle or booming sounds miles away but be unable to hear the high-pitched sound of a canary or the ring of a telephone in the same room.

Treatment   The treatment of deafness depends entirely upon the cause of the condition. If it is caused by enlarged adenoids closing off the inside of the eustachian tube, by an infection causing a redness and thickening of the eardrum, or by fluid behind the drum or a mass of wax in the outer ear canal, it can be easily corrected, as a rule, by proper medical care.

If the deafness or partial deafness is the result of permanent damage to the nerves of hearing, a hearing apparatus should be given to the child as soon as the diagnosis is made, even in early infancy. For the sooner an infant hears sounds the more aware he is of the many things around him and the greater is his chance of learning to speak normally. Much of the child's future emotional development, and possibly his education as well, depends on the early recognition and treatment of hearing defects.

With the remarkable advances in electronics, small, lightweight hearing aids of clear quality have been produced. Some of these fit into the ear, others are held against the skull behind the ear, depending on the youngster's type of deafness.

As soon as it is apparent that a child has no speech or is badly handicapped by unintelligible speech, he should have speech instruction, which may be obtained at a special school for the deaf or at a university or hospital speech clinic. In the few cases where the nerve damage is so severe that there is total deafness, the child should be taught lip-reading as soon as possible.

Vocations for the deaf   Numerous occupations are open to those who are deaf, even those who are totally deaf. Many of the totally deaf have been most successful in such fields as electronics, mechanics, laboratory work, cabinet-making, farming, photography, and accounting.

Those who are partially deaf may enter almost all professions and occupations, including law, medicine, architecture, and engineering—and most can also drive automobiles.

Parents of deaf children should realize that with early recognition of their defect, the learning of lip-reading, and a full education their children can lead successful, happy, and fulfilled lives.

Parents of children with hearing defects may get valuable information by writing to the American Speech and Hearing Association, 9030 Old Georgetown Road, Bethesda, Md. 20014.

Death, dealing with a

The manner in which a death is explained, especially to young children, is most important. To the young child, who is so greatly dependent on his parents, even the thought of a temporary separation from them can be extremely upsetting.

The death of someone outside the family should be explained differently from the death of a loved member of the family. Between the age of 2½ to 6 years, the death of a parent causes the greatest anxiety to a young child, although the loss of a loved grandparent or other close person may bring not only some sense of loss but also the anxiety that the parents might die and disappear forever.

A child should be told immediately of a death, particularly if the person is a member of the family or a beloved relative or acquaintance. Too many parents in their effort to spare the child anguish and sorrow say that the deceased is on a trip or a vacation or is in the hospital. But holding off the statement that a person has died only deceives the child and makes it more difficult to explain later.

The young child should be told simply that the person has died and will not return. But he should be reassured that his parents, or whoever is closest to him if his parents are not living, will never leave him. This is, of course, a little white lie, but is much needed by a child at this time to bolster his security.

Because parents are the individuals closest to a child, the death of a parent is not only extremely upsetting but is very difficult for young children—under the approximate age of 6 years—to understand. Since the child has no conception of the finality of death, he cannot understand why the parent he loved should have left him. He often feels the event to be a rejection, and he may combine his sorrow at being deserted with anger at the parent for having left him.

The young child who has lost one, or both, parents needs the constant reassurance that he was much loved by the parent or parents who died, and that those who remain love him very much and will always stay with him.

An older child, as a rule, has more understanding of the meaning of death, but he too needs the reassurance that those remaining who love him and whom he loves will not leave him.

Care should be taken not to associate the death with illness or with being in the hospital lest a child develop anxieties of death when any illness or hospital experiences arises. Nor should he be told that a person died in his sleep or that the deceased is sleeping and will never wake up. Many children have resisted sleep after having someone associate death with sleeping.

During the period following a death, a young child should remain in the home even if his parents and others express and display sorrow. A child must learn about these feelings, although, preferably, he should not be exposed to hysteria.

Whether or not a small child should be taken to a funeral has received considerable debate. A child over 5 or 6 years has more understanding and can usually adjust, but it is probably best for him not to view the deceased; he is better able then to remember the person as he knew him when he was living.

If the child has no previous knowledge of death, he can be told that when a living person or animal dies the body just stops working, there is no movement or feeling, and the person cannot come back again. Most children will then ask what happens to the person after he dies. If a child has a religious background it is comforting to tell him that the person has gone to heaven, or whatever is in line with the parents' belief. Otherwise he can be told that the body is taken to a cemetery where there are beautiful trees and flowers and green grass. If possible it is better not to go into details about burying the body in the earth or about cremation, for, again, young children misconceive and think a living person is being buried or burned.

Again, the important thing to remember is that a young child needs constant reassurance that those who remain and love him deeply will stay with him and never leave him.

Children over the age of 6 usually have much more understanding, and death can usually be discussed with them on a more mature level. But they also need a great deal of reassurance concerning their own as well as their parents' lives.

See also **Death as children see it.**

Death as children see it
A child's idea of death is very different from that of of an adult. The adult, realizing the finality of death, has a deep sense of loss and sorrow if the person who has died has been close to him. The young child—the child who is younger than 6 or so—has no notion whatsoever of the finality of death. To a young child, and to many older children as well, death is not final—it is just a separation. A young child may even be angry at the parent or grandparent who dies, because he or she has left him. He feels rejected—he just can't understand why a person he loved and who loved him should leave. Or, a child may feel guilt at the loss of a loved one. Remembering his own momentary angers at the person who is now dead, he believes his anger caused the death.

A young child understands death simply as a stopping of activity—and a temporary one at that. Most of them play "dead" in the course of their games. They see characters on television shot dead—but they are sure they can get up again.

Children over 6 begin to understand more and more the meaning of death—but most of them still cannot fully accept its permanence. When children reach puberty they usually understand the significance of death, realize its permanence, feel the loss, and suffer sorrow.

Deciduous teeth see **Teeth.**

Dehydrated fruit, swallowed whole see **Foreign objects, swallowed.**

Delirium
A mental disturbance in which illusions, hallucinations, and incoherence occur. In children it is often encountered in acute infections that are associated with high fever. Such conditions would include acute tonsillitis, measles, and pneumonia. The delirium itself is not serious and disappears as the fever subsides.

Delivery   see **Birth.**

Demand schedule see **Feeding schedules.**

Dental braces
Dental braces are used to bring teeth into normal position not only for appearance but also to assure that the teeth on the top jaw meet those of the lower jaw properly. Correct alignment aids in proper chewing and prevents teeth from loosening.

Braces are of the greatest importance in improving the appearance of many children. Protruding teeth may be gradually drawn back to a normal position, receding lower jaws may be brought forward, and the jaw itself may be widened.

Braces should be applied as soon as the permanent teeth are in. Since approximately two years are required to accomplish the straightening, prompt attention to this cosmetic factor will allow the removal of the braces before the child reaches adolescence. At that age, of course, children have a great need to appear at their best for their early encounters with the opposite sex.

See also **Dentist; Orthodontist; Teeth.**

Dental care   see **Teeth.**

Dental caries   see **Tooth decay.**

Dentist
A specialist trained to diagnose and treat malfunctions and diseases of the teeth, gums, and nearby tissue. The dentist is an important person in a child's life and his relationship with the child should be a good one. He should like children, enjoy caring for their teeth, and be a relaxed and unhurried person. In many localities pedodontists, dentists especially trained and interested in treating children, have established practices.

Some good children's books are available to introduce the young child to this strange new world of buzzing instruments, drills, water squirters, and elevator chairs (see **Bibliography**). The best method of introduction, however, is to take the child with you on your regular dental visit and let the youngster observe. Perhaps the dentist will even give him a ride up and down on the dental chair. A child of 2 is not too young for this initiation.

A child should have his teeth examined by a dentist by the time he is 3 years old, and routinely thereafter. The necessity for this dental care cannot be overemphasized, for good teeth are basic not only to nutrition but to general health and appearance as well.

Dentition   see **Teething.**

Depilatories
Cosmetic preparations for the removal of body hair. In the form of liquids, ointments, and creams that contain chemicals that burn the hair from the skin, these preparations are often very irritating to the sensitive skin of children and adolescents. Most dermatologists advise against their use but suggest that if a person does use them, a small area of the skin should be treated first to see if any reaction occurs.

Depression
Periods of depression are only occasionally seen during infancy and childhood but are quite common during adolescence.

During early infancy, babies who are not cuddled, loved, and handled seem to develop a form of depression that is characterized by sad, unsmiling faces, little appetite for food, and a gradual decline.

During the preschool years children may go into periods of depression, for example when their parents go away for several weeks or more on a vacation. The child feels completely lost and rejected and cannot understand why someone who loved him would suddenly disappear. Death of a parent or a loved relative may also cause a serious period of depression.

Apart from such relatively short periods, children do not usually have a tendency toward sustained depression. The rare child who is chronically depressed is usually highly anxious and extremely unhappy. A depressed boy or girl may need therapy to relieve his worry and misery.

As children approach adolescence and enter the teen years, depressions become more common. First, there is greater academic competition and its concurrent fear of failure. At times a teen-ager may feel he cannot reach the high standards expected of him by his parents. Secondly, as boys and girls endure this very difficult period of social and sexual adjustment, they may be easily depressed over minor or unrealistic worries. They may feel they are ugly, underdeveloped, homosexual. They may masturbate and feel a deep and unrelaxing guilt. They may be depressed over the modern world with its wars, hatreds, prejudice, and inhumanity, and wonder if the future holds anything real in store for them.

Children in puberty and adolescence who seem to be depressed should be studied carefully. Parents should be sure they are communicating as much as possible with the child, and should also consult the child's doctor. Many of these children require psychotherapy, in which the underlying troubles will be brought out into the open and discussed.

Unless carefully handled, some of these depressed boys and girls may attempt suicide.

See also **Suicide and suicide threats.**

Depression, postpartum see **Postpartum depression.**

Dermatitis   see **Eczema; Rashes.**

Dermatologist

A doctor who specializes in diseases and abnormalities of the skin.

Most skin conditions of infants and children can be diagnosed and treated successfully by the pediatrician. In certain stubborn cases, however, or in cases that cannot be diagnosed by the child's regular doctor, a dermatologist should be consulted.

Destructiveness

All children at one time or another are destructive—an upsetting observation to most parents. But the causes of destructiveness vary not only with the age of the child but also with his intention—whether he or she destroys innocently (unintentionally) or maliciously. Most destructiveness by small children is innocent, that is, unintentional. Rarely is it malicious or the result of anger or frustration.

The little child creeping around or starting to walk—at approximately 9 to 15 months—is at his greatest period of exploration and discovery and unless watched closely can be very destructive. He's likely to tear pages out of books, knock a vase over and break it, pull a tablecloth down from the table, usually smashing a few dishes in the process—the possibilities are almost endless. His need to explore, discover, and experiment can be satisfied, and the destruction curtailed or at least diverted, by giving him substitute materials and activities. For example, as you take away the new book he is about to "explore," say, "No, we don't tear books, but you can play with these newspapers and magazines." Given old newspapers to tear with abandon, old pots and pans to bang around and clatter, balls and rubber blocks to throw, and toys to drag and shake, his destructiveness can be seen for what it really is—endless interest and curiosity.

As children approach the age of 3 they are still destructive but in a different manner. They become very curious about the workings of things. They take clocks apart; loosen knobs from doors, tops off bottles, knobs off TV sets; dismantle flashlights. Toys that can come apart or be broken in any way won't last long. This type of destructiveness is not bad—it's a sign of healthy curiosity—and this is the time to give the child old clocks, flashlights, and toys that can be taken apart.

Children of 3 to 5 will occasionally have temper tantrums and in their excitement and uncontrolled frustration throw things on the floor (see **Temper and temper tantrums**).

When children approach the age of 5 or 6 they may still be destructive—innocently or, at times, maliciously. Tremendously active, they enjoy jumping on beds, chairs, and couches. Once again they must be given substitute activities and short but definite laws: "No jumping on couches or beds"; "No wrestling in the living room"; "No throwing balls in the house." Instead they should be given a wrestling mat for their room or the playroom; some kind of climbing apparatus; a place to throw balls, to skate, and to bicycle; and all sorts of toys that give them an opportunity for activity.

At this age a child who is jealous of or angry at another child may now and again destroy something that this child owns or has made. He may knock down another child's building of blocks or scribble over his praised drawing. If this behavior is frequent, it means that the child is unhappy; it is a signal to the parents to investigate and to alleviate the child's difficulties.

During the school-age and teen-age period certain children deface or destroy property—for example, they may smash windows, set fires, daub cars with paint, destroy gardens, let the air out of car tires. Typically these children are hostile to their parents and, by extension, the whole adult world. They may otherwise appear as normal children—often with high IQ's. But a child who is this destructive, particularly if he takes the lead in destructive activities, is a troubled child, apt to get into great difficulties in later years. It is of no help to the child to assume that this is a passing phase. Often, in fact, the child's acts are at least partly motivated by a subconscious need to let the adult know that he needs special help. The relationships of these children with their fathers and mothers must be studied first. Sometimes the conditions that are upsetting them are clearly evident—lack of parental interest, repression, overdiscipline, lack of discipline, or sibling rivalry and jealousy.

Usually guidance help is needed, for parents can rarely see themselves accurately or dissect their family life. These children often need psychotherapy to aid them in overcoming their hostilities.

Detergent poisoning see **Poisons: first-aid treatment.**

Development in the first five years

The following chart indicates the average behavior that may be expected at different age levels. Parents should remember that an average does not represent the behavior of any individual child, but of hundreds of thousands of children, many of whom vary widely from the average. Marked differences in behavior often occur among healthy, intelligent children of the same age.

DEVELOPMENT IN THE FIRST FIVE YEARS

Approximate Age	Activity	Vocal Reactions	Social Reactions
birth	stares at lights, colored mobiles, colored pictures, and nearby faces	crying is usual language	loves to be picked up and cuddled
4 weeks	starts to follow people and large objects with eyes grips objects with hands on contact enjoys bath but may object to being dressed or undressed	little throaty noises from time to time	usually calms down when spoken to, especially by deep masculine voice usually will stop all activity and listen to special sounds such as ringing of bell
8 weeks	when placed on abdomen, intermittently lifts chin and head off mattress when held in sitting position, lifts head upright but it frequently bobs forward follows dangling toys, moving people, and other large objects	vocalizes, with growing variety of sounds, especially when talked to	smile at people and some sounds enjoys being held and spoken or sung to
4 months	follows lights lifts head up and pushes body up on arms when placed on abdomen grasps and holds rattles and may bring to mouth watches his hands and fingers	laughs and coos bubbles, gurgles, may cough and make other sounds to hear own voice	recognizes his parents and others who are close to him usually smiles at people he knows enjoys being with people enjoys being pulled up by hands and sitting on parents' knees usually likes rhythm

Approximate Age	Activity	Vocal Reactions	Social Reactions
6 months	usually begins to sit up without support, although may not until 9 months<hr>rolls over by self<hr>shakes rattle and bangs it<hr>places objects in mouth<hr>transfers objects from one hand to the other	laughs, coos, and vocalizes a great deal	continues to enjoy people; may cry when they leave the room<hr>enjoys sitting up and looking around
9 months	pulls self up in playpen to standing position<hr>begins to creep<hr>sits up well<hr>may hold his own bottle<hr>often walks if held by both hands	makes many sounds and enjoys hearing own voice<hr>may say "Mama" and "Dada"	loves to play peekaboo<hr>enjoys being wheeled in carriage; sits up and looks at everything<hr>enjoys being with family<hr>if taught, will wave "bye-bye" and play "How big is the baby?"
12 months	may stand alone for a moment without support<hr>walks held by one hand<hr>short attention span<hr>enjoys throwing things down from high chair or out of playpen	usually says a few simple words such as "light," "Mama," "Dada," and "bow-wow"	may be shy of strangers<hr>responds to "No! No!"<hr>much interested in other children, dogs, autos, etc.<hr>still enjoys carriage walks immensely
15 months	walks independently without support but usually unsteadily<hr>creeps up stairs and pulls self up on low chairs and couches<hr>enjoys books with pictures and colorful magazines<hr>usually watches TV<hr>throws objects and looks to see what happens to them<hr>loves playing with boxes and pots and pans	talks a great deal, but often not understandable<hr>imitates sounds and occasionally rhythm	often points or indicates by voice what he desires<hr>may indicate by sounds when he is urinating or having a bowel movement

Approximate Age	Activity	Vocal Reactions	Social Reactions
18 months	walks well with fairly good coordination climbs easily up stairs and walks down stairs holding on throws or rolls ball pulls and pushes toys; plays with toy dolls and animals carries out simple directions	usually has about 15 words in vocabulary often names objects he sees, including objects he sees in picture books	usually very sociable
2 years	runs well with good coordination builds towers of 4 to 8 blocks walks well up and down stairs carries out directions well loves looking at books and enjoys rhythm	good vocabulary starts to make small sentences of 2 and 3 words starts to use such pronouns as "I" and "me"	watches other children; plays by them rather than with them loves rough and tumble play
3 years	uses larger blocks and makes more intricate buildings enjoys playing with toy trucks, fire engines, and airplanes also enjoys playing with dolls and doll carriages walks upstairs and downstairs using alternate feet jumps off bottom step will do simple cutout puzzles loves swings, slides, climbing ladders uses crayons more effectively and is beginning to enjoy finger paints	usually speaks very well and with a good vocabulary uses plurals and pronouns knows own sex knows full name knows songs and some rhymes constantly asks questions repeats 3 numbers or a sentence of 6 syllables	joins other boys and girls in play is generally cooperative willing to take turns will help setting the table

Approximate Age	Activity	Vocal Reactions	Social Reactions
	stands on one foot a few seconds		
	dresses and undresses self but usually needs help with buttons		
	washes and dries hands and face		
4 years	throws ball fairly well	obeys commands fairly well when told to place something "on" or "under" or "on the side"	very social
	brushes teeth		enjoys playmates and play group
	often pretends he is an animal in his imaginative play	knows one or more colors correctly	frequently quotes his mother and father as authorities
	hops on one foot	loves to sing and dance	at times may be very bossy
	uses scissors to cut out pictures	immense enjoyment of phonograph records	occasionally has imaginary playmates
	climbs well	tells a story	goes to toilet alone
		counts 4 objects	
5 years	generally well organized	listens to his phonograph records and plays them over and over	enjoys helping prepare for parties and other occasions
	can throw a ball well, rides well on his tricycle, and can walk a straight line with ease	sings many songs and nursery rhymes	plays well with other children
	can lace his shoes with ease and sews through holes in a card	often sings with his records or with TV and radio programs	loves rhythms and dancing and group singing
	enjoys drawing and painting	names 4 colors	will play housekeeping with other children
	an excellent block-builder as a rule; prefers using large blocks	counts 10 objects	enjoys pretending he is an adult
	enjoys copying letters and numbers		likes to run short errands
	enjoys routines		dresses and undresses unaided
	skips		

Developmental age

The age of a child as measured by certain physical attainments known to be normally expected at a certain age range. This contrasts with chronological age and mental age.

For instance, the first tooth appears as a rule as a rule between 6 and 9 months of age. At this age also, the child usually sits up by himself. He starts pulling himself up to a stand at 8 or 9 months; walks without support from 12 to 15 months; the anterior fontanelle (soft spot on the head) closes between 12 and 18 months. Later, a doctor can judge the developmental age of the child by X-raying his bones, especially those of the wrists and elbows, to see if they are changing from cartilage to bone at the usual time. Secondary sexual characteristics, such as breast development in girls and nocturnal emissions in boys, among other indications, are signs of the developmental age of puberty.

See also **Chronological age; Mental age.**

Dexedrine

Trade name for dextroamphetamine, one of the amphetamines. Dexedrine is a drug that stimulates, exhilarates, usually prevents sleep, and diminishes appetite. It is used medically to overcome depression; to aid at times in the initial treatment of obesity; and to treat children with mild brain dysfunction.

Dexedrine is also used by teen-agers and others taking drugs for the stimulating effects they derive. It is usually taken orally but can be injected into a vein. Overdoses can be very dangerous, especially when injected into veins.

See also **Drug abuse.**

Diabetes mellitus

A chronic disease caused by a lack of insulin from the pancreas and characterized by an excessive amount of sugar in the blood and urine.

Not uncommon during childhood, 7 or 8 percent of all diabetes cases are among children. Children under the age of 15 are most often affected, the average age of onset being about 8. The disease is probably hereditary, for about 50 percent of all children with diabetes have family histories of the disease. So far, no cure is available.

The signs and symptoms of diabetes appear rather rapidly in children, occurring usually in a matter of hours or days. They include excessive thirst, a great increase in appetite, frequent urination (the child has to get up several times a night to urinate, or bed-wets), and a rapid loss in weight.

The diagnosis can be made almost immediately by the doctor, who examines the child's urine and blood for excessive sugar. Specially prepared slips of paper that change color when dipped into urine determine whether an excess of sugar is present. Although all children over 3 should have their urine tested for excessive sugar, this procedure is especially important when there is a family history of diabetes.

The treatment of diabetes in children is somewhat more difficult than in adults but in most cases is very successful. Since children do not react to diabetic pills, they must receive insulin by injection. Although no child likes an injection, almost all except the youngest soon learn to give it to themselves. Usually a single daily injection of long-acting insulin, taken in the morning, suffices. However, if a child develops an infection, respiratory or otherwise, extra amounts of insulin may be needed.

The urine of a diabetic child is tested by the parent or the child himself several times each day to assure that the condition is fully controlled.

The dosage of insulin in the diabetic child must be carefully regulated, not only to supply the necessary body needs for insulin but also to prevent an overdose. An overdose of insulin causes a lack of sugar in the body (hypoglycemia) and may give rise to various symptoms, such as headache, drowsiness, flushing, sweating, vomiting, speech and visual disturbances, incoordination, tremors, and even convulsions.

To avoid the possibility of hypoglycemia, many pediatricians do not attempt to completely free the urine of sugar. Instead, they regulate the child's daily dosage of insulin so that a little sugar is still passed in the urine. This method assures that there is always enough sugar in the blood to prevent a dangerous lack of sugar.

Diabetic children who are on insulin therapy usually learn to recognize the early symptoms of hypoglycemia, generally headache and drowsiness. They should carry candy or an orange with them to eat in case they experience such symptoms. The candy or orange juice quickly raises the blood sugar.

On the other hand, if a diabetic child receives inadequate amounts of insulin, signs of diabetes will continue, or if they have subsided will usually reappear within twenty-four hours.

Once the child is adjusted to his daily dose of insulin, he should be treated like any other child without restrictions. Some of the world's greatest athletes have had diabetes. The child should at no time feel that he is an invalid—the insulin he takes substitutes for the insulin he lacks. He can, once he is adjusted, eat any food he desires and enjoy life fully.

Every diabetic child should wear a Medic Alert bracelet in case of accident, diabetic coma, or insulin shock.

See also **Insulin; Medic Alert.**

Diaper rash

An irritation of the buttocks caused by an ammonia burn from the child's urine. Ammonia is not found in the urine when it is passed, but when the urine is exposed to air and acted on by bacteria on the skin, it changes chemically, and ammonia is formed. When a diaper rash is severe, causing blistering and a breaking of the skin, some of the fungi normally found in the bowel movement often infect the area and cause a chronic infection of the skin.

Treatment for the prevention and curing of diaper rash includes the following:

Change diapers frequently.

Apply a waterproof ointment to the diaper area to protect the skin. Suitable ointments include Desitin, Diaperene, A and D, Diaprex, and Balmex.

Powder the baby's buttocks and thighs with a good baby powder or simple cornstarch (although this tends to cake). In applying the powder, do not shake it in the air so that the baby breathes it in. Sprinkle it on the buttocks and rub it in.

Try disposable diapers, such as Pampers, that absorb the urine, keeping the infant's skin almost dry.

Since ammonia is alkaline, another approach to the prevention and treatment of diaper rash is to include in the baby's diet some foods or food products that tend to make the urine acidic so that it will not form ammonia. This can be accomplished by including in the baby's daily intake of milk a completely safe food concentrate, such as Pedameth (di-methionine). The urine will be acidic and diaper rash will be avoided or, if present, will subside.

For long-lasting diaper rash, an ointment or cream containing hydrocortisone and Mycostatin (nystatin, a drug that kills fungi) may be prescribed, and is usually successful in clearing up the irritation. It is also advisable to let the child go without diapers as much as possible.

Plastic, rubberized, or latex pants to cover diapers should generally be avoided if a child has diaper rash (see **Pants, waterproof**).

Diapers

Any of the standard types of diaper on the market are perfectly suitable. As always, convenience costs more. Disposable diapers and disposable paper diaper liners are useful but not necessary, although disposable diapers are advisable when traveling.

If you plan to buy cloth diapers and wash them at home, at least three or four dozen are necessary. Diaper services suggest 80 to 100 diapers weekly for the first few months, although this may vary with the individual child. Even if you use a diaper service, keep a dozen of your own diapers on hand for various uses (such as covering the crib sheet so that the infant's head is not directly against the rough cloth beneath) or in case you run out of diapers.

How to fold a diaper depends on the size and shape of the diaper. The most common shape is rectangular (see illustration).

When pinning a diaper in place, always hold the diaper away from the baby's skin with two fingers of one hand. Too many babies have had diapers pinned to their skin.

Diapers are usually pinned together to hold them securely on the child.

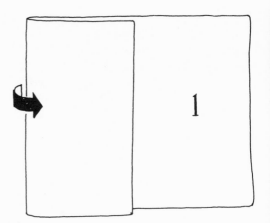

1. First step in standard fold of rectangular or square diaper, in which diaper is folded in thirds; folded piece extends ⅔ of way across diaper. 2. Continue, as if folding a letter. 3. For extra thickness, fold up from bottom; thickest section is placed in front for boys and in back for girls. 4. First step in fold of rectangular diaper for extra thickness between the legs; folded piece extends ⅔ of

way across diaper. 5. Fold this piece back on itself to within about 3 inches of edge of diaper. 6. Then fold panel on right over to left edge of diaper.

However, the use of a special adhesive tape in place of diaper pins has recently been found to be effective. One such tape is Scotch Package Sealing Tape. Some of the disposable diapers are now sold with tape already attached.

Most mothers change their infant's diaper every time they find it wet or soiled. This helps prevent diaper rash. However, immediate changing is not necessary, especially during the night or when the baby is outdoors. Most babies are not bothered by wet or soiled diapers, and it takes some hours before the skin becomes irritated. Regular use of a diaper ointment rubbed into the skin also guards against diaper rash (see **Diaper rash**).

Soiled or wet diapers should be placed in a pail with a deodorant in the cover. Wet diapers may simply be thrown into this pail. Diapers soiled with bowel movement should be rinsed in the toilet before being put into the pail.

Diapers may be washed in a washing machine, separate from other wash, or by hand with a mild soap or detergent. Then they should be rinsed thoroughly (twice in a washing machine) in plain water to rid them of all soap that may have remained in the cloth. They may be dried in a drier or out in the sun on a clothesline. Diapers should not be ironed, since this spoils the softness.

Latex, rubberized, or plastic waterproof pants are used for social reasons, such as a visit to friends or relatives. They should not be used routinely since they keep the moisture in, encourage the growth of bacteria, and thus foster diaper rash (see **Pants, waterproof**).

When a baby begins to walk, the thickness of the diaper between the legs gives him a bowlegged appearance. If the diaper seems to interfere too much with the baby's movements, you should check for unnecessary bulkiness, perhaps switching to a lighter weight diaper.

Diaphragm

The large flat muscle of breathing, which separates the chest from the abdomen. During most of the first year of life, this muscle is almost entirely responsible for the mechanics of breathing. When the diaphragm pulls down, the chest area and lungs expand, and air is inhaled. After the child is a year old the chest muscles also are used in respiration and continue to work with the diaphragm for the remainder of a person's life.

Two rare but important disorders related to the diaphragm may cause difficulty during infancy and childhood.

The first type of disorder is a diaphragmatic hernia—a congenital hole in the diaphragm, usually on the left side. The stomach and part of the small intestine protrude through the hole, often filling up the chest cavity on that side and compressing the left lung into a small, solid mass. Immediate surgery is required, and is successful in almost all cases.

The second type of disorder is a weakness or paralysis of one side of the diaphragm. This condition is caused by damage to the nerve controlling that side of the diaphragm, usually a result of the stretching of the baby's neck during birth. There is no medical treatment for this condition, and it usually causes very little or no discomfort, since in a few months the chest muscles start aiding in breathing. In some cases, however, the diaphragm muscle may become very thin through lack of use. The thin, inactive muscle, although still separating the abdomen from the chest, allows the abdominal contents to push up into the chest, thus compressing the lung. If respiratory distress, shown by rapid breathing, results, a surgical operation is performed in which the diaphragm is pulled down and folded over itself to make it smaller and thicker. This permits the lung to expand fully; the child should have no further difficulty and will breathe normally.

Diarrhea

Frequent loose or watery bowel movements. This condition is fairly common during infancy and childhood.

Diarrhea is rarely dangerous except during infancy when a water loss from watery bowel movements may cause dehydration. A doctor should always be called if more than four or five loose or watery movements occur daily, if blood or mucus appears in the movements, or if the movements are associated with severe abdominal pain.

The most usual causes of diarrhea are:

Foods to which a child is sensitive   In

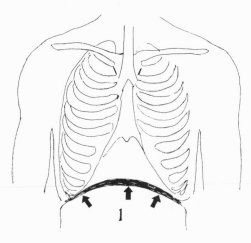

Position of the diaphragm (1), the chief muscle used in breathing.

early infancy and childhood, the body may show a sensitivity or allergy to certain foods by reacting with diarrhea. When an infant is sensitive to cow's milk, the bowel movements are not only loose but may contain mucus and occasionally blood. Relief is usually quickly obtained by giving the infant a substitute formula of a soybean or meat-base preparation (see **Milk allergy**).

Allergies or sensitivities to other foods can usually be detected by observing the relationship between the food and the onset of the diarrhea. A totally breast-fed baby may be reacting to food in the mother's diet. Most sensitivities to specific foods disappear as a child grows older. Celiac disease, a sensitivity to wheat and rye, is rare and requires a restricted diet (see **Celiac disease**).

Spoiled foods   The most common types of spoiled foods are milk that has not been properly sterilized (and in which bacteria have multiplied) and food that has spoiled through lack of refrigeration. (For methods of sterilization of milk, see **Formulas.**)

Infections or irritation in the digestive tract   Most infections of the gastrointestinal tract in infants are caused by viruses and are accompanied by fever and occasionally vomiting. Bacterial infections of the intestinal tract which result in diarrhea, are frequently caused by an overgrowth of the colon bacilli that normally live in the intestines or to certain colon bacilli that are toxic (pathogenic colon bacilli). Other rarer infections that result in diarrhea are caused by salmonella, bacteria of the paratyphoid variety, and amebas. These, as well as the bacterial infections, are usually successfully treated by specific antibiotics prescribed by a doctor.

Diarrhea may also be associated with appendicitis.

Occasionally diarrhea in children is caused by the use of antibiotics, especially tetracycline, over long periods. These antibiotics kill the normal bacteria in the intestines, allowing an overactive growth of fungi that cause an irritation and a severe, resistant diarrhea.

Other infections   Frequently when children have infections such as tonsillitis, swollen glands, pneumonia, or a contagious disease, the toxins of the organisms irritate the intestines and cause diarrhea. Such diarrhea subsides as the infection subsides.

Treatment   Specific treatment to eliminate persistent diarrhea depends, of course, upon the cause. Diarrhea in a breast-fed infant will usually subside with regulation of the mother's diet, unless it is due to an infection of the baby. However, in early infancy a general treatment of the symptom that is widely recommended and usually of great help is to put the infant on a temporary diet of boiled, diluted skim milk. To prepare, dilute skim milk with an equal amount of water and simmer for ten to fifteen minutes. Then add enough boiled water to make up for the amount evaporated during boiling. No solids are given until the condition has improved.

At times the doctor may recommend giving the digestive tract a rest for twenty-four to forty-eight hours by placing the infant on a mixture of one quart of boiled water to which is added one tablespoon of sugar and a half teaspoon of salt. Following the treatment, which usually halts the diarrhea in twenty-four hours, you can substitute the boiled, diluted skim-milk mixture and then boiled skim milk and then regular formula.

Solids that may be added gradually are rice, raw scraped apple that has been allowed to brown in the air, ripe bananas, and beef.

It may be necessary to place a child on Kaopectate (a mixture of kaolin and pectin) or a similar preparation. At times doctors prescribe medications such as paregoric to slow down the motion of the bowels and atropine or belladonna to overcome pain caused by intestinal spasm.

See also **Celiac disease; Milk allergy.**

Dick test

A test for susceptibility to scarlet fever. The Dick test is rarely used today, since penicillin quickly kills the streptococcus of scarlet fever, and the disease, which is now comparatively rare, is mild when it does appear (see **Scarlet fever**).

Diet, elimination

A limited diet to which foods are added one by one in an attempt to determine if a particular food is responsible for an allergic reaction such as chronic eczema, hives, or some intestinal upset. This procedure is used particularly when neither past experience nor skin testing has revealed the cause.

In infancy one can place the child back on the diet he received before the onset of the allergic reaction. In older children one starts with a diet of foods that rarely cause allergies. The diet must be adhered to very strictly. Once the skin or intestinal condition has subsided, new foods are added every four or five days. A good diet to use as a start is limited to:

barley	spinach
rice	carrots
rice biscuit	sweet potatoes
rice bread	lamb
grapefruit	gelatin
lemons	cane sugar
pears	salt
baking soda in	maple syrup
place of yeast	cane sugar syrup
in baking	olive oil

Nonallergic vitamins can be prescribed by your doctor to assure proper nutrition.

Diet, liquid

A doctor may advise that an ill child be placed temporarily on a liquid diet. This would include the following: water, fruit, juices, tea, carbonated beverages, clear soups, bouillon, and clear chicken broth. Some variations that could be made from combinations of these foods are jellied soups such as jellied madrilène, clear gelatin desserts, sherbet, and lollipops.

Dieting

Dieting, for whatever reason, should always be under the direction and supervision of a doctor. This is especially important in the case of teen-agers who are, or think they are, overweight. Fad and crash diets can be extremely dangerous to growing boys and girls. A well-balanced diet, limited in calories, plus increased activity, will reduce almost any teen-ager's weight.

With the exception of a well-balanced vegetarian diet, many of today's popular diets and "health" diets are not, in fact, healthy at all. They may be safe for some adults, but they are not safe for children or teen-agers who still have some growing to do and whose nutritional needs are stricter. Among the detrimental diets are: the Zen Buddhist Macrobiotic Diet, to which a number of deaths have been attributed; the Mayo

Diet (disclaimed by the Mayo Clinic); the Calories Don't Count Diet; the Hindu Guru Diet; the Air Force Diet (disclaimed by the Air Force); the Royal Canadian Air Force Diet (disclaimed by the RCAF); and the Low Carbohydrate Diet. The Stillman Diet is not only inadequate for teen-agers, but extremely difficult for them to maintain.

Vegetarian diets, which have attracted many teen-agers not for weight reduction but out of pity for animals or fear of impure food, can give full nutrition if carefully regulated. The danger is a lack of adequate protein, but if plenty of eggs, milk, cheese, and nuts are eaten, the diet will satisfy the body's needs.

Some young teen-agers, particularly girls, actually fast rather than diet. Anorexia nervosa, which occurs almost exclusively among girls, is a condition in which for psychological reasons the girl literally starves herself to death. Intense medical and psychological treatment is required (see **Anorexia nervosa**).

If a doctor prescribes pills to reduce appetite (most often one of the amphetamines) parents should be sure that the youngster is strictly following the doctor's schedule and not taking the pills on his own. Appetite-reducing pills may be addictive, and overdoses are dangerous.

See also **Obesity.**

Digestive tract see **Alimentary canal.**

Digitalis poisoning see **Poisons: first-aid treatment.**

Diphtheria
A dangerous contagious disease characterized by a severe sore throat and the formation of a white membrane that lines the throat and larynx. It is rare today because of the routine immunization of infants and children. An attack also confers immunity.

Source The disease is caused by diphtheria bacteria, which not only cause severe inflammation of the tissues they infect but also give off a poison (toxin) that is absorbed into the body.

Diphtheria is transmitted through direct contact with an infected person or with a well person who carries the diphtheria bacteria in his throat. Contrary to popular fears, it is almost impossible for the disease to be spread in milk or by some article a person with the disease has handled. A susceptible person will usually develop diphtheria in two to six days after exposure to the person with the disease or to a carrier of the bacteria. The period of contagion may last as long as one to two weeks. The infected person is considered to be no longer contagious when three successive nose and throat cultures at twenty-four-hour intervals show that no diphtheria bacteria are living.

Symptoms The child usually develops a sore throat, headache, and a fever of 101 degrees to 103 degrees. At first the throat and tonsils are red, but in twenty-four hours small white spots develop on the tonsils or the side of the throat. These spots get larger, forming a white membrane that covers the tonsils or surrounding area and rapidly spreads to the soft palate and the back of the throat and then down the throat and up into the nose. Soon there is difficulty in swallowing, followed by difficulty in breathing. The diphtheria bacteria also give off a poison, which may paralyze muscles all over the body. The child becomes extremely ill. Intensive care is required. Paralysis of muscles disappears under proper treatment, and full use usually returns.

Treatment The patient should receive an injection of diphtheria antitoxin as soon as possible. Penicillin is also injected every few hours. The doctor may have to place a tube down the throat or even do a tracheotomy (an incision in the throat) to allow the patient to breathe.

All persons exposed to the disease should have nose and throat cultures taken for several days after exposure. If diphtheria bacteria are found, oral and intravenous penicillin are administered for five to seven days.

Immunization Diphtheria toxoid is given during infancy, plus booster inoculations every few years to keep the immunization high. (See **Immunization schedule and tests.**)

Dirt-eating

Dirt-eating among children is far more common than is generally realized. It is most usually found among children of 1 to 3 years. In a study at Johns Hopkins University, it was found that out of 784 children over 7 months old attending the clinic, 27 percent of the Negro children and 17 percent of the white children ate dirt, ashes, or plaster. The children studied came from a lower economic area.

This dirt-eating is not the random tasting and putting to the mouth of any object so common among most children. Rather it is persistent and purposeful, and largely confined to dirt or ashes. It is much like the urge of many pregnant women to eat ashes or some other particular strange substance.

It seems quite definite that dirt-eating is related to poor nutrition. (The body has a need for some particular mineral, and so appetite develops for something containing that mineral.) In many cases it has been found that the child is anemic, and once he receives iron, the condition subsides.

Dirt-eating is not as a rule dangerous, since the bacteria in the dirt is destroyed by the digestive juices. But, of course, a doctor should examine the child as soon as the habit appears.

Some children eat paint or plaster chips, and this is extremely dangerous if the paint contains lead. (See **Lead poisoning; Pica.**)

Dirtiness   see **Cleanliness.**

"Dirty words"   see **Swear words.**

Disagreement see **Arguments between parents.**

Discipline

Through the years methods of discipline and attitudes toward discipline have been gradually changing with newer knowledge of a child's needs and his emotional development. Only a few generations ago discipline was strict from early childhood on, and punishment was severe, often physical—the child learned obedience through fear. Schools at that time also followed this same code in dealing with disciplinary problems. Modern methods of discipline are generally much more lenient—today's parents are usually less restrictive than their parents were, and physical punishment is much less frequent.

The more lenient approach to discipline does not mean that the child is to be free to follow every impulse. The aim is to find the best method for teaching the child the self-discipline he needs for his own happiness in childhood and adult life. Punishments that the child cannot understand, punishment that is unnecessarily severe, and restrictions that interfere with behavior that is healthy and appropriate at a given age do not encourage self-discipline. Instead, they undermine the child's sense of his worth and competence and teach him that force makes right.

But all children need discipline and must learn to accept authority. Children are unhappy and fearful when they feel that there is no order to life and no controls on behavior. They need the security of consistent and reasonable adult authority. As they learn that this authority acts not to hurt them but to protect them, they learn to respond through respect and understanding rather than fear.

The definition of discipline that is accepted today is guidance and direction. Discipline is not to be interpreted as scolding, slapping, spanking, or sending a child to stand in a corner, although these methods are still resorted to occasionally.

The infant and toddler Discipline should be at a minimum during the first year of a child's life. Almost completely helpless for the first 8 or 9 months, the child looks to his parents for his every need, and parents should meet those needs as promptly as possible. Allowing an infant to be hungry or uncomfortable does not mold his character. A bit later, when the child is just beginning to discover the world, when he starts creeping around or holding onto objects and walking, he is likely to get into trouble. A baby will tear a page out of a book, for example, or break a glass, or pull on a tablecloth, bringing all the dishes and utensils down on the floor—his reward

for these efforts at exploration and discovery is often a spanking. Even more unthinking parents spank an infant to make him stop crying (which, of course, is impossible) and slap him if he wets the carpet. At this age a child cannot understand why he is being punished; he will, however, learn one thing from punishment: fear.

When infants start to creep around, they should be watched constantly. If a child gets into trouble, it is usually the parents' fault for leaving a particular object available. The youngster's spirit of exploration and discovery should be encouraged as much as possible. He should be allowed to tear out pages from old magazines and newspapers rather than books. He should be allowed to bang—with spoons on old pots and pans rather than the furniture. Children whose parents stimulate their interest in the world around them, indoors and out, will be brighter, more alert— and happier—boys and girls than those children who have not received this stimulation. (See **Stimulating the child.**)

Usually between the age of 1 and 2, children are more understanding and can be told "No" if they cry to be given a valuable vase or a breakable object. Substitution may be tried, but if the child insists, he may be allowed to cry. A child must learn that he cannot break down his parents' authority by crying.

At the toddler stage, discipline is limited to a simple "No" and removal of the child from the scene, for example, if he is clearly contemplating hammering a peg into a wall mirror. A slap, which could give a child an unhappy association with the activity, might be in order when a child insists on doing something that might endanger his life, such as turning on the gas, trying to climb out of windows, playing with fire or electric wires, running into the street. Such occasional spankings will not upset the child-parent relationship that is generally warm and loving. The fewer the spankings, however, the more effective they are when necessary.

The 2-year-old   Special disciplinary problems related almost entirely to the stage of development usually occur when the child is about 2. Many children of this age are aggressive—kicking one another, biting, hitting, and knocking one another down. This, of course, cannot be permitted, and the child should be taught certain short rules: "No biting!" "No hitting!" "No kicking!" "No pushing!" If a child persists in these aggressive activities, he should be picked up, taken away from the other children, and be made to sit next to his mother for fifteen to twenty minutes after being told strongly, "No, you cannot play with other children if you bite,"—or push or kick. Children quickly learn with this type of discipline.

Children of this age are also very possessive, often refusing to share their toys and wanting everyone else's toys. Although a parent should not force a child so young to share his toys, neither should he be permitted to take toys belonging to another child unless the child permits it or unless he shares one of his toys with the other child.

In general, from approximately 18 months to 2 years, the child is resistant. "No" is often the most used word in his vocabulary. This is the stage when most children first try to be on their own. They want to put on their socks, shoes, and shirts by themselves, even if it takes twenty or thirty minutes. They express their negativism by not wanting to dress or go outdoors, not wanting to come indoors, not wanting to take a bath, not wanting to be taken out of the bath, and so forth—just on principle. Parents should act quickly to overcome this resistance. If a child is occupied with some interesting play, give him a few minutes warning, and at the end of that time pick him up and prepare him for bath, bed, or whatever is necessary.

Discipline is best achieved by putting every direction positively. For instance, don't say, "Would you like your bath now?" or "Don't you think it's time for bed?" but rather, "Now we'll take our bath," or, "Come, it's time for bed." (See **Temper and temper tantrums.**)

The preschool child   Although problems of discipline are generally less difficult with 3- to 5-year-olds, a great deal depends on the number of children in the home and whether or not the child attends nursery school. Up to this period the youngster has been almost completely dependent on his parents. He wants their attention and wants more than anything else to know that he is loved and wanted. When a new baby comes into the home and the attention must be divided, the older child becomes very upset and usually expresses signs of sibling rivalry and jealousy. Although this situation often requires some manner of discipline, an understanding of the child's feelings is far more important. If, for instance, the older child hits the baby, he should not be spanked, as so often happens. He is unhappy because he feels the baby is more loved or has taken too much attention; a spanking only increases his feeling that the baby is more loved. A more effective disciplinary measure is to take the child from the room, telling him that if he hits the baby he cannot be near the baby. The parent should go with him to another room and talk to him—not angrily, but with some feeling and understanding of his unhappiness. Tell him that when he was little you would never let anyone hurt him either—and tell him also that you could never love anyone more than you love him.

Preschoolers are often disciplined for bad table manners, getting their clothes dirty, messing up a room, and using "dirty" language. Parents should remember that these are little children in the process of growing up. They are not little adults and should not be judged by adult standards. (See **Cleanliness; Manners; Swear words.**)

Throughout childhood and during this period especially, it is important that only one standard of discipline be used in the home. Children of this age frequently test a parent's authority, often playing one parent against the other. A child can become extremely upset and confused if one parent is lenient and the other restrictive, or if one parent counteracts the discipline of the other.

To be effective and meaningful for the child, discipline should be consistent. Vacillation upsets children, who look to their parents for consistent strength.

The school-age child The kindergarten year has comparatively fewer disciplinary problems, although there may be some related to making an adjustment to school. Again, some problems may arise when the child brings home "dirty" words. The usual problems among brothers and sisters at home also exist. Often parents create problems for the 5-year-old by expecting him to clean up his room by himself. "If he can clean up at kindergarten, why can't he clean up at home?" Actually, at kindergarten he *is* helped to clean up; he should also

be helped at home. He is not as a rule so self-controlled that he can clean up a room by himself.

Somewhere around the age of 7, children suddenly become real individuals with ideas of their own and a resistance to their parents' ideas and authority. The child desires to make his own decisions and must be watched and checked frequently. For example, he'll go out in the cold without a coat, or in the rain without rubbers. He still needs direction and should have certain short but definite rules that must be followed without the necessity of a long discussion: "When it's cold, we wear coats"; "When it rains, we wear rubbers."

At this stage children first form groups, and among their primary desires and concerns is to be accepted and admired by the group, a situation that often gives rise to special disciplinary problems. A child may tell lies to impress his companions and his class. He may steal to further impress them with his wealth or to try to buy their friendship by treating them to candy and other goodies. He may cause trouble in class so that all eyes will be focused on him. When a child is not fully accepted, the numerous problems that arise related to his unhappiness require help and understanding as well as discipline.

During this school-age period, parents should do everything they can to develop a child's sense of pride and to encourage friendships. They should build up a child in front of his companions—more important, they should not scold, criticize, or humiliate him in the presence of his friends.

The teen-ager The adolescent is normally negative, argumentative, critical, and resistant. He wants to run his own life and objects to parental interference.

However, he is not yet ready to make important decisions and still needs direction and discipline.

Restrictions should be minimal during adolescence; the teen-ager should be given as much freedom as possible in the selection of clothes, hair style, and makeup. Restrictions should definitely be made however, on staying out late, taking drugs or alcoholic beverages, and speeding when driving a car. Parents should also be firm in seeing that adequate time is spent on studies.

Nagging is especially resented by teen-agers. Approval by parents is always wanted. Parents should give the boy or girl a feeling that they trust him or her.

Discipline of the adolescent must be reasonable and just. Although depriving a teen-ager of certain privileges usually impresses him, this method of discipline should be used rarely, mostly for a repeated misdemeanor after warnings.

Reasons for restrictions or discipline can often be discussed with a teen-ager, if the parents will try to remember that this is a new generation. Even if your child's ideas are not accepted, they should be respected.

Adolescent antisocial activities, such as stealing and drug use, must be disciplined, but the child should also be studied carefully to determine the underlying causes of the behavior. Psychotherapy is often necessary.

Some general rules   Only one standard of discipline should be used in the home. Parents should support one another on discipline.

Discipline should be consistent, so the child knows what to expect; but some flexibility as well should be allowed under special circumstances.

Punishment should be immediate for younger children. Delayed punishment is not effective. A child who is "naughty" in the morning should not be told "Now you can't see TV tomorrow night."

Whenever possible the punishment should fit the crime. For instance, a child who bites other children should be withdrawn from playing with them and made to sit aside for a period of time by himself: "You can't play with children if you bite," rather than "No ice cream for you today."

Punishment should be reasonable and just.

Never threaten loss of affection: "If you do that, I won't love you any more."

The child should not be made to feel rejected: "Get out of here. I don't want to see you any more."

Spanking, except under rare circumstances, should be avoided. Physical discipline should be used only if a child is doing something that would endanger his life or safety.

See also **Nagging; Obedience; Punishment; Scolding; Shaming.**

Disrespect

Disrespect means different things to different people. To most people disrespect in a child signifies a hostile or indifferent attitude toward parental authority and other adult authority, as well as a disregard for the feelings, opinions, privacy, and property of others. To some people it also signifies rudeness, such as interrupting conversations, calling parents uncomplimentary names, or even calling parents by their first names.

Momentary rudeness is not to be confused with disrespect, especially when children are young. We must always be careful not to judge children by adult standards. A child who in a fit of anger yells at his parents, "I hate you! You stink!" is expressing momentary anger, but usually no lasting disrespect is implied or felt by the child. Parents should let the child know they do not like this kind of talk, but there is no need for harsh punishment or angry rebuttals.

At times school-age children try to impress their parents with their sophistication. For instance, a child when told "I wouldn't do that if I were you" may answer, "Well, goody for you!" At this same age period youngsters often try to imitate the bold actions and talk of their companions; and they also tend to show off and try to "act big" in front of one another as well as adults. This usually represents a desire to break away from childish dependence and to be "bigger," even though the behavior may seem just rude and silly to adults. Such behavior is usually of no seriousness, although often it should be corrected.

Parents should also remember that each generation and each person has a somewhat different idea of which rules and values are most worthy of respect. There has always been conflict in this area, and such conflict is often for the good.

On the other hand, respect for authority is one of the basic qualities to be attained if a child is to grow up as a law-abiding citizen. He must learn to respect those rules of the family, school, or society that regulate behavior for the sake of everyone.

True disrespect involves a basic rejection of authority. It is apparent in anti-social behavior that ignores the rights and feelings of others. It is not reasoned or selective. The child is essentially resisting his parents or other adult authorities.

Parents should not expect respect simply because they are parents, and if a child is habitually disrespectful, they must try to find out why in order to remedy the situation. First, they should check their own attitudes, for if they wish to encourage respect in their children they themsleves must be respectful. Many youngsters when challenged on their disrespectful attitudes claim that their parents or teachers do not follow in practice the values they profess to respect. This is often a fabricated excuse but it is also often true. Hypocrisy is a very poor example for children.

Second, a disrespectful child may really be asking for more authority and strength from his parents. Mothers and fathers who are too weak and too permissive, who fail to correct and discipline, will often create a disrespectful attitude in their child.

Third, the child may be behaving rebelliously as an expression of a very deep unhappiness and hostility. If parents cannot on their own discover or correct the reasons for a generally disrespectful attitude, they should consider getting professional advice.

Distractibility

A child who is too easily distracted by sounds or other stimuli will have a difficult time completing any task, because his concentration is constantly interrupted. Excessive distractibility is a characteristic of general hyperactivity. Parents need worry about their child's distractibility only if it is part of a larger pattern of hyperactivity and learning difficulties.

In such a case it may be due to a condition called mild brain dysfunction. This can be diagnosed by psychological and neurological tests. Distractibility may also be associated with mental retardation.

See also **Attention span, short; Brain dysfunction, mild; Hyperactivity; Mental retardation.**

Divorce

The effect of the parents' separation on the child should always be considered when divorce or separation is contemplated, for children are always deeply hurt by this occurrence. Parents who do not love one another, however, or parents who hate one another should not stay together for the sake of their children, for this situation can be even more detrimental to youngsters.

If both parents really love their children, they should first consult a marriage counselor to explore their problems to determine if their life together can be more satisfying. The marriage counselor can aid greatly in reconstructing a potentially good marriage, or if the marriage is not salvageable, the counselor can make the separation more bearable.

Unfortunately most parents in the process of separation and divorce are so angry at one another that consciously or subconsciously they deeply injure their children by using them as pawns in their marital and postmarital struggles. A father may say, "If it weren't for your mother, we'd all be living together." A mother may say, "I can't get you children the clothes and food you should have, because your father's so selfish and gives us so little." A father may say, "Your mother's insane. I'm going to ask the judge to send her to a place for crazy people."

Often a mother, given custody of the children, will refuse to let the father set foot in the home, even if the children are ill. Children generally are loyal to both their father and mother; they are usually distressed if one parent talks against the other or attempts to have them act as spies. There are many, many similar ways in which parents hurt their youngsters to satisfy their own hatred.

To help a child during the period of separation and divorce, parents should impress upon the child that he is deeply loved by both of them, but that they are no longer happy living together and must separate. The child should know that although he will be living with his mother, he will still see a great deal of his father. (Awarding custody to the father occurs only in rare instances.)

Parents who really love their children are able to put their children's interests first, even though it is often difficult in the heat of the hatred that usually develops in such situations. The separation is easier on the children when the following rules are adhered to.

1. Avoid involving children in personal tussles.
2. Speak civilly to one another when the children are present.
3. Do not speak against one another or belittle or deride one another to the children.
4. Do nothing to keep the child away from the other parent. Do not discipline the child by threatening to keep him from talking to or seeing the other parent.

Dog bites   see **Rabies.**

Dogs, fear of   see **Fears.**

Dogs as pets   see **Pets.**

Dolls   see **Toys and play materials.**

Down's syndrome   see **Mongolism.**

Downs   see **Drug abuse.**

Drain cleaner poisoning see **Poisons: first-aid treatment.**

Dramamine   see **Motion sickness.**

Drawings   see **Art.**

Dreams, bad   see **Nightmares and night terrors.**

Dressing and undressing

Learning to dress is a gradual process that starts at about 18 months, when a child puts up his or her foot to have a sock pulled on or extends his arm for his nightgown or shirt to be put on. During the next six months he may even try to undress himself.

By about 2 years, he will attempt to put on his socks by himself and refuse all help. He will often struggle for thirty minutes before getting them on or accepting help. Often he will go through a similar process in putting on his undershirt. Given encouragement and some help he will persevere, and by the age of 2½ he can usually put on simple garments, although as a rule he is still unable to button his clothing. At this time he can generally take off his clothes if aided in the unbuttoning.

By the time he is 3, he can generally dress himself with help, put on his shoes, and unbutton his clothing. Usually at this age he is unable to distinguish the front from the back of clothes.

A parent can, at this time, aid a child in dressing himself by providing clothes that are easy to put on: pullover shirts, shorts and skirts that have elastic waistbands, and, of course, clothing with large buttons and buttonholes, for these require much less effort to manipulate.

Between 4 and 5, a child learns to dress and undress himself without assistance and can easily lace his shoes.

(The ability to tie the laces comes later, at about 6.) But because a 5-year-old has dressed himself once does not mean that he shouldn't occasionally be helped a bit, for most children still love a little of this attention from their parents until they are at least 6.

Parents can aid the child in developing self-dependence in dressing by encouraging him, by using simple clothing, and by giving him the opportunity of attempting to do the job himself as often as possible.

Dried fruit, swallowed whole see **Foreign objects, swallowed.**

Drinking, adolescent

Many parents are troubled when teenagers want to drink alcoholic beverages. Should they restrict them vigorously or allow them to drink occasionally with their friends? This is a serious question, for adolescents have strong impulses, resist authority with vehemence, and supported by a feeling that "it can't happen to me," are imbued with a daredevil attitude that sometimes prompts them to take irresponsible chances.

Of course, most boys and girls see their parents taking alcoholic drinks for social relaxation. They see them mix and serve such drinks to their friends. To these teen-agers, drinking is one sign of growing up and being socially acceptable.

Many parents from time to time allow their son or daughter to take a small alcoholic drink along with the family. They feel that if they forbid any drinking at all, the teen-ager may react by drinking behind their backs. Whether this is effective depends upon the individual case and the relationship between the parents and the teen-ager.

This does not mean that a parent

should say yes to an adolescent of 15 or 16 when he asks permission to take alcoholic drinks with his friends. The parent should suggest that he wait until he is older—until he is more or less on his own, at about 18 or 19. If a parent has had a good relationship with his son or daughter, this advice should make an impression. Although such a teen-ager may occasionally experiment with drinking, he will know that he is opposing his parents' suggestions and desires, and consequently, is unlikely to drink habitually or to excess.

An absolute ban on drinking before driving is imperative. Innumerable serious auto accidents and deaths have occurred with an adolescent drinker at the wheel. Teen-agers tend to take chances, and at times they even feel omnipotent—under the influence of liquor, they lack judgment, full coordination, and the ability to react quickly in case of emergency.

Although teen-age drinking has been labeled a medical and social problem as serious as drug addiction, this is probably not true. The likelihood of becoming addicted to alcohol varies widely among individuals and usually takes some time to develop, while the addictive and other harmful effects of strong drugs such as heroin and morphine may appear very rapidly (see **Drug abuse**). It is nevertheless true, however, that drinking among teen-agers is often associated with antisocial behavior and reckless driving. Heavy drinking on a regular basis is, of course, physically unhealthy, and may eventually develop into alcoholism. It also is probably a sign that the youngster is seriously distressed over some aspect of his life. Psychotherapy may be indicated.

Driving   see **Automobile travel with children; Automobiles and adolescents.**

Drooling
Most babies drool excessively when they are about 3 to 4 months old, because the saliva glands start secreting fully at that time and the saliva pours into the mouth. The infant knows how to swallow when he takes fluid into his mouth by sucking, but he hasn't as yet learned to swallow when fluid (saliva) just starts running into his mouth. However, he learns how to swallow saliva after a month or so.

Slightly older infants sometimes drool when they are cutting teeth, especially the molars.

Children who continue to drool for some years usually have a weakness of the tongue muscles (use of the tongue is necessary in swallowing). This condition usually subsides spontaneously, although it may take a few years.

The drooling that occasionally occurs in children with cerebral palsy is also caused by a weakness of the tongue muscles.

Drowning   see **Mouth-to-mouth resuscitation; Swimming.**

Drug abuse
The taking of drugs by teen-agers and some children even younger is a major problem facing today's parents. Boys and girls of all social, economic, and religious groups are taking drugs, including many of the brightest students. A report issued in 1969 estimated that at least 300,000 high school and college students were taking drugs, but many doctors, teachers, and sociologists feel this figure is far too low.

What causes boys and girls to take to drugs? According to Dr. Graham B. Blaine, Jr., of Harvard University, they fall into three broad groups: the experience seekers, the oblivion seekers, and the personality-change seekers.

The *experience seekers* are experimenters; many of them enjoy taking risks. Although some have been encouraged by the urging of their friends, many others, motivated by rebellion and hostility, express their anger by breaking rules and laws.

The *oblivion seekers* find the sensation of being drugged a pleasant relief from the stresses of home and world. These include those boys and girls who will take ever greater risks to escape from their unhappy environment, often eventually succumbing to overdoses.

The *personality-change seekers* are the teen-agers who feel inadequate socially and sexually. They take drugs to stimulate themselves and thus obtain a sense of feeling that they are really someone and can accomplish what they desire. These adolescents often become severe addicts.

Some of the various drugs used by boys and girls are described below.

Marijuana (grass, pot) Dried marijuana leaves are usually smoked, often in the form of cigarettes (joints). Marijuana is not addicting and its use can be discontinued without withdrawal symptoms.

Generally marijuana cannot be considered a dangerous drug, especially as compared with the so-called hard drugs, but preparations of the dried leaves may be of different strengths, so some are more potent than others. Approximately 30 percent of all marijuana smokers go on to try the dangerous drugs such as heroin, LSD, and intravenous amphetamines.

What are the effects of marijuana? At first it may stimulate exaggeratedly animated conduct, with rapid, loud talking and bursts of laughter. Later there may be sleepiness and even stupor. The marijuana smoker has poor judgment, a slowed reaction time, and a distortion of depth perception that makes driving dangerous. Concentration is diminished when smoking marijuana, and thus heavy use undermines educational attainment.

Marijuana is, of course, illegal at the present time, and the marijuana user is, consequently, breaking the law and liable to punishment. Teen-agers are more apt to be arrested than other marijuana users. Smoking marijuana may also incline a teen-ager to disrespect all law.

Marijuana is not very expensive, is widely available, and widely used.

Hashish (hash) The strongest part of the marijuana plant, hashish is a resinous substance that may be packed into blocks or balls. It is usually smoked. The effects are approximately the same as those of marijuana, but stronger. Youngsters may occasionally find this type of intoxication frightening. (This can be true of marijuana also, but is much less common.) Hashish is much more expensive than marijuana and, therefore, less commonly used.

LSD (lysergic acid diethylamide; acid) Although not habit-forming, LSD is a powerful and dangerous drug. Easily prepared and tasteless, LSD is taken absorbed in cubes of sugar, in small tabs of paper, in pill form, or dissolved in fruit juice. Often the actual strength of the drug is unknown, and frequently other drugs, such as amphetamines, are added to it. It causes hallucinations and its results are unpredictable. The user may feel that he is omnipotent and supernatural. Some users have been killed attempting to fly out of windows. Some have walked into traffic, feeling they could stop any auto. One boy under the influence of LSD set himself afire in the belief that he could not burn. (A special danger of LSD usage is the recurrence of hallucinations weeks or months after its use.)

Other effects of LSD are distortions of perception (such as seeing bright colors in all sorts of unusual shapes and patterns, hearing strange and unusual sounds, seeing oneself and others in strange shapes) and distortions of time; dreamlike thoughts; and rapid mood changes, from excited happiness to anxiety and depression.

Some evidence also exists that LSD—by breaking the chromosomes in cells—may cause abnormal births in this or the next generation. Although the breaking of chromosomes has been demonstrated, insufficient time has elapsed to determine the final effect on offspring.

LSD is inexpensive and widely available.

Amphetamines (speed, A, ups, uppers, crystal, crank)   A group of stimulant drugs, the amphetamines include Dexedrine (pep pills; chemically, dextroamphetamine), Benzedrine (bennies; chemically, amphetamine), and methamphetamine (meth). They are prescribed by doctors to relieve depression and are also used to diminish appetite in the treatment of obesity. They make tired people feel alert and have been taken by many students in order to stay awake while studying for examinations.

The habitual amphetamine user develops numerous difficult problems. The user may go without eating or sleeping for long periods of time. As tolerance builds up rapidly, the user needs larger doses to achieve the same high. In con-

tinued use, the person frequently becomes exhausted and ill, and is kept going only by the drug. Depression almost always occurs as the drug wears off; with heavy users, the depression may be accompanied by severe anxiety and suicidal feelings. Users often take barbiturates to sleep and amphetamines to get going again.

Amphetamines cause the user to become excessively active, excitable, talkative, and nervous. There is often a tremor of the hands and increased perspiration.

Amphetamine may be injected directly into a vein. Taken in this manner or even in large oral doses, it can bring about severe loss of judgment. The user may try, for example, to step out of a moving car without realizing the danger. The original feeling of exhilaration and omnipotence may be followed by a severe emotional reaction resembling schizophrenia, in which a person becomes paranoid and thinks everyone is his enemy or that he is being followed by would-be murderers. Large intravenous doses may produce hemorrhages and death.

Amphetamine is inexpensive and widely available. To some extent, youngsters themselves have turned against the drug, as witnessed by the slogan "speed kills." (This is also true of LSD, but to a lesser degree.) Nevertheless it is still commonly used.

Barbiturates (downs, downers)   Generally prescribed by doctors to calm patients and produce sleep, the barbiturates, which are classed as sedatives, are also used to control epilepsy and to counteract certain severe emotional states in mental upsets.

An overdose may cause slurred speech, staggering and falling from lack of balance, falling asleep in class, and a quickness of temper. A massive overdose may produce coma. A combination of barbiturates with alcohol may cause death.

Barbiturates often cause addiction, and sudden withdrawal may cause delirium and even convulsions. Withdrawal, which must be very gradual to avoid symptoms, may last a month or more.

Barbiturates are inexpensive and easily available.

Heroin (smack, junk, scag, H) and morphine Potentially dangerous, heroin and morphine are made from the juice of the unripe seedpods of the opium poppies. Since the drugs are addictive, they are used medically as painkillers for only short periods of time.

Although heroin and morphine may be sniffed or smoked, they are usually injected by needle into the skin (skin popping) or even into a vein (mainlining). Addicts can usually be identified by scars on their arms and legs.

Many teen-agers think they can try heroin a few times and control the habit. The drug is extremely addictive, however, and depending on psychological, physical, and environmental factors, a habit can be formed after only three doses.

Teen-agers are generally introduced to the drug through friends, although at times a dealer may make the drug available free or for only a little money to entice a beginner. The notion of a pusher seeking out new customers and corrupting youth, however, is generally misleading. Most pushers have plenty of customers.

Until a person builds up complete tolerance, heroin gives a sense of euphoria and a feeling of being beyond all daily cares. It causes a marked slowing down of mental and physical activity, accompanied by yawning and drowsiness—and anxiety, muscle twitching, cold and hot flushes, and a feeling of desperation as the drug wears off. An overdose may cause coma and death.

Withdrawal, which is painful physically and mentally, may lead to delirium, convulsions, tremors, delusions, fever, and, occasionally, death. Today, however, because most illegal heroin is drastically cut in strength, the physical symptoms of withdrawal are often much milder. Another drug, methadone, is currently being used as one method of treating heroin and morphine addiction. Administered as a substitute, it removes the intense need for heroin.

Heroin is widely available. It is expensive, however, and the price often drives the addict to crime or prostitution. The addict's life is completely organized around obtaining money for the drug, and the care of his health is ignored. Hepatitis is often contracted from contaminated needles and syringes.

Cocaine (coke) Derived from the leaves of the cocoa plant of South America, cocaine is usually sniffed (snorted). It produces a marked stimulation of the nervous system, causing feelings of exhilaration and self-confidence.

Although tolerance develops relatively slowly and withdrawal symptoms are mild compared to those of morphine, heroin, and the barbiturates, cocaine is, nevertheless, habit-forming. Quite expensive, it is used largely by those who are wealthy.

Glue sniffing The inhalation by children and adolescents of the glue used in making model airplanes, boats, and cars is a major problem. It is often the first step in drug abuse.

The glue is placed in a bag, rag, or cloth and the vapors are inhaled. The inhalation soon produces a sense of euphoria and exhilaration that may progress to hallucination, disorientation, and even coma if continued.

Recently, major producers of such glue have added mustard oil to the product to make it undesirable to sniffers.

Some signs of possible drug abuse

1. Irregular school attendance or a decline in the quality of schoolwork.
2. Unusual outbreaks of temper or unexplained elation.
3. Long periods without sleeping or eating. Sudden increases in appetite and hours of sleep.
4. Slurring or difficulty of speech, as if drunk.
5. Yawning, often in spite of a good night's sleep.
6. Weight loss and a general rundown look.
7. Disappearance of prescription drugs from the home, especially weight-reducing pills and sedatives.
8. Wearing sunglasses to hide dilated or small pupils or bloodshot eyes.
9. Borrowing money from friends and others, much more than usual.
10. Stealing money and household articles from the home, stealing from school, pawning property.
11. Syringes, cotton, needles found in drawers at home or in lockers at school.
12. Wearing long-sleeved shirts to hide needle marks. These marks are often pinpoint scabs.
13. The smell of airplane glue or the smell of marijuana (a pungent smell, somewhat like Gauloises or other European cigarettes, but sweeter). Incense may be burned to cover the smell of marijuana.

These signs are possible indications only; several of the "symptoms" may have other causes. For example, outbursts of temper and difficulties in school are common in adolescence, and parents, therefore, should not jump to conclusions. Generally, a parent who is close to his child and communicates well with him should be able to recognize when the youngster is under the influence of drugs or is troubled over the issue of drug use. Parents should not, however, discount the "symptoms" without investigation. A common complaint among people working with young drug users and among the youngsters themselves is that parents either consciously or subconsciously ignore very obvious signs and hints that drugs are being used.

What can parents do?   If you suspect or realize that your child is taking drugs, above all remain calm. Panic and screaming and scolding help little and probably not at all. Try to understand your child, find out to what extent he is taking drugs and what the reasons are. In doing this, do everything in your power to keep open a bridge of communication so that the child can talk freely and is assured of your concern.

Your child's doctor can also be a great help. He can talk more objectively to the child, advise him, treat him, and if necessary, send him to a hospital or treatment center for continued care. (There are agencies and facilities for treating drug addiction in most large communities and large hospitals.)

Do not try to frighten your youngster with scare stories about drug abuse. Adolescents are not easily frightened, and the youngster realizes, all too often, that the parent knows little about drugs and, consequently, he will not believe anything more the parent has to say on the subject. Also, do not assume that drastic measures are necessary. Not every youngster who has smoked marijuana or tried amphetamine is in need of either medical or psychological treatment (he may be, but it is advisable to have a professional opinion on this). Nor should your child be turned over to legal authorities, for such action will not only completely destroy the parent-child relationship, but will also expose the child to experiences that may be extremely harmful.

Drug sensitivities

Usually manifested by skin eruptions, sensitivities to specific drugs may occasionally cause vomiting or diarrhea in sensitive children.

Although almost any drug can cause a reaction, the most frequent offenders are aspirin, phenobarbital, sulfa drugs, penicillin, and tetracycline. Morphine and codeine and their derivatives and iodides are also occasional causes of sensitivity. Reactions may be treated by antihistamines and if necessary by cortisone derivatives.

No effective means of desensitization has been developed as yet. Avoidance of the drugs to which the child is sensitive is, therefore, required. A child who has had a severe reaction to penicillin, for example, should wear a tag around his neck or wrist (preferably from Medic Alert) warning of the sensitivity (see **Medic Alert**).

Drugs, effect on fetus and newborn

Many drugs taken by mothers during pregnancy are known to be dangerous to the unborn infant, a fact that was illustrated during the early 1960's by the thalidomide tragedy in Europe (many infants were born without arms and legs after their mothers had taken thalidomide in early pregnancy to stop nausea and vomiting). Other drugs, too, cross the placenta and enter the body of the fetus. Drugs containing iodine may cause goiter in the infant; sulfa drugs may cause jaundice; cortisone preparations may cause a baby girl to develop abnormalities of the sex organs; some drugs given to protect pregnant women against malaria may cause a bleeding tendency in infants.

Most drugs taken by mouth or injected are excreted by the kidneys or broken up by the liver. The immature, poorly functioning kidneys and liver of the newborn infant and especially of the premature baby cause drugs to be excreted and broken up very slowly and poorly. They therefore accumulate in high concentrations in the bloodstream and can be extremely harmful. Even aspirin can be dangerous.

If drugs must be given to newborn and premature babies, they should be given only under the careful supervision of a pediatrician. Very small doses of the drugs are given at lengthened intervals to give the slow-working kidneys and liver time to eliminate the drugs from the child's body and thus prevent accumulation in the bloodstream.

A pregnant woman should take drugs, including non-prescription drugs, only under the supervision of her obstetrician.

See also **Cigarettes**.

Duodenal ulcer   see **Ulcer, stomach and duodenal.**

Dwarfism

Stature considerably below normal height. Dwarfism does not include such conditions as delayed puberty—in which the rapid adolescent gain in height is much later than in the average child—or inherited, familial tendencies to short stature.

Scientific study of a child's blood, hormones, and bones can usually determine whether a child is a true dwarf and the type and course of treatment, if any is possible.

True dwarfism can be caused by many conditions, among which are the following:

1. Severe malnutrition during the early years of life when there is normally rapid growth. Although such nutritionally deprived children may later put on weight, they can never make up the deficiency in height. An inadequate amount of food is not the only causative factor, however. Diarrhea or other intestinal disorders that prevent the absorption of food by the body may also cause dwarfism.
2. Hereditary dwarfism, such as achondroplastic dwarfism, which is characterized by a normal size head and torso but very short, muscular arms and legs. No treatment is known.
3. Cretinism, which is a condition caused by an absence or severe lack of thyroid secretion. If recognized early in infancy, the child may be given thyroid orally and will develop as rapidly in height as any normal child. (See **Cretinism.**)
4. A lack of the pituitary growth hormone, which results in an adult who is very small and proportioned like a child, a midget. It can be treated by human growth hormone as soon as the lack is diagnosed.

Dysentery see **Amebic dysentery; Diarrhea.**

Dyslexia

To resolve the many, varying interpretations of the word "dyslexia" the World Federation of Neurology in 1968 agreed on the following definition: "A disorder manifested by difficulty in learning to read despite conventional instruction, adequate intelligence, and sociocultural opportunity. It is a disorder in children who, despite classroom experience, fail to attain the language skills of reading, writing and spelling commensurate with their intellectual abilities."

Only since the end of the 1950's has research on children with reading problems led to the discovery that some children see words or letters upside down, backward, or distorted in other ways; that some children have a tendency to move their eyes from right to left; that others fail to remember what the sounds of certain letters are when written down—although they can remember the sound when the name of the letter is told to them. All of these and similar reading problems are included under the term dyslexia.

Today many educators, psychologists, and physicians feel that dyslexia is usually the result of mild brain dysfunction—of some irregularity in brain functioning, often the result of a temporary lack of oxygen to the brain. The cause may have been prenatal or birth complications, encephalitis, or a fall on the head. In certain children, however, dyslexia may be familial. Many dyslexic children have parents, aunts, uncles, or grandparents who had similar reading disabilities. There are many more dyslexic boys than girls. (See **Brain dysfunction, mild.**)

Some adults now realize that they suffered the problems of dyslexia in their childhood—that it was not understood, and that they were made to feel inadequate and at times even stupid. Actually, most dyslexic people are of average or above average intelligence. Many of them have found ways of coping with and compensating for this problem; some just hide it or cover it up. A good many have handled it so well that they have become successful even in professions demanding above-average reading skills. It is only when they become tired or are under tension that some remnants of the old problems are likely to become evident.

The degree of dyslexia may vary greatly. In fact many young children demonstrate some reversing of letters or words as they first learn to read or write. This is very normal in the young child. But when a child still continues to reverse at the age of 7 or 8, it is time to check to find out whether the child is simply slow to develop in this area or whether he or she has a form of dyslexia and needs special attention.

One of the most difficult problems that results from dyslexic disability is that the child initially cannot understand why he cannot learn and feels inadequate and frustrated. His classmates may tease him, which upsets him even more. Some such children withdraw into themselves, puzzled and ashamed; others become the clowns or the problem children in class, trying to attract attention to themselves, trying to find ways of regaining their self-worth.

Since most teachers are not prepared or trained to handle dyslexic children, many schools have special classes with specially trained teachers to help such youngsters.

Parents of a dyslexic child should be particularly sensitive to his or her needs and feelings. Parents should help him work diligently on the special exercises and lessons the child may have to do. They should let the child know that they understand how frustrating and upsetting his lessons can be. And they should assure the child that he can overcome this problem and go on to college and success in life.

Dysmenorrhea see **Cramps, menstrual.**

E

Ear, foreign objects in see **Foreign objects in ear.**

Earaches

The discomforting pains of earache may be caused by an infection in the ear canal, usually a pimple, abscess, or fungus, or by an inflammation of the eardrum resulting from infections of the nose and throat.

Infections in the ear canal, although painful, are not as a rule serious and usually respond to wet dressings and antibiotic eardrops. These infections occur with equal frequency at all ages in childhood. They often follow swimming in ponds or lakes.

Infections of the nose and throat that also cause earaches are much more common during childhood than later, largely because the anatomy of the child's nose, throat, and ears is different from the adult structure. In children the eustachian tube, which leads from the inside of the ear to the throat, is connected directly to the throat and is comparatively short and wide. It is like part of the throat itself, so that when the throat is sore and congested some redness of the eardrum almost always ensues. In an adult, on the other hand, the eustachian tube is longer and narrower and branches off the throat at an angle, thus minimizing the chance of throat infection spreading to the ear.

Frequent earaches in children are also likely to be caused by enlarged adenoids that close off the eustachian tube, thus providing an enclosed space in which bacteria can grow.

Treatment Give the child aspirin to reduce pain even if he does not have a fever. A heating pad held against the painful ear often helps. The ear should be examined by a doctor, who will most likely add eardrops to further relieve the pain and an oral decongestant or nose drops in an attempt to shrink the swollen adenoid tissue. He will probably also prescribe an antibiotic to overcome the infection.

Deafness and earaches Temporary deafness, which often accompanies infections in the ear, is usually a result of the thickening of an inflamed eardrum. When the infection subsides, the drum returns to normal thickness and the child hears as well as previously. Occasionally fluid forms beneath the drum, causing some added deafness. If this fluid is composed of pus it will often rupture through the drum, causing a runny ear for a day or two. Once the eardrum ruptures, relieving the pressure beneath the drum, the pain—which may be severe—subsides almost immediately. The fever almost always drops as well. The opening in the eardrum heals and closes completely in a few days.

At times a fluid that is not pus but is more like serum collects under the drum and may remain there, causing chronic deafness. An ear specialist may make a temporary opening in the drum and even place a tiny tube through it to let the liquid flow out. He may leave the tube in the eardrum for several weeks, because the liquid within may be thick and sticky. Once the tube is removed, the eardrum heals perfectly.

Before the use of antibiotics, both discharging ears and mastoiditis (infection of the bone behind the ear) were common. Discharging ears still occur occasionally. Mastoiditis however, is extremely rare. Many parents still worry about mastoiditis as soon as a child develops an earache. Mastoiditis does not develop as a rule until an earache has been present for at least three days. Under proper treatment the infection should be under control before it has a chance to spread to the mastoid bone behind the ear.

See also **Mastoiditis.**

Earwax

Wax normally formed in the external ear canal. Its purpose is to keep the canal clear of foreign substances that might enter the ear; the small hairs lining the canal tend to move the wax out of the ear.

Mothers should not attempt to remove the wax, for they might damage the skin lining the canal, and if they poke too deeply, they might even damage the eardrum. Mothers should limit themselves to cleaning the outer ear as far as the entrance to the canal.

At times the wax thickens and often clogs the canal. It may be removed by instilling some specially prepared drops that soften the wax, and then syringing out the ear gently with a rubber bulb ear syringe. Two of the commercially prepared drops for softening and loosening the wax are Debrox and Cerumenex. Five drops are instilled into the ear

twice a day for three to four days. At the end of that time, syringing usually removes the wax with ease.

Occasionally the child's skin may be allergic to the drops. If the inside of the ear gets red and irritated, the drops should be discontinued.

ECG   see **Electrocardiogram.**

Eczema

An inflammatory condition of the skin, almost always of allergic origin. It may be caused by a food or by contact of the skin with some substance to which it is sensitive.

Eczema occurs most commonly during the first year of life, when new foods are being added to the infant's diet and when the skin is highly sensitive. The foods that are most likely to cause eczema during the first year are cow's milk, eggs, wheat, and orange juice, although it can be caused by any food or by a vitamin preparation.

During infancy the rash usually appears first on the cheeks in the form of red pimples, and rapidly spreads over the face and to other parts of the body. In older children when eczema is chronic or may appear from time to time, it most frequently involves the folds of the elbows and behind the knees. The rash usually itches, and rubbing and scratching only makes the condition worse.

Contact eczemas, which are caused by allergic reactions or sensitivities of the skin to some substance in contact with it, are common in infancy when the skin is tender. Among the common irritants are wool, bath soap, baby oil, laundry soaps or detergents in which the baby's clothes are washed, or laundry bleach that has not been thoroughly removed from the clothes. The "enzyme-added detergents" are irritating to the skin of many infants.

Unfortunately, the allergy skin tests are not too accurate in the diagnosis of food sensitivity eczema. A much more effective method is the elimination diet. For instance, if an eczema starts when a child is 4 months, put him back on the foods he was eating when he was 3 months old. After the eczema disappears, add new foods one by one every five or six days until the eczema reappears. The food that caused the eczema can then be determined and eliminated from the diet and substitutions made. When a child is older a more complicated elimination diet is followed. (See **Diet, elimination.**)

Contact eczema can be eliminated by removing the questionable object or substance. Patch tests, in which a cloth patch containing the suspected substance is held against the skin by adhesive tape for several days, are occasionally used by allergists to determine sensitivity. If the child's skin is sensitive to the substance, the skin beneath the patch will be inflamed.

Treatment The treatment of eczema depends upon the cause. If the eczema is caused by a food, the food, of course, is eliminated from the diet. Food allergies, however, can frequently be overcome. After a complete avoidance of the allergenic food for some months, it is added little by little to the child's diet, thus increasing gradually his tolerance to it. Many infants with severe eczema during the first year of life are almost miraculously free of the rash after that time. Apparently they have built up a toleration for the specific food or foods and the skin is less sensitive.

In treating eczema locally it is important to prevent the child from scratching, which only makes the condition worse. Various ointments, lotions, and baths (described below) usually relieve the itching.

Water should be used on the affected area as little as possible, since this too irritates and increases the inflammation. Often the skin may be kept clean with mineral oil. When water is used, a hypoallergenic soap should be used (Lowila, Aveeno, or Neutrogena are examples). Also, special soothing baths are often helpful, relieving the itching, and thus limiting the amount of scratching (Aveeno Colloidal Oatmeal bath, Soyaloid colloidal bath).

Many excellent creams and ointments are also available to relieve all but the most severe eczema. The best of these preparations contain cortisone products that counteract the inflammation and subdue the itching. These preparations are prescribed by the doctor, who will select the type he feels to be most effective and suitable in strength. But although these creams and ointments improve the condition, only the elmination of the offending substance will cure the eczema. Severe or persistent cases should always be under the care of a doctor.

Occasionally eczema may be infected by the child's scratching. This must be treated by antibiotic ointments.

Education
In our culture, education primarily means learning in a school situation. For the child, school opens up a new world of experience and accomplishment. Learning to read and write and work with numbers is exciting. And much of the child's future will be based

on this learning. But, of course, education also includes the full range of understanding and skills that the child gains at home and in experiences outside the home and school. Education begins in infancy when parents satisfy a baby's curiosity with new sights, sounds, and games, and continues throughout childhood as parents are able to communicate more and more of their thinking, skills, and interests to the child. (See **Stimulating the child.**)

Parents who are good educators in the home are also usually of great help to the child in his school life, because of their vital interest in their child's academic education. It is extremely important to the young student to know that his parents are concerned with all aspects of his schoolwork and want to understand and share his problems and triumphs. It is generally helpful if parents take an active role in school affairs. By this means parents are able to communicate with teachers and the school administration regarding their child; they learn the school's strengths and weaknesses; and they give their child the feeling that his parents understand and care about what he is doing all day, and are not just sending him off into the care of strangers.

Some parents, however, become too involved in their child's schoolwork. They go over every homework assignment, sometimes doing the work themselves. They want to know how the child has done on every small test. They become depressed and upset if there is a poor grade on the report card. Although children should be expected to do their best in school, parents who set unreasonably high standards can only make their children feel incompetent and miserable. And parents should also remember that in school a child should be learning to work on his own. Not every task should be supervised, even though this means that a child will occasionally take it easy and get a low mark.

All children, of course, do not attend school with the same enthusiasm, and all children do not acquire learning skills at the same rate. If a child is having problems in adjusting at school and in learning, he needs a great deal of encouragement and understanding from his parents—not punishment, scolding, or the feeling that he has failed his parents as well as himself.

Some children do poorly in school because they lack stimulation or are not at the same intellectual level as the rest of the class. At times they are too advanced scholastically for the class in which they are placed; sometimes they are below the class standard. They might have sight or hearing difficulties or mild brain dysfunction or dyslexia. (See **Brain dysfunction, mild; Dyslexia.**) At other times the class is too large and a child lacks the personal attention he needs, or the teacher is poor or is the wrong teacher for the child. But if a child is having learning problems or other difficulties that upset his schooling, it is always wise to discuss these matters with the teacher and the guidance counselor if one is associated with the school. The cooperation of parents and teacher is always beneficial to the child.

A college education or its equivalent in technical education is almost a necessity if a person desires to succeed in the competitive world. If a parent wants his child to attend college and the child seems qualified, the parent should start speaking of it and planning for it early in the child's life; most often the child then follows the suggestion as a matter of course.

Education, experimental approaches in

In recent years more and more elementary schools in the United States and Canada have followed the lead of England in experimenting with methods of education adjusted to each child's intellectual ability. Among these experiments are the unstructured, or open-space, schools and the ungraded schools. At the present time most of the unstructured, open-space, ungraded schools are for the elementary grades.

In these schools the guiding concept is that play is a child's most natural and effective means of learning. Therefore education should be based essentially on the child's interests. The theory is that children will learn all the skills and necessary knowledge for later education if they are allowed to pursue learning in areas which are of particular interest to them. Furthermore, it is pointed out that methods of teaching that force a child into activities he dislikes and shame him if he fails to meet certain standards tend to block learning rather than encourage it. Instead, it is proposed, the direction of education should differ with each child. A youngster should learn at his own pace and in his own way under the stimulation and guidance of his teacher. There should be no comparison between children and no grades.

A school based on these principles should have an abundance of materials to arouse and sustain a child's interests and a good library to which a child can readily turn. Although in many of these schools no set texts are used, texts are available for those children who wish to use them. The school library usually becomes a "learning center" with a multitude of books, tapes, records, film strips, and films which the children learn to find and use on their own.

The construction of the building in schools of this type is important to the program. Classrooms are often not enclosed but are sections of a broad area, perhaps separated by movable dividers or screens. Children can move from area to area, although they are ultimately responsible to the teacher in their own area.

Learning evolves from a project that interests the child, and the teacher encourages and guides the youngster's enthusiasm. A single project may involve reading, writing, arithmetic, science, geography, and history. In fact, the possibilities of where a child's interests might lead him are almost infinite.

In many of these schools the child outlines to the teacher what he wants to do and how he plans to carry it out. He gets the teacher's guidance. From time to time he may return for help, and in the end he will work through and evaluate the project with the teacher.

For example, a child of 6 paints a picture of a house. The teacher sees it and asks him to write "house" under it, or the teacher may show him how to write it. They discuss the number of doors, rooms, windows, and chimneys of the house. The child is stimulated to go to the library and look at books on houses. He sees log cabins, wigwams, thatched huts, igloos. The idea of living in an ice house may intrigue the child. He wonders how its inhabitants keep warm, where they live, what they eat. Depending upon the age and talents of the child, learning to find the answers to these questions and to communicate what he has learned may involve mastering a wide range of skills and absorbing a great deal of information.

Thus the child does more than simply

play. The teacher must be alert to help a child go from imaginary play or other random activity to a more structured activity. And the teacher must know when to intervene and when to let the child continue with his activity.

Formal education is not, as a rule, entirely dispensed with. The children may be given reading, spelling, or mathematical games to play among themselves or with the teacher. They may also get some drilling in phonetics and reading and writing. Often youngsters have notebooks of their own learned words which are gradually enlarged.

Under this type of education no child should be made to feel inadequate, for all children travel in different directions for their academic knowledge. Equally important, these children are learning to work independently, to seek out and find answers to questions, and to follow through and complete a project.

This open approach to education is certainly in many ways an improvement upon more conservative methods. However, parents should not assume that a school with such an approach is an automatic solution for their child. Some of these schools are less good than others: the administrators and teachers may lack the skill, experience, or resources to make the approach work successfully. Also, some children need and want a more structured environment.

See also **Montessori method.**

Educational counseling see **Counseling, educational and guidance.**

EEG see **Electroencephalogram.**

EKG see **Electrocardiogram.**

Electra complex see **Oedipus complex.**

Electric shock

Occasionally a young child chews on an electric wire, pokes a piece of metal into an open electric outlet, or puts his finger in an empty electric light bulb socket. This usually causes only a shock or a burn. If the child is standing on a wet surface, however, or is in a tub of water or at a water-filled sink, the shock is increased to such intensity that it may be fatal.

Older children and adolescents may come into contact with live tension wires, which are extremely dangerous; the shock is likely to be fatal. The same is true of lightning shock.

First-aid If the child or teen-ager is still in contact with the wire, shut off the current. If it is a tension wire, the electric company should be called as soon as possible.

Don't touch the child as long as he is still in contact with the current unless you are insulated by standing on a rubber mat, pile of dry newspapers, dry wood, or other dry nonconductive (nonmetallic) material. Rubber-soled shoes are safer than leather shoes. Remember that unless you are insulated, you too may get a shock. Push the child free with a dry nonmetallic object—a board, stick, a rolled-up magazine or newspaper.

After contact has been broken, immediately give mouth-to-mouth resuscitation, even if the child's body is stiff, his color is blue or white, and you cannot detect a heartbeat. Electricity has a paralyzing effect on the breathing center, heart, and muscles, but the victim may recover. It may take hours of artificial respiration before the child breathes by himself—possibly as much as eight hours. (See **Mouth-to-mouth resuscitation.**)

If more than one person is affected simultaneously by electric shock, immediate emergency treatment should be given to those who appear most seriously affected—even those who appear dead—ignoring temporarily anyone who is moving and breathing.

Prevention In the home, all wires should be well insulated, not frayed, and the wiring system should be in good condition, to guard against fires as well. The house should be grounded for lightning. Unused outlets should be taped over or closed with plastic plugs made solely for that purpose. Electric power tools and appliances should be checked for the possibility of shock. Toddlers should be kept away from outlets, wires, and light sockets. A youngster who persists in playing around outlets must be severely scolded or even slapped for his own safety. Older children should be helped to understand the principles of electricity and the possibility of shock. Many children old enough to understand are not told that current runs into a light socket or the wires in a toaster when the appliance is plugged in. When there is a possibility of lightning, no one should be allowed to swim, and if you are caught in the country in a thunderstorm, the safest place to be is in your car. Avoid standing under a tree.

Electrocardiogram (ECG, EKG)
A graphic tracing of the electric current produced by the contractions of the heart muscle.

Whenever a muscle contracts, a very minute electrical impulse is given off. When the muscles of the heart contract the electric impulse can be picked up by wires attached to the body. The impulses are transmitted to an electrocardiograph, where they are magnified and recorded graphically.

The normal heart produces a characteristic tracing of curves and spikes. Heart disorders produce tracings that differ from the normal tracings and give valuable clues as to the disability.

Electrocardiograms must be interpreted by a doctor with special training and considerable experience.

Electroencephalogram (EEG)
A recording of the fine electrical currents produced by the brain. The normal brain has a definite wave pattern. This pattern is usually disturbed by abnormalities in the brain, such as grandmal and petit-mal epilepsy and local irritations or tumors.

Wires from an electroencephalograph, a machine that records brain waves, are attached to the surface of the scalp. Readings are usually made on three occasions, when the child is awake, drowsy, and asleep. The procedure, which can be performed in a short time and does not require hospitalization, is entirely harmless.

Elimination see **Bowel movements; Constipation; Diarrhea.**

Elimination diet see **Diet, elimination.**

Embryo
The fetus in its early stage of development, approximately the first three months. This is the most important period in the development of a baby's body, for it is during this time that the various parts of the body are formed.

The head, torso, extremities, heart, lungs, digestive and reproductive systems, nervous system, eyes, ears, nose, and mouth develop during this period. The upper lip, which is originally in three separate parts, joins together and forms one complete lip. The palate, originally open in the center, also grows together. Then arm and leg buds sprout from the torso and these continue to grow and develop until they are completely formed.

Embryo of about 5 weeks, ⅔ of an inch long.

By the time the embryo is three months old it is well developed and looks like a baby. During this early period in the development of the baby, special care must be given so that no drug taken by the mother or infection such as German measles damages the embryo or interferes with the normal sequence of growth.

See also **Drugs, effect on fetus and newborn.**

Emotional disturbance

Every child has certain emotional upsets from time to time. Most of these are minor or passing—temper tantrums, fear of the dark, separation anxieties, resistance to authority, worry, feelings of frustration, the usual rivalries and jealousies. Most of these minor disturbances either disappear or do not remain as serious problems, as maturity in understanding and judgment develops.

Nevertheless, many children have more severe emotional upsets or severe psychiatric difficulties. They are in great need of help.

The primary cause of severe emotional disturbance is most often some factor in the home environment. A child's sense of emotional security and stability can be severely harmed by traumatic situations, such as the death of a parent, abandonment by the mother or father, divorce, or quarreling between the parents. When one or both of the parents are themselves emotionally upset, and especially if they are unable to give adequate love to the child, or when a child is constantly punished, there is a great risk that the child will be seriously affected.

Emotional distress is expressed by children in various ways:

1. Antisocial personality. Some children regularly resist the authority of parents, teachers, even law enforcement officers. They may lie and steal and show no signs of guilt. They often have very little feeling for others. They may commit criminal acts.
2. Passive and depressed personality. Some emotionally disturbed children withdraw from other people and live a lonely and depressed life. As teenagers they may become suicidal.
3. Extreme difficulty in getting along with other children.
4. Failure or low grades in school, de-

spite normal or above normal intelligence.

5. Manifestations of nervous tension, including tics, stammering, stuttering.

6. Exaggerated fears that interfere with normal activity.

7. Persistent and severe sleep disturbances.

8. Marked overeating or undereating—to the point of undermining good health.

9. Persistent patterns of compulsive behavior, such as great concern with washing the hands or avoiding dirt.

10. Behavior that is characteristic of a much earlier age level, such as bed-wetting by a 7-year-old or clinging to the mother by an 8-year-old.

11. Frequent and uncontrollable fits of crying or rage.

12. Sexual deviations, such as promiscuity, compulsive masturbation, transvestism (wearing clothes of the opposite sex), recurring homosexual activity, markedly masochistic or sadistic sex play or sexual activity, sexual exhibitionism.

13. Drug addiction or chronic drug abuse. Some basically healthy children experiment with drugs out of curiosity, but a youngster who uses drugs to the point that his health or normal activity is affected is often seeking relief from emotional tensions through escape from reality.

The treatment of serious emotional disturbance is often a long process, usually requiring the cooperation of the family to adjust the home environment and the help of a psychotherapist or other trained professional to guide the child to an understanding of his problems and a new means of dealing with them.

See also **Aggressiveness; Anger; Ano-** **rexia nervosa; Anxiety; Arson; Bullying; Compulsions; Depression; Drug abuse; Family psychotherapy; Homosexuality; Juvenile delinquency; Obesity; Passivity; Phobias; Psychotherapy; Regression; Sadism; Stuttering and stammering; Temper and temper tantrums; Tics; Transvestism.**

See also **Appendix D: Community Mental Health Centers in the United States.**

Encephalitis

Inflammation of the brain, usually caused by virus infections; among children lead poisoning is also a fairly frequent cause. The types of encephalitis most commonly found during childhood are:

Measles encephalitis A severe and damaging complication of measles that arises in about 1 case in 1,000, measles encephalitis may be fatal. More often, however, the child recovers but is left with permanent brain damage. Bright children may become retarded or dull, or a child with a warm and happy personality may become aggressive and difficult, and exhibit negative behavior. This type of encephalitis can be prevented by vaccination against measles.

Mumps encephalitis Quite common but not dangerous, mumps encephalitis, is of short duration, and children who suffer from it almost always recover completely. The symptoms usually appear about the sixth or seventh day after the onset of mumps: severe headache, followed by vomiting and drowsiness. The child also usually develops a stiff neck and back. After two or three days, the symptoms subside and the child recovers completely.

Chicken pox encephalitis Comparatively rare, chicken pox encephalitis occurs in only about 20 cases in 10,000. The symptoms, which are the same as in mumps encephalitis, appear about four to ten days after the onset of the rash. Almost all children recover completely, but in very rare instances the condition may be serious.

Polioencephalitis A dangerous complication of acute poliomyelitis, polioencephalitis is the cause of almost all polio fatalities. Fortunately, the polio vaccination has virtually eradicated this type of encephalitis.

Vaccinia encephalitis Dangerous and extremely rare (1 case in 100,000 in the United States), vaccinia encephalitis follows vaccination against smallpox. The mortality rate is high—about 40 percent. The cause of the infection has not been established. Some investigators think the vaccine is responsible, others that the vaccine activates a virus that is present, while still others feel that it is an allergic reaction.

Lead-poisoning encephalitis A dangerous complication of chronic lead poisoning, the symptoms of this variety of encephalitis start with weakness, irritability, headache, and abdominal pain. The disease may progress to convulsions, blindness, mental deficiency, and possibly death. (See **Lead poisoning.**)

See also **Sleeping-sickness encephalitis.**

Endocrine glands   see **Glands.**

Enemas

Enemas are occasionally advised by a child's doctor to relieve constipation and in rare instances to reduce high fever. They should only be given if recommended by a doctor, and should not be used routinely to treat constipation.

It is best to use a solution of bicarbonate of soda in warm water. Soapsud enemas are too irritating. For infants, use two to three ounces of water and a quarter teaspoon of bicarbonate of soda. For older children, use at least eight ounces of water and one teaspoon of soda. Commercial disposable enemas, such as the Fleet Disposable Enema, are available at drugstores. Convenient to use, a disposable enema consists of a plastic nipple and a plastic bottle filled with solution. The nipple is inserted into the anus and the bottle is slowly squeezed until the contents are emptied into the rectum. Disposable enemas are available in infant and adult size. Children are given one half to a whole of the adult enema, depending on their age and size.

If a disposable enema is not used, a *soft* rubber bulb syringe is best for infants up to about age 2. Thereafter an enema bag with a soft rubber tube may be used. Before use of either a syringe or enema bag, the tip should be lubricated with petroleum jelly or other lubricant (but not soap). Also, let out a little of the liquid from the syringe or bag to be sure that all the air has been expelled.

In giving an enema to a baby have him lie on his back on a waterproof pad, and hold his legs in the air so that the buttocks are slightly raised. Gently insert the tip of the syringe into the anus, and squeeze the bulb very gently so that the water flows in slowly. An older child should lie on his left side with his legs drawn up toward his stomach. The enema bag should be no more than eighteen inches above the child to be sure that the solution does not flow too

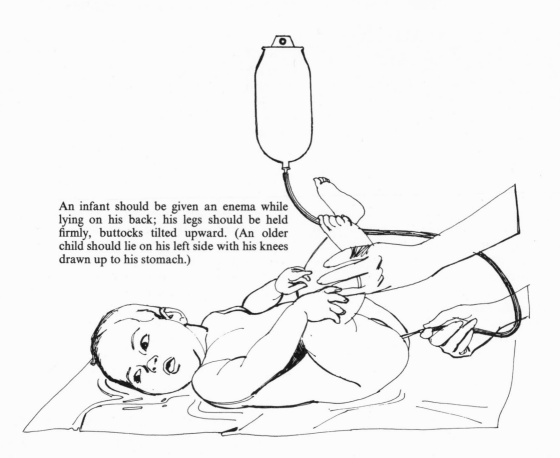

An infant should be given an enema while lying on his back; his legs should be held firmly, buttocks tilted upward. (An older child should lie on his left side with his knees drawn up to his stomach.)

quickly. Insert the tube about two inches into the rectum, and then hold the buttocks together while the liquid is flowing in. If the child complains of a stomachache or wanting to "go," slow down or temporarily stop the flow. After the enema is finished, both an infant and older child should hold in the solution if possible for several minutes. The buttocks may be held together so that the solution is retained. Have a diaper, basin, or potty at hand, or place the child immediately on the toilet once the procedure is completed.

Occasionally a child does not discharge the enema solution. There is no harm done if the solution is retained.

Entertainment see **Amusements; Books; Comic books; Movies; Television; Toys and play materials.**

Enuresis see **Bed-wetting.**

Environment

The total surroundings—persons, conditions, and influences—in a child's life. Key environmental factors are whether the child is reared by his own parents; whether the parents are together or separated; whether the parents are relaxed or nervous, permissive or punitive, loving or rejecting, sympathetic or unsympathetic. Other important factors are the number of children in the family, the child's rank in order of siblings, the economic status of the family, and the character of the community in which the family lives.

The character and personality of the adult is in large part dependent upon the total effect of all environmental influences during childhood.

See also **Heredity.**

Epilepsy

Epilepsy is not a disease but a group of symptoms caused by any of several disorders of the nervous system. There are essentially two types: a mild type called petit mal, and the more severe grand mal, associated with convulsive seizures.

Petit mal seizures consist of a momentary loss of consciousness, usually without twitching spasms, the only outward signs being staring or an upward rolling of the eyes. The child may be talking, eating, or involved in any activity and then suddenly stop for a few seconds, staring or with the eyes rolled up. He rarely falls, although at times he may drop a dish or a book he is holding. Parents often refer to these seizures as "staring spells" or "lapses." Often the child will be unaware of the momentary attack and continue whatever he was doing before the attack.

These seizures vary in frequency from only one or two a month to as many as several hundred a day.

Grand mal seizures are convulsions in which the child loses consciousness, falls and becomes rigid, and foams at the mouth. In a few moments the stiffness subsides, only to be followed by a series of violent muscular contractions. These convulsive movements may last a few minutes, after which the child lies unconscious and prostrate and falls into a deep sleep. After a while he awakens with a headache and in a state of confusion.

Fortunately, 70 or 80 percent of both petit mal and grand mal seizures can be controlled and prevented. Epilepsy, once controlled, should not disable a child. It does not affect mentality, and he or she should be able to go to the same schools and camps as other children and do just as well in adult life. Among many famous epileptics in history were Julius Caesar and Dostoevski.

Causes Although epilepsy has been known from at least 2000 B.C. and was described by Hippocrates, the great Greek physician, about 400 B.C., the cause is not known in many cases. Where an injury to the brain has occurred before, during, or after birth, epilepsy may follow. Heredity may be involved, but in most cases there is no evidence of genetic influences.

Diagnosis The nature of the seizures and the readings of an electroencephalogram determine the diagnosis. The electroencephalogram, or EEG, is a recording of the electrical currents produced by the brain. In convulsive disorders the brain wave pattern is usually abnormal.

Treatment Petit mal can usually be controlled by small daily amounts of phenobarbital. If this is not effective, another drug, such as Tridione (trimethadione) is added. The treatment is continued daily for several years. If no further seizures have occurred, the drugs may be discontinued; in most cases there is no recurrence. Petit mal sometimes disappears spontaneously.

Grand mal can be controlled by drugs, especially phenobarbital and Dilantin (diphenylhydantoin). Once a seizure has been diagnosed as epilepsy, these drugs are given and are usually continued daily for several years, whether or not the child has subsequent seizures.

Fifty percent of all cases of epilepsy can be completely controlled by medication. In another 30 percent, the seizures can be partially controlled.

The child with epilepsy should be under the supervision of a doctor, who will decide just how long treatment should continue. Treatment can often be discontinued after three to five years if there have been no seizures.

In the case of an acute attack, parents or others near the child should remain calm. The seizure cannot be stopped and will run its course. There is no advantage in trying to restrain the person or interfere with his movements. There is no reason to force anything between his teeth, but if his mouth is open, a folded handkerchief may be placed between his teeth to prevent tongue biting. After the seizure, let the child rest, and remain calm when the child awakens.

For information on epilepsy, write: Epilepsy Foundation of America, 733 15 St. N.W., Washington, D.C., 20005.

Erection, genital

A temporary rigidity, enlargement, and elongation of the penis. During infancy it is not uncommon for baby boys to have erections, usually when the bladder is full. This is of no importance.

When boys are between 3 and 5 years of age, most of them find that they can get a pleasurable sensation from handling or stroking the penis. This is a masturbatory activity and usually causes an erection. Masturbation is normal during this period and of no harm. (See **Masturbation**.)

As boys enter puberty they start to have erections spontaneously. These usually occur at night, associated with a sex dream, and are accompanied by a flow of semen through the urethra to the outside. (See **Nocturnal seminal emission.**) During adolescence frequent erections are usual and normal.

Erysipelas

An acute infection of the skin caused by streptococcus bacteria. The condition usually starts from an infection of a cut or even a surgical incision. At times it may follow the scratching of eczema or chicken pox.

The condition starts as a swollen and inflamed area around the site of infection, and then the inflammation and swelling spreads. The child develops a high fever as a rule (104 to 105 degrees) and is usually very irritable, loses his appetite, and vomits frequently.

Erysipelas, formerly a very dangerous disease, responds rapidly to treatment by penicillin. This antibiotic, given by mouth and injection, kills the streptococcus organism. Local treatment by ointments or lotions is of no value.

Erythroblastosis see Rh factor blood incompatibility.

Eustachian tubes

Narrow tubes extending up from the throat and connecting with the inner ears. Bacteria from infections in the throat often travel up the tubes, causing an inflammation of the eardrums and a resulting earache.

For proper hearing, the eustachian tubes must remain open so that air pressure is equal on both sides of the eardrums. If the tubes are closed off by the adenoid tissue in the throat or by fluid or inflammation, the child's hearing will be impaired.

See also **Earaches.**

Examination, physical see **Physical examination.**

Examinations and tests in school

School exams and tests are designed, ideally, to enable a teacher to determine how much a child knows about a given subject. Many students soon learn, however, that teachers, parents, and even classmates often attach greater importance to test grades than to all of the other work the child has done in class.

Children who are secure, self-confident, and good students usually take tests successfully. For children who fear the consequences, however, tests often become frightening and threatening. This anxiety may cause them to perform at a far lower level than that of which they are actually capable. And there are still other children who are not especially good students but who learn how to play the test-taking game. They become expert at answering multiple choice questions. They learn how to eliminate obviously wrong answers and can guess more accurately at the right answer; they learn how to pick the important ideas out of what they read—and memorize these. They do well on tests but retain only a minimal knowledge of the subject.

Test-taking has a positive side, however. Tests can motivate a child to read and study material he might otherwise ignore. They provide a structure for knowing what a teacher feels are the most important ideas to be learned about a particular subject. They give a child practice for the exams to be taken in the future for college entrance, scholastic awards, and so on.

If a child is a poor test taker, the best thing his parents can do is express appreciation for the good work he does in other areas. Parents should express sympathy for the problem, not pressure the child to improve. Improvement will come as the child relaxes and gains more experience. He will feel easier if his parents let him know that they understand how hard he has to work to do well on a test and that he probably knows more than is reflected in his mark.

Exanthema subitum see **Roseola infantum.**

Exceptional child

The term exceptional child once referred only to gifted children. In recent years it has been used to refer primarily to those children who are handicapped in some way. (See **Autism; Blindness; Crippled child, helping the; Deafness; Mental retardation.**)

Exchange transfusion see **Rh factor blood incompatibility.**

Excuses

All children, as well as adults, make excuses at one time or another. Many situations call for explanations—not having done something expected, forgetting to do something, losing something, getting home late, getting to school late, causing trouble in school or elsewhere.

Excuses that are reasonable and not too repetitious should be accepted and are generally no cause for further concern. It is the child who is constantly making excuses who needs special attention, particularly if his excuses follow a specific pattern: the aggressive child who is constantly blaming others for starting fights; the child who is frequently late for school and always has a story to explain it; the child who does poorly at school and blames it on the "poor teacher" or claims the teacher doesn't like him; the child who regularly "forgets" his chore.

Why does a child make excuses? Is he afraid of the consequences or of punishment? What is the basic reason for the behavior for which he makes excuses? Why does the tardy child always arrive late? Why is the aggressive child who blames others for his fights so aggressive? Why does the child who is constantly making excuses for not doing his chores want to shirk his responsibility?

All frequent and repetitive excuses should be carefully studied if the child is to be helped. The basic causes must be found and relieved, if possible. Sometimes parents are too restrictive or expect too much, sometimes they give the child too little love and interest, and at times a chore is too boring or too difficult.

But parents must be careful that they themselves do not also make false excuses, for they, of course, serve as examples to their children. A parent, for example, who wants to take a child away on a Friday for a long weekend and writes an excuse note to school stating that the child was ill is certainly serving as a poor example.

Once a child is secure in his relationship with his parents and his teacher the need for making false excuses should subside.

See also **Arguments children give.**

Expectant parents see **Parents, expectant.**

Expectorants
Administered to loosen the dry, irritating coughs of children, expectorants are drugs that soothe but do not cure the infected or inflamed respiratory tract.

The most commonly used expecto-rants, ipecac, ammonium chloride, terpin hydrate, and the iodides, are found in many of the common cough medicines. (See **Coughs.**)

Eye defects
Although cross-eye or improper eye motion can be detected early, usually during infancy, most vision defects are often not detected until children enter school. This is unfortunate, for it is most important that defects of the eye or of vision be detected and treated early. The following are signs that a child is having vision difficulty:

1. Holding a book too near or too far away from the eyes.
2. Excessive sensitivity to light.
3. Eyelids that are red-rimmed, crusted, and swollen.
4. Tilting the head to one side when reading a book or looking at television.
5. Frequent blinking or rubbing of the eyes.
6. Frequent attempts to brush away a blurriness in front of one or both eyes.
7. Headaches, nausea, and vomiting following close reading.
8. One eye, or occasionally both eyes, chronically crossed (strabismus), which is not to be confused with the apparent crossing of the eyes in young infants (this disappears as the bridge of the nose develops, pulling the inner corner of the eye toward the center).

All of these symptoms can be serious, and the child's eyes should be examined immediately.

Cross-eye, in which one eye looks straight at an object while the other looks to the inner side, was formerly primarily considered a cosmetic problem. Actually, the crossing often means there is poor vision in one eye. The child sees double and compensates by shifting the poor eye inwards to avoid the blur; the vision in the eye that moves closer to the nose may deteriorate, eventually resulting in loss of vision—amblyopia. The condition, however, can almost always be successfully treated if detected at an early age. But treatment must begin as soon as possible—preferably by age 2 or 3, and not later than age 6. Corrective measures include correcting the vision in the poor eye by glasses and covering over the good eye with a patch. This causes the poor eye to be used exclusively, thus improving the vision. Instead of using a patch over the good eye to force the use of the poor eye, some doctors use drops in the good eye to blur the vision. Exercises are also often used to strengthen the eye muscles and bring them into focus so that the child sees one object instead of two when both eyes are focusing differently.

Walleye, in which one or both eyes turn outward instead of inward, another and much rarer form of strabismus, is treated similarly.

Other common vision defects found during childhood and adolescence are nearsightedness (myopia), farsightedness (hyperopia), and astigmatism.

To understand nearsightedness and farsightedness, it must be understood that in the normal eye the image of an object looked at falls exactly on the retina on the inner rear of the eye.

In nearsightedness, the eye is longer from front to back than it should be. Therefore, the image falls in front of the retina and the object appears blurred. A nearsighted child cannot see objects in the distance clearly.

In farsightedness, the eye is shorter from front to back than it should be, so that the image of the object looked at is

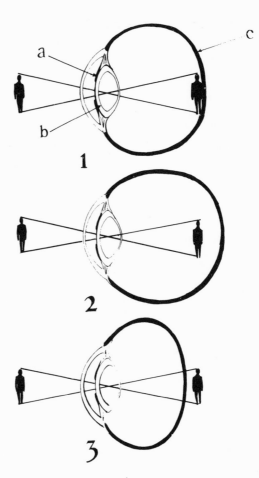

Nearsightedness and farsightedness are related to the shape of the eyeball. In (1) the eyeball is perfectly shaped, and the image transmitted by the lens (b) behind the iris (a) falls directly on the retina (c). In (2) the eyeball is deeper than normal and the person is nearsighted; the in-focus image falls short of the retina. In (3) the eyeball is less deep than the normal and the in-focus image falls at a point beyond the retina; the person is farsighted.

behind the retina. Again, the object looked at appears blurred. A farsighted child cannot see objects at close range clearly.

Both nearsightedness and farsightedness may be present in the young infant;

1 2 3

Focusing difficulties caused by astigmatism involve horizontal and vertical focus. In (1) the "T" appears as normally seen. But the person with astigmatism sees either the vertical bar out of focus (as in 2) or the horizontal bar out of focus (as in 3). He cannot keep both in focus at the same time.

usually, however, these conditions do not develop until the child is between 7 and 10. Both nearsightedness and farsightedness are hereditary.

Astigmatism is a condition of a difference in focus between the horizontal and vertical lines of an image. The vertical lines may focus directly on the retina, while the horizontal lines focus behind it—or vice versa. For example, if the child focuses on the vertical line, he sees a *T* as a strong downstroke with only a hazy crossbar, and if the child focuses on the horizontal line, he sees a *T* as a crossbar with a hazy downstroke.

Correction of nearsightedness, farsightedness, and astigmatism requires the use of corrective lenses to enable a child to see clearly at normal distances. No cure exists for these conditions; eyeglasses or contact lenses do not improve the eye defect; they only correct the defective vision. In these cases eye exercises to improve vision are ineffective.

If not corrected by eyeglasses, these defects of vision may cause headaches, fatigue, dizziness, and a burning of the eyes, and may interfere with a youngster's schoolwork.

See also **Blindness; Cataract; Color blindness; Glaucoma; Night blindness; Stye and chalazion.**

Eyeglasses

Eyes are well protected by nature, for they lie in hollows with protruding cheekbones beneath and with the bridge of the nose in the center. Eyeglasses, however, are a special hazard. Many children still wear breakable eyeglasses, and because they are children, special care must be taken to avoid breakage. In 1971 a new ruling was passed by the Food and Drug Administration that from that time on the lenses on all glasses must be impact-resistant. Children, because they are so active, are particularly prone to accidents in which glasses are damaged.

Two types of safety lenses are commonly used. One type is a highly tempered lens that is very difficult to break. This lens will crumble into granules if struck with force, not into sharp slivers as ordinary glass does. The other lens is plastic and even safer because it is unbreakable; it scratches easily, however, and requires special care.

According to the Guild of Prescription Opticians, the cost of tempered glass adds about two to four dollars to the cost of glasses, while plastic lenses add approximately five dollars—small cost for the safety they provide a child's eyes.

Contact lenses, which are even safer than ordinary eyeglasses, should be well fitted by an ophthalmologist. Since contact lenses are placed on the eyeball itself, a fairly careful technique of insertion and removal is required. They are also easily lost and expensive to replace.

Recently soft contact lenses have been developed. Although they are more comfortable and easier to fit they have at least two drawbacks: the porous lenses may provide a breeding ground for bacteria (wearers are advised to boil them for twenty minutes before each usage), and the price is much higher than that of ordinary contact lenses.

A real advantage of soft contact lenses is their use in eyes with chronic ulceration, although this condition is rare among children. Since they are still in the experimental stage, soft contact lenses should only be used under strict medical supervision.

Children can readily learn to use ordinary contact lenses as early as 7. They have been used with children as young as 5 or 6 months following the removal of cataracts. In such cases the parents have learned to insert and remove the lenses.

Eyelids, granulated

Crusting, redness, irritation, itching, and occasionally even permanent loss of the eyelashes, caused by a chronic, recurrent inflammation of the eyelid margins. This condition, also called blepharitis, is quite common.

Treatment is usually highly successful, although the condition may recur. Yellow oxide of mercury ointment 1 percent is commonly used. It is applied to the lids twice a day until at least a week after the condition has disappeared. The cause is thought to be viral. Persistent cases should be treated by a doctor.

Eyes, color of

The colored part of the eyes surrounding the pupil is the iris. The iris of newborn white infants is almost always blue, since the cells of this area contain little or no pigment. As pigment starts to form in the first few months of life, the color becomes darker. By 6 months it can usually be determined if the eyes will be brown or will remain blue. Eyes that will turn brown usually change from dark blue to greenish blue to greenish gray to greenish brown and then to brown.

Newborn black babies usually have brown eyes from birth. The eyes of albino children, who have no pigment, are pink.

The ultimate color of the iris depends on the eye-color genes of the father and mother. The dominant eye colors (the shades from brown to black) in one parent usually produce brown eyes in the child, even if the other parent has eyes of one of the recessive colors (blue, gray, and green). If, however, the brown-eyed parent has a close relative (father or mother, brother or sister) with blue eyes, the chances are stronger that he will have and pass on the recessive gene, and the child may have blue eyes. Although two brown-eyed parents usually produce brown-eyed children, they can have blue-eyed children if they both have the recessive eye-color gene.

Eyes, foreign objects in   see Foreign objects in eye.

Eyes, harmful substances in   see Poisons: first-aid treatment.

Eyestrain   see Lighting.

F

Facts of life see **Sex curiosity and interests; Sex education in the home; Sex education in the schools.**

Failure

Young children under the age of 5 usually are persistent and will attempt almost any project without thought of failure. They seem unconvinced that something cannot be accomplished.

In spite of the impossibility of achieving their goals every time, children should be encouraged by their parents to persist, to create, and to construct. If a child fails in a single project or area, he should not be made to feel incapable. Often patience and persistence may be required. With a parent's encouragement and, if necessary, help, a child will learn that he can eventually succeed in many projects that seemed doomed to failure.

Children who do not receive encouragement from their parents often develop a fear of failure as they grow older and may refuse to attempt anything unless they are sure they will succeed. At times they will give up on a project or even destroy it if it seems likely to end in failure or not meet their expectations.

Some parents set extremely high standards for a child, or apply too much pressure. The result is a child who will often give up rather than risk failure in his parents' eyes.

Fainting

Fainting, which is quite common during childhood and adolescence, may be caused by emotional stress or by a physical disorder.

Some children faint at the sight of blood, such as from the prick of their finger. Some faint when they receive an inoculation, or simply from the thought of it. Some young children, usually under the age of 5, lose consciousness momentarily if they have a sudden fright or are hurt.

In many cases, especially in older children, fainting may be caused by fatigue, a stomach upset, standing too long under a hot sun, anemia, low blood sugar, or low blood pressure. In rare instances repeated fainting attacks are caused by a basic brain difficulty and represent a mild convulsive seizure. This condition may be diagnosed by neurological studies and an electroencephalogram.

In most instances fainting is caused by a lowering of blood pressure, so that the normal amounts of blood and oxygen are unable to reach the brain.

Fainting episodes in children should be reported to the doctor for determination of the cause and possible treatment.

Treatment There are two common methods of bringing a child (or adult) out of a faint. One method is to lay the child down on a bed or on the floor and elevate the legs on pillows so that they are higher than the head. This is the most effective method of treatment. The other method is to have the child sit with his body bent forward and his head between his knees. Usually consciousness returns in a few seconds. The child should not walk until he has completely recovered.

Fairy tales

Fairy tales can give a child a colorful, fanciful, and wonderful experience, for they not only stimulate his imagination but bring him satisfaction and assurance. The good are always saved from the evil, the weak overcome the strong, the meek overcome the aggressive, virtue is always rewarded and the wicked are always punished.

Parents, however, must use their judgment in reading or telling fairy tales to young children. Long and complicated stories should be avoided, as should violent stories and tales of cruelty. Fairy tales should be especially carefully selected for a child who is anxious and fearful. Young children, it should be remembered, do not differentiate clearly between the fantasy world and the real world.

Children of 7 to 9, who are reading by themselves and are sufficiently mature, usually greatly enjoy these stories—which, after all, have appealed to children and adults for hundreds and perhaps thousands of years.

Do young children like fairy tales as much as they like stories about dogs and horses and the world they live in—the city and the country? Yes, they probably do. A place for both types of stories exists in the mind of the child, who is usually eager for all kinds of reading experiences.

Faith   see **Religion.**

Falls

Unfortunately, many babies fall off dressing tables or beds because the adult in charge is careless. Never leave an infant where he can fall, even if you are sure that the baby cannot yet roll over. If you must leave a young infant on a bed for a moment, lay the baby crosswise so that even if he rolls over he cannot roll off.

The baby who is starting to walk has not yet learned to put his hands forward to break a fall. As a result, most beginning walkers fall face forward, usually striking their noses. Very possibly, many deviated nasal septums stem from such early unbroken falls.

Every child and adolescent falls fairly frequently in the course of activity—running, skating, skiing, bicycling, playing baseball or football. Most of these falls are of no significance, possibly a scrape or bruise resulting. But contact a doctor at once if a child of any age strikes his head severely and loses consciousness, even temporarily; if he vomits or becomes sleepy; or if he sustains a deep cut or skin tear.

See also **Cuts; Head injuries.**

Family car   see **Automobiles and adolescents.**

Family psychotherapy

An approach to the treatment of emotional disturbance in a child in which the whole family is treated as a unit. It is based on the concept that the emotional problems of children are almost always the outcome of family relationships and that there are great advantages in viewing, studying, and treating the family together. By this means the causes of a child's difficulty may be more readily unearthed; and on the basis of this knowledge the therapist is better able to treat the problems successfully and to prevent further difficulties. The therapy is conducted by either a psychiatrist, a clinical psychologist, or a specially trained psychiatric social worker.

There are a number of approaches to this form of psychotherapy depending on the individual family and the specific situation.

Usually, at the first interview the whole family comes together—even infants are included, since behavior toward a baby is often significant. The therapist asks questions and observes the interreactions of the family members. Following this, arrangements are made for treatment, the approach varying according to the individual therapist and situation. Some therapists start by having the family play games, or all draw pictures, to see how they relate to one another. Often the therapist enters the activities with them. Later the therapist, or sometimes two therapists, sit down with the parents and children and start general discussions in an attempt to bring forth a picture of home conditions. It may be that children will hesitate to talk in front of their parents or vice versa. In such a case, if there are two therapists, one may take the children aside and speak with them while the other discusses home situations and relationships with the parents. The family then comes together again and further discussion continues.

As mentioned, the type of therapy is very flexible and varies with different families and therapists. At times the whole family is seen at one session, the parents at the next session, the children at the next session, and the entire family again at the fourth session.

In family therapy the therapist must be observant and alert, watching closely the interaction among members of the family. Nonspoken behavior, such as hostile facial expressions and silence, is often just as important as what the person says.

The therapist seeks to understand what makes the family work well together as a group in addition to what causes the unhappiness and tension. He or she tries to help each member of the family discover ways of breaking hurtful patterns of behavior and ways of developing new approaches to each other. By the testimony of many families and therapists, this treatment approach can be very successful not only in helping the child who is most obviously unhappy, but in improving family life for all members.

Family therapy has been widely used for only the past five or six years. Patients may be referred to Family Therapy Clinics from private doctors, from hospitals, from social agencies, or from Regional Mental Health Centers. More and more therapists in private practice are using the family approach.

Fantasy

Children, with their rich imagination, give a great deal of time to vivid fantasy. A common fantasy is an imaginary playmate who is very real to the child. The mother must set an extra serving at the table for this playmate; the child will talk to this figment of his imagination as if it were present and answer it back as if they were having a conversation.

The fantasy world of a 5-year-old might take him to a jungle, a western ranch, or a battlefield, and to the child, his few hours of fantasy experience in these places is almost as real as if it had actually happened.

As a child gets older and approaches adolescence, games involving fantasy give way to daydreaming. This is perfectly normal, for the teen-ager's world is uncertain, new relationships are building up, and a whole unknown world is before him.

In adolescence and adulthood fantasizing is often associated with masturbation and aids in securing sexual gratification.

Fantasy is one of the most important sources of creative energy and is important to the emotional development of the individual. There is no cause for worry, as a rule, if a youngster spends a great deal of time fantasizing. However, if a school-age child or adolescent seems to be spending most of his time in a fantasy world, or does not distinguish between fantasy and reality, it may be that the child is withdrawing from unhappiness in the real world. Parents should seek to discover and alleviate the cause of his unhappiness.

See also **Daydreaming; Imaginary companions.**

Farm camps and farm vacations

Many working farms and ranches throughout the country provide summer vacations for children, including preschool children. Each camp takes only a few children and provides a summer experience in a family setting and a program related to the interests of a child: learning about cows and horses, observing chickens and collecting eggs, playing in the hay, chasing frogs, and bathing in the brook.

Many of these farm camps and ranches have facilities for parents as well as their children, so that if a child is not ready for separation, the family can vacation as a unit.

A list of such farms and ranches is available from Farm and Ranch Vacations, 36 East 57 Street, New York, N.Y.

Farsightedness see **Eye defects.**

Fasting see **Anorexia nervosa; Dieting.**

Fat child see **Obesity.**

Father, need of

A father or a good father substitute is extremely important to the emotional development of boys and girls. For boys their father is the chief model of masculinity—of what a man is like and what it means to be a husband and father.

For girls too the father is the model for all men, and their relationships with boys and men later in life will be strongly influenced by their relationships with their fathers.

Good fatherhood must present a good example. Fathers of course have many personalities, but most children learn to accept difficult qualities when the general attitude of the father is one of love. The child must know that his father loves him and enjoys being with him. Love of his children is expressed by the warmth of a father's relationship with them, and by his wholehearted interest in their lives, thoughts, and what they are doing.

Today, more and more fathers have discovered the benefits (both for them and for their children) of caring for their children from infancy by taking on many of the activities known as "mothering," that is, taking care of the child's needs and playing with him. This is a welcome change in the traditional parental roles.

It is most important that a father regularly spend time with his children, and this time should be especially for the children—a time when father and children can get to know each other Finding this time may seem a difficult task for many suburban fathers who leave their homes early in the morning and return home at 7 P.M. or later. But this situation can be rectified by spending more time with the children during the weekend. The quality of the relationship with a child is more important than the number of hours spent with him.

Unfortunately, in many homes the father is absent, either through separation, divorce, or death. If the father is alive it is most important that he visit and be with his child regularly and at frequent intervals. This is especially important for boys of 6 to 12 years, although girls need this fatherly attention also.

If a boy does not have a father or good father substitute, he is handicapped in forming his own identity as a male. Recent studies have emphasized how deeply upset and unhappy a fatherless boy may be. One study from Harvard University on male suicides found that the risk was increased by 50 percent for students who had lost their fathers through death or divorce in their precollege years.

What then can be done to aid growing boys in homes where the father has died or has left the family? In such cases it is very important that a good father substitute be found—either a close male relative, a Boy Scout leader, a member of Big Brothers, a male teacher, a minister, or some other man of good character who will take a real interest in the youngster.

Similarly for little girls, a father substitute who will give the child love and attention in a stable relationship is very important. This is especially true when the girl has no brothers and only female teachers.

Father, new

Most new fathers react very positively, with pride and happiness, to the role of fatherhood. Today many new fathers have attended classes for expectant parents, and they enjoy helping their wives in the care of their newborn sons or daughters.

Formerly child care was deemed to be strictly a female occupation, many fathers showing little interest until a child had learned to walk and talk. But in recent years much has been done to build up a complete family unit, involving the father in his child's care and development as early as possible. Not only can he attend prenatal classes, but many hospital obstetrical units have rooming-in facilities, which allow the baby to stay in a crib beside the mother's bed, and the father is encouraged to visit both mother and baby and get to know his child from birth.

Sometimes a new father develops a certain amount of jealousy of the new infant who demands so much of the wife's time and attention. This can be greatly relieved when the father plays with and cares for the baby. Usually he will find this pleasurable, gain a full understanding of the needs of the infant, and even enjoy the attention his wife gives to the baby.

Of course, once a child has arrived in the home, the mode of life will be changed. But the young family usually adjusts to it and often arranges that the father can still have his night out for bowling or playing cards. Parents can still go out for social evenings, either leaving the infant with a baby-sitter or taking the baby with them to sleep in the home of their friends while they are visiting.

A new father is generally well adjusted to all the changes that must be made in his home and his married life by the time his son or daughter is 6 months old.

See also **Parents, expectant.**

Fatherless child see **Father, need of.**

Fatigue
Children show fatigue in various ways, depending largely on age. The young child, even during the nursery years, may express his fatigue by being irritable, unruly, and hyperactive, a very common behavior at the end of the day. Some young children when fatigued will lie down or become quiet, but crankiness and irritability is more the rule. Older children usually show fatigue by being less active, droopy, and listless.

Unusual fatigue may be caused by overactivity, oncoming illness, some chronic infection, anemia, lack of sleep, or some emotional difficulty. If the cause cannot be determined by the parent, it should be investigated by the child's doctor.

See also **Crankiness.**

Fatness see **Nutrition; Obesity.**

Fats see **Nutrition.**

Fears
All children develop fears at one time or another in the course of their childhood. This is entirely normal, for fear is a natural, protective instinct. Infants between birth and 12 months usually have an instinctive fear of being dropped, of loud noises, and of sudden movement.

As children grow older, new fears usually develop—some real, others imaginary.

At about 12 months, many children develop a fear of strangers. Later on, between 18 months and 3 years, many different types of fears may appear, for example, fears of airplanes, vacuum cleaners, fire engines, darkness, the toilet, unfamiliar places, doctors, dentists, police, animals, insects.

Older children also have fears, some valuable and protective, others that should be overcome. Among these are fear of fire, of being run over by an automobile, of falling from high places, of water, of an operation or a tooth extraction or an inoculation, and of punishment for real or imagined wrongdoing.

Children's fears are derived from instinct, parental example or warning, or experience.

Instinct Instinctive fears include fear of falling from high places, fear of loud or unusual sounds, fear of separation (from the need of young infants to be near the protecting parents), fear of the dark, and fear of fire. Fears of the sound of the vacuum cleaner, an airplane, or a fire engine are probably related to the fear of loud noises.

Parental fears or warnings Children often contract their fears from their parents. They are completely dependent on their parents for protection, and it is natural that they should also fear what their parents are fearful of. For example, a mother fearful of lightning and thunder who clearly shows this to the child, or a parent who is afraid of dogs and shudders or crosses the street every time a dog is in sight, will transmit these fears of thunderstorms and dogs to the children.

Warnings by parents often instill fear: "Don't go near the dog—he may bite"; "Don't climb trees—you might fall, break a leg, and have to go to the hospital"; or, to a little boy who is masturbating, the irrational warning, "If you do that, your penis will fall off."

Experience Many children develop fears based on a frightening or painful experience. An older infant's or child's painful separation from a parent may lead the child to fear other separations. A young child may be badly frightened by a barking dog or by a dog jumping on him. From a bee or wasp sting a child may develop a fear of all insects. The painful experience of an inoculation at the doctor's office may cause a fear of doctors. Fear of punishment for a lie, for doing something wrong, or for disobedience is, as a rule, based on experience.

When children are fearful of punishment in general, without having done anything very wrong, it is a sign that the parents are too punitive or shame the child too much.

Treatment of fears   The age of the child and the particular fear determines treatment. With infants, parents should avoid frightening situations, including throwing the child in the air if he responds to this with crying or a worried look, and startling him with shouts or sudden movements. Parents should be casual when a small child cries or shows fear of everyday things, such as the noise of an airplane or a vacuum cleaner or the arrival of strangers. They should be responsive to the child's fears but not overprotective.

In general, a child should not be forced to approach a situation he fears, but parents should try to make clear that the situation is not dangerous and gently encourage the child to overcome his fear. For example, the child may be willing to approach the vacuum cleaner when it isn't running or even play with it. He should be warned when it is going to be turned on. Many young children are frightened of falling into the toilet and being flushed down it. They should have their own potty and not be forced

to use a seat placed on the toilet. They can be verbally reassured that there is no danger. A child who fears strangers should not be pressured to be sociable; parents can explain to friends and relatives that it will take a little while for the child to get used to them. A child who fears the dark should have a night light in his room or a light in the hallway with the door open. Usually these fears of early childhood disappear within a few months if handled casually.

Parents who have their own fears should avoid as much as possible communicating these fears to their children. Fear is contagious and a parent's fear is easily contracted by children. This is especially seen in a parent's fear of lightning and thunder, of dogs and cats, and of insects.

A child's fear of dogs can almost always be dissipated by giving him a little puppy that offers no threat, and letting him feed it and aid in its care. This plan has been proven successful in numerous instances, regardless of the cause of the fear.

If there is fear of water or a fear of climbing, the fear should be respected and treated slowly and gradually. Fear can only be intensified by throwing a child in the water or placing him up in a tree and forcing him to come down by himself without help and encouragement.

Fear of surgery is normal but can usually be relieved by preparing the child for the uncertainty of such happenings, by explaining as much as possible beforehand, and by omitting details that may be frightening. (See **Hospitalization**.)

A deep, persistent fear that seems to have no reasonable basis may be a symptom of some emotional disturbance. If—despite reassurance and encouragement—a child remains fearful in harmless situations, parents must try to discover the underlying reasons for the fear. This may require the help of a psychotherapist.

Don't ridicule the child for his fears. Respect these fears even if they are irrational. A child should know that it's not a disgrace to have fears and that he can overcome most of them. He also should know that everyone, including his parents, has had fears that were overcome.

See also **Anxiety; Nightmares and night terrors; Phobias**.

Feces   See **Bowel movements**.

Feeble-minded child   see **Mental retardation**.

Feeding, self-demand
Under a schedule of self-demand feeding the baby regulates his own feeding times. Whether on the breast or the bottle, the baby nurses when and as long as he likes. This approach is popular today, for it is no longer believed that any advantage is gained by forcing the baby's appetite to conform to a set schedule. On the contrary, if a set schedule is markedly different from the baby's own hunger patterns, it is quite possible that the baby will suffer from harmful and entirely avoidable physical and emotional distress.

The intervals between feedings and the number of feedings daily vary considerably during the first few weeks of a newborn's life. On a self-demand schedule the infant may nurse eight to ten times daily during the first week or two. But after two weeks, although the intervals between feedings may be irregular, feedings are usually limited to six or seven daily. Most babies on self-demand feedings gradually work themselves into approximately a four-hour schedule sometime between four and six weeks of age.

The self-demand feeding procedure is especially advised for the first child, when the new mother usually has plenty of time and can be at the beck and call of the infant.

When other young children are around, family life must be more or less routinized, so a modified self-demand feeding method is usually more satisfactory. Under this procedure, a baby is placed on a regular schedule but a mother is given a leeway of one hour before or one hour after the set time. However, at no time is a baby permitted to cry for hunger. If he is on a four-hour schedule and cries at two and a half hours, he is picked up and cuddled and patted until it is nearer three hours, and then fed. This usually helps the baby's body to establish a four-hour schedule earlier than if the baby works out the cycle himself.

This modified self-demand schedule gives a mother a general idea of when feedings will be required. It gives her a chance to prepare lunch for the other children, dress them, give them baths, and so forth without interruptions for feeding or nursing the baby at the same time. This is also especially helpful in relieving somewhat the normal sibling jealousy of an older child who usually feels that the baby is getting more time and more attention than he.

Feeding problems see **Appetite, poor.**

Feeding schedules
Good timing of a child's meals depends largely on the child's age, weight, and appetite.

During the early weeks of life, the schedule varies somewhat with the size of the infant. Many mothers prefer self-demand feedings rather than scheduled feedings during these early weeks. (See **Feeding, self-demand.**)

The feeding schedule is usually determined by the infant's doctor. The tiny baby, under five pounds, is usually fed every two to three hours, approximately eight to ten feedings a day.

Children of five to six pounds are often fed on a three- to four-hour schedule, usually seven times a day: 2 A.M., 6 A.M., 9 A.M., 12 noon, 3 P.M., 6 P.M., and 10 P.M. On such a schedule babies usually are given more per feeding than they would take in the average self-demand feeding.

Babies over six pounds in weight are usually fed every four hours, usually five times a day: 2 A.M., 6 A.M., 10 A.M., 2 P.M., and 10 P.M.

The 2 A.M. feeding is usually eliminated by the time a baby is three months old, and the 10 P.M. feeding is often eliminated by the time the infant is five months old.

At five to six months, the baby may be placed on three meals a day with an added bottle of milk in midafternoon. The approximate hours are: breakfast 7:30 to 8 A.M.; lunch (usually the big meal of the day) 12 noon; milk and crackers 3 P.M.; supper 6 P.M. Orange juice is given when the child wakes up in the morning or between feedings.

For weaning techniques, see **Bottle feeding; Breast feeding**.

Feeding self

Many babies start holding their bottles as early as five to six months, and if the bottles are lightweight plastic, they usually master the technique in a few weeks.

By nine to ten months or even sooner, most infants can hold a zwieback or cracker in their hand and chew on it or even nibble on a slice of cheese. They also usually love to eat dry cereal by hand. Of course they put their hands in any kind of food.

Between 1 and 2 years many babies start playing with a spoon and usually start spoon-feeding themselves—very sloppily—at about 18 months. By the time they are 2 they can usually spoon-feed themselves fairly well, although they are still quite messy (a child cannot overcome his messiness until he is better coordinated). To encourage self-feeding, a parent should give a 2-year-old food that he can hold in his hand and chew: a chicken leg, a slice of bologna, a cooked or raw carrot, potato chips, pieces of apple, banana, pear.

Gradually, most children learn to feed themselves and strongly demand to do so. Certain children, however, insist on being spoon-fed. A good solution to this is for the mother to make a game: "Now you take a spoonful and then I'll give you a spoonful."

Feet

As all too many adults know, difficulties with the feet can cause considerable pain and annoyance. Luckily most children are free of such difficulties, but care of the feet nevertheless should start young. The following are some relatively common foot problems.

Clubfoot Clubfoot is a congenital defect (the most frequent of all orthopedic defects), caused in most cases by the position of the baby in the uterus, with the wall of the uterus pressing down constantly on the foot. The foot may be turned in badly. In some cases the child can walk only on his heel, while in other cases the heel is held high and the child can walk only on the toes or the front of the sole.

Treatment of clubfoot should be started almost immediately after birth. In mild cases, parents are shown how to stretch the feet to the corrected position. In more severe cases, corrective casts are used to hold the foot in the normal position. Results are usually excellent and the feet are entirely normal. In some cases surgery may be necessary.

Webbed toes   The webbing of toes (and fingers) is not uncommon. When webbing occurs between the toes it is of no significance and does not interfere with walking or running, nor is there any difficulty in fitting the feet with shoes.

Toeing in; toeing out   Neither toeing in (pigeon toes) nor toeing out is usually significant, but either may cause some awkwardness in walking.

Many children toe in slightly. This is beneficial rather than a detriment, for mild toeing in develops high arches and aids in producing straight legs.

If, however, the toeing in causes a child to trip over himself while walking or to be very awkward, it can usually be corrected by inserting a wedge of ³⁄₁₆ inch thickness on the outside of the sole.

Some orthopedists think toeing out or toeing in is fostered by the child's sleeping on his stomach with his toes pointing out or in. Occasionally the toeing difficulty is due to a fixation at the hip that prevents a foot from taking the normal position; in this case an orthopedist should be consulted. But in most cases, toeing in or toeing out will correct itself in time or can be relieved by wedging, which can be prescribed by a doctor or orthopedist.

See also **Achilles' tendon.**

1. The imprint of a foot having a good arch.
2. The imprint of a foot having a poor arch.

Flat feet   Since the arch of the foot does not start to develop until about 2, almost all children start life with flat feet. Occasionally the arches remain flat, and corrective measures must be taken.

To allow the development of good arch formation, parents should avoid putting shoes on the baby's feet when he is learning to walk, since in learning this procedure, the child grasps the carpet or ground with his feet and in this way exercises his arch muscles. Walking shoes are not advised until a child is able to take three or four steps by himself without support. Also, the first walking shoes should have semisoft soles so that the child still has some freedom in moving his feet. (See **Shoes.**)

If a child of 2½ or 3 years still has very flat feet, the doctor usually prescribes arch supports for the weak arches and later may even prescribe some exercises to strengthen the arches.

The exercises for weak arches can help greatly and may completely correct the condition. Very simple, they can be performed with enjoyment by most children over 3. One exercise is a game in which a dozen marbles are strewn over the floor. The barefoot child picks each one up with his toes, walks across the room still holding it in his toes, and deposits it in a plate in a corner of the room. Another simple exercise requires the child to try to make a fist of his feet and walk on the outside of his feet for a while each day. The more the child performs these exercises, the more active use his arch muscles get. The parent, as well as the child, must be persistent about these exercises and have patience; usually the results are successful.

Fetus

The term for an unborn baby during the last six months of pregnancy, when its

Fetus of about 5½ months.

body is usually completely formed. Prior to that time, the baby is spoken of as an embryo.

Fever

A temperature above normal. In children a rectal temperature above 100 degrees F. and a mouth temperature over 99 degrees is considered a fever.

Although many parents tend to judge the severity of an infection by how high the child's temperature is, this is not a sound basis of judgment.

Fever indicates that a child has an infection or inflammation of one kind or another, but a high temperature does not indicate severity. Many simple, non-dangerous viruses cause fevers of 104 degrees to 105 degrees, whereas fevers in some very severe infections, such as diphtheria and typhoid, as a rule run much lower. The way a child acts is far more indicative of severity than temperature. A child with a fever of 101 degrees who is sick, listless, and uninterested is much sicker than a child with 104 degrees or 105 degrees who is active and alert. Whenever a child has a fever, a doctor should be consulted.

Occasionally convulsions occur in certain children when they develop a high fever. These seizures, although frightening, are not as a rule dangerous and can usually be prevented; the doctor can prescribe a small amount of phenobarbital to be given with each aspirin dose. (See **Convulsions**.)

Many parents are concerned that high fevers might cause brain damage. This is rarely true. Children can develop fevers of 105 degrees to 106 degrees, and a great many do, without any evidence of subsequent brain damage. Many doctors feel that when brain damage follows fevers of 107 degrees or more, the infection rather than the fever is responsible for such damage.

Treatment   A fever is usually treated by giving the child aspirin, either by mouth or in a suppository, and by sponging the child with half alcohol and half water (see **Alcohol rub; Aspirin**), which should bring the fever down several degrees. When the temperature is very high, or if it remains high after aspirin and alcohol sponging, a cool enema may be given. The best enema solution is bicarbonate of soda in cool, rather than warm, water, the amount depending on the child's size (see **Enemas**), which usually brings down the temperature 2 to 3 degrees in about twenty minutes.

See also **Temperature taking**.

Fidgeting

Children tend to fidget, that is, make many restless movements, when they do not have sufficient outlets for their great physical energy. A child who fidgets constantly is most probably bored, restless, or too restricted.

Excessive restlessness and fidgeting may also be part of a general pattern of hyperactivity, and if the child is constantly moving about and seems unable to concentrate for more than a brief time, parents should consult the doctor.

Some children fidget in a manner that resembles a tic, with numerous small nervous motions. This may have some physical cause, such as hyperthyroidism or chorea (Saint Vitus's dance). Again, the doctor should be told of the problem.

See also **Hyperactivity; Tics**.

Fights   see **Arguments between parents; Biting, kicking, hitting, pushing; Quarrels**.

Finger paints   see **Art; Toys and play materials**.

Finger-sucking   see **Sucking, thumb and forefinger**.

Fingernails   see **Nails, biting; Nails, cutting**.

Fire-setting   see **Arson**.

Firearms   see **Accident prevention, indoors**.

Fires

Approximately six thousand deaths from fires occur in the United States each year, and of these about two thousand are children. Some fires are started by unsupervised children, but a great many fires are caused by the carelessness of parents themselves or other adults.

Fire always fascinates children, so it is extremely important that matches and cigarette lighters be kept out of their reach. Candles should also be removed, for children often use the gas stove to light candles if no matches or cigarette lighters can be found.

When possible, children should have clothes and bedding made of a fire-retardant substance. Forty percent of all home fire deaths in the United States are from clothing catching fire. Wool burns very slowly; cotton and synthetics burn rapidly. Although fabric labeling is still not adequate, some fabrics are marked nonflammable, fire-resistant, or something similar. The temperature of burning clothes may be three times the temperature of boiling water. If a child's clothing catches fire, quickly roll him in a rug, a blanket, or even a coat. Beating out the flames with your hands is usually ineffectual.

Prevention Observation of the following rules is imperative.

1. An *absolute* rule for all adults and adolescents is never to smoke in bed, even if you don't feel sleepy or tired. The danger is extreme. Imagine that the bed is soaked in gasoline and can flare up if fire is near.
2. Be sure electric cords and electric plugs are not worn out. If electric fuses blow out frequently, there is a short circuit somewhere, and, consequently, the danger of fire.
3. Do not leave gasoline or other flammable liquids around; don't let old rags and paint cans accumulate.
4. *Do not leave young children alone in the home, even for a few minutes.*

Saving lives Many children die needlessly in fires because of a lack of instruction on what to do in such emergencies. Young children, frightened by fire, often try to escape by climbing under a bed or running into a closet and closing the door. In the closet, where they cannot be found immediately by parents or firemen, they can be overcome by smoke, if not burned.

The parents, along with the children who are old enough, should work out what to do in case of fire, and each child should be instructed in emergency measures.

The prearranged plans should include the following:

1. Keep a bell or whistle in every room and use it only in the event of fire. Or work out other signals for giving the alarm and calling for help, such as pounding on the walls or on the radiator pipes.
2. Various fire alarm systems can be installed at little expense. One of these is a bell system: a bell rings loudly if the temperature rises above a certain level.
3. If possible, install a sprinkler system.
4. Children who are old enough should be taught how to telephone the fire department in case of fire and should be shown where the nearest firebox is located.
5. Work out a prearranged route of escape and a meeting place outside the house. Parents often think children are left in a burning house when they have already escaped. The escape and meeting should be practiced in a drill at least once a year.
6. Always instruct baby-sitters in the fire safety measures you have arranged.

Children should be instructed in the following particular rules on what to do if a fire breaks out:

1. Do not hide under a bed or run into a closet.
2. Never take the time to get dressed or to run back for anything—toy or treasure.
3. If you think there is a fire in the next room, open the door of your room slowly, with your body against it—be ready to slam it shut if there's a hot blast of heat and smoke.

Every family should contact the local fire department to discuss fire prevention and the best procedures to follow in case of fires of various kinds.

See also **Flammable clothing and bedding.**

Fireworks

Fireworks, which used to be sold everywhere—especially for July Fourth celebrations—are now banned from sale in most of the United States. *Every* state should ban firecrackers, however, and both parents and legislators should realize there is a potential danger in even the smallest pinwheel. Most firecrackers, explosive caps, and spectacular displays require a combination of fire and gunpowder, both of which are dangerous in the hands of children and at times dangerous to adults as well.

The danger of explosives cannot be overestimated. Many children have lost their sight from misfiring or premature explosions of firecrackers, Roman candles, or skyrockets. Fingers have been lost and faces scarred permanently. Serious fires have been started from rockets fired into trees.

If fireworks are legal and used at all, they should be handled by parents or—better still—be under the supervision of trained personnel in local communities, such as members of the fire department.

Parents are only endangering their children when they buy fireworks from clandestine dealers so that their children can have "a real old-fashioned Fourth of July."

First-aid supplies

The necessities for first aid are comparatively few. The following are suggested:

1. A nonstinging soap for cleaning a dirty wound.
2. A nonstinging antiseptic, such as Betadine (providone-iodine), and an antiseptic ointment such as Neosporin or Neopolycin (both of which contain neomycin, polymycin, and bacitracin).
3. A rectal thermometer.
4. Sterile gauze pads, 3 inches by 3 inches.
5. Sterile gauze roll, 1 inch width.
6. Band-Aids or some similar adhesive gauze pads.
7. Butterfly Band-Aids.
8. Adhesive tape, ¾ inch or 1 inch width.
9. A nonoily burn ointment, such as Furacin (nitrofurazone).

First-born child   see **Parents, expectant; Oldest child.**

Flat feet   see **Feet.**

Flattening of head   see **Head, flattening of.**

Flammable clothing and bedding

Most parents buy clothes and bedding for their children without regard for the material's flammability. But fires are among the leading causes of death in children. Of the almost 6,000 deaths from fire and explosion each year, about 3,000 are caused by the ignition of the clothing, and most of these are among children. It is estimated that the number of nonfatal burns from clothing fires is 250,000 yearly.

At present there are laws requiring that children's sleepwear be labeled as to its flammability, but few manufacturers heed them. After July 1973 all nightclothes must, by law, be labeled "Flame-retardant" or "Flammable, should not be worn near sources of fire." Bear in mind, however, that this law applies to sleepwear only, and that in making other purchases parents are on their own. Moreover, sleepwear manufactured before the July 1973 date may still be available in stores.

Wool (*pure* wool) is basically flame-resistant. When it catches fire, it burns very slowly and usually goes out by itself. Textile glass fibers are flame-retardant. All other fabrics are flammable but can be made flame-retardant. Fabrics may be made flame-retardant by chemical treatment or the addition of flame-retardant fibers—modacrylic fibers, high-temperature-resistant nylon, glass fibers. Untreated cotton, rayon, acetate, and triacetate are highly flammable. Some synthetic fibers, such as nylon, polyester, and acrylic, are only moderately flammable but are still very dangerous because they may melt and drip if not properly treated.

Concerned parents should study fabric labels and, even better, closely question sellers and manufacturers regarding the flammability of items for sale. Hopefully, the situation will improve. In the meantime special care must be taken to keep children (and adults) safe by being very careful in handling matches, cigarettes, lighters, gas jets, and all other possible causes of fire.

See **Fires.**

Flu   see **Influenza.**

Fluorides
Fluorides are compounds of the element fluorine, a nonmetallic gas. They have been used in the water supply, in toothpastes, and in other substances that are taken by mouth, to protect the teeth against decay. Fluorides strengthen tooth enamel, prevent acids from penetrating into the softer tooth structure under the enamel, and inhibit decay-producing bacteria on teeth. When fluorides are added to the water supply, they go through the bloodstream and strengthen the nonenamel portion of the teeth. Fluorides in toothpaste increase the strength of the tooth enamel.

Although some people still object to fluoridation of the water supply, the fact that fluoridation protects teeth against decay is unquestionable.

The value of fluoridation as a tooth decay preventative has been substantiated by considerable evidence. First, in some geographic areas of the United States and in other areas abroad where a sufficient amount of natural fluoride is in the water, considerably less tooth decay was experienced than in those areas having insufficient amounts of natural fluoride in the water. Second, studies to determine the value of fluoride have shown that it is an excellent deterrent against decay when taken orally—in milk, water, or vitamins—or when applied directly to the teeth in toothpaste.

Some objectors to the fluoridation of water have suggested that it may cause mottling of the teeth and kidney trouble, and shorten lives. This contention has not, however, been substantiated by scientific data. On the contrary, all studies thus far have shown that an adequate level of fluoride in the water does not affect length of life and does not cause kidney or any other physical difficulty.

Fluoridation of water has been strongly supported by the American Dental Association, the American Medical Association, the American Public Health Association, and the American Academy of Pediatrics.

Fluoroscopy   see **X rays.**

Fontanelles
Soft spots on the head of an infant at the opening between the bones that make up the skull. There are two fontanelles—the larger one, the anterior fontanelle, is just above the forehead in the midline. The smaller fontanelle, the pos-

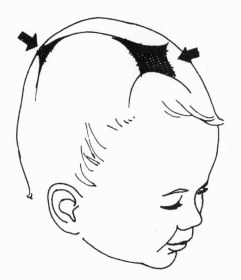

Position of the fontanelles.

terior fontanelle, is on the back of the head, also in the midline.

Contrary to popular belief there is no danger whatsoever in touching the fontanelles.

The five bones of the skull are separated in the newborn. During delivery, as the baby is passing out of the uterus and through the vagina, the bones overlap and make the head smaller so that birth will be easier. After birth, the bones start growing together, and by the time a child is 18 months old, the fontanelles usually have disappeared completely.

Food poisoning

The bacterial poisoning of food is common, usually a result of food spoiling in a warm temperature or because of inadequate refrigeration, improper canning, or a lack of cleanliness in preparing foods. The three bacteria responsible for most food poisoning are salmonella, staphylococcus, and the bacteria of botulism.

Salmonella poisoning   Meat, eggs, vegetables, milk, and water may be contaminated by salmonella bacteria. Contamination may be brought about by animals—mice, rats, rabbits, dogs, and cows—which may carry the organism normally in their bodies. Most often, however, the source of contamination is a person. The bacteria, which are in the intestinal tract, may be carried on a person's hands if he does not wash carefully after elimination. From the hands, the infected person contaminates food that he handles.

Symptoms and treatment   Symptoms, which may start from a few hours to as long as twelve days after the time the food is eaten, are usually headache, nausea, and vomiting, followed by abdominal pain and diarrhea. The stools are often watery and may contain mucus and blood. With its usual course, the diarrhea may last for some weeks.

Antibiotics are rarely used in treatment, since they subdue but do not kill salmonella, thereby lengthening the course of the disease. The treatment is usually directed toward relieving the diarrhea and being sure that the patient gets sufficient rest. The infected person is considered contagious until several cultures of the stools have ascertained that no further salmonella organisms remain alive. Persons infected with the salmonella bacteria should scrub their hands carefully after each bowel movement. Their plates and eating utensils should be kept separate and washed separately.

Staphylococcus poisoning   A common type of food poisoning, staphylococcus poisoning occurs when foods containing whipped cream, custards, certain other dairy products, and occasionally meats are kept out of the refrigerator in warm weather or are refrigerated at a temperature that is not cold enough. Staphylococcus bacteria invade the food and give off very powerful poisons (toxins). The poison is not destroyed by cooking and the food remains an extremely dangerous substance.

Symptoms and treatment Usually a few hours after eating the contaminated food the person develops nausea, vomiting, abdominal pain, and diarrhea. At times blood and mucus may appear in the stool. If the patient receives medical treatment within a few hours after the food is eaten, a cathartic of magnesium sulfate is usually given. Later, fluids must be given by vein to prevent dehydration and shock. Usually only the first day is dangerous. After that, recovery is rapid.

Botulism poisoning Although botulism is rare, it is the most dangerous and fatal of the various types of food poisoning. It is caused by bacteria that live where there is no oxygen. At present it is usually contracted from home-canned foods, although commercial products are occasionally contaminated. The powerful poisons produced by the bacteria can be destroyed by thoroughly boiling at 180 degrees Fahrenheit for ten minutes.

Symptoms and treatment The poisons act on the nerves of the body. Symptoms, which start in twelve to forty-eight hours after eating the infected food, include dizziness, weakness, drooped eyelids, the crossing of eyes, and then difficulty in breathing, swallowing, and talking. Death may occur in one to eight days. A specific antitoxin is available for botulism and should be given as early as

possible. Also, as soon as the condition is suspected, the stomach should be washed out and a cathartic given.

See also **Mushroom poisoning; Plants, poisonous.**

Foods, basic

Four basic food groups are necessary for the proper nutrition of a child. A serious lack of even one food group in the child's diet can cause a deficiency that may interfere with his proper development.

The four basic food groups are milk, meat, vegetables and fruit, and bread and cereal.

Milk group Milk and milk products, including cheese and yoghurt. Skim milk or buttermilk may be substituted for whole milk. Milk or milk products should be an important part of the diet through the teen-age years, and should be served three or four times daily. A 1-inch cube of Cheddar cheese equals ⅔ cup of milk in calcium content; ½ cup of cottage cheese is equal to ½ glass of milk.

Meat group Meat, poultry, fish, eggs; with certain nuts and dried peas or beans, such as kidney beans, as alternatives. Two or more servings daily.

Vegetable-fruit group At least two servings of vegetables and one serving of fruit daily. Include a citrus fruit or other fruit or vegetable containing vitamin C daily and a dark green or deep yellow vegetable for vitamin A at least every other day.

Bread-cereal group In addition to bread and cereal, rice, kasha, barley, pasta, cake, and so on. Three to four servings daily. One slice of bread, whole grain or enriched, counts as a serving.

See also **Nutrition.**

Foods, solid see **Solid foods, introducing.**

Football see **Sports.**

Forceps delivery

Delivery of a baby with the aid of forceps, an obstetrical instrument somewhat like small, flattened fire tongs. The ends are fitted on the sides of the infant's head. The doctor may use forceps if an awkward position of the fetus in the uterus poses a danger of damage to the baby's head or danger to its life, or if long-drawn-out labor is fatiguing to the mother.

Forceps in position to ease infant out of birth canal.

With the forceps the obstetrician can turn the baby's head into normal position, and by gentle pulling can help in the delivery. Formerly, forceps deliveries were often feared, especially because of the possibility of injuring the baby. Today, however, the dangers have been practically eliminated.

Foreign language see **Bilingual families.**

Foreign objects, inhalation of

For emergency procedures, see **Choking.**

When you suspect that a child has inhaled a bit of food or other foreign object, notify the doctor at once. Breathing in a foreign object will lead to choking, gagging, and coughing. Even if the child stops coughing after a while, the doctor should still be notified, for even though the nerves of coughing may relax, the object can remain in the breathing tube. It is often assumed that the object has been coughed up and swallowed when it has not. No further signs or symptoms may occur for a few hours or for as much as a few weeks. Then a hard, dry, brassy cough usually develops, often with wheezing and pain. If the object left in the breathing tube is vegetable matter, such as a peanut, a green pea, or a piece of carrot, a severe reaction can occur very soon, and within a few hours there may be marked inflammation and swelling of the inside of the tube, often partially closing the tube, causing great difficulty in breathing. This is very serious, and the doctor should be called or the child taken to a hospital.

Metal or plastic objects such as coins, plastic toys, closed safety pins, and bottle tops usually cause no immediate reaction after the first episode of choking and coughing. They may remain in the breathing tube for days, sometimes a week or more, before symptoms of irritation appear.

Foreign objects, swallowed

Young children are always placing objects in their mouths and often swallow these objects, including coins, rings, buttons, stones, camphor balls, safety pins, and small toys. About 90 percent of all foreign objects swallowed by children go through the stomach and intestines and are passed in the feces without causing any symptoms or difficulty.

A doctor should nevertheless be

called when a child swallows an object, for some objects, such as camphor balls, may be dangerous. The doctor may also wish to X ray the child's chest and abdomen to be sure the object has not been inhaled into the breathing tubes, which would be, as a rule, a much more serious problem.

The size of the object is rarely of any concern unless it blocks the intestines. Dehydrated fruits such as dried prunes can be dangerous if swallowed whole, for they take on fluid in the intestines and swell up to their full size, often causing blockage. Coins and small toys almost always pass through without difficulty. Nails, thumbtacks, and even open safety pins usually pass through, but parents, nevertheless, should watch the child carefully for any signs of intestinal irritation or abdominal pain. If a child has swallowed an object, the bowel movements should be observed carefully each day to ascertain that the object has been passed.

See also **Hair or wool, swallowed; Poisons: first-aid treatment**.

Foreign objects in ear

Children frequently poke foreign objects—beads, buttons, beans, peas, and wads of cotton or cleansing tissue—into their ears. Also, an insect may fly into a child's ear.

Never try to dig anything out of a child's ear unless you can see enough of it to pull it out with tweezers. Too often parents push the object farther into the ear, thus making it more difficult to remove. The object should be removed by a doctor.

If an insect flies into the ear, fill the ear canal with mineral oil, olive oil, or baby oil. This will kill the insect at once. A few minutes later the child should lie down with the affected ear toward the ground. The insect may flow out with the oil. If it does not, a doctor can easily remove it.

Foreign objects in eye

If a foreign particle enters a child's eye, try to prevent him from rubbing the eye even if it itches or feels irritated, for a particle that is free in the eye may either scratch the sensitive membrane covering the eyeball or be rubbed into it, thus making a potentially serious condition out of a simple one.

Attempts to remove the particle should be limited to the following:

1. Gently pull the upper lid out and over the lower lid several times. This may move a particle off the upper lid or cause enough tears to wash the particle into the corner of the eye. From there it can be easily removed with the corner of a clean handkerchief or a sterile cotton swab.
2. Pull lower lid down by placing a finger on the cheekbone and drawing the cheek down. The particle, if seen, can usually be easily removed.
3. To inspect the upper lid, first be sure you have a good light. Next, have ready a thin pencil, a cotton swab stick, or a thin wooden match to be placed over the middle of the lid. Draw the lid down gently and roll it back over the pencil, swab stick, or match. If the object is seen on the lid, it can usually be removed without difficulty with the corner of a clean handkerchief or a cotton swab.

Once the object is removed, or if nothing is found, gently pull the upper lid forward by the eyelashes, let go, and the lid will return to position.
4. If the object has not been found, look at the front of the eye very carefully, with a magnifying glass if possible, to

see if there is any particle embedded in the eye. If an object is seen embedded in the front of the eye, or if a particle anywhere in the eye cannot be seen or cannot be removed, the child should be taken to the doctor for examination and further care if necessary.

If a child has had sand thrown in his eyes, he should always be seen by a doctor, since in most cases the sensitive membrane of the eyes is scratched. Scratches on the eyes, if properly treated, will heal completely in two or three days. If not treated, they may become infected and cause serious and painful ulcers of the eye.

Foreign objects in nose

Small children frequently place small objects in their nostrils. These may be wads of cotton or facial tissue, beads, beans, peas, or almost any object capable of being pushed in.

If the object is cotton or paper and is close enough to the outside, it can usually be extracted with tweezers. One should not attempt to extract the solid objects, since they are very likely to be pushed farther back. If you can get the child to sneeze—have him breathe a little pepper—the sneeze may force the object out. Older children who know how to blow their noses can often expel the object that way.

If the object remains in the nose, it should be removed by a doctor within twenty-four hours. Otherwise it may cause an irritation of the mucous membrane, followed by a local infection.

If at any time a parent notices a foul-smelling, yellowish mucus—it may also be bloody—flowing from one nostril, the possibility of a foreign body in the nostril should be investigated.

Foreskin

The loose fold of skin that covers the head of the penis. In girls there is occasionally a bit of foreskin coming down over the clitoris.

If the foreskin is closed tightly over the head of the penis, either a stretching of the opening, a slit in the foreskin, or removal of the foreskin through circumcision may be necessary. It may also be necessary if the foreskin is unusually elongated.

See also **Bathing the infant; Circumcision.**

Formulas

A formula is usually a mixture of cow's milk, water, and sugar given to babies who are not receiving breast milk or as a supplement to breast feedings. It is served warm until the baby is about 6 months old, when it can be given to him cold.

Cow's milk differs from human milk in having more protein and less sugar. Water is therefore added to dilute the protein, and sugar is added to bring the sugar content to the approximate percentage of human milk.

Neither breast milk nor cow's milk contains sufficient iron for an infant over 3 months old. Even when solids are

Bottle sterilizer.

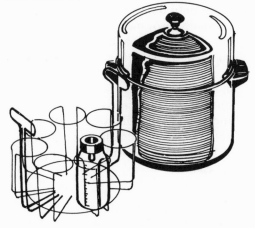

given, most infants take in too little iron and become anemic. Therefore, infants should receive extra iron either in their formulas or in their juice.

Formulas are most often prepared from evaporated milk and whole milk; many already prepared commercial cow's milk formulas, with minerals added, are also available. Among such prepared formulas are Baker's, Bremil, Enfamil, Modilac, S-M-A, and Similac. Most of these come in both liquid and powder forms.

In preparing a formula of cow's milk and water, various sugars may be added, such as granulated sugar, corn syrup, honey, or a prepared commercial sugar called dextri-maltose.

All formulas prepared at home should be sterilized and placed in sterile bottles, since bacteria left alive in the milk may multiply and upset the infant's digestive tract (for sterilization methods, see below). Once a formula is prepared it should be refrigerated until used. If possible, formulas should be prepared every twenty-four hours. Sterilization is not necessary after the baby is 4 months old. Special formulas using soybean, meat-base, or goat's milk are available for children with an allergy to milk. (See **Milk allergy.**)

Evaporated milk formulas Evaporated milk is milk that has been evaporated down until it has two times the strength of whole cow's milk. As a canned product, it is sterile and is usually easily digested. Vitamin D has been added to it. Evaporated milk is most commonly used for formula making in the home, since it is less expensive than whole milk and the cans need not be refrigerated until opened. It also has the advantage of being readily obtained in all parts of the country.

A preparation of equal parts of evaporated milk and water has the same value as whole milk, although the taste is somewhat different. Parents often switch from evaporated milk to whole milk when the baby is 4 or 5 months old. If they wish, they can continue the baby on half evaporated milk and half water for the rest of the first year or even longer.

Whole cow's milk formulas Whole milk used in formulas should be pasteurized to assure that it contains no dangerous bacteria. Most commercial milk is pasteurized, but health food stores may sell it unpasteurized. In most parts of the country vitamin D is added to whole milk and whole milk is homogenized— the fat droplets are broken up into minute particles and float evenly throughout the milk, so all portions of the milk have the same cream content.

Prepared commercial formulas Most prepared commercial formulas come in one of three different forms:

1. Completely prepared in cans or bottles. No dilution is necessary.
2. Concentrated in cans. To prepare the formula, an equal amount of water is added. The water should be boiled for ten minutes.
3. Powder form (ideal for trips). One tablespoon of the powder is added to 2 ounces of water that has been boiled for ten minutes.

How much formula? How often? The amount of formula the baby gets at each feeding depends on the desires of the baby. Usually it is best to let the baby have as much as he wants. Remember, when an infant is breast-fed, he takes as much or as little as he desires at all

feedings. The amount is usually unknown. One rule is never to force a
baby to take more than he wishes.

Any infant can be started on self-demand feeding, especially if the baby is
the first child in the family. (See **Feeding, self-demand.**) If other children demand the mother's attention as well, it is
preferable to place the new baby on a
modified self-demand schedule—setting
a definite schedule, with a leeway of one
hour on either side of the set schedule to
fit in with the infant's feeding desires.
Most infants establish a time cycle for
feeding somewhere between 4 and 6
weeks of age. The general feeding
schedule for newborn infants is approximately every three hours for babies under six pounds and every four hours for
babies over six pounds. (See **Feeding
schedules.**)

At 4 or 5 months of age, most babies

Milk Formulas

The doctor will advise on formulas, but the following are typical.

6 to 7 pounds:
whole milk....................11 ounces
water........................10 ounces
sugar........................ 1 tablespoon

or

evaporated milk............... 7 ounces
water........................14 ounces
sugar........................ 1 tablespoon

$3\frac{1}{2}$ ounces every four hours
six times daily

7 to 8 pounds:
whole milk....................12 ounces
water........................12 ounces
sugar........................ 1 tablespoon

or

evaporated milk............... 8 ounces
water........................16 ounces
sugar........................ 1 tablespoon

4 ounces every four hours
six times daily

8 to 9 pounds:
whole milk....................18 ounces
water........................ 9 ounces
sugar........................ 2 tablespoons

or

evaporated milk...............10 ounces
water........................17 ounces
sugar........................ 2 tablespoons

$4\frac{1}{2}$ ounces every four hours
six times daily, or $4\frac{1}{2}$ ounces
for five feedings daily when
baby is 6 weeks of age or
older

9 to 10 pounds:
whole milk. . . . . .20½ ounces
water. . . . . 7 ounces
sugar. . . . . 2 tablespoons

or

evaporated milk. . . . . .11½ ounces
water. . . . . .16 ounces
sugar. . . . . 2 tablespoons

> 5½ ounces for five feedings daily

10 to 11 pounds:
whole milk. . . . . .25 ounces
water. . . . . 7½ ounces
sugar. . . . . 2 tablespoons

or

evaporated milk. . . . . .13 ounces
water. . . . . .19½ ounces
sugar. . . . . 2 tablespoons

> 6 to 6½ ounces for five feedings daily

11 to 12 pounds:
whole milk. . . . . .30 ounces
water. . . . . 7½ ounces
sugar. . . . . 2 tablespoons

or

evaporated milk. . . . . .16 ounces
water. . . . . .21½ ounces
sugar. . . . . 2 tablespoons

> 7 to 7½ ounces for five feedings daily

over 12 pounds:
whole milk. . . . . .35 ounces
water. . . . . 5 ounces
sugar. . . . . 1 tablespoon

or

evaporated milk. . . . . .19 ounces
water. . . . . .21 ounces
sugar. . . . . 1 tablespoon

> 8 ounces for four or five feedings daily

can be placed on undiluted whole milk or skim milk. Many doctors prefer the latter, which contains all the value of whole milk except the fat. This limits the calories and cholesterol in the baby's diet.

Equipment required for formula making

1. Six or seven 8-ounce feeding bottles. (Pyrex or plastic preferable. Playtex plastic sterile bottles are excellent.)
2. Bottle caps and nipple covers.
3. About nine or ten nipples.
4. Funnel.
5. Bottle brush and nipple brush.
6. Can opener for evaporated milk or prepared canned formulas.
7. Large glass measuring cup.
8. Set of measuring spoons.
9. Bowl or pot for mixing and heating formula (if necessary).
10. A sterilizing pot with a rack for holding eight bottles. If possible, obtain a pot with a large hole in the center for the nipple jar.
11. A large spoon for mixing.
12. A pair of tongs to lift hot bottles from sterilizer.
13. A nipple jar. This is a wide-mouthed jar that has two covers, one perforated and the other solid. The perforated top is used while sterilizing the nipples; the solid top is used to cover the bottle containing the nipples when it is removed from the sterilizer.
14. Bottle-warmer, or any ordinary pot in which a single bottle can be set in water, to heat the formula just before serving. The temperature of the heated formula should be tested against the inside of the wrist. As soon as it feels comfortably warm (not hot), it can be given to the baby.

Sterilization of formulas   Two methods of sterilization are in general use today:

the terminal method and the aseptic method. The terminal method, which is taught to mothers in most hospitals, is probably the simplest method since the formula is prepared, placed in the bottles, and then everything is sterilized together.

After use, bottles, bottle caps, and nipples should be rinsed thoroughly in cold water and then washed in hot water with soap, and again rinsed thoroughly. If one of the sterilizing methods described below is not used, bottles, bottle caps, and nipples should be boiled for fifteen minutes.

Terminal method

1. Mix the correct amount of milk and water in a pot or bowl. Add sugar and stir with a large spoon.
2. Pour the required amount of formula into each bottle. Place the nipples in upside down. Then cap each bottle loosely so that heat can escape when the bottles are warm.
3. Cover the bottom of the sterilizing pot with about 2 inches of water. Place the bottles containing the formula on the rack in the pot and boil the water for fifteen to twenty minutes. Allow the bottles to cool slowly in the pot.
4. When the bottles have cooled to lukewarm, screw the caps on tightly and refrigerate. The formula may be kept in the refrigerator for up to forty-eight hours.

Aseptic method

1. Sterilize bottles, caps, nipples, tongs, and funnel by boiling them in a covered pot for five to ten minutes. Let them stand in the covered pot to cool.
2. Place the amount of water required for the formula, plus 2 extra ounces (for

evaporation during boiling) into a measuring cup.

3. Add sugar and stir until entirely dissolved.

4. Add the necessary amount of milk.

5. Place the whole mixture in a pot over a flame, bring to a boil, and let simmer while stirring for about five minutes.

6. Cool the mixture for a few minutes; pour the amount for each feeding into sterile bottles through a sterilized funnel.

7. Cap the bottles at once with sterilized caps.

8. When cool, refrigerate.

Foster care

If a child is an orphan or if he can no longer live at home because of conditions there (the mother may be living alone and have to work; may be ill and unable to care for the child; or may have died), then a foster home is almost always the best substitute for a real home and far superior to an institution.

The best foster homes are those that are supervised by state or private social agencies. Foster parents generally care for no more than two or three children and can, therefore, give them adequate individual attention. Kind and understanding people are sought by the social agencies to act as foster parents; they are usually paid for this care.

Although a foster home cannot really approximate a happy and successful true home, it does offer the best substitute, especially for young children. In a home atmosphere the child can relate to and depend upon a single person or couple—and these people will care for him and be interested in him.

Foster homes are almost always preferable to institutions. However, for ado-lescents who are emotionally upset and in great need of psychotherapy or guidance, a well-organized and well-staffed institution is usually more helpful.

4-H Clubs   see Recreational organizations.

Fractures

Fractures are broken bones. The type of fracture and the speed of healing varies considerably with age. The bones of children are usually softer than adult bones, and as a result, children sustain many more "green-stick" fractures—a fracture in which the bone breaks but is held together like a broken green stick—than clean-cut fractures. Children's broken bones also heal much more rapidly than adult fractures.

The usual fractures are "closed fractures," in which the broken segment of bone does not tear through the skin. Those fractures that break through the skin are known as open fractures. In the treatment of fractures of the long bones of the arms and legs, and fractures of the collarbone, the doctor attempts to set them in their original position. Even if they grow together at a slight angle, they usually straighten out perfectly in the course of a year.

During healing, the broken segments must be protected and held in position. For this reason a cast or a splint is usually applied and is kept on until the bone has healed sufficiently to prevent any rebreaking if weight is placed on it or force applied.

See also Collarbone, fracture of; Head injuries.

Fractures: first-aid treatment

A fractured (broken) arm or leg is usually easily diagnosed even when the fracture is a simple fracture, that is, a

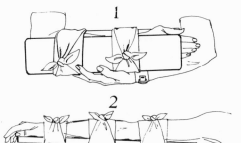

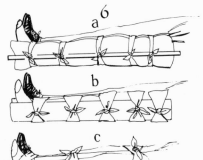

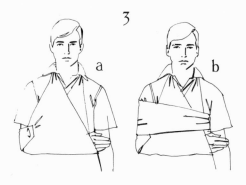

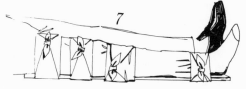

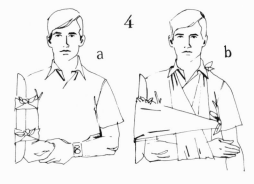

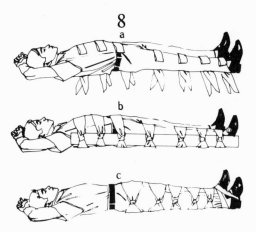

1. Splint for break in lower arm. 2. Splint for broken elbow, straight position. 3a. Sling for broken elbow, bent position. 3b. Arm bound to body to prevent jostling. 4a. Splint for break in upper arm. 4b. Arm in sling and bound to body (sling may be used for break in lower arm as well). 5. Splint and bandage for break in finger. 6a. Blanket (or pillow) and pole splint for break in lower leg. 6b. Board splints for break in lower leg. 6c. Blanket splint with legs bound together for break in lower leg. 7. Splint for broken knee-cap. 8a. Bandages in place for splinting break in upper leg. 8b. Splints in place (inner splint not visible) and bound. 8c. Blanket splint with legs bound together for break in upper leg.

fracture that has not broken through the skin. Generally the child has heard the crack of the bone. There may be some deformity, which may be felt. The child rarely uses the injured limb because of the pain. When pressure is applied over the fracture point pain may be felt. Swelling appears quickly over the fracture point.

The primary concern in first-aid treatment of a fracture is to prevent any further injury by moving or careless handling of the child. Make the child as comfortable as possible and guard against the development of shock by keeping the child warm and giving him warm drinks if necessary (see **Shock**). In general, unless you are trained in first-aid, it is important to make no attempt at all to treat or move the patient, but rather to get medical help on the scene. However, if it is necessary to move the patient, the broken bone must be splinted, and the principles of splinting are therefore given here. But *never* attempt any splinting, moving the patient, or allowing the patient to move if the break involves the back or neck. Keep the patient warm and seek help.

In splinting a fracture, several general principles must be kept in mind:

1. The splint must be firm enough and held in such a position that the broken ends of the fractured bone do not move when the patient is moved.
2. The splint should be long enough to prevent motion at the joints above and below the fractured bone.
3. All splints should be thickly padded, with the greatest padding next to the fractured part of the limb to fill in any irregularities on the surface caused by the fracture. The padding can be a pillow, blanket, newspaper, cotton or any other soft material. A folded newspaper

or blanket may substitute for a board splint. If possible, make more rigid by tying a pole, rod, or the like to the outside of the padding or, in the case of a broken leg, binding the two legs together.
4. The splints should be bandaged firmly in place but not so tightly as to impede circulation. The bandaging should be examined every thirty minutes since often the arm or leg swells, causing the bandages to become taut. In the case of an arm break, remove rings or bracelets. In the case of a break in the lower leg, gently remove or cut off shoe.
5. None of the bandages that hold the splint in place should be tied directly over the area of the fracture.

The following specific procedures are suggested for splinting common fractures:

Fractures of the wrist and lower arm   These are the most common fractures in children. Prepare two padded splints, each of which extends from above the elbow to the mid-finger region. (Folded newspaper may be used in place of boards.) Place the forearm across the chest at right angles to the upper arm. Then place one splint on the inner surface of the forearm and hand, the other splint on the outer surface, with the padded surfaces next to the arm.

Tie the splints securely but not too tightly in place with two bandages (wide pieces of cloth)—one just below the elbow and the other at the wrist. Support the arm in this position with a triangular sling.

Fracture of the elbow   This may be a serious condition since improper healing may permanently interfere with full motion of the elbow. It is urgent, therefore, to prevent any further motion until the fracture is under the care of a doctor.

The type of splinting depends on whether or not the arm is straight. If the arm is straight, place a padded splint on the inside of the arm, extending from the palm to just below the armpit. Tie the splint in three places—one at the wrist, one above the elbow, and one between the elbow and the wrist.

If the arm is bent, do not straighten it out. Place the arm in a comfortable position in a large triangular sling. Then tie the arm snugly to the body with a wide bandage passed completely around the body and over the injured arm.

Fracture of the upper arm Place the arm in a comfortable position but with the lower arm at a right angle to the upper arm.

Apply one well-padded splint on the outside of the arm, extending from the shoulder to just below the elbow. Hold splint in place with two bandages. Then tie arm closely to the side of the body with a bandage or sling.

Fracture of a finger This can easily be splinted with a padded piece of cardboard, or a splint may even be omitted and the arm placed in a sling.

Fracture of the lower leg (knee to ankle) Straighten out the leg by pulling on the foot slowly, then rotating the foot until it appears in normal position. Hold the leg in this position until proper splints can be prepared. If no one is available to help, tie the fractured leg to the normal leg at the ankle so that it is held immobile while you prepare the splints.

To apply the pillow splint (a folded blanket may be substituted), raise the leg just high enough off the ground so that a pillow can be placed underneath. It should be wide enough so that it can be used to pad the sides of the legs. Tie the pillow securely around the leg in five places. Increased stiffness may be gained by placing a stick or board on each side of the leg extending from above the knee to below the ankle.

If no pillows or blankets are available, well-padded board splints may be used, also extending from above the knee to below the ankle. These also are held to the leg by five ties. If no sticks or boards are available, place folded blanket between legs and bind the two legs together.

Fracture of the kneecap A fracture of the kneecap can usually be detected by feeling the line of the break between the two parts of the bone.

To splint, gently straighten out the injured limb and apply either a pillow splint or a board splint.

When using the pillow splint, lay the leg on a pillow (or a folded blanket) with the middle of the pillow behind the knee. Tie in place with four bandages, leaving the knee free and exposed. A board splint tied outside the pillow will provide greater rigidity.

To apply a board splint, take a well-padded board about 4 inches wide and place it underneath the leg. The splint should extend from the middle of the thigh to the heel. Stuff extra padding under the knee and heel, and tie the board in place with four bandages, leaving the knee free and exposed.

Fracture of the upper leg This is a very serious and usually very painful fracture. The patient is often in shock and should be under treatment by a doctor as soon as possible. There may or may not be any deformity at the site of the fracture, but if you are in doubt, the injury should be treated as such.

To splint, place one hand under the heel and the other over the instep. Then pull steadily and gently and rotate the limb into its normal position; continue to pull steadily while splints are being prepared. If working alone, tie the child's feet together temporarily.

Before applying the splints, prepare seven wide bandages or cloth strips, and with a small stick push them under the hollows of the ankles, knees, and back. From these positions the bandages can be worked up and down into the desired positions.

Apply two well-padded splints 4 to 6 inches wide. The outer splint should reach from the armpit to the heel, the inner splint from the crotch to the heel. Fasten splints in position by making three ties around the body over the outer splint and four ties over the outer and inner splints below the crotch.

If no splints are available, place padding between the legs and tie the legs together, using the uninjured leg as a splint.

Since shock so often accompanies fractures of the upper leg, be sure to keep the patient warm with covering blankets and give him warm drinks.

Frail child   see **Susceptibility to infections.**

Freckles
Light brown spots on the skin caused by the stimulating action of the sun on pigmentation in the skin. Freckles usually appear in blue-eyed blondes and children with red hair around the age of 5 or 6. They are of no significance and can cause no trouble. Once acquired they usually remain, becoming more pronounced each summer with exposure to the sun.

It is extremely rare for freckles to be so dark or numerous as to be considered a defect, and even in these cases the problem is usually in the feelings of the young girl or boy rather than in the child's actual appearance.

Increased freckling during the summer may be lessened by staying in the shade, wearing a broad-brimmed hat, and using a sunscreening lotion. Various methods of bleaching are not successful, but cosmetics may be used to hide the freckles.

Radical treatment such as skin peeling may be of some help but should be under the control of a dermatologist. It should be attempted only when a child is unusually disturbed over the condition. Generally, it is better to assure the child that freckles are not ugly.

Friends, close
Having close friends is not really important during the preschool years. From ages 3 to 6 years children need the companionship of other children, but there is no need for a particular friend.

But during the school years close friends become of great importance, for children feel the need to be closely in contact with other children and to have their acceptance and admiration. The child is beginning to live in a world much wider than the family, and he needs to communicate his interests and doubts to another person on his own level. Most children seek out a "best friend" (almost invariably of the same sex). In the early school years these friendships may be less intense or enduring than later, but they are nevertheless very important. There may be considerable jockeying to find the most desirable relationship, and competition and jealousy are not unusual.

In these school years a third child often invades the established close friendship of two friends and causes a triangle situation—usually a deeply upsetting experience for whichever child feels he is being deprived of his close friend. There is little that parents can do to alter the circumstances. They may try to reinforce the original friendship, or alternatively to help the youngster to find a new friend. But essentially the children themselves must work out the situation.

During the preadolescent years, when preteens and early teen-agers are developing physically and for the first time encountering boy-girl interests, a close friend of the same sex is practically a necessity. Boys usually want to talk to boys, and girls to girls, of their feelings and experiences. At this age youngsters will talk to the parents rarely or not at all about their innermost feelings. They close the door on their parents and converse for hours on the phone with their close friends.

If children have no close friends during the preadolescent or adolescent years, there is usually a reason which should be investigated. These "loners" often involve themselves in asocial interests such as chemistry, astronomy, stamp collecting, or raising tropical fish. Not that there is anything wrong with such hobbies in themselves, but they may keep a young person constantly isolated. A child with similar interests can usually be found, often with the aid of the teacher. A child who withdraws completely may need psychological help.

The need for a close friend of the same sex usually diminishes as boys and girls develop strong relationships with the opposite sex. Then the close friendship becomes one of boy-girl relationship rather than a close relationship of those of the same sex.

Parents frequently ask what to do if the close friend chosen by a child is not up to their own standards. It must be answered that the importance of close friends is so great that unless there is some very serious reason for opposing the friend—such as drug addiction, promiscuity, or the like—the friendship should not be broken suddenly. Parents may try to help cultivate other friends for their child as subtly as possible but they should avoid attacks upon the chosen friend. The friend means a great deal to the child and the criticism may be received with deep resentment. After all, parents are not only criticizing the friend but, by implication, their own child's affections and interests. In such matters, if at all possible, it is better to let the child learn for himself the qualities that make up a truly good friend.

See also **Companions.**

Frostbite

An injury to the skin and underlying tissues caused by freezing. Various degrees of frostbite occur, ranging from simple freezing without blistering or peeling, to blistering and destruction of the skin, to destruction of underlying muscles and tendons.

Mild frostbite, which is quite frequent in children, is characterized by numbness, itching, and prickling of the affected part. The skin is usually white or yellow and the feet or hands are stiff. Deeply frozen tissue is livid white. The depth of injury can only be determined by the doctor.

Treatment DO NOT rub or massage

the frozen extremity or apply ice, snow, or any other material. Instead, warm the frozen extremity with natural body heat. Tell the child to put his frozen hand under his armpit or between his legs or on his belly. Cover frozen feet with slightly warmed towels or blankets.

If the skin is deeply frozen, call the doctor at once—the condition may be extremely serious.

Fruit, dried (swallowed whole) see **Foreign objects, swallowed.**

Frustration

The unhappy, tense, or angry reaction of any child or adult when his desires or needs are blocked or unfulfilled.

Every person must learn to accept some frustration, for it is an unavoidable aspect of life. Children frequently meet temporary frustration because of their small stature, inadequate strength, lack of coordination, or lack of experience. Other frustrations must be accepted in ordinary family living and when living in an organized, civilized community.

Up to one year of age, there is nothing to be gained by letting an infant remain frustrated, for example by letting him cry for long periods when he is hungry, uncomfortable, or even bored. Unless the child develops the basic trust that his important needs will be met, he will not later develop the assurance that he can trust his parents and others when he must be restricted and suffer frustration.

Little by little, as the child grows older, he learns that some frustrations are inevitable but that others can be overcome. Children must learn that they can't have everything they want and that those things they can have they often may not get immediately.

Parents should encourage children in all reasonable endeavors and help them to overcome feelings of failure and frustration.

See also **Failure.**

Furuncle see **Abscess.**

G

Gagging

Gagging is rarely of any importance, except for the gagging that occurs when a child is nauseated, vomiting, or choking on something.

Infants gag frequently when their diet of finely pureed infant food is being shifted to semi-pureed junior food. In such cases the new food should be introduced very gradually and in small amounts.

Children also gag when forced to take food or medicines which they dislike or think they will dislike.

In many cases gagging over certain foods will disappear if the foods are prepared in a more appetizing manner. But when a child strongly dislikes a food and shows it by gagging, it should temporarily be omitted from his diet. There is no food which is invaluable or for which there is no substitute.

See also **Choking; Nausea; Vomiting.**

Gall bladder

The sac behind the liver, which stores bile until it is ready to be used.

Disorders of the gall bladder are rare during infancy and childhood.

Inflammation of the gall bladder (cholecystitis) may occur with certain bacterial infections such as typhoid fever, scarlet fever, and bacterial bloodstream infections. It can also be caused by migration into the gall bladder of intestinal parasites such as the roundworm. As in adults, the symptoms are pain in the right upper abdomen, nausea, and vomiting, usually accompanied by abdominal distention. The diagnosis is made with difficulty. If suspected, antibiotic therapy is indicated.

Gallstones in children are rare and usually cause no difficulty. But they may occur as a complication of sickle-cell anemia.

Gamma globulin

The portion of the blood that contains the antibodies which a person has built up against infections. For instance, if a person has had measles, the antibodies held in his gamma globulin make him immune to the disease in the future. Gamma globulin is given (by injection) to prevent such diseases as measles, hepatitis, and poliomyelitis in children exposed to these diseases. Children who have a total lack of gamma globulin (agammaglobulinenemia) in their blood are highly susceptible to infections. But treatment by monthly injections of gamma globulin throughout life is generally successful, and the child can live normally. Children who have a partial lack of gamma globulin (hypogammaglobulinemia) often need injections of gamma globulin for only one or two years.

Gas poisoning see **Carbon monoxide poisoning.**

Gasoline poisoning see **Poisons: first-aid treatment.**

Gastric ulcer see **Ulcer, stomach and duodenal.**

Gastrointestinal tract see **Alimentary canal; Intestines.**

Gate, safety

A wooden or metal gate to be placed above stairways or in doorways to prevent young children from passing through. Its use is an essential safety measure in all homes with stairways in which there are creeping infants and toddlers. These gates are also of use in doorways to prevent children from leaving a room.

The gates are usually made of wood and are expandable and retractable, so they can be folded to one side when not in use. There is a safety catch to hold the gate securely in position when in use.

Generosity

Generosity is a trait that is gradually developed in children. The young child, during his toddler period and often for a year or so longer, is very possessive and usually refuses to share. As he grows older, with the guidance of his parents and often his nursery school teacher as well, he learns to share his toys and possessions and begins to derive some pleasure in doing so. He finds that it brings him friendship, a need that becomes more and more important as he grows older. (See **Sharing.**)

Once children reach the nursery school age, the development of generosity goes far beyond the mere sharing of toys or other possessions. We see it developing when a child gives something he treasures, such as two shiny pennies, to his parents or to a friend. It is a token of love or warm friendship. We see it developing when children show sympathy for those who are less fortunate and are eager to help them.

You should not give your children the impression that generosity is a means of buying love. This attitude is sometimes expressed by relatives who bring a present but, if a child gets angry at them, demand that he give it back.

Generosity must be the result of a spontaneous inner feeling and should not be placed on a materialistic level.

Genes

The molecules in the chromosomes that carry inherited qualities. There are thousands of genes relating to all inherited features and characteristics of a person and his forebears—the body size, color of hair, color of eyes, shape of eyes, shape of nose, length of fingers, broadness of muscles, etc.

Certain traits transmitted by the genes may be classified as "dominant" or "recessive." An explanation of the probability of passing on such traits is given at **Heredity.**

Genetic counseling

When parents have had a child with some inherited defect such as Mongolism, cystic fibrosis, or harelip and cleft palate, they are as a rule anxious to know whether or not their next child might also have a similar defect. There are also prospective parents who have either themselves or in their family such conditions as diabetes or hemophilia. If they have a child, what are his chances of having the condition also?

To answer such questions, genetic clinics have been set up in many of the large hospitals and medical centers throughout the United States, Canada, England, and many other countries. The specially trained doctors and other scientists at these clinics will know in most cases if a condition is hereditary or not, and what the chances are of the parents having a child with the condition.

For instance, cerebral palsy is not hereditary; congenital heart disease is not hereditary; nor are blindness and deafness caused by the mother's having had German measles in the first three months of pregnancy. Cystic fibrosis, diabetes (in most cases), and hemophilia are inheritable, but they are recessive diseases—that is, they will only occur if both parents are carriers. If parents have one child with such a recessive condition, there is a 25 percent chance of the same condition occurring in subsequent children. (See **Heredity.**) In certain conditions, such as Mongolism and Mediterranean anemia, a study of the parent's blood or cell chromosomes will usually tell if a parent is a carrier.

Some genetic counseling centers are also equipped to perform amniocentesis. (See **Amniocentesis.**)

A list of genetic counseling centers is given in the appendix.

Genitals

The reproductive organs, especially the external sex organs.

In the male these consist of the penis and of the two testicles held within the scrotal sac.

The female external genitals consist of the clitoris, a small counterpart of the male penis, and the labia, which are the lips on either side of the vaginal cleft. (The internal genital system includes the uterus and ovaries.)

The genitals grow quickly from their childhood size to their adult size during adolescence.

See also **Clitoris; Foreskin; Penis; Testicles; Vagina.**

Genius

Exceptional intellectual and creative power.

It is often erroneously stated that a child or older person with an IQ of 150 or above is "in the genius class." This is not true, for although the IQ rating may give some indication of a child's intelligence, it gives no indication of what he will do with that intelligence.

The determination of genius is based on what one does with his intelligence, not how high it is. A genius must not only have intelligence but unusual creative ability as well.

The danger of branding a child as a genius is that he is too often pressured by his parents, who always want and expect him to surpass other children in every intellectual endeavor. As a result, the child may live under a cloud of anxiety and tension.

Before characterizing any child as a genius or potential genius, it should be remembered that he is first and foremost a child with a child's needs, desires, and interests.

See also **Intelligence, exceptional; Talent, exceptional.**

German measles

German measles (rubella) was once thought to be the mildest of the contagious diseases. But it is, of course, extremely dangerous to an embryo or fetus if the mother contracts the disease in the first three months of her pregnancy.

The disease, which is caused by a virus present in the secretions of the nose and throat, is of no danger to the mother or any other person who contracts it. But to the baby in the uterus it is very harmful in a large percentage of cases: it may cause blindness, deafness, bleeding conditions, cardiac conditions, mental retardation, irregular bone formation, and hepatitis.

Mothers who have already had German measles are immune to the disease. Those who have received the vaccine against it have varying degrees of immunity. If a mother is uncertain as to whether or not she had German measles or whether or not she has built up a full immunity from the vaccination, her blood may be sent for testing.

If a mother contracts German measles during her first three months of pregnancy, most pediatricians and obstetricians recommend that the pregnancy be terminated because of the danger of fetal damage.

Mode of transmission   The disease is transmitted only by direct contact with a person who has the infection.

Period of contagion   Usually from twenty-four hours before the onset of the rash until the rash fades, about three days after its appearance. However, it has been found that babies who are affected by the disease while still in the uterus can hold the live virus in their bodies for months after they are born.

Incubation period   The symptoms of German measles usually appear between fourteen and twenty-one days after exposure, most usually on the seventeeth or eighteenth day.

Signs and symptoms   These are usually mild, starting with a low-grade fever, a headache, and swollen glands on the scalp behind the ears and on either side of the back of the neck. These signs may

appear during the twenty-four hours prior to the appearance of the rash. Occasionally the eyes are inflamed.

The rash of German measles may be either mottled or composed of tiny pimples. It usually appears first over the face and neck and then works down, covering the whole body in twelve to twenty-four hours.

Treatment   There is no treatment at the present time, and there is no known sure method of preventing the disease once a susceptible person has been exposed. Some doctors have given pregnant mothers twenty c.c.'s of gamma globulin intramuscularly, but immunity produced by this treatment is far from guaranteed.

Immunization   The German measles (rubella) vaccine is now available and is highly effective in preventing the disease, although it is not yet known if it gives lifetime immunity. It should be given to all children, especially girls.

Germicide
Any substance that kills germs. See also **Antiseptic.**

Germs   see **Bacteria; Viruses.**

Gifted child   see **Intelligence, exceptional; Talent, exceptional.**

Gigantism
A comparatively rare condition in childhood in which there is unusual growth, with the child possibly reaching seven feet or more. In many cases this condition is merely an inheritance from parents or very close relatives who are unusually tall. Many basketball players exhibit this type of gigantism.

On the other hand, gigantism may be caused by abnormal conditions.

One such condition is an oversecretion of the growth hormone from the pituitary gland, which is usually due to a tumor of this gland. The extra stimulation by the hormone in children and adolescents causes a rapid growth in length of the long bones. The children affected may grow to heights of eight feet or even more. The jawbone also grows large, and the fingers and toes become long and thick. The tumor of the pituitary gland may be diagnosed by increased growth hormone in the blood serum. It may also be demonstrated by an X ray of the skull.

Treatment is by X-ray radiation of the pituitary tumor. If this is unsuccessful, or if the child develops headaches and difficulty in vision, the tumor must be removed by surgery.

In another type of gigantism, which is not well understood, there is a rapid growth in height for the child's first four or five years, after which the growth rate is normal. The amount of growth hormone in the blood serum is normal in such cases. But children with this condition usually have other symptoms as well. They are almost always retarded mentally, they have large heads, the eyes are widely separated, the jaw is large, and they are clumsy and awkward. There is no known treatment for this condition.

See also **Puberty, precocious.**

Girl Scouts   see **Recreational organizations.**

Glands
Organs in the body that secrete various substances.

There are two types. The endocrine glands secrete their substances (hor-

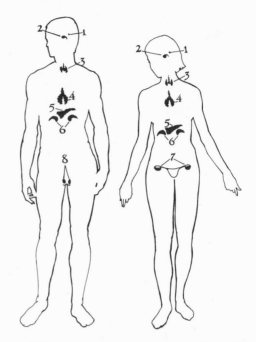

1. Pineal gland. 2. Pituitary gland. 3. Thyroid and parathyroid glands. 4. Thymus gland. 5. Pancreas. 6. Adrenal glands. 7. Ovaries. 8. Testes.

mones) directly into the bloodstream and have an important regulatory role in body functions. These glands include the adrenals, the pituitary, the thyroid, the parathyroid, the ovaries and testes, a portion of the pancreas (the Islands of Langerhans), and the pineal and thymus glands, the functions of which are not fully known.

The exocrine glands are those which open directly on the surface of the skin or mucous membrane. These include the oily glands of the face and scalp; mucous glands that open into the mucous membrane of the mouth, nose, throat, respiratory tree, and digestive tract; salivary glands; tear glands of the eyes; digestive glands of the stomach and intestinal tract, including the liver and the pancreas; and sweat glands of the skin.

See also **Adrenal glands; Ovaries; Pancreas; Parathyroid glands; Pituitary gland; Testicles; Thyroid gland.**

Glands, lymph   see **Lymph nodes.**

Glands, swollen   see **Lymph nodes.**

Glandular fever   see **Mononucleosis, infectious.**

Glaucoma

A condition of increased pressure within the eyeball. This condition is usually associated with age rather than youth, but there is one type of glaucoma (congenital glaucoma) that occurs in the newborn and children under age 2. In infants and young children, glaucoma is usually detected by a clouding over of the pupil of the eye. But the most common symptom is the child's inability to tolerate bright lights (photophobia). The eyeball also gradually increases in size because of the internal pressure.

The condition must be treated, for the constant pressure within the eye and on the optic nerve will eventually cause blindness if unrelieved.

Treatment   The increased pressure in the eyes of children is, as a rule, influenced very little by the usual antiglaucoma drops given to adults. The best results are obtained by surgical operation performed early, which is in most instances very successful.

Glue sniffing   see **Drug abuse.**

Goat's milk   see **Milk, goat's.**

Going steady   see **Dating.**

Goiter

An enlargement of the thyroid gland, which is situated in front of the lower part of the neck.

Goiters are not at all uncommon among infants and children. They occur at all ages but much more frequently in some areas in the country than in others. They may have various causes.

In areas of the country where large numbers of people are affected, the cause is almost always a lack of adequate iodine in the water or soil. The use of iodized salt for table use will prevent such goiters. In certain iodine-deficient areas small amounts of iodine are added to the drinking water.

Occasionally a goiter is seen in newborn babies, as a result of certain drugs, especially any containing iodine, that pregnant mothers have taken for one reason or another. These drugs cross the placenta and cause the baby's thyroid gland to enlarge considerably. Such goiters will usually disappear without treatment in a few weeks.

The most common goiters of childhood appear during early adolescence. These are generally of no significance and subside without treatment. However, any such enlargement of the thyroid gland should be examined by a doctor, and certain tests should be made before assuming that it is merely a simple adolescent goiter.

Other goiters occasionally seen are those caused by underactivity or overactivity of the thyroid gland. Careful diagnosis is necessary so that the proper treatment can be given. Tumors of the thyroid must also be considered, although these are quite rare during childhood.

See also **Thyroid gland.**

Gonorrhea

The most common of the venereal diseases. It is caused by a bacteria called gonococcus. In recent years there has been a marked increase in the number of adolescents contracting the disease.

In the vast majority of cases, gonorrhea is due to sexual intercourse with infected persons. Occasionally a female infant may acquire the infection from the contaminated hands of a person with the disease.

Signs and symptoms The first symptoms occur a few days to a week after intercourse with an infected person. In the male there is a burning sensation on urination, followed in a day or so by a urethral discharge of pus. In girls the initial symptoms are usually pain on urination and later a profuse vaginal discharge. In males the symptoms cause sufficient discomfort for the boy or man to know that there is something wrong and to realize that he should get treatment. Unfortunately the symptoms are much more variable in girls and may pass unnoticed. Thus, many girls and women become carriers and may be seriously injured by the disease without having ever been aware that they had contracted it. Until recently the belief that venereal disease had been "conquered" also lulled many doctors into the mistake of not testing often enough for the possibility of gonorrhea.

Treatment The disease can usually be eradicated successfully by large doses of penicillin. And recently a new drug, Trobicin (spectinomycin-dihydrochloride pentahydrate), has been found to be very effective. A single dose given by injection will cure most cases. If not treated, sterility and other painful symptoms may result.

It is now recommended that gonorrhea tests be given routinely in gynecological examinations, and they definitely should be given if there are any symptoms of discomfort or if there is a persistent vaginal discharge.

Grand mal see **Epilepsy.**

Grandparents
Grandparents almost always mean a great deal to those children who have the opportunity to be with them and know them. For grandparents give a child a very special type of love and attention, different from that received from his parents. This relationship extends the child's world and enhances his understanding of people and family life.

It is probably true that most grandparents are considerably more permissive and indulgent than the child's parents. But this is rarely of any concern unless the grandparents are living in the same home as the child and his family. Otherwise, a child soon learns that although he may have greater freedom in the grandparents' home, this is not to be expected in his own home.

In addition to complaining that grandparents spoil their children, parents also express frequent annoyance at their constant criticism of, and attempts to direct the upbringing of the children. This is probably true in many families, especially when young parents have their first child. It is often very difficult for grandparents to realize that their children have grown up and are ready to bring up their own children. Grandparents should realize that new parents must live their own lives and bring up their children as they see fit. The grandparents have had their turn; now it's the new parents' turn. And the parents should do their best to work out any difficulties so that both the children and the grandparents will not be denied the values of this important relationship.

Granulated eyelids see **Eyelids, granulated.**

Granuloma, umbilical see **Navel.**

"Grass" (Marijuana) see **Drug abuse.**

Grooming
Care of one's appearance.

The young child is rarely able to make decisions on appearance and clothing, and most of his grooming is entirely dependent on his parent's efforts.

But during the school years, and certainly as a child approaches the teen years, his appearance and his manner of dress become largely his own prerogative. He should know when he can be sloppy in dress and appearance, and when he should be better dressed and well-groomed.

Today sloppiness in the way clothing is worn and in the adolescent's appearance is the standard accepted by teenagers in many parts of the country. Uncombed hair, unkempt beards, dungarees that are cut, patched, and frayed are the style. But the same teen-agers usually, although not always, know that if they go to the opera, theater, or ballet, or to visit relatives, they should temporarily be better groomed.

Occasionally one sees an adolescent who is uninterested in personal care and appearance not because it is the style among his companions but simply because he doesn't care. Such boys and girls are almost always emotionally upset and usually depressed. They may benefit from psychotherapy to help them with their difficulties.

Growing pains
Also called "night pains." "Growing pains" is an obsolete term from a period when parents and doctors alike felt that when the bones of the arms and legs grew, there were extra pulls on the muscles that caused pain. This is not considered true today.

Doctors now feel that there is no natural pain associated with growth. So when pain arises in the joints or muscles of a growing child, some other cause is always sought. Such pain could be due to infections, muscle strain, vitamin deficiency, injury, a nerve disorder, or an allergic reaction.

Rheumatic fever and rheumatoid arthritis are among the first considerations if the pain is in the joints and especially if it is accompanied by swelling and fever. A number of tests of the child's blood will usually indicate if such diagnoses are to be considered.

Sometimes the pain is caused by a local infection somewhere in the body which gives off toxins into the blood. Such infections could be localized in the lymph glands, sinuses, or teeth.

Pain in the joints may also occasionally follow German measles. This arthritis, seen most often in teen-agers who contract German measles, continues for several weeks and then subsides completely. Such temporary pain may also occasionally occur in adolescent girls who have received the German measles (rubella) vaccine.

Muscle strain and injury are the most usual causes of growing pains. Allergic pain is rare and occurs only occasionally following injections of penicillin or horse serum.

See also **Muscle pains; Rheumatic fever; Rheumatoid arthritis.**

Growth see **Body measurements; height.**

Guidance, vocational see **Vocational guidance.**

Guidance counseling see **Counseling, educational and guidance.**

Guilt

The uncomfortable sense of shame and often fear commonly experienced when a person feels he has done something morally wrong.

The capacity to feel guilt is developed gradually as a young child learns (primarily from his parents) what kinds of behavior are considered right and worthy of approval, and what kinds are wrong and bring disapproval and punishment. All children seek approval, especially from parents. For approval assures love and care, and guarantees, for the time being at least, that the parent will stay with the child and protect him—a desperately needed assurance.

As a child grows, the values learned from his parents become "internalized"—that is, a part of his own emotions and feelings, so that whenever he does something that does not accord with these values, he feels wrong and guilty, even if no one else could know about it or punish him. This is what has been traditionally called a sense of conscience.

Children who are brought up from infancy in an institution may develop very few guilt feelings. They usually have no real parent figures from whom they learn the basic moral values on which to build their lives. Similarly, children coming from overpermissive homes, where parents have a lack of real interest, may develop very little conscience and therefore have very little basis for guilt feelings.

The development of conscience is essential to any society, for people must follow certain standards of behavior without constant supervision. Nevertheless, any child or person whose sense of conscience is so strict that he suffers excessively from guilt feelings is not well adjusted emotionally, and cannot develop to the full extent of his abilities. This is particularly true when the child is not consciously aware of what is causing his feelings of guilt and anxiety and cannot explain his worries. If the guilt is severe, he may develop symptoms of emotional disturbance. Overly intense guilt feelings may express themselves in various ways. Compulsions may arise, such as constant, washing of hands, often related to masturbation, or the endless recitation of prayers which sometimes occurs as a result of a child's deep anger toward parents.

The desire to avoid guilt feelings may also result in the "goody-goody" child, always righteous and always good, trying to live within the confines set up by his conscience.

Examples of common situations that may create excessive guilt in children include the following:

A child with sibling jealousy may wish his brother dead. The brother becomes extremely ill, and the child develops intense guilt feelings because of his destructive thoughts. A boy aged 4 or 5 secretly wishes that his father would go away so that he could have his mother all to himself. The parents divorce; the child feels responsible and is also afraid that his father will punish him by rejecting him completely. A child is caught masturbating by his parents. They scold him violently and make him feel that he has done something morally wrong as well as physically dangerous. Later the child will masturbate secretly, but will experience a deep sense of guilt which clings to him for a long time.

Fathers and mothers should guard against developing overly intense guilt feelings in a child. They should avoid being too strict or too punitive or constantly telling the youngster, "You ought to be ashamed of yourself"—that is, telling the child he ought to feel guilty. And, above all, parents should never make a child feel that he is unloved because of something he has done. They can strongly express disapproval, but they should explain why they disapprove.

See also **Anxiety.**

Gum   see **Candy and chewing gum.**

Gum boil

A localized abscess of the gum caused by an infection beneath it. The infection is almost always the indication of a dead tooth: the death of the nerve causes an inflammatory reaction in the bony socket of the jaw in which the tooth lies. An abscess results, and it works its way to the surface.

The abscess may be easily seen on a dental X-ray. Affected baby teeth are usually extracted, but permanent teeth are generally treated by root-canal work and filling plus the use of antibiotics.

The abscess usually subsides quickly once the source of the infection is removed.

Guns   see **Accident prevention, indoors; Toys and violence.**

H

Habit spasms   see **Tics.**

Hair, excess

Many newborn infants have a covering of fine hair over their bodies. This hair is often of concern to parents, especially when it is fairly evident on the forehead and the sides of the baby's face, but it falls out in the first few weeks of life.

Otherwise, marked hairiness of the body before puberty is rare and should be brought to the attention of the child's doctor. He will ascertain if there is any glandular cause for the condition.

Adolescent girls often complain of the hair on their arms and legs, even if the amount is so slight as to be hardly noticeable. Occasionally they may also complain of the fine hair on their faces. This may be justified if there is dark hair on the upper lip.

Probably the best treatment is the use of bleaching peroxide, but many girls are dissatisfied because the hair remains.

Depilatories which chemically burn hair from the skin should generally be avoided, since adolescent skin is still sensitive and may react violently with severe irritation.

If hair must be removed from the legs or arms, the use of an electric razor is best and is least irritating. Disfiguring hairs on the face may be removed by electrolysis performed by an expert.

Hair, pulling out

The habit of pulling out hair, like nail-biting, is usually a sign that the child is under some emotional strain. A tense youngster may twirl a strand of hair around a finger until the hair is pulled out.

No one is absolutely certain just why a child under tension should pull out his hair. The habit arises typically between the ages of 2 and 5 years, and some psychiatrists feel that it is a reversion to infancy—the most secure period in the child's life, when a baby held in its mother's arms felt or stroked her hair. This may be true, for a good many children who suck their thumbs pull their hair at the same time—as in infancy, when they nursed and felt their mother's hair at the same time.

There can be any number of reasons why a child might be under tension. There may be a feeling of jealousy of a younger brother or sister, or strife between a father and mother. It is important to carefully investigate the emotional state of a child who habitually pulls out his hair.

For treatment, scolding and punishing are of no value. This will make the child more tense and upset. Essentially the underlying cause of nervousness must be resolved. However, there are a couple of tricks that will usually help to overcome the habit: giving the child a sailor hat, beanie, or any popular hat, to wear at most times; and rubbing Vaseline on the hair, which makes the hair slip from the child's grasp.

See also **Baldness.**

Hair or wool, swallowed

At times young children develop the habit of swallowing their own hair or wool from toy animals, dolls, blankets, brushes, fur, or coats.

Most of the hair is passed through the intestines and excreted, but when the habit persists, a hairball may form in the stomach. There may be few symptoms at first, but later there usually is indigestion and upper abdominal pain. The mass can be easily seen on special X-ray examination. It must be removed surgically, for if it passes into the intestines, it may cause an obstruction.

Hair washing

Washing the hair of an infant or child should be no problem as long as soap is not allowed to irritate the child's eyes. This can be accomplished in various ways.

A shampoo hat helps to keep soap out of the baby's eyes.

The primary approach is through the use of baby shampoos that will not sting the eyes. Among the better shampoos of this type are Breck Children's Shampoo; Johnson's Baby Shampoo; Avon Baby Shampoo; and Korval Baby Shampoo (obtainable only at Korvette stores).

A further aid is a shampoo hat, which is simply a broad brim that surrounds the child's head and fits tightly, preventing soap from oozing through or dripping down into the eyes.

For older children who are fearful of shampoos, the wearing of snorkel masks during the procedure usually helps, keeping the soap out of their eyes and nose at the same time.

A baby's hair may be washed everyday during the bath. Later, when the child is older, shampooing once a week is usually adequate. Teen-agers should wash their hair twice a week, because the oil glands are more active at this age.

Haircut

Unless handled carefully, haircutting may be very upsetting to young children, especially if done by a stranger. A person approaches the child with a snipping pair of scissors and starts cutting away something that is part of the child.

During the early years—that is, the first two or two and a half years—it is better if the child's hair is cut by the mother. When the child is old enough, he or she can be taken to a parent's barbershop or beauty parlor to watch hair being cut and have the process explained. If possible, a child should also see other children having haircuts.

Select a barber or hair stylist who is relaxed and enjoys children. There are special children's barbershops or hairstyling shops in many cities. Often the child is given a small toy or candy when the haircut is over. In addition, parents often make the affair a happy one by taking the child out afterward for ice cream.

Halitosis   see **Bad breath.**

Halloween safety
Halloween is one of the most exciting and enjoyable of all childhood holidays. At the same time it offers certain potential dangers against which all parents must guard.

Some of the important safety rules for this holiday are the following:

1. Young children going out to "trick or treat" should always be accompanied by a parent or other responsible person.
2. Children going out in costumes after dark should not wear entirely black clothing. Too many children are run down by autos each Halloween because the drivers of cars did not see them. Reflecting material can be used, or reflectors pinned to the costumes.
3. Masks should have ample spaces for the eyes and should be adjusted so that they cannot slide down and cover the eyes.
4. Costumes should be of flame-retardant material. (See **Flammable clothing and bedding.**)
5. Children should not carry jack-o-lanterns with candles in them. These are potentially very dangerous. Electric lamps can be substituted.
6. Children should be ordered not to run across streets and not to go in dark areas and alleyways. They should stay in their own neighborhood and return home at an early hour.
7. Where people live in private houses, the porch lights should be kept on to aid in lighting up the street.

Hallucination
An apparent perception, especially a sound or a sight, for which there is no real physical or factual basis. Hallucinations are extremely rare in children, usually occurring only when children have high fevers.

However, children with schizophrenia often have visual or auditory hallucinations. These children usually live in a world of their own in which, for example, they hear voices telling them to do certain things, see their own bodies taking different shapes, or see animals crawling over them. These hallucinatory symptoms may occur in early childhood but usually appear during adolescence. Intensive medical and psychological treatment is required. (See **Schizophrenia.**)

Adolescents who take hallucinatory drugs may suffer from hallucinations, sometimes after the drug has apparently worn off. (See **Drug abuse.**)

Handedness
Numerous studies have indicated that whether a child is right-handed or left-handed is determined primarily by heredity. Environment is apparently a strong but secondary factor. There is considerable feeling among doctors that handedness is determined by a specific center in the brain—and that it is genetically determined.

Careful observation of infants' hand activity can usually detect the child's handedness. But handedness is not obvious until later, for most children are ambidextrous until about 2 or 3 years (or even 4 or 5). Then use of the dominant hand emerges.

There have been numerous methods suggested to test a child's handedness, but simple tests at home might include the following: which hand does a child use for cleaning a blackboard with a blackboard eraser, winding a clock, picking up an object from the floor, hammering a peg or a nail, drawing, cutting paper with scissors, throwing a ball?

Surveys of schoolchildren have revealed that approximately 6 to 8 percent write with the left hand.

Most doctors and workers in the field of child development believe that if a child shows a strong tendency to use the left hand, no real effort should be made to change him to right-handedness. Some advocate training a child who is ambidextrous or weakly left-handed to the use of the right hand, since this is a right-handed world with writing equipment, table settings, musical instruments, and sports equipment all designed for right-hand use.

It has been found that most of the children who habitually tend to mirror-write are really left-handed children who have been trained to write with the right hand.

At one time it was felt that stuttering might be induced in a child by changing his handedness. But the feeling now is that the stuttering comes about because of pressures from the parent that keep the child under tension.

The child who is definitely left-handed should be permitted to remain left-handed but will need special help in writing, in the use of tools and sports equipment, and in certain games of skill. But in certain sports, such as baseball and tennis, left-handedness is often an asset.

Handicapped child see **Blindness; Camps for the handicapped; Crippled child, helping the; Deafness.**

Hands, washing see **Washing the hands.**

Harelip

The upper lip of the embryo in its early weeks is divided into three segments—one beneath the nose and one on either side. Under normal conditions these segments join together and fuse between the sixth and seventh week of pregnancy.

A failure of fusion results in a cleft lip, better known as a harelip. The cleft may be only a small notch or line, or it may be so pronounced as to be a complete separation extending up and into the nostril. The harelip may involve only one side or both sides. When it is marked, the nose is pulled down and flattened. Frequently a harelip is combined with a cleft palate.

The causes of this harelip deformity are not fully known. It is probable that some infection or drug taken by the mother between the sixth and seventh week of pregnancy may stop the fusion at its normal time. This concept is held because the harelip is so often associated with other congenital abnormalities. But there is also evidence that the condition may occasionally be hereditary, since at times it occurs in successive generations and in brothers and sisters.

Treatment is surgical operation, preferably by a plastic surgeon. This is usually performed in the first few weeks of life. The cleft is stitched together and held together further with adhesive tape on the surface. Until the edges have grown together (approximately 2 weeks) the infant is fed by a dropper. If necessary, a secondary operation may be performed at 2 to 3 years. The results are usually excellent.

See also **Cleft palate.**

Harness

Bands of leather, plastic, or thick cloth

that fit over a child's shoulders and around his waist to assure his safety.

Harnesses may also be attached to carriages and strollers, and should be used when the baby is becoming active but is not yet coordinated enough to avoid falling out.

Another common harness is that used when a baby is learning to walk, or in the early toddler months. This harness has reins which an adult can hold to give the baby support and prevent him from falling when he is learning to walk. It is also of great value in preventing a toddler from running into the street when he is learning to stay on the sidewalks and not to cross the streets without an adult holding his hand.

It should always be remembered that a harness is to be used only as a safety device and never as restrictive punishment.

Hashish see **Drug abuse.**

Hate

All people hate at one time or another. During childhood and adolescence hate is normally experienced from time to time.

To the young child, hate is usually a temporary emotion. A child may hate another child, often a brother or sister, who in his mind is receiving most of the parents' attention or is better favored. Hatred may also be expressed against a child or adult who prevents a youngster from doing or attaining what he desires. But in most instances this emotion is not sustained.

Adults should remember that when a young child says, "I hate you", he is expressing aloud a momentary feeling. Usually he will be friendly and loving very soon after the temporary cause of his upset has passed. As a matter of fact, it is much better for the child to express his feelings freely than keep them within him as an under-the-surface disturbance.

Hatred may be deeper and longer-lasting in adolescence. If a teen-ager expresses feelings of hate, parents should talk this over with him. If the emotion is too violent, therapy may be indicated.

See also **Anger.**

Hay fever

An allergic reaction of the mucous membranes of the nose and eyes, which affects susceptible children and adults during the spring and summer months. It is due, as a rule, to the action of pollens of timothy, ragweed, and, to a lesser degree, plantain on the sensitive mucous membranes.

Ragweed.

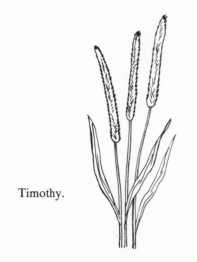

Timothy.

The other method is a scratch test. A drop of the pollen solution is placed on the surface of the skin and a scratch made through it. A white irregular border around the scratch in ten to fifteen minutes indicates that the child is highly sensitive to the specific pollen.

Treatment This varies with the severity of the symptoms. Mild and moderate cases of hay fever will usually respond to treatment with antihistamines by mouth. In more severe cases the child may be given a series of injections of the pollen solution starting months before the season. The child is given gradually increasing amounts of the extract so that he builds up a toleration for the pollen and is able to withstand its effects during the season. A recent and successful approach to the treatment of hayfever is by a single injection of a slowly absorbed pollen solution which lasts throughout the hay-fever season.

At the present time there is no cure for hay fever.

Parents of children with hay fever often want to find areas where they can spend the summer free of the irritating pollens. There are pollen-free vacation spots and camps located in most states. Many of the state health departments will send this information, or you can write to the American Academy of Allergy, 756 North Milwaukee Street, Milwaukee, Wisconsin, for a free copy of the brochure "Hay Fever Holiday" by O. C. Durham.

The agent causing hay fever can be tentatively diagnosed according to the season during which the child is affected. The pollens of trees are in the air in late April and May. The pollens of timothy and plantain are given off from approximately May 15 until July 15. Ragweed pollen is spread from about August 15 to the first frost.

Signs and symptoms Susceptible children during their period of sensitivity to the pollen in the air react by sniffling and sneezing, and usually by a clogging of the nose when they lie down. Frequently there is also an itching, burning, and irritation of the eyes. These symptoms may be mild or very severe.

Diagnosis Diagnosis is very simple, practically painless, and takes ten or fifteen minutes. There are two common tests. The first, and most accurate, is by injecting a tiny amount of a liquid extract of the pollen into the outer layer of the skin, usually of the upper arm. If a child is sensitive to the pollen, a white irregular welt appears at the site of the injection in ten to fifteen minutes.

Head, flattening of
During the first few months of life an infant may habitually sleep on only one side of the head. This causes a flattening of the skull on that side, since the skull bones are still fairly soft.

The flattening is easily remedied, using the fact that the infant of about 3 months and older wants to see what is going on in the room while he is awake. Either have the infant sleep with his head at the foot of the crib, or turn the crib completely around so that the infant in his usual lying position faces the wall. In either position he will turn his head and lie on the other side. The head usually becomes symmetrical again in a few months.

Head banging see **Crib rocking; Temper and temper tantrums.**

Head injuries
Head injuries during infancy and childhood are fairly common, ranging from simple lacerations of the scalp to concussion (a shock to the brain), and even to fracture of the skull or a tearing of blood vessels beneath the skull or in the brain matter.

Head injuries may be sustained by an infant during birth, especially when the actual birth has been difficult and forceps have been used. Usually such an injury will be diagnosed when a baby is still in the maternity nursery, and treatment will be instituted.

But in the course of infancy and the childhood years, there are occasions when a child's head may be injured.

Scalp wounds   These are usually very bloody but are rarely serious. Bleeding can generally be controlled by direct pressure on the cut with sterile gauze pads for at least three minutes. Scalp wounds usually gape and unless small may require one or more stitches. These wounds usually heal very quickly. (See **Cuts.**)

Concussions   If a child strikes his head in a fall or is hit on the head by a hard object, he may lose consciousness momentarily—probably for five to ten seconds. This is caused by a shock to the brain. He may later vomit, feel dizzy, and have a headache, also because of the shock to the brain. The doctor cannot tell without an X ray if the skull has been fractured. It is always of great importance to distinguish between a concussion and a fracture of the skull, since the cause is the same and the immediate signs and symptoms may be the same. However, if no further symptoms occur except the unconscious spell followed by one attack of vomiting, many doctors feel that an X ray of the skull is not indicated unless vomiting continues or the child develops deepening drowsiness. Treatment of concussion is complete rest until all symptoms have subsided, followed by several days of low activity.

All but the most minor shocks to the head should be reported to the doctor.

Fracture of the skull   Continued vomiting and deepening drowsiness after a blow on the head are signs of increased pressure on the brain due to bleeding of torn blood vessels or to pressure of a broken, depressed skull bone. An X ray is definitely indicated, and if a fracture is seen, the child should be placed under the care of a neurosurgeon. Fractures of the skull with pressure on the brain may be extremely serious if not treated early enough.

Head lice

Infestation of the hair and scalp by lice (pediculosis, from the name of the genus, *Pediculus*) is common among children, especially those of school age. The head louse is a tiny, crablike louse which causes severe itching of the scalp. The child scratches a great deal, which usually produces an infection of the skin.

Louse (actual size in circle).

You can occasionally see the lice, but you are more likely to find their little pearly-white eggs (nits) attached to—really glued to—the hairs. To the naked eye they look like dandruff, but through a magnifying glass they appear oval and white or gray, and they cannot be combed out.

Children pick up lice by direct contact—from the hair of other children when their heads are close together, by lying on a mat or cot that another child with head lice has recently used, or by sharing hairbrushes and combs.

Treatment   This consists of killing both the lice and their eggs. One of the most effective and rapid treatments is by the use of Kwell (gamma benzine hexachloride) shampoo. This is a four-minute treatment. The hair is wet with warm water and then about one ounce of the shampoo is lathered in for a full four minutes. Then the hair is rinsed thoroughly and dried with a towel. If necessary, a second and similar treatment may be given in twenty-four hours, but no more than two treatments should be given in any week.

Another successful treatment is the use of crude petroleum oil, either pure or mixed with an equal quantity of olive oil. It is thoroughly applied to the scalp for one or two nights, followed each morning by a shampoo with tincture of green soap or just with plain soap and water.

Head nodding

Involuntary nodding of the head accompanied by side-to-side eye movements; the movements stop when the infant sleeps or when his eyes are covered. It is fairly rare, usually occurring between the ages of 4 and 12 months and disappearing completely after a few months. Occasionally there is a temporary recurrence, perhaps during the second year. Its cause is unknown. It is not related to the intelligence of the child; it is more often observed in malnourished children than in healthy ones. There is no specific treatment and no need for the use of drugs. Once it subsides it leaves no disability of any kind.

Head wedging

Every so often a child gets his head wedged between the iron bars of a railing or between the bars of a playpen or crib.

Remember that the head of a small child is the widest part of his body, and if his head goes through, the rest of his body can go through also. Tell the child to walk through sideways or to manipulate the rest of his body through. This is, as a rule, easily accomplished. Occasionally the bar must be removed if the child is too large to pass through the space.

For safety's sake it is important to see that the slats of a crib or playpen are so close that neither the child's body nor his head can slide through—no more than 3½ inches apart.

See also **Crib; Playpen.**

Headache

Headaches are far more common in children than most people believe—and undoubtedly occur from infancy right up through adult life.

The causes are generally the same as for adults, with the greater number related to emotional tension. Such tension is at times due to anxieties and unhappiness, while at other times it may be due to simple excitement about going to school or even to a birthday party.

You should never consider a headache to be due to emotional causes unless all physical causes have been ruled out. The diagnosis should be under a doctor's supervision.

Among the many possible causes which a doctor considers are eyestrain, migraine, sinusitis, high blood pressure, infections, kidney conditions, and brain disorders, which are rare but which many parents consider first.

The diagnosis of the cause of frequent headaches should always be made by a doctor, but a few pointers may be of interest to parents. If a child complains of headaches on school days but not on weekends or holidays, the headaches are probably due to tension or eyestrain. This does not necessarily mean that the child dislikes school, but it does suggest that school makes him tense. If headaches occur only in the late afternoon or after viewing television, they may be caused by some form of eyestrain or other eye trouble. If headaches are one-sided, they may be caused by migraine or sinusitis.

You may give the child aspirin to relieve a headache, but remember that the headache is the symptom of a condition for which the cause should be sought.

See also **Eye defects; Lighting; Migraine headache.**

Hearing   see **Deafness.**

Hearing aids   see **Deafness.**

Heart

The muscular organ which pumps blood to all parts of the body.

The heart starts beating when an embryo is less than one month old—that is, less than one month after conception. In the newborn child the heart usually beats between 120 and 140 times per minute. This gradually slows down so that by the time a child is 2 to 3 years old, the beat is approximately 70 to 85 times per minute, a rate that generally continues throughout life.

1. Schematic drawing of circulatory system (stripes, blue blood; dots, red blood): The blue blood, which has given up oxygen for carbon dioxide in the body (g), enters the right auricle (a) of the heart (f); it flows through a valve into the right ventricle (c), and is then pumped to the lungs (e). In the lungs it gives up carbon dioxide and picks up oxygen, becoming red again. It is returned to the heart (f) and enters the left auricle (b); it then flows through a valve into the left ventricle (d), and from there it is pumped to all parts of the body (g). In the body, the blood gives up oxygen, becoming blue again, and is returned to the heart.

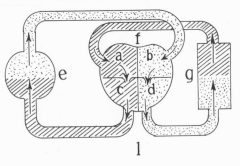

1

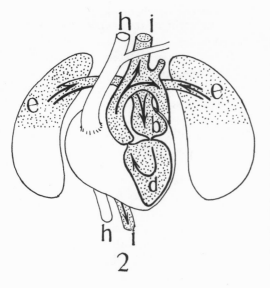

2. Circulation of red blood: From the lungs (e), red blood enters the left auricle (b), flows to the left ventricle (d) and is pumped through the great aorta (i) to the body.

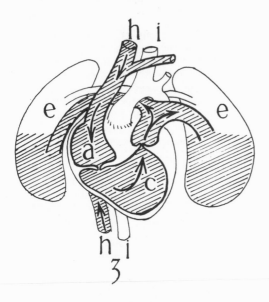

3. Circulation of blue blood: Returning from the body, blue blood flows through the vena cava (h) into the right auricle (a). From there it flows into the right ventricle (c), and is then pumped to the lungs (e).

The heart is divided into two sides by a muscular wall, the septum. The right side of the heart receives the blood which returns from the cells of the body. This blood, because it contains little oxygen, is colored bluish and is often termed "blue blood." It contains waste products from the cells.

When the heart contracts, it pumps this blue blood from the right side of the heart to the lungs, where it gives up carbon dioxide (waste gas from the cells) and takes on oxygen, becoming bright red ("red blood"). This red blood is returned to the left side of the heart, from which it is pumped out through the arteries to all parts of the body.

Heart, congenital abnormalities of

The heart is a complex organ and in the course of its embryological development may occasionally not develop normally, leading to defects in anatomy and function after the baby is born.

Fortunately many if not most of these defects can be permanently corrected by modern cardiac surgery.

Among the congenital cardiac abnormalities are such conditions as openings in the wall separating the two sides of the heart; a narrowing of the opening of the heart into one of the large blood vessels; a right-sided heart; and a mixup of the large blood vessels so that the blood from the body returns to the wrong side (left side) of the heart and the blood with inadequate oxygen is pumped out to the body from the right side.

The signs and symptoms of these congenital abnormalities vary greatly depending on the specific condition. They may vary from a simple murmur, with no outward or other symptoms, to blueness of the child caused by a lack of sufficient oxygen in the blood.

Diagnosis of the exact abnormality is made by electrocardiograms, cardiac catheterization, and X rays.

Parents who cannot afford the high cost of a cardiac operation should turn to the Crippled Children's Service in their state for assistance. They may also write for information to the American Heart Association, 44 East 23d Street, New York, N.Y. 10010.

See also **Blue baby; Heart murmur.**

Heart disease

Any dysfunction of the heart acquired after a child is born. Heart disease is fortunately quite rare in infancy and childhood, thanks to modern antibiotics.

Heart disease following rheumatic fever is due to the effects of poisons of the streptococcus bacteria. Since streptococcus sore throats are now so frequently treated with penicillin, there has been much less of this type of heart disease.

One other type of heart disease that may affect children, caused by a different type of streptococcus (streptococcus viridans), is called subacute bacterial endocarditis. This is a chronic condition in which the bacteria cause clots of blood to form in the inner lining of the heart. These clots break off and are carried by the blood to small capillaries, where they lodge and cut off the blood supply. The condition can be successfully treated by massive doses of penicillin.

See also **Rheumatic fever.**

Heart murmur

Many parents are told by the doctor that their child has a heart murmur. The term is frightening. But most murmurs are not signs of a serious condition. As a matter of fact, approximately 65 percent

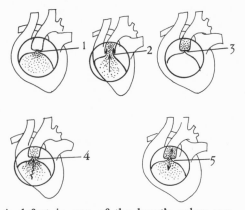

A defect in one of the heart's valves can cause a heart murmur. 1. The valve between the left ventricle and the great aorta in the normal closed position. 2. The valve in the normal open position as the ventricle contracts, allowing a free flow of blood from the ventricle through the aorta. 3. The valve in the normal closed position after the blood has been pumped out. 4. A defective valve that has not opened completely when the heart contracts, causing a back up of blood. 5. A defective valve that has not closed completely after the ventricle contracts, allowing some of the blood to flow back from the aorta into the ventricle.

of all children have a murmur at some time or other during their childhood.

There are essentially three types of heart murmurs. First, there are murmurs caused by heart defects originating before a baby is born. These are the murmurs of congenital heart defects in which the heart is not formed normally. Such defects can often be treated successfully through surgery.

Then there are the murmurs following infections. These are usually due to damage to the heart by the bacteria and their poisons. Rheumatic fever is the most common condition causing such a murmur. Murmurs of this sort have become much less common in recent years, thanks to the use of antibiotics.

The third and most common type are the so-called functional murmurs. These are of no significance. A murmur of this type may remain constantly with a child or adult, or may be heard only at certain times, especially when a child has a fever.

A mumur of the more serious type is the sound of flowing blood heard when there is an abnormality of the valves of the heart, an opening in the wall separating the two sides of the heart, or a defect in the arteries and veins leading from the heart.

Usually, when a doctor listens to a normal heart, he hears the sounds "lub-dup, lub-dup," each sound clearly defined as the various heart valves close. If a valve cannot close completely, the flow of blood through the opening causes a rushing sound, heard perhaps as "lub-duf-f-f-f, lub-duf-f-f-f." This rushing sound is called a mumur.

When there is an opening in the dividing wall of the heart, the blood flows back and forth through the opening as the heart contracts and expands, and this abnormal flow can be heard by the doctor as a to-and-fro murmur.

Diagnosis   The particular type of murmur can usually be diagnosed accurately. X rays and the electrocardiogram give a fair amount of information, although far from complete. Two new methods are fully diagnostic: cardiac catheterization and the angiogram.

During catheterization a fine tube is inserted into a vein in the arm and pushed forward until it enters the heart. Tests of oxygen from the various chambers of the heart can indicate if there is a leak or if the valves are imperfect. The angiogram is a test in which a dye is injected into the bloodstream and X rays are taken quickly as it passes through the heart. A leaking or tight valve, an opening in the wall separating the two sides of the heart, or a defective formation of the heart can usually be easily seen.

Treatment   The serious conditions that cause murmurs of the heart can usually be corrected by modern cardiac surgery.

The doctor will determine how much activity should be permitted to a child with a heart murmur. If he diagnoses the murmur as functional and concludes that no restriction is necessary, the parents should abide by his decision. Too many parents, in their anxiety, tend to unnecessarily restrict a child from sports and vigorous exercise and to give him extra rest. This is not at all required. The child should be treated as normal. Many boys and girls with functional murmurs have entered fully into the most vigorous sports, such as basketball, tennis, football, and prizefighting.

Heartbeat, rapid   see **Tachycardia, paroxysmal.**

Heat exhaustion
A disturbance of the body caused by an excessive loss of salt and fluid from sweating during extreme heat.

The symptoms, which are quite sudden, usually follow exposure to intense heat with a high degree of humidity. They start with general malaise and lassitude, headache, dizziness, and profuse perspiration and end with skin pallor and a general collapse. The skin is cold and clammy; pulse and respirations are rapid.

In severe attacks there may be delirium, unconsciousness, or convulsions.

Treatment   Remove the child to the

coolest and shadiest place possible in the vicinity and give him cold water with ½ teaspoon of salt for 8 ounces of water. He may not feel like taking much at first, but urge him to drink as much as he can.

Apply cold compresses to the forehead, neck, and chest.

Treatment should be under the direction of a doctor. He can advise for such possible complications as convulsions and delirium.

Prevention In hot, humid weather, it is always advisable to see that a child takes plenty of fluids, and also salty foods such as pretzels.

Heat stroke see **Sunstroke.**

Height
The height of a normally healthy child is largely related to family background. But although height is genetically determined, it is influenced by the total genetic inheritance more than the actual height of each parent. Short parents are much more likely to have short children than are tall parents, and vice versa. But environment, nutrition, and general health also affect height, and the vast majority of tall and short children of tall and short parents tend to reach average or normal height rather than to be shorter than short parents or taller than tall parents. Adult height can't be predicted from the height of a baby.

Many small children don't develop a growth spurt until they reach adolescence—at times as late as 14 or 15—and many tall children have a slowdown in their rate of growth after puberty that brings them nearer the heights of their contemporaries.

Occasionally a person's height is the result of an abnormal condition. This is comparatively rare. Among medical reasons for stunted growth are poor nutrition, either from a lack of food during the rapid growth periods of childhood or from an inability to digest foods properly, as in celiac disease. Chronic infections, such as are found in cystic fibrosis and bronchiectasis, are likely to slow a child's growth rate. And on rare occasions abnormal tallness is caused by disorder of either the pituitary gland or thyroid gland. (See **Dwarfism; Gigantism; Puberty, precocious.**)

Shortness Before puberty, most short children adjust fairly well to their size, but parents are often concerned when a boy is the shortest in his class or among his companions; they may unnecessarily upset the child by showing anxiety over his shortness. But as a child approaches adolescence and his friends become much taller, he, too, becomes concerned and often upset, and he needs reassurance. He should have the assurance of his doctor that he is entirely normal, that boys and girls go into their preadolescent and adolescent growth spurts at different times, and that a boy who develops his growth spurt at 15 is just as masculine as one who starts to develop at 12, just as a girl is equally feminine whether her growth spurt begins at 11 or 15.

If boys of 14 or 15 are very upset because of their small size, it may be suggested that they be given treatment with male sex hormones, which will push them into puberty in a few months. This will make the boy grow taller rapidly, but he will not grow taller than he would have grown without the impetus of the extra hormones. As a matter of fact, some doctors question whether boys forced into puberty by means of sex hormones might not eventually be a little bit shorter than they could have been. This has not been proven. Any hormone treatment should be under the careful supervision of the doctor.

It is not so easy to push a girl into puberty, since the hormone treatment might upset her whole glandular system.

Within recent years the human growth hormone has been obtained from the human pituitary gland and used quite effectively to increase the height of children who were excessively small for one reason or another. At present the use is experimental and very expensive. However, the production of a synthetic growth hormone has been reported, and it will probably be available in the future.

It is one thing to reassure a child that he or she is growing normally for his or her background, that Father, Mother, or some other member of the family grew the same way. But it is another thing for a small child to try to compete with taller, more developed children. Many small children refrain from sports and other physical activities because they feel inadequate. This is true of girls as well as boys. Even though the problem is usually less troublesome, a small girl doesn't enjoy being treated as the pipsqueak of the class, being at a disadvantage in games, or constantly having people think she is a year or two younger than her age.

In such situations it is important for the parents to do all they can to make the child feel accepted and admired by his or her friends. A small child can be taught to excel in one phase of a sport—for example, a boy can be taught pitching or catching—so that he is desired by others as a member of their team. Often skilled baseball players from nearby schools or colleges may be hired to spend one or two afternoons a week teaching the boy the finer points of the game. Or a child can be taught to be an excellent swimmer or tennis player—or even to excel at the harmonica or the guitar. The reassurance the child obtains from this help will usually carry over into adolescence.

Tallness An unusually tall boy may feel awkward at times, but as a rule he will find his height an advantage. But a noticeably tall girl is often of considerable concern to her parents, and often the girl herself is worried.

"When will she stop growing?" parents so often ask, and "How tall will she be when she's fully grown?"

The answer depends largely on what age the child is when she is abnormally tall. There is a rapid spurt of growth when girls approach puberty, but once they have had their menstrual period, the growth in height slows down rather quickly.

This accounts for the fact that girls who have their first menstrual periods at 10 years are often a head taller than the other girls in their class. But they stop growing much sooner, so that by the age of 13 or 14 the other girls catch up, and by age 15 they are often shorter than any of their classmates.

It is the girl who is extremely tall at 15 or 16 who is most apt to worry about her ultimate height. Here a great deal depends upon the height of her parents, plus whether or not she has developed her menstrual periods.

If she has not menstruated, a doctor can estimate, by examining her, when her menstrual period might develop.

There are methods of hastening the onset of menstruation by the use of hormones, but most endocrinologists hesitate to advise their use, since it might upset the whole glandular cycle.

If a girl is very tall, she should be encouraged to carry herself well and not stoop. It should be pointed out to her that many strikingly beautiful women, including many models, are taller than average, and she should be helped to appear at her best. Her parents should show pleasure in her the way she is, and under no circumstances should they express dissatisfaction with her height or joke about it.

Hemangioma   see Birthmarks.

Hemoglobin

The red coloring matter of blood cells, which absorbs oxygen from inhaled air and carries it to cells throughout the body.

A lack of adequate hemoglobin results in anemia.

See also Anemia.

Hemophilia

A hereditary condition, occurring only in males, in which there is almost uncontrolled bleeding from a simple cut, a nosebleed, or a bruise or fall (with bleeding under the skin or in a joint). Hemophilia is caused by an inadequate amount of factor VIII or factor IX, substances in the blood which are necessary for normal clotting.

Hemophilia cannot be cured, but generally can be successfully treated under the close supervision of a doctor.

A man with hemophilia does not transmit the disease to his son, but his daughter carries the tendency in her chromosomes and may transmit the disease to her son. The girl who transmits the disease shows no signs of it herself.

Usually the disease is not diagnosed until a child of toddler age has a fall and gets cut. In families with a male child in which a grandfather has had the condition, the family and its pediatrician should be on the alert.

Parents of a child with hemophilia should do everything in their power to prevent accidents which might cause bleeding. Furniture in the child's room should be padded with foam rubber, and the floor should be thickly carpeted or also covered with a layer of foam rubber. Toys with sharp edges or sharp points should be avoided. When boys get older they may participate in sports but should avoid those of violent contact, such as football, basketball, and baseball.

Superficial scrapes and small cuts may be controlled by local application of clotting substances used with a pressure bandage. Nosebleeds can usually be controlled by a firm packing, using the clotting substance. In the case of greater bleeding or if a nosebleed continues, the transfusion of blood plasma or one of the concentrates obtained from plasma is indicated. The routine immunizations against disease may usually be given with impunity, as the puncture wound is very tiny.

Treatment   The outlook for a boy with hemophilia today is excellent, and unless he is severely injured, he should usually be able to live, with proper medical care, as long as any other person. Since the hemophiliac's lifetime tendency to hemorrhage is due to a lack of adequate factor VIII or IX in his blood, the treatment consists of replacing these factors.

In the past treatment was limited to the use of blood plasma, which contained moderate amounts of these factors. Within recent years much more effective concentrates of factor VIII and of factor IX have been prepared from human blood. These concentrates stop bleeding rapidly and cause rapid healing of a bleeding area. In certain cases the concentrates have been given two or three times a week to protect against possible bleeding.

The drawback is that the concentrates are very expensive. In 1972 adequate replacement of factor VIII or factor IX in the purest concentration available cost from $10,000 to $20,000 annually, depending on the severity of the case. It is hoped that very soon a means will be found to make this medication available to all who need it.

Hepatitis, infectious

An inflammatory disease of the liver caused by a virus. Although it may be a serious disease in adults, it is rarely serious in children, and complete recovery almost always occurs within two months.

Source of infection   The virus is usually transmitted from the feces of an infected person. It gets on food or into water and enters the body through the mouth and gastrointestinal tract. Children and adults who are believed to have been exposed to the disease should receive an injection of gamma globulin. This gives protection lasting approximately four weeks.

Period of contagion   This has not been fully determined. The virus may be in a person's feces several weeks before the onset of symptoms, and it remains in the feces at least as long as the acute signs and symptoms last.

Incubation period   A susceptible person exposed to hepatitis may develop signs of the disease at any time from ten to forty days after exposure. The average onset occurs at about twenty-five days.

Signs and symptoms   At first, loss of appetite and general apathy and weakness. Then the infected person usually complains of pain in the right upper abdomen, followed by nausea and vomiting. The urine becomes dark-colored while the feces are very pale. Then jaundice appears, with the skin and whites of the eyes becoming noticeably yellowish.

Treatment   There is no specific treatment, but physical activity should be reduced and bed rest maintained during the active phase of the disease. A high-protein diet and adequate vitamins, especially B complex, are advised. In severe cases, which are rare in children, cortisone preparations are given.

Immunization   There is no vaccine available to protect against infectious hepatitis. However, children who are to travel in areas where hepatitis is prevalent should receive gamma globulin before going and every four weeks while possible exposure exists.

Heredity

The biological process by which physical and possibly some personality characteristics of parents (and their ancestors) are transmitted to their children (and their descendants).

Most of our physical characteristics are hereditary. The exceptions are variations in structure or function caused by prenatal or postnatal events such as infection or injury.

There is also evidence indicating that part of a person's temperament and per-

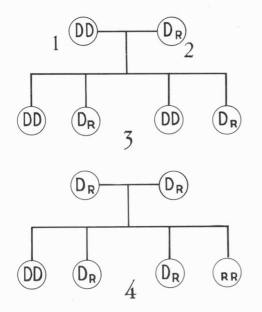

The chromosomes, when viewed through a microscope, look like tiny threads in varying shapes and sizes. There are twenty-three pairs of chromosomes (forty-six in all) in every cell of the human body with the exception of the sperm cell and the egg cell, each of which contains only twenty-three chromosomes.

Each chromosome, consists of tiny segments arranged like a string of beads. These segments are the genes, and there are thousands of them in each chromosome. It is the genes that determine all our inherited characteristics and traits.

Each gene has a specific quality for which it is responsible. For instance, there is a specific gene for hair color, another for hair curliness, another for thickness of hair. There is a gene for eye color, one for shape of the nose, another for broadness of muscles, and so on for all the features and parts of the body.

Every sperm produced by the father has its particular assortment of genes in each chromosome. It is almost impossible for any other sperm to have the same combination of genes, for all the many hundreds of thousands of inherited characteristics from parents, grandparents, and other forebears are carried by the genes. One sperm may carry the gene for red hair hair in its chromosome, while another may carry the the gene for black hair. A third may carry the gene for brown hair, and so on with all the inherited qualities.

The same is true for the genes of the of the egg cells produced by the mother. It is practically impossible for two egg cells ever to have the same combination of genes.

The genes are arranged in a definite order in the chromosomes. For example, a gene relating to eye color may be at the top of the chromosome thread, one

There are always four possible genetic combinations for matching pairs of genes from the sperm and egg cells. For example, if a person bearing a pair of matched dominant genes for a specific trait (1) marries a person bearing matched dominant and recessive genes for the same trait (2), there is a 50 percent probability that each child will carry the recessive gene (3). The recessive trait will not appear (because the dominant gene dominates), but it can be passed on to the next generation. When both parents bear a recessive gene for the same trait, there is a 75 percent probability that each child will inherit the recessive gene (4). However, there is only a 25 percent probability that the recessive trait will actually appear—this happens only when two recessive traits are matched together.

sonality may be inherited, although these personality factors are largely influenced and molded by environmental circumstances.

The basic elements which control heredity are found in microscopic particles, the chromosomes and genes, in the egg cells of women and the sperm cells of men.

for the shape of the nose may be in the center, and one for the color of hair at the bottom.

During the process of reproduction the sperm cell of the father, carrying twenty-three chromosomes, enters the egg cell of the mother, also carrying twenty-three chromosomes. Now there are forty-six matched chromosomes— half of which bear the qualities of the father, and half those of the mother.

And then a fascinating sequence follows. A specific chromosome of a particular shape and size in the sperm cell seeks out a chromosome of a similar shape and size in the egg cell. The like chromosomes line up next to one another, with the like genes side by side. The gene for color of eyes of the father's sperm lies next to the gene for color of eyes of the mother's egg, and so on with the father's genes for each particular quality—they lie next to similar genes of the mother.

Some genes are stronger than others and are known as *dominant* genes. Some genes are weaker and are known as *recessive* genes. There are also some genes that are partly dominant or partly recessive.

When a specific gene of a father meets a similar gene of a mother, they combine. The resulting characteristic of the child will depend on the dominant-recessive relationship. For example, a dark-brown-eye gene is dominant over a pure-blue-eye gene, and if two genes meet, the child's eyes will be brown. If, however, a partly-brown-eye gene meets a partly-blue-eye gene, the child may have hazel eyes or some other combination of brown and blue mixtures. If two blue-eye genes meet, or two brown-eye genes, the child will have blue or brown eyes, respectively.

Since every human being carries in his cells the genes not only of his parents but of his close relatives and forebears as well, a child may have one or more qualities not evident in either of his parents. Thus, although two dark-haired parents will usually have a dark-haired child, they can have a child with light hair if both parents have close relatives who are light-haired.

A person carrying in his cells the recessive gene for a particular characteristic or for some hereditary disease will usually not show this characteristic or have the disease himself. Nor will any of his children develop the characteristic or disease unless the cells of his mate also contain these recessive genes. With both parents carrying the recessive genes, there is a 25 percent chance that any pregnancy might result in a child with this recessive characteristic or hereditary disease. This is the case in such recessive diseases as cystic fibrosis, Mediterranean anemia, sickle-cell anemia, and Tay-Sachs disease.

Through the modern knowledge of genetics parents can now receive information on their chances of having a child with some hereditary disease which has occurred at some time in the family background. For this reason, genetic counseling centers have been set up in many cities and communities throughout the United States and Canada.

See also **Genetic counseling** and **Appendix C: Genetic counseling services.**

Hermaphroditism

The condition of having both ovaries and testes which function. This is exceedingly rare.

More frequently seen but still uncommon are the so-called pseudohermaphrodites: children born with external genitals of both sexes. For instance, the child may appear to have a normal-sized penis and female genitals as well. In past years there was considerable difficulty in determining the sex of such a child unless an abdominal operation showed whether the child had ovaries or testes.

Today, using more advanced methods, physicians can tell the sex by the chromosomes in the child's body cells. The absolute knowledge of the child's sex gives direction to necessary reparative surgery and to guiding the child toward the sex role he should follow. In many cases the results of surgery and guidance are excellent and the child grows up to have a normal marriage and sex life.

Most of the female pseudohermaphrodites are able to have children. Most male pseudohermaphrodites are sterile.

Umbilical hernia: The balloon effect is caused by the intestines pushing outward (as shown in circle).

Hernia

The protrusion of intestines through an opening in the abdominal wall.

Hernias in infants and young children are very common, and every parent of a young child should know about them, for at times they can be extremely dangerous. There are two types of hernias frequently seen in children:

Umbilical hernia A protrusion that is forced through the region of the navel. As a rule it is not dangerous, but it is undesirable cosmetically. The smaller umbilical hernias seen in early infancy will usually disappear without treatment. Larger hernias, which balloon out on the abdomen, are usually strapped down by the doctor, and most of them will recede and finally disappear. Those that remain may require surgery to close the opening through which the intestinal

mass protrudes. If surgery is performed, parents should be sure that the surgeon leaves—or forms, by plastic surgery—a navel where one normally would be. There have been many instances in which surgeons have removed the navel completely, leaving just a straight scar in its place. Teen-agers and adults with such scars were usually upset by not having a navel, and many went for plastic surgery to have one made.

Inguinal hernia A protrusion through an opening in the wall of the abdomen, usually above the crease where the abdomen meets the thighs. It occurs more often in boys, usually during the first six months of life, and appears as a swelling or lump in the lower abdominal wall on either side. This type of hernia can be extremely dangerous, for intestines pushing through the opening beneath the skin sometimes get caught in a large mass outside the opening and cannot be pushed back. This is called a strangulated or incarcerated hernia and should be treated immediately. The danger is that the sides of the opening press tightly on the base of the herniated mass and may cut off the blood supply to the portion of intestine that has been forced through—and after some hours the intestinal tissue in the hernia begins to die.

Fortunately most inguinal hernias slide in and out of the opening easily; as long as this happens and the parent can push the hernia back without difficulty, there is no immediate danger. But there is still a serious potential danger, for a real strain on the child may force a great portion of the intestine through the opening in the abdominal wall, making it extremely difficult or impossible to force it back.

If it is difficult to push the hernia back, try holding the child upside down. This will often cause the protruding intestines to be pulled back into the abdomen, but if it doesn't work, place the child in a warm bath to relax the tissues, keep him calm, and gently push back the hernia mass. This is usually very successful. But if it can't be done, call the doctor immediately. If the doctor is unable to reduce the hernia, an emergency operation is necessary.

Trusses, formerly used to hold in hernias, are rarely used for children today, since the operation is simple, safe, and curative. The child usually stays in the hospital one or two nights at the most. (See **Hospitalization.**)

Hernia, diaphragmatic see **Diaphragm.**

Heroin see **Drug abuse.**

Herpes simplex see **Canker sores; Cold sores.**

Herpes zoster see **Shingles.**

Hexachlorophene
For many years hexachlorophene was a widely used antiseptic in soaps such as Phisohex, Dial Soap and Desitin Soap, and in various baby lotions and creams. In many nurseries for the newborn throughout the United States and Canada infants were routinely bathed in Phisohex to prevent skin infections.

In December 1971 the U.S. Food and Drug Administration and the American Academy of Pediatrics cited experimental studies showing that this drug could be absorbed through the skin, and that monkeys who were bathed in solutions containing hexachlorophene and rats who received it by mouth suffered brain damage. It was further demonstrated that human infants washed with hexachlorophene solutions and soaps absorbed the drug, although no harmful results were reported.

However, in view of the effects on the brain cells of monkeys and rats, the U.S. Food and Drug Administration and the American Academy of Pediatrics have advised against the use of this drug on the skin of infants.

It should be avoided in soaps, lotions, and creams for infants, children, and adolescents unless specifically ordered by a doctor.

Hiccups
Hiccups are caused by a spasm of the diaphragm, the large muscle of breathing between the chest and the abdomen.

They are extremely common in infants during their first few months of life, usually occur after a feeding, and are of no significance. They last only a short time and can generally be quickly relieved by giving the baby warm water.

Hiccups occasionally occur in older children and if troublesome can usually be treated by having the child hold his breath as long as possible or breathe in and out of a closed paper bag while the nostrils are held together.

High chair

After a baby's back is strong enough for him to sit with ease, approximately at age 6 months, a high chair may be used for feeding.

This chair should be sturdy, with weighted, spread-out legs, so that it is impossible for the child to topple it over. There should also be a safety strap to hold the baby securely so he does not slide down and under the tray, or later stand up in the seat. A high chair also should have an adjustable footrest.

There are also low feeding tables with chairs, adjustable in height from about 20 to 30 inches above the floor. These tables have one advantage over high chairs in being low, in the child's own sphere; they also may be raised to the level of the dining table so that at times the child can sit and eat with the other members of the family.

Hip, congenital dislocation of

This is a condition occasionally found in newborns, in which the thighbone does not fit perfectly into the hip socket. It occurs seven times more often in boys. It can almost always be diagnosed by careful examination shortly after the baby is born. There are a number of signs that lead to this diagnosis, one of which is that the buttock creases (at the top of the legs and below the buttocks) are not on a line with one another. An X ray of the hips will produce definite diagnosis if such a dislocation is present.

Causes   The dislocation may have various causes: embryological maldevelopment of the hip during a mother's first three months of pregnancy; a poor position of the baby in the uterus during the last six months of pregnancy; hereditary factors which apparently play an important role, since the condition frequently runs in families.

Treatment   This should be under the supervision of an orthopedist. If the dislocation is recognized early, the legs are moved into position by manipulation and held in place, in a frog-legged position, by a plaster cast for several months. Usually excellent results are obtained by this treatment and the child walks normally. If the dislocation is diagnosed only when a child is learning to walk or later, surgical treatment is necessary, and is usually quite successful.

Hirschsprung's disease   see **Colon, enlargement of.**

Hitchhiking

In the 1960s and 1970s there has been an increase in the popularity of hitchhiking among young adolescents. It is not safe to hitchhike or to pick up hitchhikers. Too many young girls and boys have been the victims of sexual assaults and robberies in connection with hitchhiking. In some cases, however, parents may find it virtually impossible to enforce rules against hitchhiking, and they should then concentrate on minimal safety rules. No one alone, and especially no girl who is alone, should pick up a hitchhiker. The fact that the hitchhiker may look just like one of the driver's school friends in dress and style of hair does not mean that he or she could not be dangerous. It is better to hitchhike in pairs or threes than alone, and girls should never hitchhike alone or without male company.

Parents should also point out to their teen-agers that most states have laws against hitchhiking.

Hitting   see **Biting, kicking, pushing, hitting.**

Hives

Also called urticaria. An allergic reaction of the skin characterized by one or more itching wheals—slightly raised irregular pale patches of the skin. A rare type of hives is pimply hives (papular urticaria), which appears generally in young children and in which hard pimples appear, usually on the arms, legs, and face.

Causes   In children hives are usually caused by some food to which they are allergic. The hives may appear whenever the child eats a particular food or if he eats more than a certain amount of that food.

Hives may also appear during gastrointestinal upsets, probably because the mucous membrane of the intestine is temporarily weakened and absorbs more of a certain food substance than normally.

Perforation of the skin by irritating substances, such as those produced by the stings of nettles, jellyfish, and wasps or bees, may also cause hives.

Certain medicines may cause hives in children who are sensitive to them. Most frequent among these are penicillin, aspirin, barbiturates, and certain cough medicines.

Treatment   Prompt treatment with antihistamines usually brings effective relief. Benadryl (diphenhydramine hydrochloride) and Chlor-trimeton (chlorpheniramine) are commonly used. This treatment may have to be continued for several days. An injection of Adrenalin (adrenaline or epinephrine) may be necessary to obtain immediate relief in severe cases.

Of course the primary treatment consists of removing or reducing the cause of the allergic reaction. This is not always a simple problem in the case of foods. One method is to list all foods eaten in the twenty four hours prior to the appearance of the hives. After such listings have been made in association with several attacks, a particular food may appear to be the cause. It should be given to the child to see if it is responsible for the reaction.

Hobbies

Almost all children enjoy a hobby, frequently switching from one to another. Popular hobbies include collecting dolls (especially in foreign costumes), miniature statues of animals, miniature knights and soldiers, stamps and coins, comic books and sea shells, constructing and painting boats and planes; miniature cars and trains; weaving, knitting, and embroidery; photography, chemistry, electronics, or working on cars.

Hobbies change as a child develops and his interests mature. Eventually he may find one particular hobby that absorbs him and gives him pleasure through the years. Many adults who collect stamps, coins, miniature glass animals, or dolls of the world as a hobby have their interest originally stimulated in this endeavor as children.

Hobbies should be encouraged by parents as far as is practical, for they satisfy a child's curiosity and need for self-expression and relaxation.

Hodgkin's disease

A chronic and at times fatal disease in which there is a progressive, painless enlargement of the lymph nodes in various parts of the body. It is a type of cancer, and the cause is unknown. Increasing numbers of cures have been reported in recent years.

Signs and symptoms   The first signs are usually a swelling of superficial lymph nodes, especially those in the neck. This is followed by enlargement of other nodes as well. At times the size of an enlarged node may be such as to press on a blood vessel, causing a marked swelling of the body where the proper drainage of blood has been blocked. At other times there may be pain when an enlarged node presses on a nerve. Pressure of nodes may also cause hoarseness and difficulty in breathing.

The child affected by this disease usually develops fatigue, loss of appetite, and a fluctuating fever.

Diagnosis   There is no specific means of diagnosis at the present time. It is made by eliminating other causes of enlargement of the lymph nodes.

Treatment   X ray therapy produces a rapid and almost complete shrinking of the swollen nodes. But the swelling usually reappears again in a few weeks, requiring further X ray treatment. The results of the X ray treatment may become less and less effective as time goes on.

However, in recent years, a number of chemical agents have been used by mouth or intravenously in the treatment of Hodgkin's disease. When given in combination with X ray therapy, they have been more effective than X ray alone. Many cures following this method of treatment have been reported.

Holding the breath   see **Breath-holding.**

Home, broken   see **Divorce.**

Home, location of

The question of whether the city, the country, or the suburbs offers the child the greater advantages is difficult to answer. There is one basic consideration: no matter where children live and grow up, the home and the parents are the most important influences. Where the family is happiest is the first concern.

City living offers many advantages as well as disadvantages. The city child usually has better cultural facilities to supplement the schools. Among these are museums, large libraries, zoos, airfields, concerts, theaters, ballet, art exhibits. The public school systems in different cities vary in quality. Some are overcrowded, but some are first-rate, and there is more likelihood of specialized classes for the bright child, the retarded child, and the handicapped child.

Socially the city child can usually meet people of many different ethnic groups, religions, and nationalities. And at home he usually has a greater opportunity to see and be with his father than the child brought up in the suburbs whose father works in the city.

But there are disadvantages as well. The city child is usually overprotected and may have to be watched almost constantly because of dangerous street traffic, deviants or criminals, and gangs of other children or adolescents. He has limited space in which to play, and the air he breathes is likely to be dangerously polluted. (See **Air pollution.**) Schools are often too large, and sometimes triple sessions are required. In addition, for those youngsters who cannot get away either to camp or to the country, most cities during the summer are hot, uncomfortable, and boring.

One of the greatest advantages of living in the suburbs or the country is the outdoor space where youngsters can play freely and safely and not be under the constant eye of their mother. There is dirt to dig, space to plant seeds and watch them grow. There can be swings from trees and outdoor play equipment. In the suburbs there is little sidewalk or street traffic as a rule in residential areas, so that children can ride with comparative safety on their tricycles or bicycles when they are old enough. There is usually room for a workshop— a delight for boys—as well as open space nearby for a baseball game or other sports. There can be picnics and cookouts on the back lawn, and occasionally children can set up tents in the backyard and sleep out for the night. In the winter there are usually opportunities near at hand for sledding, skating, and possibly skiing. As children grow older they can visit friends by walking, roller skating, or bicycling over to their house—and their mother usually knows where they are going and how they can be reached.

In the real country, children also enjoy these advantages, except that they may be more isolated from companions. This is certainly an important consideration in the case of a child who has no brothers or sisters for playmates. On the other hand, in rural families the children generally have much more time with their father than is possible for a suburban family.

The quality of schooling varies in suburban and country areas as it does in the cities, but there are likely to be fewer children in each class and some suburban schools are excellent.

But, in spite of all the advantages of living in the suburbs or country, there are certain potential disadvantages and certain real disadvantages. There is a tendency for a rural community to be composed of people of similar ethnic, economic, and social backgrounds, and generally of like religious and political beliefs. This limits a child's experience.

Furthermore, children, and especially adolescents, in the country miss the cultural advantages mentioned earlier. To take in cultural events in the city often requires a full day's trip or is impossible except on vacations.

As children get into the teens, many of them feel restricted and envy what they consider the exciting life and freedom of boys and girls their age in the cities. They often feel bored and hemmed in by country isolation.

It is important at this time for the parents to devote a great deal of interest to their children and to work hand in hand with the school, church, and community to provide interesting and worthwhile activities for the boys and girls in their locality. Scout troops, the 4-H Clubs, the Little League baseball teams, dramatic groups, art exhibits, concerts, and dances are examples of activities to be fostered. The need of most teen-agers for social life and group activity should be understood, and adequate opportunities should be provided for such outlets.

Home movies   see **Photographs and home movies.**

Homebound child   see **Bedridden child.**

Homesickness

Homesickness is a common occurrence among children leaving their home and parents for the first time and occasionally even on subsequent occasions.

It is very frequent when children go to sleepaway camps for the first time.

The degree of homesickness and its duration depend largely on the attitude of the parents.

For instance, some parents increase the child's lonesomeness by writing letters telling him how much he is missed and how his pet dog sits sadly in the corner waiting for him, and by describing at length interesting things the family is doing. What parents should do principally is to ask about and comment on the interesting things happening at camp, with some mention of what goes on at home as well. They should ask the child to tell them fully of everything going on from day to day.

Many children are homesick at times, especially in the evenings the first week or so, and they may write or telephone their parents during these temporarily depressed periods. Parents should reassure these children and learn from the camp director or some adult in authority how they act generally. Most children lose their homesickness in a short time.

In very rare instances, when a child is deeply depressed, he should be taken home. Perhaps he is too young or not yet sufficiently mature for the experience.

Homework

The amount of homework expected of a child varies with the school and the class in which he is a student.

Parents have an important part in establishing good studying habits at home and assuring that the homework is completed. But they shouldn't nag.

The first step should be to set aside a definite time for homework. This does not have to be extremely rigid, for occasionally something of importance arises that necessitates changes. However, the child should realize that homework is the first consideration, and that TV, game playing, or hobbies are secondary.

Parents should not do the child's homework for him, but he should feel free to discuss a perplexing problem with them—although they may not be able to help, since most parents have little background, for example, in modern methods of mathematics. Parents should also consult the teacher regarding to what extent it's permissible to work with the child, since many teachers disapprove of this.

It is often advisable for parents to check the homework when it is supposedly finished in order to be sure that it has been completed. When good work habits have been established, this is unnecessary.

Homicide

Homicide is rare in children who have not yet reached puberty. In those cases that do occur, the child usually uses a gun which has been in the home, and he does so in a momentary period of anger. Fathers or siblings are usually the victims. The child under puberty rarely realizes the finality of death; he "murders" to punish his victim rather than to kill him. Studies have shown that as a rule such a child does not continue to show violence or manifest antisocial attitudes. The homicide was due to a momentary fit of anger or resentment without realization of the consequences.

In addition, there are numerous accidental homicides involving guns.

Whether the homicide is accidental or partially intentional, the child involved will bear a heavy burden for the rest of his life. Parents should therefore be absolutely sure that no child has access either to firearms or ammunition.

Sadistic or premeditated murder is

not unknown among children but is extremely rare.

Homicide by adolescents is more common, and the child at this age understands death and usually knows right from wrong. During adolescence revenge and robbery are the most common motives of homicide, and often the murder is premeditated. Poor economic and environmental conditions as well as drug addiction are the indirect causes of homicide in most cases.

Homosexuality

Sexual desire for a person of the same sex. This is not usually present until adolescence, but there is considerable evidence to show that the roots of homosexuality are to be found during childhood. But occasional homosexual experience in childhood or adolescence is quite common and not in itself a sign that the child will be homosexual.

Causative factors As far as can be determined at the present time, homosexuality is not hereditary. Nor is there any scientific evidence that it is caused by a malfunction of one or more glands of the body. Studies have demonstrated that in homosexuals there is no undersupply of hormones of their own sex, nor an oversupply of hormones of the opposite sex. Furthermore, there is no evidence that homosexuality is traceable to any prenatal difficulty.

All scientific evidence to date leads to the conclusion that usually there is no single cause, and that the multiple causes of homosexuality are emotional and brought about by factors in the child's environment.

Among the possible influences that might lead to homosexuality are:

1. Anything that prevents a child from experiencing love from a parent of the opposite sex. A boy in normal development is loved by his mother, loves her, and can later be loved by and transfer his love to another woman. The same holds true of a girl and her father. Without this love, difficulties in relationship with the opposite sex may occur during adolescence and later.

2. Fear of or hostility to either parent that causes distortion of a child's sex attitudes. For instance, a boy who hates his father and has no adequate father-substitute will have no masculine model in which to pattern the development of his sex role, and he may look to his mother as the worthwhile model to follow.

3. A dominant, strong, and overpowering mother and a weak or absent father, or a father who is constantly criticized and run down by the mother, may cause a boy to mold himself along female lines—to be like his mother rather than his father.

4. A possessive and seductive parent. A child may be so constrictively loved by a parent of the opposite sex and may return that love so deeply that he cannot later have a love relationship with any other member of that sex. For example, a boy may become so attached to his mother that when he is mature he sees her in every woman he meets. Since he knows he cannot think of himself as his mother's lover, he is unable to be any other woman's lover, and he finds his gratification in members of his own sex. For girls and their fathers the same holds true.

5. The feeling of a child that he would be better loved if he were of the opposite sex. Some parents create this feeling by their attitudes toward and treatment of their youngsters. Some children know that their parents desired a child of the

opposite sex when they were born. For example, a mother who enjoys seeing her son pretend he is a woman by dressing in women's clothing is edging the child toward homosexuality.

6. Failure of a child during the school years to be accepted by those of his own sex because of personality difficulties, physical difficulties, or other reasons. In these cases the child may find it easier to be with members of the opposite sex, may try to act and think as they do, and may even associate with them almost exclusively. In such cases, there is probably a strong underlying tendency toward homosexuality which developed during the earlier childhood years.

7. A repressive attitude toward sex at home and a fear of sex repeatedly impressed on a child during the school years and adolescence. The hazards of "necking" and "petting" and the ultimate dangers of sexual intercourse are stressed so strongly that the child may develop a negative attitude toward normal sex urges and desires.

8. Seduction during puberty or adolescence by a person of the same sex. This is rarely the definitive cause of homosexuality but may tend to establish it in a child already predisposed. Homosexual activities often take place at boys' or girls' schools during the teen years. These activities are usually only temporary and occur for lack of relationship with the opposite sex. It is only when a child already tends toward homosexuality that this becomes a real problem.

9. Parents who in their eagerness to make real boys or real girls out of their children impose on them exaggerated ideas of masculinity and femininity and attempt to force them into overly rigid molds. This causes problems for the children, who feel that they cannot meet the high standards expected of them,

and it may help to push them into a role in which they are not forced to meet these difficult standards.

Signs Signs of potential homosexuality may never be clear or may begin to appear as early as age 4 or 5. It is sometimes apparent that a young child fears or dislikes his own sexual identity and wants to take on the identity of the opposite sex. There is no single sign of this; for example, a boy who likes to cook does not necessarily want to be a woman. He is mastering a basic skill, one that more and more young boys are enjoying. However, if by the way he dresses, talks, and acts he indicates generally that he would prefer to be a girl, there may well be reason for parental concern. Often when a child has a problem with his or her sexual identity, this is apparent to other children, who may reject the child for that reason. Among boys especially, the child may be severely teased, driving him even further into unhappiness. Girls are usually teased less openly, but they may have difficulties getting along with other girls.

It was formerly felt that tomboyishness among girls was an early sign of a homosexual trend, but we know today that many tomboys are essentially very feminine. However, if a girl over a period of time makes every effort to walk, talk, and act like a boy, these may be danger signals worth investigating.

The so-called "crushes" of adolescence, when a girl falls deeply in love with an older girl, a teacher, or some other woman, are usually not evidence that the teen-ager is homosexual. The "crushes" are almost always temporary and, as a rule, dissipate when a girl forms a close relationship with a boy. (See **Crushes.**)

Treatment Any signs that a child is tending toward homosexuality should alert the parents to a need for investigating his or her environment. This is best accomplished with the help of a guidance counselor or a psychotherapist. It is important not to accuse the child, and to take this step as matter-of-factly and calmly as possible. The worries of parents on this subject are frequently entirely misplaced, and, in any case, open or underlying hysteria can only harm the child. If the therapist feels that there is indeed cause for concern, then the child, as well as his parents, are in need of psychological help—the child for treatment, the parents for direction and perhaps also for treatment.

Parents and others should always remember that homosexuality is not a disease or a breakdown of personality. It is an attempt to find love when for some reason or reasons love with a person of the opposite sex is extremely difficult or even impossible.

See **Transvestism.**

Hookworms   see **Worms.**

Hooky, playing   see **Truancy.**

Hormone poisoning   see **Poisons: first-aid treatment.**

Hormones   see **Glands.**

Hornet stings   see **Bee stings.**

Horse serum

A serum used in treatment of diphtheria or tetanus when the condition is present. It is also used for the quick prevention of diphtheria or tetanus in children and adults who have been exposed to these conditions and have never had diphtheria or tetanus-toxoid immunizations.

It is made by injecting some of the toxins (poisons) of the diphtheria or tetanus bacteria into horses, which then build up strong antibodies in their blood serum. But some children and adults are very sensitive to horse serum and may have severe, or even fatal, reactions. To prevent such reactions, the doctor tests sensitivity by skin testing or by placing a drop of the serum in the child's eye. If signs of sensitivity result, such as an irritation of the eye, the child is given a serum prepared from rabbits or some other animal which has been treated to produce the proper antibodies.

Hospitalization

Not infrequently children must be in hospitals—many for simple operations such as the repair of hernias or removal of tonsils and adenoids, others for more serious conditions and extended stays.

A child over 6 can usually understand and adjust to the situation if adequately briefed. To the younger child, the enforced separation from his parents, especially if he is in pain or not feeling well, may be extremely upsetting and may cause deep emotional damage.

This emotional harm to the young child, generally the child under 5, can be largely avoided if the mother is permitted to stay with him the first two or three nights and if there are long visiting hours during the day.

Many of the modern children's hospitals and pediatric sections of large hospitals are aware of the emotional needs of hospitalized children. Not only do they have liberal visiting hours, but they do a great deal to relieve the anxiety of the children by keeping them occupied, interested, and happy during their hospital stay. Many of the hospitals have trained play therapists who work with each child individually. And frequently there are playrooms in which these therapists direct the children in numerous activities—once they are able to be out of their beds. These playrooms have almost a nursery school atmosphere—some children painting, others modeling, some weaving baskets, some building with blocks, others playing with dolls and doll carriages or toy animals, balls, and balloons.

When a child is bedridden, the play therapists work with him when the parents are not around—finding appropriate toys for him, talking to him about his home and parents, preventing the deep loneliness that formerly was so common when little children were separated from their parents. The play therapists, aided by nurses, also work with infants, holding them frequently and giving them the stimulation they all need.

Preparing a child for hospitalization
Always be completely honest with the child, telling him why he is going to the hospital in terms that will reassure and not frighten him. Explain to the child that he is going to be helped to get well or to avoid any pain he has been having, such as with appendicitis or tonsillitis. If possible, he should meet the surgeon or other specialist who will treat him before he goes into the hospital. Explain the purpose of an operation but do not go into too many frightening details. Do, however, explain any procedures that may be especially upsetting such as anesthesia. Describe to the child everything that he will see in the hospital—doctors and nurses dressed in white, the

operating room, other children who are being treated, and so on. There are children's books about going to the hospital that can be very helpful.

Tell the child that you will be waiting to see him, and be clear about when he can expect to see you and how much time you will be spending with him.

If possible, wait until a day or two before an operation before telling a young child the exact day and time he will be going into the hospital.

Be calm and cheerful, but do not deceive the child by telling him he's going to feel just fine and get lots of ice cream to eat. If he's having an operation, tell him that it will hurt afterward but he will soon be better than before. When he is in the hospital, allow him to talk about any feelings he may have against doctors, nurses, and hospitals—it is perfectly natural to resent pain and hospital procedures.

Remember that it is most important for one or both parents to be with the child when he wakes up after surgery. They should also make every effort to be with him the first night (at least) and as much as possible during the daytime.

Hostels and hosteling   see **Recreational organizations.**

Hostility   see **Hate.**

Household chores   see **Chores.**

Humidifier   see **Moisture in the air.**

Hunger   see **Appetite.**

Hyaline membrane disease
A very dangerous respiratory condition

of the newborn, found primarily among premature infants.

It is caused by the formation of a membrane lining the inside of the air sacs (alveoli) in the lungs. This prevents the oxygen in the air breathed in from passing through the walls of the sacs and entering the bloodstream. The tiny baby struggles to get oxygen and is usually in extreme distress.

To date very little has been found to influence the course of the disease, and many children die of it. But if the baby lives through the first seventy-two hours of life he will usually recover, for at that time, for reasons unknown, the membrane starts to disappear, and it disappears completely in a few days. Babies with hyaline membrane disease are usually given oxygen in an incubator and fluids to prevent acidosis (too high a level of acidity throughout the body).

Children who recover from this disease are usually as strong as other children and show no harmful or lasting effect physically or mentally.

Hydrocele

A collection of fluid usually surrounding one or both testicles in the scrotal sac but occasionally found around the spermatic cord above the testicle.

This is very common in male infants during the first year of life and is of no danger. The swelling may persist for months and then disappear without any treatment. If a hydrocele remains for two years or more without any signs of subsiding, it may be treated surgically. This is very successful.

An important differentiation must be made between a hydrocele and a hernia which forces its way down into the scrotum. Hernias may be dangerous, so the diagnosis is important. A doctor can

usually make this diagnosis without difficulty.

Hydrocephalus

An accumulation of fluid within the skull, often causing great enlargement of the head in infancy.

Normally there is fluid formed in spaces within the brain (cerebrospinal fluid) which flows down and into the spinal canal inside the backbone. In the spinal canal this fluid is absorbed into the body.

In hydrocephalus, which usually starts developing before a baby is born, there may be too much fluid produced or, more frequently, there is a blockage preventing the fluid from entering the spinal canal. This fluid continues being formed in the brain but has no outlet, and so it is dammed back into the brain, compressing the brain and expanding the skull. If the pressure continues too long, it may squeeze the brain so much that partial or total blindness and even mental retardation may result.

It is only in recent years that a method has been devised to not only treat but actually cure this condition. A long, very narrow plastic tube is used. One end of it is inserted into the fluid spaces of the brain. The tube bypasses the blocked area, and the other end is inserted either into the abdomen, into a vein, into one of the tubes leading from a kidney to the bladder, or into some other area within the body. The tube is inlaid under the skin so that the child has no knowledge of its presence and no one can see it.

This release of fluid from the brain relieves all pressure within the brain and skull. If such treatment is instituted early, before brain damage occurs, the child will be just as normal and intelligent as if he had been born without the defect.

The tube usually remains in place for life, although it is necessary to lengthen it as the child grows taller.

Hydrochloric-acid poisoning see **Poisons: first-aid treatment.**

Hydrocortisone see **Cortisone and hydrocortisone.**

Hydrophobia see **Rabies.**

Hymen
A thin membrane covering the entrance of the vagina.

The hymen normally has an opening in the center, but occasionally there may be no opening. This causes no difficulty until the girl begins to menstruate at puberty. The flow of blood cannot escape and accumulates within the vagina, eventually causing severe lower abdominal pain. The condition can be completely corrected by a simple surgical cut.

Traditionally the intact hymen was regarded as the sign of virginity. This concern with the intact hymen is even less reasonable today than it was in the past. There are many possible causes of variations in the hymen, including the use of tampons during menstruation, which widens the opening in the membrane.

Hyperactivity
Many infants are very active almost from the first day of life. They are constantly moving around in their cribs, they sleep considerably less than the average infant, and even before 3 months of age they watch everything that is going on around them with an unusual degree of alertness.

This heightened degree of activity may be part of the child's normal makeup, and there may be no special problem, at least during the preschool years, as long as the child has plenty of opportunity and space to be freely active and energetic.

On the other hand, in some cases parents report difficulties from an early age related to their child's restlessness, shifting moods, irritability, and impulsiveness. The mother in particular may begin to feel strained and fatigued in dealing with the child.

Difficulties are more likely to arise, however, once the child is in school. Some very active children adjust satisfactorily to the school situation, but in other cases the parents get persistent reports that the child is unable to concentrate or stay still, that he is easily distracted, that he disrupts the class, interrupts the teacher, and is not learning properly. The child may also be excessively restless and disruptive outside of school. The question of what, if anything, is really wrong with the child, and what sort of adjustment or treatment is appropriate, then arises.

In recent years it was discovered that certain patterns of hyperactive behavior tend to be associated with evidence of some degree of brain dysfunction or damage, and that in some cases drug treatment greatly helped hyperactive children to settle down, concentrate, and learn. In many cases hyperactive children with severe learning difficulties were found to have average or above-average intelligence and to quickly begin learning at a level commensurate with their intelligence following treatment.

Treatment The reports of successful treatment naturally caused great interest and hope that many other children could also be helped. The term "hyperactive child" became widely, perhaps too widely, used. There is today considerable complaint that youngsters are loosely labeled "hyperactive" and referred to medical treatment even when their activity is within the normal range or their problems are primarily emotional resulting from difficulties in relationship to parents, other children, or teachers.

If parents feel or are told by school authorities that their child is hyperactive, the diagnosis and treatment recommendations should be the responsibility of a doctor, who will consider the entire range of possible causes of the difficulty; who will see to it that careful investigation of motor activity, neurological function, intelligence, and emotional factors is carried out; and who will closely supervise any medical treatment that may be indicated. In some cases it may be recommended that special tutoring and/or psychotherapy accompany the medical treatment.

The drugs that have been found to be most useful in the treatment of hyperactivity include Ritalin (methylphenidate), Tofranil (imipramine hydrochloride), Mellaril (thioridazine hydrochloride), and Dexedrine (dextroamphetamine). Given the widespread abuse of stimulants by adolescents and adults, this has raised questions about whether their use in treating hyperactive children means that we are encouraging a drug-dependent society or even addicting the children to these drugs. On the basis of studies of thousands of children so treated, there is no evidence of any child under proper medical supervision having become addicted to the drugs used in treatment of hyperactivity. Proper supervision implies that drugs will not be used unless there is clear indication that they are benefiting the child. With the right drug and adequate dosage improvement should be almost immediate. There will be careful investigation of any possible unwanted side effects, such as insomnia or loss of appetite; the treatment will be stopped or adjusted to avoid or minimize such effects; the treatment will only be used as necessary—for example, treatment may be discontinued during the summer when it is not so critical for the child to be able to concentrate closely, and when there is a much greater outlet for hyperactivity.

As a rule long-term treatment is not indicated, and the condition clears up during adolescence.

Very often the hyperactive child's difficulties are increased by the fact that he does not do well in school, feels humiliated and frustrated, and falls further and further behind. In addition, his impulsive and "odd" behavior may make him unpopular with his peers and increase his unhappiness. For this reason, it is important for parents to seek help before a pattern of failure is established.

See also **Brain dysfunction, mild; Dyslexia.**

Hyperkinesis   see **Hyperactivity.**

Hyperopia   see **Eye defects.**

Hyperthyroidism   see **Thyroid gland.**

Hypoglycemia   see **Diabetes mellitus.**

Hypothyroidism   see **Thyroid gland.**

Hysteria
A temporary state of loss of emotional

control induced by fear, fright, shock, or sorrow; or, in medical terminology, a neurotic condition in which a person has constant or recurrent physical symptoms without any physical or physiological basis.

The neurotic type of hysteria is comparatively rare in childhood but is seen not infrequently in puberty and adolescence.

Examples are a girl of 5 who started falling a great deal while walking. Careful neurological examinations revealed no abnormality. Finally it was discovered that her baby sister was learning to walk and was stumbling frequently. The condition cleared quickly as soon as greater attention was given to the older child. A boy of 14 developed a sudden paralysis of his right arm. Again no physical or physiological cause could be found. Psychiatric study brought forth the fact that he had been masturbating and had been told that it was not only very dangerous but very sinful as well. The condition disappeared quickly under psychotherapy plus a mild electric shock to the arm, which the boy was told would cure the paralysis immediately—the power of suggestion is often helpful in cases of this kind.

Hysterical symptoms are usually sudden in onset and may involve almost any portion or function of the body. Among these are impairment of vision or even blindness; impairment of walking or paralysis of an arm or leg; loss of speech; tremors or uncontrolled bodily movements; areas of numbness over the body; fits or convulsive seizures; retention of urine or frequency of urination; and partial or complete loss of voice.

Hysteria is more common in girls than in boys.

It is not to be confused with malingering, in which a child deliberately feigns a sign or symptom to deceive his parents or others.

Treatment   This involves relieving the hysterical signs or symptoms by such means as drugs (often placebos), heat, manipulation, and exercises, with the suggestion to the child that the treatment will remove the symptoms. In addition, the psychological causes must be unearthed and treated. Hypnotism has been used successfully but should only be attempted with a capable and experienced hypnotist. It is important to remember that hypnotism or any form of suggestion that focuses on the symptom alone must be supplemented with attention to the underlying reasons for the onset of the hysterical reaction. The symptom is usually only one sign of a deeper problem.

It is essential to determine the emotional causes of the hysteria, and in this investigation the cooperation of the parents is a necessity. The child's complete environment should be studied, with special emphasis on his relationship with his family and friends. Psychotherapy is often indicated. With treatment, the prognosis is good.

I

Ice skating

Every year during the winter months millions of children go ice skating. And every year hundreds of children break through the ice and drown. The prevention of these accidents is of vital importance to all parents whose children enjoy this sport. And "ice rules" are also of special importance when parents live with their children near lakes, ponds, or streams, for children are venturesome and frequently take chances walking or skating on ice to see if it will hold them.

There are means of preventing ice accidents that every parent should know—and there are also safety rules that both parents and children should learn for use in case of emergency.

Preventing ice-skating accidents

1. Beware of the first ice of the season, for it is not only thin but uneven in thickness.
2. Winter skating over lakes, ponds, and streams should not start until the ice is at least four inches thick. Many people consider a two-inch thickness as safe. This is probably true if very few people are skating, but it will not hold large numbers.
3. It is much safer to skate on ponds and small lakes where the water is no higher than waist-deep.
4. On deeper areas of water, never skate alone. A child should be under constant supervision.
5. Never skate on ice over fast-flowing

currents, for even in deep winter the ice can vary in thickness.
6. Never skate on saltwater ice.
7. Never skate where the ice borders on open water.
8. Never skate at night unless the skating area is well lighted.
9. Never gather in large groups on ice.
10. There should be simple safety equipment always available and handy near skating areas. This includes a ring buoy with a line attached, which may be thrown to a person who has fallen through the ice; a ladder which can be placed flat on the ice, and on which a rescuer can crawl; and a pole and rope to which the person in the water can cling while being rescued.

Emergency action The following safety rules should be learned by all who skate.

If you fall through the ice:

1. Keep calm.
2. Keep your chin up.
3. Do not grasp the edge of the ice, since it will only break and you will go down again.
4. Instead, extend your arms over the unbroken surface of the ice and kick as vigorously as possible, with your legs behind you. This will propel your body forward onto the solid ice.
5. When eventually your chest is on firm ice, squirm, wiggle, or roll to safety.

In rescuing a person who has fallen through the ice:

1. Don't panic.
2. Use rescue equipment as indicated previously, if it is available.
3. If you have no equipment, lie down and slide your body over the ice so that there is not too much weight on any one area of ice. As calmly as possible, instruct the person in the water on how to escape.

Ill child   see Bedridden child.

Illegitimate child

A child born out of wedlock. The term "illegitimate child" is a poor one, for it makes it appear that the fault is with the child.

There are approximately 250,000 births out of wedlock in the United States each year. This number is being reduced somewhat by the widespread use of contraceptive pills and devices and by an increase in legal abortions.

A great many of these children born out of wedlock are sent to adoption agencies. A large number are adopted by other members of the family, especially grandparents. A third group are taken care of by their mothers.

There have always been unwed mothers who have chosen to raise their own children despite social stigma, and today the stigma is much less, making life easier for both mother and child. Most unwed mothers should seek professional counseling so that they will be aware of the difficulties that they face if they keep their children.

Legally, mother and child are eligible for welfare aid if necessary, but the amount and the regulations governing it vary from state to state. All states except Texas require a known father to contribute to the support of his child. But the illegitimate child still lacks full rights under the law, for he does not receive all the rights of support and inheritance and the right to bear his father's name if he so desires later.

Of interest is the fact that a number of famous people were "illegitimate." Among these are John Audubon, Sarah Bernhardt, Alexander Hamilton, Nancy Hanks (mother of Abraham Lincoln), Jack London, and James Smithson (founder of the Smithsonian Institution).

Imaginary companions

Many children of about 3 or 4 years of age have imaginary playmates or companions who are apparently as real to them as living people.

A child will walk down the street conversing with an imaginary friend, have the mother set a place at the table for this character, and even play with him in the playroom and yard.

At times these strange activities cause parents great concern. But this behavior is very common at a period when a child's imagination is at its height. It signifies that a child is lonesome for close companionship, and he compensates for this lack by manufacturing a friend of his own design.

There is nothing to be gained by interfering with the child's enjoyment of his imaginary playmate. This is a passing phase, and most children grow out of it by themselves within a year or two. Parents should not encourage the continuance of the fantasy after this time simply because they think it's "cute."

Realizing that this is a sign of loneliness, there are means that parents can take to overcome it: encouraging friendships with, and frequent visits by, children of the same age; giving a child a cat or a dog of his own.

Imagination   see **Fantasy.**

Imitation

Children are constantly learning by imitation from early infancy and throughout the years of childhood.

The 4-month-old infant will often watch a person's mouth very closely and try to imitate its movements. A baby learns early to wave his hands "bye-bye" in imitation of his parents. The play of young children is largely in imitation of what they see their parents and others do.

As children get older they imitate parents in many ways, often copying such mannerisms as the way they talk and smile and laugh. Often adopted children so take on the mannerisms of their adoptive parents that they begin to look like them. Children learn good manners and good habits by observing their parents. They also may learn bad manners and bad habits in the same way. Imitative tendencies continue through the school-age period (approximately age 6 to 12) when the parent as a model worth imitating becomes even more important. For it is during this period that children develop their sex roles. Boys look to their fathers, as a rule, as their ideal of what a man should be like—and they try in many ways to imitate them—and girls react to their mothers in the same way.

The knowledge that children develop so many of their qualities by imitating their parents is extremely important for parents to realize. For if we expect our children to develop the qualities we admire and wish for, we ourselves must first and foremost serve as examples worth imitating.

Immunity

The state of being not susceptible to a particular disease or infection.

The actual mechanism that accounts for immunity is not well understood, but the manner of developing immunity is clear. The body either builds up or acquires antibodies against a particular disease. (See **Antibodies.**)

Although newborn infants are highly susceptible to many infections, they receive an immunity from their mothers against the infectious diseases their mothers have had. This immunity, which comes almost entirely through the placenta, lasts, as a rule, slightly over six months. Among these diseases to which newborn infants are commonly immune are measles, mumps, chicken pox, diphtheria, poliomyelitis, and German measles. If a mother has no immunity to a disease, her infant will have no immunity either during the first six months of life.

Besides this temporary acquired immunity which a baby gains from its mother's blood, there are two other types of immunity which a child can develop.

The first type, known as active immunity, is formed after a child himself has contracted an infectious disease and recovered from it. Against diseases such as chicken pox, measles, mumps, German measles, whooping cough, poliomyelitis and diphtheria, the immunity gained is almost always permanent. At times a person develops immunity to a disease from such a mild case that he has no knowlege of having had it.

Another type of active immunity is the immunity the body forms following an injection of a virus or toxin, as in the case of smallpox vaccination. The Sabin vaccine against infantile paralysis is administered orally, but contains a weakened but living virus which stimulates the body to develop an active immunity against polio.

Passive immunity to a disease may be

conferred by giving a child gamma globulin from a person who has had the disease or serum from an animal immunized against the disease. This type of immunity is called "passive" because the body does not build up its own antibodies, but depends upon the antibodies from another person or animal. The immunity is temporary.

In certain cases, such as immunization against diphtheria, tetanus, typhoid, and influenza, booster injections are necessary to keep the level of immunity high.

See also **Gamma globulin.**

Immunization schedule and tests

Doctors' recommendations vary for immunization schedules. The American Academy of Pediatrics has suggested the schedule shown at the bottom of the page.

Impetigo

A highly contagious disease of the skin, often found in epidemic form in schools, camps, and wherever children are congregated and in close contact with one another.

The condition is due to a superficial infection of the skin by a streptococcus or staphylococcus bacteria. It starts as a little red spot which quickly forms little blisters that fill with thin, watery pus. These blisters break and form crusts. The oozing from the blisters is very infectious, and the infection is rapidly spread to other parts of the body by fingers, towels, or the oozing from the lesions. It usually starts on the face, nasal openings, ears, and scalp, but any portion of the body may be involved.

Other than mild itching, there are no symptoms.

The treatment of impetigo is not difficult, and if it is followed carefully the disease will usually clear within a week. The child, if old enough, should be told of the contagiousness of the condition and instructed not to finger the infection, to wash his hands carefully, and to use only his own towel, hairbrush, and comb.

The lesions should be soaked to soften the crusts, which are then removed by scrubbing with soap and water. The area involved should be washed three or four times a day with soap and an antiseptic ointment such as Neosporin or Neopolycin (both of which con-

Approximate Age	Immunization
2 months	diphtheria-tetanus-whooping cough; oral polio vaccine
4 months	diphtheria-tetanus-whooping cough; oral polio vaccine
6 months	diphtheria-tetanus-whooping cough; oral polio vaccine
12 months	measles vaccine; tuberculin test (or combine measles-mumps-rubella vaccine)
1 to 12 years	rubella vaccine; mumps vaccine
18 months	oral polio booster; diphtheria-tetanus-whooping cough booster
4 to 6 years	oral polio booster; diphtheria-tetanus-whooping cough booster
14 to 16 years	diphtheria-tetanus booster
Thereafter	diphtheria-tetanus booster every ten years
Each year	tuberculin tests, if possible

tain neomycin, polymixin, and bacitracin).

The child should have his own separate washcloth and towel. He should be kept home from school until the condition has completely subsided and no new lesions have arisen. This is to protect his classmates and others at the school from contracting the disease.

Incubation period

The period between the time an infecting germ enters the body of a child or adult and the first appearance of signs and symptoms of the disease. During this period the person who will develop the disease is not contagious.

For instance, a child who has never had chicken pox is exposed to a person with the disease. He is infected with some of the chicken pox virus. He will begin to show signs of the disease twelve to nineteen days after exposure. The twelve to nineteen days after the exposure is the incubation period.

For incubation periods of specific diseases, see under the title of the disease.

Incubator

A plastic-covered bassinet used to provide infants, especially premature infants, with warmth, adequate moisture in the air, and increased oxygen if needed.

The goal is to maintain a child's underarm temperature at approximately 98.6 degrees Fahrenheit. To do this the air temperature inside the incubator is usually kept at 89 degrees Fahrenheit, and sometimes higher for smaller infants.

The air is kept moist to aid in maintaining the temperature and to prevent drying of the mucous membrane of the baby's respiratory tract.

Today most incubators use atmospheric air, oxygen being added only if the infant turns blue or is having rapid respirations, both being signs of a need for oxygen. Formerly all premature babies were given extra oxygen in the incubator until it was found that a high percentage of oxygen in the air could cause their eyes to develop a membrane behind the lenses that caused blindness. Today the amount of oxygen given babies is carefully regulated.

Independence see **Clinging child; Responsibility; Self-esteem.**

Independence Day see **Fireworks.**

Indulgent parent see **Overindulgent parent.**

Infant, newborn see **Newborn, characteristics of.**

Infantile paralysis see **Poliomyelitis.**

Infantilism see **Regression.**

Infections see **Bacterial infections; Rickettsia infections; Staphylococcus infections; Streptococcus infections; Viruses.**

Infections, susceptibility to see **Susceptibility to infections.**

Infectious hepatitis see **Hepatitis, infectious.**

Infectious mononucleosis see **Mononucleosis, infectious.**

Inferiority, feelings of

Many children, for one reason or another, acquire the feeling that they are less valued, less desired, less important, or less capable than other children in their home, school, or community.

The possible reasons for such feelings of inferiority are numerous. They may be caused by a feeling of being unloved, by a jealousy of, or rivalry with, brothers or sisters, or by a child's concern that he is less desired and less important because of his size, color, religion, sex, appearance, or such physical defects as cerebral palsy, poor vision, or lameness.

Whatever the reason, the problem of relieving a child of such feelings depends upon the cause or causes. In most instances it is the parents who can be the most effective, either by relieving the causes of a child's feeling of insecurity—for example correcting such unattractive defects as crossed eyes, protruding teeth, and protruding ears—or by reassuring him, building him up, and helping him to feel more loved and more capable. At times a combination of home, school, and community action is necessary to remove such insecurity as that caused by religious or racial discrimination.

See also **Insecurity; Rejection; Unpopularity.**

Influenza

An acute and highly communicable virus disease affecting the respiratory tract and occurring periodically in epidemic form.

Mode of transmission By direct contact with an infected individual or by inhaling air which contains infected droplets of saliva or mucus from the coughs or sneezes of infected people.

Signs and symptoms Influenza begins abruptly with chills, fever, headache, and general achiness of the body. The throat is usually dry and sore. The fever rises rapidly, often to 104 or 105 degrees Fahrenheit, and a dry, hacky cough develops. The nose is congested and there may be some nasal discharge. The child often feels very ill and complains of severe headache.

If uncomplicated, the disease usually lasts about four days, after which there is rapid recovery.

At times secondary infections with bacteria may occur, causing pneumonia.

Incubation period A susceptible person, exposed to the disease, will usually develop influenza within one to three days after contact.

Period of contagion Infected individuals are usually contagious from the first through the fifth day of the illness.

Treatment There is no specific treatment for influenza. Since the disease is caused by a virus, antibiotics are of no value and should be reserved for any possible bacterial complications, such as ear infections or pneumonia.

Treatment is symptomatic: bedrest; aspirin for fever, headaches and body aches; cough medicine if necessary; and plenty of fluids. Complications, such as severe coughs, laryngitis, or earaches should be under the care of a doctor.

Care of exposed persons None.

Immunization Immunization against specific types of influenza is effective but should be given several months before an expected epidemic of the particular type. A booster dose is given each year. This is especially important for children who suffer from chronic lung conditions, heart disease, kidney disease, or frequency of severe respiratory infections. Most children do not require influenza immunization unless a severe epidemic is expected.

Inguinal hernia   see **Hernia.**

Inhalation of foreign objects   see **Foreign objects, inhalation of.**

Inhalators   see **Steam treatment.**

Injections   see **Immunization schedule and tests; Pediatrician.**

Inoculations   see   **Immunization schedule and tests.**

Insect and spider bites

The bites of mosquitoes, black flies, gnats, spiders, and ants may cause a child serious discomfort and should be prevented as far as possible. Among the best insect repellents are Off and 612. In using a repellent, follow the directions carefully, and be sure it does not get in the child's eyes and is not breathed in.

Once the child has been bitten by an insect, the following procedures may be followed for relief:

1. An anti-itching preparation should be applied over the bite. Caladryl lotion—calamine lotion (zinc carbonate), plus camphor, Benadryl (diphenhydramine hydrochloride), and rubbing alcohol—or a one-percent hydrocortisone cream is especially helpful. A paste of baking soda is also very soothing.
2. Special antihistamines taken by mouth—Tacaryl syrup (methdilazine) or Temaril syrup (trimeprazine tartrate)—may reduce the itching and the resultant scratching.
3. In cases of severe itching baths may be given containing Aveeno Colloidal Oatmeal—1 cup to a bathtub of water;

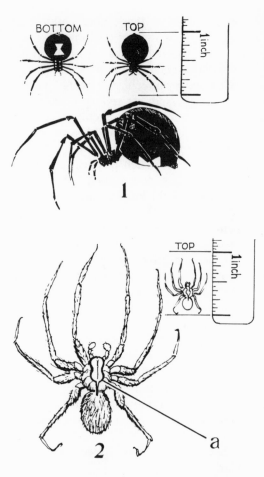

1. Black widow spider (female). 2. Brown recluse spider, also called fiddler spider after the fiddle-shaped marking (a) on its thorax.

½ cup to a Bathinette or infant tub of water. Or use Soyalid colloidal bath—1 envelope to a bathtub of water, or ½ envelope to a Bathinette or infant tub of water.

Spider and scorpion bites   The black widow spider may live in almost any part of the United States, although it is more common in the southern and western states. It prefers damp places and may be found in damp cellars, under rotting boards, in stone walls, and in outhouses. The female, which is poisonous, has an hourglass-shaped marking on its stomach that is colored red or orange.

The brown recluse spider (also called fiddler spider) is also poisonous, and is found primarily in the southern and western states. It prefers a dry habitat, and may be found in dark, dry cellars, attics, closets, and garages, and in the folds of bedding and clothing.

Tarantulas, which are large and frightening-looking, are relatively harmless and are even sometimes kept as pets. The bite is painful and should be reported to a doctor, but it produces no general symptoms of poisoning.

The bite of a black widow spider produces at first a sharp, needle-like pain, which usually subsides quickly, although it may last several hours. The child should be rushed to a hospital, and an ice pack may be held over the area of the bite on the way. In fifteen minutes to a few hours, there are usually muscle cramps in the area of the bite. As a rule, paralysis of muscles follows, and soon there is severe pain in the abdominal muscles. Restlessness, anxiety, and difficulty in breathing follow, and there may be delirium and convulsive seizures. There is an antivenin available which may be used if the child is not sensitive to it.

The bite of the brown recluse spider is less severe initially than that of the black widow but quickly becomes more severe, and the pain becomes intense within six to eight hours. By this time a blister has formed over the area of the bite. The top of the blister dries and drops off, leaving a deep-red denuded area. In a day or two this becomes a black crust, which drops off in two to five weeks, leaving a slowly healing ulcer that forms a scar. Treatment should

begin as soon as possible: it involves relieving the symptoms and sometimes performing minor local surgery at the site of the bite. While taking the child to the hospital or doctor, parents may hold an ice pack on the area of the bite.

Scorpions, which are distantly related to spiders, are found in the western and southeastern United States. Their sting is very painful and after about an hour usually induces headache, nausea, vomiting, dizziness, and an increased flow of saliva. In severe cases shock, convulsions, and coma may follow. The child should be taken to a doctor or hospital, and in the meantime an ice pack may be held over the bite. There is an antivenin, but it is made in Mexico and is not widely available. Treatment is usually confined to relieving the symptoms. At times cortisone preparations are used to reduce the reaction.

See also **Bee stings; Chiggers; Head lice; Rocky Mountain spotted fever; Scabies.**

Insecticide poisoning see **Poisons: first-aid treatment.**

Insects see **Nature.**

Insecurity

One of the primary aims of every interested parent is to bring up secure children.

In spite of this, parents often see signs of insecurity in their children, such as shyness, fearfulness, loneliness, and even at times unpopularity. More specific signs of insecurity, in children past the toddler stage, include thumb-sucking, nail-biting, tics, stammering, stuttering, and—in children over the age of 6—bedwetting, and also clinging to or staying close to the parents. On the other hand, the bully, the cruel and overaggressive child, is almost always an insecure child as well. (See **Bullying.**)

There are many possible causes of a child's insecurity. Parents who are too protective and too restrictive do not give a child the opportunity for building up self-assurance. A child who is scolded too much and in constant fear of punishment tends to be insecure, as is the child who feels unloved and rejected by his parents. Often this feeling of being unloved or insufficiently loved stems from sibling rivalry that makes a child feel less loved than a brother or sister.

Children who feel excluded because of racial or religious differences or because they are deprived economically often feel insecure. And physical conditions also can cause insecurity; obesity, acne, protruding teeth, prominent ears, poor vision or hearing, deafness.

During the school-age years and adolescence, insecurity is a source of great unhappiness to the child. For during these years one of the first needs of every child is to have friends, to be accepted by the group, and to be looked upon by his companions as an important member of the group.

The most important step in the prevention of insecurity is for a child to always have the assurance that he is very much loved and wanted by his parents. Parents should also attempt to develop in their child a sense of self-assurance and self-dependence as he grows older. Friendships should be encouraged and physical defects should be treated, whenever possible, before they upset a child. Children who for one reason or another cannot compete physically should be helped to develop some compensatory activity that will gain them the admiration of their companions.

At the earliest sign of insecurity parents should look into the child's environment and attempt to determine the causes. Is the child assured of their love and interest? Are they too protective or restrictive? Is the child subject to overly frequent punishment? What are his relations with his brothers and sisters? Has he real or imaginary physical defects which can be corrected or about which he should be reassured? Is the child excluded at school because of his race, religion, or other factors beyond his control? If the reasons for the insecurity are not apparent, the advice of the child's doctor or a guidance counselor should be sought. At times an insecure child may need professional help with his problems.

See also **Adolescent, helping to be more attractive; Rejection; Unpopularity.**

Insomnia   see **Sleep problems.**

Institutional care

The placing of children for care in institutions should be limited to those youngsters whose care at home would be extremely difficult or of possible danger to the community. This would primarily include children with severe mental deficiencies, children who are very upset emotionally, and children who are dangerously delinquent. In the past, a child without parents or from a broken home was usually placed in an orphanage for his care and education. This has largely given way to placement in a foster home where the child can have a home environment, individual care, and a feeling of receiving some personal affection and attention from a person or a couple to whom he can relate with warmth. It has been clearly demonstrated that the feeling of being loved, wanted, and cared for by one individual to whom the child can turn at all times is essential for the normal emotional growth and emotional health of the infant and young child.

The following are difficulties for which institutional care is considered.

Mental retardation During the early years mentally retarded children develop much better physically and even mentally if given the love and attention of their parents. At times, however, when a child is severely deficient mentally, institutional care is advisable, especially when there are other children at home who would be greatly deprived by the diversion of parental care and time to the retarded child.

Children who are mentally retarded but trainable or educable will do better in every way if they can remain at home and attend special classes in a local school. If no such schools are available in the community, institutional care may be necessary when children are of school age so that they may receive the appropriate special education and training. (See **Mental retardation.**)

Blindness or deafness Children with either of these handicaps will also do better in a home environment, but parents need guidance by and close cooperation with well-trained and skilled professionals. When the child is ready for schooling, he should if possible remain home and receive special treatment and education at a local school. If no such facilities exist, it may be very worthwhile to send the child to an institution for special care and education. (See **Blindness; Deafness.**)

Severe emotional disturbance At times, when children are severely autistic, or when they are a danger to others, or in need of a great deal of psychiatric help, institutional care may be necessary. Such placement should only be made after careful consideration and consultation. It should always be remembered that a child who is sent away to an institution will feel, at least to some extent, that he is unloved, unwanted, and rejected by his family. (See **Autism; Schizophrenia.**)

Insulin
A secretion produced by the Islands of Langerhans in the pancreas. It aids the body in metabolizing carbohydrates, thereby reducing the amount of sugar in the blood and urine. Diabetics lack insulin, and insulin is used to treat them.

Insulin is given only by injection. It comes in several forms—long-acting insulins ("lente" or "NPH" insulin or protamine zinc insulin) and the short-acting crystalline insulin.

Children with diabetes are usually placed on the long-acting insulin, given before breakfast. The crystalline insulin is given only in emergencies or when the child's body needs more insulin, such as times when the long-acting insulin does not last the full period for which it was given, or during the course of infections.

See also **Diabetes mellitus.**

Intelligence see **Genius; Intelligence, exceptional; IQ.**

Intelligence, exceptional
Unusually bright children who are far ahead of others their age in mental ability may occur in any family. These children have wonderful potential but also special problems. Bright children who have been stimulated by their families and environment to develop their intel-

lectual interests may also have to deal with similar problems. (See. **Stimulating the child.**)

Parents should do everything possible to stimulate and satisfy the intellectual curiosity of an exceptionally intelligent child, but should avoid making him feel self-conscious or pressured. Calling such a child a "genius," setting perfectionist standards, and above all requiring him to work or behave in a manner that is not appropriate to his age must be avoided. The highly intelligent child has the same emotional fears and needs as any other child.

In school the child should not, as a rule, be pushed ahead of his grade. Many schools have special classes for the "intellectually gifted" (I.G. classes) that allow them to remain in their own grade without being bored. Other schools are prepared to give the child who is ahead of his class extra attention and special work assignments. Parents might also want to consider entering the child in an "experimental" school in which several grades are combined. This method is designed to allow the child to find his own level of work. (See **Education, experimental approaches in.**)

If there is no way for the child to avoid boredom except by skipping grades, then this should be done as early as possible so that the child has a chance to make good friends among older children before entering high school. At this stage there is the danger that the bright child who is younger than the adolescents in his class will feel left out and isolated as a "kid" while his classmates are forging ahead physically and socially.

At all times parents should make a special effort to see that an exceptionally intelligent child has a good relationship with his brothers, sisters, and companions—that he has a normal family and social life. In addition, parents should consult with the child's teachers to be sure that everything possible is being done in the home and school to encourage the child's interests and development.

Intelligence quotient   see IQ.

Intelligent child   see Intelligence, exceptional.

Interest, stimulating   see Stimulating the child.

Interest test   see Tests.

Interrupting

Interrupting is a common habit of most children and many adults as well.

Children in their desire to express themselves, to ask questions, to focus attention on themselves, and as an expression of their natural exuberance are likely to interrupt frequently when others are speaking.

A child's desire to talk freely or ask questions should not be stifled, but nevertheless he must learn that there are times when he has to wait until another person finishes speaking. The parent should be kind in correcting a small child: "Just a second, please, until I finish speaking," or "Just a minute while I listen to Jimmy."

Gradually, as a child grows older, and if his parents adhere to the same principles, he will learn not to interrupt. He will learn it not only from his parents but from teachers in nursery school, kindergarten, and elementary school.

One should expect a teen-ager to realize that interrupting is impolite, although, like most people, he may still do it from time to time.

Intestinal obstruction

A rare but dangerous condition. In the newborn child an obstruction may be caused by a developmental closure of the intestines or by blockage of the intestine due to a hard, solid mass of meconium (the early fetal stool). This latter condition is a forerunner of cystic fibrosis. (See **Cystic fibrosis.**)

During the first few years of life, intestinal obstruction may at times be caused by intussusception, a serious condition in which one portion of the intestines envelopes another and causes a blockage. (See **Intussusception.**)

Occasionally intestinal obstruction is caused by something swallowed by a child, e.g., a whole dried prune or apricot, which when mixed with fluid in the intestines swells up and causes a dangerous blockage of the intestine, necessitating surgical removal of the object.

Intestines

A tube that forms the part of the digestive tract below the stomach. The small intestine leads from the stomach, forms many coils, and enters into the large intestine. The large intestine is wider and less coiled, and passes the leftover material (feces) out of the body through the anus.

In the small intestine food is digested and passes in solution through the intestinal walls into the surrounding blood vessels. Those parts of the food that remain undigested pass into the large intestine as a liquid mass. Here the fluid in this mass is mostly absorbed and the feces are usually passed in solid form. If the large intestine absorbs too much fluid, or if too little fluid has been taken

to begin with, the stools will be hard, resulting in constipation.

If the bowels are irritated by bacteria or viruses, by spoiled food, by foods to which one is allergic, or by certain laxatives, the motion of the intestines is rapid and diarrhea results.

See also **Bowel movements; Colitis, ulcerative; Colon, enlargement of; Intussusception.**

Intolerance and prejudice

Intolerance and prejudice are attitudes acquired usually from the parents, and often instilled in a child so young that it almost seems the child was born that way. These attitudes learned at home may be modified by later experiences in school and the wider world, but if the community itself is intolerant, there is a good chance that the child will grow up to be what can only be described as bigoted.

Children growing up in a good family environment will learn that there is a variation of opinions and beliefs. Discussion should always be encouraged, and each person's opinion should be respected. Children should have the opportunity to meet people of different ethnic and religious backgrounds. And if this is not possible, they should at least not be given the impression that outsiders are inferior.

If children show bigoted attitudes it is important that efforts be made to overcome them. This will rarely be attempted by their parents, who themselves are usually intolerant.

In school children can gradually learn to listen to others and to respect their opinions, beliefs, and differences. A great deal can be accomplished by having children read books about people of various beliefs and races. When children can get to know other children of all colors, races, and religions through integration in schools and churches, this is of the greatest value in eradicating intolerance.

Most often parents are themselves unconcerned with their own prejudices and do not see them as problems in their children. However, some parents are aware that their attitudes may be unfair or are shocked to hear their children openly express intolerant attitudes that they themselves believed they had kept hidden. In such cases parents should look into their own feelings and try to learn more about the subject. Very often they will find that their feelings are based upon misinformation or irrational fears (often picked up from *their* parents). They should also examine in what ways they have been communicating their prejudices to their children, so that they can make an effort to check this habit.

Intradermal test see **Skin tests for allergies.**

Intussusception
An obstruction of the intestine caused by the telescoping of one part of the bowel over the next succeeding segment. It is one of the dangerous emergencies of early childhood. The portion that envelopes the next portion of bowel cuts off the blood supply of the latter, and without blood the tissue starts dying. Gangrene of the bowel will set in and perforation may occur if treatment is not started in a very short time.

Intussusceptions usually occur between ages 3 months and 2 years. The cause is generally unknown, although in rare instances it follows diarrhea or constipation.

Signs and symptoms Usually there is a sudden onset of pain in an otherwise healthy infant. The pain is intense but stops in a few minutes only to return in another few minutes, continuing off and on in this manner.

The stools, containing a mixture of blood and mucus and resembling currant jelly, are usually moved within the first twelve hours after the onset of the condition, but in rare instances there may be no movement for twenty-four hours or more. Vomiting usually occurs after the onset of the abdominal pain. It may become more and more severe.

Diagnosis Careful pressure on the abdomen by a doctor will enable him to feel a sausage-shaped abdominal mass caused by the intussusception. And a barium enema almost always reveals the obstruction.

Treatment In a great many cases of intussusception the pressure caused by the barium enema, given for X ray diagnosis, will disengage the affected bowels, and the condition will clear spontaneously. If it does not clear a surgical operation is urgent, for an intussusception may result in death.

With early treatment, the child will almost always recover completely. The longer one waits, the more dangerous the condition becomes.

Iodine see **Nutrition; Poisons: first-aid treatment.**

IQ
Intelligence quotient. The IQ is a score of a child's intelligence based on one or more tests which, having been given to hundreds of thousands of children,

measure how well a child of a certain age level should be able to score. The score is a ratio of the child's test score (stated as "mental age") to his actual age and multiplied by one hundred. The result is the IQ of the child:

$$\frac{\text{IQ test score: 9 years}}{\text{Actual age: 6 years}} = 1.5 \times 100 = \text{IQ of } 150$$

The average score is 100. Children with IQ's of 110 to 119 are considered "bright"; those with 120 to 129, "very bright"; those with 130 to 149, "gifted"; while those of 150 and over are often said to be in the "genius" class (see **Genius**).

The IQ tests consist of a series of questions, problems, tasks, and puzzles. There are questions concerning the meaning of words and the understanding of situations in the child's environment; there are tests of the child's memory, mathematical ability, power of reasoning, and ability to see similarities between one thing and another. (See **Tests**.)

A child of 6 years with an IQ of 130 is likely to have the same IQ at age 8. But this score can be very markedly affected by a child's emotional state. The same child who made a score of 130 at age 8 may score 105 at age 10 if emotionally upset.

A child's success in the IQ tests depends not only on his emotional state but also on his cultural background, his environmental experiences, and, of course, his opportunities to learn normally. It is obvious that a child who is blind or deaf will not usually have had the same opportunities for learning as the normal child. A child who does not have a good command of English will have difficulties with the tests. A disadvantaged child from a poor home environment is also likely to score below par on these tests.

An inexperienced tester or poor testing conditions will likewise affect the child's score. For example, group intelligence tests are often given in schools to a whole class. They have the advantage of not requiring a trained tester and also taking less time to administer and score than individual intelligence tests. However, the IQ a child receives on a group test is not nearly as accurate as an individual test given by a trained tester. When group tests are given, children whose scores deviate from the normal levels of the class should be followed up with individual testing.

The testing of a child's intelligence should not be generally encouraged unless there is some specific reason. At times IQ tests are important in detecting cases of mental retardation, or in differentiating behavior problems from those due to mental deficiency. Certain schools require IQ ratings before they will consider accepting children as students.

It is almost invariably satisfying for the parents and the child if a youngster scores well on the tests. However, it should be obvious that since a child's score can fluctuate by twenty or thirty points at different times, the tests are not infallible. And despite all efforts to make tests "culture free" (standardized so that children from a variety of backgrounds will have an equal opportunity to score well), this has not yet been accomplished.

Most children are all too aware that parents and teachers are very concerned with the IQ results. Parents should attempt to minimize the importance of these results and should never convey disappointment to the child because of his IQ score. And the child should not be told his score. It is suspected that many competent children have been discouraged from developing their abilities because schools and parents have been too greatly influenced by IQ scores.

Parents should never attempt to test their own children and should even avoid reading books on how to figure their child's IQ. An overconcern with IQ can only make a child tense and unhappy.

See also **Intelligence, exceptional.**

Iris   see **Eyes, color of.**

Iron   see **Nutrition.**

Iron lung   see **Respirator.**

Irradiation   see **X rays.**

Irresponsibility   see **Responsibility.**

Irritability   see **Crankiness.**

Isolation of contagious persons
Strict isolation at home or in a hospital is usually necessary for a person who has typhoid fever, viral hepatitis, diphtheria, or active tuberculosis. Strict isolation generally means keeping the infected child or adult separated from contact with others, with his own dishes and towels. As a rule anyone immunized against the disease need not be separated from the patient.

Most of the contagious diseases are contracted by direct contact with the infected individual and cannot be carried by a third person. An exception to this is diphtheria, which may be carried in the throat of a person who is himself immune.

Itch mite   see **Scabies.**

Itching
A reaction of the nerves in the skin to mild or moderate irritation.

There are numerous causes of itching, and the treatment must, of course, be related to the cause of the condition.

Itching caused by local irritants, such as irritating soaps and lotions or allergy-producing wool, can usually be relieved by removing the irritant and using a soothing lotion such as calamine (zinc carbonate with one percent phenol) or caladryl (zinc carbonate, plus a little camphor, Benadryl—diphenhydramine hydrochloride—and rubbing alcohol) if necessary. The same is true of the itching associated with eczema or hives, although if these are caused by an allergy to a food, the cause of the allergic condition must be determined and eliminated from the diet. In the case of hives antihistamines are very helpful. The itching of athlete's foot requires a specific ointment. The itching of poison ivy can usually be relieved by a soothing, drying lotion such as calamine or caladryl, and the child should be taught to avoid this plant in the future. (See **Allergy; Athlete's foot; Eczema; Hay fever; Hives; Poison ivy.**)

The itching of the eyes and nose during hay fever usually responds to antihistamines given by mouth. In severe cases, however, desensitizing inoculations, given preventively, may be necessary. (See **Hay fever.**)

The itching of chicken pox and shingles can be treated locally with lotions, by mouth with antihistamines, and by special baths. (See **Chicken pox; Shingles.**)

Itching caused by insect bites can be treated locally with a paste of baking soda, and antihistamines may also be prescribed. (See **Insect and spider bites.**) That due to scabies or head lice requires the elimination of the insects. (See **Head lice; Scabies.**) Itching caused by chiggers is treated locally with calamine or caladryl and soothing baths. Antihistamines may also be given. (See **Chiggers.**)

Itching caused by pinworms can be relieved by the local application of anesthetic ointment but requires also the elimination of the worms by specific medicines. (See **Worms.**)

J

Jaundice

A yellow discoloration of the skin and the whites of the eyes, caused by excessive bile pigments in the bloodstream.

There are numerous causes of jaundice during infancy and childhood, among which the most common are:

1. Incompatibility of the mother's and the baby's blood during pregnancy. This is found in Rh incompatibility and occasionally in other cases of the mother's blood differing in type from the baby's. (See **Rh factor blood incompatibility.**)
2. Any closure or narrowing of the bile duct, which transfers bile from the liver into the intestines. In this condition the liver continues to form bile, but the blocked duct causes the bile to back up and it is finally forced into the bloodstream. When this condition exists, the urine is dark brown and the bowel movements white or gray.
3. Infections, especially during the newborn period, which either damage the liver or break down blood cells, releasing their pigment.
4. An immaturity of the liver in certain newborns, especially those that are premature.
5. Infectious hepatitis, a contagious condition caused by a virus. (See **Hepatitis, infectious.**)

Treatment Since jaundice may be due to so many different causes, the treatment varies. Jaundice caused by blood incompatibility may require exchange transfusions if the jaundice gets too intense. Jaundice caused by a closed bile duct requires surgical correction. When an infection is the cause, treatment of the specific infection is indicated.

Jaundice of the newborn child and especially the premature infant due to immaturity of the liver is successfully treated by light therapy, in which the infant is placed under a special blue or white fluorescent lamp. The rays of this lamp break down the bile pigment circulating in the blood, so that it can be disposed of by the liver.

There is no treatment at present for infectious hepatitis, but it will almost always clear up with rest and proper medical supervision.

Jealousy

The most common form of jealousy among children is jealousy of siblings. This is almost universal when there is more than one child in the family, but a parent should always try to be sure that he is making each child feel fully and equally loved and admired. (See **Sibling rivalry and jealousy.**)

It is also very common for children to feel jealous of other children because they have more toys or better clothes, are better in school or at sports, are more popular, and so forth. This is natural, but at times it may become too intense, edging over into bitterness, hostility, and self-pity. Excessive jealousy is a sign of insecurity and will disappear if the child is helped to feel better about his own attractiveness and abilities.

See **Competitiveness; Insecurity; Unpopularity.**

Jellyfish stings

Jellyfish float in the ocean looking like small, translucent umbrellas with long strings (tentacles) hanging down from the outer rim. These tentacles contain thousands of tiny stingers, and any child or adult who touches the tentacles will usually receive a very painful sting. The sting of larger jellyfish may produce not only pain but also muscle cramps, nausea, and at times even difficulty in breathing. Some children and adults may experience allergic reactions from the stings.

Treatment Wash the painful area immediately with a mixture of equal parts of ammonia and water. This will usually relieve the worst of the pain within thirty minutes, but if inadequate, then Xylocaine (lidocaine) or Nupercaine (dibucaine) ointment may be applied locally. Aspirin by mouth is also helpful in relieving pain. Allergic reactions should be treated by antihistamines orally and, if severe, by injections of adrenalin.

Jobs see **Chores; Work, full-time, part-time.**

Joint pains see **Growing pains; Rheumatic fever; rheumatoid arthritis.**

Junior bed

When children reach the age of 2 to 3 years, the time comes for giving up the crib and sleeping in a bed. This is one of the steps which gives the child the feeling that he is growing out of the infan-

tile period. And by this time most children can climb out of their cribs, so cribs are no longer useful in keeping them in bed.

The junior bed is a low bed with protective boards running from the head of the bed halfway down each side. These boards are removable and can be taken off when a child is completely adjusted to sleeping on the bed without falling off. Some parents make junior beds out of low cots or beds by placing the backs of chairs against the side or sides of the bed.

A firm mattress is always advisable. It is usually still necessary to use a waterproof pad or have the mattress covered with waterproof material. (See **Mattress.**)

One word of advice: if a new baby is expected, and will be using the older child's crib, it is advisable to move the older child to the junior bed a month or so ahead so he will not feel that he is being "evicted" in order to make a place for the new arrival.

Junior college see **College, preparation for.**

Juvenile delinquency

The definition of juvenile delinquency varies from state to state. It includes all serious offenses committed by boys and girls under age 18, such as murder, robbery, assault, burglary, auto theft, and rape. It usually also includes less serious misbehavior, such as being "uncontrollable" or "incorrigible," truancy, running away from home, smoking marijuana, and vandalism. However, in certain states boys and girls are labeled delinquent only if they are found guilty of committing offenses that would be considered crimes if performed by an adult.

There is no accurate figure available as to the number of cases of juvenile delinquency in the United States; not all cases are recorded, particularly from middle-class or upper-class families. However, over 1,500,000 cases are reported each year by the courts. Children convicted of serious misbehavior are usually sent to correctional institutions by the court. Children with minor problems—such as truancy, resistance to parents, running away, and smoking marijuana—are usually placed on probation and under professional care. There are very many exceptions to this general pattern, however; a youngster who has committed a seriously antisocial act may receive little or no care or supervision. A youngster found guilty of relatively minor misbehavior may be sentenced to an institution.

The majority of boys brought before the juvenile courts have been accused of serious crimes, whereas the majority of girls are brought for minor crimes, such as difficult behavior at home, running away from home, truancy, or petty stealing. In certain instances girls are subjected to legal proceedings and punishment for behavior that is usually acceptable for boys.

Causes The causes of juvenile delinquency are numerous, but undoubtedly the two most frequent are problems of family life and neighborhood environment.

Delinquency occurs among children of the affluent as well as in economically deprived families. In most cases the family life is unhappy and at times almost nonexistent. Often the parents show little or no interest in their children's lives and development, and there is no warmth in the parent-child relationship—in fact, communication between the parent and child may be almost totally lacking. Frequently, too, the children come from broken homes.

The delinquent often acts out his unhappiness and dissatisfaction by such actions against the adult world as arson, stealing, and smashing windows—actions that are destructive, hostile, resentful, and defiant.

Many children brought up in deprived ghetto areas are not only involved in problems at home but are exposed to established culture patterns that make it prestigious to be tough and fearless, to outwit people, seek thrills, risk danger, and resist authority.

Treatment For a condition that has so many causes and expresses itself in so many ways, no single remedy or treatment can be given. Unfortunately no treatment has been more than mildly successful.

In the area of prevention, attempts have been made to identify boys and girls who might later commit delinquent acts. Teachers in the elementary schools can often recognize children who are veering in the direction of delinquency.

Some of the characteristics which may define a predelinquent are:

Repeated resistance to authority; excessive lying, especially during the preteen and teen years; lack of respect for others and their property; constant refusal to cooperate with others; withdrawal from activity with others; temper tantrums; constant fighting; stealing and cheating; cruelty and bullying; truancy.

A teacher can usually detect, as well, those children who are neglected or abused.

In many schools a child who shows predelinquent behavior is referred to a guidance counselor, who studies him and his environment and advises the parents. This approach has met with only moderate success, probably because of the lack of trained guidance counselors and the lack of time to devote to each child and his family.

Other efforts to work effectively with predelinquent children are made by community-organized youth organizations and athletic groups such as the Police Athletic League. Also, the Big Brother Movement takes a close interest in individual boys referred by the court as predelinquents.

These preventive efforts are undoubtedly helpful in some cases, but unfortunately the treatment of juvenile delinquents has been far from successful. One review of delinquents under the age of 20 who were released from institutions in 1963 showed that 74 percent had been rearrested by 1969.

Just what happens when a child is found guilty by the courts and is judged a juvenile delinquent? In some states he is sent to jail with adult criminals. It is reported that each year in the United States more than 100,000 children under the age of 18 are held in adult jails or prisons.

There are special correctional institutions—some for first offenders, others for those convicted repeatedly—to which many of these children are sent. In some of these institutions the boys and girls may receive some group therapy, but no deep therapy is available. Rarely is any effort made to correct the home environment which is so often the basis of the child's difficulty.

The great danger of this penal system is that the delinquent child, being thrown in with others who have committed various types of crimes, learns their methods. All too often the institutional atmosphere is brutalizing—excessively restrictive without preventing violence, sexual deviation, and drug use. In many cases administrators are well-intentioned but have not been able to bring about adequate reforms.

The dangerous consequences of institutional care should serve as a strong deterrent to parents who bring their children to court as delinquents because they cannot control them at home or because the children run away, smoke marijuana, or indulge in petty stealing. Such parents are badly mistaken in their belief that the discipline of the law will correct the problems that exist. Quite the opposite is true, and these children, who, as a rule, are not really "bad," return home much worse in every way than when they left.

The best treatment is through guidance and psychotherapy of both the predelinquent and delinquent child and his parents, with an effort to alter his home environment and bring about a better and more understanding parent-child relationship. Dedicated, well-trained youth counselors are needed to work with groups of boys and girls in deprived areas to keep them actively and purposively occupied and help to deter them from possible acts of delinquency.

Institutions for delinquents should be corrective rather than penal. The children should not be locked in behind walls or bars but should be involved in interesting activities, vocational as well as educational or entertaining. At the same time, therapy is most important, and social workers should endeavor to work with the parents as well.

The approach to and treatment of juvenile delinquency must be radically altered if we are to expect improvement in this serious, ever-growing problem.

K

Keloid scars see **Scars.**

Kerosene poisoning see **Poisons: first-aid treatment.**

Kicking see **Biting, kicking, pushing, hitting.**

Kidney machine

A mechanism designed to remove wastes products from the blood when the kidneys are no longer able to function or have been removed, as in the case of tumors of the kidney. Such a machine is used as a temporary treatment until a satisfactory kidney transplant can be arranged. Children can remain on this form of treatment for years, although they grow very little during the period they are so treated. Once a kidney is successfully transplanted, some of this growth deficit is usually made up.

The method most frequently used is to place one of the fine tubes leading from the machine into one of the child's arteries and another tube into one of the child's veins. The blood flows out of the artery through the tube into the coils of the machine, where the waste products of the blood are removed. Then the blood flows back into the child's body through the tube in his vein. A single treatment usually takes four to six hours, during which time the child can read, study, or watch television. The treatment is given three times weekly.

Another form of treatment is by putting tubes through the child's abdominal wall into the abdomen and passing fluid in and then withdrawing it (peritoneal dialysis). This is rarely used, except in emergency situations or before artery-vein treatment is started.

The cost of treatment is very high, although it may be covered or partly covered by insurance. In 1972 the cost varied from approximately $7,000 a year for home treatment to $100,000 a year for hospitalization with treatment. Hospital treatment includes the cost of hospital room, nursing care, services, and so on. This cost varies from $50,000 to $100,000 a year.

Intermediate-care centers are centers to which patients can go for treatment three times weekly for four to six hours. The cost in such centers is approximately $15,000 a year.

Home care is being used in an increasing number of cases. The parents buy a machine for $5,000 (maintenance is $2,000 a year), are taught to operate it, and also are taught how to insert the tubes into the child's arteries and veins. Home care is being looked on as the future method of treatment.

Regarding the question of costs, many different groups are seeking reforms and changes so that this treatment may be available to all who are in need.

Kidney transplantation

Kidney transplantation is being done more and more frequently and with increasing success.

The most successful kidney transplants are those from identical twins, but other transplants have been successful also when blood typing is the same.

Kidneys

The kidneys are two organs located in the rear of the abdomen (one on either side) that are extremely important for the elimination of waste products of the body cells brought to them by the blood. The kidneys are also greatly responsible for regulating the volume and

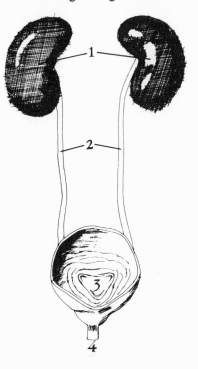

1. Kidneys. 2. Ureter. 3. Urinary bladder. 4. Urethra.

composition of the body fluids, preventing the blood from becoming too acid or too alkaline. They also regulate the salt and water balance in the body.

In the kidneys the waste products

from the blood plus the excess water from the body form urine. The urine flows from each kidney into a tube (ureter) which carries it to the urinary bladder.

Kidney insufficiency If the kidneys are not functioning sufficiently to eliminate wastes from the body, whether the cause is infection or a structual defect, then emergency treatment is required. When the kidneys fail to pass waste materials, then toxins build up in the system (uremia), and the patient's life is in danger. If there is danger of total kidney failure, a kidney transplant (see **Kidney transplantation**) or the use of an artificial kidney (see **Kidney machine**) may be recommended as a last, life-saving resort.

See also **Nephritis; Nephrosis; Pyelitis; Urinary obstruction.**

Kidneys, polycystic

A congenital condition in which the kidneys are riddled with cysts (hollow openings in the inside of the organ). Both kidneys are usually affected.

The remaining normal tissue of the kidneys can often function adequately for the child for the first year or two, but then, with growth, the kidneys gradually fail. This is one of the conditions for which a kidney machine or kidney transplant is eventually necessary to sustain life.

Kindergarten

A class in school for 5-year-olds to give them some understanding of how school works without the formality of the classes in the regular grades. Formerly this was a child's first introduction to education, but within recent years nursery school education has been generally accepted as advantageous, and for a large number of children the nursery school is their first educational experience. (See **Nursery school.**)

The program of a kindergarten is approximately the same as that of a nursery school but on a slightly higher level. There are a great variety of materials for a child to play with: building blocks and painting equipment, toys for imaginary play, books to look at and puzzles to do. And then there are dancing or rhythms, storytelling both by teacher and child, and group discussions. Those children who are ready to read may be given this opportunity as well. Most kindergartens have programs preparing children for reading.

The kindergarten class usually has space for outdoor play, and often walks and trips are taken so that the children can observe and discuss many of the things in the world around them.

Most children learn, in the course of the kindergarten year, what will be expected of them in the first grade in school, and the transition to a more formal type of education is made without too much difficulty.

Kleptomania

A compulsive urge to steal. This obsessive condition is found among children of all social and economic levels. It is not to be confused with the occasional stealing by young children who do not fully appreciate the rights of possession. Kleptomania also differs from occasional stealing as a part of a general pattern of antisocial behavior; for example, a child who will steal on a dare from his companions may well be in trouble because of the company he keeps and his recklessness, but he does not necessarily feel an urge to steal frequently. (See **Stealing.**)

The juvenile kleptomaniac is usually a child of 8 or older who habitually takes things belonging to classmates or other people, or even from stores. He may arrive home with a silver dollar, a pearl-handled knife, a pen, or any of numerous other objects and when questioned may say that he traded something for it, that he found it, that it was given to him as a present.

Why do these children have this compulsive urge to steal? It usually is not because they lack money, for many of them come from well-to-do families and would probably be given the objects they take if the parents felt that they were so greatly wanted.

In almost every instance these are unhappy children coming from homes where they feel unloved, and often where there has been a lack of real interest. Or they may come from broken homes or homes where there is constant strife.

These children are subconsciously trying to compensate for the lack of affection and attention by the pleasure gained from having something that belongs to someone else—they gain some sense of power as well as possession. They steal without restraint or remorse and as a rule have no feeling for the persons from whom the objects are taken.

Treatment It should be remembered first and foremost that kleptomaniac youngters are not bad children but sad children.

Of course the objects stolen should be returned, but without exposing the child to shame or derision.

Most important, the parents' relationship to the child, as well as the whole home environment, must be carefully investigated. In almost every instance consultation with a psychotherapist or child guidance expert is necessary to uncover the causes of this asocial behavior and to correct it.

Knock-knees

A condition in which the child stands with the knees close together and the ankles spread apart. This is fairly common in children; it is the result of poor muscle tone and weak knee ligaments,

A knock-knee stance is common in young children. Most often it will disappear as the muscles strengthen, but it should be checked by a doctor.

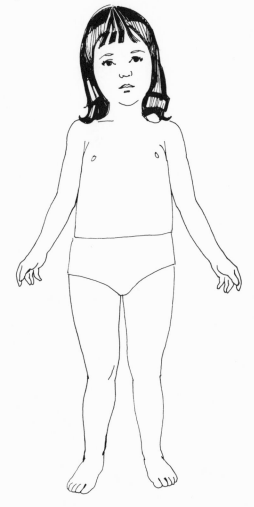

and often is associated with flat feet. It was also formerly caused by such conditions as rickets and poliomyelitis, both of which are today quite rare in this country. In older teen-age girls some knock-knee may be caused by the normal widening of the hips.

Treatment It has been shown that if the child's muscle tone is built up, the legs will straighten out by themselves. This is aided by increased activity and special toys for younger children in which leg muscles are used. Bicycle and tricycle riding, riding a toy horse, and playing a game of walking with a book between the knees can be of help.

The condition may also be treated effectively by placing wedges one-eighth of an inch thick on the inner heels and soles of the child's shoes. This tends to separate the knees and hastens improvement.

Kwashiorkor

A disease caused by severe protein deficiency, often despite the intake of adequate calories. It is found largely in the undeveloped countries, where there is no milk and very little, if any, meat in the diet. There are occasional cases in the United States as well. Kwashiorkor occurs in children who, after they are taken off the breast, receive no further milk and very little, if any, protein.

There is a retardation of growth, weakness, loss of appetite, a general swelling of all parts of the body, a greatly distended abdomen, loss of hair pigmentation, diarrhea, and anemia.

Treatment with a high-protein diet and vitamins produces fairly rapid recovery. Without treatment the children grow weaker and weaker, and usually die of some contracted infection.

L

Labial adhesions

Adhesions binding together the inner walls of the vulva are not uncommon in infants and little girls. The adhesions usually start in the rear and form a membrane gradually extending forward, covering the hymen and, at times, leaving only a small opening at the front for the passage of urine. Often the condition exists with no signs or symptoms. At other times, however, the area beneath the membrane gets irritated, probably from ammonia formed by a small amount of urine retained within it.

Formerly these adhesions were separated manually or even cut, but both forms of treatment were painful. Today creams are available, obtained by prescription, that when applied to the area will separate the adhesions without pain or discomfort.

Language   see **Bilingual families; Speech.**

Language, bad   see **Swear words.**

Language, foreign   see **Bilingual families.**

Laryngitis

An inflammation of the larynx usually associated with a respiratory infection. The larynx, or voice box, is a part of the upper end of the trachea (windpipe) and contains the vocal cords. In mild laryngitis there is only hoarseness, but if the inflammation is more severe, a hard, brassy, barky cough results and diffi-culty in breathing may develop. This severe laryngitis, known as croup, may be serious in young children. (See **Croup.**)

Treatment of mild laryngitis is by the inhalation of either warm steam or cold-water mist. The warm-steam inhalation is most commonly used, but when used it should be constantly watched to prevent possible spilling and burning. (See **Steam treatment.**) Severe types of laryngitis usually require antibiotic therapy as well as other therapy prescribed by the doctor.

Laryngotracheobronchitis see **Croup.**

Latency period   see **School-age period.**

Laxatives

Foods, drugs, or other substances that, taken by mouth, stimulate evacuation of the bowels. Stronger laxatives are sometimes called "cathartics," but this does not mean that a product called a "laxative" is necessarily mild.

Fruits and vegetables are nature's laxatives, and, if possible, should be used in preference to drugs and mineral oil in infancy and childhood. Among these, the most effective are prunes, apricots, raisins, figs, and grapes. Other laxative foods are spinach, carrots, beets, and bran.

Certain sugars are also excellent and natural laxatives. The unrefined sugars—brown sugar, dark Karo syrup, malt soup—belong in this category.

These may be added to the child's formula or milk (2 to 3 tablespoons daily of unrefined sugar, or 1 to 2 teaspoons daily of malt soup).

Laxative drugs should be avoided unless their use is suggested by the child's doctor. These are of several types:

1. Laxatives that act by drawing fluid from the blood through the intestinal wall, causing a liquid stool. Among such are epsom salts, castoria, milk of magnesia, and citrate of magnesia.
2. Laxatives that act by mildly irritating the lining of the intestinal wall, causing increased intestinal activity. In this category are cascara, castor oil, and phenolphthalein preparations such as those commonly sold in the form of chewing-gum, chocolate squares, and mints.
3. Mineral oil, which lubricates the intestines and prevents the stool from hardening. This is not given routinely because it tends to absorb vitamin A from the diet.
4. Stool softeners, which are drugs that cause the stool to hold liquid and prevent drying and hardness. Colace is such a drug.

See also **Constipation.**

Layette
Suggestions for clothing and other basic equipment for an infant's first three months are given below.

Clothes
4 cotton shirts (medium sleeves), 6-month size
3 cotton nightgowns, one-year size
2 stretch pajamas, medium size
2 cotton kimonos, one-year size
2 sacques, one-year size
2 sweaters, one of which should be warm for cool weather
2 bibs
See also **Clothing.**

Diapers
If using diaper service, 80 to 100 a week, plus one dozen for home use.
If washing at home, 3 to 4 dozen diapers
If using disposable diapers, have 50 to 100 on hand
2 waterproof panties or covers
6 safety pins (rustproof), specifically for diapers
diaper pail

Bed
1 bassinet or crib
1 firm mattress (most are waterproof)
2 large flannelette-coated waterproof sheets or waterproof sheeting covering entire top of crib mattress
3 cotton pads, if not using flannelette-coated waterproof sheets
3 smaller waterproof pads, for carriages, laps, etc.
4 crib sheets (fitted sheets preferred)
3 receiving blankets (light)
1 warm crib blanket
1 medium-warm crib blanket

Bathing needs
Bathinette or plastic tub
3 soft towels, small
2 bath towels to wrap around baby
3 soft washcloths
baby soap
baby oil or lotion
powder
cotton balls and swabs
hairbrush (soft natural bristles)

Feeding needs
This depends on whether a baby is breast-fed or bottle-fed, and on whether a formula is to be prepared each day or obtained already sterilized and bottled.

For the breast-fed baby
3 four-ounce glass or clear plastic bot-

tles for water or fruit juice (Playtex presterilized plastic bottles may be used)

3 prepared, sterilized, and bottled commercial baby formulas to be kept on hand in case mother cannot breast-feed at a particular time

For the formula-fed baby

For preparing formulas; either use the Playtex presterilized plastic bottles or the following:

a sterilizer with rack and lid
6 eight-ounce bottles
2 four-ounce bottles
8 nipples
8 bottle caps and nipple covers, or hoods
measuring spoon
tongs
glass measuring cup
nipple jar
bottle brush
nipple brush
funnel (boilable)
electric bottle warmer

For outdoors
carriage
carriage blanket
bunting
bottle bag

Other helpful equipment in baby's room
chest with deep drawers for clothing, bedding, and extra diapers
clothes-drying rack
chair to sit on while feeding the baby, preferably a rocking chair

See also **Bassinet; Bottle feeding; Breast feeding; Carriage; Clothing; Crib; Formulas; Junior bed; Mattress.**

Laziness

A healthy young child is never lazy. He is almost always active and occupied when he is awake, with the exception of times when he is listening to a story or watching television.

The term "lazy" is applied to some older children when they reach the age at which they are expected to carry out chores, do special jobs, or do their schoolwork. Then if a child resists or holds off or does the work slowly he is called lazy.

Occasionally "laziness" is due to some physical cause such as anemia or a low-grade infection. Therefore, a listless child should always be checked by the doctor. More often the cause is emotional: unhappiness, fear, anxiety, or the child's feeling that he is not appreciated even when he has fulfilled what is expected of him. Or the so-called laziness may simply be due to boredom. Also, during the school years, and even more so during adolescence, there is so much to do and to think about that at times dishwashing, mowing the lawn, or raking the leaves becomes "too much" or takes up too much valuable time.

Parents should be sure that the demands they place upon a child are not beyond his capacity or do not deprive him of too much time, limiting too greatly his normal activities and association with his companions. They should not exercise too much direction as to when or how a task is to be done and should not resort to constant nagging. Much more can be accomplished in stimulating activity by giving the child some leeway in arranging his work, giving him a knowledge of parental confidence, and expressing appreciation for the work completed.

Lead poisoning

Approximately 200,000 cases of lead poisoning occur each year among children in the United States. Most of these are young children (aged 1 to 3) who contract the condition by biting lead paint off cribs, playpens, walls, and less frequently, by biting lead toys or tinfoil (not aluminum foil). These children may stand in their cribs or playpens and bite the paint off the sides or the railing, or they may eat bits of plaster from the walls.

There are laws in most states prohibiting the use of paints containing lead in cribs, playpens, carriages, and children's toys. But only too often people use old or secondhand cribs and playpens and, to freshen them, repaint them with ordinary paint, which may contain lead.

Furthermore, children may bite the paint off windowsills, walls, and chairs. In most homes in the past these items were painted with lead paint, and often they have not been repainted or the new paint has chipped away, exposing the old paint. In 1972, however, the Federal Drug Administration moved to combat this danger by ordering lead to be banned from all household paints as of 1974.

Signs and symptoms At the outset the symptoms may be relatively mild—some weakness, irritability, loss of weight, anemia, and headache. These are usually followed by loss of appetite, abdominal pain, and vomiting. If the condition continues with added ingestion of lead, the child's brain is affected and damaged (lead encephalitis), and nerve symptoms occur, such as muscular incoordination, muscle paralysis, and finally convulsions. This is very dangerous, and the damage to the brain may be permanent.

Diagnosis The child's blood and urine are studied for abnormal amounts of lead. Under the microscope one can see little dark spots in the red blood cells, a sign that lead is in the child's system. Also, an X ray of the long bones will show a dense line of lead at the ends of the bones near the joints.

Treatment The first thing to do is to eliminate all possible danger of further lead poisoning by removing objects containing lead or by restricting the child from eating the lead. There are drugs of value in removing the lead from the child's body, but this is a long process.

Remember, lead poisoning is entirely preventable, and there is no excuse for children's contracting the condition.

Learning

From the moment an infant is born, he starts learning. He begins to respond to touch, sound, light, taste, and smell. And the learning continues every day through every experience.

All healthy children have an innate curiosity and an ability to learn about the world by observation, exploration, and discovery. In this, parents can aid greatly by stimulating and encouraging the child's interests, by providing him with numerous things to see, feel, and hear. The child who receives this extra stimulation during infancy is likely to be much more alert and interested, in later childhood, than the child who lacks this extra care and attention.

See also **Books; Imitation; Play; Stimulating the child; Toys and play materials.**

Learning difficulties

Within recent years increased interest has been taken in children who have definite learning problems, and especially in children of apparently normal intelligence who have great difficulty in learning to read, write, or spell.

Most often a child's difficulty is not apparent until he enters school. At this time the teacher may tell the parents that he is having trouble keeping up with the class. However, the child may be doing moderately well but working under a handicap that makes the lessons more difficult for him than they should be and very probably makes him tense and discouraged as well. If a learning problem arises suddenly after two or more years of schooling, it is most likely that some cause of unhappiness or emotional upset is distracting the child or that some physical problem, possibly with vision or hearing, has cropped up. In the relatively intimate situations of kindergarten and first grade, there are fewer demands on vision or hearing, but thereafter the child may find himself sitting further from the teacher and having to follow more complicated instructions, either spoken or written on the board.

Many good teachers will advise parents on what steps to take to discover the cause of a child's learning difficulties, but parents should be prepared to take the initiative themselves if the child seems to be having difficulty getting his work done or keeping up with the class. Parents should first ask the child's doctor to investigate whether there may be some physical problem. If not, they should try to discover whether anything in the child's home or school life is making him unhappy and unable to do as well as he is capable of doing. Parents should also consult with the teacher.

And they should keep in mind that some children develop more slowly than others, and may not in the early years be fully ready for the complicated task of learning to read and write. Also, not every child can be at the top of his class. If a child is doing adequate although not excellent work, and seems reasonably happy and well-adjusted, he should not be pressured by his parents to do better. Many of these children do very well indeed as they grow older and develop a more mature understanding of what interests them and what they like and want to do.

The primary causes of learning difficulties are:

Mental retardation   Children with mental deficiency vary greatly in their learning capacity depending on the severity of the deficiency. Children with an IQ below 20 will rarely attain the mentality of the average 2-year-old. Children with an IQ of 20 to 40 can be expected to reach the mentality of a 3-to-5-year-old but will rarely learn to read or write. Those with an IQ of 40 to 70 may attain a level of the 5-to-10-year-old and may learn to read and even write, but their learning rate is much slower than that of the average child. (See **Mental retardation**.)

Poor vision   Visual difficulty may cause hardship in learning to read, and should always be investigated as a possible cause. (See **Eye defects**.)

Hearing difficulty   Hearing problems may be responsible for learning difficulties, since children with such difficulties are often unable to understand directions or follow what is going on in class. Hearing difficulty should always be checked as a possible cause. (See **Deafness**.)

Brain dysfunction   This may be caused by many conditions and may be mild or severe. One of the most common forms involves difficulty in concentrating and, frequently, perceptual difficulties. (See **Brain dysfunction, mild.**)

Dyslexia   This is a general term indicating difficulty in learning to read because of difficulties in perception. The dyslexic child may not see letters and numbers in the normal way or remember what he has read and heard as well as other children. The condition may be caused by mild brain damage. (See **Brain dysfunction, mild; Dyslexia.**)

Hyperactivity   The hyperactive child who is easily distracted and full of restless energy may also have difficulty settling down in school and learning. Hyperactivity may be the result of mild brain dysfunction, and this can be diagnosed and treated by the child's doctor. (See **Hyperactivity.**)

Emotional upset   Children who are emotionally distressed may have marked learning difficulties. Their unhappiness causes them to be easily distracted and prone to daydreaming instead of studying.

Often children who have learning difficulties from other causes develop emotional difficulties because of insecurity about their ability to keep up with their classmates. These emotional difficulties compound their educational problems.

Lack of stimulation at home   All children with normal learning ability need stimulation at home during their preschool years. They need parents or others who will talk to them, stimulate their curiosity, and give them new experiences. Children who suffer from paren-

tal indifference will often have learning difficulties. (See **Stimulating the child.**)

Cultural deprivation   When for economic or other reasons boys and girls receive few or no cultural advantages at home, they often have trouble with the usual learning skills. This is often the case among children from areas where economic levels are low, where many mothers are forced to work, and where parents themselves have little cultural background and can give little or no stimulation to their children in that direction.

Left-handedness   see **Handedness.**

Leukemia
A disease that is a cancer of the blood-forming organs of the body. It is characterized by a widespread, rapid, and disorderly production of white blood cells. Recent evidence has indicated that it may be caused by a virus.

Leukemia is essentially a disease of childhood and youth. At the present time it is incurable, but recent advances which keep the disease in check for years give hopes of an eventual cure.

Signs and symptoms   Leukemia can only be diagnosed by careful blood studies. Parents must be warned against trying to make their own diagnosis, since there are other, nondangerous diseases such as infectious mononucleosis and generalized infections which may produce signs and symptoms very similar to those of leukemia.

The most common signs and symptoms are fever, weight loss, and fatigue. Bruises over the body are frequently encountered, and swollen lymph nodes may also be present. The children are pale and anemic, and bleed and bruise easily. Often there is loss of appetite, nausea, and abdominal pain.

Treatment Within recent years a number of drugs have been found to control leukemia successfully for long periods of time. However, when any single drug is used by itself, it is successful in controlling the disease only temporarily. One of the most recent treatments, as reported by the National Cancer Institute, is to use these successful drugs, capable of destroying leukemic cells, in rotation. When each drug begins to lose its effectiveness, it is supplanted by another successful drug. This approach can be continued for a period of years. Another modern treatment is by the transplantation to the child of normal, healthy bone marrow.

Lice see **Head lice.**

Lighter-fluid poisoning see **Poisons: first-aid treatment.**

Lighting
Proper lighting is important in preventing eyestrain in children, especially when they reach the reading age. The light should not be glaring directly at the child and should not be flickering. Glare and flickering can also be a problem in watching television. When children sit too close to the television, they cannot avoid seeing the flickering found in most sets. Also, there should be some light in the room in which a child watches television.

Contrary to general belief, poor lighting does not do permanent damage to the eyes. It has no influence in causing a child to become nearsighted or farsighted or astigmatic. The only harmful effect is eyestrain, which may cause headaches or interfere with a child's reading pleasure and capability.

Lightning shock see **Electric shock.**

Lip, cleft see **Harelip.**

Lip sucking see **Sucking need.**

Lips, chapped or cracked
Dryness of the lips in children is often followed by cracking. It may occur when the child licks his lips and then they are dried by the wind in cold, dry weather. And when toys or other objects to which the child may be sensitive come into contact with the lips, this may cause drying.

The dryness and cracking usually respond well to frequent applications of Vaseline, camphor ice, or one of the special preparations such as Chap Stick or Lipaid.

Chapping and cracking of the lips may also occasionally occur among teen-age girls who use lipsticks to which they are sensitive.

Lipstick see **Makeup.**

Liquid diet see **Diet, liquid.**

Lisping
A speech defect in which the letters s and z are pronounced as th. "Sing" will be pronounced "thing" by children with this defect, and "zebra" will be pronounced "thebra."

Usually this is an infantile manner of speech carried on to an older age. It is probably caused by inadequate control and use of certain muscles of the tongue, and in most cases it disappears as complete control of the tongue is gained. In some cases special speech exercises are advised to aid the child in learning to pronounce *s*.

Speech clinics are associated with many hospitals and colleges. There are also speech experts in private practice who can be referred by doctors in the community.

Parents should not regard this speech defect as "cute" and thereby encourage its continuance.

Listlessness   see Fatigue; Laziness.

Liver

A large, reddish-brown glandular organ in the upper right abdomen just under the lower ribs on that side. It is one of the most important digestive organs in the body. A person cannot live without it.

The liver has a number of functions including producing bile, the digestive juice of most importance in the digestion of fat; breaking down certain toxic (poisonous) substances that may be in a person's system; storing the products of the digestion of carbohydrates and sugars for use as energy when necessary; and storing vitamins A and D.

The liver is also the primary organ of blood formation in the fetus, and serves as a storehouse for iron during the first five months of life—an important function during a period when the baby is unable to form his own iron.

Fortunately, during infancy and childhood liver problems are rarely encountered with the exceptions of those that occur with hepatitis and infectious mononucleosis. Congenital defects of the liver causing jaundice are extremely rare.

Lobar pneumonia   see Pneumonia.

Lockjaw   see Tetanus.

Losing   see Competitiveness.

Love

Of all the qualities that make a good parent none is more important than love. Nothing is so devastating and destructive to a child as to feel unloved and unwanted.

Love is expressed in many ways, and there is no single standard by which love can be measured. Hugging and kissing, although outward expressions of affection, are not necessarily essential in the demonstration of affection. The tiny infant feels love, almost from the moment of birth, in the way the mother holds him, cuddles him, feeds him, and keeps him warm and comfortable. Soon he also recognizes affection in the sound of her voice when she talks or sings to him, in her smile and her laughter, and in the comforting touch of her hands and her enjoyment of him and his discovery of the world around him. And the father, too, should join in these expressions of affection.

As a child grows older, love is shown in many other ways. Giving encouragement and support when needed, praise and admiration when warranted, comforting when a child is hurt, understanding when he is unhappy or upset; reading to him, being interested in what he's doing, laughing with him, playing with him, enjoying him—these are only a few of the many ways by which affection is expressed.

Some parents worry that too much affection may be bad for the child—that it may spoil him, may interfere with his learning to be independent. Fathers, in particular, may want their sons to be tough, although they are dismayed if the child shows signs of being callous or cruel. Real affection, the expression of true love, cannot harm a child. If a parent will look back on his own childhood, he will realize this clearly. It is very unusual for an adult to complain that his parents loved him too much, although many complain that their parents didn't love them enough. Shows of affection, however, may sometimes be motivated by feelings other than love. This may happen, for example, when a parent feels that his or her own life has been empty and unrewarding and looks to the child to make up for this, or when a parent feels guilty for resenting having the child and tries to mask this resentment by exaggerated gestures of affection. It is only this kind of false affection that can spoil the child.

See also **Mothering; Rejection.**

LSD   see **Drug abuse.**

LSD poisoning   see **Poisons: first-aid treatment.**

Lungs
The two organs of breathing, one on either side of the chest. The right lung is divided into three lobes, the left lung into two. It is in the lungs that the inhaled air gives up its oxygen to the blood and absorbs waste gases from it. (See **Bronchial tree.**)

Prior to birth the lungs are collapsed. Immediately after birth the infant breathes in and the lungs expand. At times mucus in the breathing tubes makes expansion difficult. It is to prevent this that doctors or nurses hold babies upside down after they are born and suction out their throats with a small rubber tube to remove any mucus that might be obstructing breathing.

Lye poisoning   see **Poisons: first-aid treatment.**

Lying
Little children often do not tell the truth, but this does not mean that they're lying. Usually they simply do not distinguish between fantasy and reality when making an untrue statement. Sometimes, of course, even a young child will deliberately lie—for example, claim that the cat broke something he broke himself.

After approximately age 6 years the majority of children understand the significance of truthfulness but still lie occasionally. Usually children lie for one or more of the following reasons: to avoid punishment; to gain approval, praise, and affection; to conceal their guilt; to get some other child or person into trouble; to impress other children or adults.

Just how should parents approach the problem of a child who lies? First, they should see to it that they themselves do not lie. Of course, all of us tell white lies, which might confuse a child, but it can be explained to him that these lies are told to avoid hurting other people's feelings. Most children soon distinguish between white lies and other lies.

Second, parents should try to determine why a child lies. Have they been too critical or punitive? Have they given too little approval and too little praise? Have they placed too much emphasis on achievement? Have they set standards that are too high and too difficult? Is the child insecure and telling lies to impress other boys and girls?

At times parents can discover the causes of lying by themselves. At other times they may need professional help.

But a child should know that his parents realize he is lying and that they do not like it. A child should be made to understand that he should tell the truth, but punishment should not be so severe that the child will lie to avoid it next time. (See **Discipline.**)

There are some children who are so upset emotionally that they lie regularly and at least partially believe the lies they tell. These youngsters are in great need of psychotherapy.

Lymph nodes

Rounded masses of tissue, sometimes called lymph glands (they look like glands) situated throughout the body. They are the "glands" under the chin that swell up and become tender when a person has a sore throat; they swell up in many parts of the body in infectious mononucleosis (glandular fever) and in German measles (rubella).

The nodes serve as filtering stations, holding bacteria or other foreign substances and preventing them from spreading throughout the body. For instance, if a child or adult gets an infection of his arm or hand, the lymph nodes in the armpit on the same side will often become enlarged and tender. Unless the infection is treated with antibiotics, the nodes may form pus within themselves and in a few days discharge it through an opening in the skin caused by a breaking down of the tissue near the pus area. Or a doctor may cut through the skin above the node and release the pus in this way. As a rule the

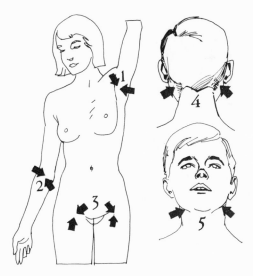

The main lymph nodes are in the armpit (1), the inside of the arm at the elbow (2), the groin (3), behind the ears (4), and in the front of the neck under the jaw (5).

infection disappears after the discharge of the pus.

All lymph-node swellings in children should be examined by the doctor for his diagnosis and treatment. In the vast majority of cases the cause will be found to be a local infection, but at other times blood studies, bone marrow studies, and microscopic studies of the gland tissue must be made to arrive at a diagnosis, for such swellings may be a symptom of rare but serious disorders, such as leukemia or Hodgkin's disease.

M

Magnesia, milk of see **Laxatives.**

Make-believe see **Fantasy; Imaginary companions.**

Makeup

Among teen-age girls fashions in the use of lipstick, rouge, eye shadow, eyebrow pencils, and mascara come and go. Often parents object to their daughter's use of cosmetics while the girl is equally determined to do what her friends are doing, to feel grown up, or to be attractive to boys. These are the normal desires of adolescent girls and should be understood and respected. But, without criticizing or ridiculing, parents may tactfully urge their daughters not to look garish.

It is true that a teen-age girl may resent her mother's or father's opinions as old-fashioned and "establishment." But the popular teen-age magazines have articles on makeup and grooming which most girls will respect. In some communities courses in grooming are given in the high school.

Malaria

A common disease in many parts of the world, especially in tropical and subtropical regions. It is transmitted to man by the bite of a mosquito (of the genus *Anopheles*) that has previously fed on the blood of a malaria-infected person.

In the United States the disease is generally confined to the southern states. Although it is not common in most parts of this country, in the areas where it is found, it is caught by almost every child. The majority of these infected children are between the ages of 6 months and 6 years.

Signs and symptoms Symptoms usually develop about fifteen days after the bite of the infected mosquito. The onset of the disease is sudden, with high fever (103 to 105 degrees) accompanied by chills and usually by convulsions in the very young. These convulsions are not dangerous in themselves.

The chills, which last approximately twenty to sixty minutes, are characterized by a shaking of the body and a chattering of teeth. Nausea and vomiting are frequent, and the child complains of pains throughout the body and a headache. After about four hours (although it may vary from two to twelve hours) the child perspires intensely and the fever drops to normal. He then usually sleeps and feels well when he awakens. However, forty-eight hours from the onset of the disease the fever, chills, headache, pains, and other symptoms return, and the pattern is continued every forty-eight hours until the child eventually recovers from the attack. If untreated, this may take a few weeks or months and there may be relapses.

Another type of malaria is characterized by the same symptoms occurring every seventy-two hours instead of every forty-eight hours.

A third type, which is rare (falciparum malaria), has irregularly remittent or continuous fever. It is the most severe type of the disease.

Diagnosis The diagnosis of malaria is made by examining under a microscope a smear of the blood of the person suspected of having the disease. The parasites causing the disease can be clearly seen in the blood.

Prevention and treatment A number of drugs are very effective today in the prevention of malaria, and they should be given to all children and adults living in or traveling through areas where malaria is present.

The drugs are given in tablet form one week before arrival in the infected area and once a week regularly thereafter, continuing for six weeks after leaving the area. Usually the dose is given on Sunday so that it is easily remembered.

Among the drugs most frequently used for prevention are Aralen (chloroquine phosphate with primaquine phosphate) and Dariprim (pyramethamine). A doctor should prescribe the dosage.

The usual dosage is: adults and children over 10 years: 1 tablet once weekly; children 4 to 10 years: ½ tablet once weekly; children under 4 years: ¼ tablet once weekly.

The same drugs are used in the treatment of malaria. They act to kill the parasites causing the disease, and complete recovery usually occurs in seven to ten days.

Prognosis Excellent with proper treatment.

Malnutrition

To most people the term "malnutrition" brings to mind a thin, undersized child. To the pediatrician this image symbolizes "undernutrition," only one aspect of malnutrition. For malnutrition can mean a lack of any of the essential vitamins, minerals, or food elements in a child's diet.

In infancy lack of protein can be critical, affecting the development of the brain. Protein deficiency is a problem among poverty-stricken families in which the mother does not produce enough breast milk, or stops nursing early, and there is not enough money to buy milk or meat. (See **Kwashiorkor.**) Infants who have celiac disease are malnourished because the intestines are not adequately absorbing food.

Malnutrition in older children may have numerous causes and does not always result in a thin, wasted child. Children who are given a great deal of carbohydrates (such as bread, spaghetti, and potatoes) but very little protein. may even appear overweight and still be weak from the lack of protein.

Poor and finicky appetites, inadequate eating habits, the dieting of adolescents, chronic infections, anemia, and emotional upsets may also cause malnutrition.

See also **Appetite, poor; Celiac disease; Dieting; Nutrition.**

Maltreated child   see **Child abuse.**

Manners

Children learn good manners largely from the example of their parents. It is difficult to force manners on them. This does not mean, however, that you cannot explain manners to a child and occasionally remind him of what is expected.

A child learns manners first by imitation. He starts eating with his fingers and later tries to copy the example of his parents by eating with a spoon and fork. He is taught to say "please" and "thank you," and he may often be reminded by his parents to use these words, but he learns primarily by hearing what his parents and others around him say.

It is not true that if manners are not taught early it will be more difficult to teach them later.

Several principles should be remembered in teaching manners to children:

1. Always set a good example.
2. Teach a child gradually, without pressure or anger or upset. Remember at all times that you are dealing with a child and not an adult.
3. Teach a child manners at home rather than outside the home. Rather than criticize him in public, say "thank you" for him if he doesn't say it at the proper time.

See also **Rudeness.**

Marijuana   see **Drug abuse.**

Marks for schoolwork

The marks a child receives for his school work may be interpreted in a number of ways, depending on the standards used by the teacher in grading. It is important to know if the teacher has based the marks on a group standard (the highest 10 percent of the class gets A's; the next 10 percent, B's, etc.), on the basis of individual performance (what the teacher considers the child able to do), or on an "absolute" standard (numerical grades may be given).

Marks may be a fairly accurate gauge of a child's academic ability. On the other hand, if for some reason a child is not working to fullest capacity, the marks will not be an accurate indication

of his capability. If the child's marks in one or more subjects are going down, parents will not help by punishing him, severely criticizing him, or appearing miserable over the subject. This kind of pressure will only make the child more tense. Rather, they should attempt to find out why his marks have declined, through discussions with the teacher, the child, and possibly the school guidance counselor. At times he may be having difficulty with a particular subject, which may require some special help. At other times his learning ability may be affected by problems with his teacher, his classmates, his school, or his health, or by difficulties in his home environment.

Only too often a parent will compare his own academic ability as a child with that of his youngster. "I always got A's in math. How come you get such low marks in it?" Even worse, parents may directly or indirectly compare children. "Your brother never got marks off for spelling. Why can't you be more careful?" These attitudes can be equally damaging in that they make the child feel inadequate and do not take into consideration the many things that may affect his ability to learn.

There are great individual differences among children in respect to their academic potential. The main emphasis should be not on marks received, but on whether a child is working up to his full potential and whether he enjoys learning. Many very brilliant and successful people, including Albert Einstein, have had mediocre or erratic school records.

Sometimes children are so fearful of a parent's reaction to poor marks that they will change the marks on the report card or forge the parent's signature. This is a sure sign that an unhealthy amount of pressure is being put on the child. Rather than scolding or punishing the child, parents should reexamine their own behavior toward him regarding achievement in school.

See also **Examinations and tests in school.**

Mastoiditis

An inflammation of the inner bone behind the ear, caused by a bacterial infection.

Fortunately it is now extremely rare, since the use of antibiotics can almost always overcome infections in the ears before they invade the mastoid bone. It usually takes an ear infection approximately three days to cause mastoiditis.

The condition can be diagnosed by tenderness and swelling of the mastoid bone behind an infected ear and by X rays which show the inflammation.

Treatment involves the use of antibiotics depending on the bacteria involved. At times surgery is necessary to drain the abscess.

See **Earaches.**

Masturbation

Manipulation of the genitals to gain pleasurable satisfaction. This is a normal, almost universal activity in young children and adolescents, and is not harmful.

Although infants often find that they can gain some pleasurable sensation from touching or handling the genitals, or possibly even by rocking while sitting up or on hands and knees, there is rarely any notable activity until approximately the age of 3.

During the period from ages 3 to 6, masturbation is very common and is practiced in various ways: handling the genitals; placing a soft toy animal or other soft object between the thighs and rocking the body from side to side; ly-ing face down and rolling the genital area over a soft object; straddling the leg of a table and sliding up and down. Not infrequently the activity induces an orgasm.

Usually masturbation is considerably less during the period of approximately 7 to 12 years. During puberty and adolescence there is a great increase in masturbatory activity in both boys and girls. It is a means of releasing sexual tensions which arise at this time.

It is true that a great many adults have been brought up in homes where masturbation was generally frowned upon and even prohibited by parents. Therefore, although fathers and mothers today are reassured by their pediatricians that this activity does no harm, it usually disturbs them to see their young children masturbating. In such cases it is much better to distract the child than to scold him or prohibit the activity. For it should be remembered that the only real harm in masturbation can come from the guilt feelings and fears a child may develop when he feels that he is not only disobeying his parents but is doing something that they feel is harmful or immoral.

Most children condemned by their parents for masturbating will nevertheless continue the activity, but away from parental observation and under great tension lest they be discovered.

When a child masturbates excessively—that is, to the exclusion of other normal activities—it is usually an indication that he is emotionally distressed and in need of psychotherapy.

Maternal care   see **Mothering.**

Maternity blues

A brief period of edginess or depression that many mothers experience following childbirth. The depression is apparently associated (in a way that is not understood) with the beginning of the flow of milk into the breasts. This usually occurs on the third day after childbirth, and the mother may feel emotionally depressed for a day or two. The condition is exaggerated when she has to entertain many well-meaning visitors. It is, however, a fairly common and passing mood. It should not be confused with postpartum depression, which is comparatively rare but more serious and of much longer duration.

Mattress

A mattress for an infant or child should be firm and not give way permanently under the child's weight. For a bassinet or crib, it should be waterproof. This is not necessary for the bed of an older child. A mattress should also be able to withstand the acrobatics and jumping up and down of an active child.

An inner-spring mattress is firm and not only retains its shape, but can best stand the jumping and other punishing activity of children.

A foam-rubber mattress consists of a single piece of foam which is firm and retains its firmness and shape well. But it may not stand up quite as well under intense activity as the inner spring type, and the covering may slide on the foam beneath, making it less neat than other mattresses.

A hair mattress was formerly made of horsehair, which is curly, resilient, and usually keeps its shape, especially when inner springs are added. However, today hog's hair is used, which has to be curled artificially and may later lose its curl. This type of mattress does not as a rule, stand up as well as the inner-spring or foam mattress, and it also has the disadvantage of causing allergic reactions in certain children.

Measles

A very contagious disease caused by a virus, and characterized by a rash and fever.

Mode of transmission Measles is caught by direct contact with a person having the disease. It cannot be carried indirectly to another person by someone who has visited a child with measles, nor can it be carried on books, toys, letters or clothing.

Period of contagion From four days before, until five days after, the appearance of the rash.

Incubation period A susceptible person exposed to measles will usually develop the disease between seven and fourteen days after the date of exposure—the most likely day being the tenth. The exposed child who is incubating the disease is not contagious the first seven days after exposure.

Signs and symptoms Usually there is fever for three or four days, followed by a runny nose, red eyes, and a dry, hacky cough. Then tiny white pinpoint spots called Koplik spots appear upon the gums, palate, and inner cheeks. Next the rash appears, and the fever usually reaches a height of 104 to 106 degrees. The rash is blotchy, red, and slightly elevated; it usually appears first over the face and neck and in approximately twenty-four hours covers the chest and abdomen as well. In another twenty-four hours it also covers the arms and legs. Then it starts fading from the head down. The fever continues as the rash develops, though not as high as before. Then the fever drops, the eyes clear, the nose stops running, the cough subsides, and the rash fades. The rash usually lasts five or six days in all.

Treatment   There is no specific treatment for measles, but antibiotics are often used to treat accompanying complications such as infected ears and swollen glands.

In an exposed person measles can be prevented or modified by injections of gamma globulin given during the incubation period. The gamma globulin must be given early; it is of no value once the symptoms have appeared.

Immunization   Measles vaccine is very effective and will immunize a child for a long period of time—possibly for life. A few children may develop fever, and occasionally a mild rash, seven days after the inoculation.

Immunization against measles is very important, for the complication of measles encephalitis, although not common, is extremely dangerous and may cause death or damage the brain of a child permanently. Other possible complications of this disease are pneumonia and ear infections.

Measurements, body   see **Body measurements.**

Meat
Meat is an excellent source of protein as well as being high in iron and vitamins.

Since it has been shown infants digest meat easily, meat is now often added to a baby's diet in a pureed form as early as age 3 or 4 months.

Specially prepared meat for infants may be obtained already pureed in bottles or cans. Or it may be prepared at home: Put ½ cup of cooked meat (cut into one-inch pieces, with bone and fiber removed) into a blender; add about 4 tablespoons of liquid, preferably meat broth or milk; process in the blender until smooth, and add more liquid if desired.

When a baby gets older—that is, from 8 or 9 months on—he can eat the prepared junior meat in bottles or cans. Or use the blender to chop the food to the desired size. Other methods of preparing meat for children of this age are by scraping the meat after searing it on both sides in a hot pan, or, in the case of beef, having the top-round beef double-chopped by the butcher. It is seasoned with a pinch of salt, formed into a cake or patty, and broiled in a dry pan until it is well seared or brown. Then a little water is added to soften the meat before offering it to the baby.

Throughout childhood meat is necessary for furnishing the protein the body needs, unless adequate protein is received in other forms, such as from milk, eggs, lima beans, peas and cereal, and food prepared from soy beans.

See also **Solid foods, introducing.**

Meconium   see **Bowel movements.**

Medic Alert
There are children who have medical problems that should be known to doctors, police, and others giving them first aid in emergencies. In some instances the knowledge of these problems may save a life; in others it may prevent serious reactions.

Among such conditions are epilepsy, diabetes, penicillin allergy, insect-sting allergy, heart conditions, hemophilia, and the wearing of contact lenses.

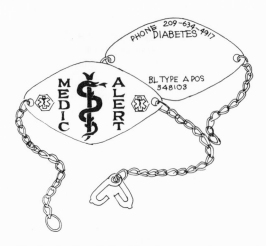

The back of a Medic Alert bracelet gives the possible cause of an emergency situation, the person's blood type, the telephone number of Medic Alert for further medical information, and the identification number of the person's medical file.

It is most important that children with such problems wear a bracelet or pendant with a warning disk stating the condition that should be known in first-aid situations.

The bracelet or pendant can be made individually, but one of the best known and most effective sources for obtaining it is a nonprofit organization, endorsed by many medical groups, called Medic Alert, Turlock, California 95380.

Not only does the disk state the condition to be known and, if desired, the blood type, but it lists the medical file number of the child and the telephone number of the office of Medic Alert Foundation. By telephoning this number (collect) one can learn the name of the child, his doctor, and his nearest relative.

The importance of the bracelet or pendant in the safety and proper treatment of children with certain medical problems cannot be overemphasized.

Medicine cabinet see **First-aid supplies.**

Medicines, giving

Many medicines for children, both in liquid and tablet form, are flavored so as to make them more palatable. This is of great advantage in assuring that they will be taken with no resistance, or with much less resistance. However, because of the attractive taste, there is always the potential danger that a child may drink too much of the medicine or chew up flavored tablets. For this reason, flavored medicines, like all medicines, should be securely locked up.

There are several ways in which unflavored medicines can be made more palatable. They can be mixed with a teaspoon of sugar, jam, or honey. They can be diluted in a drink of juice, cola, or ginger ale, but the child may not take all the liquid and therefore may not receive the full dose of medicine.

If the medicine comes only in tablet form and does not dissolve, it can be placed on the back of the tongue and swallowed with a drink, or it can often be broken up and powdered and placed in jam, honey, or apple sauce. Capsules can also be swallowed in most cases by placing them on the back of the tongue and having the child swallow a glass of water or juice. Many parents give a piece of candy or a lollipop after the child has taken medicine.

If the child puts up fierce resistance to a medicine that must be given: hold the child's nose; give him the medicine, continuing to hold the nose until it is swallowed—and follow up with a treat.

Giving medicines by rectal suppositories is not generally advised for children. However, in cases of severe vomiting or high fever, it may be necessary to give rectal suppositories to control the vomiting and aspirin suppositories to control fever.

Mediterranean anemia

Also called thalassemia. A hereditary form of anemia in which the red blood cells are poorly formed and are destroyed at a rapid rate, and hemoglobin (the red coloring matter in the red cells that carries oxygen) is also chronically deficient. It is found largely among children of northern Mediterranean (Greek and Italian) extraction, although occasionally in other children as well.

Thalassemia minor is a mild type of the disease. Although the person subject to it lives with a moderate degree of anemia, he has no other signs or symptoms except pallor, and he can live normally.

Thalassemia major is a severe type. The red cells are rapidly destroyed. Children with moderate to severe types of Mediterranean anemia are pale and slightly jaundiced. They have mongoloid features with high cheekbones. The spleen is greatly enlarged. The child requires transfusions every few weeks or months, depending on the rate of blood destruction, to maintain an adequate amount of red blood cells and hemoglobin. At times the removal of the spleen seems of benefit in slowing down the process of blood destruction.

See also **Anemia.**

Meningitis

An inflammation of the membrane covering the brain and the spinal cord.

There are many types of meningitis, since the term does not imply a specific disease, but rather an inflammation which may be caused by any of a number of different bacteria or viruses.

The most common type of meningitis is that caused by bacteria called menin-gococcus. Among other types are tuberculosis meningitis, pneumococcus meningitis, influenzal meningitis, and virus meningitis. However, when one refers to meningitis it is usually taken to mean the type caused by meningococcus bacteria.

Meningococcal meningitis The infection is transmitted from the nose and throat secretions of an infected person, and only by direct contact with that person. The bacteria inhaled by a susceptible person pass through the mucous membrane of his nose and throat into the bloodstream and are taken to the brain, where they cause an inflammation.

Signs and symptoms Many of the cases start with a nose-and-throat infection. After a few days the usual symptoms of fever, severe headache, and vomiting appear. There is almost always a stiffness of the neck. Unless treated, the symptoms continue to delirium and coma. In some cases, during the period when the bacteria are in the bloodstream there are red spots on the skin scattered over the body.

Diagnosis Although the signs and symptoms just described are strongly indicative of meningitis, the only definite means of accurate diagnosis is to examine the spinal fluid. The number and type of cells in the fluid and the amount of sugar, proteins, and chloride are of the greatest importance not only in establishing the presence of meningitis but in diagnosing what type it is. A culture of the bacteria in the spinal fluid is also of great value.

Treatment The use of penicillin or the sulfa drugs in the treatment of meningococcal meningitis is highly successful in curing the disease, especially if given in the early stages.

Period of contagion As long as the bacteria remain in the nose and throat of the infected person. This varies with the speed of treatment. There are, however, certain people who are carriers of the meningococcus in their nose and throat without being ill themselves. They are usually not detected unless people exposed to them develop the disease and cultures are taken of all persons with whom they came in contact.

Incubation period The time between the day of exposure and the onset of symptoms of meningococcus meningitis is usually three to seven days, although symptoms can commence as early as one or as late as ten days after exposure.

Care of exposed people Sulfonamides or penicillin taken by mouth in dosages prescribed by the doctor.

Immunization No medical means at present. One attack of the disease usually confers permanent immunity.

Meningocele see **Spina bifida.**

Menstrual cramps see **Cramps, menstrual.**

Menstruation
The monthly discharge of blood from the uterus of adolescent girls and women. The onset of menstruation usually occurs at some time between the ages of 10 to 16 years.

Once a girl becomes fully adolescent, an egg is produced approximately every twenty-six to thirty days. This egg, if fertilized, will develop into a baby within the uterus. The uterus has numerous blood vessels in its walls. Every month, when an egg is released from an ovary, the uterus prepares for it with an extra supply of blood and a lining ready to receive the egg if it is fertilized.

For about ten days after the egg has been released the uterus remains ready for it. Then, if no sperm fertilized the egg, there is no further use for this extra blood and the lining membrane, and they are discharged out of the uterus and flow from the body through the vagina.

Menstruation usually lasts three to five days and is often spoken of as the menstrual period or the monthly period.

When girls first start to menstruate, their periods may not be regular, often skipping months at a time or coming more frequently than once a month. It often takes as long as two years from the onset of menstruation until the normal monthly cycle is established. (Normal irregularity should not be confused with amenorrhea, which means an absence of menstruation. This may occur as a result of severe dieting, chronic debilitating disease, or severe depression or anxiety.)

When a girl is 8 or 9, parents should be sure that she understands the facts of menstruation—that this is a healthy function of the mature body that has nothing to do with being sick. Girls may be normally active during menstruation, and may swim or take baths.

Prior to menstruation a girl should be taught how to use either an absorbent gauze pad called a sanitary napkin which is held in place by a narrow sanitary belt (certain types of napkins come with adhesive strips so that no belt is necessary), or a tampon (the smallest size to begin with), which is inserted into the vagina and absorbs the menstrual flow internally. Tampons may be safely used from the time a girl starts menstruating, but she should be instructed how to insert and remove them.

There may be some pain during the first day or two of the period. Usually this can be easily relieved.

See also **Cramps, menstrual; Tampon, vaginal.**

Mental age
The measure of a child's intellectual development according to an intelligence test. If a child whose chronological age is 5 scores as well as the average 6-year-old on an intelligence test, his mental age is said to be 6.

See also **IQ; Tests.**

Mental health centers
In 1963 Congress passed and President John F. Kennedy signed the Community Mental Health Center Act for the creation of mental health organizations throughout the United States regulated on the basis of population.

The Mental Health Centers are dedicated to the prevention and treatment of behavior disorders in children and adults. The centers are funded by the U. S. government and the individual states. Although there is a fee for treatment, it is on a sliding scale depending on the economic status of the family. No person is turned away because of a lack of money.

The centers offer a variety of services:

Preventive services For the early detection of emotional problems before they can develop into severe forms of psychoneuroses. Children may be referred by nursery schools, schools, or doctors, or brought by parents themselves when behavior difficulties are in their early stages.

Treatment services Organized into various categories:

1. Emergency care, for the immediate care of urgent cases.
2. Outpatient care, when children and adults with behavior difficulties are treated routinely on a clinic basis.
3. Inpatient care, when intensive care is indicated or removal of the child from his environment is deemed important.
4. Rehabilitation care, in such places as halfway houses (where those almost ready to be discharged have residence) and social centers.

Consultation and educational services To the community at large. Each Mental Health Center has a licensed psychiatrist as the director. Treatment and services are performed by psychiatrists, clinical psychologists, social workers, and other specially trained professionals.

Treatment is given either individually or in groups, depending on the patient.

Parents who have children with behavior problems may apply individually or be referred by a doctor, child health clinic, school, or the community health department.

For information on the location of the Community Mental Health Center in any particular area, a parent is advised to communicate with the local branch of the National Association of Mental Health or the state or county Department of Mental Health. A listing of the centers is also given in this book. (See **Appendix D.**)

The facilities of the Mental Health Centers vary from state to state. In one well-organized center in New York State there are facilities for family therapy, group therapy, individual therapy, family counseling, educational tutoring, and treatment of mental problems with drugs when indicated. It should be mentioned further that in this center every child admitted for treatment in the clinic must receive a psychiatric examination by a licensed psychiatrist.

Such standards differ from state to state, but careful review of the individual case by the clinic staff is a uniform procedure.

If a Mental Health Center is not capable of treating a child for his particular behavior problem, it will refer the parents to a licensed clinic.

Mental illness see **Autism; Emotional disturbance; Schizophrenia.**

Mental retardation

Mental retardation or mental deficiency is a condition of those children or adults whose intelligence is considerably below the average for their age level.

It is estimated that in the United States 1.5 percent of the population is mentally retarded. This would approximate 3 million individuals, although some authorities would place the number as high as 6 million.

Mental retardation cannot as a rule be detected at birth—with the exception of children born with Mongolism (Down's syndrome), in which the face, eyes, hands, and chromosomes of the child's cells differ so markedly from those of normal infants as to make diagnosis definite.

Causes There are numerous known causes that may occur before birth, during birth, or after birth. Causes before birth include hereditary factors; infection of the mother—for example, by German measles; damage to the fetus through drugs or through X rays or other radiation given to the mother; damage to the fetus through blood incompatibility; or malformation of the fetus, as in hydrocephalus. During birth the prime danger is lack of oxygen reaching the infant's brain if there are difficulties in the birth process, such as premature separation of the placenta or a winding of the umbilical cord around the infant's neck. Injury to the skull and brain during delivery may also cause brain damage. Causes after birth include inflammation of the brain, as in measles encephalitis; damage resulting from injuries or toxic substances (as in lead poisoning); malnutrition; and thyroid malfunction, which causes cretinism.

Prevention A great deal can be accomplished in preventing mental retardation through early and good obstetrical care during pregnancy and combined obstetrical and pediatric care during and after the birth of a baby.

Good obstetrical care can prevent many of the problems that arise during pregnancy and birth. Genetic counseling may prevent pregnancies with a high possibility of mental retardation. Chromosome studies and amniocentesis can detect certain hereditary forms of retardation, including most cases of Mongolism. (See **Amniocentesis; Genetic counseling.**) An abortion can then be performed if the parents so desire. Cooperation between obstetricians and pediatricians will prevent most of the retardation caused by Rh and other blood incompatibilities. Mental retardation caused by PKU can be prevented by detection immediately after birth and by giving the infant a special diet. (See **PKU.**) Retardation from hydrocephalus can usually be prevented by new surgical techniques. Measles encephalitis as a cause of retardation should be completely eliminated by routine vaccination against measles during infancy. Most of the retardation of cretinism resulting from lack of thyroid secretion may be avoided by the daily administration of thyroid tablets given by mouth from early infancy throughout life.

With the exception of thyroid used in the treatment of cretinism, there is no drug at the present time that will elevate the mentality of the retarded child.

Care of the retarded child Should a retarded child be cared for at home or sent to an institution? It is strongly felt that most of these children, with the exception of the most retarded, will do much better at home where they can receive the attention and love of their parents. When old enough for training or education they should be sent to the special classes in schools in their locality. Most schools or communities have such classes. When children become older, particularly when they are approaching the teen years, they may be sent away to one of the special training schools for their education, or they may attend special training classes provided by the Association for the Help of Retarded Children.

Education of the retarded child The aims of educating the retarded child are essentially the same as those for the normal child—to teach him to use all his capabilities to the fullest extent and to become a useful and, if possible, self-sufficient member of society. He should also be taught to make worthwhile use of his leisure time.

Children with an IQ below 25 are usually totally dependent, unable to direct their own lives or make decisions alone. Children with an IQ of 25 to 50 are trainable but generally not educable.

The term "trainable" implies that the child can learn basic self-care, such as dressing and undressing, self-feeding, and being toilet-trained. He can be trained in occupations such as housework, farm work, and work in a stock room. Most children with an IQ of 50 to 80 are both trainable and educable. The degree of education—including, among other things, writing and figuring—varies with the individual child.

Retarded adolescents Retarded children entering adolescence, although retarded mentally, are usually normal physically and have the same needs as normal children for a social life, for achievement and admiration, for feeling loved and wanted. It is most important that these needs be met as fully as possible. Parents of mentally retarded teenagers should be warned, however, that these children are often molested sexually, since their understanding of such dangers is usually low and their resistance poor. They should be under watchful supervision to avoid such problems.

In many large communities most of the social needs of retarded teen-agers can be satisfied through the activities of the Association for the Help of Retarded Children. This organization groups young people according to their age, similarity of backgrounds, intellectual capacities, education, and level of functioning. The children meet one another at organized social events, dances, and theatre parties. Bowling, swimming, cooking classes, and fishing are among their activities. There are also summer camps for retarded children. This organization also has workshops to keep these young folks occupied and teach them suitable trades.

Employment opportunities for the retarded Many jobs are open to mentally retarded children, depending largely on their mental ability. Listed below are tasks that children of specified mental ages are usually able to perform. As with all children, mentally retarded children have varying abilities and often will function greatly above or below their mental age in particular areas.

Mental age 5. Simple household and manual work, such as scrubbing and polishing floors, washing dishes, sandpapering furniture, and paring vegetables.

Mental age 6. Simple manual and crafts work such as mowing lawns, simple laundry work, crocheting, weaving rag rugs.

Mental age 7. Simple crafts work, including some carpentry and shoe repairing, hand ironing, knitting ties and scarves, simple mending.

Mental age 8. More difficult labor and handiwork, such as farm work, painting houses (both exterior and interior), cutting hair, garden work, making dresses from patterns by others.

Mental age 9. Simple piecework or shopwork, such as repairing furniture, painting toys, running a foot-powered printing press, high-grade shoe repairing, mattress and pillow making, pattern making, cutting out and making clothes, knitting socks and stockings.

Mental age 10. More difficult and detailed work, such as shellacking and varnishing, painting signs, detailed laundry work and garden work, farm work and dairy work, setting and sorting type, operating sweater and stocking machines,

fancy cooking and fancy laundry work, canning foods, weaving.

Mental ages 11 and 12. Can become proficient stockkeepers and janitors, lawn caretakers, small storekeepers, factory workers, and can do simple library work, power sealing in bottling or canning plants.

Aids to the parents of retarded children There are a number of national and local organizations which can offer invaluable help in caring for and educating mentally retarded children:

National Association for Retarded Children. This organization, located at 420 Lexington Ave., New York, N.Y. 10017, publishes advice for parents and presents reading lists on the subject of retardation. It also devotes itself to the formation of parent groups throughout the country in which fathers and mothers of retarded children can cooperate and exchange ideas for the betterment of their children.

Association for the Help of Retarded Children. This is an organization dedicated to working for, and directly with, retarded children. There are branches of the association in every state and in most large cities. They either run their programs by themselves or work through state facilities. They provide training programs for retarded children as well as sheltered workshops to keep them happily occupied and possibly learning a trade. They also foster social groups and social affairs for retarded adolescents and in many states conduct camps for retarded children. Information concerning the location of a particular branch of the Association for the Help of Retarded Children may be obtained by writing to the National Association for Retarded Children at the address given above.

Mental testing   see **IQ; Tests.**

Middle child
Often, when there are three children in the family, the middle child meets the greatest problems. Of course, a great deal depends on the relative ages of the children, the attitude of the parents, and the sex of the child.

It is true that in many families the second child, who will later be the middle child, has temporary advantages until the third child arrives. The first child has cleared the way for the second, and the parents are more experienced and relaxed in his care. But often, to counter these advantages somewhat, the older child develops a feeling of jealousy and rivalry in relation to the younger child, who, he thinks, is receiving too much attention and affection.

Now a third child is born; the second child becomes the middle child and often feels that he is in a vise. In many instances this is true, for he lacks the privileges and certain advantages of the older child and may even be bullied by him. To add to his problems, he may now find himself jealous of the infant who has taken his place as the baby in the family and is demanding and receiving so much of the attention he feels should be his.

Middle children finding themselves in this situation react in various ways depending on the individual child, his relationship to his siblings, and his relationship to his parents. Some react by being disobedient and aggressive, forcing attention upon themselves even if it means being scolded or punished. Some react by being sullen and depressed and feeling that nobody knows they exist; others, when young, may revert to infantile habits such as soiling and wetting.

Parents observing such reactions of the middle child should be sympathetic and understanding, and try to relieve as much as possible the anxieties that the child harbors. They should reserve for the middle child his due share of attention, and offer him a great deal of praise for his accomplishments and the knowledge that he is much loved and wanted. He should also be given a chance to be alone occasionally with one or both parents for outings or special treats.

Parents should also check the frequent aggressions of the older child, not only by prohibition but by working with him to relieve his feelings of jealousy and rivalry.

See also **Sibling rivalry and jealousy.**

Midget   see **Dwarfism.**

Migraine headache
A special type of headache that is repetitive, occurring irregularly at intervals of weeks or months. Migraines are probably much more common in children than is generally realized, possibly because children are unable to describe their symptoms fully.

A migraine headache is usually preceded by some dizziness and distortion of vision; the sight is marred by bright zigzag flashes, spots, and partial blurring. After these first symptoms have lasted for twenty or thirty minutes, a severe headache arises which is usually limited to only one side of the head. At times the headache is accompanied by a ringing in the ears, sensitivity to light, or dizziness. After a few hours the headache may be accompanied by nausea and vomiting. In many cases the patient falls into a deep sleep for several hours, after which he awakens free of pain. However, in some cases the headache and vomiting may last several days.

The cause of migraine attacks is not actually known. It seems to be partly hereditary and may possibly be triggered by tension, anxiety, eyestrain, allergy, constipation, fatigue, or hormonal activity.

Treatment   If the headache is generally preceded by dizziness or derangements of vision, the child should be given aspirin at the first sign of such symptoms. This will often prevent the attack or greatly reduce the headache which follows.

The drugs that seem to be most effective in the treatment of migraine attacks are Cafergot and Wigraine, combinations of ergotamine and caffeine. They should be taken only on prescription and under the supervision of a doctor.

Mild brain dysfunction   see **Brain dysfunction, mild.**

Miliary tuberculosis   see **Tuberculosis.**

Milk, cow's
Cow's milk contains the same number of calories as breast milk but differs from it in other important aspects.

It has much more protein and much less sugar than breast milk. Therefore, when cow's milk is used in formulas for young infants, water is added to reduce the amount of protein, and sugar is added to bring the values near to breast milk. All the commercial formulas prepared from cow's milk make such a change in an effort to make their prepa-

rations as close to breast milk in composition as they possibly can.

In spite of the effort to prepare cow's milk to make it simulate breast milk in its component parts, there are still a good number of infants who are sensitive to cow's milk and cannot tolerate it.

See also **Milk allergy.**

Milk, evaporated
Cow's or goat's milk which has been evaporated to half its original volume. It is only the water which evaporates, so that the remaining milk has twice the food and calorie value of undiluted milk. It is sterilized, so it contains no living bacteria. After its preparation it is placed in hermetically sealed cans which may be stored at room temperature until opened and used. Once exposed to air it must be refrigerated. It may safely be kept refrigerated for up to forty-eight hours.

It is a convenient and inexpensive preparation for infants' formulas. (See **Formulas.**)

Milk, goat's
For many years goat's milk was used as a formula for children who were allergic to cow's milk. It is still used today by a fair number of parents for their milk-allergic children. It is readily available as evaporated milk (Meyenberg), and when diluted with an equal amount of water has the same strength and caloric value as whole cow's milk.

Formulas of evaporated goat's milk are prepared in the same manner as those of evaporated cow's milk.

Soybean preparations and meat-base formulas superseded goat's milk when it was found that many infants allergic to cow's milk were also allergic to goat's milk. However, it is worth trying goat's milk as a substitute for cow's milk and then shifting to one of the soybean or meat-base formulas if necessary. Its advantage is that it is comparatively less expensive than these other preparations.

See also **Formulas; Milk allergy.**

Milk, witch's   see **Witch's milk.**

Milk allergy

Allergy to cow's milk occurs quite frequently during infancy. The symptoms include eczema, colic, and vomiting or diarrhea (often with mucus and blood). These symptoms usually develop during the first few weeks of life.

Treatment   Formerly goat's milk was substituted for cow's milk, and it is still occasionally used, but a good many children are sensitive to goat's milk as well. At the present time various milk substitutes made from soybean have been found highly effective. These have almost exactly the same amount of protein, fat, carbohydrates, and minerals as breast milk. There are some children, however, who react to the soybean formulas too. These children are placed on a formula prepared of meat (Meat-base or Lambase formulas). Like soybean preparations, these have essentially the same qualities as breast milk.

Most infants outgrow their milk sensitivity within one or two years. A rare person carries the sensitivity over into adult life.

Milk crust   see **Cradle cap.**

Milk of magnesia   see **Laxatives.**

Milk sensitivity   see **Milk allergy.**

Minerals   see **Nutrition.**

Minimal brain dysfunction   see **Brain dysfunction, mild.**

Mirror writing

Reversal of writing words and letters—from right to left rather than from left to right. This is frequently seen when children are first learning to write.

In most children the tendency disappears very quickly, except in those who are left-handed. It is possible that this is the normal and most comfortable means of writing for the left-handed child. But when mirror writing is continued by the right-handed child, it usually indicates some confusion in the visual and language centers of the brain, and at times is related to both reading and writing difficulties.

It has been found that most of the right-handed children who continue to be mirror writers are really left-handed children who have been trained to write with the right hand.

Training a child to discontinue mirror writing often requires forcing his attention to the shape of each individual letter and guiding his hand as he writes. He might also be taught to write individual script letters rather than words, and later to connect the letters in the writing of words. At times professional help is necessary.

Probably the most famous mirror writer in history is Leonardo da Vinci, who continued the habit in adult life as part of a private code system.

See also **Dyslexia; Handedness; Perceptual difficulties, neurological.**

Mites   see **Chiggers; Scabies.**

Moisture in the air

Adequate moisture in the air is important not only for comfort but also as an added protection against respiratory infection. This is a problem during winter months, for cold air normally contains much less moisture than warm air. Modern heating methods dry the air still further—and this air, when breathed in, dries up the mucous membrane of the nose, throat, and breathing tubes, making them greatly susceptible to infection.

To correct this difficulty, the use of a cold-steam humidifier is advised. This is usually a large container of cold water with an electrically operated mechanism that throws microscopic droplets of water into the air of the room, raising the humidity considerably. A humidifier differs from a hot-air steamer (vaporizer). The humidifier blows fine droplets of water into the air, whereas the steamer produces a small flow of water vapor (steam), which rarely moistens the air in the room adequately. Nor is it completely satisfactory—although it is helpful—to use pans filled with water or to leave water in the bathtub.

Moles
The common brown pigmentspots on the skin of children and adults. They vary in color from light brown to almost black. They are rarely present at birth. In most children they start appearing at about age 15 months and continue to appear on the skin throughout childhood and adolescence.

There has long been a general belief that moles located on areas of the body subject to irritation, such as under a belt or brassiere strap, might eventually become malignant and should therefore be removed. However, there is no scientific evidence that such malignancies do occur.

A mole should be brought to the attention of the doctor if there are changes in its size or shape; if there are surface changes such as scaliness, bleeding, crusting, or ulceration; or if the mole becomes firmer or darker. Although very rare in children, these changes may be signs of malignancy. Malignant moles must be removed—an operation that is safe and relatively painless.

The most usual reason for removing moles is cosmetic. Any mole on the face that is disfiguring or unattractive should be removed if possible.

Money see **Allowances; Chores; Savings accounts; Work, full-time, part-time.**

Mongolism
Also called Down's syndrome. A condition of mental retardation. It can be diagnosed at birth, for mongoloid children are born with almond-shaped eyes, a flat bridge of the nose, and usually a short neck. Their muscle tone as a rule is very poor.

Mongolism is almost always caused by the presence of an extra chromosome in the child's cells. In many cases the condition is hereditary, and the possibility of having a child with Mongolism can be estimated by studying the cells of the prospective parents. The occurrence of Mongolism is also related to the age of the mother. Mothers under 30 years of age have one chance in 3,000 of having a mongoloid child. At age 35 to 39 the chances are one in 280; at age 40 to 44, one in 70; and at age 45 to 49, one in 40. This age tendency is only related to the age of the mother, not the father.

A modern method of preventing the birth of a mongoloid child is through amniocentesis, a process in which a needle is inserted through a pregnant mother's abdomen in the eighth to the twelfth week and amniotic fluid is withdrawn.

This fluid, which surrounds the baby, has some of the infant's skin cells floating in it. The cells are cultured and examined, and if the extra chromosome is found, signifying that the baby is mongoloid, termination of the pregnancy is advised by the doctor.

Children with Mongolism usually have an IQ of 50 to 70. Most of them are trainable, with those at the upper level being educable as well.

See also **Mental retardation.**

Mononucleosis, infectious

Formerly called glandular fever. An acute infectious disease, only mildly contagious. It is rarely seen in infancy, most usually affecting children over 5 years of age. It is caused by a virus and characterized by an increase in certain types of white blood cells known as monocytes.

Signs and symptoms Infectious mononucleosis usually begins with grippe-like symptoms: a headache and a fever which may rise between 102 and 103 degrees. Soon afterward, a sore throat develops, and the child feels weak and fatigued. As a rule there is a marked enlargement of the lymph "glands" (lymph nodes) in the neck, armpits, and groin. It was because of this "gland" enlargement that the disease was formerly called "glandular fever." One other common sign of this infection is an enlargement of the spleen. In some cases a red, spotty rash may appear over the body or there may be a mild hepatitis.

The disease is practically never dangerous and usually runs its full course in two to four weeks. During this time the child feels quite fatigued, eats poorly, and may have a nearly continual low-grade fever. Once the disease has sub-sided completely, there are no aftereffects. A second attack of the disease is extremely rare.

Diagnosis Diagnosis can only be made by a doctor through special blood studies which may not be indicative until the child has been ill for about a week. These blood studies, if positive, not only show the increased number of monocytes in the child's blood but also detect antibodies which the body has manufactured to fight the disease.

Treatment There is no specific treatment for infectious mononucleosis. Antibiotics are of no value, since the symptoms are those of a virus infection, and viruses do not respond to antibiotics.

Bed rest is advisable during the fever period, and then limited activity until the fatigue has disappeared. The child may return to school when the temperature has dropped to normal and the feeling of fatigue has subsided. But vigorous activities should be limited for several weeks afterward.

No restriction or special care is indicated for exposed individuals.

Mode of transmission Thought to be a face-to-face exposure, although this has not been proved as yet. It has been said that mononucleosis is transmitted by kissing, but this is only because it occurs largely during adolescence and young adulthood—"the kissing period." It is so mildly contagious that two cases in the same home or the same school class are extremely rare. The incubation period is approximately eleven days, although it may vary considerably.

Montessori method

A method of education for children between the ages of 3 and 6, originally formulated by Dr. Maria Montessori, an Italian pediatrician who became interested in child education.

The children are educated in an ungraded classroom and are allowed to play with any toys or objects they desire. Each child in the group can be working on a different project at the same time and at his own pace.

The children are presented with numerous special toys, games, puzzles, and types of apparatus designed by Dr. Montessori to teach a youngster to read, write, and think, and at the same time to develop coordination, sense perception, and muscular ability.

Among these specially designed materials are the famous sandpaper letters—letters cut out of cardboard and covered with sandpaper so that children can not only see the letters but can trace them with their fingers and try to form words with them.

Also there are pegs, or rods, of different standard sizes and colors corresponding to a full peg, ½ peg, ¼ peg, etc., to teach mathematical relationships; there are picture puzzles; buttoning and lacing frames for physical coordination; and map puzzles, designed to improve manual dexterity, improve perception of visual relationships, and teach some geography at the same time.

In the Montessori schools of the United States, certain supplementary activities, such as easel painting and clay modeling, have been added to those originally recommended. Montessori teachers today are also often more liberal in their view of what constitutes appropriate behavior in a classroom. In particular, they may no longer hold to the original Montessori belief that the children should use the classroom materials only for the purposes for which

they were specifically designed. (For example, the square blocks of increasing sizes are to be used for tower making and are not supposed to be pushed along the floor as freight trains. This strict adherence to the original method affords children little opportunity for imaginative and creative play). But basically the approach of using materials that appeal to vision and touch to allow the child to discover abstract concepts remains the same.

Children educated by the Montessori method usually learn to read, write, and count at an early age, although this was not its original object.

Permitting children to carry through their individual interests is not only an effective educational process but also tends to develop their attention span and their initiative—valuable assets in later school years.

In Dr. Montessori's words, the children educated in this manner "are thoroughly disciplined in the highest sense of the term, having developed and become masters of themselves through liberty."

Since the mid-1960's there has been a great increase in the number of Montessori schools in the United States and Canada. Most of these follow the principles of Dr. Montessori. Some, however, are using the name under false pretenses.

It is important, therefore, that parents planning to enter their child in a Montessori school be assured that the school is affiliated with either the American or European Montessori Societies. Parents may also want to ascertain whether the school is conservative or liberal in its attitudes toward play or classroom behavior.

See also **Education, experimental approaches in.**

Morphine poisoning see **Poisons: first-aid treatment.**

Mosquito bites see **Insect and spider bites.**

Mothball poisoning see **Poisons: first-aid treatment.**

Mother, working

There are a great many mothers in the United States who work, and many of them wonder if they are depriving their children greatly by doing so. Their reasons for working vary, although in most cases the motivation is economic. In some homes there is no father around and the mother must of necessity work. At times, because of illness or disability, the father is unable to work, and so the mother becomes the earner. At other times a mother works to add to the family income for buying a home in the suburbs or contributing to the future education of the children. There are mothers who want to finish their education, and so take courses during the day. And there are active, skilled, successful women who really dislike housework and want to work at their profession.

Are the children of these mothers deprived?

There is no simple answer, for it is certainly true that during the early years of life, and especially during the first two years, a child needs a great deal of mothering. On the other hand, a mother who has to work to support her child has no choice in the matter. A mother who would be unhappy and irritable without an outside job will be a better mother if she goes ahead and works. Her resentment at being tied to the house will surely be felt by the baby.

If a mother is working simply to do her share toward buying a house or saving for the future college education of the children, it is much more advisable to wait until the children are at least of nursery school or school age before going to work. The first few years of a child's life are so important that a mother desiring to finish her education would also be advised to wait until these formative years have passed, unless she can arrange her courses for only a few hours a week.

Also, a working mother may find that she can work at home or part-time, and this is usually preferable to working full-time if at all possible.

But even if the mother works full-time, she can have a relationship to her child that will be satisfying to both of them. She can arrange to be with the child during the most significant times of the day—in the morning, as he starts his day, and at supper and bedtime—and she can be available at home if he awakens in the night. On the days that she isn't working, her love and interest can be fully expressed.

It is very important that the person who takes care of the child while the mother is working be carefully selected. A warm, affectionate person who will spend a great deal of time playing with the child is much more important than a good housekeeper. The sitter should also be experienced and responsible, and have a good relationship with the mother. A working mother must make every effort to assure herself that all is well while she is away, and that the child is not being neglected or harassed. Once a good sitter is found, it is important, if possible, to continue with this person. It is confusing and upsetting for a child to be cared for by a series of different people.

If the mother cannot find or afford a good sitter, a well-run day care center can be an excellent solution. (See **Day care centers.**)

Mothering

The special warm and loving care a mother gives her child. To the child, the mother's presence—her voice, her touch, her interest, her concern—is vitally important. The need for mothering is biological as well as emotional, and exists practically from the moment a baby is born. The newborn child needs handling, cuddling, warmth, smiles, talking-to, and love. If a baby lacks this completely, he will become unhappy and unresponsive and may deteriorate physically as well as emotionally.

The sooner mothering starts, the better it is for the child—and if possible it should start at birth. It is for this reason that many hospitals have instituted the system of rooming-in, under which the baby is with its mother from the moment it is born, rather than occupying a crib in the newborns' nursery. Breast feeding, while not essential for mothering, can bring with it one of the warmest and most satisfying relationships between a mother and her child.

There is no need for a mother to fear that too much loving, cuddling, and satisfying her baby's desires during the early months of life will spoil the child. On the contrary, an infant thrives on it and gains a feeling that he is deeply cared for and that his needs will be satisfied. This feeling of being wanted and the knowledge that he can depend on his parents give a child a firm base of security as he grows older.

Mothering does not cease once a child grows out of infancy, but continues during the succeeding years of childhood. It no longer involves the same intensive care, for the child attains more and more the ability to do things by himself and for himself. But although the demands on the mother are less, the children still need her attention, care, and protection. Also they need her direction and reasonable discipline.

An interested and good mother is one who throughout their childhood and teen-age years meets the needs of her children, both physical and emotional, as well as she can, and helps them to develop self-dependence and self-discipline as they mature.

This does not mean that a mother must necessarily be tied down to her home and children, especially once the youngsters are of school age—many mothers work—but she should leave adequate time to be with and enjoy her children. (See **Mother, working.**)

To be mothered is a necessity for the child's normal emotional development and a primary right of every infant and child.

Motion pictures for children see **Movies.**

Motion pictures of children see **Photographs and home movies.**

Motion sickness

Dizziness and nausea resulting from the motion of a car, plane, train, or boat. It is thought to be caused by a disorder of the balance center of the inner ear. It can usually be prevented by one of the antinauseant drugs prescribed by a doctor. This may be given one hour before departure and is usually effective for six to eight hours.

A number of preparations suitable for children are available. There is a liquid preparation—liquid Dramamine (dimenhydrinate)—of which ½ teaspoon should be given to a child of 1 to 3 years, 1 teaspoon to a child of 3 to 6 years, and 2 teaspoons to a child of 6 to 12 years. Dramamine is likely to make a child sleepy. There is also a flavored chewable tablet called Bonine (meclizine hydrochloride); ¼ tablet should be given to a child of 1 to 3 years, ½ tablet to a child of 3 to 8 years, and 1 tablet to an older child. Another preparation in tablet form, Marezine (cyclizine lactate), is also very helpful in preventing motion sickness. Its dosage is the same as for Bonine.

If a child tends to become motion-sick, parents should try to see that he gets plenty of air during the trip. The child should be neither too hungry nor too full. Light snacks should be provided.

Motor Development see **Development in the first five years.**

Mouth

For infants and very young children, the mouth and lips are the most sensitive organs of touch. Almost as soon as an infant gains full use of his hands for grasping and learns to move his hands purposefully, he will start putting practically anything and everything he can hold in his mouth. In the early months it is the lips and mouth that discover the qualities of objects—hardness, softness, cold, warmth, and so on.

This tendency to put almost everything in the mouth continues through the creeping stage and early walking period, usually subsiding at about age 15 months. It is extremely important for the child's safety that the mother be aware of this tendency. There are so many objects inside and outside the playpen to watch out for. Certainly no toys should be given that are small enough to be taken into the mouth and swallowed or inhaled. These include small dolls, very small toy autos, sea-shells, coins, and marbles. Pencils, sticks, spoons, and lollipops are also dangerous, for children often fall while holding these in their mouths, tearing the palate or perforating the back of the throat.

See also **Choking; Foreign objects, inhalation of; Foreign objects, swallowed; Sucking need.**

Mouth breathing see **Breathing through the mouth.**

Mouth-to-mouth resuscitation

An emergency treatment to restore

Mouth-to-mouth resuscitation: 1. Tip head back, push jaw forward. 2. Clear mouth and throat of any obstructing substance or object. 3. Pinch shut nostrils; with an infant, skip this step and place your mouth over both the nose and mouth of the baby. 4. Place your mouth over victim's mouth and blow vigorously for an older child or adult, gently for an infant—every three seconds for an infant or young child, every four to five seconds for an older child or adult. 5. Check for exhaling by victim while you are inhaling another breath. If there is no air exhaled, try pressing down on the chest following each breath. If this does not work, quickly turn victim on side (or over your knee if an infant) and slap hard between shoulder blades to force out anything that might be choking him. Then continue as before.

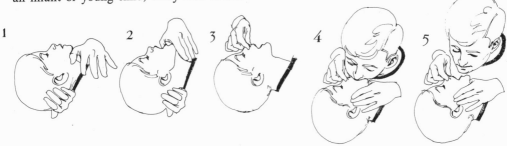

breathing. Mouth-to-mouth resuscitation should be studied by every person so that he is prepared in the event of an emergency.

The most common accidents requiring artificial respiration are drowning, electric shock, carbon monoxide poisoning, and gas poisoning.

If a child has drowned, you should begin mouth-to-mouth resuscitation without worrying about fluid in the lungs. The water will be absorbed or come up in the course of the procedure. Mouth-to-mouth resuscitation should be continued until regular breathing is fully established. At times breathing will suddenly stop again, so the person giving resuscitation should remain nearby, ready to institute it again if necessary.

Hospitalization for observation is usually advised for at least two days for a person whose breathing has been restored by this method.

Movies

Most children in the United States over the age of 6 or 7 years go to the movies. Occasionally younger children are taken by their parents and others to movies, but this usually is not a good idea unless the pictures are short and specially selected for such young boys and girls. Young children, as a rule, have a fairly short attention span and will rarely be able to sit through a feature film without becoming restless. Furthermore, the young child has a fertile imagination and tends to become closely involved in the action, which may, at times, upset him deeply.

However, as children grow older, there is much to be gained by attending selected movies. Children want very much to see what their friends are seeing so that they can discuss it among themselves or even imitate certain of the actors. Furthermore, during the later grade school years, and certainly during the high school years, going to the movies with friends becomes a matter of great social importance.

But throughout all these age levels, parents should supervise the movie the child or teen-ager plans to attend. Today, fortunately, in almost all communities movies are rated as to their suitability for viewing by children. However, parents should remember that violence is less strictly rated than sex, even though it can be especially upsetting to a child.

The ratings nationally accepted are:

G (General): for all ages.
PG: All ages admitted. Parent guidance suggested.
R (Restricted): Admittance under 17 requires accompanying parent or adult guardian.
X: No one under 17 admitted (age limit may vary in certain areas).

In limiting children to certain of these categories of motion pictures, it is important that parents assure themselves that their children do not see "R" movies by asking some adult on the ticket line to take them along. If a parent knows that his child is eager to see an "R" rated movie and fears that he will gain entrance with a stranger, it is better that the parent arrange to go with the child.

Movies, home   see Photographs and home movies.

Moving day

When families move to a new home, older children will usually take it in their stride, even if they have lost their friends. But to young children, those under the age of 3, it can be a very frightening and upsetting experience.

Even if his parents remain close to

him, moving can be very disturbing to a young child. If he remains around while the moving men are at work, he is likely to see his bedroom—his place of security—being literally taken apart. His familiar pictures are taken off the walls; his bed or crib is dismantled; his toys are put in boxes and carried out of the house and placed in a big truck.

However, parents can prepare a young child for moving day.

First, if at all possible, show the child the new home ahead of time. Let him see his room, and place a few of his familiar toys in it to build the association.

Then, when moving day comes and the present home is being dismantled, let the child's room remain intact until the last minute—and take him outside, or at least away from his room, while its contents are being moved. At the new house, set up the child's room first and arrange it as much as possible like his original room, so that when he lies in his bed or crib he will see the familiar pictures in approximately the same loca-

tion and, if possible, even the window in approximately the same position.

It is also a worthwhile plan to introduce the children of all age levels to children in the new neighborhood, even before you have moved. This always makes the transition easier.

See also **Home, location of.**

Mucous membrane

A type of thin, shiny membrane that lines the inner nose and mouth, the throat, esophagus, stomach, intestines, breathing tubes, urinary bladder, and inner lining of the genitals. This membrane contains microscopic glands which secrete mucus as a lubricant. They secrete increasing amounts when irritated.

Multiple births

Births of twins, triplets, quadruplets, and quintuplets have become more frequent during recent years with the use of "fertility pills"—hormone preparations which, for reasons not fully under-

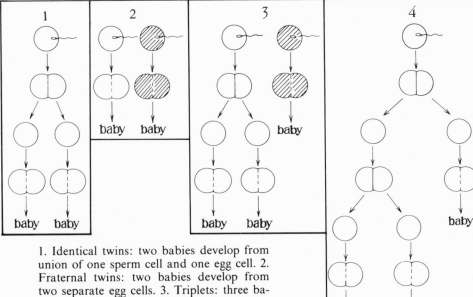

1. Identical twins: two babies develop from union of one sperm cell and one egg cell. 2. Fraternal twins: two babies develop from two separate egg cells. 3. Triplets: three babies develop from two egg cells, two babies are identical and the third is fraternal. 4. Identical triplets: three babies develop from the union of one sperm cell and one egg cell.

stood, stimulate multiple births. The type of hormone most widely used in the United States is the female hormone estrogen. Estrogen increases tenfold the possibility of having twins. However, it does not increase the likelihood of quadruplets, quintuplets, and other groups that occurs when the hormone perganol—widely used outside the United States—is taken.

Twins (and very occasionally triplets, quadruplets, and quintuplets) may be identical—that is, both infants are formed from the same sperm—or twins may be fraternal, the result of two different sperm cells. Identical twins are always of the same sex; fraternal twins may or may not be.

Triplets, quadruplets, quintuplets, and other multiple groups are usually the result of two different eggs joined by two different sperm—although occasionally they may be identical.

Babies born of multiple births are usually full term but smaller than the average newborn, since the nourishment before birth must of necessity be divided.

See also **Twins.**

Mumps

A contagious disease caused by a virus, in which the salivary glands, most frequently the parotid glands (in front of and below the ears) are swollen, giving the face a "fat" appearance.

Mode of transmission   Mumps is transmitted by direct exposure to a person who has the disease.

Incubation period   It takes between fourteen and twenty-one days after contact for a susceptible person to develop the first signs and symptoms of the disease.

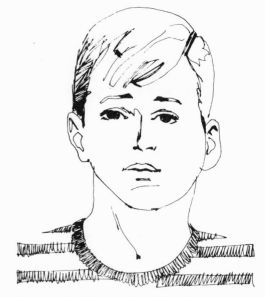

Mumps affecting one side of the face.

Signs and symptoms   The disease usually begins with fever, headache, vomiting, and general malaise, followed in one or two days by a swelling of the salivary glands in front of and below the ears. In approximately 50 percent of the cases, only the glands on one side of the face are swollen, the swelling on one side may precede that on the other by two or three days. The swelling of the glands usually takes place by the third day, after which the fever subsides and the swelling gradually disappears within three to seven days. The child is considered no longer contagious and may return to school when the swelling has completely subsided.

Treatment   There is no special treatment for mumps. The child can do as much as he feels up to doing, although he should not be in contact with adolescents or adults who may be susceptible.

Complications   Occasionally, about

seven days following the swelling of the glands, a child may develop a severe headache, vomit, and become very drowsy. This is due to mumps encephalitis, an inflammation of the brain by the mumps virus. It is not in any way serious. It subsides completely in a day or two and leaves no aftereffects.

Another occasional, rare complication, seen only in adolescent boys and in men, is an inflammation of the testicles (orchitis). This is a painful and serious condition that may (in about 13 percent of the cases) permanently impair fertility. Potency, however, is not affected. Inflammation of the ovaries occurs in about 7 percent of the adolescent girls who contract mumps. As far as is known, it does not impair fertility.

Care of exposed persons   No effort to prevent the disease is usually made when susceptible children are exposed, with the exception of adolescent boys, or occasionally if children are going on a vacation. Then they are given an inoculation of mumps hyper-immune globulin—taken from the blood of people just recovered from mumps. This is a temporary immunization lasting only three to four weeks.

Immunization   Longer-lasting—possibly lifetime—immunity can be conferred by a modern mumps vaccine that should be given to all children other than those who have been recently exposed. It is not applicable for use with exposed persons, since it produces immunity in a few weeks rather than immediately.

Murder   see **Homicide.**

Murmurs   see **Heart murmur.**

Muscle pains

Muscle pains are experienced at one time or another by every child. Among the many possible causes are infections, sudden overuse of muscles, excessive strain on a muscle, rheumatic fever, and injury.

One of the first types of muscle pains a child may experience is that which for lack of a better name is called "night pains" (or sometimes, inaccurately, "growing pains"). These occur in arm and leg muscles of children aged approximately 2 to 5 at night after they are already asleep. They occur almost always before 1:00 A.M., causing the child to wake up crying. Usually massaging the sore muscle or applying heat will relieve the pain, and the child will generally return to sleep within twenty minutes. These pains are probably muscle cramps caused by an unequal pull of different muscles as they relax.

Muscle pains which occur during infections are fairly common. They are especially pronounced during influenza or virus infections when a child aches "all over," but they usually subside quickly under treatment with aspirin.

An excessive pull on certain muscles may also cause pain. Certain children have a short Achilles' tendon. When a child runs a good deal this pulls on the calf muscles, resulting in pain. (See **Achilles' tendon.**)

The suddenly increased use of muscles after relative inactivity is a common cause of muscle pains. Such pains occur when children start ballet, modern or acrobatic dancing, or seasonal sports activity such as tennis, baseball, or football.

Muscle spasm may also be a cause of pain in children, although this is comparatively rare as compared with adults. The cause may be vitamin B deficiency.

Rheumatic fever may also cause muscle pains, although in this case the joints are usually much more involved. Pains that occur only at night, or pains occurring only in the muscles of one extremity, are not caused by rheumatic fever. But repetitive or constant pains in muscles and joints should always be investigated by a doctor for the possibility of rheumatic fever. (See **Rheumatic fever.**)

Muscular dystrophy

A disease characterized by progressive weakness and wasting away of the outer muscles of the body. Among the muscles involved are those of the arms, legs, chest, and back.

Muscular dystrophy is usually hereditary, with only an occasional case having no known family background. It occurs predominantly in male children, the ratio being three to one over female children. In girls it is likely to be less severe.

The most common type, pseudohypertrophic progressive muscular dystrophy, has its onset when the child is between 3 and 6. The first symptoms are in the legs—difficulty in walking and a waddling gait. Later the trunk muscles are involved, and the child has great difficulty in rising from a reclining to a standing position. The muscles of the arms and legs may become enlarged, although considerably weakened. The condition gradually worsens over five to ten years until respiratory failure or pneumonia terminates life.

There is no specific treatment or cure known at the present time, although several very optimistic reports have recently been published by investigators in Chicago and Japan. Intensive physical therapy may aid by strengthening and improving the use of unaffected muscles. The aim is to minimize painful muscle spasms and deformity. A high-protein diet and supplementary vitamins are advised.

There are other types of muscular dystrophy that have their onset later in life (usually from age 6 to 20). These progress more slowly, and the patient may live out a normal life span.

Mushroom poisoning

There are numerous species of mushrooms and only a few are poisonous. However, the danger is so great and it is so difficult to distinguish the poisonous from the nonpoisonous species that it should be a firm rule that no wild mushrooms be picked by children or other members of the family for food.

None of the popular "rules" for distinguishing poisonous from nonpoisonous mushrooms are safe or even true. One "rule" states that if the skin can be peeled from the top of a mushroom it is nonpoisonous. Another is that a silver spoon or coin added to a pan in which mushrooms are cooked will darken if poisonous species are present. Both of these are false.

Symptoms of mushroom poisoning Usually there is acute abdominal pain, diarrhea, and vomiting several hours after the mushrooms have been eaten. After about twenty-four hours the child may go into shock, have convulsive seizures, and go into a coma. Death may follow in several days.

Treatment The child should be made to vomit as soon as you realize that he has eaten a mushroom or any part of a mushroom. For methods of inducing vomiting, see **Poisons: first-aid treatment.** Call the doctor or take the child to a hospital immediately.

Music in the home

Children of all ages react strongly to music, and nearly all love it in one form or another. Parents, by encouraging this love, give their children a wonderful source of pleasure, a means of making friends, and an excellent means of self-expression and emotional release. In addition, parents may find that music calms a restless or overexcited child, stimulates a bored or withdrawn child, and entertains children at times when there is "nothing" for them to do.

All babies are born with a natural response to rhythm and sound, and as they get older enjoy music more and more. They are calmed by quiet songs (thus the universal use of lullabies to put babies to sleep); they will smile or laugh at peppy, bouncy songs; and frequently they will move their bodies, rocking or bouncing, in response to music.

One of the earliest forms of involving the child himself in music is through playing little action games such as "Pat-a-cake" and "Ride-a-cock-horse."

It doesn't matter whether the music was written for children or not. Some children prefer rock or jazz or Beethoven to "Twinkle, Twinkle, Little Star." But most children like any music that has a rhythmical beat.

What is important is that the parent play music to the child or sing to him. The baby will soon indicate his special preferences.

When a baby is demanding attention or play, a busy mother may find that singing a song or playing a record will keep him interested and happy.

Toddlers can have their own records, and they love to listen to them over and over again. They will sing with these records, march around to the beat, and "dance," twisting or turning around and around. Toddlers also love it if their mothers sing directions for them to follow, such as "Run, run, run around," "Clap, clap, clap your hands," or "Jump, jump, up and down." A mother can even do this while performing some household task. A parent can help a child to find the record he wants by marking records with different colors or pictures.

Children of nursery school age sing, make up songs, dance to music, and skip and run and jump. They love to play rhythm instruments and they love to sing with the family. They act out the meaning of songs and make up their own words. They can have their own record players as well as their own record collection, and know the specific song on each record.

Many children of nursery school age have even started to pick out tunes on the piano or whatever musical instrument is available and playable by a child so young.

In elementary school, children who show a special interest in music often start taking lessons. Parents should encourage them without pressure. Practice is, of course, necessary to attain proficiency but must not be forced against violent objections. It is much better for the child to continue enjoying his playing rather than to build up negative reactions.

Classical music, semiclassical music, folk songs, country music, jazz, rock, show music, and children's songs are all valuable in maintaining a child's interest in music and building up his potential for the full enjoyment of music in all its forms.

See also **Music lessons; Rhythms and dance; Talent, exceptional.**

Music lessons

Some young children show a special

musical aptitude: they pick out tunes on a piano, make up songs, sing on pitch, or demonstrate an unusual degree of rhythmic sensitivity.

Many parents react to this early interest and aptitude by wanting to give their child lessons when he is as young as 5 years of age. Some children that young even beg to be given lessons.

There is no particular age that is right for all children to start music lessons; while 6 years might be appropriate for one child, it could be totally unsuitable for another. In general, age 7 or 8 years is a good time to start lessons. Children who start taking formal lessons too early usually lose interest, for they do not as yet have the concentration or muscular coordination necessary, and it is difficult to persuade them to practice.

Prior to the approximate age of 7 years, children can still enjoy themselves playing on various, usually simple musical instruments, and they may join rhythm orchestras in which youngsters are directed by a teacher.

The choice of an instrument depends largely upon a child's age, his interests, and his reason for wanting to play. The piano is the most popular of all instruments, but it is basically a "one-man" instrument. The study of the flute, violin, clarinet, cello, or various other orchestral and band instruments can lead to a most rewarding experience—participation in group music: bands, orchestras, chamber groups, or even pop and rock music groups.

The string instruments will usually present an interesting challenge to the child with a good ear and good coordination. For the youngster who enjoys singing, the guitar may be an appropriate choice.

Pianos and other instruments may be rented until you are sure that the child will continue on the instrument.

The selection of a teacher is also very important. A good teacher must like children and have an understanding of their needs and interests at various age levels. The teacher should also be aware of the capabilities of a specific youngster.

The teacher who uses his imagination and ingenuity, and who can establish a good rapport with the child, will almost surely be much more effective than one who insists on rigid drilling and overemphasis in perfecting details.

Of course, proficiency in playing an instrument requires practicing. To make it easier for the child to organize his time, a certain defined practice period should be set aside each day, preferably one that does not compete with other interests such as ball playing or similar after-school activities.

The youngster should receive a great deal of encouragement and a minimum of nagging. At times children will become bored with their practicing. During such periods the pressures of enforced improvement should be relaxed, and the children should be permitted to "tread water" rather than forced to drop the lessons entirely. Only too often in later years, many a child has been severely critical of his parents: "Why did you let me stop my lessons?"

Myopia   see **Eye defects.**

Mysophobia   see **Phobias.**

N

Nagging

Constant bothering and fault-finding by parents is annoying and upsetting to all children. Often it is parents who are unhappy and upset who take out their irritability on their children by nagging and apparently never being satisfied.

Nagging rarely produces the result desired. The child resists and feels that his parents are not happy with him. A child who is nagged may do what his parent wants at the time but will not be motivated to do better on his own.

It is much more effective to encourage a child and praise him or show approval for what he has done well or for an honest effort. And it is important that parents break the habit of nagging even if this means that some things do not get done for a while.

Nailpolish-remover poisoning see Poisons: first-aid treatment.

Nails, biting

Many boys and girls bite their nails—usually when watching television, reading a book, or just standing around. These are tense children who relieve themselves to some degree by nail-biting. Such behavior is similar to that of children who relieve their tension and anxieties by thumb-sucking or chewing gum constantly.

Many parents try to prevent nail-biting by putting adhesive tape on the fingertips or having the children wear gloves or mittens. These methods are generally of no help whatsoever and just make the child more tense. Bad-tasting medicine on the fingernails is also of no help unless a child, trying to break the habit, asks for it himself.

The best method of treating nail-biting, although far from easy, is to uncover the causes of the tensions and anxieties and relieve these as much as possible. Often they are due to some situations at home—such as a child's jealousy of a brother or sister; quarrels between parents; overdemanding, restrictive, or nagging parents; parents who belittle a child or set standards too high for him to attain. School and outside situations may also be responsible, and should be looked into for causes of unhappiness.

Parents should do the best they can to help the child be more relaxed, and remember that continuing to bother him about nail-biting will have just the opposite effect.

Often children of school age may make a real effort to overcome the habit of nail-biting, and in this parents can help. Girls may be permitted to use fingernail polish if they will let their nails grow. Boys, also, can be offered some special inducement. Permitting children to chew gum will also usually help in overcoming the habit.

Nails, cutting

The fingernails of a new born child may be so long that within a day or two there are scratches on his cheeks.

The nails should then be cut while the baby is still in the nursery or as soon as

Blunt-edged manicure scissors are strongly recommended for cutting an infant's nails. There is less chance of an accident.

he is brought home. And throughout infancy and childhood, fingernails and toenails should be regularly trimmed.

Unless performed correctly, nail-trimming can be a fairly dangerous operation. Infants, especially, and fingers, particularly, are always moving, so unless the proper scissors are used, as well as the proper technique, the child's fingers or toes are likely to be stuck or cut in the process.

Use a blunt-ended nail scissors. Take the whole hand or foot of the infant in your hand and hold it securely. When cutting a nail on the hand, let one of the baby's fingers protrude at a time, and cut the nail. When the nail is on a toe, separate as far as possible the toe you are working on from the other toes. Continue in this manner until all nails are cut.

Name-calling see **Teasing by children; Teasing by parents.**

Naps

Once a child is approximately 6 months old, he is awake most of the day but takes two or three naps. The times at which he takes these naps, as well as their duration, vary with the individual, and the pattern changes constantly.

Usually from age 5 or 6 months up to approximately 1 year, children take two naps a day. Between ages 1 and 2 many children give up the morning nap and sleep one to two hours in the afternoon.

The need for naps diminishes between ages 2 and 5, and many children, as they near 3 years of age, start resisting the nap. However, the rest period is still needed, and although napping cannot be forced, you can read quietly to the child or involve him in some quiet occupation such as crayoning, looking at books, stringing beads, or listening to music.

At times children aged 1 to 3 may nap so long in the afternoon that they are not sleepy in the evening and strongly resist going to bed. In such cases you may wake the child after a nap of one hour. But sometimes this causes him to become very cranky in the late afternoon and at suppertime. In such situations it is necessary to experiment in order to reach the best solution.

See also **Sleep.**

Narcotics see **Drug abuse.**

Natural childbirth

Childbirth with very little or no anesthesia. Various methods are used to prepare the mother so as to minimize the pain through education, relaxation, and physical exercises.

The original concept was presented in the 1940's by Dr. Grantley Dick Read of England in his book *Childbirth Without Fear.* In it he discussed and described what would happen during labor and delivery so that a mother would know what to expect. A great many mothers, he felt, had been culturally conditioned to expect pain during the birth process and had almost looked upon the whole happening as an illness rather than a normal, natural physiological process. Mothers, following Read's method, gave birth with little or no anesthesia.

Within more recent years the Lamaze method of childbirth, developed by Dr. Fernand Lamaze of France, has become the most popular approach. Mothers are not only carefully instructed in almost every detail of pregnancy and the birth process, but are given explicit exercises to prepare them to breathe and push effectively during the uterine contractions that precede the birth of the baby. Lamaze felt that ill-timed pushing by the mother led to difficulties and that proper breathing gave her more oxygen, a lack of which was in part responsible for painful uterine contractions. Expectant mothers are also given regular exercises to perform to increase the strength of the abdominal muscles, to limber up the joints that will stretch during labor, to increase the elasticity of the area between the legs through which the baby passes during birth, and to teach relaxation.

The husband goes to the classes with his wife, learns what she is doing and why, and also learns the breathing, pushing, and relaxation exercises. He stays with her during labor and acts as a coach, aiding her in breathing and pushing according to the practiced plan. He, in his way, experiences the labor with her and strengthens her by being close to her at such a meaningful time. He goes with her into the delivery room and is next to her during the birth of the baby.

Most modern pediatricians approve highly of the Lamaze method of childbirth. The lack of anesthesia makes it safer for the newborn, since he is not at all narcotized. Also, the preparation of the mother physically, aiding in the speed and ease of delivery, often helps to make the birth safer and easier.

There are branches of the American Society for Psychoprophylaxis in Obstetrics (natural childbirth) in most major cities. (See **Appendix E: Agencies for Parents.**)

Nature

All children are fascinated by nature. They are interested in animals of all types, from the animals on a farm and in a zoo to butterflies, ladybugs, fireflies, and spiders. They love flowers and trees, with their variously shaped leaves, and the flaming autumn colors. They enjoy catching and watching frogs, turtles, salamanders, and snakes. They collect rocks of different colors and odd shapes. They are fascinated by the sky, the wind, the stars, the moon, and the snow. Their interest in nature is endless.

Whether a child is in the city or country, parents can do much to make his life more enjoyable by fostering and helping to maintain these interests. The country or the seashore is an exciting source of natural interest, as are parks with their flowers and trees and lakes.

A walk in the country with a child during the summertime will often be an adventure. Ask a child to look around and make discoveries, and the results will be exciting to the adult as well as to the child. Under the eaves of a house or barn, he may find the mud nests of the mud wasp. Walk along a brook with a child and let him turn over the rocks on the side of the stream, and often he will discover salamanders, or fascinating nests of ants who hasten to hide their little white eggs. The child will look further and usually find frogs and turtles and see occasional fish. Wild flowers and leaves can be collected and brought home for identification and pressing. Birds can be observed, and often nests can be seen in trees and bushes. Of all animals in the world, none are more interesting or more numerous than the insects. Very few insects bite or sting, and children can learn to recognize those that do—the bees and wasps, mosquitos, biting flies, a very few ants, bedbugs, and a few of the larger spiders. Practically all the others, including all the butterflies, moths, dragonflies, damselflies, beetles of all sizes, the weird walkingsticks, praying mantises, locusts, and cicadas, are entirely harmless and can be handled without fear.

There is also gardening, which children enjoy immensely. Planting seeds and watching them grow into flowers or vegetables is extremely exciting. Children should have flower pots or boxes of their own or, if possible, a small plot of ground to plant and care for and watch.

There are excellent books for children about all areas of nature—birds, insects, turtles, snakes, animals of the seashore and water, wild flowers, and trees.

Enjoying nature fully will make a child's life more worthwhile, fulfilling, and meaningful, as well as more enjoyable and satisfying.

Nausea

Nausea is a common complaint in childhood. It usually occurs before a child vomits, but at times it is a symptom by itself.

There is no single cause of nausea. It is just a symptom of something that has affected the nervous system of the stomach. It may precede or accompany any of numerous infections, whether they be infectious diseases, influenza, or bacterial conditions. It may be a simple stomach upset caused by a food reaction or food allergy. It may be caused by some digestive disturbance in the intestines.

In attempting to treat nausea do not force the child to eat or drink, lest vomiting follow. However, old remedies are still effective. Give the child nothing by mouth for an hour. Then start with just a tablespoon of sugar water or medium-strength tea with sugar, or a cola drink or ginger ale. Increase by ½ tablespoon every twenty minutes. After four tablespoonfuls have been reached and the nausea has subsided, give broth and crackers, and then go on to apple sauce and cereals.

If the nausea continues, and especially if vomiting or fever ensues, call the doctor. He may prescribe a special medicine given by mouth or suppository, or possibly the injection of an anti-nauseant drug. He may also want to determine the cause exactly.

See **Vomiting.**

Navel

Immediately after birth the doctor ties and cuts the umbilical cord, leaving a few inches still attached to the navel of the baby. This portion dries in a few days and usually drops off in seven to ten days.

The navel is slightly moist after the cord drops off but dries completely in several days. Most doctors advise that a baby not be tub-bathed until the navel is dry. (See **Sponge bath for the newborn.**) There is no need to cover the navel with gauze pads or to put on a binder. It will dry much sooner if exposed to the air.

If the navel continues to be moist, the doctor will usually advise the use of a dressing of 95 percent alcohol or else a sterile powder to help the drying process.

In certain instances the navel still continues to discharge, and close observation will reveal a small, moist, red mass within. This is of no seriousness. It is an overgrowth of healing tissue on a tiny stem, much like a cauliflower, called an umbilical granuloma. If small, the doctor will touch it with a silver nitrate stick, and it will dry up and disappear. If the granuloma is fairly large, he will tie it off at its base, and it will dry up and drop off in a few days.

If shortly after birth or shortly after the cord has dropped off the navel appears inflamed and swollen, the doctor should be called at once. This may be an infection and should be treated immediately.

If, after the cord drops off, the navel balloons out, this is called an umbilical hernia. When small, it will usually get smaller and disappear by itself. However, if it is large, the doctor will usually strap it with waterproof adhesive tape. With this treatment the hernia usually disappears before the child is one year old.

See also **Hernia.**

Nearsightedness see **Eye defects.**

Neatness see **Cleanliness; Grooming; Orderliness.**

Neck, wry see **Wryneck.**

Negativism

All normal children exhibit negativism during their childhood and adolescence. It is especially characteristic at certain specific age levels—at approximately 2 years, at about 7 years, and during adolescence. At each of these stages the child is attempting to gain a new level of freedom.

The period from approximately 2 to 3 years of age is a time when a great many children are typically resistant. They resist every suggestion, whether it is to put on a coat, take off a coat, take a bath or get out of the bath, go to bed, etc.

There are a number of approaches in the handling of this resistance that are usually very helpful. First, put everything in the positive form: "Tommy, it's time to go to bed," rather than "Tommy, don't you think it's time to go to bed?" It is often amazing what a difference this will make.

The second suggestion is always to give a youngster a few minutes advance notice rather than stopping him abruptly if he is occupied in some interesting project. Tell him, "All right, you can play a few minutes longer and then you must stop." At the end of the few minutes, do what you planned to do even if the youngster resists. Sometimes, setting a timer for the time allotted makes things easier.

The third suggestion is not to let the child feel or learn that by throwing a temper tantrum he can gain his way. Carry out your intention as calmly and quickly as possible despite any screams or kicks. (See **Temper and temper tantrums.**)

Between the ages of about 3 and 6 children are generally less rebellious than during the preceding period or the years that follow. During this preschool period, however, there will be occasional testing of parents' authority, making it important that parents set one standard of discipline and support one another in carrying out any disciplinary measures. At this period, as throughout childhood, orders and restrictions should be held to a necessary minimum. There is no value in provoking resistance over unimportant issues.

During the early school years another period of resistance appears, usually starting around the age of 7 years. This is most often related to a child's desire to do what his classmates and companions are doing. This is the period when children very much want to be accepted in a group of their peers, and often this means more to them than orders and demands by parents.

Children during this school-age period often make up their own minds on what they want to do or how they want to do it. They are constantly active, busy, and energetic, and haven't time to waste. They will run out on a cold day without a hat or coat, or on a wet and rainy day without rubbers. Here again, in spite of the youngster's stubborness, parents should not give in on important matters, especially if a child's health is involved or if he wants to do something of which the parents strongly disapprove. The child should be told why he must—or must not—do a certain thing, without going into a long-drawn-out discussion. "When it's cold out we wear coats so that we don't catch colds." The short explanation and the authority with which it is stated should be sufficient.

On other issues, parents should consider whether it's worth insisting. Perhaps the child doesn't really need to wear a hat. Maybe it really is more important that he have the chance to see a popular movie with his friends than that he stay home to greet visiting relatives. Perhaps, in general, too much is being demanded of the child.

Negativism is normal as children enter adolescence. At this stage boys and girls are trying to be on their own and break the ties that bind them to their parents. And so the natural reaction to a parent's orders and demands, or even simple requests, is to say "No." Here again, but more than at any time during childhood, demands and restrictions should be limited to those that are really necessary.

See also **Adolescents, understanding; Discipline.**

Nephritis

An inflammation of the kidneys. During childhood it is most commonly seen following streptococcus infections such as scarlet fever or a streptococcus sore throat. The most frequent of the obvious signs and symptoms is blood in the urine, causing the urine to be either blood-red or—more frequently—a smoky brown. In some cases there may be a reduction in the amount of urine passed and a puffiness around the eyes either before or during the time blood is present in the urine. Often there is an increase in the blood pressure. At the onset of acute nephritis there may be fever and a severe headache. A moderate anemia may develop. Often, however, the child does not appear or feel as ill as he is—making it difficult for parents to appreciate the seriousness of the condition.

The diagnosis should be made by a doctor, who will study the chemistry of the child's blood and the microscopic appearance and cell content of his urine. Improvement generally starts within one to two weeks. The urine returns to normal color in this period of time, although microscopically it contains red blood cells until approximately six weeks after the onset of the condition. A much more delicate test (Addis count) shows extra red blood cells remaining in the urine for an average of four to eight months. Blood pressure usually drops to normal after a week, and blood chemistry within two weeks.

There is no specific treatment for nephritis, although penicillin is usually given. Rest in bed is essential during the acute stages of the disease and until the urine clears.

Many doctors continue children on penicillin two to three months after the onset of nephritis to lessen or prevent the chance of infections which might aggravate the condition.

Nephrosis
A disease of the kidneys occurring generally during the childhood period. It is characterized by a swelling up of the body and excessive albumin in the urine. There is only rarely blood in the urine, and only occasionally is the blood pressure elevated. It is estimated that about 7 out of 100,000 children under age 5 have nephrosis.

The cause of nephrosis is not actually known, although it has been found to follow certain infections, toxic reactions to chemicals, bee stings, and even severe poison ivy attacks.

The most common and obvious symptom is the swelling of the body from the retained fluid which is not removed by the kidney. The child's appetite is poor and he is droopy and irritable.

Children with nephrosis are extremely susceptible to infection.

A specific diagnosis of the disease and how far it has progressed can be made by a doctor from a study of the child's blood and urine.

Treatment of nephrosis is largely aimed at preventing infections, ridding the body of the swelling by stimulating kidney activity, and righting the disturbed body chemistries. Cortisone therapy has been widely used in treatment but should be under the constant direction of the doctor. This diminishes the amount of albumin passed in the urine, thus stimulating the flow of urine and so reducing the body swelling.

Nephrosis is a recurrent disease, often subsiding only to reappear again. Cortisone therapy may have to be repeated with each new attack. Recovery is attained in most children only after months and at times years of treatment.

Neuroblastoma
One of the most common malignant tumors of infancy and childhood. It is a condition that occurs early in life, with three-fourths of all cases appearing before age 5 years. It is the most common tumor found at birth.

This tumor usually arises from an adrenal gland, although it may originate in other parts of the body. It is usually discovered by a doctor, who feels a firm mass in the child's abdomen.

Treatment is by immediate surgical removal followed by treatment with anticancer drugs such as Cincovin (vincristin sulfate) given intravenously and Cytoxan (cyclophosphamide) given orally or intravenously.

With immediate removal and subsequent treatment in children under age 1 year, there has been a 76 percent survival rate; survival is considerably lower in older children.

Newborn, characteristics of
As a baby is being born, the skin is a dusky, bluish color. Almost immediately the infant starts crying and breathing. Within seconds after the onset of breathing, the color of the skin turns to its normal pink. The baby is now living on its own.

The skin at birth is covered with a greasy, white material called vernix caseosa. This is usually washed off by the

Newborn infant.

The skin of the newborn infant also is very thin and especially prone to irritations and infections. During the early weeks of infancy, little pearly blisters may often be seen on babies' faces. These are caused by clogged sweat glands and usually disappear in a week or two.

The head of the newborn has the greatest circumference of any part of the body, assuring that once it has passed through the birth canal, the chest and abdomen will follow without difficulty. The head is usually one fourth the size of the body at birth, as compared to the adult head, which is one seventh the body size. And, because a baby is born

nurses in the newborn nursery. Fine, silky hair may be present on the forehead, down the sides of the face, and on the arms and legs. This hair (lanugo) usually disappears within a few months.

The majority of babies show a red discoloration of the skin at the base of the skull in back where it joins the neck. Many babies have red flushes on the eyelids and on the forehead just above the bridge of the nose. These flushes gradually fade and usually disappear by the time a baby is one year old.

The skin of the newborn reflects not only the maturity of the child but its state of nutrition. In premature babies there is a lack of fatty tissue in the skin, but the skin is generally tight. In dysmature infants—who are small because the source of food through the placenta has been inadequate—the skin is loose, wrinkled, scaly, and glossy.

Peeling of the skin of the newborn normally occurs in twenty-four to forty-eight hours after birth. There is little or no peeling prior to that time. Peeling immediately at birth, however, may occur with dysmature infants.

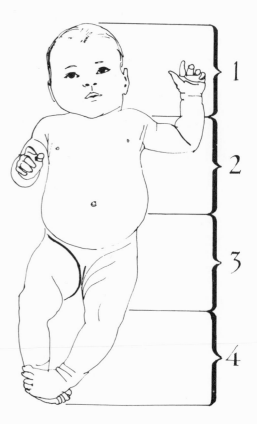

A baby's head is one-fourth of its total length.

with a comparatively large brain, the forehead and portion of the skull above the ears usually take up half its face and head. The bones of the skull are not rigidly joined. This makes it easier for the baby to pass through the birth canal, and also allows flexibility as the brain expands in normal growth. (See **Fontanelles.**)

The face of the newborn infant will often disappoint parents. The nose generally has very little bridge and is flattened down between the eyes. At times, following birth the end of the nose is turned down, but it usually turns up in a week or two. The newborn usually breathes through its nose unless clogging with mucus makes it difficult.

The eyes of the newborn white child are usually a grayish blue color of varying intensities. They may change color and will usually have their permanent color by the time the baby is 5 or 6 months old. The eyes of the newborn Negro child are usually brown at birth. There is often puffiness around the eyes following birth, especially following long-drawn-out labors. This puffiness should disappear within a day or two. There may be some discharge from the eyes, usually caused by the antiseptic eyedrops that have been used following birth. Occasionally a small hemorrhage may be seen in the whites of one or both eyes. These blood spots are caused by a rupture of capillaries in the eyes, most frequently during a difficult labor. They are of no importance and usually disappear within a month.

The features of the baby are rarely motionless, even when it is asleep. There is a flickering of an eye, a motion of the mouth, an occasional frown, and, when the baby is awake, yawns are frequent. A very slight smile may occasionally be noted at age 1 or 2 weeks, and usually the smile becomes pronounced by age 4 to 6 weeks. These are real smiles and are not due to gas as so many people have believed.

Usually, during the first few weeks, the baby lies in a position similar to that it had within the uterus, with legs flexed, head bent forward, and back arched forward as well.

Vision is present at birth, but the clarity of vision probably varies with the individual child. Certainly all newborns with normal eyes differentiate light from darkness. But, contrary to general opinion, a great many babies a day or two old actually see large objects around them and will stare at these objects and often follow them. Most babies a few days old will look steadily at the face of the person holding them, as if studying the features.

Hearing also is present at birth.

The neck of the baby is short compared to that of an older child. Its chest is comparatively much deeper in a front-to-back direction than it will be in later childhood and adult life. The newborn breathes largely with its abdominal muscles, so comparatively there is very little motion of the chest during respiration. (See **Diaphragm.**)

The abdomen of the infant becomes moderately protuberant shortly after birth because of air which fills the stomach and intestines. Later the abdomen often becomes very prominent after feeding, giving some mothers the erroneous impression that there is something wrong with the child. (See **Abdominal distention.**)

The genitals of the female newborn may appear unusually large. This is due to the fact that they are temporarily enlarged by stimulation from adult sex hormones of the mother. They usually reduce in size within two weeks. In the male, both testes have usually already descended into the scrotal sac. (See **Testicles.**) The foreskin covers the penis and is usually adherent to it.

The stump of the umbilical cord is attached to the navel and begins to dry and shrivel within twenty-four hours. The cord, usually leathery in color and texture when dry, drops off in approximately seven to ten days. No attempt should be made to remove the dry cord before its normal separation. (See **Umbilical cord; Navel.**)

The arms and legs of a newborn continue to move freely as they have previously been doing in the uterus. As a rule, the hands are clenched but will firmly hold any object placed in them.

Newborn babies frequently hiccup after feedings. This is of no importance and in no way upsets the baby. Newborns also sneeze from time to time. This, too, is of no significance.

The bowel movements of the newborn are a sticky black or dark green substance called meconium that continues to be passed for three or four days. The stools then change to a greenish or brownish color, which in a day or two changes to the normal yellow color. (See **Bowel movements.**)

The baby may regurgitate a little milk from time to time. This may be due to air coming up from the stomach that brings up a little milk with it. (See **Bubbling [burping] the baby.**) Or it may be due to a temporary incomplete closure at the top of the stomach, so that some of the milk is forced out as the stomach contracts in the process of digestion.

The strongest drive in the newborn is for sucking and feeding, and the closeness and warmth that he experiences as the mother feeds him is the beginning of the positive and strong relationship between parents and child. (See **Mothering.**)

Niacin   see **Nutrition.**

Nicotine (cigarettes) poisoning   see **Poisons: first-aid treatment.**

Night blindness
A condition in which sight is perfectly normal during the day but badly impaired or entirely deficient in darkness or even in semidarkness.

It is comparatively rare during childhood and adolescence. It is occasionally caused by certain retinal diseases. More often it is caused by a lack of vitamin A in the diet or a lack of vitamin A absorption.

In such cases increased vitamin A is given in liquid or tablet form and also in the diet. Carrots, sweet potatoes, and egg yolk are especially high in vitamin A.

The child should not receive mineral oil regularly by mouth, since this absorbs the vitamin A and takes it out of the body.

Night pains   see **Muscle pains.**

Night walking   see **Sleep problems.**

Nightmares and night terrors
These are both severe disturbances of sleep, especially common from the ages of 2 to 5. The nightmare is a frightening dream, and the child often awakes very much upset. He can usually remember the details of the dream and may recall them the next day. If nightmares are frequent, the child may become afraid to go to sleep.

A night terror makes the child scream and thrash around in his sleep. He kicks and strikes out. When aroused, he is completely disoriented. He does not recognize his parents or other people present, and cannot relate the dream. He usually goes back to sleep in a few minutes and cannot remember the violent experiences the next day.

The causes of these disturbances are essentially the same, for they can both be due to emotional upsets, tensions, excitement, and overstimulation. Some children are upset and overstimulated after viewing an exciting or distressing television program; some are upset because of tensions and fights between their parents or others at home. At times there is intense sibling rivalry and jealousy which upsets the child.

The prevention of most nightmares and night terrors lies in preventing or relieving overstimulation, excitement, and tension. Be sure that the child's surroundings are quiet and relaxed for an hour or so before he goes to bed. Preferably, television should be turned off. There should be no overstimulation by active games or jouncing around. For younger children, a quiet story should be read before bedtime. In most cases this is all that is needed to overcome the tendency to nightmares and night terrors. If the child has special fears regarding darkness, he should have a night-light, or the door to his room can be left open.

However, if the problem persists, it will be necessary to look carefully into the home situation to see if the child is under tension, and, if so, to try to relieve this as much as possible. Occasionally the doctor may advise the use of a non-habit-forming tranquilizer before bedtime for a few weeks to break the pattern. Sometimes he may advise parents to seek professional help in providing a more secure atmosphere for the child.

Nits   see **Head lice.**

Nocturnal seminal emission

When boys reach puberty, usually between 12 and 15, their testes enlarge and start producing semen, the fluid in which sperm cells swim. When there is excess semen, some of it must leave the body through the penis. This usually occurs during sleep. Because seminal emissions are almost always associated with sexually exciting dreams, they are also called "wet dreams." These emissions occur at irregular intervals, and there is no way by which a boy, his parents, or a doctor can determine when they will occur. Nocturnal emissions should be explained to every growing boy before he enters puberty. The youngster should be reassured that they are normal signs of maturing, so that he will have no worry or guilt feelings.

Nodding spasm   see **Head nodding.**

Nodes, lymph   see **Lymph nodes.**

Nodules of the breast   see **Breast development.**

Nose, development and shape

The nose of an infant has little or no bridge. This makes the upper part of the nose rather flat on the face and usually makes it appear that the eyes are widely spread apart, as well as frequently giving the erroneous impression that the eyes are crossed.

One cannot tell at birth, or even during childhood for that matter, what the eventual shape of the nose will be. Occasionally, immediately after birth, the nose may look pushed down, for it has been forced down that way in passing through the birth passages. In such cases it generally returns to its normal cute baby shape in three or four days.

The bridge of the nose starts to really form at approximately age 2, but the real shape of the adult nose does not begin to form until approximately age 13 or 14. For this reason plastic surgery, if necessary or desirable, should be delayed until the youngster is at least 17.

See also **Nose, plastic surgery on.**

Nose, foreign objects in   see **Foreign objects in nose.**

Nose, plastic surgery on

Occasionally plastic surgery of the nose is desired by a teen-age child and his or her parents. Usually they feel that the shape or size of the nose is a social handicap. This is most frequently the case with girls. Boys most often desire surgery to correct a fracture of the nose which has bent it down or to one side.

There are some adolescent boys and girls who focus so much on their appearance that even if they have normal noses they may feel that they are too long, too large, or too curved. Usually, as these boys and girls become more successful socially and more stable emotionally, this intense desire for a different nose subsides.

The nose does not take its mature shape until late in adolescence. Plastic surgery should not be attempted until the cartilage and bone are fully developed. 1. One year. 2. Five years. 3. Twelve years. 4. Fifteen years. 5. Nineteen years.

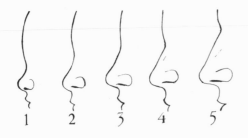

1   2   3   4   5

If plastic surgery of the nose is to be performed, it should be postponed until the child is at least 17, when the nose is fully grown. If performed too early, the continued growth of the nasal bones may spoil the original results and, at times, even make a second operation necessary.

Since a perfect result is so important, these operations should always be performed by plastic surgeons skilled in this particular technique.

Nose blowing   see **Blowing the nose.**

Nose drops

Nose drops should only be used if a child's nose is badly clogged and then only on the advice of a doctor. They should not be used for a simple running nose.

Most of the clogging of a nose is caused by the swelling of the tissues within it, and nose drops shrink these tissues. The effect of the drops, however, is only temporary, and in many cases the swelling of tissues returns even more pronouncedly once the effect has worn off.

The use of nose drops may be indicated when:

1. An infant finds sucking extremely difficult with the nose clogged.
2. The appetite of the child is greatly diminished. Most of the sense of taste is due to smell, and with the nose stuffed, smell is greatly decreased or absent.
3. A child is sleeping very restlessly because of a clogged nose.

Nose drops for very young infants should be mild; the doctor may prescribe Otrivin (xylometazoline hydrochloride) pediatric drops or Neo-synephrine (phenylephrine) ¼ percent—two drops in each nostril five minutes before a feeding. The nose drops given older children should be ephedrine or ephedrine-like preparations in water solution. Oily nose drops or mineral oil should *not* be used, for they may be inhaled and cause a dangerous and chronic condition of the lungs called lipoid pneumonia.

Antiseptic nose drops, formerly used frequently, are ineffective, for they cannot invade or affect the tissues that are infected beneath the mucous membrane.

Nose drops should not be used more often than every three or four hours. A good plan is to instill them in the nostrils five minutes before feedings and before bedtime.

Older children who object violently to nose drops may be given a nasal spray or, better still, one of the liquid or tablet decongestants by mouth.

One word of warning—nose drops used for one child should not be used for other children or even for the same child during subsequent infections if the dropper used for instilling the drops is placed back in the bottle. The solution may become contaminated by the bacteria from the child's nose. These bacteria live and multiply in the nose drops.

See also **Colds.**

Nose picking

Many young children pick their noses, probably for no other reason than that the nostrils are openings in which fingers may be inserted. Some may get a pleasurable sensation from it. Most children give up the habit after being reminded a few times by their parents that "it doesn't look nice."

Some children start picking their noses if they are irritated and even itchy because of colds or allergy. With proper medical treatment of the condition, the inflammation will subside and the nose picking cease.

There is no rationale at all to the old belief that nose picking is an indication that a child has worms.

Nosebleed

Nosebleeds in children are usually caused by a breaking of one or more of the small blood vessels in the mucous membrane of the septum, which divides the nose into its two sides. They may follow a blow on the nose, a cold or other infection which dilates the blood vessels, or may be caused by the child's picking the nose.

The quickest treatment of nosebleed that is successful in the vast majority of cases is to hold the nostrils together with the fingers for three to five minutes by the clock. The hold should not be released at any time during this period. Blood is usually completely clotted within three to five minutes. Pressure should be withdrawn slowly and the child instructed not to blow, rub, or pick his nose. A scab remains at the bleeding point and can easily be rubbed off, reestablishing the bleeding.

Other methods of stopping the bleeding are by applying an ice pack or cold compresses over the bridge of the nose. This causes a contraction of the bleeding blood vessels.

You can also insert a plug of cotton with Vaseline up the bleeding nostril, letting it remain there for four hours.

If the bleeding continues or if it recurs frequently, the doctor should be called so that he can locate the bleeding point. Cauterizing the bleeding point may be necessary, and the doctor may also want to make a blood study.

Nurse, infant's

An infant's nurse can be a help to a mother during the first few weeks after the baby is brought home. She can teach the inexperienced mother techniques and routines, and assure the mother of adequate rest while she is regaining her strength.

Occasionally a grandmother can help instead of a nurse, but this only succeeds fully if there is a warm relationship between the young parents and the grandparent. If difficulties arise or differences of opinion exist, a grandmother cannot be fired.

It is important that the nurse have a warm personality so that she will not upset the home. She should let the mother take care of the baby as much as possible. The mother should feed, clothe, clean, and bathe the baby as much as she is able to and as soon as she desires—and the nurse should encourage rather than discourage her in these efforts. Some practical nurses not only care for the baby, but also do light housework and simple cooking.

In selecting an infant's nurse, the parents should if possible telephone for her references rather than accept the written words. Far more information can be obtained from talking directly to a reference—often much that is not included in the letter.

The nurse should be hired far enough in advance to assure her presence once the baby arrives home.

If a mother cannot afford the services of an infant's nurse and cannot or prefers not to have the help of a grandmother, she can usually arrange to have a public health nurse visit her for the first few days after coming home. This nurse will usually bathe the baby, prepare the formulas, and aid in many other ways.

Nursery rhymes

All young children enjoy the rhythm, rhyme, and nonsense of nursery rhymes. They may not fully understand some of the nonsense but they enjoy it nevertheless. Some of the concepts of fantasy amuse them, as, for instance, a cat playing a fiddle as a cow jumps over the moon and a dog sits by laughing.

There are adults who have lost the ability to view and enjoy the world as children do. These are the people who call nursery rhymes silly, worthless, and even harmful. However, the fact remains that children love these rhymes with their amusing concepts and especially if accompanied by fanciful, child-oriented pictures.

All young children should have the opportunity to enjoy nursery rhymes, and all parents should have the joy of reading them to the children.

Nursery school

The role of the nursery school in stimulating the development of the child between age 3 and 5 is almost universally accepted today.

However, there are still many mothers who question the value of such preschool experience:

"Aren't most nursery schools no more than baby-sitting groups—just to give mothers a rest?"

"Isn't going out to the park every day and playing with other children just as beneficial?"

"I love taking care of my child—isn't that much better than the care of a teacher?"

In the first place, a nursery school does not and cannot take the place of a mother—but a good nursery school can offer a great deal to complement all that a mother can give. It is considered best for the child to spend only half a day at the nursery school, so that he has the values of mother care plus the additional benefits of the nursery school education.

What is a good nursery school and what are its special benefits?

A good nursery school is one that is well organized and well equipped, and has a well-trained, capable director and well-trained, mature teachers. There are, however, many successful cooperative nursery schools where mothers take turns helping the director. These mothers usually enjoy and learn through the experience. In some areas the nursery schools are sponsored by the state.

A good nursery school helps children to adjust to one another, to learn to respect each other's rights and feelings, and to take turns and share. It provides a great deal in the way of equipment and materials to help a child develop his creative abilities as well as aiding him physically, socially, and intellectually. The program may include rhythms, singing and playing various instruments, and story telling, painting, and small trips to the park or zoo.

A good nursery school is very much interested in the individual child and tries to help him with such problems as attention-seeking, shyness, and bossiness.

When children enter nursery school for the first time, many of them will cling to their mothers until they make an adjustment and are willing to accept the teacher as a mother substitute. Most good nursery schools realize this and permit mothers of new children to remain in the classroom the whole first week while the children are adjusting. After this time most youngsters have formed a relationship with other children in the class and with the teacher, and although they may cry when their

mothers leave, they will stop within a few minutes and join the class activities. If a parent feels that her child is unhappy and not adjusting to nursery school after at least three weeks, she should consult with the teacher before considering his withdrawal. The child may be too immature, or the mother herself may be making it difficult for him to adjust.

Today nursery schools can be found in most suburban and larger communities. There is a great deal to be gained from a child's attending one—but before he is enrolled the parent should investigate it and also go there as an observer.

Nursing   see **Breast feeding; Bottle feeding; Mothering; Nurse, infant's.**

Nutrition

The food we eat should provide a healthy balance of protein, carbohydrates, and fat and the essential vitamins and minerals. During the growing years of childhood and adolescence it is absolutely essential to maintain good nutrition. If not, permanent harm may be done to the normal development of muscles and bones, and growth may be retarded and never made up. The harmful results of poor nutrition are often not recognized until there is already damage such as a lack of normal growth, lack of stamina, poor bone formation, cavities in the teeth, susceptibility to infection, and constipation or diarrhea.

Protein   This is the most important nutrient in the food of the growing child and adolescent. Proteins, which are combinations of amino acids, are essential constituents of all living organisms. They are necessary to the growth and repair of the cells of the body, and a lack of protein will cause the death of body cells. Protein is also very important to the formation of hemoglobin, enzymes, hormones, and antibodies. To some degree, protein is also utilized as a source of energy for the body. Excess protein is converted by the body into fat and stored.

Milk, eggs, meat, fish, poultry, and cheese are the chief animal sources of protein. The best vegetable sources are soybeans and other dried beans and peas, cereals, nuts, and lentils.

Protein deficiency causes weakness and eventually may cause a debilitating condition called kwashiorkor. (See **Kwashiorkor.**)

Carbohydrates These chemical compounds, which compose the starchy foods and sugars, provide the body with energy and heat. If more carbohydrates are absorbed than are needed for immediate energy, the carbohydrates are converted into fat and stored under the skin. A child, who needs relatively more energy than an adult, can eat proportionately more carbohydrates without becoming fat. However, children should not be permitted to fall into the habit of dining exclusively on carbohydrates. This is not healthy, and may harm the teeth. (See **Candy and chewing gum.**)

Among the sources of carbohydrates are potatoes, rice, bread, noodles, cookies, cakes, most cereals, honey, and all types of sugar.

Fats Fat, whether consumed directly in the form of animal fats or vegetable oils or converted from other foods and stored in the body, is an excellent source of energy. A certain amount of fat is essential for normal functioning. It is nature's reserve of food for periods of illness or hunger. It provides a packing to hold the abdominal organs in place and to shield the blood vessels, nerves, muscles, and bones. It insulates against the cold.

About one-eighth of the body weight of infants is fat, and this is healthy and normal. However, the view that the fatter the baby, the healthier the baby is mistaken. Recent research indicates that children who are overfed and develop a relatively high percentage of fat cells in the body will retain these throughout their lives. In other words, the fat infant or young child is likely to have an obesity problem all his life.

An excess of fat, especially animal fat, is not healthy in anyone's diet. Large amounts of animal fat may be conducive to arteriosclerosis in adult life, and excessive fat slows down the activity of the stomach and intestines.

After 4 or 5 months of age infants do not need fat in their formulas, and skim milk can be used.

Minerals The most important minerals in a child's diet are iron, calcium, iodine, and phosphorus.

Although iron is found in only small amounts in the body, it is essential to health. It is important in the production of hemoglobin (the red coloring matter in the red blood cells). It is the hemoglobin in the blood that absorbs oxygen in the lungs and carries it to all parts of the body.

As neither breast milk nor cow's milk contains adequate iron, some supplement must be given after a baby has used up the supply absorbed from its mother during pregnancy. This supply is usually used up by the time a baby is 3 months old.

Meat, liver, eggs, green vegetables, and modern enriched cereals are excellent sources of iron. Nevertheless, many infants and toddlers are mildly anemic and should be given iron drops or tablets, or iron-fortified milk. (See **Anemia.**) An excess of iron is of no danger, although at times it may cause some diarrhea.

Calcium is required for the formation of bones and teeth. A lack of calcium causes weakness and decay of the teeth and rickets, a condition in which the bones are soft and grow slowly. (See **Rickets.**) Insufficient calcium may also lead to tetany, a condition of nerve irritability, and can interfere with normal blood coagulation.

Foods high in calcium are milk, cheese, green leafy vegetables, and salmon. For calcium to be adequately absorbed, the child must also receive a good supply of vitamin D.

Iodine is necessary for the functioning of the thyroid gland. It is usually obtained (in the minute amounts needed) in drinking water. In areas where the water does not supply adequate iodine, it must be added to the water supply or to the salt used (iodized salt). A lack of iodine leads to the development of goiters. (See **Goiter; Thyroid gland.**)

Phosphorus, too, is needed for the proper development of bones and teeth. It is also important in cell metabolism and the transmission of nerve impulses. It is obtained from milk and milk products, egg yolk, meat, beans, nuts, and whole grains.

Vitamins   Almost all parents give their children vitamin drops or tablets daily, but many of them wonder just how necessary vitamins are if their children are also receiving a well-balanced diet. Very few children, however, routinely receive such a complete diet. Vitamin drops or tablets, given daily, are health insurance—a guarantee that there is no lack of these essential needs.

Parents should not, however, dose children with vitamins on their own or increase the dosage if the child seems run down. This can be harmful. If you think your child should be getting more or fewer vitamins, discuss this and the child's nutrition in general with a doctor.

The usual vitamin drops or chewable vitamin tablets contain vitamins A, B_1, B_2, C, D, and niacin. All of these are important for good nutrition. Some vitamin preparations contain B_6 and B_{12} as well.

Vitamin A   This vitamin is found in milk and butter, egg yolk and the coloring substance of carrots (carotene), which is converted to vitamin A in the body. Vitamin A prevents night blindness, roughness of the skin, and certain infections of the skin. It possibly aids as well in protecting against colds and sinusitis.

Vitamin B   This is a complex vitamin composed of, among others, vitamin B_1, B_2, B_6, niacin, and B_{12}. These are found especially in yeast, whole-grain cereals, liver, pork, and peanuts.

Vitamin B_1 (thiamine) stimulates appetite and regulates the gastrointestinal tract. Severe deficiencies of vitamin B_1 may cause beriberi, a disease that is rare at the present time. The disease results in restlessness, loss of appetite, vomiting, and constipation. The child is pale, apathetic, and drowsy, and the liver is enlarged. Treatment with vitamin B_1 results in dramatic improvement.

Large amounts of *vitamin B_2 (riboflavin)* are found in liver, kidney, brewers' yeast, cow's milk, cream, ice cream, cheese, eggs, and leafy vegetables. Cow's milk contains about five times the amount of vitamin B_2 as breast milk. A lack of vitamin B_2 causes cracks at the outer angles of the mouth, dryness of the lips, and a slimy tongue. The child deficient in this vitamin also has general malaise and is weak.

Niacin is present in good amounts in meat, liver, whole-grain cereals, and peanuts.

A lack of this vitamin causes a debilitating disease named pellagra, which is still found occasionally in southern United States and wherever children are malnourished.

Pellagra is a severe deficiency disease that affects all parts of the body, especially the skin, gastrointestinal tract, and the nervous system. Although the signs and symptoms of pellagra are numerous, the primary signs are a marked redness of the hands and wrists, diarrhea and vomiting, and nervous conditions such as depression, insomnia, disorientation, and delirium.

Children with pellagra respond rapidly to treatment with niacin plus a well-balanced diet.

Vitamin B_{12} (a blood-stimulating vitamin) and *vitamin B_6* (a vitamin necessary for normal nerve function, but found generally in a child's diet) are not usually included in the routine daily vitamins unless the doctor feels there is some special need for them.

Vitamin C   This vitamin is found in citrus fruits and juices, in tomatoes, potatoes, and leafy vegetables.

An inadequate supply of vitamin C causes the disease scurvy, a very painful condition characterized by bleeding under the lining of the bones and into the joints. There may also be bleeding of the gums. (See **Scurvy.**) Some scientists feel that a lack of sufficient vitamin C produces a susceptibility to infections although to date there has been no proof of this.

Vitamin D   This essential vitamin, required for the normal development of bones and teeth, is usually not found in natural foods in the amounts needed by children. There is some vitamin D in eggs and fish and liver, but far too little to satisfy the needs of the body. Although the body forms its own vitamin D by exposure to sunlight, the sunshine most children receive during the few summer months available is not sufficient. Formerly children were given large daily doses of cod liver oil, which is high in vitamin D. Then halibut liver oil was also found to contain high levels of vitamin D. Today, however, children receive their vitamin D from milk, whole or evaporated, which is fortified to contain the required daily minimal amount (400 international units). Each quart of milk contains this amount. The usual multi-vitamin drops and tablets also contain 400 international units of vitamin D in the daily dosage.

A lack of adequate amounts of vitamin D causes the disease rickets, which is characterized by a softening of the bones and poor teeth. Children with rickets usually have bow legs, a very slow closure of the fontanelles, and late development of teeth, which have poor enamel and are prone to cavities.

Parents should be warned that giving vitamin D in excessive doses makes a child lose his appetite.

Vitamin E   As far as is known, this vitamin is not required for children. It may have some beneficial effect on fertility in women, but this has not been proven scientifically. It is found in wheat germ and in unsaturated fats, such as the corn, soy, and safflower oils.

Vitamin K This is an antihemorrhage vitamin. It is found in ample quantities in the child's natural diet. Green leafy vegetables, egg yolk, and liver contain large amounts.

In the rare instances when a newborn has "hemorrhagic disease of the newborn," the condition is quickly cleared by injections of vitamin K.

Dosage The usual vitamin drops or tablets given to children contain the following, with variations in different products:

Vitamin A—3000 to 5000 units
Vitamin C—50 to 75 mg.
Vitamin D—400 units
Vitamin B_1—1 to 2 mg.
Vitamin B_2—1.2 to 2.5 mg.
Niacin—8 to 20 mg.

Some doctors prescribe drops or tablets containing only vitamins A, C, and D, depending on other foods in the child's diet as sources of vitamin B. In areas where the water lacks adequate fluoride, fluorides are added to the vitamin drops or tablets.

Home and Garden Bulletin No. 72, prepared by the U.S. Department of Agriculture, lists many common foods and gives, in addition to calorie content, their protein, fat, and carbohydrate content and vitamin values. The pamphlet can be obtained for 30 cents from the Superintendent of Documents, U.S. Government Printing Office, Washington, D.C. 20402.

See also **Cereals; Meat; Orange juice.** For information on a balanced daily diet see also **Foods, basic.**

O

Obedience

This is a quality necessary to some degree throughout life, but parents should attempt to develop in their children intelligent and understanding obedience rather than blind obedience.

Of course, when a child is very young we must insist on certain habits, and the child, who does not as yet understand reasons, must simply obey. He must not run into the streets, touch the hot radiator, play with fire, climb on windowsills, or the like.

As the child grows older, a certain amount of obedience will be necessary not only for his health and safety, but also for his own welfare and social adjustment. But the parents' authority cannot be arbitrary, and the child must be given the reasons (without overly involved explanations) as soon as he is at all capable of understanding. As he grows older, he will be able to understand more and more why he can't bite, push, or kick other children, why he can't watch television as much as he desires, why he must get to bed at a certain hour, why he must wear rubbers on rainy days and wear a warm coat when it is cold.

Children should always be given the opportunity to express their opinions and discuss them freely with their parents. Obedience should be based on trust of, and respect for, the parents' authority and not on fear. This respect for authority will be carried over in relation to schools and the laws of the community.

As children grow into their teen years, the need for parental authority diminishes, and those who have had a background of understanding obedience based on respect rather than fear will usually obey most of the rules and laws of their schools, colleges, and communities without difficulty. But they should have the knowledge that they can assert themselves and discuss the issues openly if they feel that changes should be made. Many young people will rightly question regulations they feel are unfair or inappropriate.

See also **Discipline**.

Obesity

Obesity is a serious problem among Americans: Twenty to thirty percent of them are overweight when entering adolescence. Eighty percent of obese children develop into obese adults.

There have been numerous theories about the cause of obesity. Why is it that some children are overweight and become overweight adolescents and adults, while others remain thin or of normal build?

Some writers and researchers have blamed obesity on heredity, some on family background. Others have said it results from lack of activity. Psychiatrists have claimed that obesity is often caused by a person's attempt to gain satisfaction from food when he is unhappy in life. Obesity has been blamed on imperfect body metabolism and on glandular disturbances.

But with all these theories, two facts stand out: First, most overweight people eat too much food, and the foods they eat are the high-calorie ones. Second, overweight people are generally much less active than those who are thin or of normal weight. It has been found that overweight children spend 80 percent of their time sitting or lying down.

Recent studies have indicated that much of the obesity in older children and adults may be the result of over-feeding in infancy and early childhood. These studies show that all children are born with approximately the same per-centage of fat cells, and that extra fat cells are built up by overfeeding during the rapid-growth period of infancy and early childhood. The researchers con-clude that once a person's body has these extra fat cells they remain there for the rest of his life, and he may have an obesity problem all his life unless he continues to diet.

Obesity itself is not inherited, al-though the tendency to become obese may be familial. Often parents set a pat-tern of overeating by providing meals of high-calorie foods that they themselves enjoy and relish.

Many parents think first of glandular trouble as a cause of their children's obesity. This is rarely the case. A study of obese children a few years ago dem-onstrated that in only 2 out of 100 such children was there any evidence of a glandular cause. A doctor can deter-mine very easily if obesity is caused by poor functioning of the thyroid gland or by pituitary-gland activity.

Much of the obesity which develops in children over 3 years old is the result of unhappiness or anxiety. A child who is unhappy will often try to gain com-pensatory pleasure and satisfaction from eating. Often such a child feels unloved, rejected, or unwanted. Or the child may be living in a home where there are family conflicts or other difficulties. Compulsive overeating at any age, with the possible exception of the normally voracious appetites of rapidly growing adolescents, may usually be considered a sign of emotional trouble.

In the treatment of obesity in chil-dren, there are three avenues of ap-proach:

1. Regulating diet so as to satisfy hunger but reduce calories at the same time.
2. Increasing the child's physical activ-ity. Vigorous activity such as swimming, tennis, running, bicycle riding, and dancing can use up considerable num-bers of calories. Unfortunately, inactiv-ity is very often tied up with the child's emotional problems. He may feel un-popular, and so doesn't join in games; the fatter he becomes, the less capable he feels of performing in such games, and the more isolated he becomes from other children. The child should be en-couraged to join in family activities, such as bicycle riding, and may be given exercises and exercise equipment to work with on his own. He should be complimented on any improvement in his appearance or physical strength. In severe cases, parents may want to talk over with the child the possibility of attending a camp for obese children where everyone follows the same diet and exercises together.
3. Seeking to uncover possible emo-tional causes for overeating, and reliev-ing or eliminating such causes. Parents may need expert psychological guid-

ance; psychotherapy may be indicated for the child.

Regulation of diet Obesity in almost every instance is caused by the eating of foods containing an excess of calories for the specific needs of a particular child. It is obvious, then, that if parents are to succeed in limiting the calories and reducing their child's weight, they must know the approximate caloric value of foods. With this knowledge they can prepare lower-calorie foods to substitute for those that contain more calories and still satisfy the child's appetite. (See **Appendix B: Calorie Chart.**)

Since the bodies of almost all children except the very young require more than 2,000 calories daily (see **Calorie**), a diet limited to 1,200 calories daily will in almost every case produce a loss in weight. The meals should be well balanced and nutritious. Fad diets, popularly advised for adults, should be avoided. The child should be encouraged not to omit breakfast or any other regular meal. The foods prepared and offered do not have to be dull or uninteresting or tasteless. There are numerous low-calorie cookbooks and numerous low-calorie foods on "diet shelves" in groceries and supermarkets. And low-calorie snacks can be used in place of those fattening snacks so often taken.

Diet pills should be avoided unless advised by and used under the supervision of a doctor. At times they may be helpful, if used for a short period only, to aid boys and girls who find adjustment to the new diet difficult. However, it should be remembered that diet pills are almost always stimulants—amphetamines—and can become habit-forming. They are the same pills that are commonly called "speed" or "pep pills" and are responsible for much drug addiction.

The overweight child should have the full cooperation of the parents in his efforts to reduce. There should be no nagging or obvious restriction, and, if possible, low-calorie but satisfying meals should be prepared which all members of the family can eat.

Eating is a pleasure that satisfies a physical and often a psychological need. However, the social, psychological, and physical consequences of obesity are such that every effort should be made to aid the overweight child by satisfying his appetite while reducing calories, encouraging increased activities, and doing everything possible to assure that he is generally happy.

See also **Dieting; Nutrition.**

Obscene words see **Swear words.**

Obsessions see **Compulsions.**

Obstetrician

The obstetrician is responsible for the care of the mother and fetus through pregnancy; he delivers the child, and he is usually involved in early follow-up care, including difficulties the mother may have in breast feeding. An expectant mother should take care in selecting her obstetrician and be completely satisfied that he is concerned, careful, willing to take time, and sympathetic. She should then be scrupulous in following his advice. In selecting an obstetrician, a mother may ask for the recommendation of her regular doctor and also ask other mothers in the community. The obstetrician should be affiliated with a good hospital.

A good obstetrician has a warm understanding of the emotions involved in parenthood; has a rule of using drugs as little as possible during pregnancy; has an agreeable attitude toward natural childbirth, including permitting the husband to be present during the birth of the baby; has a flexible approach to breast feeding—encouraging all mothers who so desire to nurse their babies.

See also **Prenatal care.**

Obstinacy see **Negativism.**

Obstruction, intestinal see **Intestinal obstruction.**

Oculist see **Ophthalmologist.**

Oedipus complex
Often children between the approximate ages of 3 and 6 tend to have an especially close and loving relationship with the parent of the opposite sex.

Freud called this the Oedipus complex, after the Greek myth in which the infant Oedipus, son of the king of Thebes, was left to die by his father because of a prophecy that the child would grow up to kill him. Oedipus, however, was saved, and he met his father (without knowing who he was) and killed him in a quarrel. Thereafter he married his widowed mother, unware that she was his mother.

Referring to girls, the term Electra complex is sometimes used. Electra was the daughter of King Agamemnon. She helped her brother, Orestes, kill their mother, Clytemnestra, after Clytemnestra and her lover had killed Agamemnon.

In Freudian theory the Oedipus complex is held to be responsible for the appearance of neurotic symptoms if not satisfactorily resolved through the development of healthy and mature relationships within and outside the home.

Freudian theory has been modified in many ways, but it is widely recognized that Freud was right in observing that this is a critical stage in development. It is not uncommon to hear a boy of between 3 and 5 years say to his mother, "Mommy, when I grow up I'm going to marry you." And little girls often speak to their fathers in the same manner. The little boy may want his mother to himself, may want to be her favorite, and may resent the attention the father gives the mother, while the little girl, in the same way, wants her father, desires to be his favorite, and resents the attention the mother gives the father.

This attitude must be understood by the parents and handled carefully, for if these strong emotional ties continue, children may grow up with no desire to leave the home and often with no desire to be married. They may fear that they can find no one who measures up to the adored parent. Or they may be able to relate only to older, parent figures. Or they may feel guilty in normal sexual relations, identifying all lovemaking with incestuous feelings. This is felt to be one cause of homosexuality. Unfortunately, some parents enjoy this deep devotion of their children and help foster an overly close relationship rather than temper it.

In the normal home the parents continue to be affectionate and close to one another throughout the stages of their children's development. They support one another in matters of discipline and do not let the children come between them—even though they still are deeply devoted to their children. The child is reassured that he has the love of both parents, and that when he grows up he will find someone to love and marry. Feelings of resentment against a parent of the same sex should be accepted as normal, and the parent should respond as an understanding adult, not with anger and threats. It should be remembered that the child does not feel only hostility toward the parent of the same sex; this parent is also the object of love and admiration. As the child accepts this parent as a model, hostility subsides.

Gradually, as children enter the school years, the vast majority give up excessively strong emotional ties to the parent of the opposite sex. The boy realizes he cannot supplant his father in his mother's eyes, and the girl realizes she cannot supplant her mother. The secure child begins to look confidently beyond the home for a life of his or her own.

Oil, baby   see **Baby oil.**

Oldest child

Today the oldest child in the family enjoys little or none of the deference shown the first child several generations ago. He has special advantages when he is the only child, but as soon as the second child arrives this changes abruptly. In many cases the older child is overwhelmed by jealousy of the new baby. It is more important that parents do everything possible to minimize this upset. (See **Sibling rivalry and jealousy.**)

As the firstborn child becomes older, he is faced with what he considers inconsistent discipline. He finds himself being scolded for the same misdeed accepted of his younger brother or sister. It is difficult for him to realize that with age comes more responsibility and that therefore more is expected of him.

It is important for the older child that he be given some special privileges, such

as staying up a little later—even if it is convenient for parents to put all the children to bed at the same time. And besides special privileges, he should always have a slightly larger allowance than the younger children.

The oldest child should not be made responsible for the care of his younger brothers and sisters. It not only puts an undue strain on him, but usually interferes with his relationship with the younger children. Many older children, constantly left as baby-sitters, have lost a great deal of the freedom and enjoyment of playtime.

The oldest child should always receive praise, approval, and support from his parents whenever the chance arises. This will help overcome some of the problems inherent in being the firstborn.

See also **Middle child; Youngest child.**

Only child

As a rule, the only child has a certain advantage in having the undivided attention and love of his parents. But his situation also presents problems for the child as well as the parents during the course of the years. Too often the parents are overindulgent, overpermissive, and overprotective. The child often grows up in an adult's world, and, of course, is the center of attention.

This may cause difficulties in learning to share, to socialize, and to become one of a group when the child enters nursery school or kindergarten. In some areas he may be accustomed to privileges that other children don't have. On the other hand, he may be more restricted.

What can parents do to avoid these problems as much as possible? First, they must make every effort not to be too indulgent and too protective. But their main object should be to make up for the lack of brothers and sisters. It is important that the parents invite other children over frequently and arrange for their child to make visits as well. Cousins and friends of the child's approximate age should be invited to stay overnight, and the child should have the opportunity to play with these children, share toys with them, and in some sense share the parents as well. When the only child becomes about 3 years old, attendance at a good nursery school is much more important than it is for children with brothers or sisters. When the child is older, parents should consider sending him to a good camp in the summer. In adolescence only children often benefit from boarding school.

With intelligent handling, an only child doesn't have to be spoiled and have problems. The situation does, however, require extra care and good management by the parents. This does not mean that parents should torment themselves with worries over whether they have struck exactly the right balance. It is reassuring to note that although the difficulties involving only children are widely recognized and talked about, a number of surveys have shown that these youngsters do as well as or better than average in adult life.

Open-space school see **Education, experimental approaches in.**

Operations see **Hospitalization.**

Ophthalmia neonatorum see **Blindness.**

Ophthalmologist
Also called oculist. A doctor of medicine skilled in and specializing in the examination of eyes, the detection of vision defects, and the treatment and correction of abnormalities or diseases of the eyes.

An ophthalmologist is different from an optician or optometrist, who is not a medical doctor but makes glasses for remedying vision defects, usually in accordance with the prescription of the ophthalmologist.

Although many optometrists examine vision and prescribe glasses, it is always important that a child with possible sight difficulty or any eye defect should be examined by an ophthalmologist. For poor vision can be caused by numerous conditions, many of which can only be detected through the careful examination of a well-trained ophthalmologist. (See **Eye defects.**)

Opiate poisoning see **Poisons: first-aid treatment.**

Opium derivatives see **Drug abuse.**

Optician
A person who makes and sells glasses (not a doctor). (See also **Ophthalmologist.**)

Optometrist
A nonmedical person trained to examine and treat certain optical defects by correctional lenses and other methods.

Orange juice
This is generally added to an infant's diet at any time between ages 2 and 5 months. It is an excellent source of vitamin C.

Because about one third of young infants are sensitive to orange juice, many pediatricians hold off until a baby is 5 months old before adding it to his diet. By that time the sensitivity has, as a rule, subsided. If a child remains sensitive or allergic to orange juice, tomato juice or pineapple juice may be substituted, although these are not as high in vitamin C content.

However, the usual daily dosage of multivitamins given to a child contains an adequate amount of vitamin C for his general body needs and for the prevention of scurvy.

Orderliness

Orderliness as demanded or expected of a child is usually a reflection of parental attitudes. As such it varies greatly from family to family, some parents placing more emphasis on it than others.

The young child is usually not upset by a room in disorder. He may prefer it that way. Neatness and orderliness are learned slowly through example and experience.

Most parents today realize that a child at play should be allowed to make a mess. Many modern schools recognize this as well. But a child can learn that at certain times his belongings must be put into order. If a child is at play, disorder should be overlooked, but when the time comes to discontinue this activity, the toys should be put back in their proper place. The parent should usually help in the cleanup with children under the approximate age of 7. There should be adequate storage space for toys, books, and clothing.

As the child grows, he will usually learn orderly habits, and parents can help by observing the following principles:

Their own example will have the greatest influence on the child.

Children should not be nagged. Most often they should be reminded, encouraged, and helped to keep their things in order. At times it may be necessary to be firm—for example, to say that a child cannot go out to play until he has picked up his room. However, if the job is really too much for the child, the parent should give him a hand with it.

Parents should not impose arbitrary standards of orderliness on a child, but should consult with him regarding his ideas on how best to keep order. If the plan for orderliness meets the child's own needs, there is a better chance that it will be adhered to.

Parents should remember that orderliness is not one of the prime virtues in life. An active, happy child is more to be valued than a neat room.

In adolescence many previously neat children become disorderly and sloppy. This is also the age of spontaneous massive cleanups. At this time it is especially important not to nag, unless the disorderliness is interfering with the activities of others in the family. The messiness is usually a passing stage.

Organic brain syndrome   see Brain dysfunction, mild.

Orthodontist

A dentist who specializes in treating problems involving the shape of the jaws and palate and the proper alignment and proper meeting of teeth of the upper and lower jaws.

An orthodontist may be recommended for numerous conditions including:

1. Tooth decay with premature loss of baby teeth. When baby teeth decay so badly that they either disintegrate or must be removed, an empty space remains. In such a case, and especially in the case of the larger teeth, the molars, the teeth on either side of the space move together and either partially or completely close the space. When the permanent tooth is ready to erupt, it is

forced out of position by lack of space. To prevent this deformity, a dentist will usually insert a small bridge called a spacer to hold the teeth on either side of the space in position and prevent them from moving together.

2. Thumb-sucking that continues after the child is 5. This may cause a pushing forward of the upper teeth while forcing in the lower teeth. To prevent this, many dentists and orthodontists fasten a metal attachment behind the upper middle teeth. This gets in the way of the finger and prevents satisfaction from thumb-sucking. Restrictive measures to keep a child from putting the finger in his mouth should be avoided. (See **Sucking, thumb and finger.**)

3. Finger-sucking, tongue-sucking, and lip-sucking. These can also cause protrusion of the upper teeth. The only method of overcoming these habits is by frequently reminding the child—without constant nagging or scolding—and by explaining in simple language to the child that this habit may spoil his good looks.

4. Wide spacing between teeth. This should be corrected not only for cosmetic reasons, but also because it may interfere with normal closure of the jaws.

5. Certain habits, such as always sleeping with the face against an arm, open hand, or fist. This may push the side teeth in and even cause an asymmetry of the face.

6. An orthodontist may also be consulted in connection with: cleft palate (see **Cleft palate**); harelip (see **Harelip**); irregular jaw development, such as a receding or protruding upper or lower jaw, or jaws that are too narrow; and problems that may arise when the child has fewer or more than the normal number of teeth.

The age at which orthodontic treatment should be started depends entirely upon the condition being treated. For instance, spacers which hold teeth apart when a tooth between them is missing may be inserted as early as age 4 or 5. The appliance to discourage thumb-sucking is usually attached at age 5. Braces to bring teeth into alignment and to correct an improper meeting of the upper and lower teeth may be applied as soon as the permanent molars are in position, usually by age 7—depending on the decision of the child's dentist.

If possible, braces should be applied early enough so that they can be removed by the time a child enters adolescence—a period when every child desires to be as attractive as possible and often feels disfigured when wearing braces.

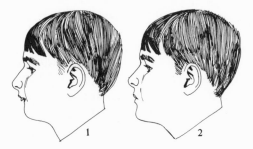

Timely treatment by an orthodontist can bring about a dramatic change in a youngster's appearance. For example, a severe malocclusion (1) can be corrected by braces, as shown in (2).

Orthopedist

A doctor who specializes in the medical and surgical treatment of ailments involving the bones, joints, and muscles.

There are many conditions in infancy and childhood for which a pediatrician would advise the expert care of an orthopedist. Among those found at birth are congenital dislocation of the hip, clubfoot, incurving of the feet, fracture of the collarbone, and torn or stretched nerves of the arms.

In infancy, childhood, and adolescence the injuries most frequently treated by the orthopedist are fractures, sprains, strains, and walking difficulties such as toeing in, toeing out, and flat feet.

Otologist

A doctor who specializes in the diagnosis and treatment of ailments of the ears. These include deafness and other hearing defects, as well as earaches, discharging ears, and infections of the mastoid.

See also **Deafness; Earaches**.

Out-of-wedlock birth see Illegitimate child.

Ovaries

Two small, oval-shaped glands, situated one on each side of the lower abdomen in females. The ovaries have two functions: to provide egg cells and to secrete the female sex hormones, estrogen and progesterone.

The ovaries are essentially inactive until a girl reaches puberty, at about 11 to 13 years of age. Then they start functioning by secreting their hormones and forming egg cells, usually one a month.

The hormones are responsible for the growth and development of secondary female sex characteristics: for the maturation of the breasts and the filling out of other parts of the female body to form the adult figure, and the growth of pubic and axillary hair. The hormones also control the process of menstruation and the maturing of the sex organs.

They also stimulate the development of sex interests and desires.

The ovaries continue to produce egg cells from puberty (early adolescence) until a woman is approximately 45 to 50 years old, the period of menopause. At this time there is also a decline in the production of the ovarian hormones.

Overactivity   see **Hyperactivity**.

Overanxiety   see **Anxiety**.

Overeating   see **Obesity**.

Overindulgent parent

An overindulgent parent is one who gives in to almost every wish and whim of a child. This attitude on the part of parents is just as detrimental to the child as overprotection or overrestriction.

The overindulgence can be the result of overaffection on the part of the parent—the so-called "smother love"—or, at times, a consequence of the parent's guilt feelings. Overaffection is easily understood, for many parents love their children so much that they cannot stand to see them cry or in any way be unhappy. The guilty parents who overindulge are those who feel that they are not good parents, either because they resent the child or because they are deeply involved in work or other outside interests. They compensate by giving their children everything they wish. An example is certain working mothers who give their children innumerable treats and special privileges when they are spending time with them.

Eventually overindulgence by the parents brings problems to the children as well as to the parents. The overindulged child later expects to get everything he desires. He insists on a quick response and is angry and frustrated if his desires are not met immediately. As a rule he has difficulties with his friends and other children, who do not always accede to his wishes. He is also likely to lack incentive to work for what he desires or hopes to attain.

It is important that parents who feel deeply for their children and are looking ahead to their happiness refuse to give in to unreasonable demands. The children should work to gain some of their desires—for example, save some of their allowance to pay partially for things they want—in order to develop self-dependence and self-confidence.

See also **Discipline; Spoiling the child.**

Overpermissive parent

An overpermissive parent is one who hesitates to say "no" to a child and hesitates to discipline him. The child has almost complete leeway to do what he wants. The motives may be an excess of affection or feelings of guilt, as discussed previously. (See **Overindulgent parent.**) But they may also involve a lack of interest in, or concern for, the child—it is simply easier to let him do what he wants, even if this isn't in the child's best interests. Sometimes overpermissive parents are following some theory of child care—or, most often, their own misinterpretation of that theory.

It is true that in certain respects and for certain specific age levels modern methods of child care are more permissive than in prior generations. We are today more relaxed in the feeding schedule of infants, in their weaning, and in their toilet training, and this has proven to be beneficial.

But many parents, believing that restrictions might thwart the full emotional development of their children, have given them almost complete freedom. They give them anything they want and let them do what they wish—such as letting them crayon the walls and floors, tear pages out of books, or watch television until midnight.

This almost complete lack of direction and restriction becomes a greater and greater problem for both parent and child as the youngster grows older. For all children in the course of normal development, need the authority and guidance of their parents. When children are not at home, when they are in nursery school, and throughout the school years, they need limits and restrictions. They need these if they are to get along well with other children and meet the normal challenges of life successfully. The child of overpermissive parents finds it extremely difficult to face these demands and usually becomes either a disciplinary problem or reacts by giving up if things don't go his way.

Thus parents should realize that although saying "no" may bring temporary conflict, it is very much worthwhile in the long run. Restrictions are necessary in the lives of all human beings, young and old, and the intelligent parent must find the balance between permissiveness and overrestriction.

See also **Discipline.**

Overprotective parent

Protection of children is a normal part of parenthood, but the appropriate degree of protection varies with the age of a child and the environment in which he lives.

Complete protection of a young child is most important. He has no experience, no judgment, and very few fears.

Obviously he must not cross streets by himself, he must not play with knives, he must not lean out of windows, he must not play with electric wires or electric outlets.

But as children grow older they must gain self-confidence, self-dependence, and self-reliance. The overprotective parent, usually an insecure and anxious person himself, never lets a child gain an adequate degree of self-confidence and self-reliance. The child may become fearful and anxious, afraid to attempt many things. Such parents are frequently observed in playgrounds:

"Don't climb on the jungle gym. You might fall down and get hurt."

"Stay away from the sandbox. It's full of germs."

"Don't go near the dog. He may bite you."

"I don't want you to ride a two-wheel bicycle; it's too dangerous."

The overprotective parent of a city child will often continue to take him to and from school as late as 12 years of age.

The overprotective parent also may try to protect a child from a knowledge of anything sorrowful or unhappy such as death, calamity, and war. This does not help the child, who must grow up with some understanding of the world in which he lives. If he is later to be a responsible and involved citizen, he must understand events and be able to form opinions. He must know the tragedy of war, the harm of drug addiction, and the suffering of the poor and underprivileged. Only in this way can he as an adult work confidently to overcome these devastating problems.

Overweight see **Obesity.**

P

Pacifier

A rubber nipple for an infant to suck on. Pacifiers are made without holes so that the baby does not suck in air and with rubber or plastic guards to prevent them from being swallowed.

Within the last twenty years pacifiers have come back into popular use since it has been shown that infants relax greatly when sucking pacifiers or fingers. Apparently infants have a need for sucking that must be satisfied. (See **Sucking need**.)

Infants generally discover their thumbs and fingers at about 6 to 8 weeks, and those who have a sucking need, if not given the pacifier first, will suck their fingers. Once they begin this, they will reject the pacifier. Pacifiers are usually given up by children spontaneously at 15 months to 2 years—when the need for sucking has subsided. If not, the pacifier can be taken away at 2 years and the child will not resort to finger sucking. The child who has become a thumb or finger sucker, however, may continue sucking his finger past the age of 5, when the permanent teeth appear, posing the possibility of malformation of the teeth.

All in all, much can be gained by giving the child a pacifier if he seems to need it. The baby, and probably also the parents, will be more content. And there is nothing to be gained by letting an infant become tense for lack of sucking

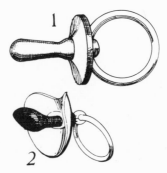

1. Standard pacifier with nipple, mouth guard, and ring for grasping. 2. Nuk Sauger pacifier, sometimes recommended by orthodontists. Shape is designed to insure that sucking does not affect correct development of the teeth.

or letting him develop a finger-sucking habit. In selecting a pacifier, consult with your doctor. Some types have a small part inside the nipple that could be swallowed if the pacifier comes apart; others are filled with edible plastic and are not recommended. Also, some doctors feel that a non-standard-shaped nipple, such as the Nuk Sauger, is preferable in order to avoid any possibility of pushing the teeth out of line and raising the palate.

See also **Sucking, thumb and finger.**

Pain in joints see **Growing pains; Rheumatic fever; Rheumatoid arthritis.**

Pallor

The child who appears too pale may simply be so because the blood vessels lie deep under the skin, which is a hereditary trait, or he may be pale because he is anemic. It is very simple for a doctor to determine if a child is anemic or not. If so, he can direct the treatment.

See also **Anemia.**

Palsy, cerebral   see **Cerebral palsy.**

Pancreas

A soft, elongated gland lying below and slightly behind the stomach. It has a duct (the pancreatic duct) that leads into the first (upper) part of the small intestine.

The pancreas has two functions. It produces and secretes the most powerful of the digestive juices (pancreatic juice) directly into the intestines through the pancreatic duct. One part of the pancreas, the islands of Langerhans, also produces insulin, which is secreted directly into the bloodstream. A lack of adequate insulin causes diabetes. (See **Insulin.**)

Panic, adolescent   see **Adolescent panic.**

Pants, waterproof

Waterproof pants, made of nylon, plastic, or rubber, are used by parents to cover diapers. Such pants are handy when visiting or traveling or on other occasions when it is important to keep the baby's and the adult's clothing from getting wet. But waterproof pants should not be used too frequently or too constantly. By holding in the moisture they tend to cause diaper rash.

Waterproof pants should not be worn at night when wet diapers are so rarely changed.

Even if a child does wear waterproof pants when visiting or on a trip, the diapers still should be changed from time to time to prevent irritation of the baby's skin.

Paper diapers   see **Diapers.**

Parasites   see **Head lice; Scabies; Worms.**

Parathyroid glands

Four small glands, each pair of which is located at the outer margins of either lobe of the thyroid gland.

The parathyroid glands secrete a hormone called parathormone, which regulates the use and balance of calcium and phosphorus in the body. As the producers of this hormone, these glands are controlling factors in the strength and structure of bones, in coagulation of blood, in nerve-muscle activity, and in the regulation of the heartbeat.

Undersecretion by the parathyroid causes twitching and even convulsive seizures in newborn infants. In older children, undersecretion is rare. It may cause symptoms such as headache, vomiting, and muscular pains and cramps that progress to numbness, stiffness, and a tingling of the hands and feet. Convulsive seizures may occur that at times are difficult to distinguish from epilepsy.

Emergency treatment of undersecretion which is causing convulsions requires intravenous injections of a solution of calcium gluconate followed by a large, daily, oral dosage of vitamin D. Less severe cases can usually be successfully treated solely by oral vitamin D.

Oversecretion of the parathyroid glands is very rare in children and is usually caused by a benign tumor of the gland or to an overgrowth of glandular tissue. Children with an oversecretion of parathormone may be prone to fractures of the bones, kidney stones, blood in the urine, and eventually loss of kidney function.

Treatment is by the surgical removal of any tumor of the parathyroids or removal of some of the tissue if there is an overgrowth.

Paregoric

A tincture of opium, paregoric is often used in pediatrics in the treatment of diarrhea or for numbing the gums during the teething of infants. (It acts in diarrhea by slowing down the rapid action of the intestines.)

It should only be used under the direction of a doctor. It is less used today than in previous years but still has its place.

Parent, death of see **Death, dealing with a.**

Parent, foster see **Foster care.**

Parent, step see **Remarriage.**

Parent-teacher relationship see **Teacher-parent relationship.**

Parents, expectant

The knowledge that a wife is pregnant usually ushers in the beginning of a wonderful and exciting experience for the future father and mother. This is especially true for new parents who have never before gone through the numerous discussions, arrangements, and adjustments that normally arise during the nine months of waiting.

The primary concern is that the baby be born healthy and have a good start in life. For this reason it is important to see an obstetrician early and follow his directions carefully, especially in regard to the taking of drugs and the treatment of infections. If natural childbirth is desired, this should also be discussed. (See **Natural childbirth; Obstetrician.**)

Now is the time also to start learning about babies and their care. Many good books that advise on the various items that will be needed in the infant's room and necessities for the care of the baby are available.

Within recent years classes for expectant parents have been established in many of the hospitals throughout the country. Such classes are also sponsored by the American Red Cross, the Maternity Center Association, and by most large medical centers. Both prospective fathers as well as mothers attend these classes, where there are discussions with pediatricians and nurses. They learn of the development of the fetus, the procedures at birth, and many details on the emotional as well as the physical care of the baby. They usually practice child-care techniques with life-size dolls, although there may also be infants for them to hold, bathe, diaper, and occasionally even feed.

It is advisable for expectant parents to spend time in the selection of their future pediatrician. They may interview a number of pediatricians to determine what their attitudes on child care are, to see if they can relate well to the pediatrician, and to ascertain that he will have time to talk with them when they feel the need.

See also **Pediatrician; Prenatal care.**

Paroxysmal tachycardia see **Tachycardia, paroxysmal.**

Parties

Almost all children love parties. In addition to birthday parties, it is often fun to have parties on other special occasions or holidays, which lend a theme to the party itself.

The type of party, number of children invited, amount of adult supervision needed, and specific activities differ at different age levels.

For younger children it is important not to make a party too long or over-stimulating. At this age only a child's closest friends should be invited. More than six to eight preschool children can become extremely difficult to manage. It might be helpful if one or two mothers are invited to stay and assist. The games and activities planned should be simple and not too competitive. For example, a peanut or marble hunt in which children are given bags in which to collect the pre-hidden items; games such as But-ton-button, Who's Got the Button?, Go-ing to Jerusalem, or Pin the Tail on the Donkey are also appropriate.

The food for a preschool-age party should depend largely upon the time at which the party is given. If a party be-gins in the early afternoon, then three o'clock ice cream and cake is usually adequate. However, if the party begins midmorning or midafternoon, it is prob-ably wisest to plan a simple meal such as hamburgers or hot dogs and a vegeta-ble, followed by ice cream and cake.

As children get older, the activities and types of parties can become propor-tionally more complex. The child is now old enough to help in the planning and preparation. Trips to the zoo, theater, beach; picnics, skating, bowling, and so on, are all appropriate and popular ac-tivities for the school-age child. Once again it is important that enough adults be present to aid in supervision.

During the teen-age years boys and girl can assume almost total responsibil-ity for the planning and preparation of the party. Many teen-agers prefer or demand to run their own parties without direct parental supervision. However, it is usually important in the case of young teen-agers that a parent be somewhere on the premises and available should any need arise.

There may, of course, be protestations such as, "It's not fair; all the other par-ents go out." But this does not mean that a parent should be swayed by this argument. The other parents have prob-ably heard the same words and given in. It is a parent's privilege to follow what he himself feels is the proper course of action.

Passivity

The passive child is one who simply goes along with whatever is asked of him. He never gets really excited about anything. He never gets really angry over anything or at anybody. He is quite unemotional. He has learned that he may be hurt if he lets others see the emotions he feels and so keeps these within himself. The emotions may be so deeply repressed that the child himself is not in touch with his own feelings.

Some children are by nature more passive than others, but extreme passiv-ity is usually created by harmful envi-ronmental situations and is not a healthy condition.

If a child at approximately one year of age acts very passively and rarely expresses emotions, it is important to have the doctor check him thoroughly for possible mental as well as physical problems, such as poor vision or poor hearing, which might be limiting the child's emotional development.

Children who have been reared in an institution, or foster children who have passed from one home to another, often become quite passive, for they have been exposed to many unsettling and frightening situations. Children who have been exposed to a traumatic experience within the family, such as a difficult divorce, may also become passive. They have learned that it is safer not to let oneself respond too strongly—that love may be withdrawn. The feelings are there but adults cannot see them; they may in turn interpret the child's passivity as a rejection of themselves and react by rejecting the child. Passivity can in this way become a vicious circle. The passive child needs more warmth and care than most other children and needs to have his emotions lured to the surface. It is important for the parent to discover what things have real meaning for such a child, to stimulate his interests, to express excitement and appreciation for things the child does or achieves.

Patch test see **Skin tests for allergies.**

Pediatrician

A medical doctor specially trained in the care of children from infancy through adolescence. It is advisable for parents to interview a doctor before selecting him to care for their children. A great deal can be learned from this interview. Can the parents relate well to the doctor? Has he a warm attitude toward children? Is he interested in the child emotionally as well as physically? Will he have adequate time to talk to the parent? Will he make house calls if the child is really ill, or send another doctor—or at least will he be willing to direct the parent fully over the telephone? Also, is he connected with a good hospital? A well-trained pediatri-

cian is usually accredited by the American Board of Pediatrics. He may also be a Fellow of the American Academy of Pediatrics.

As time goes on many children become fearful of visits to the doctor. This fear, of course, is generated by their associations with the doctor, which are not always happy ones: the child remembers injections, which no one enjoys, and he remembers seeing the doctor when he was sick—and possibly having received an injection at that time as well.

But there are a number of steps parents can take to aid in the development of a warmer relationship between a youngster and his doctor:

Never threaten a child that if he doesn't do so and so you'll call the doctor. Doctors should be presented as helpers to keep a child well or make him well.

If your child is fighting and yelling at the doctor's office, don't scold and berate him. Try to reassure and calm him. Let the doctor handle the child.

Try to become friends with the child's doctor, for if so, you'll speak of him in friendly terms and the child will follow suit sooner or later.

Injections are a prime cause of difficulty. No one likes to receive an injection and most young children cry when they receive one. But the attitude of the parent and the doctor will determine if the reaction to the pain is just a momentary episode or if the child will develop an intense fear of receiving further inoculations. Some children who have developed such fears scream in terror when taken to the doctor's office for any reason.

Parents should follow these simple rules:

Never let a child be injected while he is sleeping or not expecting the shot.

Never tell a child he will not receive an injection when he is due to receive one. It is much better to say, "We'll have to wait and ask the doctor."

Never say, "It won't hurt a bit," when it might or will hurt. Rather say, "It might hurt a little but only for a minute."

Reassure the child and hold his hand or even hold him in your arms if he wishes when he receives the injection.

Never comfort a child after an injection by saying, "Bad doctor! Mommy won't let him hurt you again."

Don't be squeamish and show pain and terror in your face when the child receives an injection.

Tell a child that the injections keep him strong and well and that is why doctors give them.

Most children adjust to the doctor by 18 months of age, but some may take as long as three years. The rapidity of adjustment depends upon the doctor, the parents, and the attitude of friends of the child.

See also **Physical examination.**

Pediculosis   see **Head lice.**

Pellagra

A disease widespread in Egypt, India, and the southern countries of Europe. It has also been found among children and pregnant mothers living in some of the southern states of the United States.

It is a chronic disease caused by a deficiency in the diet of niacin, one of the parts of the vitamin B complex. Corn and cereal are very poor sources of niacin, so that in areas where these are basic foods and there is little meat, poultry, or fish, pellagra is likely to oc-

cur. If children have pellagra they often have other diet-deficiency diseases as well, since frequently their diet is also deficient in proteins, other vitamins, and minerals.

Signs and symptoms The early signs are usually irregular but may include weakness, loss of appetite, irritability, and apathy. After a long period of niacin deficiency, the characteristic manifestations appear. These involve skin, digestive tract, and nervous system.

Lesions on the skin, which are often brought out by exposure to intensive sunlight, start as a redness of exposed areas, especially the backs of the hands, the forearms, face, neck, ankles, and knees. They often resemble and may be mistaken for sunburn. But in more severe cases the red color becomes darker, and the skin gets dry and scaly. The irritated area is sharply demarcated from the normal skin, often giving the hands the appearance of having red gloves. There is also inflammation of the mucous membrane of the mouth and of the tongue, vomiting, and diarrhea. Manifestations of disorder in the nervous system include insomnia, depression, and sometimes delirium.

Treatment Children suffering from pellagra are rapidly cured with a full, well-balanced diet supplemented by niacin given in tablet form. Brewers' yeast is also an excellent supplement.

It should be noted that a well-balanced diet, which includes meat, vegetables, eggs, and milk, contains adequate niacin to prevent pellagra.

Penicillin allergy

Allergic reactions to penicillin, although

not infrequent in adults, are comparatively rare in children. It has been estimated that less than 5 percent of children are sensitive to penicillin. The most frequent signs of this sensitivity are flushing, itching all over the body, or hives, which can be very disturbing. In rare instances such parts of the body as the ears or lips or even the whole body may swell, and there may be a swelling of the throat, a dangerous complication that may cause difficulty in breathing.

The signs and symptoms of penicillin allergy may appear anywhere from twenty minutes after a penicillin injection to even a delayed reaction of several days to a week or more.

A doctor is usually able to relieve the symptoms quickly by the injection of adrenalin or a cortisone preparation if the allergy is severe, or by the use of oral antihistamines in less severe cases.

Skin tests can determine if a child is really sensitive to penicillin. This knowledge is important in certain cases where penicillin is the drug of choice in the treatment or prevention of a condition. For instance, no other antibiotic or drug is more effective than penicillin in destroying streptococci, the causative agent of rheumatic fever and most cases of nephritis. If a child is definitely sensitive to penicillin, other drugs that are almost as effective can be substituted.

Children who are allergic to penicillin should wear a bracelet or necklace identifying him as "Penicillin Sensitive," for occasionally a child may be in an accident and taken to a hospital where he may routinely be given a penicillin inoculation to prevent infection.

Such bracelets or necklaces may be obtained by writing to Medic Alert Foundation, Turlock, Calif. (See **Medic Alert**.)

Penis

The penis of the newborn male infant is usually about an inch long. In some infants it may appear considerably smaller when the shaft of the penis is embedded in a fat pad above. In almost every instance the embedded penis, which looks so short in early infancy, will be of normal size when the boy reaches adolescence.

The end of the penis in the newborn is covered by a sheath of skin, the prepuce or foreskin, with an opening at the end. Removal of the foreskin (circumcision) is rarely necessary except as a religious ritual, unless it is too tight and cannot be retracted over the head of the penis or is too elongated. If circumcision is to be performed, it should be done within the first ten days of life (see **Circumcision**). If there is no circumcision, the foreskin should be pulled back over the head of the penis each day at bath time and the area cleaned (see **Bathing the infant**).

During infancy most boy babies have occasional erections of the penis. These usually occur when the urinary bladder is full and are of no medical or other significance.

Occasionally there is an irritation at the end of the penis at the opening of the urinary tube (urethra). This is caused by an ammonia burn from urine. It usually will clear up very quickly if a little boric acid ointment is applied under the direction of the doctor.

Between approximately 3 to 6 years of age, boys normally tend to masturbate. This produces temporary erections that are of no consequence. There is less masturbation during the school-age period, but it becomes more frequent again during adolescence (see **Masturbation**).

The size of the penis increases greatly

as a boy goes into adolescence, usually between 13 and 15 years of age. The final mature size may vary from 2 to 6 inches in length, varying with body build and familial background. Many boys with shorter than average penises are concerned about their masculinity and their sexual ability. They should be assured that they are completely normal and that the size of the penis has nothing to do with sexual capability.

Perceptual difficulties, neurological

Difficulties resulting from the brain's misuse of the sensory impressions (of sight, hearing, touch, etc.) that it receives. This does not include difficulties caused by defects of the eye, ear, or the nerves of touch and motion.

The brain decodes sensory information received via the nerves. Thus stimuli conveyed by the nerves do not cause any perception until they reach the brain. It is the activity in the brain itself that causes us to perceive colors, shapes, pain, sounds, and so forth. The brain also stores sensory impressions for future use, which is essential to all learning. Gradually a network of associations is built up: an infant learns to associate the sound of the mother's voice with comfort, an older child associates the symbol "2" with two things, and so forth. At the same time the child learns to respond to his perceptions with effective action. An infant sees something he wants and reaches out for it. An older child sees a dog and learns to draw it as he sees it.

These abilities must all be present and working well if a child is going to read and write at the usual time, and remember and understand what he reads and writes.

A child with perceptual difficulties may be able to see perfectly but cannot

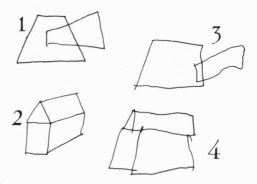

Designs 1 and 2 were drawn by Dr. Levine; designs 3 and 4 are attempted copies by a 7-year-old boy who had mild difficulties in the perception of spatial relationships and in coordination, and a history of hyperactive disruptive behavior in school.

remember what a symbol means when he sees it later and especially when two symbols are placed together. The average child of 6 years soon learns that D-O-G stands for the animal he knows so well and calls "dog." The child with perceptual difficulties may have problems remembering the sounds of the individual letters and much greater problems remembering the meanings of letters strung together. He may have a problem in learning to write, for he may not be able to make his hands write down correctly what he sees. He reverses letters or skips them. Some children have great trouble remembering what they have just read in a paragraph but remember very well when the paragraph is read to them: visual memory is impaired, but hearing memory is normal.

If a child has perceptual difficulties, this may be diagnosed with special tests by the doctor or by a specialist in the school.

Successful treatment of this condition involves working with specially trained teachers. Most good schools provide such tutoring for children who need it.

See also **Brain dysfunction, mild; Dyslexia.**

Perfume poisoning see **Poisons: first-aid treatment.**

Period, menstrual see **Menstruation.**

Peritonitis
An inflammation of the peritoneum, the membrane that lines the inner walls of the abdomen as well as lining the exterior of all the organs in the abdomen and intestines.

Peritonitis, which is a very severe and dangerous condition, may occur from bacteria brought to the peritoneum by the bloodstream, or, more commonly in children, from the rupture of the appendix or a tear of the stomach or intestines in an accident.

Treatment Large doses of antibiotics may be used against the bacterial infection; surgery is required for the repair of ruptured organs or the removal of the infected appendix.

Whereas approximately 20 percent of children with peritonitis died in the period prior to antibiotic therapy, the mortality rate today is less than 3 percent, most fatalities being in debilitated infants and children.

Permissiveness see **Overpermissive parent.**

Pertussis see **Whooping cough.**

Petit mal see **Epilepsy.**

Pets
If at all possible, every child should have a pet animal to enjoy, care for, and even at times to serve as a companion (although they should never substitute for real companions).

The care of the animal should in part be the responsibility of the child as soon as he is old enough, although parents must as a rule aid considerably.

Probably dogs are the best of pets because of their intelligence and the fact that they are loyal and devoted. Dogs can be taught to fetch and return, to do various tricks such as sitting, begging, and lying down when ordered, and they add greatly to the richness and adventure of a child's life. But dogs require taking out and exercise—and in the city much of this falls to the parents. In the country this rarely presents problems.

Cats are also wonderful pets and have the advantage of not having to be taken out of the home. They can be cuddly, warm, affectionate, and express their love and satisfaction by purring. They have the special quality of being soft and small enough to be held and cuddled in one's arms.

Other animals useful as pets, although certainly not as exciting as dogs and cats, are rabbits, guinea pigs, hamsters, gerbils, turtles, fish, and parakeets. All of these can be enjoyed by children, and as in the case of dogs and cats, a child's sense of responsibility can be developed by the care the pet requires.

At times children are cruel to their pets. Sometimes, when they are young, they may not know better, but occasionally when they are angry and upset, they may take out their feelings on the animal. Parents should not permit this cruelty and should teach a child kindness in the care of his pet. If a child is constantly cruel to a pet, it is very possible that he is emotionally upset and guidance should be sought.

Having a pet in the home is often the occasion of necessary discussions regarding pregnancy, birth, and death. Many city parents, in particular, feel that it is valuable for children to have the chance to observe and learn about these natural processes in the animal world. It certainly is a wonderful experience for children to observe the birth of puppies or kittens, but parents should be careful to warn children of the possibility that not all offspring will live. In one family a pregnant hamster, who had been unwisely promoted as a symbol of motherhood, killed her offspring after giving birth, causing great consternation and upset. Parents should try to be realistic and matter-of-fact in discussing animal behavior, and not depend too much on references to animals as a substitute for explaining what happens with human beings.

The death of a small pet, such as a goldfish, is usually not too distressing to a child, but he will certainly have questions. Parents must explain that the animal has died and that he cannot be brought back to life. The child may want to bury the animal, and should be allowed to do so. Some parents are tempted to remove the remains and say simply that the animal disappeared or went away. Usually the child suspects that something is being hidden, and in any case this only postpones to a later, and possibly more difficult time an explanation of death.

The death of a beloved cat, dog, or other pet can be an extremely upsetting experience for a young child who has enjoyed the companionship and love of the animal. Many parents are inclined to run out and obtain another animal to replace it at once. The advisability of such a move depends entirely upon the reaction of the child. If a youngster is very unhappy, no other animal can take the place of his pet for the time being. It is best to wait, possibly several weeks, before securing a "substitute." In the meantime, let the child talk freely about his pet.

Many young children need the assurance that, although death came to their pet, their parents will stay with them and not leave them.

Phenobarbital

A most valuable sedative used in the treatment of certain childhood conditions. It should only be given to a child on the advice of and under the direction of a doctor. In combination with atropin, phenobarbital is often used in the treatment of colic or pylorospasm. When so given, it is prescribed in very small amounts so that it will not sedate the baby but will only relax the muscles of the stomach and intestines. It is the drug of choice in the initial treatment of petit mal and grand mal epilepsies. In a great many cases, this drug alone is adequate in controlling seizures.

Phenobarbital is one of the safest drugs, with only very rare toxic reactions. Occasionally there may be some drowsiness, which will require regulation of the dosage by the doctor.

In rare instances, phenobarbital may excite a child rather than sedate him. And occasionally, again in rare instances, a child may develop a rash from a sensitivity to the drug.

It should always be remembered that large doses taken over long periods of time may be habit-forming (see **Drug abuse**).

Phobia, school   see **School phobia.**

Phobias

Unwarranted and very powerful fears of

something or some situation. Among these are: fear of being shut in a small or closed space (claustrophobia); fear of heights (acrophobia); fear of open spaces (agoraphobia); and fear of dirt and infection (mysophobia).

These irrational fears cannot be removed by explanations or reassurance by the child's parents or others whom he trusts and loves. The reassurance is ineffective because the deep underlying fear has usually little if anything to do with the object or action of which the child appears so fearful. A true phobia generally involves the displacement of fear from one object to another, for example, the fear of being abandoned by one's mother might be expressed as fear of open places.

While many children outgrow phobias, others may require investigation as to the cause and possibly psychotherapy.

Although most parents are not capable of uncovering the deeper causes for these phobias, they can aid the child in overcoming the phobia by being casual and giving the child the opportunity of gradually becoming acquainted and familiar with the feared object or situation, and by reassuring the child and letting him express or discuss his fears.

The parent of a child with phobias should not force the child into contact with the feared object or situation, nor should they ignore his fears.

In treating phobias the child must eventually be convinced that his fear of a specific object or situation is unreasonable. But, as mentioned, if the phobia is severe, if it does not diminish, and if it interferes with the normal activities of a child's life, it warrants psychiatric care.

See also **Anxiety; Fears; School phobia.**

Photographs and home movies

Almost all parents enjoy taking photographs and/or home movies of their children, and these do provide an exciting and vivid record of the child's life.

For better and more meaningful photographs and home movies:

1. Don't ask a child to pose. The best pictures are taken of a child reacting normally. And don't ask a child to smile. A thoughtful, interested, alert face is just as enjoyable and memorable as a smiling face.
2. Try for action shots of a child—in the swings at the park, playing with pets and friends, swimming, enjoying a birthday party, and so on.
3. The commonplace things in a child's life are excellent subjects—eating at the dinner table, listening to a bedtime story, taking a bath, playing with toys.

Physical examination

The routine physical examination is an important aspect of good child care. The frequency of the examination varies with the age of the child. During the first year, when there is such a rapid gain in weight and height and in general development, examinations are usually given every one to two months. During this period, the doctor not only checks the infant's growth but examines for any abnormalities of the heart, lungs, liver and spleen, for signs of anemia (common in the early months), for the normal closing of the fontanelles, and for the normal appearance of the teeth. The doctor also is interested in the child's activity development—when he sits up, when he stands up and starts to walk—and in the child's emotional development as well.

The child should receive a physical examination three or four times during the second year, and at least twice a year from 2 years of age until 6. After the sixth year, the examination should be given at least once a year, taking special note of vision and hearing. The doctor will not only keep the child up to date in his immunizations, but from time to time he will examine the child's urine for excess of sugar and albumin and the possibility of infection, and he will conduct routine tuberculin tests.

Physical fitness

The improvement of the physical fitness of our children has become a national effort in the United States, for tests have shown that American children are far less capable physically than European children.

Most American parents make very little effort to develop their children physically. We let our children sit for hours before the television set instead of insisting on outdoor play. We give them toys that require little or no effort to operate.

There are very few chores today that require any real physical effort. For example, boys formerly mowed a lawn with a hand mower, which required real strength. Now little or no effort is required to mow a lawn with lawn mowers driven by a gasoline motor or electricity. And whereas in former years children walked to school, today they are most often driven by bus or car, or they travel in the city by subways.

What can parents do to aid in the physical fitness of their children?

First, limit their television time. An hour in the evening should generally be adequate. See that they get plenty of outdoor activity in which they make good use of their muscles. Swimming is an all-around muscle developer. Give them activity toys and encourage them

to use these toys, which should make the child work against some type of resistance.

A list of suggested activity toys would include play equipment to develop arm and shoulder strength (climbing bars, chinning bars, punching bags or knock-down dummies, jump ropes, Irish mail, basketballs with baskets, baseballs and bats, tennis balls and rackets, bowling balls, tetherballs, swings) and toys to develop the lower extremities and increase agility (bicycles, tricycles, and other foot-operated toys, skates, Pogo sticks, skip ropes, seesaws, kites).

Today most schools, aware of the problems faced by American children, have changed their physical education activities to improve the physical fitness of their students.

Pica

The habit of eating non-food substances. Almost all very young children put any substance or object into their mouths, but some children develop a craving for non-food substances, or at least a habit of eating them. Some children eat dirt regularly. This may reflect a nutritional lack (see **Dirt-eating**). Many children eat paint chips or plaster chips, which could be dangerous if the paint contains lead (see **Lead poisoning**). The habit may be related to hunger or to a desire for sweets, since the plaster chips often have a slightly sweetish taste similar to candy.

Picking the nose   see **Nose picking.**

Picnics and cookouts

These are fine family experiences in which everyone can and should have a role and some degree of responsibility relative to his individual ability. Even the smallest toddler can carry a bag or collect wood or aid in spreading out a tablecloth.

The participation of children in planning a picnic or cookout not only adds to their enjoyment but makes them feel an important part of the venture. They may aid in suggesting foods and even in picking them out at the store. If sandwiches are to be made, children can often aid in making them, wrapping them, and packing them. If a child's suggestion is not acceptable, parents should explain why and offer alternative ideas. A child might, for instance, suggest something that is too expensive, too difficult to handle, or out of season.

Picnic meals, generally, are much more enjoyable if they are simple menus, quickly and easily prepared. Children who have to wait around for long periods of time while an elaborate meal is being created often become completely frustrated and lose their picnic enthusiasm. A young child rarely has the patience for foods that require a great deal of preparation and complicated cooking processes, but at times older children do enjoy this procedure. A child over the age of 3 usually prefers to cook his own frankfurter, although the cooking should be supervised. Hamburgers are more difficult for a child to cook himself.

The picnic grounds should not be too far away from home, for youngsters become weary with too much travel time. The picnic area should be large enough so that the children can spread out and play within appropriate boundaries. If there is a swimming area, parents should determine the depth of the water and the condition of the bottom, that is, whether it is free of such things as broken glass, open cans, and barbed wire.

Picnics and outings also can become an important learning experience for children. There is much to admire, investigate, and discover about nature—the birds and their sounds, insects of all kinds, water animals as well as land animals, wild flowers, trees, and trails. (See **Nature**.)

And lessons in the preservation of the land can also be learned. Children should learn that the natural habitat of plants as well as animals should not be destroyed or disturbed; that the picnic area should be cleaned up completely before departing; and that you should be absolutely sure that no sparks or fire remains where the food was cooked.

Pigeon toe see **Feet**.

Pilonidal cyst
A deep cyst situated above the base of the spinal column. It is connected to the surface by a narrow canal. During the embryonic stage, there is a deep, narrow opening at the base of the spine just above the cleft of the buttocks. This usually closes over before birth, but in some few children this tract remains open and appears as a very deep dimple. Matter collects here, forming a cyst, and in early adolescence the collection of matter may become infected. There is pain, swelling, and redness, and eventually pus is discharged. When infection occurs, the cyst should be removed by surgery.

Pills see **Barbiturate poisoning; Poisons: first-aid treatment.**

Pimples see **Acne**.

Pink eye see **Conjunctivitis**.

Pinworms see **Worms**.

Pituitary gland
Probably the most important gland in

the body, the pituitary is situated underneath the brain. It is truly the master gland, for it regulates the thyroid gland, the adrenal glands, the ovaries, and the testes, besides being responsible for the growth of the child and controlling other functions.

The pituitary produces several hormones, each of which has a different function:

1. The growth hormone regulates the growth of an individual. Too little of the growth hormone might result in the child's being a midget, while too much might produce a very tall child or a giant.
2. A thyroid-stimulating hormone, too much of which produces an overactivity of the thyroid gland, resulting in exophthalmic goiter, and too little of which produces a lack of adequate thyroid secretion, resulting in subthyroid sluggishness and, in severe cases, even cretinism.
3. An adrenal-stimulating hormone, ACTH, which regulates and controls the functioning of the adrenal glands. Too little makes a person extremely weak, while too much may make a person extremely obese or may cause excessive hairiness.
4. Testes- and ovaries-stimulating hormones, of which an excess produces precocious puberty, while too little leads to a lack of sexual growth and maturity.
5. A lactation hormone that stimulates the mammary glands and controls the flow of milk once the baby is born.
6. An antidiuretic hormone that prevents the excessive loss of fluids from the body through the kidneys. When there is a lack of this particular hormone, the child drinks many quarts of fluid each day and urinates very frequently as well. The condition is called diabetes insipidus, but is in no way related to the more common diabetes mellitus. Diabetes insipidus can be treated effectively with hormone injections.

PKU

An abbreviation of phenylketonuria, a hereditary disease that occurs in approximately one out of every 10,000 births in the United States. It is caused by a recessive gene. It is estimated that about one out of every 50 people is a carrier of this recessive gene.

PKU is caused by a metabolic disturbance in which phenylalanine (present in all natural proteins) is not broken up by the body's digestive juices. It accumulates in the blood and damages the brain of the child, causing mental retardation.

Children with PKU appear normal at birth, and if they are not treated within the first few months begin to show mental damage which becomes very apparent between ages 2 and 3. This mental retardation remains throughout life.

The disease can be diagnosed almost immediately after birth by a simple test of the infant's blood or urine. This test is given routinely to newborns throughout the United States, and most pediatricians repeat it at age one month.

Treatment   If a test for PKU indicates that a child has this condition, a special milk substitute is given that is low in phenylalanine. A low-phenylalanine diet is continued for a few years, after which the child is gradually placed on a normal diet.

The diet must be given very early in infancy to prevent brain damage, and a child so treated is usually normal mentally.

Placenta

An organ attached to the inner wall of the uterus containing blood vessels of the mother and the infant. It is connected to the baby by the umbilical cord.

In the placenta the blood vessels of the mother and the fetus lie side by side. There is no mixing of the mother's and the baby's blood. Normally none of the mother's blood passes into the baby and none of the baby's blood into the mother. Food and oxygen from the mother's blood pass through the walls of her blood vessels and enter the walls of the baby's blood vessels. The carbon

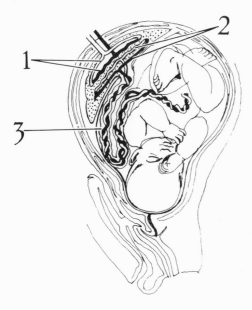

In the placenta the blood vessels of mother and baby lie side by side. 1. Mother's blood vessels. 2. Baby's blood vessels. 3. The umbilical cord containing the blood vessels of the baby; it runs from the placenta to the baby's navel. The unshaded blood vessels carry food and oxygen from the mother's blood to the baby. The shaded blood vessels carry waste products and carbon dioxide out of the baby to be eliminated by the mother.

dioxide and waste products from the baby are transmitted through the cord to the placenta where they pass through the walls of the baby's blood vessels and into those of the mother.

The placenta remains attached to the wall of the uterus until after the baby is born. If the placenta separates prematurely it cuts off the supply of oxygen and food to the infant and may cause its death. At times there is a partial separation of the placenta with some bleeding, which causes some diminution in the amount of oxygen received by the baby, but usually the baby is born without any resulting difficulty.

Plantar warts   see Warts.

Plants, poisonous

Parents should be aware that there are many plants, including common household varieties, that are poisonous when the leaves, roots, or berries are eaten.

Among these are the English holly, azaleas, laurel, rhododendron, oleander, lily of the valley, milkbush, dieffenbachia, philodendron, caladium, autumn crocus, iris, poinsettia, the rosary pea, jimson weed, rhubarb leaves, the leaves of the water hemlock and poison hemlock, and the precatory beans (the black and red beans from the tropics often made into necklaces).

The berries of the English holly when eaten produce violent diarrhea and vomiting and may cause death if twenty to thirty berries are eaten.

The flowers (nectar) and the seeds of the Jimson weed are poisonous, causing symptoms in a few minutes to a few hours: thirst, disturbance of vision, hyperirritability, delirium, fever, convulsions, coma.

Poinsettia is fatal if its leaves are

eaten; and one chewed seed of a rosary pea is fatal.

Azaleas, laurel, and rhododendron leaves may not only cause vomiting and diarrhea but cardiac failure and irritation of the brain and nervous system as well.

The roots and lower parts of the stem of water hemlock or poison hemlock may cause symptoms within fifteen minutes: excessive salivation, tremors, severe convulsions. Prognosis is excellent with early vomiting.

Oleander, lily of the valley, and milk-bush leaves can also cause cardiac symptoms, and the leaves and roots of autumn crocus and iris may cause kidney failure.

The leaves of dieffenbachia, philodendron, and caladium may cause swelling of the mouth and throat and severe ulcers in these areas.

Rhubarb leaves may cause abdominal pain, vomiting, and weakness.

If parents are unable to identify a plant of which a child has eaten leaves or berries, it is much safer to consider it poisonous and induce vomiting at once (see **Poisons: first-aid treatment**). Also call your doctor or local poison control center.

See also **Poison ivy; Poison oak; Poison sumac.**

Plastic bags

The thin, transparent bags of the type used by dry cleaners to cover clothes. Unless these bags contain numerous perforations throughout the plastic, they are of great potential danger to little children who love to put them over their heads. Soon the oxygen within is used up, the plastic clings to the child's face when he inhales, and the child may get panicky and lose consciousness. Unless rescued promptly, the child may die.

If the child is unconscious, start mouth to mouth resuscitation immediately and do not stop until the child is breathing normally. Have someone else call a doctor, hospital, or rescue unit. (See **Mouth-to-mouth resuscitation.**)

The potential danger of this "toy" can be eliminated, of course, by seeing to it that all such bags are either liberally perforated or destroyed immediately on being brought into the home.

Play

Play is one of the most vital factors in a child's development, for through it the child learns to test out and master his environment, and he gains a great deal of pleasure as well.

Children must be able at times to play without dependence on or interference from adults, and parents should arrange opportunities for such play.

For the infant, play is a form of exploring his surroundings. As he develops physically, he gains more mobility, and so is better able to explore his environment and make use of things he encounters. From early infancy parents should provide interesting, colorful, bright, shiny, moving objects for the baby to watch and focus on. These toys stimulate the child's interest and curiosity and encourage him to observe. Later, when he is more active, he will reach for, grasp, and play with these toys.

As the child grows older and creeps and then walks, his opportunities for play increase greatly. Toys are greatly enjoyed at this age. He continues his explorations and handles almost any object he can move.

At first, a child's play is usually by himself, with very little interest in what other children are doing. But at about 18 months, children begin to watch other children. While not yet playing with them, they play alongside of them, usually attempting to imitate their play activity. At approximately 3 years, children play cooperatively with other children.

Prior to the age of 3 or thereabout, children in their play are inquisitive, experimental, at times destructive, but rarely "constructive," as adults use the term. Children will throw blocks simply to hear the sound and see what happens. They are interested in tearing things up and pulling them apart. This is not, however, because they deliberately want to ruin things. They are learning what things feel like, how they work, and what can be done with them.

As boys and girls approach the age of 3, their play usually becomes much more constructive. Blocks are piled on one another and even "houses" are built; modeling clay is now used to make familiar objects.

As the child grows more mature, he learns how to use different toys in many ways, and he observes more and more how things in his environment work and what people do in their everyday lives. He sees Daddy put on a hat each morning—he wants to do the same and feel like Daddy. He sees firemen whiz by in their bright red engines. He plays fireman, for he wants to experience the firemen's activities himself. He may not fully comprehend, but he can imitate what he has seen.

Through the nursery-school period and even later, children enjoy imitative play, pretending they are fathers, mothers, babies, and other people—often re-enacting the pattern of their own home. Their building with blocks becomes more complex; they enjoy painting and simple musical instruments.

During the school-age period, play begins to involve more and more games of skill and competition. Physical activities may still be mixed with fantasy. For example, forts are built by young pirates and cowboys. Or the play may be intellectual, as in checkers, chess, and similar games. In all ways—physically, emotionally, and intellectually—the child uses play to develop and test himself, to try out different roles, to attempt previously impossible feats. It is essential to his individual and social growth, and the child who has too little time or place to play or no one to play with is greatly deprived.

It should be emphasized that throughout childhood it is the parents' duty to see that a child's play is safe. Toys or objects that are dangerous should be removed and kept out of reach of children; activities that are dangerous, such as playing with fire and climbing trees with weak or dead branches, must be absolutely forbidden even if discipline must be stronger and more severe than usual.

See also **Toys and play materials**.

Play groups

Groups of children organized by parents or others to give children an opportunity to spend time profitably with youngsters of their approximate age level. These groups are usually of two types—those for preschool children and those for children of the school-age years.

For the preschool age, play groups help children develop socially and cooperatively in play—sharing, taking turns, and adjusting to the care and direction of other adults outside the home. Cooperative play groups for preschool children have been successfully organized in many areas by groups of four to six mothers with children of approximately the same age. Each mother arranges to take the children for one day or part of a day every week. The mothers should not simply turn this into a baby-sitting situation but should plan activities and outings appropriate to the abilities and interests of the children. Occasionally a second mother aids in supervision. These parent-directed play groups can become not only a very rewarding experience for the children but also for the mothers if they will take the time to discuss, plan, and share ideas with one another.

For children of school age, play groups are often organized for after-school activity and for Saturdays as well. These are usually under trained supervision. The children are taken to parks, swimming pools, athletic fields, and entertainments, as well as partaking in such activities as bowling and skating. Such programs are usually privately organized and charge a fee, but they may also be run by communities, housing projects, churches, settlement houses, and, in some larger cities, by the Police Department.

Play therapy   see **Psychotherapy.**

Playing hooky   see **Truancy.**

Playmates   see **Companions.**

Playpen
Various types of playpens are available. One variety has sides of wooden bars similar to the bars of an infant's crib; another has cloth-mesh sides to prevent the infant from hurting himself if he falls. The upper rail is sometimes covered with a plastic strip—a so-called teething rail—for the baby who is teething to bite when he is standing up. All playpens are raised off the floor, and all have a soft waterproof mat that covers the boards beneath. For safety, the bars on a playpen should not be spaced more than 3½ inches apart.

Playpens are enclosed areas designed to keep an infant safe while the mother is occupied around the house or relaxing. But they are not supposed to be miniature prisons from which a child constantly cries to be taken out and in which he is always upset. This violent and negative reaction is harmful to the child if it occurs too frequently or over too long a period of time. The child, young as he is, may feel rejected. Such upsetting reactions often occur when a baby is introduced to a playpen too late and has already learned to enjoy the freedom of creeping around and playing on the carpet.

The playpen should be introduced when the baby is about 5 months old. Even though he is not yet able to sit up without support, he will usually find pleasure being in it. Put his favorite toys in with him. When he is 6 or 7 months old and is sitting up, playing in the playpen will be even more pleasurable. Later he will hold on to the sides and enjoy pulling himself up to a standing position. However, he may need help at first in learning how to sit down again.

At times a child who is perfectly satisfied in the playpen if his mother is in the room or at least within sight cries if she leaves the room and disappears. This does not mean that he must be picked up the minute the tears start, especially if the mother plans to return soon. But if she is going to work in the kitchen or be in some other room for any extended time, and the child wants to be near her, it is better to take the child out of the playpen and let him sit in a high chair.

When the weather is nice, the playpen may be moved to the porch or yard.

A word of warning: never place a

child in the playpen as a form of punishment. If a parent wishes to use it for the child as a place of safety, he should do all he can to make it a place of interest and pleasure rather than unhappiness.

Pleurisy

Inflammation of the pleura, the membrane lining the inner chest wall and covering the lungs.

The pleura consists of two layers: the outer layer under the chest wall and covering the big muscle of breathing (the diaphragm) below, and the inner layer that covers the lungs. The space between these two layers is called the pleural space.

When the pleura is irritated it usually exudes a fluid very much like serum. If the irritation is caused by a virus, a tumor, tuberculosis, or an irritation of the lung beneath the inner pleura, the fluid is usually sterile. If the irritation is caused by a bacteria, as in the case of pneumonia, the fluid may be mixed with pus. The fluid collects between the two layers of the pleura within the chest and may at times compress the lungs.

Symptoms and treatment The most common symptoms of pleurisy are a dry cough, fever, and occasionally difficult breathing. A viral or tuberculous pleurisy will clear by itself as the inflammation subsides. A pleurisy with pus requires intense antibiotic therapy and often surgical removal of the fluid as well. Pleurisy may last from several weeks to several months, depending on the cause, intensity, and treatment.

Pneumonia

An inflammation of the lung caused either by bacteria, viruses, fungi, or by some irritating substance that has been inhaled.

The most common pneumonias are those caused by bacteria or viruses. The term lobar pneumonia designates an inflammation that is confined to one or possibly two lobes of a lung, causing the whole area to solidify. The term bronchopneumonia designates an inflammation that is scattered and patchy, involving areas of the lung surrounding the bronchial tubes. Bacterial pneumonias may be either lobar or bronchial in type, whereas those caused by a virus, fungus, or an irritating substance are almost always bronchial.

As a rule, pneumonia in children is not a dangerous disease when properly treated, and recovery is complete.

Signs and symptoms of bacterial or viral pneumonias These pneumonias are almost always preceded by a cold or influenza, although the inhalation of food may cause the illness, especially in weak and debilitated infants; an operation during which a child may have vomited under anesthesia and inhaled the vomitus may also result in pneumonia.

Pneumonia usually starts with a hard, repetitive cough, a rapid rise in temperature, occasional chills, and often rapid breathing. The diagnosis can easily be made by a doctor and confirmed by X rays.

Treatment Bacterial pneumonias are treated by antibiotic therapy, which is usually very effective and clears the condition within a few days. No specific treatment is used for virus pneumonia, the main effort being to relieve the severe cough and make the child more comfortable. If a child is having great difficulty breathing, the use of oxygen will be helpful in relieving the distress.

Signs of virus pneumonia may persist for several weeks. The doctor should determine when a child is ready to return to school and engage in full activity.

Chemical pneumonias These pneumonias are caused by the child's inhalation of substances that are irritating to the lungs. Among such substances are kerosene, benzine, and lighter fluid; oily materials, such as from oily nose drops or oily vitamin preparations (at times inhaled when drops are forced on a resisting child); and zinc stearate, a powder formerly used to prevent diaper rash.

Signs and symptoms of chemical pneumonias These are usually limited to coughing and the production of sputum. In severe cases there may be difficulty in breathing plus rapid respirations.

Treatment There is no specific treatment for chemical pneumonia. Treatment is limited to the use of antibiotics to prevent secondary invasion by bacteria—that is, infection by bacteria from the outside.

Poison ivy

A common plant, whose leaves contain an oily substance that on human skin usually produces a severe itching reaction.

In almost all areas in the United States the poison ivy plant is easy to recognize—its notch-edged leaves grow in clusters of three with a leaf in the center and one on either side. However, in the Southwest United States, there is a five-leaf poison ivy.

The first time a person is in contact with poison ivy there is usually no skin reaction. But some of the oil is absorbed through the skin and causes the body to be sensitive to it. From that time on, contact with the plant produces within

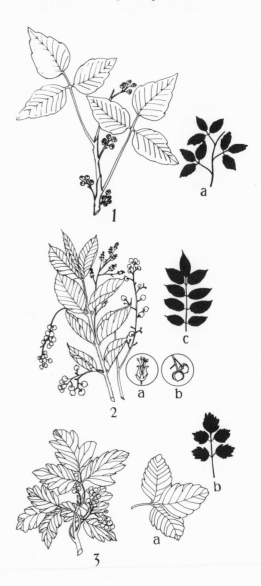

1. Poison ivy: (a) general leaf configuration. 2. Poison sumac: (a) flower; (b) fruit; (c) general leaf configuration. 3. Poison oak, eastern variety; (a) leaf of western variety; (b) general leaf configuration, eastern variety.

twelve to twenty-four hours a pimply, blisterlike eruption that itches intensely. The person scratches and quickly spreads the rash, often extending its blisterlike pimples in a line along a scratch and then, rather quickly, the rash is spread to other parts of the body as well by subsequent scratching.

One attack of poison ivy seems to make a person more sensitive to its poison. Many people are so sensitive that they react to poison ivy oil in the smoke of burning plants, or from the hair of pets who have wandered through the plants. It is important never to burn poison ivy if there is a chance of the smoke being inhaled, for the reaction may be very severe.

Treatment   The best treatment is preventive. Avoid the plant and destroy those in the immediate neighborhood. If a child is suspected of having handled or walked through poison ivy, a good scrubbing with strong soap and water immediately after will often remove the oil from the skin before it starts to irritate.

Treatment of the rash is designed to prevent the itching. Usually effective in mild cases is a thick paste of baking soda and water or an application of calamine lotion (zinc carbonate with one percent phenol) or Caladryl (zinc carbonate, plus a little camphor, Benadryl—diphenhydramine hydrochloride—and rubbing alcohol). In more severe cases a doctor's advice should be sought. He will probably prescribe the oral hydrocortisone in liquid or pill form, which usually stops the spread of the rash and causes the lesions to dry up and disappear within five or six days. Clothes worn by a child when he went through a poison ivy area should be well washed to remove any poison ivy oil.

Prevention or treatment of poison ivy by injections of the poison ivy oil or by taking small amounts orally has not been very effective.

Poison oak
Poison oak grows as a vine or shrub, and is closely related to poison ivy. Generally poison oak has three leaves, as does poison ivy, but it may have five.

The poison that irritates the skin is closely related to that of poison ivy and produces a reaction on human skin similar to that of poison ivy. Treatment is the same as for poison ivy (see **Poison ivy**).

Poison sumac
This shrub grows up to 15 feet in height, and differs from the nonpoisonous sumac plants in that the bright green leaves do not have sawteeth on their margin. The leaves are compound with seven to eleven leaflets. The fruits of the poison sumac plants hang down and are a glossy pale yellow or cream, whereas the nonpoisonous types have erect red fruits.

The reaction is similar to that of poison ivy and the treatment is the same (see **Poison ivy**).

Poisoning, food   see **Food poisoning.**

Poisoning, lead   see **Lead poisoning.**

Poisonous plants   see **Plants, poisonous.**

Poisons: first-aid treatment
During infancy and early childhood, poisoning is one of the most frequent accidents and is a common cause of death. Seventy-five percent of all deaths from poisoning occur before children

are 2 years old. All of these accidents could have been prevented by adequate precautions. Almost all deaths could have been prevented by adequate preparation for such emergencies.

Prevention of poisoning Keep all the household products and medicines that might be poisonous out of the reach of children. The safest method is to lock them in a cabinet or closet.

Household products include disinfectants, cleaning fluids, lye, ammonia, drain cleaners, insecticides, gasoline, benzine, kerosene, bleaches, detergents, mouse and rat poisons, and cigarette lighter fluid.

All medicines are potentially dangerous, including aspirin, cough medicines, laxatives, sedatives, tranquilizers, alcohol, and antiseptics.

Precautions in case of poisoning

1. Keep the telephone numbers of a poison control center (see **Appendix A**), a doctor, and a hospital prominently displayed near the phone.
2. Keep three ounces of syrup of ipecac on hand at all times to induce vomiting if necessary (but keep it out of the reach of children).

First steps if poison is swallowed If you see a child swallow a substance that might be poisonous, or if a child states that he has swallowed such a substance:

1. Get the container, if possible. If it is missing, try to have the child describe what he has taken.
2. Read the list of ingredients in the substance that is given on the container. The ingredients are important. One drain cleaner, for example, may be strongly alkaline, while another is acid,

and the treatment in each case is different. Sometimes first-aid treatment is given on the container.
3. If the antidote is indicated on the container, give it to the child at once. Then call a poison control center, a doctor, or a hospital immediately. If the antidote is not given and you are not absolutely certain how to proceed, call a poison control center, doctor, or hospital. Remember that all medicines should be vomited up, according to the method given below. Other poisons may be diluted by giving the child milk or water, olive oil, or another vegetable oil.

To cause vomiting Give the child syrup of ipecac: 1 teaspoon for a child under one year, 1 tablespoon for a child one year or older, followed by a glass of water. If no vomiting results, repeat only once again in twenty minutes.

Or give the child 6 to 8 ounces of milk; then turn him upside-down, or have him sit or lie with his head down, to avoid inhalation of the vomitus; and put a finger down his throat.

Do not make the child vomit
A. If he is unconscious.
B. If he has swallowed **petroleum distillates**, such as:

Kerosene	Spindle oil
Gasoline	Stoddard solvent
Benzine	Diesel oil
Turpentine	(Petroleum distillates
Crude oil	are common
Mineral seal oil	ingredients in
Naphtha,	household
high-boiling	polishes and
Summer black oil	waxes.)

Give 1 to 2 ounces of olive oil or other vegetable oil. (Do not force, as this may cause vomiting.)

POISONS: FIRST-AID TREATMENT 369

Then call a poison control center, doctor, or hospital at once. Prepare to rush the child to the hospital.

C. If he has swallowed **strong alkalis,** such as:

Lye (sodium   Drain cleaners
   hydroxide,   containing sodium
   potassium   hydroxide
   hydroxide)   Washing soda
Ammonia   (sodium
                        carbonate)

Give 1 part vinegar to 4 parts water (give 4 to 7 ounces); or lemon juice, 3 to 7 ounces; or orange juice, 4 to 10 ounces.

Follow any of these by up to 8 ounces of milk, olive oil or other vegetable oil, or egg white.

Then call a poison control center, doctor, or hospital at once. Prepare to rush the child to the hospital.

D. If he has swallowed **strong acids,** such as:

Hydrochloric acid   Drain cleaners
Nitric acid   containing sodium
Sulfuric acid   bisulfate
Battery acid

Give milk of magnesia, 4 to 10 ounces; or bicarbonate of soda, 1 tablespoon to 8 ounces of water; or 4 to 10 ounces of a mild soap solution (not a detergent).

Follow any of these by up to 8 ounces of milk, olive oil or other vegetable oil, or egg white.

Then call a poison control center, doctor, or hospital at once. Prepare to rush the child to the hospital.

Drain cleaners
   containing sodium
   bioxalate

Give 6 to 10 ounces of milk or chalk solution (powdered blackboard chalk in water, to make a soupy consistency).

E. If he has swallowed **disinfectants containing carbolic acid (phenol),** such as:

Lysol
Creosol
CN

Give 7 to 10 ounces of milk; or 3 to 4 ounces of olive oil or other vegetable oil.

Then call a poison control center, doctor, or hospital at once.

Dangerous common household substances The following is a list of common household products which may be poisonous when swallowed by children. First-aid treatment is given for each substance. Again, if you are in doubt about ingredients in a substance, check the container for the antidote or call a poison control center. In case of delay give milk, water, or olive oil or another vegetable oil. **Always call a poison control center, doctor, or hospital at once for follow-up treatment.**

After-shave lotion
   Induce vomiting.
Alcohol
   Induce vomiting.
Aminophylline (found in medicine for treatment of asthma)
   Induce vomiting.
Ammonia
   Do *not* induce vomiting. Give 1 part vinegar to 4 parts water (give 4 to 7 ounces); or lemon juice, 3 to 7 ounces; or orange juice, 4 to 10 ounces. Follow any of these by up to 8 ounces of milk, olive oil or other vegetable oil, or egg white. Prepare to rush the child to the hospital.

Anacin
Induce vomiting.
Antidepressants
Induce vomiting.
Antifreeze solutions
Induce vomiting.
Antihistamines
Induce vomiting.
Ant poison
Induce vomiting.
Appetite suppressants
Induce vomiting.
Arsenic
Induce vomiting.
Aspirin
Induce vomiting.
Asthma medicine
Induce vomiting.
Atropine
Induce vomiting.
Barbiturates
Induce vomiting.
Battery acid
Do *not* induce vomiting. Give milk of magnesia, 4 to 10 ounces; or bicarbonate of soda, 1 tablespoon to 8 ounces of water; or 4 to 10 ounces of a mild soap solution (not a detergent).

Follow any of these by up to 8 ounces of milk, olive oil or other vegetable oil, or egg white. Prepare to rush the child to the hospital.
Belladonna
Induce vomiting.
Benzene (Benzol)
Induce vomiting.
Benzine
Do *not* induce vomiting. Give 1 to 2 ounces of olive oil or other vegetable oil. (Do not force, as this may cause vomiting.) Prepare to rush the child to the hospital.
Birth control pills
Induce vomiting.
Bleaches
Read the label. Call a poison control center. Ajax, Clorox, and other chlorinated bleaches (often containing hypochlorite) should be treated with sips of milk. Do *not* induce vomiting. Some bleaches are alkali—may contain sodium peroxide or hydrogen peroxide—not usually very dangerous, but induce vomiting.
Bluing
Induce vomiting.
Borax
Induce vomiting.

Boric acid
Induce vomiting.
Bromides
Induce vomiting (usually spontaneous vomiting occurs if a large dose has been taken).
Caffeine (in most over-the-counter stimulants)
Induce vomiting.
Camphor
Induce vomiting.
Carbon tetrachloride (Carbona)
Induce vomiting. Prepare to rush the child to the hospital.
Chlorpromazine (Thorazine)
Induce vomiting.
Cigarettes and cigars
Induce vomiting.

Cleaning fluids (read the label)
   Acetone
   Induce vomiting.
   Amyl acetate
   Induce vomiting.
   Carbon tetrachloride
   Induce vomiting. Prepare to rush the child to the hospital.
   Methyl alcohol
   Induce vomiting.
   Trichlorocythlene
   Induce vomiting.
   Benzene, Kerosene, Naphtha, Petroleum distillates, Stoddard solvent
   Give 1 to 2 ounces of olive oil or other vegetable oil. (Do not force, as this may cause vomiting.) Prepare to rush the child to the hospital.

Cleaning powders (such as Ajax)
Do *not* induce vomiting. For Ajax and Clorox give sips of milk. See also in this list: Bleaches, Detergents.
Clorox
Do *not* induce vomiting. Give sips of milk.
Codeine
Induce vomiting.
Cold pills
Induce vomiting.
Cologne
Induce vomiting.
Cough medicine
Induce vomiting.
Crayons (if they are not labeled as nontoxic)
Induce vomiting.
Creosol
Do *not* induce vomiting. Give 7 to 10 ounces of milk or 3 to 4 ounces of olive oil

or other vegetable oil. Prepare to rush the child to the hospital.

Creosote
Do *not* induce vomiting. Give 7 to 10 ounces of milk or olive or other vegetable oil.

Crude oil
Give 1 to 2 ounces of olive oil or other vegetable oil. (Do not force, as this may cause vomiting.) Prepare to rush the child to the hospital.

DDT
Induce vomiting.

Decongestants
Induce vomiting.

Deodorants
If large amounts are taken, induce vomiting.

Deodorizers (room, refrigerator, toilet bowl)
Do *not* induce vomiting. Give 7 to 10 ounces of milk.

Depilatories
Induce vomiting.

Detergents (granules or cakes are usually stronger than liquids)
Do *not* induce vomiting. Give 7 to 10 ounces of milk or water. Follow with 2 to 3 ounces of olive oil or other vegetable oil, or with 2 tablespoons milk of magnesia. Detergent granules for an electric dishwasher may be quite strongly alkaline. A poison control center may recommend giving dilute vinegar, dilute lemon juice, or orange juice.

Dexamyl, Dexedrine
Induce vomiting.

Diesel oil
Give 1 to 2 ounces of olive oil or other vegetable oil. (Do not force, as this may cause vomiting.) Prepare to rush the child to the hospital.

Diet pills
Induce vomiting.

Digitalis
Induce vomiting.

Dishwashing liquid
See in this list: Detergents.

Dishwashing-machine detergent granules
See in this list: Detergents.

Disinfectants containing phenol (carbolic acid), such as Lysol, Creosol, CN
Give 7 to 10 ounces of milk or 3 to 4 ounces of olive oil or other vegetable oil. Prepare to rush the child to the hospital.

Drain cleaners
Do *not* induce vomiting. Read the label for ingredients and antidote.

Cleaners containing sodium hydroxide
Give large amounts of dilute vinegar (1 part vinegar to 4 parts water); or lemon juice, 3 to 7 ounces; or orange juice, 4 to 10 ounces.

Cleaners containing sodium bioxalate
Give 6 to 10 ounces of milk, water, or chalk solution (powdered blackboard chalk in water, to make a soupy consistency).

Cleaners containing sodium bisulfate
Give milk of magnesia, 4 to 10 ounces; or bicarbonate of soda, 1 tablespoon to 8 ounces of water; or 4 to 10 ounces of a mild soap solution (not a detergent).

Eyebrow pencil
Induce vomiting.

Eye shadow
Induce vomiting.

Fire-extinguisher fluid
Induce vomiting.

Freckles remover
Induce vomiting.

Furniture polish
Do *not* induce vomiting. Give 1 to 2 ounces of olive oil or other vegetable oil.

Gasoline
Do *not* induce vomiting. Give 1 to 2 ounces of olive oil or other vegetable oil. (Do not force, as this may cause vomiting.) Prepare to rush the child to the hospital.

Hair dyes, tints, colorings
Induce vomiting.

Hair-setting lotion
Induce vomiting.

Hair sprays
Induce vomiting.

Hair straighteners
Induce vomiting.

Heart medicines
Induce vomiting.

Holly berries
Induce vomiting.

Hormones
Induce vomiting.

Hydrochloric acid
Give milk of magnesia, 4 to 10 ounces; or bicarbonate of soda, 1 tablespoon to 8 ounces of water; or 4 to 10 ounces of a mild soap solution (not a detergent). Follow any of these by up to 8 ounces of milk, olive oil or other vegetable oil, or egg white. Then call a poison control center, doctor, or hospital at once. Prepare to rush the child to the hospital.

However, the dilute hydrochloric acid

given by mouth for stomach disorders is not dangerous.

Hydrogen peroxide
Not usually dangerous in household strengths, but induce vomiting if a large amount is swallowed.

Ink, stamping ink, laundry ink
Induce vomiting.

Ink eradicator
Do *not* induce vomiting. Give 6 to 10 ounces of milk or chalk solution (powdered blackboard chalk in water to make a soupy consistency).

Insecticides or insect repellents
Induce vomiting.

Iodine, tincture of
Give 1 to 2 tablespoons of flour or cornstarch in a glass of water; or give bread; then induce vomiting.

Kerosene
Do *not* induce vomiting. Give 1 to 2 ounces of olive oil or other vegetable oil. (Do not force, as this may cause vomiting.) Then call a poison control center, doctor, or hospital at once. Prepare to rush the child to the hospital.

Laxatives
Induce vomiting.

Leather polishes and dyes
Do *not* induce vomiting. Give 1 to 2 ounces of olive oil or other vegetable oil. Prepare to rush the child to the hospital.

Lighter fluid
Give 1 to 2 ounces of olive oil or other vegetable oil. (Do not force, as this may cause vomiting.) Prepare to rush the child to the hospital.

Lipstick
Induce vomiting.

Liquid makeup
Induce vomiting.

Liquor or beer
Induce vomiting.

LSD
Induce vomiting.

Lye
Do *not* induce vomiting. Give 1 part vinegar to 4 parts water (4 to 7 ounces); or 3 to 7 ounces of lemon juice; or 4 to 10 ounces of orange juice. Follow any of these by up to 8 ounces of milk, olive oil or other vegetable oil, or egg white. Prepare to rush the child to the hospital.

Matches
Induce vomiting.

Metal polishes
Do *not* induce vomiting. Read the label for ingredients and antidote. The polish may be acidic, e.g., containing oxalic acid or cyanogen, or it may contain petroleum distillates such as benzine or turpentine. Do not treat unless you are certain of the antidote. Call a poison control center. In case of delay give 1 to 2 ounces of olive oil or other vegetable oil, or 2 to 3 ounces of milk. Do not force.

Mineral seal oil
Give 1 to 2 ounces of olive oil or other vegetable oil. (Do not force, as this may cause vomiting.) Prepare to rush the child to the hospital.

Mistletoe berries
Induce vomiting.

Mole poisons
Induce vomiting. If the poison contains strychnine, rush to the hospital: EMERGENCY.

Morphine
Induce vomiting.

Mothballs
Induce vomiting.

Mouse and rat poisons
  Warfarin (Pival, Valone)—most commonly used
  Induce vomiting.
  Arsenic* (rarely used)
  Induce vomiting.
  Strychnine* (rarely used)
  Induce vomiting and rush to the nearest hospital: EMERGENCY.
  Phosphorus (rarely used)
  Induce vomiting.

Mouthwash
Induce vomiting.

Mushrooms (any wild mushrooms should be considered)
Induce vomiting.

Nailpolish
Induce vomiting.

Nailpolish remover
Induce vomiting.

---

*Activated charcoal, if available, may be given (mixed in water to a soupy consistency) to absorb the remaining arsenic and strychnine after vomiting has occurred. This traditional remedy is effective in absorbing many poisons and will very probably be more widely used in the future.

Naphtha

Give 1 to 2 ounces of olive oil or other vegetable oil. (Do not force, as this may cause vomiting.) Prepare to rush the child to the hospital.

Naphthalene (mothballs, moth flakes, deodorant cakes)

Induce vomiting.

Nicotine

Induce vomiting.

Nitric Acid

Do *not* induce vomiting. Give milk of magnesia, 3 to 10 ounces; or bicarbonate of soda, 1 tablespoon to 8 ounces of water; or 4 to 10 ounces of a mild soap solution (not a detergent). Follow any of these by up to 8 ounces of milk, olive oil or other vegetable oil, or egg white. Prepare to rush the child to the hospital.

Oven cleaner

Do *not* induce vomiting. Read the label for ingredients and antidote. Easy Off and most other oven cleaners contain sodium hydroxide (lye). Give 1 part vinegar to 4 parts water (4 to 7 ounces); or 3 to 7 ounces of lemon juice; or 4 to 7 ounces of orange juice. Follow any of these by up to 8 ounces of milk, olive oil or other vegetable oil, or egg white. Prepare to rush the child to the hospital.

Some oven cleaners are acidic. Give milk of magnesia, 3 to 10 ounces; or bicarbonate of soda, 1 tablespoon to 8 ounces of water; or 4 to 10 ounces of a mild soap solution (not a detergent). Follow any of these by up to 8 ounces of milk, olive oil or other vegetable oil, or egg white. Then call a poison control center, doctor, or hospital at once. Prepare to rush the child to the hospital.

Paint

Induce vomiting.

Paint removers

Do *not* induce vomiting. Read the label. If no antidote is given, call a poison control center. In case of delay give 3 to 4 ounces of milk or olive oil or other vegetable oil. Prepare to rush the child to the hospital.

Paint thinner

See in this list: Paint removers.

Paregoric

Induce vomiting.

Perfumes

Induce vomiting.

Permanent-wave solutions

Induce vomiting.

Peroxide

See in this list: Hydrogen peroxide.

Pine oil

Give 7 to 10 ounces of milk or 3 to 4 ounces of olive oil or other vegetable oil. Prepare to rush the child to the hospital.

Plants

Identify the plant and call a poison control center if in doubt about how to proceed. Induce vomiting.

Plant food

Induce vomiting.

Polishes, waxes

Read the label and call a poison control center. Give 1 to 2 ounces of olive or other vegetable oil.

Rat poison

See in this list: Mouse and rat poisons.

Reducing pills

Induce vomiting.

Rheumatism medicine, such as Whink, naval jelly

Induce vomiting.

Rust remover

Do *not* induce vomiting. Check the label for ingredients and antidote. Give large amounts of water followed by egg white. Prepare to rush the child to a hospital.

Sedatives

Induce vomiting.

Shampoos

Usually not dangerous. Induce vomiting.

Sleeping pills

Induce vomiting.

Soaps (see also Detergents)

Usually not dangerous. Induce vomiting of strong soaps.

Spindle oil

Give 1 to 2 ounces of olive oil or other vegetable oil. (Do not force, as this may cause vomiting.) Prepare to rush the child to a hospital.

Spot remover

See in this list: Cleaning fluids.

Stoddard solvent

Give 1 to 2 ounces of olive oil or other vegetable oil. (Do not force, as this may cause vomiting.) Then call a poison control center, doctor, or hospital at once. Prepare to rush the child to a hospital.

Sulfuric acid

Do *not* induce vomiting. Give milk of magnesia, 4 to 10 ounces; or bicarbonate of soda, 1 tablespoon to 8 ounces of water; or 4 to 10 ounces of a mild soap solution (not a detergent). Follow any of these by up to 8 ounces of milk, olive oil or other vegetable oil, or egg white. Prepare to rush the child to the hospital.

Summer black oil
Give 1 to 2 ounces of olive oil or other vegetable oil. (Do not force, as this may cause vomiting.) Prepare to rush the child to a hospital.

Suntan lotions
Induce vomiting.

Thorazine
Induce vomiting.

Tobacco
Induce vomiting.

Toilet-bowl cleaners
Do *not* induce vomiting. Read the label for ingredients and antidote. If you are not certain of the antidote, call a poison control center. In case of delay give 7 to 10 ounces of milk or water. Do not force.

Most toilet cleaners are acidic. Give milk of magnesia, 4 to 10 ounces; or bicarbonate of soda, 1 tablespoon to 8 ounces of water; or 4 to 10 ounces of a mild soap solution (not a detergent). Follow any of these by up to 8 ounces of milk, olive oil or other vegetable oil, or egg white.

For cleaners containing lye (sodium hydroxide, potassium hydroxide), give 1 part vinegar to 4 parts water (give 4 to 7 ounces); or lemon juice, 3 to 7 ounces; or orange juice, 4 to 10 ounces. Follow any of these by up to 8 ounces of milk, olive oil or other vegetable oil, or egg white.

Tranquilizers
Induce vomiting.

Turpentine
Give 1 to 2 ounces of olive oil or other vegetable oil. (Do not force, as this may cause vomiting.) Then call a poison control center, doctor, or hospital at once. Prepare to rush the child to the hospital.

Varnish
Induce vomiting.

Vitamins
Induce vomiting if more than six pills are taken.

Warfarin
Induce vomiting.

Washing soda
Give 1 part vinegar to 4 parts water (give 4 to 7 ounces); or lemon juice, 3 to 7 ounces; or orange juice, 4 to 10 ounces. Follow any of these by up to 8 ounces of milk, olive oil or other vegetable oil, or egg white. Then call a poison control center,

doctor, or hospital at once. Prepare to rush the child to the hospital.

Wintergreen, oil of
Induce vomiting.

Inhaled fumes or gases If the child is overcome by dense smoke from fires, fumes from an auto accident, poisonous chemicals, or fuel gases:

1. Get the child into fresh air.
2. Loosen his clothing.
3. If the child is not breathing, start mouth-to-mouth resuscitation immediately (see **Mouth-to-mouth resuscitation**). Do not stop until he is breathing normally or help arrives.
4. Have someone call a doctor, hospital, or rescue unit.
5. Get the child to a hospital as quickly as possible.

Contact with poisonous substances
Eyes

1. Remove contact lenses if worn. Never permit the eye to be rubbed.
2. Gently wash out the child's eye immediately with a great deal of water (or milk if no water is available) for at least five minutes, with eyelids held open.
3. Call a doctor, hospital, or poison control center, and take the child for further treatment to the doctor or hospital.

Skin (with acids, lye, other caustics, pesticides)

1. Wash off skin immediately with a large amount of water; use soap if available.
2. Remove all contaminated clothing.
3. Call a doctor, hospital, or poison control center for further advice.

See also **Bee stings; Food poisoning; Lead poisoning; Mushroom poisoning; Plants, poisonous; Rabies; Snakes and snakebites.**

Poliomyelitis
Infantile paralysis. An infectious disease caused by a virus, occurring primarily in children and young people. This disease affects the nervous system and in many cases produces a paralysis of various muscles and may, by paralyzing the respiratory muscles, even cause death. It is preventable with poliomyelitis vaccine.

Poliomyelitis is transmitted by direct contact with the patient or with water or food contaminated by the feces of the patient. The virus may be present in the secretions of the nose and throat for approximately five days after the onset, and in the feces for a period of several weeks. The incubation period usually lasts between seven and fourteen days after exposure to the infection.

Symptoms and treatment The first symptoms are usually fever, vomiting, headache, and irritability. These may last several days and then subside for two or even three days. Then the fever rises again to 102 or 103 degrees. There is a severe headache and a stiffness of the neck and back and pain in the affected muscles. Paralysis of the muscles follows in approximately 10 to 15 percent of all cases.

No specific treatment is available. Symptoms are treated as they arise. Children who develop a weakness or paralysis of the breathing muscles are placed within a tank-like respirator, commonly called an iron lung. This expands and contracts the chest until the weakened muscles regain strength.

Care of exposed children and immunization Although gamma globulin has been administered to children who have been exposed to the disease, this treatment is of questionable value.

Immunization against the disease is achieved by either the Sabin live poliomyelitis vaccine (given orally in three monthly doses followed by booster doses at approximately four-year intervals) or the Salk killed poliomyelitis vaccine (given by injection and followed by booster inoculations every two years).

See also **Sabin vaccine; Salk vaccine.**

Polishes and waxes, poisoning by see **Poisons: first-aid treatment.**

Politeness see **Manners.**

Pollens
The usually tiny fertilizing elements of flowering plants. Pollens are to the plants what the sperm cells are to animals. In many plants the pollen is scattered by the wind and so during the period of pollination the air contains many pollen particles.

A large number of children, and adults as well, are sensitive to these pollens in the air they breathe. Especially important are the tree pollens, which are given off in late April and May; the pollen of timothy grass and (although less important) the pollen of plantain, from about May 15 to July 15, which cause early hay fever or "rose fever"; and the ragweed pollen, which is in the air from approximately August 15 to the first frost.

People sensitive to these pollens have irritated and discharging noses as well as red and irritated eyes. Treatment includes antihistamine therapy or inoculations to desensitize against specific pollens.

See also **Hay fever.**

Pollution, air see **Air pollution.**

Polycystic kidneys see **Kidneys, polycystic.**

Poor appetite see **Appetite, poor.**

Popularity

Strongly desired by boys and girls, popularity usually becomes important during the school-age years when it means a great deal to a child not only to be a member of a group but to be admired and looked up to. This does not mean though that to be happy a child must be popular with the whole class or group of children he associates with. A child can get along very well with one or two good friends with whom he can communicate freely and share interests. As a matter of fact, some children prefer this.

Parents should do everything reasonable to aid their children in establishing and maintaining friendships. During the school years the children's friends should be invited over, taken on special trips or to theaters, and if possible, invited to sleep over.

In adolescence, a youngster wants not only to be popular and to have friends, but also to be certain of being as attractive as possible. If there is anything parents can do to help their teen-ager to be more attractive, they should certainly do so (see **Adolescent, helping to be more attractive**).

Parents, of course, cannot arrange for their children to be popular. Some children are and remain unpopular, despite all the usual efforts parents make to help them in this area. The unpopularity may reflect a psychological or physical problem of the child's or, in some cases, it may mean that the child is being unfairly discriminated against. In such cases parents must make even greater efforts to reassure the child and get to the root of the problem.

See also **Unpopularity**.

Port-wine stains   see **Birthmarks**.

Postmature baby

It is only within recent years that obstetricians and pediatricians have realized that there are real dangers to an infant when a mother is two weeks or more overdue.

The postmature baby is usually larger, often weighing 9 or 10 pounds, and the large size presents problems before and during birth.

First, these big babies apparently cannot get adequate nutrition from their mother's blood. As a result they are often somewhat malnourished with a lack of fatty tissue beneath the skin. The skin is loose, dry, glossy, and scaly at birth. Instead of being stronger babies, they are generally weaker at first.

These large babies may also occasionally not be able to get adequate oxygen from the mother's blood because of their size, and may develop mild brain dysfunction (see **Brain dysfunction, mild**).

A primary danger, of course, for large-size babies is that their passage through the birth canal is usually much more difficult than that of the infant of normal size. As a result, the obstetrician may have to use forceps to aid in the delivery or may even need to perform a Caesarian section.

The postmature baby will usually respond very quickly to food and plenty of fluids, but for safety's sake the present policy of good obstetrics is to induce labor, thus bringing on the birth of the baby artificially when a pregnancy has reached forty-two weeks, that is, two weeks over the due date.

Postnasal drip

A postnasal discharge of mucus or mucus mixed with pus is not uncommon in childhood. The condition is usually indicated if a child coughs when he lies down. During the day he automatically swallows the discharge, while at night it collects in the back of his throat and causes him to cough.

The cause of postnasal discharge should be determined by the child's doctor. Generally, the discharge is the result of infections or allergic reactions of the adenoids or the sinuses. If caused by an infection, the condition can usually be treated successfully by antibiotic therapy. If caused by an allergic reaction, the condition can be treated successfully by removing the agent responsible, by oral antihistamine therapy, or, occasionally, by injecting small amounts of the offending agent, increasing the amount gradually, at intervals of a few days to a week, until the body builds up a toleration.

See also **Allergy**.

Postpartum depression

A type of severe depression that may affect a new mother following the birth of her baby. The time of onset varies from as early as three days after the baby's birth to as late as three to twelve months following its birth. The depression may last from a few weeks to a few months, or longer.

Postpartum depression is not to be confused with "maternity blues," a milder depression that often occurs on about the third day after birth when the breast milk is coming in. This only lasts a day or two and subsides spontaneously (see **Maternity blues**).

Often the psychological stress of the pregnancy appears to be the cause of the condition, for in many cases of postpartum depression the mother has been fearful of the pregnancy and even opposed to it. This may lead to conflicting feelings toward the infant, and perhaps even to a hostile attitude toward both the baby and the husband. There may be an underlying anxiety concerning femininity and the responsibilities of motherhood, and there may be a fear of having been physically harmed by the birth of the baby.

Sometimes, it appears that a latent tendency to emotional depression has been brought to the surface by the strain of pregnancy and birth. In such cases, it seems that it is not so much the pregnancy that has caused the depression, but that the woman was in a basically vulnerable emotional state in which depression could be triggered by any of a great number of possible experiences.

In rarer instances, the depression is the result of toxic bodily conditions caused by malfunctioning kidneys or severe episodes of vomiting.

It is important that depression not be dismissed without treatment, for the mother may be desperately unhappy and even harm herself or the baby. Treatment consists of psychotherapy and the use of antidepressant drugs. It is usually very successful.

The psychotherapist gives the mother support and reassurance and helps her to work through her problems—hostile and guilty feelings toward her child and husband; conflicts concerning motherhood and femininity; fears concerning bodily damage from the birth; and fears of the responsibilities facing her.

Posture

The posture of a child varies with his age, physical health, muscle tone, and emotional state.

Up to the age of 3, many young children stand with the abdomen protruding and the back swayed in. Termed

A child under the age of 4 may appear to have poor posture. But this is normal; as the muscles strengthen, the child will stand straighter.

"infantile posture," it is usually the result of poor muscle tone at that stage of development. As children become more active, the abdominal muscles strengthen and hold in the abdomen, and the youngsters carry themselves more erect.

Another age period when posture is often poor is during early adolescence, a time during which the child is growing rapidly in height and the muscles have not as yet adjusted to the growth. This is the age when so many children are constantly nagged to "sit up straight."

Good physical health is important in the development and maintenance of good posture. A child who is frequently ill or who has a chronic infection is not likely to have good muscle tone and may be depressed emotionally as well. Such a child will often droop in posture until he is healthy and happy again.

Most poor posture in children is caused by poor muscle tone. Today the American child sits for hours watching television, does few or no chores requiring muscle activity, and often, even if he is active, uses only the muscles of his legs, such as in bicycle riding, skating, running, jumping rope, and so on. More attention to swimming, tennis, and baseball, activities that strengthen the muscles of the arms and shoulders, should improve posture considerably (see **Physical fitness**).

Children who are bored, unhappy, or emotionally upset are often droopy and have poor posture. Many of these same children when actively occupied and enjoying some sport or other activity will carry themselves very well and often with great coordination and grace.

In aiding children to develop improved posture, one should avoid constant nagging—"Sit up straight," "Hold your head up," and so on. Much more can be accomplished by encouragement—for example, complimenting a child on his appearance when he is standing straight. Parents should also try to understand the cause of the poor posture. If it is due to lack of exercise, the child should be encouraged to be more active.

See also **Spine, curvature of.**

Poverty

It has long been recognized that poverty

often causes deep and long-range difficulties in the life of a child. Among these are learning difficulties, delinquency, and vocational and career problems.

The child born to poverty is frequently a disadvantaged child, who lacks in a multitude of ways the opportunities available to children who are on a higher economic level. The mothers as a group get inadequate prenatal care, poorer obstetrical care, and less direction and follow-up in the care of their children. As a result, families of poverty have a higher rate of prematurity and a higher rate of congenital abnormalities and mental retardation.

The newborn infant is subject to a much higher rate of disease, partly because of poor physical conditions, malnutrition, and lack of medical care.

Poverty does not necessarily mean that a child will be deprived of parental love and care, but it often means that a mother must work (frequently in a job that is boring and depressing), thus limiting the time and energy she can give to the child.

The child often grows up in neighborhoods where drugs and crime are commonplace, and because of this proximity, he is likely to become involved in this lifestyle.

Certain children forge ahead in spite of family and personal disadvantages, but poverty is, generally, a great waster of youthful talent and potential.

The answer to most of the problems related to poverty is to eliminate poverty itself, to educate the parents as well as children, to maintain day-care centers where children are well cared for physically, medically, and emotionally, and to develop a means of detecting and helping as early as possible the "problem children" of poverty.

Praise

All children need approval and praise from their parents. Parents too often are quick to criticize a youngster for something of which they disapprove, but fail to praise him when he deserves it. Praise should always be given for accomplishments that are well done, and praise should be given as encouragement when a child is engaged in a worthwhile project or has shown a definite degree of improvement in his schoolwork, some skill, or even his appearance. It should also be given if a child has been helpful, kind, thoughtful, or generous. Praise is part of a general atmosphere of approval that means so much to the child.

It is not wise, however, for parents to praise a child when little or no praise is warranted. Praise must be sincere. For instance, a parent may decide to build up a child by giving him extra praise. The child brings home a picture that he has made at school, a picture that he considers a poor effort. If the parents praise the picture, without conviction, and pin it up on the wall for all to see, the child will realize their insincerity.

Almost all children have at least one ability or talent which deserves praise and encouragement.

Praise can give a child a sense of self-worth and self-esteem. Parents should always be alert for opportunities to give praise when praise is due—it is always a great incentive to the child.

Precocious child see **Intelligence, exceptional; Talent, exceptional.**

Precocious puberty see **Puberty, precocious.**

Prejudice see **Intolerance and prejudice.**

Premature baby

All newborn infants under 5 pounds were once considered premature. Today most physicians classify as premature a small baby born a month or more before its expected birth. For instance, a full nine-months'-pregnancy triplet weighing 3 pounds is a small baby but is not premature. However, a 4-pound 8-ounce baby born at the end of an eight-month pregnancy would be considered premature.

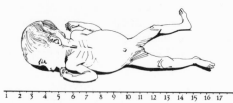

Baby girl born when mother was 6½ months pregnant. Note the lack of fatty tissue. The distension of the abdomen is due to lack of muscular development. But this was a healthy baby, who developed normally in every way.

The care of a premature infant depends largely upon the individual child. Many prematures must be kept in a heated bassinet or incubator, for their bodies are not yet able to regulate their own temperatures. The air in the incubator is kept moist to prevent drying of the mucous membrane of the infant's respiratory tract. Then, also, certain premature infants need extra oxygen or they will turn blue. The amount of oxygen is carefully controlled, since an excess might injure the child's eyes. Some tiny prematures are much too weak even to suck and must be fed through a small tube passed down the throat and into the stomach.

Given excellent care in a modern hospital unit for premature babies, most infants of seven- and eight-month pregnancies will survive. Unfortunately, however, hyaline membrane disease, the most dangerous of all ailments for the newborn, occurs primarily among prematures (see **Hyaline membrane disease**).

Most premature babies grow up to be as strong, tall, and intelligent as any full-term child of normal weight. However, it sometimes takes them at least three years to catch up to full-term children developmentally. A few, especially the early prematures of six and seven months, may have special difficulties, such as hearing or vision impairment, mental retardation, or cerebral palsy. The doctor checks for these potential problems during routine examinations as the infant grows older.

Some well-known prematures who lived long and successful lives were Winston Churchill, 91 years; Charles Darwin, 73 years; Albert Einstein, 76 years; Victor Hugo, 83 years; Sir Isaac Newton, 85 years; Mark Twain, 75 years; Voltaire, 84 years; and Daniel Webster, 70 years.

See also **Incubator.**

Prenatal care

The care of a baby begins at the onset of pregnancy, for the early stages of embryo and fetal development are vital to the normal formation and functioning of the child's body. The mother should carefully follow her obstetrician's directions regarding drugs, the type and amount of food, the type and amount of activity, and the advisability of traveling. Most modern obstetricians advise mothers to refrain from taking any drugs during pregnancy if at all possible. They also advise mothers against smoking cigarettes or, at least, to smoke no more than five or six a day. Although no specific abnormality in, or danger to, infants of cigarette-smoking pregnant women has been reported, it has been demonstrated that their babies are generally smaller than babies of non-smoking mothers. Pediatricians and developmental scientists feel that anything that thwarts the normal growth of an infant cannot be considered harmless. Mothers should also make every attempt to avoid infections during the first three or four months of pregnancy, most especially, of course, German measles (see **German measles**).

The pregnant mother must not only deal with the protection of her unborn infant but also must prepare for the birth of the baby and the care of the child after it is born.

Preparation for the infant's birth is important, since exercises in proper breathing for use during labor and exercises for muscle development may relieve much of the pain and avert the need for drugs or even anethesia in many instances (see **Natural childbirth**).

In preparing for care of the infant after it is born, a mother who plans to nurse her baby should start preparing her breasts under the supervision of her obstetrician (see **Breast feeding**). Attendance at prenatal classes for mothers and fathers is not only very informative but enjoyable as well. Such classes are given by most of the hospitals with large obstetrical units, by the American Red Cross, and by various maternity organizations. Lectures for prospective parents are also valuable in bringing them the most recent concepts of child care. Standard books, pamphlets, and magazines on child care and development are also helpful. It is also a good policy to visit the pediatrician ahead of time—not only to meet him and see that you can relate well to him, but also to ask any questions that have come to mind.

Prepuberty see **Puberty.**

Preschool period
The period of development following the toddler stage and continuing until approximately 5 years of age. It is a very important and exciting time in the child's life.

During this period the child is developing coordination and new physical skills. He is learning how to relate to other children, how to play with them and how to share. He learns confidence and assurance in his dealings with adults outside the home. His language skills are developing rapidly and his thinking is becoming more complex. He is curious about himself sexually and usually develops a recognition of sex differences. The child also begins to learn right from wrong, and anxieties may appear at this time (see **Anxiety**). A boy begins to identify with his father and a girl with her mother.

Certain personal characteristics also start developing—dependence or independence, aggressiveness or passivity, and initiative and a desire for achievement. The child still demands attention, and if a younger child is born in the family at this time, parents can expect outbursts of extreme jealously (see **Sibling rivalry and jealousy**). And this is the age period of the onset of the Oedipus complex, when a child may at times show clear hostility toward the parent of the same sex (see **Oedipus complex**).

In order to help the child make the transition from living almost exclusively within the family to living a great part of his life in school, a nursery school or a play group is often a great benefit. It helps a child to gain in independence, sociability, the ability to relate to adults other than his parents, and a sense of security in the knowledge that there are others who will look after him and meet his needs when his parents are not present (see **Nursery school**).

Prickly heat

A common condition of infants and young children, characterized by small pinpoint red pimples and occasionally tiny blisters. These usually appear when the air temperature is high or when the child is overdressed. It is caused by a slight inflammation around the openings of the ducts of the sweat glands. It usually affects the skin of the neck, the shoulders, and the chest.

It can be prevented by avoiding overdressing and by frequent bathing.

Treatment consists in keeping the area dry, especially by powdering with absorbent powders such as Ammen's powder or cornstarch (although this tends to cake). The irritation can also be treated by patting the area with calamine lotion (zinc carbonate with one percent phenol) or Caladryl lotion (zinc carbonate, plus a little camphor, Benadryl—diphenhydramine hydrochloride—and rubbing alcohol).

Privacy

There are times in everyone's life when privacy is desired, the need for it varying with the individual person. Children also desire privacy at times.

Privacy is rarely demanded by the preschool child unless the youngster is engaged in a project to surprise a parent or some other member of the family. However, during the school years many children do not want anyone walking into their rooms without permission. At this age period also, many children want their own area to play in or to be in with their friends, and do not want to be disturbed or annoyed by a younger or older brother or sister or even at times

by their parents. Parents should respect these desires and do what they can to enable a child to have his privacy. If a child cannot have his own room, partition off part of a room by screens, curtains, bookcases, or room dividers, or if the room is large enough, by a wallboard partition. During the school years also, most children demand toilet privacy, following their parents' example.

During prepuberty and the teen-age years, privacy becomes very important for most children. They want to telephone their friends in private and insist on getting their mail unopened. They often close the door when their friends are with them. Some of them write diaries and lock them away in drawers. A child's diaries or letters should never be read by parents unless the child so desires. Parents should always respect their child's privacy and do everything they can to insure it.

Profession, guiding child toward   see **Career, guiding children toward.**

Projectile vomiting   see **Vomiting.**

Promiscuity   see **Sexual behavior in adolescence.**

Prostration, heat   see **Heat exhaustion.**

Protective parent   see **Overprotective parent.**

Protein   see **Nutrition.**

Protein deficiency   see **Kwashiorkor.**

Psychiatrist, Psychoanalyst, and Psychologist

Child psychiatrist   A child psychiatrist is a doctor who has had special training in the emotional development of children, family relationships, and the causes of behavior disorders. He has also received training in the treatment of personality problems. Through his medical background he is further skilled in treating children with brain damage, and in differentiating symptoms that are due to physical causes from those that are largely due to emotional causes.

The training of a child psychiatrist qualified by the American Board of Psychiatry includes four years of medical school, a general internship of one or two years, two years of full-time training in a psychiatric hospital, and two years of full-time work in a child psychiatry clinic or mental health center. Then he must have two years of practice and pass an examination before he is qualified as a child psychiatrist.

Child psychoanalyst The child psychoanalyst may be either a child psychiatrist or psychologist. He should also have had training in one of the schools of psychoanalysis. Unfortunately, in most states there are no necessary qualifications for the title of psychoanalyst or psychotherapist. Any person can assume the title, even without the proper background or training. A parent seeking a psychoanalyst for his child should carefully check his credentials.

Freudian analysis relates much of a child's behavior problems to his experiences during infancy and early childhood, and to the conflict between a child's instinctual desires and his difficulty in satisfying these desires. It is held that behavior problems reflect subconscious feelings of anger and fear that were provoked by such an early conflict and have never been resolved. Other schools of analysis, while not rejecting the importance of early childhood experiences, give relatively more attention to

social and cultural factors and day-to-day events and pressures in a child's life. In the course of psychoanalysis the analyst studies the child's drawings and play activities and talks with him about his dreams and his feelings toward his family, friends, and teachers. The child eventually discloses the basic reasons for his problems. Once these are unearthed and discussed, the behavioral difficulties will usually subside.

Psychoanalysis, because of the method used, is somewhat more time-consuming than psychotherapy.

Child psychologist A child psychologist may be a testing psychologist, school psychologist, or clinical, or treatment, psychologist.

Every certified child psychologist must complete a Ph.D. program in educational or clinical psychology and have special training of one to two years in the particular area in which he plans to work.

Testing psychologist. Also called psychometrician, he is trained and skilled in testing a child to determine his level of intelligence at the time of testing, his level and adequacy of emotional development, the possible causes of his emotional problems, and his interests and aptitudes. A testing psychologist can also determine whether there may be some neurological disorder influencing the child's behavior.

The tests are for diagnosis only and not for treatment. They may lead, however, to recommendations for treating a child's emotional problems, handling his educational difficulties, or placing him in special schools more attuned to his mental capacity or personality, or schools concentrating on some particular learning problem such as that caused by mild brain dysfunction (see **Tests**).

School psychologist. He limits his activity, as a rule, to students' learning problems and emotional problems. He aids in diagnosing the causes of these problems through testing and observation, and advises the teachers on how to help children who are having difficulties. He often counsels these children and gives guidance to their parents. He rarely gives psychotherapy to the pupils.

Clinical, or treatment, psychologist. He specializes in psychotherapy for children. Parents considering turning to a treatment psychologist should ascertain that he has had special training in therapy with children. The local Mental Health Association will provide this information.

Psychosis see **Autism; Schizophrenia.**

Psychosomatic ailments

The word psychosomatic derives from the terms *psyche,* referring to the mind (as in psychology and psychiatry), and *soma,* referring to the body. Psychosomatic conditions are aches and pains and other physical disorders largely caused by the mind rather than by physical causes.

Psychosomatic ailments are very common during childhood and adolescence. Stomachaches, nausea, and headaches are the most common of these conditions. They are usually in response to some tension or anxiety. They may occur on school days, especially before going to school in the morning. This type of ailment does not typically occur on weekends or holidays unless there is some other cause for tension—even the excitement of going to a birthday party may cause headaches and stomachaches

in some children. These psychosomatic aches and pains are real.

There are other common ailments that are influenced by psychological factors. Asthma and other allergic conditions can be brought on or exaggerated by emotional upsets and tensions. Ulcers and colitis are also related to tension. Another common psychosomatic condition is frequent urination, in which the child must go to the bathroom twenty or thirty times during the day but does not awaken at night to go and does not bed-wet.

All conditions that appear to be psychosomatic should be reported to the doctor to rule out first the possibility that the symptoms may be caused by some real physical conditions.

See also **Hysteria.**

Psychotherapy

The treatment of emotional disorders. Psychotherapy does not include the treatment of behavior disorders resulting from an organic cause, such as the sullenness and apathy of a child whose thyroid gland is not functioning adequately.

Emotional disturbance in childhood is usually caused by some distressing situation within the family or the child's misrepresentation of some situation. A child may feel that his parents love a baby brother more than he is loved. He becomes anxious and upset and may show it by anger, disobedience, aggression, cruelty toward other children, or he may become subdued, depressed, and withdrawn. Whatever the child's symptoms, the aim of the psychotherapist is to discover and uncover the cause of his emotional problems and to remove, as far as possible, the disturbing influence.

In the case of young children who cannot adequately express their anxieties the psychotherapist may use play therapy to uncover the worries that are upsetting the child. Children of approximately 3 to 10 years who cannot or will not talk about their feelings will frequently reveal the problems on their minds while playing with dolls, paints, or other toys and play materials in the permissive and accepting environment of the therapist's office. The play-therapy room typically contains toys, games, art materials, dollhouses, dolls, doctor and nurses kits, darts, and so on, which are both interesting and stimulating to the child. As the child plays much of his tension is released.

The therapist is able to understand the child's problems by the way he plays. For example, a child playing with dolls representing members of a family can reenact family situations—the fights between children, the behavior of his parents, sibling rivalry, and so on. With the release of tension, the child, with the aid of the therapist, is able to face and examine some of his problems. As a consequence he feels differently and is usually able to change his behavior.

With older children, the psychotherapist also establishes a warm rapport, discussing a wide range of subjects with them and gradually learning the conditions that disturb them.

The child is encouraged to express himself freely. This release of cooped-up feelings is often very helpful in relieving the child's anxiety. Further discussions with the therapist may bring to the child a new understanding of his environment and help him to learn more effective ways of dealing with it.

The psychotherapist may also want to meet the parents to talk over the whole family situation (see **Family psychotherapy**).

As a rule, psychotherapy is far more successful and of shorter duration in children than in adults. A child's problems are often less deeply ingrained and he is usually much less inhibited.

Ptomaine poisoning   see **Food poisoning.**

Puberty

The point in development when boys and girls are considered to be sexually mature, that is, when girls have their first menstrual period and boys begin to have nocturnal seminal emissions. In girls it is usually between 12 and 14 years, in boys between 13 and 15. It can be considered as the point between prepuberty and adolescence.

Prepuberty starts in girls as a rule between 9 and 11 years with the gradual development of the breasts and the growth of pubic and axillary hair. In boys, prepuberty usually starts at about 12 with enlargement of the penis and testes.

Adolescence is that period of growth from puberty to adult physical maturity. In girls it usually ends at about 18, while in boys it may continue to 21.

See also **Adolescence.**

Puberty, precocious

A condition in which children start developing the physical signs of adolescence at an unusually early age, at times even before 2 years of age.

In girls, breast development is the first sign, followed by the development of the external genitals, the appearance of pubic hair and hair under the arms, and finally by menstruation.

In boys there is enlargement of the

penis, the development of pubic and axillary hair, an increase in the size of the testes, and a change in voice.

In both boys and girls there is a fairly marked increase in weight and height during this period of development. But although these children develop sexually much earlier than usual, their mental and emotional development remains on a level with children of their own age.

For a time, the child who is experiencing precocious puberty is often much taller than his fellow classmates. For instance, such a child at 8 years may be 7 or 8 inches taller than the other children in his class. But after the first fast surge of growth there is a marked slowing down in height gain, and in several years there is no further growth in height. Often in this condition the child who has been the tallest child in the class becomes the smallest child.

The causes of precocious puberty are numerous, and in each specific case diagnostic tests must be made. Among the common causes are tumors of the adrenal or pituitary gland, or of the ovaries or testes, which must be treated surgically. But in some cases no cause can be found. This is called functional precocious puberty.

It is usually very important that both the child and his parents receive psychological help. In little girls especially, there are extra problems because of the development of the breasts, which in a 7- or 8-year-old can be very upsetting. These children must also be guarded against sexual attacks by teen-age boys and men.

Often the parents of the child need much more psychological support than does the child. If the cause is a tumor and it can be removed surgically, the signs of puberty will subside and, if diagnosed early enough, will affect the growth in height only slightly if at all. Where no cause can be found, parents must be reassured that the child is in no danger, that he will not remain the very tallest in the class, that at 12 or 13 years he will probably be about the same height as his classmates, and that he will be capable of normal sexual functioning.

Pubic hair

The hair over the lower abdomen above the genitals. It may appear in girls as early as 9 or 10 years, the average age being approximately 11. In boys, pubic hair usually starts appearing at 12 or 13 years, the average age being 13.

The time of appearance varies with the individual. Some normal and healthy boys and girls do not develop pubic hair until 15 or even 16.

Hair under the arms usually appears one to two years after the appearance of pubic hair.

Pulse

The rate of the heartbeat. This varies greatly during the growth and development of a child. In the newborn infant, the pulse is very rapid, the average rate being 120 to 140 beats per minute. It may even normally go as high as 170 when the baby is crying. As the child grows older, the pulse rate becomes slower but is still very changeable, rising rapidly with physical activity or under emotional stimulation.

The pulse is generally determined by gently pressing the fingertips of the third and fourth fingers of either hand just below the child's inner wrist, under the base of the thumb where an artery comes close to the surface. In infancy it is usually easier to count the pulse by watching the beat of the blood vessels in the baby's neck or on the side of his head while he is sleeping.

Any continued pulse of over 150 in infants or over 120 in older children should be investigated.

The normal approximate pulse rates of children at different ages are shown in the following chart.

Age	Sleeping or Quiet	Average	Active or Emotionally Stimulated
Newborn	100	120	170
1–11 months	80	120	160
2 years	80	110	130
4 years	80	100	120
6 years	75	100	115
8 years	70	90	110
10 years	70	90	110
12 years	70	90	110
14 years	65	80	105
16 years	60	75	100
18 years	55	70	95

Punishment

Ideally, punishment is used to discipline, to correct, and to guide. At times, however, parents use punishment simply as an outlet for their own anger and impatience.

Punishment includes such disciplinary measures as slapping and spanking; depriving a child of some pleasure or privilege, such as watching television or going on an outing with his club; separating him from contact with others, as when he is sent to his room; restricting his activities, such as making him stay home after school; or making him do something he doesn't like to do, such as sending him to bed early or forcing him to write "I will not lie" five hundred times.

Physical punishment should be avoided entirely or, possibly, used only when a child does something that might endanger his life or the lives of others, for example, playing with fire, running into the streets, turning on the gas stove, or climbing up on unguarded windows. In such cases a slap or spanking may be necessary to impress the child with the seriousness of the matter. Generally, however, physical punishment only demonstrates to a child that "might makes right" and that a parent controls only because he is stronger, not because he is right—a very poor lesson for a child to learn.

Some families make a ritual of spanking. The spanking is performed at a set time and in a particular manner. If there is any justification for hitting or slapping a child, this can only be on the grounds of emergency action. Corporal punishment in cold blood, so to speak, is virtually useless as discipline. It leads typically to deviousness or rebelliousness. The child may sullenly learn to accept the humiliation and pain, biding his time until he is too large for the parents to control him in this manner.

As for other types of punishment, it should always be remembered that punishment may have detrimental effects; for example, a child punished for hitting his little brother may desist at home but take out his aggressive feelings on younger children outside the home. Punishment sometimes creates anxieties as to loss of the parents' love. Some children react with abiding resistance and hostility. Often a child will continue to do what he wishes and accept punishment each time as absolving him of guilt. Some children actually seek punishment to focus attention on themselves when they feel adequate attention is lacking.

Does this mean that parents should never punish their children? Of course not, but it does mean that they should keep a close watch on how often they must resort to punishment and whether it is having the effects they seek. Certain rules are also helpful. The parents should always explain clearly to a child why he is being punished. Punishments should be few and reasonable. The punishment should, if possible, fit the "crime." For example, it would be unfair to take away a youngster's treasured bicycle for a week because he hit his little brother; it would probably be more appropriate to make the child go to his room until he settled down. But the bicycle would properly be taken away if the child continuously rode dangerously in traffic.

A word of warning. It is not advisable to punish a child by making him do something that you hope he will develop a liking for. Some parents punish their children by making them practice extra time on the piano or memorize a poem. They feel that at least the child will be engaged in a worthwhile activity. But very probably the price will be a growing dislike for that activity. Above all, remember that approval, rewards, and attention may prevent many of the child's actions that call for punishment.

See also **Discipline; Scolding; Shaming.**

Purpura

A bleeding disease characterized by the appearance of bluish areas, similar to bruises, over the body.

There may be various reasons for this condition. The most common type occurs two to three weeks after an infection; it may also be a response to an allergic reaction. The clotting elements in the blood are greatly reduced, and the walls of the tiny blood vessels (capillaries) in the skin are weakened. Thus bleeding readily occurs beneath the skin.

The condition usually subsides in several weeks to a few months, but at times the child may receive medication and even transfusions. A child with purpura should be under the care of his doctor.

Pushing   see **Biting, kicking, pushing, hitting.**

Pyelitis

Also called pyelonephritis. An infection of the kidney and the outlet of the kidney leading into the tubes that go to the urinary bladder. It is most frequently found in children between 2 months and 5 years of age, and is six times as common among girls as among boys.

The bacteria causing the infection usually enter from the outside through the opening into the bladder, although they may enter from the bloodstream or adjacent tissues directly into the kidney. Congenital abnormalities associated with obstruction to urinary flow may predispose to pyelitis.

The onset of pyelitis may be gradual or sudden. There is usually a fever, which may spike and rise as high as 104 degrees or more. There may be a frequency of urination and pain on urination. There often is a dull pain in the back over the kidney areas. The child may be very irritable and occasionally may be anemic, very weak, and vomit frequently.

The condition can be definitely diagnosed by laboratory studies of the child's urine.

Treatment is largely through chemotherapy and antibiotics continued for weeks and even months. Congenital abnormalities may have to be corrected by surgery.

Pyloric stenosis

The pylorus is the opening of the stomach into the intestines. It is surrounded by a circular muscle which contracts when food is being churned in the stomach and relaxes when food is ready to be passed into the intestines for further digestion. Pyloric stenosis is a condition in which the pylorus is closed by an increase in the size of the surrounding muscle, resulting in a firm mass. Food cannot pass from the stomach into the intestines.

Pyloric stenosis occurs in early infancy, although the primary symptom—projectile vomiting—does not usually appear until the infant is 2 to 3 weeks old. It is five times as common in males as in females.

Signs and symptoms   After a few days of occasional vomiting, the vomiting becomes more frequent and more forceful, sometimes projecting the vomitus 3 to 4 feet from the baby. It usually occurs shortly after a feeding but it may occur an hour or longer after feeding. There is no nausea and the infant takes another feeding avidly after vomiting. The vomitus contains only milk and no bile.

The baby is badly constipated since little or no food passes out of the stomach into the intestines. As the vomiting continues, the baby starts to lose weight, and if the condition is not treated, the weight decreases so rapidly that the skin becomes loose and inelastic. This, plus the dehydration, makes the infant look like a withered, miniature old man.

A definite diagnosis can be made by a physical examination and X rays. Often the doctor can feel the mass of muscle at the end of the stomach by pressing down on the infant's abdomen. He may also be able to observe signs of the stomach's contractions in the form of wavelike movements across the abdomen. X rays indicate that food cannot leave the stomach.

Treatment   The condition is treated successfully by surgery in which the muscle fibers that form the mass closing the pylorus are cut. The infant improves very rapidly following this operation.

In former years attempts were made to treat pyloric stenosis by giving atropine and thick cereal feedings. This treatment rarely gave results and during the attempted treatment the babies would lose weight, dehydrate, and at times become so emaciated that surgery was dangerous. Today surgery is performed while the child is still in good physical condition. In the hands of a good surgeon the operation is not dangerous.

Pylorospasm

In this condition the circular muscle surrounding the pylorus (the opening of the stomach into the intestines) goes into spasm and closes the opening.

The condition occurs, at times, in hyperactive infants or in those who are sensitive to cow's milk formula. It usually starts within the first few days of life, and causes projectile vomiting

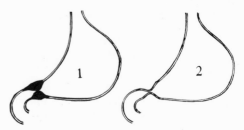

In pyloric stenosis (1) there is a thickening of the muscle between the stomach and the intestines. In a pylorospasm (2) a constriction of the muscle blocks the passage.

shortly after the formula has been taken.

Pylorospasm can be relieved in almost every instance by giving the baby oral atropine shortly before each feeding, which relaxes the muscle, or shifting the baby to a substitute formula that does not contain cow's milk. The condition usually subsides before a child is 3 months old.

Pylorospasm differs from pyloric stenosis, in which the circular muscle enlarges and forms a mass that closes the pylorus—a condition that almost always requires surgery.

Q

Quadruplets see **Multiple births.**

Quarantine
Strict isolation, often regulated by law, to prevent the spread of a contagious disease. Up to about the 1940s, before antibiotics were widely available, quarantine laws were in force in most towns and cities. A sign was placed on the door of a home when a member of the household had such diseases as measles, scarlet fever, diphtheria, whooping cough, or chicken pox. Quarantine and the identification of such houses with signs have largely been discontinued. Most children are now immunized against diphtheria, whooping cough, measles, and poliomyelitis, and a great many are also immunized against German measles and mumps as well.

See also **Isolation of contagious persons.**

Quarrels
Quarrels among children are common and normal. The most common cause is rivalry between children in the same family. Other causes may be unhappiness, boredom, fatigue, or illness.

Generally, if children are to express themselves and defend themselves and their belongings, one must expect a certain amount of quarreling. Quarrels between children in the same family or between children and their friends usually last only a short time and the opponents become friends again. It is much better for parents to let children work out their own quarrels and arguments rather than to intercede in an attempt to settle or stop the dispute.

However, a child who constantly quarrels should be observed carefully. He may feel unloved or be generally unhappy or run-down physically, and the cause should be discovered.

The treatment, of course, depends upon the cause. Usually much can be done to relieve or even remove the causes, but it may at times be a gradual process.

If the quarreling is caused by boredom, parents can attempt to keep the child occupied. Sometimes a punching bag, a knockdown dummy, a hammer board, and other active play equipment that allows a child to rid himself of cooped-up energy and aggression is helpful. An older child can be given materials to arouse his interests in such hobbies as photography, painting, model building, and so on.

Parents should also be certain that the child is getting adequate rest and is in good physical condition. Cultivating the child's friendships is also important—a younger child who lacks friends should not be allowed to interfere with an older child and his friends, or vice versa. Parents should always remember, however, that with normally active, healthy, and even happy children, quarreling will inevitably take place.

See also **Sibling rivalry and jealousy.**

Questions   see **Curiosity; Sex curiosity and interests; Sex education in the home.**

Quinsy sore throat

An abscess complicating tonsillitis. Early treatment with antibiotic therapy has almost eliminated the condition.

The abscess in a quinsy sore throat must be lanced and drained. The condition is extremely painful, and the swollen glands (lymph nodes) in the front of the neck are also very tender.

R

Rabies

An almost always fatal disease, rabies is caused by the bite of a rabid animal (most often a dog, cat, squirrel, fox, wolf, or bat). The first recovery from the disease was reported in 1971 after intensive treatment.

Rabies is caused by a virus in the saliva of the infected animal. The virus cannot penetrate the intact skin, but once the skin is bitten and torn, the virus gets into the bloodstream and attacks the nerve system of the body. At first there is general excitation and spasms of the muscles of the throat on any attempt to take food or water— hence the term hydrophobia, or fear of water. Later there are severe convulsive seizures, often at the slightest sound.

Prevention Since the disease is almost always fatal, prevention is of the utmost importance. First, if a child is bitten and the skin torn even the slightest bit, the bite should be carefully washed with soap and water. The doctor or a hospital should be notified, and the animal that bit the child should be found, if at all possible, and placed under veterinary observation. A rabid animal is usually quite sick and dies within a week. A sick stray animal will be killed so that the brain can be examined for signs of rabies.

If the child was bitten by a squirrel or other wild animal, the local health officer will advise on the possibility of rabies.

If the animal cannot be found or is pronounced rabid, the child must receive immunization with hyperimmune anti-rabies serum or with anti-rabies vaccine. The hyperimmune serum is given in one or two doses within twenty-four to forty-eight hours after the child is bitten. The rabies vaccine is usually given by injection under the skin once a day for fourteen days. The child can, however, continue his normal activities during treatment.

The bites of pet animals never, as a rule, cause rabies unless the pet has been bitten by an animal that has the disease. Nevertheless, the wound should be carefully washed and kept clean, and the doctor should be notified.

Racial prejudice see **Intolerance and prejudice.**

Rage see **Anger; Temper and temper tantrums.**

Ragweed see **Hay fever.**

Rapid heartbeat see **Tachycardia, paroxysmal.**

Rashes

The numerous rashes of infancy and childhood vary greatly in cause, appearance, and treatment:

1. Contact rashes, which are caused by some substance irritating to the surface of the skin. Among these are diaper

rash, rashes from soap sensitivity, wool sensitivity, and poison ivy.

2. Allergic rashes, which are caused by a food, medicine, or other substance that the child has swallowed. Typical of these are eczema, hives, and the rashes resulting from drug sensitivity.

3. Rashes that accompany various contagious diseases, such as chicken pox, measles, German measles, and scarlet fever.

4. Rashes caused by bacteria on the surface of the skin or in the bloodstream. Pustular dermatitis (tiny pimple pus heads) is a common surface infection in infants. Among the rashes resulting from bloodstream infections are those of meningococcosis, typhoid fever, Rocky Mountain spotted fever, and rat-bite fever.

5. Rashes of unknown origin. Typical among these rashes are psoriasis and pityriasis rosea. The doctor should be consulted to diagnose and to prescribe treatment for a rash of unknown origin.

Rat-bite fever

Resulting from the bite of a rat, this disease is fairly common among children living in poor and congested areas. It is caused by spiral-shaped bacteria that enter the system through the wound. Not all rats are infected with these bacteria, but many are.

Symptoms   At first the wound heals. This is followed in one to four weeks by a painful swelling of the area. The tissue then breaks down, leaving an open ulcer. At the same time the lymph glands in the area swell up and fever suddenly appears, rising from 102 to 105 degrees. Then a spotted, purplish, blotchy rash appears, especially over the face and trunk. The child has nausea and vomit-ing, general achiness, and occasionally delirium and convulsions.

After about three or four days, the symptoms subside. No fever occurs for three to five days, and then all the symptoms reappear. Fever may develop off and on for some months before completely disappearing.

Diagnosis and treatment   The spiral-shaped bacteria may be identified by microscopic examination of the serum obtained from the area of the bite.

Penicillin usually brings a prompt cure of the disease. If untreated, the child may become severely anemic, debilitated, and may even die.

Reading   see **Books; Dyslexia; Learning difficulties; Reading readiness.**

Reading, difficulties with   see **Learning difficulties.**

Reading to child   see **Books.**

Reading light   see **Lighting.**

Reading readiness

All children have individual patterns of acquiring learning skills. Reading ability is one area in the learning process in which wide variations exist in the age at which children are ready to acquire this skill.

This variation exists because all the skills—physical, intellectual, visual, language, listening, social, and emotional—must be developed to a certain point before a child is ready to be able to read. In addition, the amount of stimulation, discussion, and experiences in a child's life also increases the level of readiness for reading. For example, reading to the child, conversing with him, offering him varied experiences and discussing them with him are all helpful in the development of the child's reading readiness. (See **Books; Stimulating the child.**)

It is important, however, that parents do not overpressure a child in their enthusiastic efforts to aid him in his preparation for reading. This can cause resistance on the child's part and may delay his learning to read.

Certain signs indicate reading readiness. When children start recognizing letters, recognizing their own names and the names of their friends, start reading signs on storefronts, or on food packages, it indicates they are ready to begin reading.

There are also reading readiness tests prepared for schools to aid in gauging the proper time for a child to begin reading instruction.

Recreational organizations

Many organized recreational groups for children are available. The most widely known which are described below, have benefited countless millions of children in the past. These and other recreational organizations may be particularly enjoyable for only children or for children who do not have the companionship of others their own age. Parents should explore the range of organizations in their community to find those that fit the interests of their own child. The addresses of local groups can usually be found in the local telephone book; national headquarters addresses are included at the end of each description.

American Youth Hostels The American branch of a worldwide organization of overnight accommodations—farms, homes, camps, community centers, churches, or schools—for hikers and bikers.

Hostels provide separate sleeping quarters and washrooms for boys and girls and a common kitchen. They supply beds, blankets, cooking utensils, and cleaning equipment. The hostelers buy and cook their own meals and do their own cleaning up. Beer and other alcoholic beverages are not allowed on hostel property. Most hostels are supervised by houseparents.

Traveling from hostel to hostel is enjoyed by many teen-agers. It is most usually a weekend or a vacation trip. The daily distance is usually 15 to 40 miles for cyclists or 8 to 10 miles for hikers.

Hostels have been established in thirty-two countries, including hundreds in the United States and Canada. They are open only to members of one of the hosteling organizations. Members receive a pass allowing them to use any hostel facility in the world, a handbook describing the location and facilities of each hostel, and lists of planned group trips.

The national headquarters of the American Youth Hostels, Inc., is 20 West 17 Street, New York, N.Y. 10011.

Boy Scouts A worldwide, nonsectarian, nonpolitical organization of boys aged 8 to 17. The purpose of the organization is to improve mental, moral, and physical development, to increase knowledge of the outdoors, and to train for responsible citizenship. There are more than 4 million Boy Scouts in the United States and several million in other countries, organized in troops composed of boys who live in the same locality or who go to the same school, church, or synagogue. They are under the supervision of trained adults, usually volunteers.

The Scouts offer numerous activities involving many special skills. Among the activities are swimming, hiking, camping, photography, music, electronics, canoeing, arts and crafts, riflery, archery, horsemanship, skiing, and small boat sailing. These activities offer the opportunity for learning the principles of conservation, lifesaving, woodsmanship, first aid, map reading, cooking, and astronomy, as well as many other subjects.

Junior Boy Scouts, aged 8 to 10, are called Cub Scouts. Their groups are usually led by a mother of one of the boys (a Den Mother). The youngsters join in games, cookouts, picnics, and other constructive activities.

The National Council of the Boy Scouts of America is at North Brunswick, N.J. 08902.

Camp Fire Girls   A nonsectarian, interracial organization devoted to developing the interests and capabilities of girls aged 7 to 18. There are three age groups.

The Blue Bird Program (ages 7 and 8) undertakes simple creative projects, such as crafts, dancing, singing, and games.

The Camp Fire Girls (ages 9 through 11) can choose to develop individual skills in seven fields: home, outdoors, creative arts, science, business, sports, and games.

The Horizon Club (high school girls) offers activities more directly related to the girls' future. They explore career possibilities, engage in coed activities, do volunteer work for the community, and take special trips and expeditions across the United States. Some go to foreign countries to learn how other people live.

Most of the group leaders are volunteers. The Division of Field Services of the Camp Fire Girls, Inc., is at 65 Worth Street, New York, N.Y. 10013.

4-H Clubs   An organization primarily for boys and girls in rural areas of the United States and Canada, aged 9 to 19 (in the Canadian provinces of Ontario and Alberta, aged 12 to 21). The 4-H stands for Head, Hands, Heart, and Health. The emphasis is on learning—about science and scientific methods, farm production, and home management—by doing, to prepare members for their adult lives.

Recently the 4-H Clubs have become active in cities as well, with outings, projects, and activities especially designed for children who may have little chance to travel out of their neighborhoods and few outlets for their energy. The organization also brings animals into the city for children to see, and tries to acquaint them with farm life.

More than 96,000 4-H Clubs are active in the United States with a membership of about 3 million under the leadership of more than 360,000 adult volunteers. Each club meets at least once a month, and each meeting has some educational feature—movie, lecture, discussion. The clubs also hold picnics, athletic events, hikes, and dramatic presentations, and many have bands and orchestras. There are also 3,000 4-H Club camps, attended each year by about 262,000 boys and girls.

Members select their specific projects. In most states members can choose one project from a group of about fifty. Among the projects are cattle raising, cotton growing, crop production, forestry, seeds, health and fitness, home management, soil, wildlife and nature. Each year many members compete for prizes in crop or cattle raising, sewing, and preparing foods.

The projects are supervised in the United States by the Federal Extension Service, U.S. Department of Agriculture (Washington, D.C. 20250), which works in conjunction with the state agricultural colleges.

Girl Scouts A worldwide, nonsectarian organization of girls with the same aims as the Boy Scouts, for girls from 7 through 17. Almost 4 million Girl Scouts in the United States and hundreds of thousands in other countries are organized in troops of from eight to thirty girls. They are under the supervision of at least two adult leaders. The troops are divided into three age groups, which pursue projects related to their interests and capabilities: Brownies, age 7 to 9; Intermediates, age 10 to 13; and Senior Girl Scouts, age 14 through 17.

Among the activities offered the Scouts to develop their interests or to find new interests are those related to the home and the arts—dancing, music, dramatics, literature—as well as arts and crafts, science, nature, health, safety, and the out-of-doors. Camping trips are planned and encouraged for fun, for learning new skills and learning about nature, and for developing resourcefulness, self-reliance, and cooperation.

Girl Scouts of the U.S.A. is at 830 Third Avenue, New York, N.Y. 10022.

YMCA, YWCA, YMHA, YWHA Worldwide community center and recreational organizations primarily for young adults but offering many services for children and teen-agers, depending on the size of the facilities of the individual institution.

The Young Men's and Young Women's Christian Associations have branches in almost all larger communities. The Young Men's and Young Women's Hebrew Associations are found in the larger cities and in towns and cities that have a large Jewish community. The facilities and services of all Y groups are nonsectarian and are open to all regardless of race or religion. Both the Christian and Hebrew Y's, however, aim at wide social services in the context of a Christian or Jewish ideal.

The range of activities for children may include (depending on the individual Y) swimming lessons; karate and judo; gymnastics; basketball and handball; square and social dancing and modern dance; dramatics; music lessons, orchestras and bands, and choral groups; tutoring for children with learning problems and counseling for emotional and career problems. There are many coed clubs. In the larger cities relatively inexpensive hotel-like accommodations are available.

The Young Women's Christian Association of the U.S.A. is at 600 Lexington Avenue, New York, N.Y. 10022; the National Council of the Young Men's Christian Association at 291 Broadway, New York, N.Y. 10007; the World Federation of YMHAs and Jewish Community Centers, at 15 East 26 Street, New York, N.Y. 10010.

Rectal fissure see **Anal fissure.**

Rectal temperature see **Temperature taking.**

Regression

A return to a less mature level of behavior, which usually occurs in response to a frustrating or threatening situation. Almost all children, and adults as well, regress to earlier forms of behavior at one time or another. The regression releases tension and returns the individual to a stage in his life when such behavior satisfied his needs and calmed him down.

For example, many 3- or 4-year-olds regress considerably when a younger brother or sister is born. The new baby, of necessity, receives a great deal of attention, and the older child, often justifiably, feels neglected and jealous. In an attempt to gain his parents' attention, he becomes, like the new baby, infantile in his behavior. He frequently soils and wets again, sucks his fingers, uses baby talk, and at times even creeps.

An adolescent who is unable to express or communicate his feelings may fly into a rage, screaming and crying as a 3-year-old would, and storm out of the room.

Although the regression itself is an indication that the child is unhappy and needs parental help, it is only when regressive behavior becomes too frequent or lasts so long that the child has difficulty returning to his normal state that the parent should have real concern. It is usually advisable for the parent to seek the help of the child's doctor, a psychological counselor, a child guidance clinic, or some other counseling agency if regression persists.

Regurgitation

The common "spitting up" done by many infants during or shortly after a feeding. It is of no consequence unless large amounts of milk are regurgitated. Usually, however, only a small amount is pushed out of the stomach by a gas bubble during a burp.

Sometimes the spitting up results from an incomplete closure of the top of the stomach that allows some of the contents to be forced out when the stomach pumps during digestion. The condition almost always subsides spontaneously and completely before a child is a year old.

Regurgitation, unlike vomiting, in which the stomach contents are often projected some distance from the child, is usually without force.

See **Rumination; Vomiting.**

Rejection

All children, understandably, frequently feel rejected by their parents during their infancy and childhood. Much of the time there is no real rejection—although there may be unintentional rejection. But there may be rejection in the true sense of the word—at times from neglect, at other times because parents think primarily of themselves and their own pleasures.

Feelings of rejection frequently revolve around separation. An infant under a year of age, for example, often cries and screams if his mother walks out of the room. During the toddler stage, many children feel rejected when parents leave the home to go shopping or to spend an evening out. Also, if a parent must be away because of necessity, such as going to a hospital or being on a business trip, the child may feel rejected and deserted in spite of accustomed baby-sitters and even grandparents. And if a home breaks up through divorce or separation, the child feels rejected by the person who leaves. The same may be said about the death of a parent. The young child does not understand why a parent should leave—and he takes this disappearance of someone he loves as a desertion and rejection (see

Death as children see it; Divorce; Separation).

Another common cause for a child's feeling of rejection is related to the birth of a new baby in the family, especially when the older child is between 2½ and 5 years of age and has become accustomed to receiving most of the parents' attention. The time and care that must be devoted to the new baby often makes the older child feel that the infant is more loved—and so he feels badly neglected (see **Sibling rivalry and jealousy**).

Real rejection occurs when parents of young children, especially children under 5, go away for pleasure trips of a week or more, leaving the children at home feeling deserted and unloved—even if they are with their grandparents or their favorite baby-sitter. Real rejection also occurs when parents spend their weekends golfing, playing cards, or visiting friends without showing attention to their children or giving them a sense of being wanted and belonging. There is also serious neglect and rejection when parents pay little or no attention to their child's progress in school, when they show little or no approval or praise, when they show little or no interest in what a child is doing, where he is, and who he is with. There is inevitable rejection—often subconscious—when for some reason the parents are disappointed in the child or find him a burden.

Rejection and neglect of children know no economic or social class and cause great suffering. Rejected children may become resentful, asocial, and even delinquent; or they may become withdrawn and discouraged, feeling inadequate, insecure, and unwanted.

Feelings of rejection can be alleviated—or avoided—of course, by letting the child really know and feel that he is loved and wanted, by offering him encouragement and approval and praise when it is warranted, and by showing him that you are deeply interested in him and his activities. Often, however, once the child has developed a deep insecurity and resentment, his feelings of rejection are difficult to dislodge. Parents should face up to the difficulty and psychotherapy should be considered for the child, and similar help for themselves to try to repair the family situation. Prompt action may avoid a great deal of unhappiness for both the parents and the child.

Religion

A common question of parents who do not have strong religious commitments is whether to bring up a child with a particular religious background or to wait until he is a teen-ager or even older and let him decide on a religion of his choice or no religion at all.

For deeply religious parents who rear their children in a religious tradition from the time they are very young the question poses no problem. Although religion cannot be forced, it can be encouraged, and a religious education with its teachings and practices is usually accepted by children from families with a religious tradition. Occasionally, however, children in the United States do not follow the religion of their parents when they grow up. The great variety of religious beliefs, or the lack of any religious belief at all, sometimes contributes to a break in the family's religious tradition. It is regretful when such a break brings bitterness and discord, for religion should be, and often is, a source of love and hope among people.

For parents who are not strong believers themselves, however, the question of a religious education remains.

Should they familiarize the child with the traditions and concepts of religion in general or with the particular religion associated with their family background, or wait and let the child decide for himself? The answer is difficult. For parents to pretend a religious concern that they do not really feel, for the child's sake, will not work. A child is quick to recognize a lack of sincerity in his parents' feelings and interest. Parents must follow their conscience and be honest with the child, for an insincere commitment is a poor introduction to religion.

No evidence exists that children with a religious background are any better adjusted emotionally or morally than children without this background. Ethical behavior and principles largely depend upon the child's total experience and the living example of his parents.

Often adolescents without any religious background will seek some form of religious affiliation. Or adolescents raised in one religion may turn to another. At this age, youngsters are seeking security and asking profound questions, and many feel the need for religion. Parents should respect the young person's right to freedom of feeling and thought. In any case, attempts to interfere will usually have an effect exactly opposite to that sought by the parents.

Religious prejudice see **Intolerance and prejudice.**

Remarriage

How a child reacts to the remarriage of a parent varies greatly depending on the child's age; the situation which caused a separation of the parents (death or divorce); whether it is the father or mother who is remarrying; the length of time between the parents' separation and the stepparent's assumption of a parental role; the child's relationship to the parents; and the reaction of the child to the stepparent and vice-versa.

The problems involved are usually more acute when it is the parent with whom the child lives who is remarrying. At times a child may want a new parent to fill out a lack in his home and his life. But very often a boy or girl resents anyone's taking the place of either of his parents, and can make life in the home very upsetting for both parent and stepparent.

A similar situation also frequently arises when there has been either no father or no mother for a long period of time and the child is jealous of the new relationship, which interferes with the closeness he has had with his remaining parent.

Children who resent their new parents will often do everything in their power to make them unhappy. They may refuse to talk to them; make nasty, uncalled-for remarks; refuse to obey them ("You're not my father. I don't have to obey you!"); or actually tell the stepparent, "Get out. I don't like you!"

Too many stepparents, in the face of this resistance, fight back, at times to such a degree that they endanger their marriage. It is far better for them to absorb this temporary hostility, realizing that they are dealing with a child and not an adult. It also will help greatly in relieving the situation if the stepparent remains friendly and lets the parent of the child exert the authority when it is necessary. An occasional present to the child from the stepparent, without overdoing it, is also helpful. With this approach, the resentment of the child wanes rapidly and acceptance of the relationship is usually gained.

To avoid serious trouble, it is always

advisable for a child to have time to get to know a potential stepparent before the marriage. The child's real parent should take care to discuss why he wants to get married. The child should also be encouraged to discuss his feelings on the subject. But although full sympathy should be given to a child's natural feelings of unhappiness and doubt, the child should not feel that the marriage depends upon his reaction. This is too heavy a responsibility to place on a child; it can only make him feel more anxious, and possibly very guilty.

In the case of a divorce, the worst thing that a parent who is remarrying can do is to let the situation in any way interfere with the child's relationship with the absent parent. This will surely poison the child's attitude toward the new marriage.

Report card   see **Marks for schoolwork.**

Resistance   see **Negativism.**

Respect   see **Disrespect.**

Respirator

An apparatus to produce artificial respiration. There are two types in common use for children: the face-mask respirator and the "iron lung."

There are two kinds of face-mask respirators: one that forces air under pressure into a child's lungs at a rhythmic rate and another in which the delivery of air is triggered by the slightest breathing-in of the child. These respirators relieve the child of any effort of breathing and are used in the treatment of such conditions as drowning and electric shock.

The iron lung is a large, tank-like apparatus that causes a person to breathe in and out when the muscles of respiration are paralyzed or very weak.

The body of the patient is enclosed in the machine with his head protruding from one end. An airtight collar is placed around his neck. The air is withdrawn from inside the respirator, sucking the chest wall out, which expands the lungs, thus drawing air in through the patient's nose and mouth. Then air is pumped into the machine, compressing the person's chest, causing him to breathe out. The amount of suction can be regulated as well as the number of respirations. Children in respirators are very comfortable, as a rule, breathing with the help of the machine.

Respiratory tract

The parts of the body that are involved with the process of breathing. The respiratory tract includes the nose, pharynx, trachea, bronchial tubes, and the air sacs (alveoli) in the lungs.

The nose, pharynx, trachea, and bronchial tubes are lined with mucous membrane, which secretes mucus when irritated. This is one of the body's efforts to rid the breathing tubes of irritating substances. The mucus is supposed to catch the irritating substance, which is then removed from the body by sneezing or coughing.

The air is breathed through the trachea, the bronchial tubes, and into the microscopic air sacs in the lungs. These air sacs are lined with capillaries which absorb oxygen from the air and discharge their waste gases (carbon dioxide) from the body.

See also **Bronchial tree; Lungs; Trachea.**

Responsibility

A responsible child is one who can be

trusted or depended on, whose actions are based on good judgment and thinking, and who is able to act capably without constant guidance.

As in so many other phases of child development, the acquisition of a sense of responsibility is a gradual process, with the parents serving as models for their children.

The building of responsibility starts early in life, when children can be given simple chores to perform, such as bringing the napkins to the table or emptying wastebaskets. Approval from the parents is a great stimulus. And it is at this early age that parents should begin to pay attention to whether they are promoting true responsibility or inadvertently building resistance. A child who is expected to do too much or act too grown up may feel unfairly burdened or may possibly think that his parents are rejecting him in the sense that they want him to grow up quickly so they needn't care for him. A child who is constantly directed in the details of a task for which he is supposedly responsible quickly senses that the parents do not really want to share responsibility. Through trial and error, however, most parents learn to strike the right balance, and most children are eager to be accepted as responsible in new areas.

As they get older, children may be given more and more responsibilities in keeping with their age and understanding. During the preschool years they can learn certain fundamentals such as picking up paper and leftovers after a picnic, hanging up their outside clothing when they come in, and throwing scrap paper in the trash basket. During the school-age years, they can learn to be responsible for the orderliness in their rooms, for coming home after school unless their parents know of other arrangements,

and for obeying the rules at home and at school and the laws of the community.

Responsibility is especially important during the teen years when there is so much social life and such striving for independence. Boys and girls still have the responsibility of letting their parents know where they are going, with whom they are going, and when they expect to return. They also, for the first time, bear a great deal of the responsibility for their own well-being. They must make decisions largely on their own regarding responsible sexual behavior and drug and alcohol use, and often whether to continue schooling and what studies to pursue.

A parent's display of responsibility will usually set the pattern for his child. Responsibility to the home, to the community, and to the government are all important. With this type of background, the child will usually absorb a strong sense of responsibility.

Resuscitation see **Mouth-to-mouth resuscitation.**

Retardation see **Mental retardation.**

Retrolental fibroplasia
A man-made disease, found only in premature infants, causing blindness in one or both eyes. Before the cause of this condition was discovered, it was the primary source of blindness in children. Today, knowledge of its cause has virtually eliminated the disease.

Retrolental fibroplasia is the result of an overdose of oxygen given to an infant while he is in an incubator. The excess of oxygen affects the immature blood vessels in the premature's eyes (mature blood vessels of older infants are not affected). In addition, a thick layer of cells may grow behind the lens so that no light can enter, and there may be a detachment of the retina. There is no treatment. The condition is prevented by limiting the amount of oxygen in incubators.

Rewards see **Bribes and rewards.**

Rh factor blood incompatibility

A condition in which the mother's blood conflicts with that of the baby, causing destruction of the infant's red blood cells. The condition in the baby is called erythroblastosis. Modern methods of prevention and treatment have greatly reduced the incidence and serious effects of this condition.

The Rh factor is an inherited substance normally found in the blood of 86 percent of the population. When the substance is present the blood is called Rh positive blood. The remaining 14 percent who do not have this factor have Rh negative blood.

The difficulty occurs when an Rh negative woman marries an Rh positive man and their baby has Rh positive blood. While the baby is still an embryo or a fetus inside its mother's body, a few of the baby's Rh positive blood cells get through the placenta and into the mother's bloodstream. These Rh positive cells are foreign to the mother's blood, and so her body tries to protect itself from the foreign substance by building up antibodies against them. These antibodies in the mother's bloodstream go through the placenta easily and start destroying the baby's blood cells.

Usually, the first Rh positive baby escapes without harm or difficulties, for the mother has not built up enough antibodies to destroy many of his blood cells. But each subsequent Rh positive baby will build up more antibodies in the mother's blood, and the danger to the newborn with Rh positive blood becomes more serious with each successive pregnancy. Babies that are Rh negative are not affected, for they have the same Rh type as the mother.

Symptoms of affected baby The intensity of red-cell destruction in the baby's blood, caused by the mother's antibodies, determines the severity of the symptoms. The baby becomes anemic, the degree of anemia being related to the intensity of the condition. Jaundice appears within a few hours after birth and increases rapidly, again depending on the severity of the disease.

Treatment If the jaundice increases rapidly and other tests of the baby's blood show that there is a significant destruction of the red blood cells, an immediate exchange transfusion is necessary. For if the jaundice becomes too severe, it may damage the infant's brain permanently, resulting in mental retardation, cerebral palsy, or both.

In an exchange transfusion, the blood of the baby containing the dangerous antibodies is withdrawn little by little and replaced by blood that has no Rh antibodies. Although there are certain dangers inherent in an exchange transfusion, most transfusions are highly successful. The babies quickly lose their jaundice and thrive just as well as other normal babies.

Prevention Two methods of prevention are currently in use.

1. Rh negative mothers who are giving birth to their first Rh positive baby may now be protected against the build-up of antibodies by injections of a new, specific gamma globulin. This treatment

must be given within thirty-six hours after the birth of the baby. The next Rh positive baby she has will then be entirely safe because the mother's blood will not build up sufficient antibodies to damage the child's blood cells. But the special gamma globulin must be given after the birth of each Rh positive baby.

2. New methods are also available to Rh negative mothers already sensitized by the birth of one or more Rh positive children. The pregnant mother's blood is tested from time to time to see if there is a rising formation of antibodies. If the antibodies are rising rapidly, a needle is inserted in the mother's abdomen, through the wall of the uterus, and some of the amniotic fluid surrounding the baby is withdrawn and examined to see if the baby is already suffering a severe breakdown of blood cells (see **Amniocentesis**). In some cases the baby will even receive a transfusion through the mother's abdomen to make up for the destruction of its own cells. Some obstetricians, finding a very rapid rise in the mother's antibodies, will even advise that labor be induced so that the baby can receive exchange transfusions before too much damage has been done.

With the use of the new gamma globulin, however, the disease erythroblastosis should be eliminated.

Rheumatic fever

A serious, chronic inflammatory disease that causes arthritis (pain and inflammation of the joints) and may damage the heart as well. The incidence of this disease has been greatly reduced through the use of penicillin for streptococcus infections. Rheumatic fever follows a streptococcus infection—usually of the throat—but this occurs in only one or two children out of a hundred who have such an infection. Scarlet fever, which is caused by a streptococcus throat infection, is one of the common causes of rheumatic fever.

The initial attack of rheumatic fever is infrequent in the preschool child, common in the school-age child, and rare in the adult.

Symptoms Approximately 50 percent of the children with acute rheumatic fever have a history of a sore throat or some respiratory infection two to three weeks before the onset of the illness.

Then they develop fever and pains, a swelling and redness of the large joints—the ankles, knees, hips, wrists, elbows, and shoulders—usually involving only one joint at a time and jumping from joint to joint.

The heart may be affected. A heart murmur may result, as well as changes in the electrocardiogram, which often show damage to the heart muscle and one or more of the heart valves. Occasionally a child with rheumatic fever develops St. Vitus's dance.

Blood studies, especially for sedimentation time and for evidence of a recent infection by streptococcus, aid the doctor in making the diagnosis.

Treatment

1. Rest in bed is important during the active phase of the disease while there is fever and swelling of the joints.

2. Aspirin is usually effective in relieving the pain and fever.

3. Cortisone therapy rapidly relieves the pain and swelling of joints. It should be continued for a week or more under a doctor's direction.

4. Penicillin should be given as soon as possible in fairly large doses, and continued as long as the doctor feels necessary.

5. The urine should be examined from time to time during the course of the disease, since the same streptococcus that causes rheumatic fever causes nephritis.

Most children recover from their first attack of rheumatic fever without damage to the heart. However, since serious cardiac damage usually follows repeated severe attacks of the disease, it is of extreme importance to prevent any future attacks. Children who have had rheumatic fever will escape future attacks if they are protected from streptococcus infections of the respiratory tract, especially sore throats. Penicillin quickly kills all streptococci, so it is the drug of choice. So important is it that streptococcus infections be prevented that many doctors advise that following an attack of rheumatic fever penicillin be given every day throughout childhood to prevent any possibility of a streptococcus infection. Others advise giving pencillin at the first sign of any infection, and continuing it until cultures of the throat have demonstrated that no streptococci are present.

Rheumatoid arthritis

A generalized disease of the body characterized usually by fever, rash, and pain or swelling of one or more joints. The cause of the disease is not known. It is not related to rheumatic fever.

Fever with wide variations (from 99 to 105 degrees or more) is usually found and may persist for long periods of time. It may occur before any pain or swelling of the joints occurs.

A rash usually occurs at the onset of the fever and disappears quickly when the fever subsides. It appears primarily on the trunk and extremities and consists of small, irregularly shaped salmon-pink patches with pale centers. The rash varies in intensity and is increased by being rubbed or by heat.

Many children, especially in the pre-school years, develop initially pain only in a joint, with the swelling of the joint occurring only long after the onset of the illness. In other children, the swelling of a joint may increase so slowly as to be almost imperceptible. The pain and swelling are most frequently localized in a single joint. This differs from the pain and swelling of rheumatic fever, which usually jumps from joint to joint. If more than one joint is involved at the same time, it is usually the same joint on the opposite side. Swelling of other joints may follow.

The knee is the joint most usually affected—in approximately 95 percent of the cases. Swelling of finger joints occurs in about 75 percent, while swelling of the ankles and wrists occurs in approximately 30 percent of the affected children.

The disease is chronic and is characterized by the appearance from time to time of symptoms that gradually disappear only to reappear at some future time. An episode may last from a few weeks to a year or longer. In many cases, the disease quiets down before adolescence, although occasionally the symptoms recur after that time. In some cases the condition recurs from time to time in adulthood.

Diagnosis The diagnosis is difficult since there are no specific tests for the disease. It is made on the basis of the pattern of the child's symptoms and by ruling out other diseases, especially rheumatic fever.

Treatment There is no specific medical treatment. The symptoms must be treated as they arise. The prognosis is quite good. At least 50 percent of the children with rheumatoid arthritis recover completely. In rare instances the swelling of the joint remains and crippling occurs.

The best therapy requires the combined efforts of the parents, the pediatrician, the physical therapist, and the child's teacher.

Rhythms and dance

Almost every child has a sense of rhythm. Many babies, almost as soon as they can sit up, sway back and forth rhythmically when music is played. The toddler listening to music often stands with his legs spread wide and rocks back and forth from one leg to the other or turns slowly around. The 2- or 3-year-old may even try to improvise dances to music or the beat of a drum, running, jumping, swaying, stamping, and tiptoeing.

Dancing to rhythms and music may be interpretive, expressing the feelings evoked by the music or the beat, or it may be imitative of things the child is reminded of—a horse, an airplane, skaters, a merry-go-round—the possibilities are endless.

Rhythmic activities are a wonderful form of expression and exercise for a child, and parents should play records, play an instrument, sing, or beat on a drum to encourage the child in the natural pleasure he feels in this activity. Many elementary schools include rhythms as a part of the curriculum until children are 10 or 11 years old, for this type of dancing involves all the muscles of the body and develops grace and coordination as well.

For the child who seems especially talented, and who perhaps has no opportunity to dance at school, parents may consider dancing lessons. But care should be taken in this decision. For young children it is wise to avoid any emphasis on technique and best to choose a teacher who is primarily concerned with helping children to have fun through music and dance. Lessons should not be considered if the child objects.

Many little girls, on seeing a ballet performance, romantically dream of being ballet dancers. Ballet, however, is exacting, confining, and restricted to specific movements that must be learned and followed. In the beginning at least, ballet rarely gives a youngster an opportunity for interpretive response and is not really pleasurable. It is not, therefore, advisable to begin ballet lessons until a child is at least 7 or 8 years old. Then, if both the child and the parents are still interested in trying ballet, it is most important to select a teacher who is well trained in working with children.

Children should never be forced to dance against their will or to show off for relatives and friends. This is the quickest way to destroy the child's interest and pleasure in dancing.

See also **Music in the home.**

Riboflavin   see **Nutrition.**

Rickets

Resulting from a deficiency of vitamin D, rickets is characterized by a softening of the bones that is caused by a poor absorption of calcium from food. Improvements in nutrition have made this once common disease rare in industrialized countries except among the poorest families where children receive too little vitamin D (see **Nutrition**).

Because of the lack of calcium, the teeth appear late, the fontanelles close late, and bowed legs usually develop from the softness of the bones. Children with rickets also are usually shorter than average and have poor muscle tone.

During the early stages of the disease, the oral administration of vitamin D or ultraviolet therapy will cause rapid healing. In severe, untreated cases, however, the bowing of the legs and the short stature as well as other signs remain and are irreversible.

See also **Bowlegs.**

Rickettsia

Microorganisms that cause certain infections in human beings. Rickettsia are smaller than bacteria and larger than viruses. They commonly live in the intestinal tracts of certain insects such as mosquitoes, ticks, and mites, and are transmitted to man through the bites of these insects.

Among the diseases caused by rickettsia are Rocky Mountain spotted fever, typhus (virtually nonexistent in the United States), rickettsialpox (very rare and not serious), and Q fever (a mild disease, found mostly in animals). Serum tests are used to make a definite diagnosis.

Treatment The antibiotic tetracycline has been used effectively in the treatment of rickettsial diseases. The drug is continued until the child's temperature is normal for forty-eight hours, which generally takes about five to nine days after treatment is instituted.

Ringworm

A skin disease caused by a fungus infection. In spite of its name, it has no relation to worms, being called ringworm only because of its circular appearance on the skin. It may occur on almost any

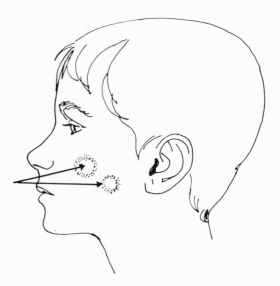

Characteristic circular growth of ringworm.

part of the body and is usually contracted from other children or pets.

Ringworm first appears as a red spot or pimple and spreads outward; the center clears, causing the inflammation to appear circular, like a ring.

The various types of ringworm are:

1. Ringworm of the skin: This condition is usually seen as a circular lesion, clear at the center with tiny, pimply blisters along its margin. It is usually contracted from other children but may be contracted from pet dogs and cats. It responds to treatment with any ointment that kills fungi, such as Whitfield's ointment.
2. Ringworm of the scalp: This condition causes a temporary loss of hair in patches on the scalp (see **Baldness**). It is very resistant to any form of local treatment but can be cleared up readily by a comparatively new drug, griseofulvin, given orally.
3. Ringworm of the foot (see **Athlete's foot**).

Rituals

Children often develop ritualistic patterns of behavior beginning at about 2½ or 3 years of age. When they go to bed, the glass of water must be on exactly the same spot on the night table, the cleansing tissue must be next to it on the right-hand side, the flashlight must be next to the tissue, and the one special Teddy bear that is allowed to sleep with the child must always be in the same place on his bed. If any of these objects are out of place, the child will not go to sleep. Such rituals are usually only temporary, lasting less than a year. However, if an older child persists in following rituals—for example, if he must touch every piece of furniture in a room before he can relax—a doctor should be consulted, for this kind of ritualistic behavior is almost invariably a sign of emotional disturbance (see **Compulsions**).

Rivalry   see **Competitiveness; Sibling rivalry and jealousy.**

Rocking the infant

For many centuries rocking has been recognized as one of the quickest and most effective ways of soothing and quieting an infant. Babies slept in cradles that could be rocked by hand or even by foot while the mother or father sat nearby. The modern era, however, has taken to immovable bassinets and cribs, although springs that fit into the base of the crib's legs, and make the crib rock whenever the baby moves, are available. Today's baby carriages, however, still have springs and are still rocked by mothers to quiet their restless infants.

The quieting reaction of rocking is in all probability related to the bobbing of the baby while it was still in the uterus and floating in the amniotic fluid. Rocking causes a reversion to this earlier experience and has a calming influence. Many parents have noted that their infants quiet down when riding in an automobile, only to wake and fuss when the car has to stop for a red light.

The question often arises as to whether rocking an infant to put him to sleep is habit-forming and difficult to discontinue without great upset. No evidence exists to prove this supposition. The need for rocking as a calming influence is usually of limited duration and rarely is demanded after the first five or six months.

Rocky Mountain spotted fever

An infectious disease caused by the bite of an infected tick. A person with Rocky Mountain spotted fever is not contagious. An attack of the disease sometimes, but not always, confers immunity in the future.

Tick (actual size in circle).

Symptoms and treatment   Fever, chills, headache, and pains in the joints and bones appear two to twelve days after the tick bite. On the fifth or sixth day, a mottled, bright red rash appears, first over the wrists and ankles, later becoming darker and covering the abdomen and back, then gradually fading. Fever may remain high for as long as three weeks. Children with severe cases may develop convulsions and even coma.

The drugs tetracycline and chloramphenicol are effective, especially if given early. In severe cases, hospitalization may be necessary.

Immunization and prevention An effective vaccine against Rocky Mountain spotted fever, given in three injections, one week apart, is available. Boosters should be given annually.

Children going into tick-infested areas should receive immunization beforehand, and a tick repellent, such as Off spray (diethyltoluamide) or 612 spray (ethyl hexanediol), can be used on clothing. Children's skin and scalp should be checked every night and any ticks found removed immediately. Pets living in or visiting tick-infested areas should be de-ticked every few days.

Ticks can usually be easily removed from the skin, but care should be taken in handling the ticks. They should not be removed with the naked hand—rubber gloves, heavy paper, or tweezers may be used. A gentle pull removes the tick without leaving the mouth parts in the skin. Or one can apply kerosene, cigarette lighter fluid, oil, butter, petroleum jelly, or alcohol to the tick's body, which will usually cause it to let go. After removal, the skin should be washed thoroughly.

Rooming-in

The meaning of this term varies in different hospitals, but essentially it means that a mother may have her newborn infant in the room with her a great deal of the time during her hospital stay rather than only at feeding time.

Among the various types of rooming-in are:

1. The baby stays with the mother twenty-four hours a day. This usually means that the mother must tend to all the needs of the infant from the start, both day and night. This plan usually restricts visitors to the father and the grandparents.

2. The baby is with the mother during the daytime hours but spends the night with the other babies in the nursery.

3. A drawer-type arrangement, which allows the mother to bring the baby into her room when she wants it and return it to the nursery when she desires. In this situation, the drawer slides through a wall separating the mother's room from the nursery.

A number of pros and cons exist in regard to rooming-in. On the pro side:

1. It allows the new mother to gain confidence in the handling of her infant while they are still in the protective atmosphere of the hospital.

2. It permits the mother who has other children at home to devote herself completely to the new baby for the few days in which she can give it her undivided attention.

3. It familiarizes the mother with her baby's behavior from the very start, forming a close bond between her and the infant.

4. It gives a father the opportunity to have contact with the baby almost from the moment it is born.

On the con side:

1. Some women feel that they will have a great deal of responsibility once they return home, especially if there are other children, so they appreciate an opportunity to have time to rest and sleep at will.

2. Some women, after a long labor and a

tiring birth, are in no condition to care immediately for the newborn. They may need a complete rest the first few days.

It should be said that most mothers enjoy rooming-in immensely. Not only do they have the opportunity for the close and early care of the baby, but in many hospitals they are in a room with several other rooming-in mothers and enjoy talking with them and "comparing notes."

Rorschach test   see Tests.

Rose fever   see Hay fever.

Roseola infantum

Also called exanthema subitum. A disease of infancy and childhood caused by a virus and characterized by three or four days of high fever that ends abruptly, only to be followed by a mottled rash over the child's body. It is probably contagious, although no proof of this presently exists. Nearly all children contract this disease during their early years. An attack confers immunity in the future.

Symptoms and treatment   The onset is sudden with the fever rising abruptly to as high as 103 to 105 degrees, and remaining high for three or four days. Usually no symptoms occur during this time, with the possible exception of an occasional red throat. Generally, the child does not appear too sick in spite of the high fever. A blood count indicates a viral infection, and antibiotics, consequently, are of no value.

At the end of the three or four days of high fever, the temperature suddenly drops to normal, and after this a reddish, mottled rash appears over the body. The disease is now at an end, and

although the rash may last one or two days, the child is healthy and may even be taken out of doors. The fever does not return once the rash has appeared.

No specific treatment is required, with the exception of aspirin to lower the fever, plus phenobarbital if the child has a tendency to develop convulsions with high fever.

Roundworms   see Worms.

Rubber pants see Pants, waterproof.

Rubella   see German measles.

Rudeness

Interrupting, disrupting, belittling, name-calling, talking back, sneering, not listening, grabbing, pushing, and disregarding another person's feelings—almost all parents complain about such behavior in their children at one time or another.

What may be considered rude at one age level, however, may be entirely acceptable at another. A 2-year-old who talks back when reprimanded may appear cute and cause adults to laugh at his responses. A 4- or 5-year-old who demonstrates the same behavior is frowned on and considered rude.

Likewise, what is considered rude in one situation may be considered inoffensive in another. For example, it is often acceptable to interrupt in a lively family conversation but not when a guest is talking.

Learning not to be rude is based on learning good manners and self-control. As such, it is largely dependent on the example set by the parents.

Parents should always explain to a child why a behavior is not acceptable.

For example: "When you say that, it makes Mrs. Green feel very sad"; or "Don't interrupt. We want to hear what you have to say, but people have to take turns talking."

When a young child sticks out his tongue or thumbs his nose, it is better to simply tell a child that you don't like it and then ignore it. If you make too much of it, a child may repeat this behavior whenever he wants attention.

Once a child is able to understand the feelings of others and to realize why he should not be rude, it is important that the attitude of the parents remains consistent. He should not be allowed to be rude to Mrs. Smith who isn't liked by the family, while being corrected for being rude to Mrs. Green. And, above all, parents must be consistent in their own behavior. Too many parents are rude to their own children, interrupting them, seldom saying "please" or "thank you," and walking into their rooms without knocking. This sets a very bad example.

See also **Manners.**

Rumination

The bringing up and mouthing of food that has already been in the stomach. A rare condition, rumination occurs generally only in young infants. It usually begins a half hour or so after feedings. The child starts with chewing movements and soon some of the partially digested food is brought up and may be held in the mouth for a while. Some of it may at times come out of the mouth.

Rumination is not to be confused with regurgitation, in which some of the food is brought up during or immediately after feedings, or with vomiting, which causes the food to be expelled from the stomach with considerable force.

Rumination is rarely of any seriousness unless the child brings up all food swallowed and spits it out. In the great majority of cases the condition does not need treatment, for enough food remains in the stomach to nourish the child properly.

Although the cause of rumination has not been determined, some observers feel that rumination occurs primarily among children whose lives lack stimulation, such as institutionalized children. Food may be one of their only pleasurable stimulations, and thus they attempt to make it last as long as possible.

See also **Regurgitation.**

Running away from home

Children between the approximate ages of 7 and 12 often threaten to run away from home and occasionally attempt to do so. Over the age of 12, the threat becomes more common and is more frequently carried out. What are the causes of these threats or acts?

In children under the age of 12, threats of running away are usually the result of some argument or discipline by a parent. As a rule, the child wishes to punish the parents and make them feel sorry for what they have done. The threat is rarely carried out, and when it is, the child usually comes home after a short walk. A child so young is still largely dependent on his parents and has no real idea or plan of what he's going to do if he runs away. However, the occasional child who really runs away is almost always a child who feels unloved and is desperately trying to find love and satisfaction. This is especially true of the child who runs away repeatedly.

The many arguments with parents that occur during the teen-age years are a normal part of growing up and gradually breaking the cord that has up to this time so securely tied the youngster to the family. During such arguments a great many teen-agers threaten to leave and gain their freedom and seek a place where they will be understood—but they rarely do so if the home environment has been essentially a good one.

When a teen-ager runs away from home, in almost every instance the parents lack understanding, adequate interest, and affection for the child. Often there is a breakdown in the ability of the child and the parent to talk openly and honestly to one another, and this gap widens as the child grows older.

Boredom with one's life and community is also a frequent contributory cause of teen-agers' running away from home. For as they grow older, they become aware of the excitement, activity, and diversity of all that is happening outside of their homes and their communities.

When a child has run away, a serious crisis exists. The parents, of course, want to find the child. In addition to the help that is given by the police, local groups in various cities try to help runaway teen-agers. If the parents have an idea of where the youngster has gone, they can try to contact one of these groups.

In most cases, however, the child will get in touch with the parents on his own within a couple of days or weeks. Often the child returns home. And all too often, he or she runs away again. After a brief period of reconciliation, the child realizes, perhaps, that nothing has changed. When this happens, the parents must recognize that something has gone seriously wrong within the family. There must be a major effort in which both the parents and the child try to create new patterns of communication and a better relationship. Very often this cannot be done without professional help from a psychotherapist or a family counselor, for it is extremely difficult for people to see what is wrong with their usual ways of behaving even when they do recognize that something must be wrong. Also the runaway youngster may be too upset to explain clearly or even to understand all the things that have been bothering him.

Runny nose   see **Colds.**

S

Sabin vaccine

An oral vaccine against infantile paralysis (poliomyelitis) perfected by Dr. Albert Sabin. It was licensed for use in 1961.

This is a living virus vaccine composed of weakened viruses, and it is given by mouth to infants and children. Three doses are usually given, starting when a baby is 2 months old, with subsequent doses at 4 and 6 months. (See **Immunization schedule and tests.)**

This vaccine, because of its ease of administration and its ability to produce a high degree of immunity, has largely supplanted the Salk vaccine, which is given by injection. In fact, it is recommended that even those children who have received the Salk vaccine be given the full dose of Sabin vaccine.

Sadism

The tendency to take pleasure in hurting persons or animals. There are some sadistic children whose behavior goes beyond normal aggressiveness or the frequent thoughtlessness of most children. Children who habitually hurt or torture animals or deliberately harm other children are almost invariably in need of psychological help.

Sometimes, with children of preschool age, sadistic tendencies can be worked out through aggressive play, such as hitting a punching bag, hammering, or "messing around" with clay. But when this is not adequate, deeper therapy is indicated to uncover and adjust the source of the child's violent feelings.

It may be that the child feels rejected by his parents, particularly in favor of another sibling. He then behaves sadistically toward that sibling or some other (substitute) child. Very often sadism in children reflects sadism in their parents, and cannot be treated unless there is an adjustment in the home environment.

The role of comic books and television as a cause of cruel and sadistic behavior has been cited by some psychiatrists. It is undoubtedly true that cruelty and sadism seen in these media may stimulate an upset child. It is very doubtful, however, that these would provoke similar behavior in a basically stable and sympathetic youngster.

See also **Aggressiveness; Bullying.**

Safety see **Accident prevention, indoors; Accident prevention, outdoors;**

Toys and safety.

Safety gate see **Gate, safety.**

Saint Vitus's dance

Also called chorea. One of the complications of rheumatic fever. A child with this condition is unable to stay still and constantly makes purposeless movements with his head, arms, legs, mouth, eyes—all parts of the body. He is unable to control these movements. At times speech becomes slurred and walking becomes very awkward. Handwriting becomes very poor and irregular.

Usually this condition is benign, and it generally disappears in about one to three months without any evidence of the cardiac damage that is occasionally found with rheumatic fever.

Treatment is bed rest, and sedation when the condition is severe.

Salicylate poisoning see **Poisons: first-aid treatment.**

Salk vaccine
The first vaccine found to be effective in the prevention of poliomyelitis. It was developed by Jonas Salk and introduced in 1955. It is given by inoculation in four doses, the first three at one-month intervals and the fourth six to twelve months later.

In the United States and many parts of the world, the Salk vaccine has been supplanted by the oral poliovirus vaccine.

See also **Sabin vaccine.**

Salmonella infection see **Food poisoning.**

Santa Claus
Many parents wonder whether or not they should tell their children the story of Santa Claus and instill in them a belief in this long-loved fantasy. Will it make it difficult for a child to differentiate reality from fantasy? Will he feel he's been duped when he learns the truth?

Many, many years of experience have proven that the story of Santa Claus can do children no harm. It is quite normal for little children to listen to, and believe in, fairy tales during that wonderful period when the imagination is so fertile. Many children between the ages of 3 and 6 years have their imaginary playmates. Belief in the child-loving Santa Claus is held in the same way.

As the child grows older, his mind grows out of the period of fantasy and he accepts the reality without difficulty. Almost all children love the story, even when they later learn that Santa Claus was created as a symbol of giving and of love and happiness.

But parents must never use Santa Claus as a threat: "If you hit your brother again, Santa Claus won't bring you any toys"; "If you don't finish your milk, Santa Claus will forget to fill your stocking."

Children today still look forward to Santa's visit with the same joy and eagerness that children have felt for so many centuries.

Savings accounts
Although many children receive allowances as early as age 5 or 6, it is rare that a child will understand and enjoy having a savings account until he is about 9 or 10.

Many parents initiate the savings-bank account by starting it with a small deposit. The child then is encouraged to add a little bit of his allowance each week to build up toward something he wants to buy. Most children enjoy watching the figures in the bank account increase—some children save money in a "piggy bank" at home to add to this account.

Also, there is great value gained by a child paying something himself for things he wants. For instance, a boy wants a baseball bat and saves for it. In many instances parents will pay half the cost when the child saves the same amount. This is far better than always giving a child outright anything that he wants.

Scabies
An infestation of the skin by a tiny insect commonly called the itch mite. This mite, so small it can hardly be seen with

the naked eye, lives on the skin. The female insect burrows into the skin, laying its eggs underneath. On the skin where the insect has burrowed, pimples, pus-heads, and crusts form. Itching is intense, especially at night.

The parts of the body most usually involved are the areas where the skin is softest and thinnest—the skin between the fingers, the inner surfaces of the wrist and elbow, the armpits, the navel, buttocks, penis, and between the toes.

Treatment   This is twofold: first, destruction of the parasite, and, second, relief of the itching.

There are many preparations useful in destroying the parasite. Probably the most effective is a substance called benzyl benzoate which comes in a liquid or cream (a good commercial preparation is Kwell Cream or Lotion). The liquid or cream is applied liberally over the affected areas and left on for twenty-four hours. Then the body is washed thoroughly, and freshly laundered clothing is put on. Repeated application is rarely needed, but if necessary, application may be repeated in four days.

Usually the treatment will aid quickly in relieving the itching. If itching is severe, one of the antihistamines may be given by mouth. If the lesions are infected, they should be treated with antibiotic ointments.

Scalp   see **Abscess; Baldness; Cradle cap; Dandruff; Head injuries; Head lice.**

Scarlet fever

Also called scarlatina. An infection caused by a streptococcus inflammation of the throat. It is characterized by a rash of the skin due to the circulation throughout the body of the toxins of streptococcus bacteria.

Signs and symptoms   The disease is first manifested by a severe sore throat, fever, and vomiting. Usually this is followed within a day or two by a red rash of the skin.

The rash, which usually develops first on the chest and abdomen, appears as a red flush. However, when examined closely, it is found to be composed of many small red pimples close together. The rash usually spreads to the arms, legs, and face also, but there is rarely any rash around the mouth, giving what is called a "circumoral pallor." The tongue is usually bright red and may have tiny elevations over it, making it what has been termed a "strawberry tongue."

The rash fades in about one week, followed by a peeling of the skin where the rash was present, as well as peeling of the skin on the palms of the hand and the soles of the feet. This peeling on the hands and feet is one of the diagnostic signs of scarlet fever.

Incubation period   The streptococcus sore throat causing scarlet fever is usually spread through close contact or drinking from the same glass or cup. The sore throat of a person catching the disease will usually develop in three to five days after contact.

Period of contagion   The person with scarlet fever is contagious until the sore throat has completely subsided, usually within ten days. Scarlet fever is not really a distinct contagious disease, but is essentially a streptococcus sore throat with a toxic rash. People who have had scarlet fever may get the same type of sore throat many times but will not develop the rash. In other words, many people with streptococcus sore throats may transmit scarlet fever, even though they have no rash.

Treatment   Scarlet fever is quickly and successfully treated by penicillin, which kills the streptococci.

Also, many doctors place an exposed child on daily doses of penicillin for a period of five days, which will usually prevent the disease.

Complications   These are rare since the advent of antibiotics. They included nephritis, abscessed ears, and swollen glands.

Scars

There are many different types of scars, some only temporary (such as most of the superficial scars of chicken pox or minor cuts) and some more or less permanent (such as the scars due to deep cuts, deep burns, operations, or smallpox vaccination).

There are a few facts that are of importance regarding scars. The first is that deep scars contract when they heal. This can be very serious when children get burned deeply over the inner elbows or behind the leg. The healing of these burns must be carefully followed by the doctor, for the resulting scar may cause the forearm to be contracted upward or the leg to bend backward at the knee.

Another fact is that certain children form keloid scars when their flesh is cut or injured. These are thick, elevated, lumpy scars. They rarely will subside by themselves and may have to be reduced by radiation if they are disfiguring. If a child has the tendency to form keloid scars, he should limit his activities to those in which there is less chance for injury to the skin of his face.

A further important consideration is that dirty wounds may leave permanently dark scars. For this reason dirty wounds, especially those on the face, should be scrubbed with soap and water—preferably by a doctor—until completely clean, even if it is temporarily painful.

Gaping or irregular cuts, especially those on the face, should always be treated by a doctor to gain the best cosmetic results.

See also **Burn; Cuts.**

Schedules, feeding   see **Feeding schedules.**

Schick test

A test formerly used commonly to determine if a child is susceptible to diphtheria.

A very small amount of the toxin (poison) of the diphtheria bacillus is injected into the outer layer of the skin of the inner forearm. If the child is susceptible to diphtheria, the area will turn red in twenty-four to forty-eight hours.

The Schick test is rarely used today, since almost all children receive diphtheria toxoid inoculations in their routine medical care, and receive booster injections to hold their immunity against the disease at a high level.

Schizophrenia

A psychosis that typically first appears in adolescence or early adulthood; it is rare in early childhood.

The most common symptom is a marked withdrawal from the world. The youngster is no longer interested in his friends, parents, school, books, or hobbies, or in radio or television. Often he will sit for hours on end playing with a string of beads or with a colored pencil, or singing a tune over and over again while rocking back and forth. Some affected children may sit rigidly, looking straight ahead. Others are hyperactive—for example, rocking back and forth rapidly.

Other symptoms include visual hallucinations or aural hallucinations, often voices; compulsions, such as a need to wash constantly; and paranoid fears, such as that someone or some group is seeking to kill the patient.

The exact cause of schizophrenia is not known, although there is some evidence that it is influenced by heredity and is of prenatal origin. Studies of twins show that schizophrenia appears six times more frequently in both identical twins than in both nonidentical twins. Also, the condition often seems to run in families.

Often the child seems to be emotionally normal and then suddenly the death of a beloved parent or some other severe shock will precipitate the onset of schizophrenia.

Some psychologists and psychiatrists feel that a schizophrenic is born with a predisposition for the condition, but that it may be avoided if the child receives a great deal of parental love and attention and does not experience any severe emotional shocks, or traumas. Whether it can be prevented completely is not known, since there is no way of diagnosing potential schizophrenics.

The prognosis for children with schizophrenia is variable. About 25 percent seem to improve greatly with treatment and to make a good social adjustment later. Others require continuous care and treatment throughout their lives.

Treatment of this condition is usually through the use of drugs plus psychotherapy. The drugs are used to quiet the patient, to give a feeling of well-being, to relieve anxiety, and in general to make it possible to communicate sufficiently well with the patient so that psychotherapy can be undertaken.

Psychotherapy can be given either individually or with a group. Both of these methods of treatment seem to aid some patients considerably in the relief of anxiety.

Research into the causes and treatment of schizophrenia continues constantly.

School see **Boarding schools; College, preparation for; Education, experimental approaches in; Nursery school; School problems.**

School phobia
A type of anxiety that becomes apparent when a child refuses to go to school. Although called school phobia (fear of school), it is usually basically a separation anxiety resulting from a great need of a child to be near his mother. This phobia also expresses itself in other separations from the home or mother such as going to camp or going on trips without the parents. Only occasionally is the child's anxiety really related to a fear of school—a fear of a teacher or teachers, a fear of other children, a fear of not being able to meet the standards expected of him, a fear of failure.

Often the mother, whether consciously or unconsciously, transmits to the child her own need to have him near her. To satisfy her need she usually hinders a child from developing a sense of self-dependence and self-assurance. She is overprotective and keeps him home at the slightest provocation. The child responds with such complaints as headaches, stomachaches, muscle pains, and sore throat—anything to make staying home seem indicated.

At other times, the problem derives from the child's feeling rejected at home, especially when there is a younger child not yet at school. He feels that he is being pushed out of the home and consciously or unconsciously fears that his parents prefer not to have him there. And so he feels more secure remaining home.

Treatment   This is often extremely difficult but can be accomplished with care and persistence. First, everything possible should be done to have the child continue at school. This is most important. But if the child stays home and refuses to go to school, then efforts should be made to maintain contact with the school. Parents should see to it that the child receives and does his homework regularly, and if possible that the teacher occasionally brings the assignments to the child and tells him that she hopes he will return to school soon.

Also, it is very helpful if the teacher or one or more of the child's classmates call for him each morning and ask him to accompany them to school—if this can be arranged. Parents can rarely accomplish what the teacher and classmates can do.

Often the mother, as well as the child, will need psychotherapy to break the tie that binds mother to child and child to mother.

School phobia resulting from fear of teacher, classmates, or failure can usually be handled most successfully by close cooperation between parents, teacher, and guidance counselor.

With careful handling and understanding of the child's fears and problems, school phobia can usually be overcome within a few months.

School problems

When children have problems at school, whether it is with their studies, their relations with their classmates, difficulties with the teacher, inattention, upsetting the class, or lack of interest, it is important that parents attempt to find the reasons and correct the situation.

The possibility of a physical cause should always be considered. Poor vision, defective hearing, chronic infection, anemia, malnutrition, fatigue—any of these can make a child incapable of working effectively. All can be easily diagnosed and corrected. Mental retardation can also be determined by psychological testing, and the child can be placed in an appropriate class with specially trained teachers. Mild brain dysfunction and any other type of neurological difficulty that affects perception or concentration is often more difficult to diagnose, but most pediatricians today are alert to this possibility. With treatment or special tutoring great improvement is possible.

Unhappiness very often interferes with a child's ability to get along in school. The cause may be upsetting home conditions such as parents who are constantly fighting, divorce, rejection or lack of interest by parents, jealousy of brothers or sisters, separation from parents, alcoholism or drug addiction of a parent. Or the unhappiness may be directly related to a problem at school such as being unpopular with the other children or a feeling of being disliked by the teacher.

Rejection by classmates is extremely troubling to all children, for, during the elementary school years and into adolescence, being accepted by other children is of primary importance to almost all boys and girls. (See **Unpopularity**.)

The feeling of being disliked by the teacher is also very destructive. At times this is a false impression and the child is simply demanding more individual attention than the teacher can give. But the child may really be disliked for one reason or another. He may be a disciplinary problem. Or it may simply be that he does not get along well with one particular teacher.

Many children fall behind in their classwork because their life outside school does not encourage an interest in studying. The child may have lacked intellectual stimulation before entering school, and there may be a continuing lack of parental interest in the child's learning. The youngster may have time-consuming responsibilities at home or an after-school job. Possibly he has no quiet place to study.

Keep it in mind that a child may be having difficulty in school even though his marks are good and there have been no very disturbing comments from the teacher or the school administration. If a child seems depressed before or after school, never seems enthusiastic about school activities, or often has headaches or an upset stomach on schooldays, this may be a sign that something is wrong. You should then make every effort to discover what is bothering the child.

Since a child's experience in school is such a large and important part of his life, it is very important that school problems be worked out as quickly as possible. You should discuss matters with the child, the teacher, the child's doctor, and if necessary the school principal. Be careful not to jump to the first plausible conclusion, but rather to investigate the problem thoroughly. A positive and understanding attitude toward the teacher's goals and difficulties and the aims of the school in general will help to enlist the cooperation of school personnel in helping the child.

See also **Examinations and tests in school; Learning difficulties; Marks for schoolwork; School phobia; Teacher-parent relationship; Truancy.**

School-age period

The period from 6 to 12 years. This is the stage when children are moving out into the world—for the first time they spend a major part of their day outside the home. They have acquired basic competence in many areas, and are constantly learning new skills. They learn to relate to authorities other than their parents, and they learn to get along with their peers.

This is the stage that Freud called the latency period, referring to the fact that there appears to be a diminishing in sexual interest, at least compared to the stages before and after this age. The child has already resolved the strong feelings toward the parents that characterize the so-called Oedipus complex. He has yet to face the burgeoning sexual interests of adolescence.

At this age children typically form friendships with members of their own sex, and acceptance by the group is extremely important. But despite a strong need to be accepted by their companions, children of this age are also working hard to establish their own identities, and it is at this age that one feels clearly that the youngster's full character is becoming apparent. Boys and girls are now looking not only to their fathers and mothers, but also to their peers to learn what behavior is appropriate and what behavior they want to emulate.

Many parents and teachers find this stage one of the most agreeable in the development of the child, for it can be a time of striking growth in creative activity, intellectual interests, and social maturity, with a minimum of stress and conflict. However, for this to be so, it is necessary that the school experience, which plays such an important role in the daily life of the child, be a good one.

During this period the child builds the basic strengths of personality that will carry him through adolescence and into adult life.

Schoolwork, marks for see **Marks for schoolwork.**

Scolding
This is a necessary form of discipline in bringing up children, for there are times when a parent must show disapproval. Occasional scolding is not at all harmful to children who look to their parents for direction and expect to be corrected from time to time.

It is only when scolding is too frequent or too harsh, and when parents spend too much time scolding and too little time praising, that it becomes damaging to the child. It is far better for a child to receive some appropriate, simple, temporary punishment, such as depriving him of some activity or pleasure, than to be exposed to incessant scolding. As a matter of fact, some children who are constantly being scolded build up a wall against it and take the scoldings without reaction.

There are also certain children who receive too little attention (or who feel that they are receiving too little attention) who actually try to provoke scoldings. They prefer to receive negative attention rather than no attention at all. When children are constantly being scolded, parents should pause and consider what can be done to avoid so much conflict. Most often if parents reward good behavior with praise and recognition and try also to keep scolding to a minimum, the situation will improve rapidly. If the conflict and scolding continue, professional counseling may be indicated to help the parents find new ways of handling the child.

See also **Discipline; Nagging; Shaming.**

Scorpion sting see **Insect and spider bites.**

Scrapes
The rubbing off of the surface of the skin by friction, such as when a child falls and scrapes his knee.

Scrapes should be cleaned with soaps and water to remove any dirt or surface bacteria which may have been rubbed in. Then an antiseptic such as iodine or Betadine (povidone-iodine), which does not sting, should be applied to avoid possible infection. The scrape should be covered by a loose gauze pad, held in place by adhesive tape or a gauze bandage.

See also **Cuts.**

Scratch tests see **Skin tests for allergies.**

Scrotum
A loose sac of skin (scrotal sac) hanging behind the penis in boys and men.

It contains the two testicles. With very few exceptions the testicles are already within the sac by the time a male infant is born. (See **Testicles.**)

The scrotal sac contains elastic tissue which causes it to change in size from a loose, hanging sac to a tight, drawn-up sac, in reaction to certain stimuli, such as coldness.

Scurvy

A disease caused by lack of adequate vitamin C in the child's food. It may occur at any age but is most common between ages 7 months and 2 years. It is rare in the United States, although occasionally found in poor families.

Signs and symptoms The child becomes progressively irritable, especially when handled. The child's legs, which are usually extremely tender due to hemorrhages under the lining of the bones, are held in a froglike position. The gums are purplish and swollen, more so around teeth in the process of erupting. Occasionally there are bluish areas in the skin from the rupture of small blood vessels.

Diagnosis Readily made by X rays, which show typical bone lesions.

Treatment Ascorbic acid or adequate amounts of orange juice cause a very rapid disappearance of symptoms—almost always within forty-eight hours. Grapefruit, tomato, and pineapple juice may also be given, but since they are not as high in vitamin C content as orange juice, larger quantities are necessary.

Recovery is usually complete.

Seasickness see Motion sickness.

Second child

A second child lives in a very different environment from that of the first child—in spite of having the same parents and often the same home. He has certain advantages and certain disadvantages as compared to his older brother or sister.

The parents are usually more relaxed, having had some experience, which makes them more sure of themselves in their handling of the child. They are also usually more settled in their relationship with each other, and finances are usually more stable.

On the other hand, there are certain disadvantages in being the second child. He is frequently in competition with the older child, who is often jealous of the attention given the younger member of the family. He has never had the advantage of having his parents solely to himself. He is frequently being compared with the first child, both at home and at school, and needs to do a great deal more than the older child to establish his own identity. His mother is more likely to be overworked and tired. And the child also has, as a rule, many hand-me-down clothes and toys.

In general, parents must work toward two goals with the second child. He or she must be protected from the hostile impulses of the older sibling without being unfairly favored. And especially when the second child is of the same sex as the first child, it is important that the youngster be encouraged to develop his own personality and interests. Too many second children feel that they are weaker, less competent versions of the older child—and also less important in the parents' eyes. Both children should have a chance to spend time alone with the parents.

See also **Middle child; Sibling rivalry and jealousy.**

Secondary anemia see Anemia.

Secondary sex characteristics see Sex characteristics, secondary.

Security see Insecurity.

Security blanket see Security object.

Security object

Typically, a blanket or part of a blanket or a stuffed toy that a child has kept since infancy or early childhood, and which he clings to when he is anxious. Such objects seem to give to children a feeling of security associated with some period during the first two years of life. Children often take a security blanket to bed with them at night, as well as on trips or overnight visits, or to nursery school for comfort and relaxation during the nap period.

Some children may need the security of having such an item with them when they enter a new and unfamiliar situation. It is important for the parent and teacher to realize that this item is "special" and to protect the child's right not to share it. Another child should be told, "This is Johnny's special bear; you can use some of the other things he has," giving the other child an alternative and Johnny an example of how to handle the situation in a socially acceptable manner. Of course the teacher should be told about the special meaning of the item. Once a child has adjusted, he should no longer have need of the special item. At first the teacher can keep it for him in a safe place without letting other children use it or play with it. Later, his mother can explain to him that if he chooses to bring it to school, he really should let other children play with it also. If he doesn't wish to share it—he should leave it home.

Security objects are often given up by children spontaneously before they are 5 years old, but they may be retained after that time. Parents should remember that this can be an extremely important matter to the child. The parents' possible annoyance at the child's devotion to a blanket should be weighed against the upset he may feel if it is suddenly removed. The security blanket may become a dirty rag but it is not wise to wash it unless the child agrees. Most children want the blanket as it is, with its friendly old look and feel. By no means throw the blanket away and get a new one without the child's full consent.

If you want to encourage the child to give up a security object, a casual, gradual approach is best. You may suggest buying a new teddy bear or similar toy. If the child is ready he will give up the old one. Blankets can often be cut down little by little without the child's objecting. Eventually the child gives up the remaining scrap.

Sedatives

Drugs that tend to quiet a person down and produce sleep.

Sedatives are rarely prescribed during infancy and childhood.

They may occasionally be used in the treatment of sleep disturbances when a child has a great deal of difficulty going to sleep. In these cases it is best to use non-habit-forming sedatives, such as some antihistamines like Benadryl (diphenhydramine hydrochloride), and certain non-habit-forming motion sickness medicines like Dramamine (dimenhydrinate). These drugs are safe but should be used only under the direction of the child's doctor. They are given every night in the dosage that will make a child very sleepy. The maximum dosage is given for a week or so and then gradually decreased and discontinued.

The stronger sedatives—the barbiturates and chloralhydrate, for example—are often given to allay a child's anxiety prior to certain medical procedures, such as surgical operations and electroencephalograms.

The indiscriminate use of sedatives during infancy and childhood should be definitely avoided.

See also **Phenobarbital.**

Seizures see **Convulsions; Epilepsy.**

Self-demand feeding see **Feeding, self-demand.**

Self-discipline see **Discipline; Responsibility.**

Self-dressing see **Dressing and undressing.**

Self-esteem

A child's self-esteem is based on the feeling that he is valued and loved and wanted—a feeling that he is important as a person.

Every parent wants his child to grow up to be secure and self-reliant, and much of this is based upon his feeling of self-esteem. It is the parents themselves who are most responsible for the desired results. To accomplish them: Make the child feel that he is very much loved and wanted. Praise the child whenever praise is warranted; let him know you are proud of him. Avoid being overprotective. Avoid being overpermissive. Aid the child in making and retaining friends. Encourage his talents.

Most important of these is making the child feel very much loved and wanted. For if he feels rejected and unloved, he cannot develop a sense of personal pride and self-assurance. All of us need approval, primarily from our parents and later from our friends, contemporaries, and teachers. But parents must be careful not to give their children "smother love" by being overindulgent, overpermissive, and overprotective. No child can develop self-esteem if he cannot build up self-confidence, self-assurance, and a degree of self-dependence.

A child of overprotective parents, who is not permitted to climb trees or jungle gyms, who at 8, 9, and 10 years of age and even older is not permitted to cross streets that are not dangerous, who is restricted from entering athletic competition and active games for fear of being hurt, cannot develop a sense of self-esteem because he is made to feel inadequate.

It is also important to the child to gain and maintain friendships—to feel and know that another child or children like him and value his friendship. Every child needs at least one good friend during school years and adolescence, and the parents should do all in their power to aid the child in attracting and holding friends.

The self-esteem established during the preschool and school years is the basis for self-assurance and self-esteem during the teen-age years and adult life.

See also **Companions; Friends, close; Overindulgent parent; Overprotective parent; Rejection.**

Selfishness see **Sharing.**

Seminal emission see **Nocturnal seminal emission.**

Separation

From approximately a year of age and through the preschool years, the most upsetting experience a child can suffer is separation from his parents. Such separation, whether it is due to parents going on a vacation of several weeks, the death of a parent, or the child's being forced to stay in a hospital for an extended period of time, almost always causes the youngster great distress and unhappiness.

In our culture little children are almost entirely dependent on their parents. They look to them not only for food, clothing, and protection, but for love, approval, and attention. If parents of young children leave, even if only for a week or two, the children usually feel deserted, rejected, and unloved, and often they are not sure that their parents will return.

Such children often show their anxiety by not mentioning the parents while they are away, by being indifferent to them and resentful when they return, and at times by waking during the nights, bed-wetting, stammering, stuttering, or developing tics.

These are reactions of secure as well as insecure children when faced with separation. The fact is that these children are just not old enough or mature enough to understand that a parent who apparently loves them very much can just leave them and disappear for a long period of time.

If parents must leave for a period of time, a warm parent substitute must be found. The best parent substitutes as a rule are the grandparents, if the children know them well and love them. Grandparents usually give the children a great deal of attention and affection. Otherwise some person whom the children know and like could be a substitute.

While the parents are away, a number of steps may be taken to relieve the young child's anxiety. First, the parents should leave their pictures displayed prominently around the house and leave some of their clothing, shoes, and hats around so that the child gets some feeling of their presence. And secondly, it helps a great deal if a collection of toys

is left, one to be given to the child every morning or every other morning so that he feels his parents have not forgotten him. Parents should also write frequently—daily if possible—and phone once in a while.

But if separation of young children from their parents can be avoided, it is well worthwhile.

Once children are of school age and more secure and self-dependent, most of them can go to sleep-away camps without any real upset. They are now secure in the knowledge that their parents will not desert or reject them.

See also **Death as children see it; Death, dealing with a; Divorce; Hospitalization; School phobia.**

Serum, horse   see **Horse serum.**

Sex characteristics, secondary
These are the external physical characteristics that develop in boys and girls during pre-puberty and adolescence and are specific for each sex. (Primary sex characteristics are the external genitals that distinguish one sex from the other.)

In girls the secondary sex characteristics include the development of breasts, hair over the lower abdomen and in the armpits, widening of the hips, and a filling out of the arms and legs.

In boys they include not only the development of hair over the lower abdomen above the genitals and under the arms, but the growth of hair on the cheeks, above the lips, and on the chin, as well as on the chest, arms, and legs. There is also a broadening of the shoulders and a marked increase in the size of the muscles of the arms and legs. And finally there is a change in the boy's voice from the high pitch of childhood to the lower tones of maturity.

Sex curiosity and interests

These manifest themselves when children are still young infants. In the course of exploring their own bodies, children find and handle their genitals and discover that they are areas of pleasurable sensation when touched.

Preschool children From approximately ages 3 to 6 years this interest in their own genitals is quite pronounced in most children. They ask numerous questions about their bodies and about their sex organs in particular –questions that call for honest and direct answers geared to the child's level of understanding. (See **Sex education in the home.**)

During these preschool years youngsters are also curious about the bodies of other children. They become very much interested in the difference between boys and girls and in the similarities that exist between themselves and other members of their own sex.

It is very worthwhile and important for boys and girls of this early age level to have opportunities to see one another in the nude. They should learn that boys and girls are made differently from each other—that all boys are made the same sexually and all girls are made the same. And it often gives little girls a sense of pride to know that their bodies are made the way they are so that when they are grown up they can have babies—something boys cannot do.

A boy and a girl of 5 or 6 years will often go off together, undress, and examine one another. This is perfectly normal and should not be discouraged unless too much time is being spent in the activity.

During the preschool period most children masturbate considerably, and

this is also entirely normal and should be accepted as such. This degree of masturbation subsides markedly during the period from approximately age 6 years until about age 12. (See **Masturbation.**)

School-age children During the school-age period (approximately 6 to 12 years) there is still considerable sex curiosity. The physical differences between the sexes are still of great interest to boys and girls at the early school ages of 6 or 7. And although children of opposite sexes tend to expose themselves less to one another after this age level, there is a good deal of voyeurism (peeping to observe nudity) during the years that follow.

The sex interests of children from 7 to 10 years are now extended to discussions of the sex act. These discussions are almost always between members of the same sex, for at this time boys generally go with boys and girls with girls.

Many children will come to their parents with questions concerning the sex act. Others will gain their information from books on the subject. Still others will obtain their facts (often incorrect) from their close companions or other boys and girls.

Most girls hear about menstruation as early as age 8 or 9 years and are highly curious concerning it. At this age great interest is also shown in sexual development, especially in girls, since they start developing a year or two before the boys.

As boys and girls start approaching puberty, at approximately age 10 or 11 years, early signs of interest in the other sex begin to appear. Boys will tease girls, and talk loudly and show off in front of them. Girls, for their part, will stand around in giggling groups when boys are present. Sex jokes are often told among members of the same sex and at times are even told to parents, either as an attempt by the young person to demonstrate his maturity or to gain some explanation.

In the latter grade-school years, as children approach puberty, girls once more invite boys, and boys invite girls to their parties, and there may be innocuous kissing games such as "spin the bottle." This is experimentation, for until puberty arrives there is, as a rule, no real sexual urge directed toward individuals of the opposite sex.

There is, generally, less masturbation during the school-age period as compared with the preschool level and adolescence. There may, however, be some masturbatory experimentation as boys and girls approach puberty.

Adolescence   As boys and girls enter puberty the functioning of their sex hormones, which become fully active at this time, brings with it a sudden and often intense arousal of sex interests, desires, and urges.

It is for this reason that if brothers and sisters sleep in the same bedroom, it is advisable for them to be separated when the girl, if older, starts to develop, or the boy, if older, reaches approximately 12 years of age.

The onset of sex interests in adolescents varies considerably with the individual. Most boys and girls have developed such interests by age 14 years, but a good number of normal teen-agers do not develop these interests until age 15 or 16.

When sex interests develop fully, girls dress up and try to make themselves attractive to boys, and boys make comparable efforts to attract girls. What was once mostly curiosity is now a real desire to be close to members of the other sex physically.

If no boys are available, girls will sometimes focus their sexual interests on other females. (See **Crushes.**) And when girls are unavailable boys will occasionally indulge temporarily in homosexual practices. (See **Homosexuality.**)

During adolescence there is a normal tendency to masturbate. It is during this period also that boys and girls are often concerned about their sexuality and worried about homosexuality.

See also **Sexual behavior in adolescence.**

Sex differences

Boys and girls are, of course, physically and physiologically different. Not only does the anatomy of their bodies differ, but the chromosomes throughout their bodies differ as well. In male infants the chromosomes show the male variation; in female infants, the female variation. These differences remain with a child throughout his life.

Today the sex differences, apart from biological differences, are less clearly defined. Women can dress like men; many men wear long hair; women compete successfully with men in almost all the fields of business or professional life; many men give a great deal of "mothering" to their children and take an active role in the household.

The question of whether there are inborn psychological differences between the sexes has not been finally settled. But as far as is known, emotional differences are not innate or inherited, but are the result of cultural patterns impressed on children from birth. Parents generally treat girls more tenderly than boys and expect them to be more passive, gentle, and ladylike. And boys are trained by their parents to develop traits of aggressiveness, leadership, and strength.

Today there is considerable controversy over whether this is the "right" way to raise children. Without getting into details, it can be said in general that raising a child in a way that interferes with his or her potential as a human being is not in the best interests of the child or society. A man who is embarrassed to be gentle or tender has stifled very rich human emotions. A woman who is afraid to develop her intelligence or to make decisions on her own is denying herself and others the benefit of all that can be accomplished by an intelligent and independent person. Being a man or woman does not depend upon such narrow interpretations of appropriate behavior. The goal to aim for is to allow a child to have an understanding of the full range of activity and accomplishment open to men and women, without confusing the child with notions as to what is masculine and what is feminine.

It is important for the sake of a child's future happiness and sexual adjustment to realize that both sexes are equally important and valued; boys should grow up happy that they are boys, and girls should grow up happy that they are girls, and they should have respect for one another. This is an extremely important factor in a healthy adult personality.

Sex education in the home

Most parents today are aware of the value of sex education for their children. "When should it start?" "How much should I tell them?" "What can I tell them about their father's role in reproduction?" These are some of the most common questions.

Preschool child Sex education usually starts somewhere between ages 3 and 5 years, when a child will almost always ask, "Mommy, where did I come from?" or "Where do babies come from?" These are almost always the first questions and should be answered simply: "Babies come from their mommies." There is no need for further discussion unless the child asks for more information. Sooner or later the next question will come: "Where in their mommies?" —and the answer, "In their mother's belly, in a special place just for babies below the mother's stomach, or tummy." Too many people confuse children by answering only, "In their mother's stomach, or tummy," which gives the child the impression that the baby is in the same place as the food that is eaten.

The questions will usually continue to come from that time on if they are answered by the parent. But, in answering these questions about birth and reproduction, there are four main rules for parents to remember:

1. Always tell the truth.
2. Use the correct terms.
3. Never put off answering.
4. (For children under the approximate age of 6) Answer only as much as the child asks and no more.

Children of the preschool age should also know the physical differences between boys and girls. If no child of the opposite sex is in the house, parents should be sure that the child has the chance to see other young children or infants in the nude. Children should know that all boys are built the same and grow up to be men, and all girls are built the same and grow up to be women. Little girls, who occasionally envy the boys for their external genitals, should be told that girls are built the way they are so that they can have babies when they are grown up. (See **Sex curiosity and interests; Sex differences.**)

Good books on the subject will usually help parents greatly. (See **Bibliography.**)

School-age child   The school-age child is generally much readier to receive sex education than children who are younger. The primary principles of sex education—to tell the truth, use the correct terms, and answer when asked a question—still hold. However, a parent can and should explain much more to a child over 6, for there are many basic facts of birth and reproduction that every school-age child should know.

If children at this age level do not ask questions concerning sex, discussions may be brought about in various ways. Visiting the newborn infant of a friend, or having pregnant animals such as guinea pigs, hamsters, white mice, cats, or dogs, will usually provide the necessary springboard. Taking children to farms where they can observe the habits of farm animals is also helpful as a starting point.

If parents find the subject difficult to handle, there are well-written, well-illustrated books that may be read with the child.

At about age 9 years, menstruation should be explained to girls. They should learn that menstruation is normal and healthy, one of the signs of maturity in girls and a preparation for motherhood. (See **Menstruation.**)   At about age 11 or 12 boys should be told of nocturnal seminal emmisions. (See **Nocturnal seminal emission.**)

See also **Sex education in the schools.**

Sex education in the schools
Sex education in the schools is now being undertaken in many parts of the country. This has come about largely in response to the knowledge that children today are being brought up in a world of changing sexual mores. For example, on television, children all too frequently see stories of broken marriages, illicit love affairs, and adultery. Nationwide, there has been a marked increase in the rate of divorce; abortions by teen-age girls have reached high levels; and there has been a great upsurge in the number of cases of venereal disease.

Studies have shown that sex education of high school students tends to lower not only the incidence of venereal disease but the number of illegitimate pregnancies.

Although ideally sex education should come from the home, unfortunately very few children receive adequate information from their parents. Most parents shy away from the subject because of their own upbringing and inhibitions; some parents know the answers but lack the words for adequate explanation; and some parents lack the answers.

Practically all authorities on child development and education, and practically all social agencies and religious leaders, have come to a common conclusion that schools must take some responsibility for the basics of sex education.

This does not imply that sex education should be given as a specific course by itself or that it should, as many people erroneously feel, be specifically devoted to a discussion of the sex act. Sex education deals with birth and reproduction, sex differences, the relations of men and women, sex identity and sex roles, and teen-age boy-girl relationships.

With this format, sex education can start in the kindergarten and primary grades of school in the general activities of the class: planting vegetable seeds, caring for classroom pets of both sexes—and their babies, learning that life comes from life and that in practically all animals and all human beings there must be a father and a mother before a baby can be born.

And throughout the school years that follow, sex education can be correlated with the general curriculum. In English class good books portraying loving family relationships can be read and discussed. In geography and social studies children can discuss the customs of other countries relating to family life and marriage. Civics can cover courts and laws relating to marriage, family responsibilities, laws to protect the unborn child, laws concerning equal rights of men and women.

In junior high school and especially in high school, sex education is most important, for this is the period when growing boys and girls suddenly develop new sex interests, urges, and desires. They need reassurance that these new drives are normal, and they need direction. Here, the teacher must be specially trained to deal intelligently and capably with the many questions asked by these teen-agers.

Often this area of sex education is given in a course under such titles as "Problems of Modern Living," "Preparation for Married Home Life," and "Looking toward Marriage."

The teacher must gain the confidence and respect of the students through be-ing mature, informed, and able to inspire an understanding of responsibility in sexual behavior.

Often the teacher can do a far better job of sex education than can the parents. Not only can he be more objective, but he receives little or none of the automatic negativism that teen-agers frequently direct at their parents' views.

Sex offenders, protecting child from

All parents are concerned about possible dangers to their children from sex offenders. They want their children to be friendly to people and not fearful. But at the same time they must strongly warn them of danger.

It is not necessary to go into any frightening or gruesome details. It is usually enough to warn young children that there are some people who are bad, and who take children away from their parents or hurt them.

There are also important rules that should be impressed on the child:

Never go with strangers or anyone else unless your mother or father tells you to do so.

Never accept candy or gifts from strangers.

Never take rides with people you don't know, or anyone else, unless your parents know it.

Never go with strangers who ask you for directions.

Never go with anyone who offers you a job with pay.

Never play alone in alleys or deserted buildings.

Always take a companion with you when you go to movies, stores, etc.

Try to get the license number of the car of anyone who tries to get you to enter his car. Take a stone and scratch the number on the sidewalk.

What should the parent do if the child has been, or the parent thinks he has been, involved in an incident with a stranger? In the first place, the parent should not scold, shame, or punish the child. Nor should the child be subjected to hysteria, harrying questions, or the like. If parents or other adults become very upset, and convey feelings of fear and disgust to the child, this can do more harm than the actual experience. It is essential that the child not be burdened with deep feelings of guilt or fear.

On the other hand, the subject should not be dropped as if nothing had ever happened. Without pressuring the child, give him or her plenty of opportunity to talk about the experience and get it out of his system. Parents who feel that some psychological damage may have been done should seek professional guidance on the subject.

As for community prevention, the following steps may be taken:

Report all offenders.

Organize mothers to take turns watching children.

Set aside certain sections for children at movie theatres.

See that streets are adequately lit in the evenings and at night.

Arrange to have discussions on the subject at churches, clubs, and schools, and distribute literature on the subject.

Note: There is no way a parent can distinguish a sex offender by sight, or usually even by acquaintance. Certainly, the stereotype of an aggressive or wild-eyed individual does not hold, for more often than not the offender is timid and withdrawn.

Sexual behavior in adolescence

As boys and girls enter adolescence, they begin to take a deep interest in the opposite sex. Often quite suddenly they develop an intense desire to be near one another, to touch one another, and sooner or later to have sexual relations with someone of the opposite sex. This is all physically, emotionally, and sexually normal.

All parents have without doubt been through this stage in their own development, but the adolescent codes of boy-girl relationships, of conduct, of ethics, and of morals have changed greatly during the past two decades. It is not clear whether there is a significant change in the amount of sexual activity, but certainly attitudes have changed greatly. There are far more sexually stimulating books and movies available to both adults and teen-agers, and there is in general a greater emphasis on sexuality. There is greater frankness in discussing sex, and teen-agers today want to talk openly about problems that formerly they would have kept to themselves. Many of them also want to integrate their sexual feelings with feelings of love and respect. For example, the former pattern of boys satisfying their sexual desires with prostitutes rather than with their girl friends seems to be waning. More teen-agers are required at a younger age to make difficult decisions regarding their sexual feelings.

There was a time, only a few years ago, when parents felt they could rely on warnings against the disastrous experience of teen-age pregnancy and the great danger of venereal diseases. But the use of birth-control pills and other contraceptive measures, the comparative ease of obtaining abortions in many communities, and the use of antibiotics in the treatment of venereal disease have greatly weakened such arguments.

How is a parent to act in the face of current adolescent morality, according to which premarital sex experiences are so often accepted rather than condemned? Many parents attempt simply to forbid sexual activity, but this is usually ineffective, for the adolescent is normally resistant to the parents. Religious education and lectures on morality have been equally ineffective.

The best approach is through building and maintaining a close relationship between parent and child. The teen-ager must feel that his parents have a deep interest in him and an understanding of his attitudes and needs. The subject of sexual relationships should be discussed without the parents' showing anger, derision, or disgust. If good communication exists between the teen-ager and the parents, the boy or girl is more likely to act with responsibility.

But the fact that parents should help their children to feel they can be frank with them does not mean that they should be afraid of expressing their own views, even if they are opposed to the youngster's. A parent should state his views and explain his reasons. Every child wants to know that his parents care very much for his well-being, and many teen-agers are in fact looking for good reasons not to get involved in relationships for which they do not yet feel ready.

In addition to a good relationship between parents and child, it is generally of great help to adolescents if sex education has been available in elementary school and if there is a good program in high school. Sex education as part of a high school curriculum has been shown to have effectively reduced the number of pregnancies and cases of venereal disease.

There are some parents who simply throw up their hands in the face of present-day sexual behavior. These parents will provide a daughter with birth-control pills or have her fitted with a diaphragm as soon as she starts going out with boys or goes away to school. This attitude is to be condemned, since it gives parental consent and even encouragement to promiscuity. It conveys to the young girl that her parents assume she will not be able to make a reasoned and responsible decision on sexual behavior and that, moreover, they do not care what decision she does make.

On the other hand, if a teen-age girl going steady with a boy comes to her mother for information on birth control, she should receive it. At the same time, the mother should talk to the girl and frankly advise her. It may turn out that the girl is seeking the general advice as much as the birth-control information. But when parents react by refusing information and even actively interfering in the relationship, the result is all too often exactly the opposite of what they hope, and the girl becomes pregnant.

Many sex educators today feel that sex education courses given in the high school curriculum should include information on birth-control practices, since many young people have serious misunderstandings on this subject. The last two years of high school are years when there are a great many pregnancies (and cases of venereal disease) in all parts of the country and in all types of schools—public, private, and parochial.

It should be noted that there is no real evidence to show that boys and girls who have had premarital sex during their teen years are any less happy or well-adjusted during their marriage years than those who abstained. This, of course, does not include the emotionally upset, promiscuous teen-ager who seeks sex activity as a compensation for deep unhappiness.

Sexual development   see Adolescence; Puberty.

Shaming

Parents who try to change a child's behavior by making him feel that he is inferior to others—naughty, selfish, stupid, etc.—are doing more harm than good. They may effectively change the surface behavior, but they are also changing the child's basic image of himself.

Gestures, facial expressions, derogatory words, and tone of voice—all are sometimes used to shame a child.

It is of primary importance that the young child feel his parents love and respect him. And so parents must find ways of changing a child's undesired behavior without making him feel self-conscious and inadequate.

Parents should attempt to understand just why a child is acting as he does. The first reaction to a child's behavior may be that it is undesirable and rude, but calling him a "dope" or a "little pig" in a disdainful tone of voice will have no positive, lasting effect. In essence, the parent is passing judgment on the child without carefully investigating the reasons for the behavior. If the parent will only speak with the child and find out why he is acting as he is, then alternate ways of behavior can be discussed.

With adolescents, fathers and mothers may break down communication if they try to shame them into their adult standards of behavior. At this age period the behavior standards of friends and companions are extremely important. Parents who make the adolescent feel that they do not respect him or his judgment risk losing the confidence and sharing of ideas that they have hopefully tried to build up over the preceding years.

Once again, discussing values and ideas openly; listening to the adolescent's ideas and his reasons for them; trying to understand the basis for his values; respecting his reasoning but at the same time letting him know how you feel and why you feel a certain way—such efforts and attitudes build up his own self-respect rather than causing him to suffer the humiliation caused by shaming.

Shampoo, swallowed   see Poisons: first-aid treatment.

Shampooing   see Hair washing.

Sharing

For young children the concept of sharing is difficult to accept. They may feel very unhappy and upset when another child plays with or borrows their toys or wishes to take a turn on a piece of play equipment that they have been using.

In our society "property rights" are quite important. The young child learns very early, "These are Daddy's books; don't touch." In this case the parent will usually substitute some of the child's books and say, "Here, these are your books; you may read them."

Later, the same day, a small friend may visit, and when Junior doesn't want the other child to touch his books, Mother's response will most likely be, "You have to learn to share," or "Give your friend a turn to read your books." This can be very confusing for the young child. If he cannot play with Daddy's books, why must someone else play with his?

As a child grows a little more socially mature and has more contact with other children of his age, he will meet an increasing number of situations in which trading toys, taking turns, and borrowing something for a few minutes can become mutually satisfying experiences. He will learn that his friend can play with his ball while he tries out the friend's new bike; that he can slide down the slide and wait until the next child has slid down before he does it again himself. He begins to be able to feel how the other child or person feels because he recognizes in him some of his own feelings.

When children do not have the opportunity of playing with other children of their own approximate age, it is difficult for them to learn how to share, take turns, or respect another's property. This is one of the reasons that nursery schools or small play groups are especially advisable for the child who does not have companions of his own age.

However, there may be a certain toy, article of clothing, or other possession which is very special to a child—a baby blanket, a certain stuffed animal. (See **Security object.**) A child should not be pressured to share this especially treasured item.

Gradually, through the guidance and examples of his parents and others, a child learns how to share and take turns.

Shingles

An infectious disease characterized by a line of burning and itching pimples and small blisters around one side of the chest. It is caused by the same virus that causes chicken pox, and chicken pox may occur following exposure to shingles. It is believed that an attack of shingles confers immunity in the future.

The virus affects one of the nerves of the skin that run from the backbone around to the front of the chest.

The earliest signs are burning, itching, and pain around the chest on one side. Within a few days the typical rash appears and the diagnosis is definite. Pain diminishes, as a rule, after the eruption appears.

In children the disease is relatively mild: the pimples and tiny blisters dry up and crust rather rapidly, and the whole condition disappears in two to three weeks. In adults the condition may be very painful and debilitating.

There is no treatment other than efforts at relieving the pain and keeping the child comfortable.

Shock

A temporary state of physiological distress or collapse usually following a severe accident or loss of blood.

The severity of shock varies from the minor symptoms that may follow the slamming of a finger in a door to the major shock following a serious accident or an extensive burn.

With minor shock, which follows a simple accident such as the finger-slamming, the child becomes pale, and cold sweat appears on his forehead and hands. He feels very weak and may become nauseated and vomit. These symptoms usually last only a few moments, and no treatment is necessary.

In cases of severe shock the signs and symptoms are similar but of greater intensity. They may occur immediately after an accident or may develop minutes or even hours later. The cause of these symptoms is a disruption of proper blood circulation.

Signs and symptoms of severe shock

1. The child's face is pale, and there may be a bluish tinge to the ears and lips. The eyelids are partially closed, and the eyes stare vacantly.

2. Cold perspiration stands out on the forehead, and the palms of the hands are cold and clammy.

3. The pulse is weak and very rapid. At times it is so weak it cannot be felt.

4. Often the child develops a chill with chattering teeth and shaking body.

5. Nausea and vomiting usually occur.

6. The child shows little or no interest in his surroundings, or may be unconscious. If he is conscious, he may have to be spoken to several times before he responds.

7. The child's breathing is irregular and varies in quality. There are often a few long, deep breaths followed by a series of short, shallow breaths.

Emergency treatment

1. Heating the child's body is most important, since the body is unable to keep itself warm with an inadequate flow of blood and a weak pulse. Cover the child warmly with blankets and apply external heat if possible. Electric pads, hot-water bottles (if you are on the road, hot water may be obtained from auto radiators), or heated bricks should also be used, taking great care that the child is not burned.

2. Let the child remain lying down with the head low. The blood pressure is very low, and sitting up may not let adequate blood go the brain.

3. Stimulants are especially helpful in minor cases of shock. Coffee and tea, both of which contain caffein, are excellent, given as hot as can be comfortably taken. Aromatic spirits of ammonia, 1 teaspoon in ½ glass of water, is also a good stimulant.

4. In severe cases medical care is urgent, not only to give the child plasma or blood if necessary, but to be sure there is no internal bleeding, fractured skull, or other injury which may not be evident.

Shock, anaphylactic see **Anaphylaxis.**

Shock, electric see **Electric shock.**

Shoes
When babies pull themselves up to a standing position in the playpen or crib at about 8 or 9 months of age, most parents start thinking about the first pair of shoes.

But there is no rush to put walking shoes on an infant until he is over a year old and taking a few steps by himself without support. Until that time he should walk barefooted on carpeted floors and wear booties or soft-soled shoes to cover his feet when out-of-doors.

When a baby is standing without shoes and pulling himself around—holding on to chairs, the side of the crib, or a parent's hand—he is constantly grasping the floor with his feet. This exercises the arch muscles, especially when the surface is resilient rather than hard.

The first pair of shoes should have semisoft soles so the child's feet still get a fair amount of exercise. However, even though a child has walking shoes for use out-of-doors to protect his feet, he should still go barefooted or with stockinged feet at home so that his feet get plenty of active exercise. (During the summer months, if a child is in the country or at the shore, he should walk without shoes on the grass or sand, if the ground is free of objects that might be injurious.)

Good sneakers may also be used for toddlers and older children. They are cool, flexible, and have rubber arch supports. It is not necessary for a child to wear high shoes, since the support of the foot comes from beneath and not from the sides.

In the early years children's feet grow rapidly, so that new shoes may be necessary every two to three months. Parents themselves can usually tell when the child has outgrown his current pair of shoes. The foot should not be tightly cramped in the shoe, and the longest toe should be half an inch from the tip of the shoe.

See also **Feet.**

Short attention span see **Attention span, short.**

Shortness see **Height.**

Shots see **Immunization schedule and tests; Pediatrician.**

Showing off
The child who has a tendency to show off constantly is usually a child with a problem. Either he lacks attention, feels that he lacks attention, or feels that he is not liked or loved. Constant demands for attention differ greatly from an occasional demonstration by a child of a new accomplishment: "Watch me tie my shoe," or "Look how well I can climb a tree."

Sometimes when a young child does something cute, parents encourage him to show off in front of friends and company. But often this cute behavior of a young child is annoying and displeasing if continued two or three years later.

During the school years the show-off is often an unaccepted, unpopular child who feels inferior. He is the child who is unruly in class, making noise, throwing things across the room, and talking back to the teacher—all in an attempt to gain the attention and admiration of the class.

If a child continues to show off, parents should try to understand why he needs to make this bid for extra attention, and, if at all possible, they should aid him in overcoming his problem. Such a child requires help and building up rather than scolding and punishment.

Another type of showing off, which is of no seriousness, occurs frequently during the preadolescent and early teen-age years. This is showing off in an attempt to gain the attention and admiration of the opposite sex.

Generally, showing off subsides as children get older, if they have been helped through their problems and have become more secure.

Shyness
A very shy child is almost always insecure, fearful, has little or no self-confidence or self-esteem, and withdraws from or avoids what he considers threatening situations or people. Situations which are threatening to the shy child may not seem so to others.

Many young children are normally shy between ages 12 and 18 months. They cling to their mother and hide behind her when a stranger approaches. This is usually just a transition from the period when a child is completely dependent on his parents to an awareness of and uncertainty about others who appear from time to time.

There are a number of possible contributing causes of shyness in an older child. If the parent is overprotective and gives the child no opportunity to develop self-assurance and independence, the child is likely to be shy and fearful.

The child may not feel capable of being on his own or of asserting himself.

A child may have been so overindulged that he has rarely had to work things out for himself. Often adults step in and prevent a child from building up his own social relationships. He feels inadequate in his relationships with other children and shies away from them.

An overdemanding parent, who expects more than a child feels capable of doing, causes the child to feel less and less adequate—eventually causing withdrawal.

Overstrict parents, who punish youngsters for every little thing, will cause many children to withdraw rather than stand the chance of being punished for a possible blunder.

When a child of preschool age and older is extremely shy, the cause should be sought and corrected.

Sibling rivalry and jealousy

Almost always when parents have one child between about 2 and 5 years of age and a new baby is born, the older child becomes upset and jealous. This occurs in practically every home—although it may take some months before the jealousy of the older child for the baby become evident.

The older child has for some years been the center of attention in the home and the focus of the parents' love. Then the new child arrives, and the attention and love of the parents must be shared. Relatives and friends arrive to see the baby and bring presents for it—and again the attention is focused on the newcomer.

Frequently the older child cannot be convinced that he is loved just as much as he was previously, and he will often express his sense of rejection openly:

"Why did you bring home a new baby? Wasn't I good enough?"

As the children grow older, the rivalry and jealousy usually continue in varying degrees. The older child still feels that the baby is more loved and has certain advantages. For example, the older child will build a building with blocks, of which he is proud—only to see it knocked down by the creeping baby. He pushes or slaps the baby—and gets scolded. The baby who started it is cuddled to calm its crying. And so on and on.

Many children below age 5, seeing the attention given the baby, will revert to infantile habits in an effort to be a baby again. They will often start soiling and wetting again; some will creep instead of walking; others will ask for their milk in a bottle; still others will start using baby talk again; some will jump into the baby carriage or crib once the baby is taken out. (See **Regression.**)

Many jealous children hold it within themselves but show their unhappiness in diverse ways. For example, some have nightmares or night terrors; some will knock down or push younger children they meet in the street, the park, or nursery school.

As time goes on, rivalry and jealousy are not confined to the older child. When the younger child becomes assertive and often aggressive, he is frequently jealous of the older child, who gets special privileges. He also may compete with him for the parents' attention, trying to do everything the older child does.

If the family grows larger, there is often less sibling rivalry and jealousy because, as a rule, the parents cannot focus special attention on any individual child.

Parents should realize that some degree of rivalry and jealousy between brothers and sisters always exists, but should try to minimize it as much as possible. How can this be done?

The older child and the newborn

1. Give the older child presents from the mother while she is in the hospital.
2. If possible, bring the older child to the hospital to accompany Mother home with the new baby. Let the older child sit with the mother.
3. If the older child is at nursery school, let him stay home when the baby arrives and remain home a few days during the period of adjustment.
4. Give the older child special attention at home, and tell relatives and friends who come to see the baby to pay attention first to the older child.
5. It is important not to place the baby's bassinette or crib in the parents' bedroom, for the older child will usually assume that the baby is favored more and loved more. It is better to place the infant in another room—even if it has to be the living room. The mother will always wake up if the baby cries—for a baby's crying is a mother's best alarm clock. Of course, a mother can take the baby into her room to nurse it or change it.
6. Let the older child help with the baby as much as possible and receive appreciation for it. Let him also imitate the mother's care of the baby with a doll, doll bottles, and doll carriages.
7. Emphasize to the older child over and over again, "I could never love anyone more than I love you."

To minimize sibling rivalry and jealousy in older children

1. Show no favoritism.
2. Make no comparisons which might be derogatory to either child.
3. If an older child is taken to something special, such as a movie, the ballet, or a ball game, the younger child should be taken to something on his level, such as the zoo or a special playground.
4. The older child should have special privileges, such as going to bed later and getting an allowance first. At the same time, the younger child should know that he also will receive these privileges and benefits when he reaches that age.
5. When the older child starts school and a younger child is left home, the school child often worries that his brother or sister at home is getting all the attention. To relieve this anxiety, parents should show a great interest in the older child's doings at school—asking questions each day and pinning up his school paintings or crayonings so that they can be seen by everyone.
6. When bringing a present for one child, a present should be brought for the others as well—except of course in the case of birthdays, graduation, and similar occasions.
7. Older children should be prevented from hurting a younger child and, as far possible, from habitually teasing or bossing him. And, as far as possible, a younger child should be prevented from playing with or destroying the older children's belongings and interfering in their activities.

Parents should, of course, realize that all fights and arguments between children are not caused by sibling problems. Fighting is usually an occasional accompaniment of all close child relationships at home and among companions. There may be fighting one minute and happy playing the next. In many if not most situations brothers and sisters can work out their own arguments. (See **Quarrels**.)

Sometimes when parents read about the problems of sibling rivalry and jealousy, they wonder if they should have more than one child. The answer is that the benefits of companionship, learning to share, and not being the sole focus of attention far outweigh any of the difficulties of sibling rivalry and jealously.

See also **Oldest child; Only child; Middle child; Second child; Youngest child.**

Sickle-cell anemia

A hereditary disease of the blood which occurs almost entirely among Negroes. It is estimated that 10 percent of American Negroes have this genetic trait. It is characterized by red blood cells which are crescent- or sickle-shaped and which break up easily, causing anemia. Because of the irregular shape of the cells,

Blood cells greatly magnified. The normal red blood cells are round, somewhat resembling doughnuts. In sickle-cell anemia, there are sickle-shaped or new-moon-shaped cells mixed with normal cells.

they tend to tangle and clump, forming clots that can lead to severe pain.

Children with this condition have recurrent attacks of anemia, weakness, loss of appetite, abdominal pain, jaundice, and gallstones. There is also an enlargement of the liver and spleen. These attacks are often precipitated by an acute infection. Damage to the liver and kidneys often causes death before 20 years of age.

There is no cure for the disease. Treatment involves relieving the symptoms when they occur. Transfusions are often helpful in reducing the anemia and temporarily preventing a breakdown of the child's red blood cells.

Prevention can only be effected at the present time through genetic study and advice. A blood test has recently been perfected to quickly determine whether a person is carrying the sickle-cell trait. Research on treatment is continuing. (See **Genetic counseling**.)

Sickly child   see **Susceptibility to infections.**

Sinusitis

An inflammation of the sinuses, hollow cavities in the skull connected to the nasal passages.

Not all of the sinuses present in adults and older children are already present when a baby is born. The sinuses in the cheekbones and behind the eyes are usually large enough at birth to harbor infections. The frontal sinuses, those in the forehead above the eyes, rarely develop before age 6, but from that time on they may become infected during colds and other inflammations of the nose and throat. Chronic sinusitis is found in relation to allergies, enlarged adenoids that close the sinus openings, and infected teeth.

Sinusitis in children is usually of the acute variety, occurring during infections of the nose and throat and subsiding as the infection subsides.

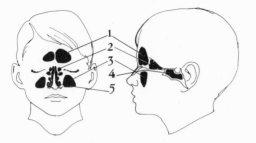

1. Frontal sinuses. 2. Ethmoid sinuses. 3. Maxillary sinuses. 4. Sphenoid sinuses. 5. Turbinate cartilage.

Signs and symptoms Headache, localized tenderness, nasal discharge, at times fever, and puffiness over the infected sinus.

Diagnosis is easily made by X rays, which show definite clouding of the involved sinuses.

Treatment Essentially the same as the treatment for infection of the nose and throat. This may include antibiotics plus the use of decongestants given either orally or by nasal spray.

Sitters see **Baby-sitters.**

Sitting up

The average infant enjoys being pulled by his hands to a sitting position when he is as young as 3 or 4 months. This activity is safe as long as it does not put a strain on the baby's spine and back muscles. This can be avoided if parents keep holding the baby's hands while pulling up, so that his full weight is not on his spine.

When the infant is 5 months old he may be placed in an almost upright position, leaning slightly back on a pillow or other support. In this position he begins to adjust to the sitting position.

Between ages 6 and 7 months most babies will sit almost upright with their hands forward and down on the mattress or floor to maintain balance. They will sit well in a high chair or propped up in a carriage or stroller.

The average infant of 7 to 8 months is able to sit up a few minutes without support, and by 8 months may sit as long as 10 minutes unsupported. It should be noted, however, that many perfectly normal babies may not support themselves in a sitting position until age 9 or 10 months.

Between 8 and 9 months, with increased mastery of their muscles, most infants can pull themselves up into a sitting position, and often are beginning to pull themselves up from a sitting to a standing position. This stage of development, like all others, also varies with the individual child.

If an infant does not sit unsupported by age 10 months, consult the doctor. The child may be heavier than the average infant and so have more weight to support. Or the late development may result from a temporary lack of muscle tone or a lack of adequate thyroid functioning. In rare instances, in conjunction with other signs and symptoms, it may be caused by mental retardation or some nerve disorder.

Skin, harmful substances on see **Poisons: first-aid treatment.**

Skin and skin disorders see **Abscess; Acne; Birthmarks; Blackhead; Chafing; Chapped skin; Cold sores; Erysipelas; Newborn, characteristics of; Prickly heat; Warts.**

Skin tests for allergies

When a child develops allergic signs and symptoms such as sneezing, red and itchy eyes, runny nose, asthma, or eczema, the doctor will attempt to find the causes for these reactions.

The most common method of diagnosis is through allergic testing of the child's skin. This is performed by making extracts of substances to which the child might be sensitive and either injecting a small amount into the outer layer of the skin, placing a drop on the skin and scratching through it with a sterile needle, or, when the doctor suspects that the condition is caused by something that has touched the skin, placing the substance on the skin.

Intradermal test This is considered the most accurate of the skin tests. With a syringe and a fine needle a small amount of the solution is injected into the outer layer of the skin. A small, white, round lump results. If the child is sensitive to the substance injected, a large white hive with an irregular, jagged border appears in ten to fifteen minutes. This often itches. The reaction disappears within an hour, as a rule. If the child is not sensitive, the small injection lump subsides in a few minutes.

1. Intradermal test: puncture and area of reaction. 2. Scratch test: scratch and area of reaction. If the person is very sensitive, an irregular welt appears around the puncture or scratch.

The doctor always has adrenalin on hand in case the child responds to the test with a severe allergic reaction.

Scratch test This is a simpler test but not considered as sensitive or accurate. A drop of the solution is placed on the skin, and a scratch is made through the solution with a sterile needle. If the child is sensitive to the substance in the solution, a white, irregular swelling appears along the needle line in five to ten minutes. This usually subsides within an hour.

Patch test This is used to diagnose allergies the doctor suspects are caused by something that has been in contact with the skin, such as wool, a skin lotion, a powder, a soap.

Usually the gauze on a Band-Aid (or similar adhesive bandage) is wet with an extract of the substance, and the tape is placed on the skin. If a fabric is suspected, a piece of it may be directly taped to the skin. The Band-Aid or fabric is removed after about forty-eight hours, and the skin beneath the patch observed. An irritated area indicates that the child's skin is sensitive to the substance.

Intradermal or scratch tests are usually effective in diagnosing the cause of allergy due to substances inhaled, and patch tests are often effective in diagnosing skin rashes due to substances in contact with the skin. Skin tests are not very effective, however, in diagnosing the cause of eczema or gastrointestinal allergies. Elimination diets are much more reliable in detecting the cause of these conditions. (See **Diet, elimination.**)

Skull fracture   see **Fractures.**

Slang   see **Swear words.**

Slapping see **Discipline.**

Sleep

Sleep patterns vary with the individual child and are related to the child's age as well. One child may sleep lightly, constantly moving around in his crib or bed. Another may sleep very deeply and move very little. One child may require more sleep than another. One child sleeps lying on his stomach; another child sleeps on his back or side.

How long should children sleep? This of course varies, but until about age 6 months children sleep approximately twenty to twenty-two hours a day. Between 6 months and 1 year of age, most children sleep through the night and have two naps a day. Somewhere between 1 and 2 years of age, one of these naps is given up, leaving a single morning or afternoon nap. This nap may be a daily occurrence until the child is about 5 years old, although some youngsters will later just rest quietly without really sleeping. (See **Naps.**)

The preschool child should generally be in bed by 7:30 or 8 P.M., except for special occasions. The school-age child should generally be in bed by 8:30 or 9 P.M., with lights off half an hour later. After age 12 the child needs eight to nine hours of sleep every night.

See also **Bedtime hour.**

Sleep problems

These are the most common complaints brought by the parents to the pediatrician. Crying at night, resisting sleep, waking frequently during the night, waking up too early, demanding that parents be present, wanting to sleep in the parents' bed, refusing to go to bed— these are just some of the numerous sleep problems that occasionally arise.

Infants crying at night The most common causes of night crying during the first year are abdominal pain, hunger, sucking need, cutting teeth, being wet or soiled, fearing the dark, and desiring the attention of the parents.

Colic is a common cause of crying in infancy, but usually, if an infant cries only at night and rarely during the day, it is not due to colic. Occasionally there is regular nighttime abdominal pain when the child is given something to which he is sensitive—such as his daily vitamin drops—in the evening only. In such cases, the offending substance may be withdrawn and a substitute given.

Hunger is a common cause of crying at night that can be easily diagnosed by giving the child more nursing or formula. Older infants, those of approximately 6 months to a year, occasionally get into the habit of awakening and crying for milk at 3 or 4 A.M. This can usually be relieved by one of two methods. The first is to give extra food at the last feeding at night in the hope of better satisfying the baby's appetite and aiding him in sleeping through. The other method, which is often successful, is to continue to give the infant milk at 3 or 4 A.M., but gradually to dilute it more and more with water until the child is receiving only water. This method is based on the assumption that when a baby is accustomed to receiving a feeding at a certain time, the stomach juices come out at that time and hunger results. If the child receives less and less food content at a particular time, eventually the flow of digestive juice will subside and hunger at that time will cease.

All babies have a need for sucking satisfaction, a need that is entirely separate from the sucking to satisfy hunger. Many but not all infants who are breast-fed and nurse thirty to forty minutes satisfy this need and are relaxed and quiet between feedings. However, bottle-fed infants often finish their formulas within ten minutes and derive too little sucking satisfaction. If they are given a pacifier or if they suck a finger, they will stop crying almost immediately. If an infant's crying at night is caused by a desire for sucking satisfaction, it will be relieved at once by giving him a pacifier.

Cutting teeth is a fairly common cause of night crying after the age of 5 months. It can usually be relieved by rubbing the gums with an anesthetic ointment or solution or with paregoric—as prescribed by the doctor. Aspirin, usually a single infant dose, will also help relieve the pain. This can be repeated in four hours if necessary. (See **Aspirin**.) Apparently during the day the infant is so occupied by the world around him that he is less bothered by the pain in his gums. (See **Teething**.)

Being wet or soiled is a rare cause of night crying, but there are occasional children who are sensitive to wet or soiled diapers and cry when these are against them. A simple change of diapers will relieve these children of their discomfort.

As infants grow older and are more aware of their surroundings, many of them dislike the complete darkness of night. Crying will usually be readily relieved by having a dim night light in the child's room, or leaving a light on in the hallway with the door ajar.

Resisting sleep This is very common after children have passed age 6 or 7 months. The infant may cry vigorously, but as soon as the parent arrives the cries change to smiles, and the child loves to be lifted up and cuddled.

It is best not to let infants cry it out until they near one year of age, when they are more understanding. Prior to that time, when a child is so completely dependent on his parents, he cannot possibly understand why they will not come and relieve his unhappiness. He cannot help but feel ignored and rejected. However, when the baby nears a year of age, he can be cuddled, placed in the crib, kissed good night, and told to go to sleep. The child will usually cry but can be permitted to cry for a half hour, at which time the parent should come in, calm him down, and put him to bed again. The child will usually cry again. The parent returns every half hour and calms him down. The child will cry less and less each successive night, and the problem is usually completely solved within a week.

Children during the toddler and preschool years may also resist going to sleep, but then the reasons are usually quite different. First, they have learned that an interesting life is going on while they are in bed, and they want to be part of this life. Second, young children, especially during the toddler years, are easily overstimulated—sometimes by the father, who comes home and plays vigorously with them; sometimes by watching an exciting television program; sometimes by just jumping around. These children should have a quiet and relaxing hour before going to bed.

Children of this age sometimes take long naps during the day and consequently are not tired when bedtime arrives. These youngsters should either have a shorter nap or a later bedtime.

One further common cause of a toddler's resisting sleep is the fear of the dark. This is easily corrected, as during infancy, by a dim night light in the room or by a hall light with the door left ajar.

During the preschool period emotional problems may also contribute to sleep problems. For example, this is the age when many children react to separation from their parents (as when parents take an extended vacation without them) by resisting sleep. When the parents return, they will often resist sleep and then wake frequently during the night to make sure that they have not disappeared again. The same reaction occurs when some familiar person has died or disappeared (as when a nurse or maid who has been with the family leaves, or when a father leaves for an extended business trip or duty in the armed forces).

Nightmares, night terrors, and sleepwalking These are most common during the preschool period and are caused by anxieties. (See **Nightmares and night terrors; Sleepwalking.**)

Sleeping with parents During the preschool period many boys and girls attempt to sleep in their parents' bed. They will awaken in the middle of the night, walk into the parents' room, and climb into their bed. This should not be permitted in spite of the fact that the child may cry vigorously, for once the habit of sleeping in a parent's bed is established, it is extremely difficult to break. The child should be told that he has his own bed and that this is Mommy and Daddy's bed. He should be picked up and brought back to his own room every time he comes to his parents' bedside. If he still attempts it, the parents should open their door slightly but block it with a doorstop, so

that the child can no longer enter their room.

Imaginary animals At approximately age 5, when imagination is at its height, many children have anxieties about imaginary animals that are in their closets or looking in their windows. This is only a passing phase, generally disappearing within the year. The child should be shown that there is no animal in the closet and that no animal could possibly be at his window, and a light should be left on in the room. The explanation usually helps very little, but the fear disappears rather quickly if not too much is made of it.

Older children During the school years, in most instances, sleep problems usually relate to a child's wanting to stay up to see some popular television program—or simply wanting to assert his independence.

During early adolescence and adolescence, difficulty falling asleep is a very common problem. Boys and girls of this age have many real concerns and problems—their bodily changes; their new body functions; their new sex urges, interests, and desires; their social adjustment. So much is on their minds. One method of relaxing these concerned young folks is to let them have a radio on in their room while they are falling asleep. It takes their mind off their problems and eventually lulls them to sleep. The parents can turn off the radio later.

Persistent problems If a child at any age continually has difficulty getting to sleep or staying asleep, parents should consult with the doctor, especially if the child seems upset about the situation or upset in other ways. It may be that the trouble is passing and not serious, but it is also possible that the child is emotionally distressed. The cause should be discovered.

See also **Bedtime hour.**

Sleeping on side of head   see **Head, flattening of.**

Sleeping-sickness encephalitis

This is a lay term for various forms of encephalitis transmitted to human beings by the bite of a mosquito. It includes the so-called St. Louis encephalitis and the equine encephalitis of which there are several types in the United States: the Eastern, the Western, and the Venezuelan.

In spite of the local names associated with these conditions they may be found in occasional epidemics in all parts of the United States. The term "sleeping sickness" is derived from the symptoms of the disease.

There are three types of the St. Louis variety, of which two are characterized by fever, headache, convulsions, drowsiness, delirium, and coma. In the third type the symptoms are merely headache and neck rigidity, and the condition can only be diagnosed by studies of the blood for antibodies. The mortality varies, in some epidemics being as high as 20 percent.

About one-fifth of those surviving St. Louis encephalitis suffer permanent brain damage such as partial paralysis, disorders of speech, aphasia, tremors, and mental deterioration.

The equine encephalitis is a severe encephalitis affecting horses and cows. The mosquito bites the infected animals and then transmits the infection through its bite to human beings.

With the exception of the milder Venezuelan type the symptoms are similar to those of St. Louis encephalitis but much more severe. The child suffering from this condition may be stuporous within a few hours after the onset of symptoms. The death rate in children is approximately 75 percent. Those who survive almost all show evidence of serious brain damage. Among the residual effects may be mental deficiency, blindness, deafness, loss of speech, and paralysis.

No effective treatment of encephalitis is known.

Sleepwalking

The child who sleepwalks gets out of bed (with eyes open, as a rule) and wanders about the house as if seeking something or going somewhere. Apparently sleepwalkers have excellent mental and muscular coordination, for they may walk down steep stairs or out onto roofs, but they rarely injure themselves. When helped back to bed they sleep, and usually they awaken in the morning with no knowledge of the episode.

The cause of sleepwalking is not usually obvious—but in some cases it can be definitely associated with an upsetting incident, film, or television program, or some deeply upsetting emotional experience such as a separation from a parent, difficulty in school, the birth of a new baby, or sibling rivalry or jealousy. In some cases it may be related to curiosity regarding the sex act.

Sleepwalking at puberty or in adolescence often reflects the worries young folks have about themselves and growing up.

Treatment   First, if the child is an avid television watcher, the programs should be limited to those that are not exciting or overstimulating. The same goes for films.

Then parents should carefully investigate the child's environment to see if they can uncover and relieve upsetting influences and difficulties, such as fights between parents, sibling rivalry, school problems, or adolescent problems.

At times the doctor may prescribe a mild, non-habit-forming antihistamine which sedates, such as Benadryl (diphenhydramine hydrochloride), or one of the safe sedative medications used to prevent motion sickness, such as Dramamine (dimenhydrinate). Such medication may break the pattern. In severe cases professional guidance should be sought.

Smack see **Drug abuse.**

Smallpox
A very serious contagious disease, extremely rare in most industrialized countries but still found in parts of the world where vaccination against it has not been carried out as a routine public health measure.

Superficially, smallpox looks like severe chicken pox, with many small pimply blisters scattered widely over the body. These blisters differ from those of chicken pox in that they are firmer and have a dimple in their centers. The scabs of smallpox are much deeper than those of chicken pox, and when they fall off they leave permanent scars.

In 1971 the United States Public Health Service recommended that routine smallpox vaccination be discontinued in the United States. This recommendation was fully supported by the American Academy of Pediatrics, because the disease is now so rare in the United States and because the vaccination occasionally causes severe reactions.

Smallpox vaccination is still recommended, however, for children who may be travelling in areas where smallpox is existent or where vaccination is required.

The vaccination is very effective. The doctor places a small drop of the vaccine on the surface of the skin and makes either four to ten pricks or a scratch through it. In about five days there is a pimple or a blister at the site of the vaccination. A few days later the blister forms a scab, which drops off in two to three weeks. Occasionally there is some fever about seven to ten days after the vaccination. If there is no skin reaction from the vaccination, it should be repeated in a month or two.

Children with eczema should not be vaccinated and should not be exposed to recently vaccinated persons until the eczema has cleared, since an allergic reaction might result in vaccination blisters, scabs, and scars all over the body. Also, children with poison ivy reactions or impetigo should not be vaccinated until the condition has disappeared.

Smoking see **Cigarettes.**

Smoking during pregnancy see **Prenatal care.**

Snacks
In spite of the general impression that eating between meals is detrimental and destroys the appetite, this is not always the case. It has been demonstrated that the active preschool child eats his meals with greater appetite if he is given a glass of milk or orange juice plus a cookie in the middle of the morning and something in the middle of the afternoon as well, several hours before his actual mealtime. Apparently the stomach tires with the rest of the body and

the child loses his appetite as a result. The in-between snack buoys up the child, relieves the fatigue, and thus improves his appetite.

It is not advisable, however, to fill up a child with sweets or snacks shortly before a meal, for this often spoils his appetite and takes away from his enjoyment of the meal. If children receive three good meals a day plus the aforementioned snacks, they will rarely feel the intense craving for extra in-between snacks. (See **Candy and chewing gum.**)

As children get older, and especially when they are entering puberty and during early adolescence, the body starts growing rapidly, and these children need and usually demand in-between snacks.

The overweight child who eats almost constantly between meals is a special problem. (See **Obesity.**)

Snakes and snakebites

Most people have a dread of snakes and a desire to kill every snake they see. This is very wrong, for the vast majority of snakes are harmless—and really beneficial, since they eat mice and rats, which can be very destructive.

There are only four types of poisonous snakes in the United States: the rattlesnake, the copperhead, the water moccasin, and the coral snake. Rattlesnakes and copperheads are found in all

1. Poisonous snake and bite marks; the fangs leave distinct puncture wounds. 2. Nonpoisonous snake and bite marks. 3. Copperhead. This snake, like the rattler and water moccasin, is a type of pit viper, characterized by a large, heart-shaped head and a hollow on each side of the head below the eye. 4. Water moccasin or cottonmouth. 5. Coral snake; the bands are colored red, yellow, and black. 6. Prairie rattler.

the states; the water moccasin (also called cottonmouth) is found in the southeastern states; and the coral snake ranges from South Carolina down to Florida, west through the Gulf states, Mississippi, Texas, and parts of Arizona.

Three of these poisonous snakes—the rattlesnake, the copperhead, and the water moccasin—have heads that are broader than their bodies and are triangular or like an arrowhead in shape. (Most, but not all, nonpoisonous snakes in the United States have heads the same breadth as the body or slightly larger.) The coral snake has a comparatively small head but is easily recognized because of its bright red, yellow, and black stripes. The nose is black. The red stripes are bordered on either side by yellow stripes. The harmless king snake has the same colors, but the red stripe is bordered on each side by a black stripe. Therefore the old adage: "Red against yellow, kill the fellow./ Red against black, venom lack."

The rattlesnake is easy to recognize because of its arrowhead-shaped head and the rattlers on its tail. The copperhead is a hazel-brown snake with chestnut-brown or orange-colored bands, usually shaped like an hourglass, narrow on the top of the back and widening out at the sides. The water moccasin is dark-colored, usually gray or brown. Its head is wider than its body, but its most distinctive feature is the cotton-white appearance of the mucous membrane inside its mouth.

Other distinguishing features of rattlesnakes, copperheads, and water moccasins (not very helpful on most occasions) is that the pupils of their eyes are vertical slits, whereas the pupils of other American snakes are round, and they have an indentation (pit) between their eyes and their nostrils. For this reason they are also called pit vipers.

Snakebites The rattlesnake, copperhead, and water moccasin have fangs located on the upper jaw. These snakes strike suddenly and inject the venom (poison) through the fangs. The bite of these snakes is recognizable, with two fang-marks above and the typical teeth-marks as shown in the illustration.

The coral snake does not strike, but bites and hangs on, sucking in the fangs with a chewing motion.

Symptoms of poisonous snakebites The bite of a rattlesnake, copperhead, or water moccasin causes severe pain almost immediately. There is a swelling of the skin in the area and purplish discoloration. The marks of the two fangs can be easily seen unless a child is bitten on the finger, in which case only one fang-mark may show.

Following the bite, the child grows weak rapidly, develops a shortness of breath, becomes nauseous and vomits, has a rapid pulse, and may become unconscious.

The bite of the coral snake does not produce the severe local pain, swelling, and purplish discoloration of the skin, but the symptoms, similar to those of the other poisonous snakebites, appear rapidly and are very severe.

Treatment

1. The child must get to a hospital or a doctor as soon as possible, but must not be allowed to walk. He should be carried lying down on a stretcher or as immobile as possible in your arms.
2. If any pain, discoloration, or swelling is present, a tourniquet should be applied—a handkerchief, rope, belt, or

necktie can be used, with wider materials preferred (a handkerchief rather than a cord). *The tourniquet must not be too tight.* You should be able to slip your finger between the tourniquet and the skin. The aim is to cut off the flow of blood in the veins and lymphatic system, but not to cut off the flow of arterial blood. If the extremities begin to turn blue, loosen the tourniquet slightly. The tourniquet can only be used if the bite is on the hand, arm, foot, or leg. It should be placed above the wound. If the swelling begins to extend to the tourniquet, move the tourniquet further up the limb. Ice, if handy, may also be packed around the wound.

3. If the area of the wound is clearly swollen, discolored, or painful, the venom should be removed by suction. Make small cuts (⅛ of an inch deep, ½ inch long) through the fang marks and at the edge of the swelling. Suck out the poison (this cannot harm the person who sucks unless he has an open sore in his mouth). Continue making cuts (twenty to forty may be necessary) and sucking out the venom for half an hour. Then continue to try to get medical help. If medical aid cannot be reached quickly, and swelling, pain, nausea, or vomiting indicate a worsening of the condition, make further cuts and continue to suck out the venom. Remember that the most effective treatment is antivenin injections; therefore, when in doubt about whether to continue first-aid or to head for a hospital, try to get to the hospital.

4. Do not give the child any stimulants, especially alcoholic drinks, since these cause increased absorption of the venom.

Note: Whenever there is a possibility of snakebite in an isolated area, you should have a snakebite kit at hand. This will include a rubber suction bulb, a sharp blade, a tourniquet, and other first-aid equipment.

Prevention About 75 percent of poisonous snakebites are on the legs of children and adults. Most of these could be prevented by the use of high shoes or boots and thick socks when walking through "snake country."

When picking flowers and berries, or climbing cliffs or ledges in snake-infested areas, great care should be taken to assure that no snakes are near.

Sneezes

A sneeze is a reflex action of the body to get rid of irritating substances in the nose.

Sneezes are very common in young infants, who often regurgitate and occasionally get some of the milk plus digestive juices from the stomach into the back of the nose.

When a child is older, sneezing is usually either associated with colds, when the mucous membrane of the nose is irritated by the infection, or with allergic reactions.

The allergic sensitivies are usually caused by pollens of grasses, ragweed, or trees, but they can be caused by dusts, molds, tobacco smoke, or at times even face powder. If a child has frequent attacks of sneezing of unknown origin, consult a doctor.

See also **Allergy.**

Soap poisoning see **Poisons: first-aid treatment.**

Soiling, chronic

This refers to almost constant fecal soiling by children who are already toilet-trained. It occurs primarily in children of the preschool years. The child continually oozes loose fecal material.

In almost every case, the child has a history of constipation and occasionally passes a large, massive stool with considerable difficulty.

Rectal examination by a doctor reveals a large, firm, constipated fecal mass filling the rectum. Loose, watery stool from the intestines above flows down along the sides of the mass and oozes out through the anal opening.

The treatment is very simple and rapidly effective. It consists of first clearing the rectum by enemas, and then placing the child on a laxative diet or giving some mineral oil or medication which will keep the stools soft.

The cure of the soiling is immediate, but it may take some time before the constipation is completely relieved.

See also **Constipation.**

Solid foods, introducing

Many pediatricians advise introducing solid foods to infants as early as 4 to 6 weeks of age. However, there is no evidence that babies fed solid foods before age 3 months gain any faster or in any way do better than babies receiving only breast milk or formula.

Most babies will take solid food very well from a spoon when it is offered to them, but some infants reject it. Either they do not know how to take it from a spoon or they are not as yet ready to take solid food.

You can easily test if a child is ready for solid food but unable to take it from a spoon. Just cut a large hole in the end of an ordinary rubber formula-nipple, fill it with the prepared cereal or fruit, and offer it to the baby. If he enjoys taking it by sucking on the nipple, then he will soon learn to take it from a spoon. If he resists the solid food through a nipple, then he is not yet ready for solids and you should wait several weeks before offering it again.

Usually pureed fruits and cereals are the first solid foods offered, followed by pureed vegetables and meats. Each new solid food offered should be given for four or five days to assure that it will not cause any upset. (See **Cereals; Meat; Vegetables.**)

If an infant reacts against any solid food by violently resisting it or developing a rash, colic, diarrhea, or vomiting, that food should be omitted from the diet—for the time being, at least.

By the end of the first year, an infant should be eating almost as wide a variety of foods as older members of the family.

Solid food is given to young infants mushy or finely pureed. Home-prepared foods or those commercially prepared may be used. More coarsely pureed food (Junior Foods in commercial preparations) are usually given at about 9 months. After 11 months most babies enjoy eating the family food cut into small particles.

Every pediatrician has his own method of adding solid foods to an infant's diet. One method is as follows (with milk or formula given after the solid food).

1 to 2 months
Cereal: barley or rice, 1 teaspoon, increasing gradually to 2 tablespoons of the prepared cereal at 10 A.M. and 6 P.M.

Ripe banana (skin flecked with brown) or Banana Flakes: 1 teaspoonful, increasing gradually to 2 tablespoons, at 2 P.M.

2 to 3 months

All cereals: 2 to 3 tablespoons at 10 A.M. and 6 P.M.

Fruit (applesauce, pears, or bananas): 2 to 3 tablespoons at 10 A.M., 2 P.M., and 6 P.M.

3 to 4 months

All cereals: 2 to 3 tablespoons at 10 A.M. and 6 P.M.

All fruits: 2 to 3 tablespoons at 10 A.M., 2 P.M., and 6 P.M.

First vegetables: carrots, spinach, peas, 1 to 3 tablespoons at 2 P.M.

4 to 5 months

Cereal, fruit, as preceding month.

Give all vegetables at 2 P.M.

Add yolk of egg, ½ increasing to 1, either at 10 A.M. with the breakfast or at 2 P.M. A good method is to grate hard-boiled yolk over the vegetables. Commercially prepared egg yolk may be used.

Add beef, 1 tablespoon increasing to 3 tablespoons, at 2 P.M.

5 to 6 months

(Usually a new feeding schedule is started at this time.)

Breakfast: 7:30 to 8 A.M. Cereal, 2 to 3 tablespoons; yolk of egg; fruit, 3 or 4 tablespoons; plus milk.

Lunch: 12 noon. Add to foods already given:

Liver and lamb, 2 to 3 tablespoons.

Soups and broths (vegetables should be in these), 3 to 4 ounces.

Mashed potato (including sweet potato), 1 to 3 tablespoons.

Jell-O and junket, 3 to 4 tablespoons (may be given as dessert at any of the meals).

Snack: 3 P.M. Milk, plus a cracker made mushy with some of the milk or water (Graham cracker, arrowroot cracker, or zwieback).

Supper: 6 P.M. As in previous month, or vegetables or soup may be substituted for the cereal.

6 to 8 months

Add to the diet:

Chicken, 2 to 3 tablespoons.

White of egg (½ hard-boiled, increasing up to 1).

Soft-boiled egg (may be given at breakfast or lunch).

Custard, 3 to 4 tablespoons.

Tapioca, 2 to 3 tablespoons.

Boiled rice, 2 to 3 tablespoons.

Rice pudding, 2 to 3 tablespoons.

8 to 10 months

Add to the diet:

Pastina, noodles, spaghetti, macaroni.

Pot cheese, cottage cheese, sour cream, cream cheese, American cheese.

All meats, including bacon.

10 to 12 months

Add to the diet:

Fish: cod, flounder, halibut, haddock, sole, tuna (packed in salt water).

Sore throat

A generalized infection of the throat (acute pharyngitis) or an infection of the tonsils (tonsillitis).

Sore throats are usually caused by an infection with streptococcus or staphylococcus bacteria, or by viruses.

A sore throat should not be taken lightly and just treated with aspirin, gargles, or throat lozenges, for at times the side effects may be much worse than the sore throat itself. Scarlet fever and the dangerous diseases rheumatic fever and acute nephritis are caused by streptococcus sore throats. The extremely rare but very serious disease diphtheria is manifested by a severe sore throat (today practically all children receive inoculations against this).

It is therefore important that a doctor's advice be sought in every case of a sore throat in children. Many doctors will take a throat culture to ascertain if the condition is caused by a streptococcus.

Signs and symptoms These vary greatly according to the severity of the condition, the organism involved, and the age of the child. The throat usually hurts considerably when the child swallows. Infants will cry and refuse solid food. Older children will complain and often act quite ill. There is usually fever, which may range as high as 104 to 105 degrees rectally. In many cases the onset is accompanied by a headache and vomiting.

With the sore throats caused by bacteria, the throat is usually fiery red and white patches may develop on the tonsils in one or two days. The lymph glands in the neck under the chin swell up and may be very tender.

With the throat infections due to viruses, the throat, although painful, is not usually very red, and the lymph glands may be only slightly swollen.

Treatment This depends largely upon the cause. If the condition seems at all likely to be due to a streptococcus infection, most doctors will place the child at once on penicillin or some other antibiotic that will kill streptococci before even waiting to see the result of a throat culture. In cases of streptococcus infection, the antibiotic should be continued for at least ten days to assure that all the

harmful bacteria will be destroyed. Staphylococcus sore throats, while not as dangerous as the streptococcus throat, may be treated by various antibiotics. Virus infections do not respond to antibiotics and clear up, as a rule, in a few days.

See also **Colds.**

Spanking see **Punishment.**

Spasms see **Convulsions.**

Speech
Learning to communicate through speech is probably the most complex and important stage in a child's development. Unlike other aspects of development—such as sitting, standing, and walking—speech requires a great deal of learning, through hearing, imitation, and experimentation.

Somewhere between ages 2 and 3 months most infants find that they are able to make various sounds, and they enjoy doing this. They may cough or coo repetitively or make certain vowel sounds to entertain themselves. They may even purse their lips and blow through them, producing a "raspberry." And if you listen carefully, you can often hear a baby trying out his new vocal ability in different intensities and pitches.

From 6 months to a year the baby vocalizes more and more, and his vowel sounds are usually clear and defined. He soon finds that by opening and closing his lips and saying "ah" he can produce "wa-wa-wa-wa-wa" and later "mamamamama," and by touching his tongue to the front of his palate he can say "dadadadada."

During this period children often imitate sounds and even, at times, songs and rhythms. From this time on, the parents become the teachers of speech, and the child soon learns the meaning of certain words and what is expected of him when they speak a certain way. He learns to wave when a parent says "Bye-bye" and to look toward a lamp or up at a ceiling light when a parent says "light." Soon he learns to recognize the words for his ears, nose, mouth, and other parts of the body.

Most children are saying a few words by age 14 or 15 months and by 18 months have approximately fifteen words in their vocabulary. The list of words and the use of consonants increase with the youngster's growing control of his tongue and lips, and by age 2 years most children use fifty to two hundred words in speech.

Between ages 2 and 3 years children start using sentences, and by 3 years they may have as many as 750 to 1,000 words in their vocabulary.

See also **Speech delay; Stuttering and stammering.**

Speech delay

Parents are often disturbed if their child doesn't speak at the average time or speaks so badly that he cannot be understood.

If a child is past age 2½ and has said practically nothing or speaks very poorly, consult a doctor. In most instances the child is just slow in learning to control his muscles of speech or has had too little stimulation from his parents. Often a child gets what he wants without having to ask for it in words. But the doctor will consider all other possibilities. Is the child's hearing normal? Has he had some nerve injury that interferes with the proper use of his tongue? Is his intelligence up to par?

Has he emotional problems that upset his speech? Has he some abnormality of the mouth that interferes with normal speech?

A well-trained pediatrician can usually make an accurate diagnosis himself, but occasionally he may desire consultation with specialists. An expert may perform a test for hearing; a psychologist will test the child's level of intelligence; a neurologist will examine for nerve damage; a speech specialist will make a definite diagnosis as to the cause of the difficulty and advise further on treatment.

If the child is normal, speech will often improve quickly if the parents take the time to speak the name of an object when handing it to him and to talk and read to him frequently. Also, placing the child with a group of children who already speak will provide a stimulation to speech development.

If there is some physical reason for the difficulty in speech, treatment can almost always be very helpful.

See also **Aphasia; Cleft palate; Deafness; Harelip; Stuttering and stammering.**

Speed (amphetamine) see **Drug abuse.**

Spider bites see **Insect and spider bites.**

Spina bifida

A condition in which the spinal column (backbone) that covers the spinal cord is open in some area, exposing the spinal cord, which is composed of nerves coming down from the brain. Spina bifida is caused by a defect in the embryological development of the spinal column. Normally the bones in the spinal column come together to protect the spinal cord.

In spina bifida these bones do not come together completely.

In one type of spina bifida, although the backbone has an opening, the cord within is normal and the skin covering the opening is normal. This is not dangerous.

In another type, often serious, some of the nerve fibers of the spinal cord pass out through the opening. In this latter type there is a swelling on the back of the newborn baby which contains within it some of the fibers of the spinal cord plus spinal fluid, and the inside of the swelling is lined by the membrane that normally covers the spinal cord. The swelling is called meningocele (from *meninges,* the membrane lining the spinal cord, and *cele,* meaning a cavity).

Because many of the nerves that should go down to the legs have been sidetracked into the meningocele, the baby's legs may be paralyzed and the baby may have no sensation in his legs either—no sensation of heat or cold, pinpricks, or pressure. At times the child may also have no control of his bladder or bowels. Sometimes the baby may also develop hydrocephalus, which is a rapid enlargement of the head.

Treatment The infant should be placed at once under the care of a neurosurgeon. In the past almost all babies with meningoceles would die. However, modern surgery makes it possible for the bulge to be removed and the exposed nerves buried beneath the skin. Unfortunately, the paralysis of the legs remains, as does the loss of sensation. Hydrocephalus can usually be prevented or stopped by surgical methods as well.

In spite of the leg disability, many of the children with spina bifida have been able to grow up and live active, happy, and productive lives.

Spine, curvature of

Curvature of the spine is quite often seen in children, especially as they approach and go through adolescence. The most common type is scoliosis—lateral curvature.

Often no cause can be found, although there are those who feel that it may sometimes be caused by sitting on

Lateral spinal curvature (scoliosis) in an adolescent girl.

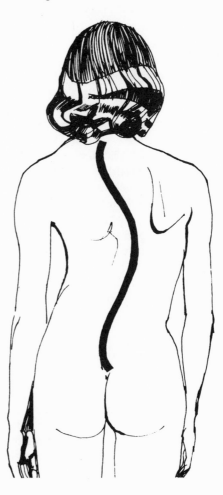

one leg while studying or watching television, or by always carrying schoolbooks under the same arm.

In many cases prompt orthopedic treatment of scoliosis is important, for unless it is corrected or further curving of the spine is prevented, the condition may become more pronounced.

Spine, tuberculosis of see **Tuberculosis.**

Spitting up see **Regurgitation; Vomiting.**

Splinters
Superficial splinters, close to the surface of the skin, can usually be easily and almost painlessly removed. The skin should be washed well with soap and water and then wiped with alcohol. A sterile needle is used to slit the skin along the length of the splinter, which then can be easily dislodged and removed by splinter tweezers. The needle can be sterilized by holding the point in a flame until it is red-hot.

An antiseptic such as iodine or Betadine (povidone-iodine), which does not sting, should be applied next, and an adhesive gauze pad applied.

Splinters that have been forced directly down into the skin and into the tissue beneath, and those forced under the fingernail or toenail, should be removed by a doctor.

Spoiling the child
It is practically impossible to spoil a child during most of its first year of life. The baby during this period is completely dependent on his parents and thrives on love, attention, and the satisfying of his needs. Both mother and father can cuddle a baby all they want and pick him up every time he cries

more than a few minutes, or sooner if they desire.

But as a child gets older and approaches a year of age, he understands much more and is beginning to become independent. He can now creep or walk, holding on to things by himself.

It is at this time, if parents are not careful, that a child can begin to be spoiled. Parents can avoid spoiling by, for one thing, encouraging the child's self-confidence so he will not expect others to do everything for him. At the same time they should assert reasonable authority, guiding the child to the understanding that he can't do everything he wants, can't have everything he wants, and that at times he must wait for the satisfaction of his needs. After the approximate age of 12 months an infant resisting sleep at night can be permitted to cry it out—with parents coming in every half hour to calm the child down for a few moments so he doesn't feel deserted and rejected. In almost every instance the baby will start sleeping through the night within seven days. (See **Sleep problems.**)

Parents who overindulge a child are spoiling the child, as are parents who are overprotective and oversolicitous. Then there are parents who give in to a child's demands too readily. Spoiled children are quick to learn methods of forcing parents to give in to them—often by whining, annoying, nagging, crying, or even by having temper tantrums. These are children who almost always get what they want when they want it and do what they desire whether or not it accords with their parents' wishes or their own best interests.

Older children can learn to work for some of the things they want. For instance, if a child wants a guitar, it is good for him to earn some of the money that is used to buy it—unless of course he is to receive it as a present.

The spoiled child is rarely a happy child. He often finds it difficult to respond to directions and to play harmoniously with other children, especially when it comes to sharing and taking turns. And he is usually a problem for the nursery school teacher as well as his parents.

See also **Temper and temper tantrums.**

Sponge bath   see **Alcohol rub.**

Sponge bath for the newborn
For a few days or longer after the newborn baby arrives home, a sponge bath is usually suggested by the doctor. Once the umbilical cord has fallen off and the navel is dry, and circumcision (if performed) of the boy baby is completely healed, the infant is usually ready for a tub bath.

The sponge bath should be given in a warm room (temperature 70 to 75 degrees) with the windows closed. The necessary items are:

1. A basin of warm water 100 to 105 degrees.
2. A mild soap.
3. 2 washcloths.
4. A baby bath towel. Some of these towels have hoods.
5. Cotton.
6. Baby oil.

The infant may be placed in a Bathinette, or on a padded table or chest of drawers. Keep the baby wrapped in the towel; expose, wash, and dry individual parts of the body one at a time.

A good plan is to first wash the face with plain water, without soap, and pat it dry. Next soap up one washcloth and wash the scalp. Using the other wash-cloth, rinse with clear water and dry. Then, in order, follow the same procedure on the neck, chest, abdomen, and arms and legs. The buttocks and genitals are washed last. With girls, wash the genital area softly from front to back, using soft cotton moistened with water or baby oil. Do not use the same piece of cotton twice. For uncircumcised boys, also use cotton; pull back the foreskin from the head of the penis, and cleanse with water or oil. Then apply powder or baby lotion (recommended by the doctor) to the infant's body.

Sports
Involvement in sports is a healthy outlet for a child's need for activity and also for the competitive drive that most children develop. But athletic activities should be related to a child's stage of physical and emotional growth and development.

Preteen children should be withheld from violent contact sports such as tackle football, boxing, wrestling, judo, and karate. It has long been realized by pediatricians that these sports are potentially dangerous for such children because the growing ends of the bones are not yet ossified, nor are they yet covered by adult protective muscles. Injury to these growth areas of the bones may produce a shortening of a limb and may handicap or terminate a child's future participation in many sports. These dangers have been emphasized by the American Academy of Pediatrics.

In the case of football, parents often meet strong objections when they try to prevent their children from playing this popular game. Young children can play at football, wearing the padded uniforms and nose protectors, and learn many of the skills of the game. Tackling, however, should still be forbidden. In high school a parent should investigate the football program carefully. A teenager should be allowed to participate only if the parent is sure that the coach understands the importance of good conditioning, is well trained in the techniques of conditioning and safety for adolescents, and puts the well-being of the players above winning games.

There are many nonviolent sports in which the young child can participate. These include baseball, basketball, swimming, tennis, volleyball, skating, soccer, and track.

Children should not be subject to severely competitive pressures which develop in them an interest only in winning and make it impossible for them to enjoy a sport for its own sake. Under highly organized competitive sports programs many children meet bitter disappointment which they are not yet ready to sustain. Children should learn to accept defeat as well as victory, and to realize it is not always possible to win.

See also **Competitiveness; Physical fitness.**

Sports, safety in see **Bicycles; Ice skating; Swimming.**

Sportsmanship see **Competitiveness.**

Sprain
An overstretching, with tearing, of some of the muscle fibers or ligaments that hold a joint together. Sprains are fairly common during childhood, because children are so active. Sprains of the ankles and wrists are among the most frequent, as is the so-called "baseball finger"—an outstretched finger hit forcibly on the tip and bent backward. (See **Baseball finger.**)

Usually, immediately following the sprain, a swelling of the surrounding tissue takes place rapidly. At this time it is best to apply ice. The joint should not be strapped for at least twenty-four hours, for if it is strapped too soon, the increase in swelling under the strapping often causes extreme pain.

If the area of the sprain becomes bluish, it should be examined by a doctor to ascertain whether or not a chip of bone has been pulled off, or whether a fracture exists as well as the sprain.

The doctor will advise when a child can walk on a sprained ankle—usually once it is strapped. Sprains of the wrist and fingers can be simply bandaged by a doctor.

Stammering see Stuttering and stammering.

Standing up
The average age when a baby first pulls himself to a standing position in his crib or playpen is 8½ to 10 months. A few babies stand up earlier, and a good many later. A lot depends on the weight of the child, his degree of activity, and his muscle tone.

Many parents are worried if their child is late in standing up. The doctor will investigate for possible physical causes, but there is usually no need for concern; the child will stand at a year of age or shortly thereafter.

Some parents try to force a child to stand as early as age 5 months by pulling him to a standing position. If this is done, the weight of the child's body should never be rested on his legs, or the bones of the legs may bow.

Once a baby has learned to stand, let him progress at his own pace, but give him plenty of opportunity to walk from place to place holding on to objects or people.

See also **Walking.**

Stanford-Binet intelligence test see **IQ; Tests.**

Staphylococcus infections
Infections caused by the staphylococcus bacteria range from the milder infections, such as impetigo and the common stye, to serious conditions such as staphylococcus pneumonia.

Most of the staphylococcus infections respond readily to antibiotics. But there are certain virulent strains, such as the "hospital strain," which newborns and, frequently, operative patients contract in the hospitals, that are resistant to the usual antibiotics. These must be treated with certain specific antibiotics, such as nafcillin, oxacillin, and methicillin. If a doctor suspects one of these strains in an infection which an infant or child has, he will culture some of the pus from the lesions or swab the throat for a culture. Then the staphylococcus found on the culture is tested with many antibiotics to find which will kill or suppress the organism.

Skin lesions such as impetigo respond to antibiotic creams or ointments. Boils caused by staphylococcus may have to be lanced and drained.

Stealing
The young child, under the approximate age of 6, has a very poor concept of ownership and will at times take a toy or other possession of another child. This is normal.

But by the time a child reaches the age of 7, he should have already formed a clear concept of ownership and of what is right. A child who steals at this age or later is almost always an unhappy child. His problems may have any number of causes, including his relationships with his parents or his brothers and sisters, or with other children, or at school.

Some children feel unloved by their parents, and steal money from them. There is a dual motivation: to get something in the place of the love that is wanted, and to express hostility to the parents. If the thefts are very obvious, it may be that the child is also trying to draw attention to his unhappiness. This situation frequently occurs when a child feels that he is less loved than a brother or sister.

Some children feel rejected by their schoolmates and companions. These children will often steal either to appear important in the eyes of the other children or in an attempt to buy friendship, by treating boys and girls to sodas and candy.

Some children, who feel unloved and unwanted, have a chronic compulsion to steal to substitute the good feeling of possession for the affection they lack. These are the kleptomaniacs. (See **Kleptomania.**)

Parents should see to it that the property is returned to its rightful owner without too great an upset to their child. But more important, they must uncover and relieve the causes of the stealing. Often professional guidance is necessary. If not corrected, this type of stealing may lead to juvenile delinquency.

During adolescent years, the use of drugs may be associated with stealing, for the youngster may want or need a large amount of money to buy drugs. Stealing during the teen years is one of the signs that a child may be taking drugs.

Steam treatment

There are two types of steam treatment.

The first is the time-honored hot-steam inhalation. Steam from a vaporizer or kettle, from hot sink-water, or from a hot shower is inhaled—usually with the mouth open. This is especially valuable in the treatment of laryngitis or spasmodic croup. The steam is not only soothing to the inflamed tissue, but also tends to relieve the spasm of the laryngeal muscles. But if a hot-steam vaporizer is used, it must be watched constantly. Too many children upset the vaporizer and are burned.

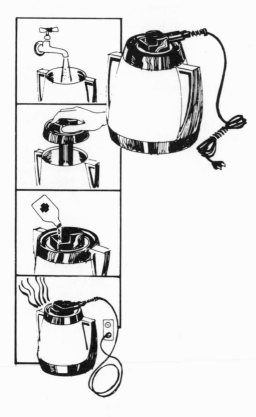

A vaporizer should be sturdy, stable, and have parts that fit tightly together to minimize spilling if it should be knocked over.

The second type of treatment is with cold steam. This is not really steam but very fine water droplets, much smaller than the droplets produced by an atomizer. These tiny droplets moisten the mucous membrane lining the breathing tubes and loosen the thick, tenacious mucus which clings to the wall of the trachea or bronchial tubes when the lining is dry. The use of cold steam is especially effective in the treatment of the serious form of croup. The cold-steam humidifier used in so many homes to add moisture to the air may be used for inhalation therapy when needed.

See also **Moisture in air.**

Stepparents   see **Remarriage.**

Sterilizing formulas   see **Formulas.**

Steroid therapy

Steroids are cortisone derivatives—hormones produced by the adrenal gland. These hormones are among the most valuable of the modern drugs. Prednisone is the one most frequently used, since it may be given by mouth.

The steroids, if given in the proper dosage, are highly effective in relieving intractable asthma, severe hives, nephrosis, rheumatic fever, and poison ivy. Steroids in creams or ointments are excellent treatment for eczemas.

These hormones should only be taken under the supervision of a doctor, since they may produce severe side effects when taken over a period of time. When taken in large doses steadily for periods of weeks or months, steroids may cause the face and other parts of the body to swell up from retained fluid; may slow down the child's growth; light up infections; cause stomach ulcers; and suppress the body's own production of steroids. The dosage and duration of treatment varies with the condition for which the steroids are given.

Stimulating the child

Parents can dramatically influence the development of their children's capabilities by paying a great deal of attention to them, by giving them love, and by stimulating them in many ways from the moment they are born.

Placing a colored mobile above an infant's crib to excite his interest, talking to him, picking him up and cuddling him, carrying him from place to place so that he has a change of scenery, and, when he is old enough, reading to him and showing him numerous objects and happenings in the world around him—all of these awaken the child's senses and mind. Above all, a constant expression of interest in the child and pleasure in his accomplishments (without pressure) will encourage him to develop his intelligence and talents.

All infants and children enjoy the sound of their parents' voices, and you should talk to the child at every opportunity about his interests—at first simply and later more fully, as the child's understanding and vocabulary grow.

When the child sits up (at perhaps 6 months) he can be given paper to tear, pots and pans to bang, balls to throw and roll, old cereal boxes, adhesive-tape rolls, cloth, fur, cellophane to crackle—the list is endless, and it all adds to the child's learning about the world.

During the creeping stage the child should be given the opportunity to crawl around and explore what interests him—chairs, tables, lamps (the infant should be watched carefully in his wanderings, and safety precautions should be observed). It is not sufficient to let a baby just sit outside in the carriage so that he is getting air and sunshine. What is invaluable is pushing the carriage or stroller on a walk while the child observes other children, cars, dogs, houses, trees, store windows, the exciting colorama of a supermarket.

As soon as a child is able to understand, beginning about age 2, you can begin pointing out to him shapes and proportions, textures and colors, rhythms and sounds. By making up games or encouraging art activities that involve making discriminations among such experiences, you help the child to grasp and enjoy the world around him. Even before the child can speak himself, he can enjoy games with words and sounds, music and nonsense jingles. When he is old enough, parent and child can share the games.

During the preschool period books become very important. Reading to a child stimulates his imagination and maintains the close and warm relationship with his parents. The same walks that the child took earlier in the stroller can now give him a chance to look at the cranes and bulldozers, street repair, garbage collection. Trips to the market or the zoo are exciting and valuable. Fathers should join mothers in as many of these activities as possible, or take the children on these walks without the mother.

As the child grows, you should encourage him to speak about his interests and concerns, and listen to what he has to say. His questions should be answered, but when possible he should also be taught how to find answers for himself. When the child is in school, he needs your support and interest in what goes on there and the work he is doing. In addition, you should find time to take the child to museums, concerts, technical exhibits, or whatever might open new avenues for him. In adolescence youngsters should be helped to find exciting projects to work on—helping in a political campaign, for example—and should travel away from home, if possible.

Stings, insect   see **Bee stings; Insect and spider bites.**

Stomach   see **Abdomen.**

Stomach, foreign bodies in   see **Foreign objects, swallowed.**

Stomach ulcer   see **Ulcer, stomach and duodenal.**

Stomachache   see **Abdominal pain.**

Stools   see **Bowel movements.**

Stories

Stories told by parents and other adults are enjoyed by all children. Whether stories are read or told, this activity is one that brings parents and children close together.

Young children of 2 to 5 love to hear stories of themselves when they were young or of Daddy and Mommy when they were young. Children of 2 to 3 especially like stories of themselves doing familiar things: going to the market, taking a walk in the park, visiting Grandma.

Children of 3, and up to 7 or 8, besides loving stories of when their parents were younger also love to have stories read to them, such as animal stories, stories of children in other lands, stories of everyday happenings they have experienced, and fairy tales.

Stories before bedtime should not be too frightening or too stimulating.

See also **Books.**

Strabismus   see **Eye defects.**

Strain

An overstretching of a muscle or tendon.

Strains differ from sprains, in which there is a tearing of muscle or tendon fibers. With sprains there is usually a great deal of swelling around the injured muscle or joint, and often discoloration as well. Strains, however, are rarely swollen and cause no bleeding under the skin.

Strains occur quite frequently in children during the course of their great activity. The child experiences a sharp pain at the time of injury, followed by soreness and stiffness at the affected area.

Treatment is simple and consists of heat given by a heating pad, a heat lamp, a hot water bottle, or a warm bath. Massage is also helpful.

Strains usually clear up in a few days.

Strangulated hernia   see **Hernia.**

Strawberry marks   see **Birthmarks.**

Strawberry tongue   see **Scarlet fever.**

Streptococcus infections

Infections by streptococcus bacteria are among the most serious infections during infancy and childhood. Although they cause streptococcus sore throats and scarlet fever, the main danger is in secondary conditions such as rheumatic fever and nephritis. It is important, therefore, that every streptococcus infection be diagnosed promptly and treated at once with penicillin or some other antibiotic.

The streptococcus bacteria are killed by penicillin, making it the drug of choice. Most other effective antibiotics stop the growth of the bacteria but do not kill them. If a child is sensitive to penicillin, erythromycin or lincomycin may be substituted.

Stroke, heat   see Sunstroke.

Stroller
When an infant reaches the sitting stage, and especially when he has begun to walk and run around, a stroller can take the place of a carriage for outings. The child sits up in it while his mother wheels him to the park, the market, on visits, or at times just for a walk.

There are many types of strollers of varying prices. Many contain different gadgets, such as a basket attached to the handle for carrying diapers and bottles or a wire shelf underneath for packages. Or the seat and its sides can be lifted out, forming a carrying case; many strollers can be folded up compactly, and there is one type that can be folded up and carried over the arm like an umbrella.

What type of stroller is best depends on how it will be used. If it is only to be used for transporting a child to the park or on walks, the simplest stroller will do. If it is to be used as a carrier after marketing, a more complicated stroller would be helpful. If the stroller is to be transported quite frequently by car, the type that folds would be advisable. For safety, a stroller of any type should be checked for sturdiness and stability (so that it can't be easily toppled over). And younger children should always be strapped in.

Stubbornness   see Negativism.

Stuttering and stammering
Although differing somewhat in mean-ing, the words stuttering and stammering are used interchangeably today. Stuttering is the most common speech defect among children (and adults as well). Studies show that there are approximately 1,500,000 stutterers in the United States alone.

Stuttering is a very frequent occurrence among children between the ages of 2 and 3 years. As a rule, it disappears within a few months unless the child is under unusual stress.

The actual cause of stuttering is not fully known. It may begin because the young child is trying to speak faster than he is able. But continuing problems seem to be related to tensions and pressures in the young child—especially those associated with toilet training. Stuttering is not inherited, but apparently there is some familial tendency. In virtually every case the onset is during childhood—after 9 years of age stuttering will usually not develop. In both child and adult stutterers who have learned to control the condition, it tends to recur during periods of stress.

There is no absolute pattern among stutterers, but most stuttering occurs with words that begin sentences, especially words that start with consonants and are longer than the average word. It is interesting to note that stutterers do not stutter when they sing. This has been explained by the theory that stress and tension are reduced during this activity.

Treatment Realizing that tension and anxiety are primary factors causing the stuttering, the first efforts in treatment should be directed at bettering the parent-child relationship and the home environment in general.

Therapy includes both psychotherapy and speech training directed at teaching a stutterer how to avoid the difficult words.

There are two schools of thought concerning when to commence treatment. One group feels that the condition should be treated as soon as possible, before the stuttering becomes too ingrained. Another group advises investigation and treatment only if the condition lasts more than two years, since two-thirds of all stutterers recover completely and spontaneously within two years.

Most severe stutterers remain stutterers throughout their lifetime, but learn by themselves or are taught means of controlling their difficulty by the selection of easier words or by prefacing a sentence with a few inessential words.

Stye and chalazion

A stye is a small, localized infection on the margin of the eyelid where an eyelash enters the lid. A chalazion is an infected cyst in the mucous membrane under the upper or lower lid. Styes and chalazions are usually caused by staphylococcus bacteria. Styes are probably caused by the rubbing of the eyes when the hands are not especially clean. Some doctors have felt that eyestrain is one of the common causes, but this is probably because a child with eyestrain rubs his eyes frequently.

Treatment of a stye is usually threefold. First, wet compresses of plain water—warm or tepid—should be applied for about twenty minutes every four hours. This should help bring the stye to a head. Second, during the night an antibiotic ointment, prescribed by the doctor, should be applied on both the upper and lower lids. This probably will not affect the stye, but may prevent the bacteria from starting infections in other

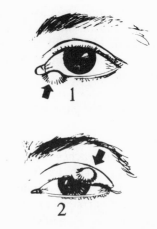

A stye (1) is always situated at the margin of the eyelid, at the base of the lashes. A chalazion (2) is situated on the interior of the eyelid.

hair follicles. Third, if the stye is severe enough to cause considerable inflammation and fever, antibiotics are given by mouth or injection to overcome the bacteria causing the inflammation.

The treatment of a chalazion is similar, except that antibiotic eyedrops may be prescribed instead of ointment. Also, the chalazion may have to be removed by local surgery, especially if it is pressing on the cornea.

Suburban home see Home, location of.

Sucking, blanket

The habit of sucking a blanket is sometimes retained by children who have a strong need for sucking and who gained satisfaction from sucking on a blanket in early infancy. In the same manner, some children suck on a special towel, diaper, or often a pacifier.

When a child is about 2, the need for sucking has disappeared in most cases and continuing the activity is maintaining a habit rather than satisfying a need.

At that time the blanket can be taken away and the child will easily do without it after a few days of moderate unhappiness. It is helpful to give the child a doll or stuffed animal to cuddle during this possibly upsetting period. If taking away the blanket or towel suddenly seems too cruel, gradually cut the blanket down until it becomes smaller and smaller and finally disappears.

See also **Security object.**

Sucking, thumb and finger

Many babies find their thumbs and fingers at age 6 to 8 weeks and start sucking on them as the natural result of the need to suck. This thumb-sucking may continue until a child is age 4 or 5, sometimes even older, as a habit, although the sucking need generally subsides around age 2. (See **Sucking need.**)

Sucking on a finger or a pacifier relaxes babies greatly. Many so-called colicky babies quiet down greatly if given a pacifier or permitted to suck on their thumb.

The only known method of stopping finger-sucking without upsetting the infant is by offering a pacifier before the habit has been established. But once a child has found its fingers and is sucking them, he will rarely accept the pacifier.

Tying the hands, covering them with aluminum or plastic mitts, or restricting elbow motion are all very frustrating to the child and only make him very unhappy and nervous. Any restrictions of this kind should be avoided.

Apparently sucking a finger before age 5 will only very rarely harm the shape of the jaw. However, when the permanent teeth appear, thumb-sucking may force the upper central teeth forward and push the lower central teeth backward. This impairs the bite and may affect the child's appearance.

There are various ways of attempting to stop a child who is approaching age 5 from finger sucking. Children are more cooperative at that age than previously. Girls may stop if their nails are polished, and boys and girls if motivated may stop sucking if some strong-tasting substance is placed on the nails to remind them when the finger goes in the mouth. Others will permit the use of adhesive over the finger's end. Some dentists put an attachment inside the upper teeth which meets the finger when sucking is attempted.

See also **Pacifier.**

Sucking need

Sucking is an instinctive activity of the infant when anything touches his mouth, and it commences almost at birth.

Sucking has two distinct and definite functions. The first is to enable the infant to obtain nourishment from the breast or bottle. The second is to fulfill the need for oral satisfaction which all babies have almost from the moment of birth. The intensity of this need varies greatly in different infants, but apparently all babies need a certain amount of this lip-and-mouth stimulation for relaxation. Babies who lack an adequate amount will cry and cry until given a pacifier or until they can suck on the breast, the bottle, or their lips, tongue, thumb, or finger. These babies do not need or want extra milk. They are not hungry—what they need is the oral stimulation.

Babies who nurse on the breast need pacifiers, thumbs, or fingers much less than those who are bottle-fed. Breast-fed babies, nursing thirty to forty minutes, may receive adequate satisfaction. Bottle-fed babies, on the other hand, often empty their bottles in five to ten minutes and do not satisfy their sucking need.

At about age 2 the child has less need of sucking gratification. But sucking habits sometimes persist after the need is lessened. For example, some children and infants put their tongue between their lips and suck it for a long time or at frequent intervals. Others occasionally suck or bite their lips, usually starting at about age 5 months. Both these activities usually stop at about age 2, but either may return when the child is anxious, tense, or embarrassed. Some adults, too, bite their lower lip or suck their tongue when tense or excited.

These habits may subside if the child is made aware of them. Vaseline or one of the special chapped-lip preparations may be used if the lips start peeling or become dry and cracked when the child is going through a phase of sucking.

See also **Mouth; Pacifier; Sucking, thumb and finger.**

Sudden infant death syndrome   see **Crib death.**

Suicide and suicide threats
Many times children, when unhappy or discouraged, say, "I wish I were dead," and a good many boys and girls attempt suicide, the majority of these being adolescents. Approximately 60,000 young people under the age of 20 attempt suicide each year in the United States.

The knowledge of the full meaning of suicide and the reasons for attempting it vary with the age of the child. A child between the ages of 7 and 12 years may at times feel very unhappy or unloved; or perhaps he got bad grades in school and fears a severe scolding. He either wants to punish his parents or make them feel sorry for him. But he doesn't fully realize that death is final. He's played cops and robbers, he's seen peo-

ple shot and killed on television and in the movies—he thinks of death as temporary and expects to come to life again. Or, like many adults, the child expects to be rescued. A child may turn on the gas, take a lot of pills, and call his parents or doctor stating that he is committing suicide. One child called the doctor to say there had been an accident and then shot himself. This child did not really understand that this act was final.

Adolescents, on the other hand, usually fully understand the meaning of death and are much more proficient in their efforts to commit suicide—and when they threaten suicide, whether one thinks they mean it or not, they should be taken seriously.

Is there any way of detecting the potential suicide? Studies of large numbers of attempted suicides showed that a great many of these boys and girls were friendless and unable to communicate with their parents. One study showed that three out of four adolescent suicides were preceded by threats or previous attempts at suicide. The children were usually very withdrawn and rebellious, and often did poorly in school, although many of them were bright. Occasionally there were teen-age love problems.

All teen-age children who are potential suicides need help desperately and should immediately begin psychotherapy. Children of school age who threaten suicide also need help very much although as a rule the situation is not as critical.

Sunburn
Sunburns are very common among infants and children, since their skin is much softer and more sensitive than that of adults.

Sunburn should and can be avoided if

parents will gradually adjust their children to the sun, or if they use protective lotions or creams—not tanning lotions but screening lotions.

Infants can be gradually adjusted to the sun by starting with a two-minute exposure front and back the first day and increasing this by two minutes every succeeding day. This is not so necessary with older children unless they are very blond and have unusually sensitive skin.

The lotions and creams that protect against sunburn are known as sunscreens. Among such preparations are Uval (10 percent sulisobenzone) and Pabanol (5 percent para-aminobenzoic acid). These contain chemicals that shut out the burning rays of the sun while letting most of the tanning rays penetrate. They can be used on infants as well as older children. However, if a child swims, the lotion or cream should be applied again, since water washes it off the skin. It will also wear off with excessive sweating, and should be reapplied every hour or so.

Treatment Ointments and creams containing local anesthetics are usually very effective in relieving the pain of most sunburns. If the burn is unusually severe, causing fever and swelling of the skin, it should be treated by a doctor.

Sunstroke

Also called heatstroke. A condition caused by prolonged exposure to high temperature.

Signs and symptoms High fever which may go from 104 to 108 degrees; very hot, dry skin with no sweating; rapid, weak pulse; rapid breathing; weakness; mental confusion and very often unconsciousness. The onset is often sudden, with the loss of consciousness as the first symptom.

Treatment The primary treatment is to reduce the high temperature. Place the child in a cool, shady place; remove his clothing, sprinkle him with water, and fan him. Immerse him when possible in cold water or wrap him in sheets wet with cold water, using electric fans to blow on the wet sheets. An ice pack may be placed on the child's head, and an ice-water enema used as well.

Continue all measures to reduce the fever until the temperature is down to 102 degrees. Then discontinue all fever-reducing measures. Repeat only if the fever rises again.

Call a doctor.

Avoid immediate reexposure to heat. The child may be unable to tolerate high temperature for several months or longer after the attack of sunstroke.

See also **Heat exhaustion.**

Suntan-lotion poisoning see **Poisons: first-aid treatment.**

Superior child see **Intelligence, exceptional; Talent, exceptional.**

Suppositories, rectal

Conical or cylindrical masses of glycerin or cocoa butter containing medicine, for insertion into the anus.

There are several types of suppositories used for different conditions during infancy and childhood. Their primary uses are to treat constipation, to give a child aspirin when he cannot take it by mouth because of nausea, and to stop vomiting.

Glycerin suppositories for the treatment of constipation may be recommended occasionally if a baby or older child is quite constipated. They should not be used frequently, for the anal sensation they cause is rather strong, and the child may form the habit of moving his bowels only when he feels this sensation.

Aspirin suppositories come in various strengths and can be used instead of aspirin by mouth when a child has a high fever and is vomiting or nauseous. The dosage by rectum is double that given by mouth, since all of it is not readily absorbed. (See **Aspirin.**)

A number of suppositories to stop vomiting are in use at the present time. Among these are Phenergan (promethazine hydrochloride), Tigan (trimethobenzamide hydrochloride), Thorazine (chlorpromazine hydrochloride), and Compazine (prochlorperazine). The strength given should be prescribed by the doctor.

Suprarenal gland see **Adrenal glands.**

Surgery see **Hospitalization.**

Susceptibility to infections
It has long been recognized that there are certain children who are much more susceptible to infections than the average child. They are frequently affected with sore throats, ear infections, bronchitis, and at times even pneumonia. These infections handicap a child greatly, not only by dragging him down physically, but by preventing him from attending school regularly and entering fully into usual childhood activities.

In such instances of repeated infections it is always necessary to search for the causes. It is no longer acceptable to merely state, "He's just a sickly child," or, "This is nature's way of building up his immunity." Present scientific knowledge enables doctors, in most instances, to locate the cause of a child's general susceptibility and treat it effectively.

There are common causes that are easily determined; common causes usually overlooked; and rare conditions often difficult to discover that make a child extremely susceptible to infections.

Common causes easily determined include such conditions as greatly enlarged adenoids, which force a child to breathe through his mouth, often causing a dryness of the mucous membrane of the throat and breathing tubes. This obstruction of normal breathing through the nose prevents the moistening of the air which usually occurs when it is breathed through the nasal passages. The dryness of the mucous membranes makes the tissues more susceptible to infection. Enlarged adenoids also may close the openings of the Eustachian tubes that connect the inner ear with the throat. When this occurs, infections may develop in the tubes and in the ear as well.

Chronically diseased tonsils and chronic sinusitis are also sources of frequent infections. Severe anemia also makes a child more susceptible to infection.

Certain common causes of susceptibility are often overlooked. Studies in immunity have led to the discovery that a person requires a certain level of gamma globulin in his body to successfully build up resistance to disease. The treatment of susceptibility due to too little gamma globulin or poor gamma globulin is by giving injections of gamma globulin every three to four weeks during the colder months of the year, when there are more infections. Some children may go through temporary periods of inability to form adequate gamma globulin, but this has not been scientifically determined.

One other group of children who develop frequent infections are those who have allergies of the respiratory system throughout the year. (This does not include hay fever.)

Rare conditions causing increased susceptibility include cystic fibrosis, agammaglobulinemia (a total lack of gamma globulin in the body), and certain congenital malformations of the lungs.

See also **Allergy; Cystic fibrosis; Gamma globulin.**

Swallowing foreign objects see **Choking; Foreign objects, swallowed.**

Swallowing hair or wool   see **Hair or wool, swallowed.**

Swallowing pills   see **Aspirin poisoning; Barbiturate poisoning; Poisons: first-aid treatment.**

Swear words

Almost all children, sooner or later, learn so-called "swear" words or "dirty" words. And also, sooner or later, they find they can excite the attention of their parents and others by using these words.

Young children of nursery school age often hear crude words or phrases. They quickly see that these words draw attention and even laughter, so they bring them home and try them out on their parents.

Whether children continue to use these words or not depends largely upon the parents' reaction. The more excited or upset parents get over the words, the more it will impress them on the child's mind. It is much better to ignore the objectionable word, or to ask quietly, "What does that mean?" or to say casually, "We don't use that word." Washing a child's mouth out with soap and water only increases the importance of the forbidden word or words.

Older children often use "dirty" words and bad language as a means of showing their maturity and worldliness. They enjoy exchanging dirty jokes with their peers and will even tell some of these jokes to their parents to impress on them that they are growing up and entering the world reserved for adults alone.

Usually the adolescent will use the accepted language of his friends and companions when he is with them. This should be recognized as his need to be accepted by his peers. But the teen-ager will minimize the use of "dirty" words at home if parents make very little of them or simply say in a casual voice, "Cut it out" or "Don't try to impress me."

But, above all, if parents wish their children to avoid the use of bad language, they themselves should be very careful of their own speech in front of their children.

Swearing   see **Swear words.**

Swimming

Swimming is one of the healthiest activities for both children and adults. It helps to build all muscles of the body, including the arm and torso muscles, which in children are often less developed than the leg muscles. It strengthens the heart and lungs. Moreover, many youngsters who are not able to compete effectively in other sports because of their size, because of eye problems, or for other reasons can do well in swimming if they practice.

However, safety rules must be observed when swimming, for there are more than 7,000 deaths from drowning in the United States each year, and most of these are among children. The peak age of drownings is 2 years.

Almost all these deaths are preventable, and directly the result of improper supervision by parents or other adults. Children fall into swimming pools, lakes, and streams, or are carried into the ocean by an undertow—and during the winter they often fall through the ice. (See **Ice skating.**)

No young child and no child unable to swim should be permitted to go unsupervised near deep or semideep water. Many small children have been drowned in water as shallow as eighteen inches.

Besides the close supervision, several other very important steps should be taken to overcome the dangers of water:

1. Every child should be taught to float or swim as early as possible, preferably during the nursery school years.
2. Swimming should be avoided when children have just eaten or are overtired, or when a storm is approaching.
3. Barriers should be placed around all swimming pools and the gates kept fastened unless an adult swimmer is around. (There is an excellent pamphlet, *Kidproofing the Backyard Pool,* published by the Injury Control Program, Public Health Service, Cincinnati, Ohio.)
4. Ropes, poles, and life preservers should be readily available.
5. All members of the family should learn mouth-to-mouth resuscitation, because trained people may not be available in an emergency. (See **Mouth-to-mouth resuscitation.**)

All children should obey the following rules outlined by the American Academy of Pediatrics:

1. Never swim alone.
2. Use the buddy system whenever possible.
3. Swim only in supervised areas.
4. Before diving into water, be sure it's deep enough and that the bottom is free of glass, stones, or other dangers.
5. Do not swim among anchored boats or in motor-boat lanes.
6. Do not swim during storms or when there is lightning.
7. Use floating devices and toys with care, since they may carry you far from shore or may deflate. They should not be used as life preservers.
8. Do not swim too far from shore. If you do, remain calm, rest, tread water, or float on your back until help arrives. Keep your hands under the surface of the water for better body position, balance, and aid in floating.
9. If you are caught in a current, do not buck it. When the current runs outward from shore, partially drift with the current, swimming diagonally across it. You will soon reach water where there is no current or perhaps a current toward shore.
10. Do not try to swim underwater without instruction.

Additional rules for children who are unable to swim or are poor swimmers:

1. Don't go out in water over your head.
2. Don't ever clown around in water.
3. Don't go out in boats unless you are wearing a life jacket or a life preserver.

Swollen glands   see **Lymph nodes.**

Syphilis
A venereal disease caused by a spiral-shaped bacteria, *Treponema pallidum.* There are two forms of this disease:

1. The acquired type—contracted through sexual intercourse with an infected person (and only very rarely by other means). It starts 10 to 90 days after contact (but most often in 2 to 3 weeks), usually with a hard open sore on the penis or vulva, called a chancre. This is followed within six weeks to three months by a mottled rash over the body. After this there may be no more symptoms for several years, but the disease is present in the body and may eventually affect all parts of the body, often leading ultimately to nerve disorders, insanity, and death. It is therefore essential that the condition be treated in its early stages.

The incidence of acquired syphilis has increased seriously in recent years. The initial symptom, the chancre, may not be noticed, especially if it appears inside the vagina rather than on the vulva. During this time the disease can be transmitted to someone else. It is important that all young people be educated in the facts of venereal disease and have access to a doctor to whom they can turn with any questions or problems.

2. The congenital type can occur among infants whose mothers had a syphilitic infection just prior to or during pregnancy. The bacteria pass from the mother's blood through the placenta and into the baby's blood during the latter five months of the pregnancy.

The first symptoms of congenital syphilis appear within the first six weeks of life, and include a rather profuse nasal discharge of a mixture of mucus, pus, and, occasionally, blood; a skin rash of red blotches and pimples, usually heaviest over the buttocks, back, and thighs; bleeding cracks and ulcers at the corners of the mouth and around the anus.

Rapid treatment of congenital syphilis will produce a complete cure, with normal growth and development of the child. If, however, congenital syphilis is not treated, there may be severe effects, including blindness and infection of the brain leading to mental retardation.

The increase in recent years in the number of cases of syphilis and gonorrhea among teen-agers is one of the reasons that sex education is so important. Ignorance bars the way to effective prevention and treatment.

Syrup of ipecac see **Poisons: first-aid treatment.**

T

Table manners see **Manners.**

Tachycardia, paroxysmal
A condition in which there are occasional attacks of very rapid heart beat. The condition may occur at any age during childhood. The cause is unknown but may occasionally be secondary to an infection or related to some congenital heart defect.

Signs and symptoms The child is pale, sweats, has difficulty in breathing, may vomit and have fever and a bluish color to the skin. The pulse is very rapid, ranging from 180 to 400 beats a minute. Sometimes it is difficult to count because of its rapidity. The heart is often enlarged, and murmurs are present in one third of the cases.

Diagnosis is made by hearing the extremely rapid heartbeat and taking an electrocardiogram (EKG).

Treatment The doctor should be notified at once.

Some simple, mechanical measures that will at times stop tachycardia are pressing on the eyeballs of the child, or causing him to gag or vomit.

Drugs such as digitalis or quinidine may be prescribed by the doctor.

Prognosis Attacks usually disappear as the child grows older unless the condition is associated with a congenital heart defect.

Taking turns see **Sharing.**

Talent, exceptional
Many children as early as 3 to 5 years of age show unusual talent. They may dance with unusual grace and rhythm, paint fascinating pictures, model exceedingly well in clay, or, if they have a special musical aptitude, carry tunes, recognize rhythms at a very young age, and at 3 or 4 may even pick out tunes on the piano and make up songs. The child with musical aptitude learns songs quickly, sings on pitch, and generally shows a highly developed response to music.

Fathers and mothers in their excitement and pride over such accomplishments may desire to start giving the child lessons at once. If lessons are started, they should be relaxed, simple, and informal, for these children are far too young to be placed under the pressures of a formal regime with the practicing it entails. The talent can often better be cultivated at home by encouraging the child in his interests and praising his accomplishments.

While exceptional talent in any of the arts is relatively rare, a great many people are definitely musical or artistic, and they enjoy music or painting or sculpting or dancing enormously.

An artistic child should be offered plenty of paper and various art materials such as crayons, poster paints, and finger paints. A musical child should hear a great deal of music at home and should be given rhythm instruments such as drums, tambourines, and triangles. If there is no piano available, a simple toy xylophone of good quality will suffice.

When a child reaches age 7 or 8, he or she may be given lessons, but the pressure should not be so great that it dampens the child's interest.

How is a parent to know if his child has a significant talent as he grows older? Although there are tests for musical and artistic talent—notably the Seashore Measure of Musical Talent, the Kwalwasser-Dykema Musical Talent Tests, and the Meier Art Judgment Test—these are of limited value in identifying the child with unusual talent. The child's progress in music or painting; his skill in playing an instrument, singing, or sketching; the teacher's assessment of his ability; the judgment of other musicians or painters—all these will give the parent a better idea of just how talented the child is.

By no means should the parents' ambition to foster a child's talent cause them to separate the child from normal contact and friendships with other boys and girls. Too many parents pressure talented children in order to satisfy their own unfulfilled ambitions.

In general, parents should remember that there is no demonstrable advantage in pushing a talent at a young age. The youngster should, of course, be helped to get the most pleasure possible from his talent, but it isn't necessary to aim for professional accomplishment. If the early talent continues to be an important part of the child's world as he grows, then the lessons can continue, or he can be sent to a specialized camp. In adolescence a youngster may wish to attend a school that specializes in his area of talent, and if this can be arranged, such a school may gradually prepare him for an adult career without isolating him from other young people.

See also **Art; Intelligence, exceptional; Music lessons; Rhythms and dance.**

Talking see **Speech.**

Tallness see **Height.**

Tampon, vaginal
A cylindrical plug of cotton and soft rayon inserted into the vagina to absorb the menstrual flow. Tampons are available in several sizes and absorbencies.

Many girls prefer tampons to sanitary napkins, for there can be no odor and there is no visible outline.

Girls must be taught how to insert the tampon properly. This is easier the first time after a warm tub bath, when the muscles are more relaxed. Instructions that come with the tampons are good, but many girls appreciate a mother's or a doctor's advice.

Tampons are changed every two or three hours on days of heavy flow, and less often when the flow is lighter. Many teen-age girls use both tampons and sanitary napkins the first day or two.

Girls may go swimming and take part in other sports while wearing tampons.

Taste
Taste is present at birth, the infant being able to differentiate liquids that are sweet from those that are sour.

By age 2 to 3 months, the sense of taste is quite acute, and the infant is quick to notice varying changes in the taste of a formula. He has already formed likes for certain foods and dislikes for others. By age 5 months, an infant will put almost everything in his mouth—to feel and to taste.

When a child is older, taste and appetite and the sense of smell are closely allied, since most of taste is dependent on smell. It is for this reason that appetite is so poor when the nose is completely clogged by greatly enlarged adenoids, a heavy cold, or a severe allergy.

TAT see **Tests.**

Tattling

Every child will now and then bring a bit of news to a parent or teacher to get someone else into trouble. This is different from the usual story telling of young children, in which they tell all the news and everything else that is on their minds.

Usually the news of a tattle-tale is insignificant: "Mommy, Johnny didn't brush his teeth," or, "Mommy, Mary just stuck her tongue out at you."

When a child indulges in tattling frequently, it is usually a sign of jealousy—most often between brothers and sisters or classmates. Or it may be outward evidence of a need for parental or other adult approval by a child who feels he is receiving too little attention.

If a child, through tattling, usually gains his desired result,—i.e., the parent's scolding or otherwise punishing the child "tattled on"—he will continue to tattle. Also, if the parent or other adult praises him for spying and reporting, the child is likely to repeat his activities. However, if he does not get the results he seeks and is told, "We don't like tattling," the tattling will usually subside in a short time.

Note: The child who tattles when another child is doing something dangerous, such as playing with matches or climbing out onto the roof, must be given approval. It can be explained to both children that the rule against tattling doesn't hold when someone could get hurt. Children can understand this in most cases.

Tay-Sachs disease

Also called amaurotic idiocy. A hereditary condition occurring almost exclusively among Ashkenazi Jews. It usually appears when a child is between 1 and 2 years old. The child, who has appeared normal both physically and mentally, starts to deteriorate rapidly. The muscles become weak and finally paralyzed. Intelligence declines until a child previously bright becomes severely retarded. Vision also gradually disappears and blindness occurs. There is no treatment at present; the disease is invariably fatal, death usually occurring before the child has reached age 3.

This disease is due to a recessive trait in both the father's and the mother's family. It will not occur if the condition has occurred in the family background of only one parent. If both parents have the tendency, the chance of having a child with this disease is 25 percent.

Prevention   A process of blood testing has been perfected for determining if a parent carries this recessive trait. Also, through amniocentesis, in approximately the fourteenth week of pregnancy, it can be definitely determined if the fetus is affected. If so, termination of the pregnancy is usually advised.

Teacher-parent relationship

Hopefully both parents and teachers have the same goal—the best possible learning experience for the child. A close relationship should exist between them in attempting to attain this goal. Unfortunately, only too often a gap exists. The parents are often afraid of the teacher and may feel that the teacher does not understand their child. The teacher, on the other hand, may feel that the parents are not helping the child or are helping him too much, that they are not cooperating, that they are not seeing or not acknowledging behavior patterns that are present, or that they are overreacting to the child's behavior.

At times the parents may blame the teachers for so-called problems of their children that are really developmental, such as talking back, using obscene language, becoming aggressive, and even expressing ideas strongly contrary to those held by the family.

However, for the sake of the child, there must be developed a team relationship between the parents and the teacher. There should be complete freedom of the parent to get in touch with the teacher and vice-versa.

At the outset of the school year, the parents should go to the child's school to meet the teacher and express their desire to develop a cooperative relationship. The parents must assume that the teacher is going to do her or his best.

Later, if a child has difficulties in studies or social relationships at school, the parents should discuss the whole subject with the teacher to obtain the teacher's point of view and to learn in what ways they can cooperate.

Parents should not expect the teacher to solve problems that are an outgrowth of the home environment. Nor should they expect a teacher to focus on their child alone.

There may be times when a parent is critical of a teacher, but this should not be expressed openly in front of the child.

If problems arise, a parent should always go to the teacher first rather than to the school principal. The principal should only be approached as a last resort.

Remember, if a parent antagonizes or creates difficulties for a teacher, the teacher may (often unconsciously) make life more difficult for their child. And a parent should never threaten a teacher.

It is most important that parents attend parent-teacher meetings—to get an understanding of the educational objectives of the school, to learn what progress their children are making, and to become familiar with new ideas in education. Furthermore, the meetings give parents an opportunity to talk informally with the teachers afterward.

Tear ducts

Tiny passages connecting the inner corner of the eyes with the nose. Normally, tears are being constantly formed in the eyes and flowing down through these ducts.

Occasionally, in the newborn child, the ducts are too narrow or are closed. In such cases the tears run down the child's cheeks. If the tear ducts are too narrow they will usually widen by themselves to a normal size before a baby is a year old. Otherwise the ophthalmologist may put a tiny probe through a duct to widen it. When there is a complete closure of a tear duct, it may be necessary to have it opened surgically, usually not before a year of age.

Teasing by children

Children tease other children, often cruelly. When there is sibling rivalry or jealousy, the teasing often gets out of hand. An older child, full of hostility to a younger brother or sister, may torment the younger child by teasing almost as much as by physical attacks. A younger child, who is protected by the parents, may take advantage of this by teasing an older child. Parents should protect the child who is the object of the teasing, but often this cannot be done effectively unless the child who is doing the teasing is reassured of his parents' love, interest, and appreciation of his difficulties and accomplishments. (See **Sibling rivalry and jealousy.**)

A child may be teased by other children because of his physical appearance, emotional problems, economic status, race, and so on. Children will call each other hurtful names such as Fatso, Smelly, Eagle Beak, and Stupid. Parents should make every effort to discover why their child is being teased and to help him to be more popular. If the child is in school, they should consult with the teacher. Physical problems should be minimized or eliminated under the direction of a doctor. The child should be helped to appear attractive, to wear what the other children are wearing. If a personality problem is involved, it may be that the child is emotionally upset and in need of special professional guidance. If the problem is the result of prejudice and bigotry, parents should see if the situation can be improved through consultations with teachers or other authorities. They should do everything possible to explain the situation to the child and reassure him. In some cases, however, it is best to remove the child from the situation.

Many children tease thoughtlessly, not having an appreciation of how this hurts another child. A parent who finds his own child engaging in this sort of teasing should make it clear that this behavior is unacceptable because it is unnecessarily cruel. Unless the teasing child has special problems, he will gradually develop sympathy for the feelings of others and refrain from malicious teasing.

Teasing by parents

Most children enjoy friendly teasing and joking, but teasing that belittles a child is destructive.

One type of teasing amuses the young child by the absurdity of the statement: "You're a big monkey!" "Are you sure that one and one aren't three?" Most children love this type of teasing, for it puts them in the superior position of knowing the right answer when the assertion is completely wrong. But you must be sure that a child is ready for this type of teasing. A young child may not get the joke if you ask, "Isn't your name Pretzel?" and may answer, "No! My name is Susan!" and give you a dark and angry look—for to many young children, their name is a valuable possession.

Parents at times tease their children without considering the harmful effect of it. Often they call a child uncomplimentary names such as Shorty, Stupid, or Lazybones. In most instances they do not use these terms in a malicious way and do not realize how much they are hurting the child by labeling him so unfavorably. But such terms usually hurt a child deeply. It should always be remembered that all children want, seek, and need approval.

Remember, too, that children may even live up to the names they are called. A child called Stupid will often act stupid and do poorly in school. A child called Slowpoke will consider himself as such and usually continue to be slow.

Some parents talk about a child in an uncomplimentary way while the child is present. A mother bringing a child to the classroom on the first day of school may remark to the teacher, "I'm bringing you the dumbest child in your school. He's yours." Such a remark cannot make a child feel that he is admired.

It is especially wrong to tease children because of their fears and anxieties. For instance, when a child shows fear of separation from his parents when first entering school, he may be told, "Oh, we've got a little baby again." Sometimes parents tease their children because of their appearance or some unbecoming behavior. They may tease them because of bed-wetting, nose-picking, thumb-sucking, blinking, and such.

Parents should avoid this malicious teasing. It can only make the child more insecure and unhappy.

Teen-ager see **Adolescence.**

Teeth

Good teeth are important for a child's proper nutrition, and good nutrition is necessary in order to have good teeth.

There are two sets of teeth during childhood. The first set, the baby teeth (milk teeth or deciduous teeth), usually start appearing between ages 5 and 8 months. The second set, the permanent teeth, begin appearing at approximately age 6 years.

The age of the eruption of the first teeth varies in different children and probably depends on heredity. In rare instances an infant will cut his first tooth as early as age 4 months. Many other normal, healthy babies are late teethers, some having only one or two teeth at age 1 year.

1. Lower central incisors, 5-8 months. 2. Upper central incisors, 8-10 months. 3. Lower lateral incisors, 10-12 months (note, the upper lateral incisors sometimes come in first). 4. Upper lateral incisors, 12-15 months. 5. Anterior molars, 12-15 months. 6. Canines, 18-24 months. 7. Posterior molars, 24-30 months.

The slow cutting of teeth is not, as a rule, due to poor health—with the exception of rickets, caused by a lack of vitamin D in the child's diet, or cretinism, when there is a lack of adequate thyroid secretion.

As a rule the first teeth to appear are the two lower central incisors (cutting teeth), which appear between ages 5 and 8 months. These are followed between ages 8 and 10 months by the upper central incisors, and between ages 10 and 12 months by the lower lateral incisors. At age 1 year the average child has six teeth, all incisors.

By age 15 months usually all the incisors are in, and the pre-molars, the first of the chewing teeth, are starting to push through the gums at the rear of the mouth. And between ages 18 months and 2 years the canines (tearing teeth) cut through the gums.

The so-called "two-year molars" arrive between ages 2 and 2½. Now the child has his complete number of first teeth.

All of these baby teeth are important, not only for biting and chewing but for maintaining the shape of the jaw so that the permanent teeth will later meet one another in normal apposition.

Children should learn to brush their teeth by age 2½ years, and should be taken to the dentist by at least age 3 years. It is very necessary that the baby teeth be kept in good condition and free of cavities by routine visits to the dentist; by daily tooth-brushing after meals with a fluoride toothpaste; by drinking fluoridated water or taking vitamin drops with fluorides; and by avoiding sugar in drinks and candy.

If teeth are lost or must be removed, space retainers should be applied by the dentist to hold the space. Otherwise the teeth on either side of the opening will close in, obliterating the normal place for the eruption of the permanent tooth beneath.

The permanent teeth usually start appearing at about 5½ or 6 years of age. The central baby teeth start loosening, then fall out; and soon afterward the permanent teeth appear beneath them. At the same time the six-year permanent molars appear on the gums at the rear of each row of baby teeth.

By the time children are 12 years old, all the baby teeth have dropped out and permanent teeth have taken their place. Then the twelve-year molars push through the gums on either side in back of the six-year molars. Now the children have twenty-eight permanent teeth. Later many of them will get the so-called "wisdom teeth," which appear in back of the twelve-year molars at about age 18 years or older. But some people never have these teeth.

See also **Dentist; Orthodontist; Teething; Toothache; Tooth decay.**

Teething

Most babies are not greatly troubled by the cutting of their first eight teeth in front of the mouth. They must have some minor discomfort, however, for they get some real satisfaction chewing on teething rings and hard or cold objects. And a few babies do show some discomfort with this early teething, even crying off and on during the month before the first tooth erupts.

Many parents have the mistaken belief that the outpouring of saliva at about age 3 months indicates the onset of teething. This early drooling occurs because the salivary glands start secreting at that time, and the baby, instead of swallowing, lets the saliva run out of his mouth. However, many babies also salivate each time they cut a tooth.

Most babies really suffer from teething when they start cutting their molars—the flat chewing teeth at the rear of the gums. The flat surfaces do not cut the gum as do the cutting teeth in front. These flat teeth, in pushing through the gum, stretch the surface, which causes pain. This stretching of the gums seems to affect the whole digestive system of many babies, causing them to spit up occasionally or even to develop diarrhea. It is for this reason that for generations mothers called the molars "stomach teeth."

The onset of teething causes a swelling and stretching of the gums. When molars are being cut, there is at times a blue discoloration of the gum caused by the tearing of a capillary, which bleeds under the surface. Some babies may be unusually irritable and may sleep restlessly or awaken frequently from sleep with a sharp cry.

A teething baby often stands up and chews the paint off his crib or playpen. It is for this reason that all paint for children's furniture is required by law to be lead-free. Repainted children's furniture should also have lead-free paint. (See **Lead poisoning**.)

To treat the discomfort of teething, give the child something firm to chew on—a rubber teething ring (some types are designed to be chilled in the refrigerator), a bagel, a zwieback, a hard cracker or teething biscuit. A teething child often enjoys drinking his orange juice or some milk from a thick glass, cup, or mug, for he chews on it while taking the liquid.

For the relief of pain, rub the gums with Anbesol, Numzit, Tot's Teething Cream, Ora-jel (all of which contain the local anesthetic benzocaine), or any other product designed to numb the gums. These are sold by all drugstores.

Paregoric has been used for many years since it also numbs the gums, but it is a morphine derivative and should only be used when advised by a doctor. Many pediatricians feel that the effectiveness of paregoric is due to the fact that a good deal of it is swallowed and acts as a sedative.

With very few exceptions, no fever is caused by teething. However, some doctors feel that the baby's resistance is somewhat lowered while he is cutting teeth, making him more susceptible to respiratory infections.

Television

Under proper control and supervision by the parents, television can be of great educational advantage to a child from early preschool age on. It can arouse many new interests, broaden his knowledge and concepts of the world and its peoples, and teach him a great deal about nature. It can also increase his vocabulary and teach him many games and songs to play and sing with children on the television screen or with other children at home.

Today there are a few good programs for children of preschool age, and many more for children of approximately ages 5 to 13.

But there are definite potential disadvantages of television as well:

1. Unless carefully regulated by the parents, children usually spend so much time watching television that they do not get enough physical activity, do very little reading, and neglect their schoolwork.
2. Programs may be overstimulating and at times so frightening that children are unable to fall asleep, or if they sleep are very restless, some even having nightmares.

3. Children are too often exposed to scenes of violence, fighting, and killing, as well as to programs dramatizing marital discord, broken families, divorce, and adultery.

It is obvious that the proper use of television requires serious thought on the part of the parents. Certainly they must regulate not only the time spent but the type of programs watched.

Television should not interfere with a child's schoolwork. It should not deprive the child of outdoor activity. It should not prevent a child from reading. Studies have shown that many children, even as young as age 5 or 6 years, will spend as much as three or four hours a day watching television unless limits are set by the parents. Limits, however, should be reasonable, for discussing television programs is one of the important social activities among children. And, of course, exceptions to the limits may be made for special programs of value and on rainy weekend days when children are confined to the house. As a rule, however, an hour a day (and not more than two hours) is enough.

How is a parent to judge if certain programs are suitable for children or not? Probably the greatest help is a rating of 300 television programs that is available for $1 a copy from the National Association for Better Broadcasting, 373 N. Western Ave., Los Angeles, Cal. 90004.

If the family can afford it, should a child have his own television set? Yes, as long as its use can be controlled. Only too often there are conflicts during the evening hours between the parents' and the child's desires. An extra set generally makes the house more peaceful.

Temper and temper tantrums

Temper is a violent reaction to frustra-tion or upset—often so violent that it is greatly disturbing to others.

Temper tantrums are a young child's method of coping with an unhappy or frustrating situation. They differ from outbursts of anger, which are usually directed at someone, and during which the child maintains a degree of self-control. In a temper tantrum, a child often loses virtually all control of himself—throwing himself on the floor, screaming, kicking, and hitting out. By this means a child tries to solve a crisis or a situation that makes him feel helpless.

Some children bang their heads on the ground in their rage. This rarely does any harm, but is frightening if the child is banging his head on a hard surface. The parents can simply pick up the child and hold him, or they can put him on a rug or other soft surface.

Temper tantrums are not at all unusual in the young child, and very rarely are an indication that a child is seriously disturbed emotionally. It is only when the child has them repeatedly or finds that through them he can control his parents that the problem of temper tantrums becomes serious.

Temper tantrums usually disappear by the time a child is 5 years old, but older children in their anger will occasionally lose control and throw things around the house, overturning chairs, breaking dishes, tearing books and magazines, knocking over lamps.

Just what are parents to do? Should they give in? Should they ignore the child during these periods, or should they be unyielding, letting the child know that violent tempers and temper tantrums will not succeed?

It is wrong to give in to a child simply because he has a temper tantrum—even if it is in the supermarket or some other public place. If, for instance, a child throws a temper tantrum in a store because his mother denies him a lollipop, she should just pick him up firmly and carry him out of the store. Preferably she should take him to some quiet place where he can calm down.

There is nothing to be gained by arguing, scolding, or slapping when a child is temporarily out of control with a tantrum. The parent should be as calm as possible, should attempt to quiet the child down and divert his attention, and should be warm rather than punitive. But the child should always feel and know that the parent is in control.

This attitude should also be maintained in the case of teen-agers, who frequently resist adult authority with fits of temper. A parent should not be forced to submit because of his adolescent child's fury. He should not fight back, but must prevent destruction of property in the home.

See also **Breath-holding.**

Temperature taking

Taking a child's temperature correctly is a necessary skill, for if a child is ill or irritable, the doctor will almost always ask for the temperature.

The rectal thermometer has a rounded bulb containing mercury at its end. The mouth thermometer has a narrow elongated tip containing mercury at its end. It is not safe to be used rectally on a struggling active child, for its narrow end may stick into and injure the mucous membrane of the anus, or may even break off in the anus or rectum. Temperature should always be taken rectally in a child under the age of 6 years.

A mother should buy a rectal thermometer and learn to read it when the baby is still young and before she is forced to read it because the child is ill. In selecting a thermometer look for one that is easy to read. If you are not famil-

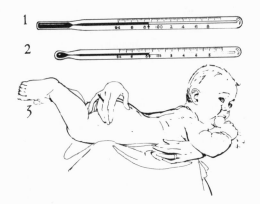

1. Oral thermometer. 2. Rectal thermometer. 3. Infant is lying on stomach; mother keeps hold of thermometer and baby.

iar with reading one, practice repeatedly using warm (not hot) water and shaking the thermometer down between each try. (A good thermometer should give an accurate reading in three minutes.)

What is normal temperature? Most thermometers are marked with every other number from 92 degrees Fahrenheit to 106 degrees or higher. An arrow points to 98.6 degrees, indicating that this is a normal temperature; many thermometers have the numbering in red above this line.

Usually the temperature by rectum is a half to a whole degree higher than the temperature by mouth. It is important, therefore, in reporting a child's temperature to a doctor, to mention if it has been taken by mouth or by rectum.

Rectally, 98.6 degrees is actually lower than normal for a young child. The temperature of children is not stable and normally varies up and down through the day from 98.6 to 100 degrees. Most pediatricians consider 100 degrees rectally as a high normal for children.

Often after a child has been ill, with

fever, and has returned to a normal temperature, the heat-regulating system of the body is still unstable. Although the child is completely over the infection, activity will often raise the child's temperature to as high as 101 degrees. This is called action temperature. Its nature can be definitely established if you let the child lie quietly for forty-five minutes, reading a book, crayoning, or watching television. If the fever is action temperature, it will return to normal during that period of time. If, however, the fever still persists, it is an indication that an infection is still present.

How to take a child's temperature

Take a baby's or young child's temperature rectally while he is lying across your lap, or stomach-down on a bed or other flat surface, so that he can be easily controlled. Older children can be asked to lie on one side, drawing the knees up slightly to the abdomen. The buttocks can then be spread slightly apart and the thermometer inserted in the anus.

Never take the child's temperature when he is lying on his back. The child may sit up suddenly, breaking the thermometer off in his rectum. And *never take your hand off the thermometer while it is in the child's rectum.*

The thermometer should be shaken down to at least 97 degrees and then well lubricated with petroleum jelly (Vaseline) before insertion into the rectum. It should be inserted about one-third of its length.

Children over 6 who are cooperative may be taught to use a mouth thermometer. This takes a little practice before a child is capable of keeping the thermometer under his tongue, holding his mouth closed, and breathing through his nose for a period of three minutes.

If a small child violently resists having his temperature taken rectally, or if rectal manipulation is not advisable because he has diarrhea, the temperature may be taken by holding a rectal or oral thermometer in the child's armpit, with the arm held tightly down against the chest. This should give a normal temperature of 98.4 or 98.6 degrees if the thermometer is left in position for three to five minutes.

See also **Fever.**

Terrors see **Nightmares and night terrors.**

Testicles

Also called testes. The olive-shaped sex glands of boys and men, normally held in the scrotal sac (see **Scrotum**) behind the penis. The testes not only secrete the male sex hormones, but also produce the sperm cells which carry the chromosomes of the father.

During the fetal period the testicles are located low in the baby's abdomen. In most newborn male infants, the testes have already descended from the abdomen into the scrotal sac.

When they are undescended, efforts are made to bring them down into the sac, either by hormone injections or surgically, before a boy is 7 years old. If there is too long a delay, i.e., past age 10 years, before correction, the testicles, although descended, may not be capable of producing sperm.

Two difficulties involving the testicles occasionally occur. The spermatic cord attached to the testicle may twist, cutting off the testicle from an adequate blood supply. Immediate operation for correction is necessary. In teen-age boys an inflammation of the testicles may occur as a complication of mumps. (See **Mumps.**)

Tests

There is a great deal of controversy surrounding the administration and interpretation of tests of all sorts. Described below are a few of the tests and types of tests a child may take at one time or another. It should be remembered, however, that tests, although often useful are not infallible. Their value depends upon the basic quality of the test (and almost all tests could be further refined); the ability of the tester to administer the test correctly; intelligent interpretation of the results; and the health and emotional state of the child taking the test.

Achievement test Any test designed to measure an individual's level of skill or amount of knowledge. Achievement tests are used by schools to assess a child's academic progress and to determine whether the child is achieving in school to the degree of his intelligence (See **Examinations and tests in school.**)

Aptitude test Any test designed to measure not present level of skill or amount of knowledge but ability or potential to do well in a given area.

Aptitude tests have been found to be more accurate than intelligence tests in predicting success or failure in different fields.

Such tests are often used during junior high school to determine the type of high school a child should enter. They are also used during high school years to help in decisions about further education and the selection of a career.

Interest test Any test designed to assess a person's likes or dislikes—of literature, art, music, science, types of people, sports, and so on. This shows interests only, not ability. Such tests are used most frequently in vocational counseling.

The child's pattern of interests is compared with those shown by people successful in various occupations to see which occupations his interests seem most closely related to.

It is always advisable that the child take aptitude tests as well, since one's interests do not always match one's potential ability.

Inkblot of the type used in Rorschach test.

Rorschach test A test designed by the Swiss psychiatrist Hermann Rorschach (1884-1922) to evaluate personality characteristics. Many psychologists consider this one of the most important of the personality tests. It is frequently used by psychologists and psychiatrists when a person is being considered for treatment. Usually the child (or adult) is sent to a psychologist with special training in administering Rorschachs, for a great deal depends upon the test being properly presented and all relevant reactions—including laughter, hesitation, exclamations, and so on—being recorded and intelligently interpreted.

The test consists of ten ordinary inkblots on cards (the same blots are always used). The child is asked what the blot looks like to him, and he is given as much time as he wants to answer, can turn the card whatever way he wants, and can give more than one answer. There are, of course, an infinite number of possible answers, but some occur again and again. Since the answers primarily reflect themes in the mind of the child, the results, when properly interpreted, should reveal many important aspects of the child's personality. The tester evaluates the nature and strength of the child's emotional responses; the strength and direction of his drives and ambitions; his emotional maturity; how he handles problems and makes adjustments.

Stanford-Binet intelligence test   A test first formulated by Alfred Binet (1857–1911), a French psychologist. It was later revised and improved by psychologists at Stanford University. This revision is called the Stanford-Binet test. The Stanford-Binet was one of the first individual intelligence tests used in this country. The 1960 Stanford-Binet Intelligence Scale is the updated version, which is presently in use.

The test is arranged according to age levels, and the tasks become progressively more difficult. A child is started at a level at which he is able to answer all the questions correctly and accomplish all the given tasks. He is then given all the questions and tasks for succeeding age levels until he reaches the level at which he is unable to get any correct answers or perform any tasks.

The questions and tasks in this test have been given to a large number of children in a broad population across the United States. Those questions and tasks which the majority of children of a certain age level dealt with correctly are

used in a given age category on the test. In this way, the child taking the test is being compared with a large population of children his own age.

The IQ is scored by dividing the mental age (computed from the number of questions answered correctly at each age level) by the child's actual age, and multiplying the result by 100:

$$\frac{\text{Mental Age}}{\text{Actual Age}} \times 100 = \text{IQ}$$

As an example: If a 4-year-old passes all the tests the average 6-year-old passes, the scoring would be as follows:

$$\frac{\text{Mental Age: 6 years}}{\text{Actual Age: 4 years}} \times 100 = \frac{600}{4} = 150 \text{ IQ score}$$

See also **IQ.**

Thematic Apperception Test (TAT)   A personality test consisting of thirty cards with a variety of different pictures on them. The person taking the test is asked to tell a story about each picture—what he sees and thinks is happening. The theory behind the test is that the person taking it will, in the course of telling a number of stories, present certain patterns of thought. This will enable a skilled examiner to determine some of the things which may be affecting a person's feelings, emotions, attitudes, and—in turn—his behavior.

There is a similar test specifically for children between the ages of 3 to 10 years (Children's Apperception Test, or CAT) in which the cards are simplified, picturing animals in various activities. Since children of this age level are very much interested in animals, they often will talk more freely about animals than about people. The child may have real fears or problems of which he is unable to speak, but in telling stories relating to the pictures, he will often reveal enough to enable the examiner to pick up cues about the causes of his behavior.

WISC (Wechsler Intelligence Scale for Children)   An intelligence test with items divided into two categories, verbal and performance.

The verbal section measures vocabulary, information, general comprehension, memory span, arithmetic, reasoning, and similarities.

The performance section is based on:

1. Block design (accurately copying a given design with colored blocks).
2. Picture completion (detecting missing parts in a picture).
3. Picture arrangement (arranging a series of pictures in sequence of a story theme).
4. Object assembly (putting together a picture puzzle).

The two separate categories, verbal and performance, are scored individually and then as a whole. By this means the tester can often uncover specific learning problems a child may have. Also, because there is a performance score separate from the verbal score, children, often from deprived or isolated areas, who have had less opportunity for gaining vocabulary, information, mathematical knowledge, and other acquirements will be judged more fairly than in many other intelligence tests.

Tests for allergies   see **Skin tests for allergies.**

Tetanus
Also called lockjaw. An infectious, non-contagious disease caused by the teta-nus bacillus, which usually enters through a wound. It is rare today, since almost all children receive tetanus toxoid as an immunization against the disease.

Signs and symptoms   It takes between three to twenty-one days after an injury, with an average of ten days, for a susceptible person to develop the disease. The first sign is a stiffness of the jaw caused by spasm of the muscles. This increases until the person is unable to open his mouth. For this reason the disease has been called lockjaw.

Later there is stiffness of the neck and back. The patient is restless, irritable, has difficulty in swallowing, and often has severe convulsions. Convulsions are started even by the slightest sound or slight touch. The muscle spasms of the body, which occur from time to time and last five to ten seconds, are extremely painful.

Treatment   Effective with adequate doses of tetanus antitoxin.

Immunization   Very effective through the use of tetanus toxoid. Booster doses must be given from time to time to keep the immunity high. (See **Immunization schedule and tests.**)

Tetany of the newborn
A temporary condition of the newborn, characterized by increased irritability, twitching, and convulsions. It is caused by a temporary insufficiency of hormone from the parathyroid gland, which causes an insufficient amount of calcium in the infant's blood. The condition sometimes occurs in infants fed with cow's-milk formulas. It rarely occurs in breast-fed infants.

The treatment, prescribed by the child's doctor, is to give calcium: intravenously at first, and then in extra amounts by mouth.

The recovery is usually rapid and complete.

See also **Parathyroid glands.**

Tetracycline

One of the common and most effective broad-range antibiotics, used especially in the treatment of acne in teen-agers. It should not be taken by mothers during pregnancy or given to infants and children under the age of 12 years, for it can invade a child's teeth during their period of formation and cause them to be permanently darkened.

Teen-agers using tetracycline for acne should know that the antibiotic makes the skin especially sensitive to sunburn. An oil-free sun-screening lotion such as Pabafilm or Sundare should be used during prolonged exposure to sun.

Diarrhea and fungus infections around the anus and genitals are sometimes caused by tetracycline. This is rare among teen-agers but is fairly frequent with adults.

Thematic Apperception Test see **Tests.**

Therapy see **Family psychotherapy; Psychotherapy.**

Thermometer see **Temperature taking.**

Thiamin see **Nutrition.**

Thinness

A thin child is often the cause of concern to parents who are in the habit of associating good health with robust, broad-muscled, and solidly built children. But being thin does not by any means imply that a child is malnourished or otherwise unhealthy. In most instances the child's thinness is simply the result of a familial build. Children who are normally thin seem to have fewer colds and other respiratory infections than heavier or overweight children.

It is not fair to the child, and may even be greatly disturbing, if a parent openly shows unhappiness over the child's thin body. And it is doubly upsetting if the parent insists on forcing the child to eat more than he desires.

If the child is thin because of malnutrition, it may be due to one of a number of conditions: poor appetite; a chronic, debilitating condition or infection; a worm infestation, as in tapeworm or hookworm; or an emotional condition, as in anorexia nervosa.

It should be left to the doctor to determine whether the child's build is normal or whether he is suffering from malnutrition.

See also **Anorexia nervosa; Appetite, poor; Worms.**

Threats see **Discipline.**

Throat, sore see **Sore throat.**

Thrush

An infection of the mucous membrane of the mouths of young infants, caused by the fungus Monilia. In most cases the infection occurs while the baby is being born, the fungus coming from the mother's body. It may also be contracted from poorly sterilized nipples on bottles in the hospital nursery or at home.

It appears as pearly white spots on the inside of the cheeks, the palate, and the tongue. These often look like milk

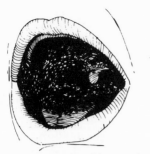

Thrush begins as small white spots on the tongue, palate, and inside of the cheeks. If untreated, the spots will spread into thick patches. This is quite a severe case.

curds. It can usually be diagnosed by mothers, for milk curds can be easily pushed aside by a cotton swab, while the white lesions of thrush remain attached.

The condition is apparently quite painful, for many babies are cranky and nurse very badly when they have thrush. Usually it is of no danger unless it extends down the esophagus and invades the stomach, intestines, and other parts of the body. But this is extremely rare, occurring usually only in weak, debilitated babies.

Treatment As a rule treatment is very effective and simple. The mother simply swabs the baby's mouth three times a day with a watery solution of gentian violet or a new, colorless preparation called Mycostatin (nystatin). The condition usually clears after treatment for a few days.

Thumb-sucking see **Sucking, thumb and finger.**

Thyroid gland
The thyroid gland is located in front of the portion of the neck just below the larynx. It is composed of two lobes, one on either side of the neck, with a con-necting strip of thyroid tissue between. This gland is one of the most important of the endocrine glands. It secretes the thyroid hormone that controls the metabolism of the body.

If too little thyroid hormone is formed (hypothyroidism), the child gains weight and may be sluggish, or even backward mentally. If very little or no hormone is formed, the child may become a cretin and be permanently retarded mentally unless treatment is started in early infancy. (See **Cretinism.**)

If too much thyroid hormone is produced (hyperthyroidism), the child becomes nervous, loses weight, has insomnia, perspires profusely, has a rapid heartbeat, and often has heart palpitations. The child eats a great deal but still cannot maintain his weight.

Diagnosis Diagnosis of whether a child's thyroid is secreting too little or too much hormone is through a blood test (the PBI, protein-bound iodine), although the doctor may wish to do other tests as well, including studies with radioactive iodine.

Treatment Children with a lack of or an insufficient supply of thyroid hormone are treated with tablets of thyroid extract or pure thyroid hormone taken daily by mouth. Treatment is very effective.

Children with too much thyroid secretion can be treated quite successfully by drugs. In rare cases, when such therapy is inadequate, surgical removal of a portion of the thyroid gland is indicated.

See also **Goiter.**

Tick bites see **Rocky Mountain spotted fever.**

Tics

Tics, or habit spasms, such as repeated eye-blinking, nose-twitching, shoulder-shrugging, and throat-clearing are fairly common in children and teen-agers. These habit spasms are characterized by the involuntary, repeated movement of a muscle or a group of muscles while the child is awake. They disappear during sleep.

The tic movements differ from the body movements of chorea (Saint Vitus's dance) in that they are motions over and over again of one group of muscles, whereas in chorea the child moves muscles all over the body indiscriminately. (See **Saint Vitus's dance.**)

Tics are almost always outward signs of some emotional disturbance which the child is experiencing. They are a warning to parents that there is some anxiety or tension upsetting the child.

Most children are able to control their tics temporarily if commanded to do so, and some can stop them completely, only to have other, different tics replace them. But calling attention to a tic, ridiculing the child, or forcing him to stop it is not advisable and may even be harmful.

In most cases the tics subside by themselves without treatment. In all cases the child should be helped to relax. In some cases doctors prescribe mild sedatives or tranquilizers for several weeks. Usually, if the cause is not too deeply rooted, this treatment will relieve the condition. If the tic continues, parents must look closely into the home or school situation to discover what is upsetting the child, and must make special efforts to lessen pressures on the child. If there is no improvement, psychotherapy may be necessary.

See also **Fidgeting.**

Timidity   see **Shyness.**

Tiredness   see **Fatigue.**

Toddler period

The period between 1 and 2 years of age. It is one of the most exciting and important stages in all the years of child development, for the youngster is learning for the first time to walk by himself, to understand speech, to talk, to control bowels and bladder, to feed himself, and to gain a sense of independence.

He still is largely dependent on his parents, and although he is gaining an early degree of autonomy and independence, these are both very unstable.

He explores constantly and learns tremendously, but in doing so needs considerable guidance and direction. He still wants a great deal of the parents' attention—will often even resent his mother's using the telephone—but does not desire to be held as much as previously. He is usually satisfied to have his mother or father nearby and since he can now understand a great deal, loves to have the parent talk with him.

He has a tremendous degree of energy and activity, and loves pull-toys and toys that make noise. He especially enjoys pots and pans that he can bang together. He needs ample outlets for his great energy.

He does not, as a rule, play with other children, although he may play near them and is interested in them. As a matter of fact, he can be very jealous, and is usually greedy and egocentric.

At this stage also he begins to take an interest in his bowel movements and at times will even play with them. These stools interest him tremendously, for he has made them himself—they are part of him. Some youngsters are upset on seeing their stools flushed down the toilet.

Because the toddler is a great explorer, discoverer, and experimenter, there is a great chance of accidents or destruction of property if he is not closely supervised. Parents must keep breakables out of the way, as well as books and new magazines, until a child learns better self-control. They must also plug up electrical outlets, put guards on the windows, keep medicines and poisonous preparations well out of the child's reach, cover radiators, and watch that he does not pull down on himself cups of hot tea or coffee or pots of hot liquids. (See **Accident prevention, indoors.**)

The toddler is going through one of the most educational years in his life but needs a great deal of guidance to go through it safely and successfully.

Toeing in and toeing out   see **Feet.**

Toenails   see **Nails, cutting.**

Toes, webbed   see **Feet.**

Toilet training

The control of bowels and urine are among the most important developmental steps in a child's progress. As a rule children are bowel trained before they are completely bladder trained.

Bowel training   At what age should bowel training be started? Formerly many mothers and nurses prided themselves on having trained their infants before age 1 year. But the experience of pediatricians, child psychiatrists, and child guidance experts shows that toilet training too early can cause a great deal of later trouble in the form of emotional difficulties often associated with constipation or soiling.

One should wait until a child shows readiness to toilet-train before attempting to help him attain this step in development. Although the usual time of readiness is somewhere between 18 months and 2 years, there is no specific time to begin, for each child is an individual and develops his own readiness for toilet training—and if not pressured or forced, he will usually train himself with ease. It is another normal developmental stage, like sitting up, standing up, and walking, but in bowel training, parents can aid in making the process easier.

During the whole training process a parent should do everything he can to relax the child when he is sitting on the potty: staying with him, talking to him, reading to him. Of course, if a child has a movement in the potty, he should gain the parent's approval. At no time should he be scolded for his difficulties or "mistakes" during training.

A child is probably approaching the bowel-training time when he starts soiling at approximately the same time each day. He may also make some special sound or give some other indication that he is going to have a bowel movement.

Then the child should be quietly placed on a potty or a potty chair (be sure the seat is warm) for a few minutes. A potty chair or potty is preferable to a seat high up on the toilet, for the chair on the floor is on the baby's own level.

There are other reasons also for using the potty or potty chair. At the age of toilet training, most children know that things get flushed down the toilet, and many children, sitting on the toilet, fear that they may fall in and be flushed down also.

Furthermore, at this age the child realizes that he has made the bowel movements himself and often is very proud of them. They are, to his mind, part of him, and he is somewhat possessive about them. If he is using a potty, he sees them in the pot—and they can be flushed down the toilet later without his observation. On the other hand, when he is using the toilet during the training period, he usually sees the movements flushed down the toilet and may be disturbed by it, and may not want to have a movement on the toilet.

Under no circumstances should a child ever be forced to toilet-train. The old method of using a suppository once or twice a day and then placing the child on the potty or toilet seat is very upsetting to the child and usually starts a resistance to the whole process.

Holding a child on the seat or otherwise forcing him to sit there also builds up resistance and makes training take much longer. Also, a parent should never use terms like "nasty," "dirty," and "filthy" in referring to the stools, whether a child passes them in his diaper, pants, or on the floor. Too often the youngster, in his effort to gain approval and not to do anything "nasty," "dirty," or "filthy," will withold his movements and develop constipation which may even become chronic. Often it is recommended that a child who has become frightened of being "dirty" should be encouraged to play with mud, finger paints, and clay to learn that it's all right to be dirty and messy.

Some children who are resisting the pressures of bowel training will go in a closet or behind a screen and have a movement in their diapers or on the floor. Apparently they are attempting to withhold it from their parents. They should not be scolded, but reminded, "We have the potty for that."

If any serious resistance appears, either the child is not physically ready yet or the parents are doing something wrong. Bowel control requires considerable muscular coordination, and a few lucky episodes may have led the parents to believe that the child is ready, when in fact his control is still weak. Or the child may have adequate control but simply be asserting his independence by resisting. This frequently happens when a child senses that the issue is especially important to his parents. He is testing his power not to do what the parents want him to do. There is nothing to be gained by fighting the child. Instead the parents should respond with greater casualness. Efforts at training can be given up for a while; or efforts to make the child sit for more than a few minutes on the potty can be given up—don't ask the child to stay on the potty if he wants to get up. Parents should also consider whether by words, facial expressions, or gestures they are communicating disgust to the child. Whatever the difficulty, remember that the child will learn control sooner or later even without guidance, and the less emotion and time put into this cause the better.

Once a child has gained some control and is past age 2 years, training pants may be used during the day instead of diapers. (Diapers may be continued at night as long as necessary.) Many children depend on the diapers to have their movements, and will not have a movement standing up or running around unless they feel the diaper in place. A child may at first object to the pants, but parents should not give in. If the child soils the pants, don't scold him or punish him, but clean him up and encourage him: "Next time tell Mommy, and we'll use the potty."

All children react to the approval of parents, and usually, with encouragement and patience, the child will be bowel-trained in a few months.

Bladder training An infant or young child cannot control urination: when the bladder is full it voids automatically. However, somewhere between 1½ and 2 years of age, mothers will usually notice that the interval between a youngster's wetting periods grows longer—to approximately two hours. Eventually the time comes when most mothers can guess when a child is ready to void.

As with bowel control, children will eventually learn to control their bladders by themselves. However, they can acquire this ability earlier with the assistance of the parents. When the mother is able to estimate the approximate time interval between the child's voidings, she can bring the child to the potty at these times. The potty should be warm, so that it is comfortable, and the youngster should be told that it is used for "weeing." If he does urinate in the potty, he should be praised.

Boys usually first learn to urinate sitting down. Later, when they see other boys or their fathers standing up while urinating, they soon follow their example.

Most children do not mind going to the potty or toilet to urinate, unlike their frequent resistance to bowel training. There are several reasons for this. The whole process takes only a few minutes, and, as a rule, brings immediate physical relief. Probably most important, the urine is a liquid, not a solid mass as is the bowel movement. Many youngsters feel that the bowel movement is a part of their body and do not want to see it flushed down the toilet.

Most children are fairly well trained to daytime bladder control by 2½ years, although there may be occasional lapses. At these times, when a child wets his pants, he should not be scolded, but should be reassured that he will soon be able to stay dry. A child who does not have daytime bladder control by the age of 3½ to 4 should be checked by a doctor.

Nighttime bladder control is somewhat more difficult for youngsters to attain. Most children are dry at night by age 3 years, but a good many continue wetting at night for a year or two longer. The age at which a child stays dry at night is largely dependent on the size of the urinary bladder, which in some children takes longer to reach normal size. Emotional factors may influence bedwetting as well.

In the early stages of training at night, it is generally a good plan to take the child to the bathroom at 10 P.M., but only if it does not upset the child. This not only trains the youngster to sleep dry, but also prevents a relatively small bladder from filling completely during the night. Later this P.M. toileting can be discontinued.

When children are still bed-wetting past the age of 6 years, special steps should be taken to aid in bladder training.

See also **Bed-wetting; Soiling, chronic.**

Tomboyishness see **Homosexuality.**

Tongue-sucking see **Sucking need.**

Tonsillectomy
In former days children's tonsils were

immediately removed if they appeared enlarged to the doctor or if a child tended to have sore throats.

Today most pediatricians advise against removal of tonsils unless a child is getting a series of severe sore throats that are preventing him from attending school or from enjoying the usual childhood activities. In rare instances removal of tonsils is advised if they are so large that they prevent a child from swallowing solids. Tonsils are seldom removed before a child is 3 years old, for if removed too early, there is often a regrowth of tonsillar tissue.

Many pediatricians feel that the tonsils serve a useful purpose by holding infections in the throat and aiding in preventing them from invading the bronchial tree and the lungs.

A further reason for avoiding tonsillectomies is the emotional strain which many young children suffer from any operation.

If a tonsillectomy must be performed, it is important that the child's doctor, his parents, and the surgeon work together to reassure and help the child through the emotional hazards of the operation. (See **Hospitalization.**)

Tonsils

Two rounded or oval masses of lymphatic tissue, located in the throat, one on each side, behind the soft palate. Like the adenoids, the tonsils work to defend the body against infection. If the defense mechanism breaks down, the tonsils themselves may become vulnerable to frequent infections.

Tooth decay

Also called dental caries. This is almost a universal condition among children, and adults as well. It is especially marked between the ages of 5 and 18.

Most dental decay is caused primarily by bacteria, which, in contact with certain carbohydrates, cause the production of acids that destroy the enamel and then eat into and destroy the body of the tooth itself. The decay may be slow and long-drawn-out, or it may be acute and rapid, eating into and destroying teeth in a very short time.

Caries may be effectively inhibited by the use of fluorides in the water, in vitamins, in the formula, or applied directly to the teeth by the dentist or through the use of fluoridated toothpaste. A great deal of scientific research has proven that this fluoride treatment not only strengthens the enamel of the teeth, but prevents the penetration of acids into the softer tooth structure under the enamel. Recent studies have also shown that the growth and action of bacteria is inhibited on teeth coated with fluoride.

Dental decay can also be held in check by preventing a child from taking sweets and drinks containing an excessive amount of sugar, for the sugar that remains in the mouth ferments, producing acid which destroys the enamel and the tooth itself. (See **Candy and chewing gum.**)

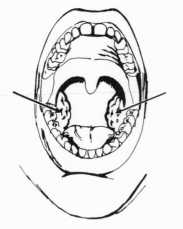

Tonsils vary considerably in size. These are quite prominent, protruding from either side of the throat.

A good diet, high in calcium and vitamin D; brushing of the teeth after each meal; and routine visits to the dentist are also necessary to prevent dental decay. The dentist will locate the tiny beginnings of cavities and fill these when they are still small. This will cause a minimum of discomfort to the child and will prevent severe damage to the teeth.

Toothache

A toothache almost always indicates that there is an infection of the tissues of the jaw beneath a tooth that is decayed, dead, or filled. Occasionally in children an exposed nerve may also cause a toothache.

A toothache should always be treated by a dentist, who will see if an infection is present and relieve the condition causing it.

If the pain is caused by an infection at the base of the tooth, it is worthless for a parent to attempt to relieve it by aspirin or other pain-relieving drugs, or by antibiotics.

Occasionally, what seems to be a toothache is actually the reflection of some other inflammatory process nearby, such as mumps, an ear infection, a canker sore, or infected sinuses.

See also **Tooth decay.**

Torticollis see **Wryneck.**

Tourniquet see **Bleeding time; Cuts; Snakes and snakebites.**

Toxoid

A bacterial poison that has been transformed so that it is no longer poisonous.

Many infections produce toxins (poisons) which are of great danger to human beings. These toxins are treated chemically to destroy their poisonous effects. But when the resulting nontoxic products, called toxoids, are injected into the body, they are capable of stimulating the body to build up a resistance against the specific infections that originally produced the toxins.

The toxoids that are given to children in their routine immunizations are those of diphtheria and tetanus. They give very effective protection, but booster injections of the toxoids are needed every few years to keep the immunity high.

See also **Immunization schedule and tests.**

Toys and play materials

From the earliest months of life toys and play materials contribute significantly to physical, intellectual, and emotional development.

Infancy The infant begins to learn about the world around him partly through his playthings. He enjoys colored mobiles hanging above his crib, and in time will reach for them and even hit them. When approximately 3 months old, he learns to hold objects such as a rattle or a cuddly animal. When he is able to sit up, he makes new discoveries every day through playing with pots and pans, large spoons, cereal boxes, adhesive-tape rollers, discarded magazines and newspapers, and other household objects. Among the standard toys he uses and enjoys are balls, large colorful blocks, cloth or cardboard books containing pictures of familiar animals and objects. At this age also, he begins to very much enjoy floating toys for his bath.

1 year to 18 months Once the baby stands up and starts walking, more complex toys help him to develop his skills. He can increase his powers of observation and coordination by placing wooden or plastic rings on a stick and setting large pegs in holes. He can now play with simple put together-take apart toys. He can push blocks ahead of him and can even make a simple pile of blocks. He begins to imitate the world he has observed and loves small wagons, small baby carriages, toy animals on wheels, and musical or chime pull-toys.

18 months to 3 years   At this age toys and play materials provide a child with a wide range of new experiences. He begins to be much more outgoing physically, climbing up on slides and sliding down, playing on seesaws, riding tricycles, throwing balls, shoveling in the sand, splashing around in a wading pool, and riding on hobby horses.

He is also gaining greater coordination of the small muscles of his hands and fingers. He can usually do simple cutout puzzles, arrange nested blocks, and place variously shaped pegs in their proper holes, and he is quite capable with pounding toys. He loves to play with blocks and will attempt to build houses or constructions.

He now greatly enjoys imitating adult activity. He likes to dress up in adult clothes and begins to play with brooms, sinks, play stoves, ironing boards, and play houses—all activities which will be carried on more fully in the preschool period, ages 3 to 6 years.

A real interest in music is also evident at this 18-month-to-3-year level as children play with simple musical instruments. They bang on toy pianos, blow harmonicas, shake tambourines, beat drums, and enjoy marching, running, jumping, and "dancing" to music. They also love phonograph records and quickly learn to select the records they most enjoy.

3 to 6 years   Children of this age generally enjoy all the toys of the children a year or so younger but use them to better advantage. They greatly enjoy acting out adult parts and activities, especially if costumes can be arranged. They are doctors and nurses, cowboys and cowgirls, firemen and policemen, soldiers, Indians. They will spend hours playing store, enjoying doll houses, having miniature tea parties with small dishes and utensils, and playing with toy soldiers, knights, and cowboys. The child's imagination is at its height during this period, and, given the opportunity, he makes full use of it in his play activities.

He still plays with blocks but now uses blocks of all shapes and builds houses, bridges, boats, garages, and towers, often using intricate designs and making amazing balances.

This is also the age when most children become fascinated with transportation toys such as trucks, trains, boats, autos, airplanes, cranes, fire engines, tractors, and ditch diggers. Play with toy animals of the farm, zoo, and circus is also popular.

Children of this age level delight in using their muscles. They will use backyard swings, ladders, and other climbing apparatus such as jungle gyms and climbing bars. They ride their tricycles and later begin to ride a two-wheeler; they learn to skate and even ski. They enjoy throwing balls and running with kites. They have what has been described as "action hunger," and their toys and play materials should satisfy this need and build up their physical strength and coordination.

Children of 3 to 6 years usually love to cut things out with scissors and to paste, especially using colored paper. Old magazines with pictures to cut out are greatly enjoyed. Sawing, hammering, and nailing are also pleasurable activities, and crayoning and painting give the child added opportunities for self-expression.

6 to 12 years   These are years of increased physical activity and sociability. Children still enjoy many of their previous play activities but in a more mature fashion. They are ready to work with carpenter sets, weaving equipment, erector sets, toy sewing machines, and other craft equipment.

Team sports become popular, and children can become skilled in baseball, touch football, soccer, basketball, hockey, volleyball, tennis, bowling, golf, skiing, skating, swimming, and many other sports. Punching bags, jump ropes, pogo sticks, Irish mails, help to develop the muscle tone of both arms and legs. Bicycles are among the most used and prized possessions.

From approximately ages 6 to 9 years children enjoy more difficult puzzles and play avidly at games of chance or skill. Weaving and beadwork sets, and erector sets, are also popular.

At approximately ages 9 to 10 years many children begin hobbies which may last into adult life. Among such hobbies are photography, stamp collecting, coin collecting, leather and metal work, stone collection, shell collection, and costume-doll collecting.

Science toys are also enjoyed by children in the later school years. These include chemistry sets, real microscopes, telescopes, and planetariums.

Interest in dramatic play increases greatly during this period. Both boys and girls usually enjoy puppets and marionettes; they make stages with props, design and make their own costumes, and create and act in their own plays.

Interest and competence in the arts may flourish. Painting, sculpting, ceramics, and playing musical instruments are favorite activities of many children.

It is obvious that the main use of toys and play materials is to have fun. Play activities, however, are of primary importance in almost all areas of child development. They involve gathering of information, development of the body, expression of feelings, gaining of friends, learning how to share and cooperate, understanding the outside world, and strengthening of family relationships.

See also **Art; Blocks; Music in the home; Music lessons.**

The following list of toys and play materials indicates the *types* of toys (not all the toys) that are enjoyed at different age levels. Children will almost always continue to enjoy some toys associated with a younger age group. Many children may want and be ready for some toys associated with older age groups.

Birth to 12 months

Brightly colored mobiles to attach to crib and carriage or string across playpen, some of which sound when hit by hand or foot

Soft, cuddly dolls and animals

Rattles

Squeaky rubber toys

Brightly colored plastic disks

Strings of large, light beads to bang or chew

Teething rings

Floating toys for the bath

Rubber blocks, some of which chime when moved

High-chair toys, such as brightly colored objects on springs that fasten by suction cup

Washable cloth books with colored pictures of familiar objects

Large colored balls

Baby bouncers, such as Jolly Jumpers

Busy box, with wheels to be turned, doors to be opened, and the like

Big wooden spoon and saucepan, pots, cereal boxes

Paper and old magazines to tear

12 months to 2 years

Push-pull toys

Strings of large beads

Colorful books with pictures, rhymes, and jingles

Small doll carriage

Music box

Drums

Nested blocks

Pots and pans

Balls

Peg box

Pegboard

Balloons

Records of nursery rhymes and children's songs

Kiddy Kart

Smallrocking chair

Animals on wheels

Floating toys

Hammer board

Small truck, fire engine, bus—to be straddled

Sandbox

Sand toys (pail, shovel)

Small xylophone

Toy telephone

2 to 3 years

Hobbyhorse

Tricycle

Small, low slide

Dishes and cooking utensils

Play furniture

Dress-up clothes

Stuffed animals

Dolls (no fancy dresses needed)

Doll furniture

Puzzles with a few pieces

Clay, Play-Doh

Pencils, crayons, chalk, blackboard

Colored paper

Books

Phonograph records

Take-apart and put-together toys

Finger paint and easel paints

Blunt scissors

Small broom, carpet sweeper

Small gardening tools

Playhouse

Boat for bathtub or pond

Small trucks and trains

Rubber farm animals

Large trucks, fire engines, buses—to straddle

Large cardboard boxes

Soap-bubble pipes

3 to 6 years

Doctor kits

Additional dress-up clothes and costumes

Hand puppets

Pegboards

Storekeeping toys, including scales, cash register

Larger baby carriage

More complicated blocks for building

Village sets

Talking dolls

Doll families

Dress-up dolls

Kaleidoscope

Coloring books

Trucks, autos, planes, trains

Easy construction sets
Puzzles with more pieces and shapes
Larger tricycle
Wagon
Sled
Knock-down dummies and punching bags
Beginners' skates and skis
Magnet
Wheelbarrow
Swing
Slide
Climbing bars
Simple carpentry tools and work bench
Wading pool
Clay
Paints and brushes
Easel
Colored cloth
Needles and thread
Matching-picture games
Jumprope
Colored paper
Paste
Better scissors
Scooter

6 to 9 years

Masks and joker items
Disguise kit
Gyroscope
Dolls with sets of doll clothes
Doll house and doll furniture
Paper-doll sets
Toy typewriter
Printing outfit
Jump rope
Marbles
Tops
Kites
More items for store play
Climbing bars
Chinning bars
Pogo sticks

Hoops
Stilts
Games of chance and games of simple skills
Bicycle
Irish mail
More difficult puzzles
Harder construction sets
Baseball, football equipment
Electric-train sets
Simple sewing and embroidery sets
Simple weaving material and equipment
Dominoes
Lotto
Garden sets
Swimming fins
Masks, snorkels
Racing cars and tracks
Magic sets
Croquet sets
Better tools

9 to 12 years

Model kits for boats, airplanes, etc.
Handicraft sets for jewelry, beadwork, metal, leather, sewing, embroidery
Hobby kits
Space toys
Table tennis
Archery
Basketball with baskets
Card games and board games
Checkers, chess
Anagrams
Tether balls
More intricate construction sets
Character dolls
Jigsaw puzzles
Sculpturing materials
Marionettes
Chemistry sets
Magic sets
Camera
Telescope

Toys and safety

Parents should take great care when selecting toys to be sure each toy is entirely safe when used by the child at his
particular age. A toy which may be safe
for a 5-year-old, such as a marble, may
be very dangerous when given to a 2-
year-old.

It is very important also to make sure
that a toy has no sharp or pointed
edges, and that it cannot be broken easily. A cheap rattle for a baby may be
broken, and the infant may eat the pel-
lets or other particles within that cause
the sound of rattling.

Toys that are potentially dangerous
include animals and dolls with detacha-
ble eyes, especially eyes on pins; flammable toys and play costumes; cheap toys
that can break or splinter; electrical toys
that do not bear the the seal of the
Underwriters' Laboratory (U.L.); toys
that can endanger the eyes or can pierce
the skin, such as bows and arrows, BB
guns, and darts; ill-balanced toys that
topple easily, such as some hobby
horses; toys painted with lead paint;
cap guns that produce noises so loud
they can damage the eardrum.

Parents must be aware that toys get
broken during use. They should examine toys from time to time to assure that
there are no sharp or cutting portions
that might be of potential harm.

Toys should not be left lying on the
floor where they may be tripped over.
They should always be put away at the
end of the day.

Toys and violence

Often parents ask whether toy guns or
other war toys are harmful to children
by leading them to violence in later
years. There is no evidence that such
toys are conducive to violence.

For many generations children have
enjoyed playing with knights in armor,
toy forts, bows and arrows, toy soldiers,
guns, battleships, popguns, and the like.
The evidence shows that it is not toys
that cause later cruelty or savagery, but
rather upbringing and environment.

Nevertheless, there appear on the
market from time to time some toys that
are totally unjustifiable and harmful.
There is no good reason for buying a
child a miniature torture set, for example.

Trachea

The trachea is the large breathing tube
leading from the throat downward. At
its bottom it divides into two tubes, the
right and left bronchi, going to the lungs
on either side of the chest.

The bronchi are lined with mucous
membrane that is very sensitive to any
foreign body or irritating substance.
When a foreign body is inhaled, the
immediate response is the production of
a cough in an attempt to force it out.

Likewise, in the case of a bacterial,
viral, or allergic irritation of the inner
wall of the trachea, the response is repeated coughing and the formation of
mucus in an effort to rid the tube of the
irritating substance. The trachea is also
involved in the severe type of croup.

See also **Bronchial tree; Croup.**

Tracheotomy

An emergency opening into the trachea,
or large breathing tube. This is accomplished by making a cut in the lower
central portion of the neck. Its purpose
is to permit air to be breathed into the
lungs when there is an obstruction
above.

The most common emergencies requiring tracheotomy are when a round
object (such as a sourball or a marble)
inhaled by the child into the breathing

tube cannot be dislodged, thus cutting off all air; or when a child has severe croup, in which the combination of thick mucus, inner swelling of the larynx, and spasm of the inflamed area causes complete obstruction.

In the tracheotomy opening, the surgeon inserts a tube (tracheotomy tube) through which the child can breathe without difficulty. This is left in place until the obstruction above is removed or disappears. There will be complete healing, and only a small scar will remain.

Tranquilizers

Tranquilizers are used only occasionally in the treatment of children with certain specific disorders. They are not to be confused with sedatives such as the barbiturates, which make a child sleepy or slow.

Tranquilizers are used if a child has severe anxiety that prevents him from functioning effectively. Such a state of anxiety is extremely rare during childhood, but occurs occasionally among adolescents. Occasionally tranquilizers are used in the treatment of tics, which are almost always a reflection of a child's hidden anxieties and tensions.

A tranquilizer should be used only when prescribed by a doctor and only under his continued supervision.

Tranquilizers, poisoning by see Poisons: first-aid treatment.

Transplantation of kidney see Kidney transplantation.

Transvestism

A persistent desire and tendency to dress in clothes of the opposite sex. This is more frequent among boys than girls, and usually appears first between the ages of 4 and 6. Transvestism is not necessarily a sign of oncoming homosexuality—although a certain number of transvestites are homosexuals as well. (See **Homosexuality.**)

The reasons why a boy wants to dress as a female vary with the individual. A boy may be the only male in a family of women or in a family of which the father is often away. He may want to be more like the women who play such an important part in his life. Frequently this dressing up is ignored or dismissed by his family. Among many male transvestites there is a history in their childhood of an older girl or woman dressing them in girl's clothing.

Many children occasionally dress in the clothes of the opposite sex, but a boy who persists in doing so should be discouraged, and the underlying causes for this behavior should be sought and corrected as soon as possible. The help of a psychologist or psychiatrist may be necessary.

Traveling with children see Automobile travel with children.

Trichinosis

A disease acquired by eating inadequately cooked meat infected by the trichina worm—almost invariably the infected meat is pork. It often goes unrecognized. The larvae of the worm are eaten in the meat, and the capsules, or cysts, surrounding the larvae are digested in the stomach and upper intestine. The larvae are freed and become adult worms in five to seven days. The male and female worms meet, and, after fertilization, the males pass out of the body through the intestines in the stools. The females give birth to live larvae and deposit them in the walls of the intestines, from which they enter the lymph vessels and the bloodstream; eventually they are carried to the muscles throughout the body. The adult female worms die in the intestines and are passed out in the stools.

Signs and symptoms   Usually the child has symptoms of gastrointestinal upset, with vomiting, nausea, cramps, gas pains, and diarrhea. There may be chills, fever, and weakness, and very often swelling of the face around the eyes. There is also usually pain and tenderness in the muscles resulting from cysts in the muscle fibers caused by the worms.

Diagnosis   This is usually made by a specific skin test (which gives a positive reaction if the child is infested) plus a blood count (which shows an increase in certain of the white blood cells).

Treatment   Until recently, hydrocortisone or one of the cortisone preparations was used effectively to give relief from the symptoms of muscular pain and tenderness.

However, within the last few years a new drug, thiabendazole, has been found to kill the larvae in the muscles throughout the body. It does not kill the adult worms, but these are passed out of the intestine and never enter the body proper. The drug, when properly administered by mouth, is considered entirely safe.

The disease, under treatment, clears up quickly and recovery is complete. Without treatment, although the disease eventually clears, there may be months of severe muscle pains.

Prevention   Since the cysts of the trichina worm are tiny and difficult to see, one must always assume they may be present in pork, including pork sausages. The parasites can be killed by cooking pork to 175 degrees Fahrenheit, and pork should never be eaten if it is pink. The meat should be white or gray. A careless butcher may let bits of ground pork get into other ground meat from the grinding machine, so it is important to deal with a reliable butcher.

Triplets   see **Multiple births; Twins.**

Truancy
Many children now and again take a day off from school without telling their parents. Some find ways to cover up their truancy; others are reported absent by school authorities. This sort of occasional truancy is not very serious. It must be discouraged, of course, and it should be explained to the child that it is not safe for no responsible adult to know where he is. Parents should also try to find out what the child was doing; typically truants go to the movies, a ball game, or the like, but the parents should assure themselves that the child hasn't been getting into trouble. They should also try to find out if the child is having special problems in school.

Some children are frequently truant, and this *is* serious. In such cases it must be assumed that the child is facing special problems. He may be doing poorly in school, may feel hopeless about his chance of doing better, and may be resentful of constantly appearing "dumb." Such a child needs reassurance from his parents and special help with his schoolwork. Teacher and parents should work together to find the reasons for the child's difficulties, to help him do better, and to minimize his embarrassment.

Sometimes a truant is bright, and is bored in school. Again, there should be a cooperative effort to find ways of making school more satisfactory for such a child. The bright child can often be successfully involved in special classroom or extracurricular projects that give an outlet for his abilities.

A truant often has a background of unpopularity with his classmates, and some means must be found to help him become more popular. Again, parents should consult with the teacher to discover and remedy the cause of the child's difficulties. (See **Unpopularity.**)

Sometimes a truant has difficulty getting along with the teacher and prefers to avoid the conflict by staying out of school. Very often such a situation will improve if parents will take the time to talk with the teacher and discuss mutual goals for the child.

Many truants are unhappy at home, where they feel they are rejected and unloved. They are bitter against all adults and authority in general. These young people need special professional attention, usually in the form of psychotherapy. Punishment will only make them more resentful, unhappy, and antisocial.

Tuberculin test

A skin test to determine if a child has ever had the germs of tuberculosis in his body. The skin becomes sensitive to tuberculin (an extract prepared from cultures of the tuberculosis bacillus) between three to six weeks after the germs of tuberculosis enter the body. The test does not indicate if an infection with tuberculosis is active at the time of testing or if the body has overcome the disease. Once the skin is sensitive to tuberculin, the test usually remains positive throughout life.

Today most doctors give routine tuberculin tests to children every year or so, and in many communities these tests are given in the public schools.

There are various ways of performing the test. The two methods most frequently used are the intradermal skin test and the Tine test. In the intradermal test a small amount of tuberculin solution is inoculated into the upper layers of the skin. In the Tine test four tiny needles, each coated with dry tuberculin, are fastened on a buttonlike object and then pressed for a moment into the skin.

If a child has ever had the germs of tuberculosis in his body, his skin will be sensitive to tuberculin and the area where the test has been given will become red and swollen in forty-eight to seventy-two hours. The swelling is the real sign of previous infection. The redness is not important.

If the test is positive, the doctor will order an X ray of the lungs to determine if there is active tuberculosis or not. If the X ray shows tuberculosis or if the doctor is suspicious, he will place the child on INH (isoniazid) to cure the condition.

See also **Tuberculosis.**

Tuberculosis

A chronic, potentially dangerous disease of the lungs and other parts of the body, caused by the tuberculosis bacteria.

Transmission Tuberculosis is usually contracted by the inhalation of tiny droplets of sputum coughed up by a person suffering from the severe type of the disease in which there are one or more tuberculous cavities in the lungs. These droplets contain the living bacteria of tuberculosis. It may also be contracted by inhalation of the dust from a room in which a person with severe active tuberculosis has been coughing.

Formerly the disease was frequently contracted by drinking milk from infected cows, but the tuberculin testing of cows and the pasteurization of milk has practically eliminated this source of infection in the United States.

Tuberculosis is not inherited and only in very rare instances are the bacteria transmitted from a tuberculous mother to her unborn child.

Types of tuberculosis in children   There are two definite types of tuberculosis: the primary, or first infection, type and a much more dangerous type called the reinfection type.

The primary, or first infection, type occurs when the germs of tuberculosis are inhaled by a child who has never before had the tuberculosis bacilli in his body. This is the type most usually found in children. Untreated, it can be very dangerous during the first two years of life, but it is not dangerous if the condition is diagnosed and treated with INH (isoniazid), a drug that effectively kills the tuberculosis bacteria. Untreated primary tuberculosis is not as dangerous in children between the ages of 3 and 12 years.

The reinfection type of tuberculosis is rarely seen in children but is not infrequent among teen-agers and adults. Tuberculous cavities are often formed in the lungs, and the sick person coughs up sputum contaminated by tubercle bacilli. People with cavities in their lungs are usually contagious and should be isolated and treated until the sputum no longer contains tuberculosis bacteria.

The primary, first infection type of tuberculosis is rarely dangerous except during the first two or three years of life and during adolescence. The reinfection type of tuberculosis is dangerous at any time.

Signs and symptoms   These vary greatly, depending on the type of tuberculosis from which the child is suffering. During the primary type of tuberculosis there may be few, if any, signs and symptoms. An infected child might have a slight fever and a slight cough, and there is usually general malaise—the child doesn't seem to feel as well as usual. There are usually no physical signs by which a doctor can diagnose the condition. He must resort to skin tests and X rays of the lungs. (See **Tuberculin test.**)

With the reinfection type the signs and symptoms of some underlying infection are more definite. There are usually a progressive loss in weight, night sweats and fever, a persistent cough, and occasionally the coughing up of blood. The diagnosis is made by a combination of the tuberculin test, X-ray findings, and cultures of the sputum for the tuberculosis bacteria.

Complications of tuberculosis in children   These occur when some of the tuberculosis bacteria are transmitted by the bloodstream to other parts of the body. This is particularly common during the first two years of life, when young children have been infected with the disease and have not been treated with the modern anti-tuberculosis drugs.

Complications include miliary tuberculosis, when there is a massive spread of the tubercle bacilli to all parts of the body; tuberculous meningitis, when the lining membranes of the brain and spinal cord are infected; tuberculosis of bones and joints; and tuberculosis of the kidneys. Another complication is a tuberculous pleural effusion, when a collection of fluid exudes between the lungs and the wall of the chest. This latter condition is not serious and usually subsides without treatment. Occasionally, also, the lymph nodes in the neck become infected, usually from minute lesions in the mouth and throat.

Treatment Tuberculosis in children responds very readily to the drug INH (isoniazid), given by mouth. There should no longer be any deaths from tuberculosis in children unless the disease has advanced too far before diagnosis is made. This is extremely rare, for even cases of miliary tuberculosis and tuberculosis meningitis almost always subside under INH therapy. In severe cases many doctors give, in addition to INH, the drug streptomycin by injection and the drug PAS (para-aminosalicylic acid) by mouth.

If a healthy child is found to have a positive tuberculin test for the first time and has a normal X ray of the lungs, most doctors today prefer to give INH daily for a year to take no chances that an infection is at an onset or smouldering somewhere in the body.

It is not necessary to keep children in bed when they have the primary type of tuberculosis unless they have a fever, which is rare except during the early weeks. And even if the X ray shows signs of tuberculosis in the lungs, the children may still be up and even attending school, for they are not contagious and will do very well if they are receiving INH therapy.

Children and teen-agers suffering from the reinfection type of tuberculosis may need bed rest as well as intensive therapy. They may be contagious and should be withheld from school unless tests show the sputum to be entirely free of tuberculosis bacteria.

Treatment of children exposed to tuberculosis A child known to have been exposed to a person with tuberculosis should have a tuberculin test given at once. If this is negative, the test should be repeated in six weeks, since it often takes three to six weeks for the skin to become sensitive after tuberculosis bacteria enter the body. If the test is still negative, it is evidence that no tuberculosis bacteria were inhaled. If the test is positive, treatment should be started at once.

Prevention Children who are likely to be exposed to tuberculosis should receive a prophylactic inoculation with BCG, or should be withheld from contact with a person suffering from an active form of the disease. (See **BCG vaccination; Tuberculin test.**)

Turns, taking see **Sharing.**

Turpentine poisoning see **Poisons: first-aid treatment.**

Twins

The birth of twins is always an exciting event. Physically, twins may be smaller than other children at birth, but they usually catch up between 1 and 2 years of age, if not sooner. If they are premature, it may take three years before they equal other children in weight and height. Intellectually, twins are just as bright as any other children.

Identical twins, coming from the same egg, are usually similar not only in appearance but in temperament as well. They are generally much easier to bring up than nonidentical (fraternal) twins, who may differ in temperaments, likes and dislikes, intelligence, and physical activity. There are likely to be many more problems with fraternal twins than with identical twins.

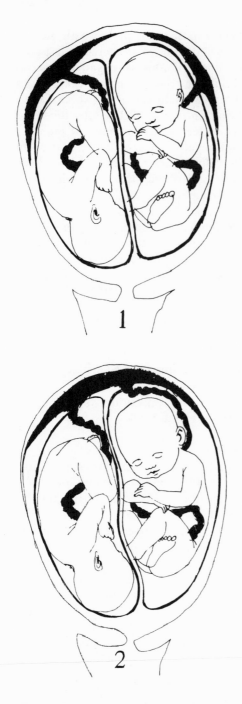

1. Fraternal twins in uterus. Umbilical cords run to separate placentas. 2. Identical twins in uterus. Umbilical cords come from same placenta.

But regardless of whether the multiple newborns are identical or fraternal, they do necessitate additional work on the part of the mother. The mother's primary task is to organize her time so that it is used to the best advantage. What about breast feeding or bottle feeding both babies? Can both be bathed at the same time? Can you get them to sleep at the same time? These are some of the questions most frequently asked by parents of twins.

Many mothers have nursed both twins successfully, and a few have successfully breast-fed triplets without the use of formulas. Some mothers prefer to nurse one baby and give the other a formula, alternating at successive feedings. Some twins and other multiple-birth babies are entirely formula-fed.

However, a regular schedule is possible after the first two or three weeks following birth, for with the help of the mother most babies establish a feeding cycle at intervals of about four hours before they are 4 or 5 weeks old, and by that time they have established a sleeping cycle as well.

This will give the mother time to rest and do necessary household duties while the children sleep. Twins can certainly be bathed together when they are able to sit up. They usually enjoy this very much. And in almost every instance, they can be put to bed at the same time. It is true that it may be some months before a mother of twins can keep her house as clean and as orderly as it was before the babies were born—but the special pleasure gained by handling the babies and watching them grow and develop will be ample compensation.

As twins get older and become more aware, they often are easier to handle than a single baby. They entertain each other and usually become very companionable. But in spite of this, a twin has the same basic needs of any child—of being loved for himself, cuddled, and made to feel wanted. Twins should be held a great deal, especially during feedings, and carried from place to place to satisfy their ever-widening interests.

But there are certain problems found more frequently among twins than among other children in families:

1. They are almost always being compared with one another at home, in school, at camp, and elsewhere. This becomes a greater and more difficult problem in the case of nonidentical (fraternal) twins, since one may be stronger, taller, better coordinated, and even brighter than the other.
2. Because of the comparisons, there is likely to be more competition and more sibling rivalry and jealousy than among brothers and sisters of different ages.
3. Since twins are always so much together, they often develop a dependency on one another and feel insecure when separated. This is especially true of identical twins or fraternal twins of the same sex, and it may become a problem when they attend school, if they are placed in different classes.

To overcome this tendency of twins to be dependent on one another, parents should encourage their individuality and develop their separate talents and interests. This brings up two questions frequently asked by parents of twins: Should twins be dressed alike? Should they be placed in the same class in school?

Although many parents enjoy dressing their twins alike, this should generally be avoided. Parents should attempt in every way to make each twin stand out as a distinct person. This does not

mean that from time to time twins shouldn't dress alike, for many twins enjoy doing this occasionally.

As far as school is concerned, it is better, if at all possible, to place the twins in separate classes. This is a rule today in many schools which have several classes in the same grade. The separation restricts comparison and competition, both of which are undesirable.

One supposed advantage of having twins is that they learn to share earlier than most children. This is undoubtedly true, but parents should see to it that each child has his own possessions, and his right to these should be protected. Once again, this aids in individualizing each child.

When there is an older child or older children in the home, there may be considerable sibling jealousy because of the great amount of attention twins usually receive, not only from outsiders and relatives but from the mother as well. However, twins usually suffer less from the jealousy of older children than would a single child, for they support one another, and this mutual support blunts the effect of any teasing or other onslaught. Twins are also less affected by younger children, because they usually keep one another interested and occupied and therefore have less desire for the attention which the mother must, of necessity, give to the younger child.

The same principles that apply to the upbringing of twins apply to the raising of triplets and quadruplets. They will be happier, more fulfilled human beings if they are encouraged to be individuals during their childhood.

See also **Bibliography; Multiple births.**

Typhoid fever
A dangerous contagious disease caused by an infection with typhoid bacteria.

Typhoid is rare in the United States but relatively common in some other parts of the world. An attack confers immunity.

Source of the disease   Typhoid is contracted through touching an object contaminated by the feces or urine of a person who either has the disease or carries the typhoid bacteria in his body. The bacteria get on the hands of a susceptible person and, if the hands are not thoroughly cleaned, are carried to his mouth on food or simply by touching the mouth.

Incubation period   Signs and symptoms usually start appearing between seven and twenty-one days after the typhoid bacillus enters the body of a susceptible person. The average incubation period is fourteen days.

Signs and symptoms   The infected person usually first develops a high fever, headache, and loss of appetite, and has a general malaise. This is followed by vomiting, abdominal pain, and occasionally chills. In many cases there is diarrhea as well. At times a pink spotted rash develops, especially over the abdomen (rose spots). The signs and symptoms may last one to three weeks.

Diagnosis   Diagnosis is made by finding the typhoid bacteria in the feces of the infected person.

Care of exposed persons   There is no special care except the examination of the feces and, if typhoid bacteria are found, treatment at once to rid the body of them.

Period of contagion   This lasts as long as the infected person has typhoid bacteria in his stools.

Treatment   The antibiotic chloramphenicol is the most effective treatment for typhoid fever. Ampicillin is the next choice for treatment.

Immunization   Three doses of typhoid vaccine given at weekly intervals provides a high degree of protection. A booster dose should be given every two years to those living or traveling in typhoid areas.

U

Ulcer, stomach and duodenal

Although comparatively rare in children, ulcers of the stomach and the duodenum (the part of the small intestine adjacent to the stomach) do occur and much more frequently than previously thought.

Symptoms   A stomach ulcer may produce pain in the center of the abdomen, while a duodenal ulcer produces pain in the right upper abdomen. The pain in both cases is often relieved by eating. At times there is no pain. The stools, however, may be dark, almost black from the digested blood within them, which signifies that internal bleeding has occurred.

Diagnosis and treatment   X-ray examination, using swallowed barium, will often, but not always, demonstrate the ulcer.

Treatment, which is usually successful, consists of medication and a special bland diet. Emotional factors apparently play a large part in the production of gastric ulcers, for many children with the condition have anxieties and are under tensions. These emotional factors should, of course, be investigated and relieved.

See also **Colitis, ulcerative.**

Ulcerative colitis   see **Colitis, ulcerative.**

Umbilical cord

The cord connecting the unborn infant to the placenta. Only the blood of the embryo (not the blood of the mother) flows through the umbilical cord, to and from the placenta. The blood flowing from the placenta contains the food and oxygen necessary to the development of the embryo, while the blood flowing from the embryo to the placenta contains the carbon dioxide and other waste products of the embryo.

Once the baby is born, the obstetrician ties and cuts the cord. If a newborn needs an exchange transfusion, as in some cases of Rh factor blood incompatibility, it is given in the blood vessels of the umbilical cord.

After the cord is cut by the doctor, the stump, which remains attached to the infant's navel, dries up and usually drops off in eight to ten days.

The manner in which the cord is cut has nothing to do with any development of an umbilical hernia, as is often erroneously believed.

See also **Hernia; Navel; Placenta.**

Umbilical granuloma   see **Navel.**

Umbilical hernia   see **Hernia.**

Underweight child   see **Thinness.**

Undescended testicles   see **Testicles.**

Undulant fever

Also called brucellosis. A disease of cattle, goats, and hogs that may be transmitted to human beings by direct contact with the infected animal, by handling its flesh, or, most usually, by drinking unpasteurized milk from a cow or goat with the disease. It is caused by brucella bacteria. Undulant fever is quite rare today, but people who, for whatever reason, drink unpasteurized milk should be aware that they run a greater risk of infection.

Symptoms   The first symptom, which does not appear until five to twenty days after exposure, is a low grade fever that occurs only in the evenings. In the course of a few days to several weeks, however, it may rise to 104 degrees. The fever undulates each day from low to high—hence the name undulant fever. It is usually accompanied by general malaise, sweating, pains in the joints, and an enlargement of the spleen.

Diagnosis and treatment   Specific skin and blood tests determine the diagnosis.

At the present time, tetracycline is the drug of choice. Streptomycin is occasionally added in severe cases. The results are excellent.

Ungraded school   see **Education, experimental approaches in.**

Unpopularity

During the elementary school period and the teen years, some children are unpopular and unaccepted. This situation is very destructive to the excluded children, for during these years acceptance by classmates and other boys and girls is one of the basic elements in the development of pride, self-assurance, and happiness.

Just what makes a child unpopular is not always easy to determine, for there are many possible causes, including the following:

1. Behavior problems. A child who is bossy or selfish or one who cheats or is a poor loser is often unpopular. Sometimes the unpopular child is self-centered; he dominates class discussions, is not willing to listen to others, and cannot feel or understand the needs of others. At times the unaccepted child is overly aggressive and even cruel, pushing and hitting other children.
2. Physical problems. A child who is very overweight or very frail and thin is often excluded. At times children with cerebral palsy or disfiguring birthmarks or marked cases of acne are shunned by classmates.
3. Color, religion, national origin, or economic background. Unfortunately prejudices are often the cause of unpopularity.
4. Being an outsider. At times, when a new child enters a class where friendships are already established, the children in the class may be cliquish and keep the newcomer on the outside— through no fault of the new child himself.
4. Objectionable personal habits or appearance. A child who has a body odor from lack of cleanliness, bad breath, or a chronically runny nose may often be excluded.

It is extremely important, for the sake of the child, that parents learn the causes of their boy's or girl's unpopularity and do everything in their power to correct whatever problems exist.

Usually the class teacher can discern in the classroom why a child is unpopular, and can be of the greatest aid in working with the parents to help him. A teacher can often help a shy, insecure, or unpopular child by praising him in front of the class when he merits praise, giving him responsible jobs, and displaying his paintings or other works if they are good or superior. But above all the teacher can help by explaining to parents the extent of their child's difficulty with other children, and what the possible causes may be. An experienced and sensitive teacher usually has more understanding than parents of how children relate to each other in groups and what causes certain children to be treated with hostility or indifference.

If the cause of the unpopularity is obviously a physical problem, such as obesity, parents, in consultation with the doctor, should make a major effort to correct the difficulty. If the problem cannot be corrected—for example, if the child has cerebral palsy—then the parents must look to the teacher to educate the other children in the class, and they must also give a great deal of support to their child. The child may also benefit from supportive psychotherapy with a specialist who is sensitive to the needs of handicapped children.

If the cause of the unpopularity is behavioral, as in the case of extreme bossiness and aggressiveness, the parents should consult with the doctor to rule out possible contributing physical causes. If no such causes exist, the probability is that some underlying emotional unhappiness is interfering with the child's ability to get along with his peers. Often the difficulty lies in the child's home situation, and parents may themselves be so emotionally involved that it is difficult for them to discover or remedy the causes of the child's upset. In such cases the advice of a psychologist or psychiatrist should be sought.

If the child is simply new to the group, parents should (but without pressure) encourage one or two friendships. They should be sure that other children are generally welcome in their home, and they should help their child to plan outings with one or two other children. A trip to a popular movie or a ballgame can often help a new child in a school or neighborhood to make friends. This approach is usually also helpful when the unpopularity has other causes. But if the problem is severe, not too much hope should be pinned on such plans. Often the child fears with good reason that his invitations will be rejected. In such cases parents should not press the issue, but should investigate all other means of making their child happier and helping him overcome his difficulties. (See **Emotional disturbance.**)

If the cause of the child's unpopularity is truly prejudice on the part of the other children, the teacher's help should again be sought. The parents must also try to support their child and explain matters as best they can, telling him how they themselves have coped with similar problems. However, at times the best remedy is to remove the child from the situation. (See **Intolerance and prejudice.**)

Unstructured school   see **Education, experimental approaches in.**

Ups   see **Drug abuse.**

Upset stomach   see **Nausea; Vomiting.**

Ureter
A narrow tube connecting the kidney with the bladder.

The ureters are of great importance to the normal functioning of the kidneys. If there is a blockage of a ureter, there will be back pressure on the kidney, which may be very dangerous. Also, urine that puddles above the blockage may become infected and, in turn, infect the kidney.

Diagnosis can usually be made by an intravenous pyelogram (dye injected into the blood that outlines the ureters as it passes down out of the kidneys). Dye injected into the bladder is also an important diagnostic aid.

See also **Kidneys.**

Urethra

The passageway that carries urine from the bladder to the outside.

The male urethra (which runs through the penis) varies in size as the child grows, from about 2 inches at birth to about 8 or 9 inches in adolescence. There is rarely any difficulty with the male urethra except an occasional narrowing of the opening at the end of the penis. A urologist can easily correct this by performing minor surgery that takes a minute or two.

The female urethra is a straight, short tube from the bladder to the outside. It varies in size from about ½ inch at birth to 1½ inches in adolescence. Because of its shortness and direct connection to the outside, it can easily be the path of infections from the outside into the bladder. It is for this reason that girls get urinary bladder infections eight times as frequently as boys.

See also **Cystitis.**

Urinary obstruction

An obstruction to the flow of urine from the kidneys. Occasionally there may be a blockage of one or both of the tubes which carry the urine down to the bladder, or there may be an obstruction below the bladder. The back pressure on the kidneys, plus the fact that the urine which collects above the blockage may become infected, gradually destroys the kidneys.

Symptoms of urinary blockage may be entirely lacking or there may be colicky abdominal pain in the kidney areas or mid-area of the abdomen. Occasionally a mass in the lower abdomen may be felt by a physician or even by the mother. If the obstruction is below the bladder, a mother may note that the child has difficulty voiding, may void in a thin, weak stream, or at times may be unable to void.

Urinary obstruction can usually be diagnosed with ease by the doctor and can be relieved by clearing the infection, by dilatating an obstructing passage, or by surgery.

See also **Kidneys.**

Urine and urinary difficulties

Throughout childhood and adolescence urine is normally clear and straw-colored. At times, when the child has taken too little fluid or during periods of fever, the color becomes darker. Occasionally, when a child has eaten beets, the urine may be slightly pink. Otherwise changes in the color of the urine are almost always abnormal.

Urine has a very slight odor when passed from the body. However, when left in contact with the air, as in the case of wet diapers, it is broken up by the bacteria to form ammonia, giving it the characteristic strong odor.

Examination of the urine microscopically and chemically by the child's doctor is one of the most important parts of the complete physical examination. Such conditions as diabetes, nephritis, cystitis, and nephrosis may be discovered through the routine examination of urine by the doctor.

Urinary difficulties   Signs of urinary

difficulties may often be detected by observant parents. When urine is red or smoky brown in color, this is usually an indication that it contains blood. This occurs especially during cystitis (an inflammation of the bladder) or nephritis (an inflammation of the kidney). During an attack of jaundice the urine is usually dark amber in color. (See **Cystitis; Jaundice; Nephritis.**)

Difficulty in urination may be caused by some obstruction of the bladder opening that leads into the urethra (the tube from the bladder to the outside), or by an obstruction in the urethra itself, or at the outside opening of the urethra. (See **Urinary obstruction.**) In boys, if the urethral opening is too narrow, the urine emerges in a very fine stream. (See **Urethra.**)

Frequency of urination is very often emotional in origin, especially when it occurs during the day but not at night. However, frequency of urination day and night might also be a sign of cystitis, pyelitis (kidney infection), or diabetes insipidus, a condition caused by a malfunction of the pituitary gland. (See **Diabetes mellitus; Pituitary gland; Pyelitis.**)

Pain on urination may be caused by cystitis or occasionally pyelitis, or simply by a local irritation of the urethra. It may also be caused by an inflammation of the urethra, such as is commonly found in gonorrhea. (See **Gonorrhea.**) Occasionally girls may have temporary pain on urination if they have injured their genital region in a fall.

Pain in the lower abdomen should always be investigated for the possibility of a urinary bladder infection.

Fever of unknown origin may be an indication of pyelitis or, especially in girls, of cystitis.

Any unusual urinary sign should be reported immediately to the child's doctor.

Urticaria   see **Hives.**

Uterus

The hollow, muscular organ in the abdomen within which a fertilized egg develops to a fully formed infant.

On the inner wall of the uterus, where the fertilized egg becomes attached, the placenta forms. Through the placenta, oxygen and food from the mother's blood are transferred to the baby's blood, and waste products from the baby's blood are transferred to the mother's blood for disposal by her body.

When the time arrives for the baby's birth, the muscles of the walls of the uterus start contracting and push down stronger and stronger, finally forcing the baby down into the vagina and out.

See also **Placenta.**

V

Vacations

Every summer most school children have a vacation of two months or more, and most working parents have two to four weeks' vacation.

How to best spend these periods is a subject of importance to most families. Much depends upon the age of the children and the economic circumstances of the individual family, as well as personal preferences.

Generally speaking, there are four types of worthwhile vacations for children:

1. Family vacations at home with planned trips to the seashore, or country, family picnics and other outings, visits to friends and relatives.
2. Family vacations away from home. These may vary considerably. The family may spend the vacation period at the seashore, in the mountains, or in the country. A vacation at a farm is especially enjoyable for young children. (See **Farm camps and farm vacations.**) Also, within recent years camping trips have become very popular.

Some families take trips, by car or otherwise, to places of special interest throughout the country or abroad. (Many families also camp out during these trips.) Such trips usually are enormously interesting and educational, especially for older children—that is, over the age of about 9 years. But these trips must be carefully planned and not fa-tiguing if they are to be completely enjoyed.
3. Camp vacations. These are of two types, at day camps and at sleep-away camps. The day camps are of special value for children of 5 to 8 years: the children still remain with their parents but have their days filled with enjoyable activities. These camps may be in the city or connected with summer resorts.

The sleep-away camps are especially rewarding for older children, for they usually offer a well-rounded program of supervised physical activity, arts and crafts, and nature and science study—a program that also provides an opportunity to build up self-reliance, self-dependence, and self-assurance. (See **Camps.**)
4. Travel groups through North America and abroad or individual experiences abroad are most enjoyable and worthwhile for young people of 15 years or older. For those over 16, arrangements can be made to live with families in foreign countries. Such arrangements can be made through the American Field Service, which has chapters in most communities and a great many high schools throughout the country. Boys and girls accepted for such family living abroad must first be screened by their local chapters before their application is referred to the main office in New York City.

Another experienced organization in arranging family living for boys and girls in foreign countries is the Experiment in International Living, 1 West Hill, Putney, Vermont 05346.

Vaccination   see Immunization schedule and tests.

Vagina
The tubular passage in the female body leading from the uterus to the outside.

The opening of the vagina is covered by a thin membrane, the hymen, which normally has a small rounded opening in it. (See Hymen.)

During the first few days after birth, the vagina may discharge mucus or a bloody secretion, or may have a bit of mucous membrane protruding from it. These occurrences are of no significance, merely the infant's reaction to some of the mother's hormones that have passed through the placenta and into the infant's body. Usually the discharge ceases and the mucous membrane tag shrinks and disappears into the vagina within a few days.

Vaginal difficulty during childhood and adolescence is rare, except for an occasional inflammation causing a discharge. (See Vaginal discharge.) Occasionally little girls will insert objects in their vagina. This usually has no sexual connotation but is only part of a child's tendency to put objects in any body opening, such as the nose and ears.

See also Labial adhesions.

Vaginal discharge
Infections of the vagina may be caused by bacteria or other microscopic organisms. In rare instances, infections are caused by foreign bodies forced up the vagina by the child. The irritation of the mucous membrane of the vagina causes a discharge. A non-specific vaginal discharge occurs in many girls during the six months prior to the first menstrual period.

Generally, infections of the vagina are of two types: the common non-gonorrheal type and that resulting from gonorrhea.

The common type of vaginal infection can occur at any age. It often occurs during upper respiratory infections and subsides as the girl recovers from the cold. It also occurs quite frequently when the child's hygiene is poor or when she is undernourished or debilitated.

The discharge in the common vaginal infection may be scanty or abundant, thin or a mixture of mucus and pus, and often is malodorous. It can be easily differentiated from the gonorrheal type by a vaginal smear, stained and examined microscopically by the doctor.

Treatment, which is directed at removing the cause of the infection and treating the inflammation, should be under the supervision of the child's doctor.

See also Gonorrhea.

Vaporizer   see Moisture in the air; Steam treatment.

Varicella   see Chicken pox.

Variola   see Smallpox.

Vegetables
Vegetables are an excellent source of roughage, which keeps the intestines working properly, and also a source of vitamins and of iron and other minerals. (See Nutrition.)

Vegetables are usually added to an infant's diet somewhere between 2 and 6 months of age. They are usually given in pureed form to babies up to the approximate age of 9 or 10 months. Following this, chopped vegetables are given (Junior Foods in the commercially prepared bottles or cans). This accustoms the baby to more solid foods.

Some infants reject vegetables. This is not a great handicap as long as the child eats fruits, which serve the same purpose. Vegetables should not be forced on a child who resists them. Give him the one or two vegetables that he likes and try to substitute others every few weeks. But it certainly is not vital if all vegetables are refused. Most children develop a taste for them later on . Older children may prefer raw vegetables that they can eat in their hands.

Occasionally in the young infant, the vegetables, and fruits as well, will appear in the stools. This is not significant if it is not accompanied by diarrhea and mucus. Remember that beets color the stool red. There is no cause for concern.

Venereal diseases see **Gonorrhea; Syphilis.**

Viral infections
Viruses are responsible for many diseases of infancy and childhood including mumps, measles, German measles, roseola, poliomyelitis, hepatitis, influenza, and infectious mononucleosis. The common cold is also usually caused by a virus infection.

Virus infections and bacterial infections usually produce different blood counts. Whereas in bacterial infections the number of white blood cells is increased, in virus infections the number is usually unchanged or diminished. Also, viruses call forth a different type of white cell to fight infections than do bacteria.

There is no specific drug or antibiotic therapy of value in the treatment of virus infections as there is with bacterial infections. Treatment usually consists of relieving the symptoms of the condition.

Many viruses can be cultured, and vaccines against the infections produced. Such vaccines include those against poliomyelitis, measles, mumps, and German measles.

Viral pneumonia see **Pneumonia.**

Viruses
Microscopic organisms capable of causing disease that are very much smaller than bacteria—so small that they pass through the finest filters and cannot be seen through ordinary microscopes. The poliomyelitis virus, for example, is only a millionth of an inch in diameter. Many viruses, however, can be seen through the electron microscope.

See also **Viral infections.**

Vision see **Blindness; Eye defects; Eyeglasses.**

Vitamin poisoning see **Poisons: first-aid treatment.**

Vitamins see **Nutrition.**

Vitiligo
Occurring occasionally in children, vitiligo is a loss of pigment in the skin in which white patches appear in normally pigmented areas. It is especially noticeable in summer when the exposed parts of the body tan. The cause of this condition is not known. It is of no real importance except from a cosmetic point of view.

Drugs called the psoralens, given orally, seem to bring back a good deal of the pigment in many cases, but must be given with great care and under the close supervision of the doctor. Usually the condition is treated cosmetically by the application of tinted, waterproof preparations (such as Covermark) that match the coloring of the normal skin.

Vocational guidance

As a child grows into the high school years, he begins to think about and plan for his future. Often he is unaware of the many career and employment opportunities available. He may also be unaware of the skills necessary for a specific job and how his personal skills match up.

Vocational guidance counselors aid students in choosing appropriate academic courses to meet their stated interests. They administer aptitude and interest tests to teen-agers who are unsure of what is appropriate for them. Intelligence and achievement tests are also sometimes administered in an attempt to discover if the necessary skills are present for a specific profession. For instance, a teen-ager who is weak in vocabulary and self-expression might have difficulty in law school.

Vocational counselors, on the basis of these tests, discuss at length the various alternatives they consider best for the student in choosing his future occupation.

A good vocational counselor can be a great help to a youngster. However, as is often pointed out, some counselors are unduly influenced by what they feel are social limits on a child's future. A counselor might discourage a girl intent on a career in the man's world of engineering, for example, or discourage a child from an impoverished family who aspires to medical school. Some counselors assume that certain professional careers are possible only for qualified youngsters whose families can support them in postgraduate education. Parents and youngsters should remember that guidance counselors are not infallible. Finances alone should not limit educational goals, for many scholarships and loans are available to qualified students.

Voice

The voice, normally high-pitched during childhood, becomes lower pitched in both sexes during adolescence. This is particularly marked in boys where, during the teen-age years, a distinctive lowering in pitch occurs, resulting from an increase in the size of the vocal cords and the larynx, or voice box.

Adolescent girls usually experience an increase in range of three notes above and three notes below their former levels. In boys the range drops as much as an octave. Usually the change in voice takes place within six months.

Occasionally, in children and adolescents, voices other than normal may be encountered, which may result from physical or emotional causes.

The quality of the voice may be changed by various physical conditions. For example, hoarseness may be caused by an inflammation of the larynx resulting from infection; from using the voice badly, as when a cheerleader yells all afternoon; or occasionally from a small growth on a vocal cord. Loss of vibrance in the voice occurs when the nose is completely stuffed during a head cold or the adenoids are greatly enlarged or an allergy is acting up. And a voice may have too much nasality, as when a child has a cleft palate.

Emotional causes of changes in voice quality are rare during childhood and adolescence. Occasionally a teen-age girl will adopt a soft, breathy manner of talking when she thinks it is attractive.

Changes in pitch are usually emotional in origin. Voices of anger, tension, or upset, as when a child whines, are usually high-pitched. A monotonous voice may result from hearing difficulties or depression.

Intensity in a child's voice—loudness or softness—may be influenced by psychological or physical conditions. A voice may be exceptionally loud if a child hears poorly or if he feels he has to attract attention. A voice that is too soft may result from a physical condition affecting the larynx or vocal cords, such as a thickening of the vocal cords or a growth on the vocal cords. Both can be treated successfully. Frightened children and children who are passive and retiring speak in a low voice or almost a whisper.

Vomiting

Vomiting may have different characteristics. There is projectile vomiting, in which the stomach expels the vomitus with such force that it is often projected a foot or more from the body. This is typical of pyloric stenosis and occasionally pylorospasm.

The color of vomitus may be green if bile is sucked into the stomach from the intestines—this in itself is not serious; the color may be red or brownish if blood has been swallowed or if there has been bleeding in the stomach; the color may also be brown in the severe vomiting of intussusception, where fecal material may be vomited.

Vomiting may result from various causes, including gastrointestinal virus infections; food poisoning; an obstruction in the gastrointestinal tract; motion sickness; concussion or skull fracture; bacterial infections or inflammation of the gastrointestinal system; liver disorders, as in hepatitis; allergic reactions to certain foods; the onset of any acute infections, such as scarlet fever, measles, pneumonia; or emotional tension. Unless the cause is known, as in motion sickness or an allergic reaction, a doctor should be consulted.

See also **Intussusception; Pyloric stenosis; Pylorospasm.**

Treatment   Until a doctor can be reached, simple vomiting in children over 1 year can be treated as follows:

1. Give nothing by mouth for at least one hour after the last episode of vomiting.
2. Then give ½ tablespoon of a cola drink, weak tea, ginger ale, or water.
3. Increase the amount every twenty minutes by ½ tablespoon until the child is receiving 4 tablespoonfuls.
4. Then give small amounts of applesauce or Jell-O or toast and broth, and continue with light foods.

If the child vomits again, begin treatment again, but still get in touch with the doctor.

See also **Regurgitation; Rumination.**

Vulval adhesions   see **Labial adhesions.**

W

Walking

Most children have pulled themselves up to a a standing position by the time they are 9 to 10 months old. By 11 to 12 months they are walking with support, holding on to adult hands, a chair, or whatever is nearby. By 13 to 14 months, the child is starting to walk by himself. Most children during this procedure hold their legs rather widely apart and point their feet outward to give themselves better support.

Gradually, as they learn balance and coordination, the legs are brought closer together and the feet straighten out.

A child who does not walk at all by 16 months of age should be examined by his doctor. Usually, however, the slowness in walking is not abnormal and the child will soon walk by himself.

A child who starts walking with a limp should be checked for the possibility of a congenital dislocation of the hip.

See also **Hip, congenital dislocation of; Shoes; Standing up.**

Walleye (external strabismus) see Eye defects.

Warts

Pinhead to bean-sized rough protuberances of the skin that are caused by virus infection of the tissue. Warts are slightly contagious, either contracted from another person or spread from one wart on a person's body to other areas on the body.

The two types found most often in children are the common elevated warts, usually on the hands, and plantar warts, which occur on the soles and heels of the feet.

Common warts These warts occur as single or multiple rough, elevated lesions. They usually do not cause discomfort, but they are unsightly. Common warts are occasionally knocked off in the course of active play and do not return. Otherwise they may be removed either by daily applications of acid, as prescribed by the doctor, or by surgical removal.

Plantar warts These warts are flat, resemble calluses, and are usually quite painful. Rarely found in young children, they are quite common on the feet of preadolescent children and teen-agers. They are most often contracted from walking barefoot around swimming pools or in contaminated shower rooms.

The surgical removal of plantar warts is quick but also painful, and the child may have to stay off his feet for a few days. But the warts can usually be removed effectively and painlessly by the application of 40 percent salicylic acid plaster, cut to the size of the wart and not covering the surrounding healthy skin. The plaster is changed every day, and the dried white surface of the wart should be rubbed off each day (pumice stone may be used). The procedure may take seven or eight weeks.

Washing   see **Cleanliness.**

Washing the child   see **Bathing the infant; Hair washing; Sponge bath for the newborn.**

Washing the hands
Children should be taught to wash their hands before eating and after using the toilet. Parents should insist that this procedure be followed. Aside from the esthetic quality of having clean hands at the dining table, clean hands prevent the spread of such parasitic worms as pinworms and roundworms, which are quite common among children.

Some children develop the need to almost constantly wash their hands. This a symptom of emotional disturbance and requires psychological treatment (see **Compulsions**).

Wasp stings   see **Bee stings.**

Water, drinking
Young babies do not usually need water since their fluid requirements are satisfied by the fluid in breast milk or formula. Some babies, however, desire water between feedings, especially during the hot summer months. A between-feeding bottle of water should be given no closer than two hours before the feeding to avoid interfering with the baby's appetite. The water should be boiled for ten minutes, at least during the first four months of life. If you are uncertain about the purity of the water, boil it before giving it to any child under a year old.

Water on the brain   see **Hydrocephalus.**

Waterproof pants   see **Pants, waterproof.**

Wax, ear   see **Earwax.**

Weaning   see **Bottle feeding; Breast feeding.**

Webbing of toes (or fingers)   see **Feet.**

Wechsler Intelligence Scale for Children   see **Tests.**

Wedged head or body   see **Head wedging.**

Weight
The body weight of children varies with the individual child, although there are certain averages for children of a specific age and height (see **Body measurements**).

The factors influencing body weight depend largely upon hereditary qualities that determine the body build of an individual—broad muscles or slender muscles, heavy or narrow bones, tallness or shortness. Other factors that influence body weight include overeating, malnutrition, glandular problems, certain kidney and heart conditions, and certain chronic debilitating diseases.

A parent who is concerned about the weight of a child should consult a doctor before attempting to alter the child's eating habits.

See also **Obesity; Thinness.**

Weight at birth   see **Birth weights.**

Wet dreams   see **Nocturnal seminal emission.**

Wet dressings
Various childhood skin conditions require treatment with wet dressings. Plain gauze pads or gauze bandages are the most useful. On most parts of the body the dressings may be kept wet dur-

ing the night by covering them with a thin plastic wrap, such as Saran Wrap.

Wet dressings of plain water, Burow's solution, or Epsom-salt solution are often used to bring such infections as boils to a head, at which time they will open spontaneously or be lanced by the doctor (see **Abscess**).

Wet dressings of plain water are used to keep infected areas moist, to keep a wound open so that it can drain, and to remove crusts from infected skin lesions. Wet dressings of witch hazel may be used to treat insect bites.

Most wet dressings are used at room temperature. Warm wet dressings are used occasionally to bring boils to a head.

Wetting   see **Bed-wetting; Toilet training.**

Wheezing

Wheezing occurs when the air being breathed in and out must pass by an accumulation of mucus in the breathing tubes. Mucus is formed when the mucous membranes of the trachea and bronchial tree are irritated, especially by allergies or infections. In rare instances, wheezing occurs when a child has inhaled some foreign body that has irritated the mucous membrane of the bronchial tubes.

Although wheezing often occurs when a child has a virus or bacterial infection that irritates the trachea or bronchial tubes, the most common cause of this disturbance is allergy. The wheezing may result from an allergen in the air to which the child is sensitive, or it may result from an allergic reaction to the products of a bacterial or viral infection, or in rare instances to some food to which the child is highly sensitive. For instance, some children wheeze when

they're in contact with a cat, while others wheeze almost every time they have a cold.

Steam inhalations and specific cough medicines prescribed by the doctor often help to alleviate wheezing. If the condition results from an infection, treatment, of course, involves clearing up the infection. If the wheezing results from an allergy, such as in asthma, treatment includes the administration of special drugs to relieve the spasm of the bronchial tubes, the removal of the irritant, or the building up of a child's toleration to the irritant. Which method of treatment is appropriate to your child's condition will be recommended by the doctor.

See also **Foreign objects, inhalation of.**

Whining

Whining can be without purpose or it can be intentional. Often when children are tired, frustrated, or annoyed, their voices reflect this by taking on a whiny tone, often a very annoying quality.

Many parents become extremely irritated by whining, and the child, realizing this, may use the technique whenever he or she wants to rouse the parent. The child who calls and calls and gets no response from his parents often starts whining. He quickly learns that he can get more attention, even if it's negative, by whining than by calling. This kind of whining may be the expression of an unhappy child seeking his parents' love and interest.

Scolding or mimicking does not help. It can even cause an exaggeration of the whining. It is better to figure out why the child is whining. If it is the result of fatigue, boredom, or hunger, the answer is obvious. If it is more than that and is fairly frequent, the parents must try to discover the underlying cause. The doctor can look into the possibility that some physical condition is causing the child to be irritable. But more often the child is unhappy over some aspect of his home life.

See also **Crankiness.**

Whooping cough

Also called pertussis. An acute infectious disease of the respiratory tract caused by the pertussis bacillus. It is characterized by severe, repetitive episodes of coughing ending in a whoop on inhalation. A person who has had whooping cough is immune to it.

The disease is transmitted either directly from contact with a person with whooping cough, from the inhalation of droplets from the cough, or indirectly through freshly contaminated articles. It is generally felt that the disease is contagious for six weeks from the onset of the cough. It is most contagious in the early weeks. A susceptible person exposed to whooping cough usually develops the disease in five to twenty-one days after exposure, the most usual time being about ten days. Pneumonia may occasionally develop.

Signs and symptoms The disease is generally divided into three stages. The first stage manifests itself by a simple, dry cough with signs of a head cold. This occurs both day and night. As the disease progresses, the cough becomes more severe. The second stage starts about the third week, during which the cough becomes very severe, especially at night. There are spells of repetitive coughing so marked that the child cannot get his breath and often gets blue in the face. This severe coughing, which may last half a minute, ends with a whoop as the child at last inhales. Vom-

iting often occurs. The third stage is one of improvement from the fifth week on.

Treatment and immunization Strong cough medicines may be of some help in relieving the cough. Erythromycin and tetracycline are the antibiotic drugs of choice. Severe cases are occasionally helped by the hyperimmune pertussis gamma globulin.

Pertussis vaccine is very effective in building up the body's immunity against the disease. It is usually given to infants in three doses at one-month intervals. Generally it is combined with the toxoids of diphtheria and tetanus in the DPT vaccine. For immediate immunization, the hyperimmune pertussis gamma globulin is effective for a period of four or five weeks.

Wilms' tumor

A malignant tumor of the kidney—one of the most common tumors of early childhood, but nevertheless quite rare. Two-thirds of the cases of Wilms' tumor occur before a child is 3 years old.

The primary physical finding is a firm, non-tender mass felt in the abdomen upon examination. Occasionally there is abdominal pain caused by pressure of the tumor on other organs. The tumor can be seen on an X ray, and some distortion of the kidney's shape is shown on an I.V.P. (intravenous pyelogram—an X ray following an injection of dye into the bloodstream which delineates the tubes from the kidney to the bladder and the bladder itself).

Treatment Treatment involves immediate surgical removal of the affected kidney within forty-eight hours after the condition is discovered. Even before the operation, if a Wilms' tumor is suspected—and after the operation, if it is found—the drug actinomycin D is given. X-ray irradiation is also given.

Prognosis is quite good with early detection of the tumor and removal of the kidney. In one series of fifty-three cases, 89 percent of the children were pronounced cured when no further evidence of the tumor was found after two years. A person with a single kidney can live a normal life in every way.

Windpipe see **Trachea.**

Winning see **Competitiveness.**

WISC see **Tests.**

Witch's milk
Within a few days after birth, newborn babies of both sexes may develop tense, swollen breasts from which milk may ooze. This milk, called witch's milk, is a normal physiologic reaction resulting from the baby's absorption of hormones from the mother before birth. It is of no significance and will subside by itself in a few days. An old folk legend advises that in girl babies the milk should be expressed so that they will nurse better when they become mothers. This, of course, is false and may lead, instead, to the formation of breast abscesses.

Womb see **Uterus.**

Wool, swallowing see **Hair or wool, swallowed.**

Word blindness see **Aphasia.**

Word deafness see **Aphasia.**

Words, bad see **Swear words.**

Work, full-time, part-time
Most children want extra spending money and are interested in working for it. This interest should be encouraged, for it adds greatly to the self-confidence of girls and boys to discover that they can earn money on their own. And work experiences are usually interesting and maturing as well.

Youngsters may begin to try to earn money by setting up a lemonade stand or selling their old comic books. As they get older, the more enterprising ones will mow lawns, shovel snow, deliver newspapers, and baby-sit. Some teen-agers have or want regular part-time jobs after school, but this is frequently too heavy a burden and generally should not be encouraged unless there is a financial need.

During vacation, especially summer vacations, there is no reason, though, why a teen-ager shouldn't work full time. This is certainly preferable to having nothing to do. Many teen-agers work as camp counselors, mother's helpers, and waiting on tables at country resorts.

Summer jobs may be hard to find, and if a teen-ager wants to work in the summer, he should be advised to start looking at least two months ahead of time (some camp jobs are taken almost a year ahead of time). In some cases, his school may help in locating appropriate employment. Volunteer community work (in a hospital, for example) is also fine experience for the teen-ager and helpful to others as well.

Whatever money a young person makes should be his own, unless there is a definite need for part or all of it to be contributed to the family budget. It is certainly advisable, though, to try to see to it that the money isn't squandered.

Parents should help their teen-ager open a savings account and discuss with him what portion of his earnings should be saved.

Working mother   see Mother, working.

Worms

The most common worms that infest children in North America are pinworms, roundworms, and hookworms. They all live, during their adult stage, in the intestines of human beings.

The old tale that worms are indicated by the grinding of teeth at night is not true.

Pinworms *(Oxyuris)*   Very common among children of all social and economic groups, pinworms are tiny thread-like worms about ⅛ inch to ½ inch in length. In the evening or nighttime, when the child is going to sleep, they can often be seen moving around on the skin outside the anus. The worms live in the large bowel. When the female worms become distended with eggs, they migrate out through the anus at night and lay their eggs in the skin surrounding the anus, which causes intense itching at the time the eggs are laid.

Signs and symptoms   The most usual sign is intense itching around the anus, primarily at night when a child is in bed and ready for sleep or just going to sleep. Such itching should always make a parent suspicious of pinworm infestation. Often the children sleep poorly and are cranky during the day.

Diagnosis and treatment   The worms can usually be easily seen moving outside the anus if the buttocks are spread widely apart. Observation should be

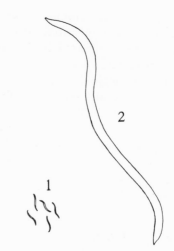

1. Pinworms. 2. Roundworm. Roundworms grow to 8-14 inches in length. Pinworms are approximately the size shown here.

made on five or six succeessive nights, since worms may not be present every night.

The eggs of the worm can be recovered by touching the skin around the anus with clear cellophane tape. The doctor will examine the tape microscopically for pinworm eggs that have stuck to it. If no eggs are found the procedure should be repeated for six or seven days. Neither the eggs nor the worms are generally found in the bowel movements.

The doctor may advise using a medication called Povan (pyrvinium pamoate), which is available in liquid or tablet form. The dosage is one tablet or one teaspoonful for every 22 pounds of the child's weight. The total dosage is given at one time and repeated again in one week's time. Another medication is Antepar (piperazine), which is given every day for seven days. This medication comes in a syrup, in tablets or flavored wafers. The usual daily dosage prescribed for pinworms is:

	Syrup	Wafers or tablets
Up to 15 lbs.	½ tsp.	—
15 to 30 lbs.	1 tsp.	1
30 to 60 lbs.	2 tsp.	2
Over 60 lbs.	4 tsp.	4

After a one-week interval, the treatment is repeated for seven days.

Many doctors advise treating all members of the family if one person has the worms, since the condition is so contagious.

During treatment, the following precautions should be taken:

1. The child should wear underpants at night to prevent, as much as possible, contamination of the bedclothes and sheets.
2. The bedclothes, sheets, and underclothes of the child should be washed carefully and separated from the rest of the laundry.
3. An ointment, prescribed by the doctor, to stop the itching should be rubbed into the anal region every evening to prevent scratching.
4. Most important, the child should be taught to wash his hands very carefully after each bowel movement, preferably scrubbing with a special brush. Should he have worm eggs on his hands, he could easily reinfect himself by putting his hands to his mouth or on food. Careful hand washing protects others from contracting the worms as well.

Mode of pinworm transmission The spread of pinworms results from poor hygiene. When a child or adult with the condition cleans himself after a bowel movement, he may get some of the worms' eggs on his hands. If he does not wash his hands or washes them carelessly, some of the eggs remain there. From his hands they may be transferred to food or to some object. When another person eats that food, he will swallow the eggs. Or if he touches the same object, some of the eggs may get on his hands and eventually to his mouth when eating or just by putting his hands to his mouth. The eggs are swallowed and the worms develop in the intestines.

Occasionally worm eggs are found in the dust of a room frequented by a person with pinworms.

Roundworms (Ascaris) A very common infestation of the intestines of children, especially those living in the southern parts of the United States. Roundworms look very much like earthworms. They are 8 to 14 inches long.

The eggs of the worm are swallowed in food, drink, or other contaminated substances. The eggs develop into worms, which live in the small intestines. Occasionally a worm gets down into the large intestines (bowels) and is passed out of the body in the child's bowel movement. The adult lays new eggs in the intestines, which are passed in the stool.

Symptoms Although symptoms do not always appear, they may include a loss of appetite, crankiness, nervousness, a protruding abdomen, and occasionally nausea, vomiting, and abdominal pain.

Diagnosis and treatment Even if an adult worm is not passed in the bowel movements, a microscopic examination of the movements will reveal worm eggs. A single female worm can lay 150,000 to 300,000 eggs a day.

Antepar (piperazine) is effective and can usually rid the body of the worms in two days. The usual daily dosage for roundworms is as follows:

	Syrup	*Wafers or tablets*
Up to 30 lbs.	2 tsp.	—
30 to 50 lbs.	4 tsp.	4
50 to 100 lbs.	6 tsp.	6
Over 100 lbs.	7 tsp.	7

Only the child with the worms is treated, since the infestation is not transmitted from one person to another by contact or touch.

Mode of roundworm transmission The eggs of the roundworm develop in the soil, not in the human body. They are spread when people with worms move their bowels on the ground instead of using a toilet. The eggs develop in the ground, and later children, playing in the soil or handling something that touched the infested soil, get some of the eggs on their hands. These eggs get to their mouths on food or by placing the hand to the mouth and are swallowed. Prevention involves general hygiene—the use of toilets and personal cleanliness, especially washing the hands before cooking or eating.

Hookworms *(Necator americanus)* These worms are found largely in the southern, warmer regions of the United States, where children go barefooted much of the time.

The infestation starts when a person who harbors the worms in his intestines has a bowel movement on the soil in the open. Numerous eggs are deposited in the feces and develop on the ground. Later, when a barefooted child or adult walks on this ground, the larvae of the worms burrow through the thin skin between the toes and enter the bloodstream. Eventually, after a circuitous route through the body, the worms enter the small intestine, where they attach themselves to the inner wall and suck the person's blood. The adult worm is approximately ¼ inch to ½ inch long.

Symptoms The child is usually pale, for there is an anemia caused by the sucking of his blood by the worms. He gets out of breath quickly, fatigues easily, and becomes dull mentally. Physical growth and sexual development are frequently delayed. Often the stools are loose and are almost black from the partially digested blood in them.

Diagnosis and treatment A microscopic examination of the stools will reveal the eggs.

A number of effective treatments are available, all of which must be given under a doctor's supervision. Tetrachloroethylene is the drug of choice.

Hookworm can be prevented or eradicated by observing the following measures. In areas where infestation with hookworm is prevalent, shoes should always be worn. Toilets should be easily available, and the use of them enforced. A search should be made for all people infested with hookworm so that they may be treated.

Wryneck

A condition in which certain muscles of the neck are shortened, resulting from a muscular defect or a muscle spasm that pulls the head to one side.

Wryneck has various causes. It sometimes appears shortly after birth and is generally caused by an overpull on a muscle on one side of the infant's neck during birth. This often results in some bleeding or damage within the muscle and a spasm of the muscle as well, causing a tilting of the baby's head to the injured side. In a week or two a hard lump can usually be felt in the muscle.

Generally, it disappears within a month or two and the infant then holds his head in the normal position. Occasionally orthopedic correction is necessary.

Wryneck can also occur in older children and teen-agers. It most commonly results from a spasm of the muscles on one side of the neck caused either by inflamed lymph glands under the muscles or by the irritation of or pressure on a nerve going to these muscles. The child's head is pulled over to one side and attempts to move it to the other side are painful. This condition ordinarily lasts for only two or three days.

Treatment Locally, the muscle in spasm should be treated by the application of heat, either a heat lamp, electric heating pad, hot water bottle, or wet dressings.

If the cause of the muscle spasm is an inflamed lymph gland, treatment should include controlling the infection responsible for the inflammation of the gland.

X

X rays

Among the most important diagnostic measures available, X rays contribute substantially to the diagnosis of vast numbers of medical and dental conditions, thereby aiding in directing treatment.

During childhood X rays are used in the examination of bones for fractures, including those of the skull; the lungs for diagnosis of such conditions as pneumonia, tuberculosis, and the inhalation of foreign objects; the stomach and intestines in suspected cases of intussusception, ulcers, swallowed foreign objects, and ulcerative colitis; and the teeth for evidence of decay and root abscesses.

Since the approximate age at which cartilage changes to solid bone is known, doctors also often use X rays to determine whether a child is growing normally. They can also determine how much growth in height may be expected.

It became evident in the past twenty years, however, that radiation from X rays could be potentially dangerous, especially to growing children. Old X-ray machines could be extremely harmful, for during X-ray examinations of the teeth the radiation could spread to the thyroid gland in the neck below the jaw. Routine X-ray examinations of chil-dren's teeth are still necessary, however, and the new machines that have been developed are essentially safe. They focus on a very small area instead of spreading radiation to the surrounding tissues. They also use a very sensitive film that reacts with a much smaller dose of X ray. Furthermore, lead barriers are used to provide additional protection against any possible spread of radiation. With these newer X-ray techniques, children receive one-tenth the radiation they formerly received. Pediatricians today are careful in seeing that children are not too frequently X-rayed. Almost all hospitals and almost all doctors taking X rays in their own office are using the modern machines with their built-in safety measures.

X-ray therapy, which is rarely used during childhood, is confined to the treatment of Hodgkin's disease, certain tumors, and keloidal scarring.

Fluoroscopy, in which the X ray is used to view body structures on a screen, should be avoided as much as possible, because of the large amount of radiation the body receives. Shoe fluoroscopes, formerly commonly used in shoe stores to visualize the correct fitting of shoes, are a definite hazard and can be extremely dangerous.

Y

Yellow jacket stings   see **Bee stings.**

Youngest child
The effect on a boy or girl of being the youngest in the family varies greatly, depending on many factors. Among these are the years intervening between his or her birth and the child directly above, the age of the parents, and the sex of the child.

Generally, if the age difference between the youngest child and the next older child is less than three years, he is likely to get much the same care and attention as the older child or children. However, he is usually the object of rivalry and jealousy from the older children, especially the one directly above.

If, however, there is a fairly long period between the birth of the youngest child and the next older one—say five to eight years—conditions and reactions may be quite different. The child may be babied and overindulged not only by his parents but often by the older children as well. They may do so much for him that they slow down his progress toward self-reliance and independence. On the other hand, older children often enjoy teaching the youngest child to read earlier than usual, and he may gain many valuable early experiences by tagging along after older children, doing or trying to do what they are doing.

If eight to ten years intervene between the birth of the youngest child and the next older child a very different situa-tion often exists. First, because of the length of the intervening years before his birth, the youngest child is usually treated much like an only child, and has been called by some the "pseudo-only" child. Like an only child, he may be fussed over, indulged, and overprotected. Then, too, the parents are considerably older and may have lost much of their resilience and even physical strength—they may not even have wanted this child. As a result of this situation, the child may be less relaxed than the child of younger parents.

If the youngest child has a brother or sister not too much older, parents must take extra care that the older child, out of feelings of envy and jealousy, doesn't harass the youngest (see **Sibling rivalry and jealousy**). If the sibling or siblings are old enough to enjoy pampering the new child, parents should be sure that the youngest also has ample experience in playing with children his own age or even younger—the youngest child should have experiences that teach him that he cannot always be the center of attention. In the case of a "pseudo-only" child, parents must take the same precautions as with an only child to be sure the child doesn't lack companions or the opportunity to develop a healthy independence (see **Only child**).

Y's (YMCA, YWCA, YMHA, YWHA)   see **Recreational organizations.**

APPENDIX A:
Locations and Telephone Numbers of Poison Control Centers in the United States*

CITY	ADDRESS	TELEPHONE

ALABAMA

State Coordinator	State Department of Public Health Montgomery	265–2341
Anniston	Anniston Memorial Hospital Pharmacy Department 400 E. 10th St.	237–5421
Auburn	School of Pharmacy Auburn University	826–4740
Birmingham	Children's Hospital 1601 6th Ave., S.	323–8901
Dothan	Southeast Alabama General Hospital	794–3131
Florence	Eliza Coffee Memorial Hospital 600 W. Alabama St.	764–8321
Gadsden	Baptist Memorial Hospital 1007 Goodyear Ave.	492–1240
Mobile	Mobile General Hospital St. Anthony & Broad Sts.	473–0341

ALASKA

State Coordinator	State Department of Health and Welfare Juneau	586–6311

* Derived from *Directory: Poison Control Centers*, U.S. Department of Health, Education, and Welfare, 1971.

CITY	ADDRESS	TELEPHONE
Anchorage	Alaska Native Medical Center Public Health Service	279–6661
Fairbanks	Fairbanks Community Hospital 119 North Cushman	456–6655
Juneau	Greater Juneau Borough Hospital 419 6th St.	586–2611
Ketchikan	Ketchikan General Hospital 3100 Tongass Ave	225–5171
Mount Edgecumbe	Alaska Native Hospital Public Health Service	966–8347

ARIZONA

CITY	ADDRESS	TELEPHONE
State Coordinator	University of Arizona Tucson	884–0111
Douglas	Douglas Hospital 610 9th St.	364–2421
Flagstaff	Flagstaff Hospital 1215 N. Beaver St.	744–5233
Ganado	Project Hope Sage Memorial Hospital	755–3411
Kingman	Mohave General Hospital 301 W. Beale	753–6132
Nogales	St. Joseph's Hospital Target Range Rd.	287–2771
Phoenix	Good Samaritan Hospital 1033 E. McDowell Rd.	252–6611
	Maricopa County General Hospital 3435 W. Durango	272–6611
	Memorial Hospital 1200 S. 5th Ave.	252–5911

	St. Joseph's Hospital 350 W. Thomas Rd.	277–6611
	St. Luke's Hospital Medical Center 525 N. 18th St.	258–7373
Prescott	Yavapai Community Hospital 1003 Willow Creek Rd.	445–2700
Tucson	Pima County General Hospital 2900 S. 6th Ave.	624–2721
	College of Pharmacy University of Arizona	884–0111
	St. Mary's Hospital 1700 W. St. Mary's Rd.	622–5833
	Tucson Medical Center E. Grant Rd. at Beverly Blvd.	327–5461
Winslow	Winslow Memorial Hospital 116 E. Hillview St.	289–2821
Yuma	Parkview Hospital Avenue A & 24th St.	782–1811

ARKANSAS

State Coordinator	State Board of Health Little Rock	661–2242
El Dorado	Warner Brown Hospital 460 West Oak St.	863–3161
Fort Smith	St. Edward's Mercy Hospital 1411 Rogers Ave.	782–3071
	Sparks Regional Medical Center 1311 S. Eye St.	782–2088
Harrison	Boone County Hospital 620 N. Willow St.	365–6141
Helena	Helena Hospital Hospital Dr.	338–6411

CITY	ADDRESS	TELEPHONE
Little Rock	Department of Pediatrics University of Arkansas Medical Center 4301 W. Markham St.	664–5000
Osceola	Osceola Memorial Hospital 611 Lee Ave., W.	563–2611
Pine Bluff	Jefferson Hospital 1515 W. 42nd Ave.	535–6800

CALIFORNIA

State Coordinator	Department of Public Health Berkeley	843–7900
Fresno	Fresno Community Hospital Fresno & R Sts.	233–0911 Night: 233–7547 439–3527 439–3539
Los Angeles	Thomas J. Fleming Memorial Center Childrens Hospital of Los Angeles P.O. Box 54700 4650 Sunset Blvd.	664–2121
Oakland	Alameda-Contra Costa Medical Assn. 6230 Claremont Ave.	652–8171
	Children's Hospital of East Bay 51st & Grove Sts.	654–5600
Orange	Orange County Medical Center 101 S. Manchester Ave.	633–9393
San Francisco	Central Emergency Hospital 135 Polk St.	431–2800
	Children's Hospital 3700 California St.	387–8700
San Jose	Santa Clara Valley Medical Center 751 S. Bascom Ave.	293–0262

CANAL ZONE

Balboa Heights	Gorgas Hospital	2–2600

COLORADO

State Coordinator	State Department of Public Health
Denver	388–6111
Alamosa	Alamosa Community Hospital
1st & Creston Sts.	589–2511
Aurora	L.K. Professional Pharmacy
9240 E. Colfax Ave.	366–1531
Cortez	Southwest Memorial Hospital
925 S. Broadway	565–3448
Denver	Department of Health & Hospitals
6th & Cherokee Sts.	893–6000
	St. Anthony's Hospital
4231 W. 16th Ave.	825–9011
	University of Colorado
Medical Center
4200 E. 9th Ave.	399–1211
Grand Junction	St. Mary's Hospital
7th & Patterson Rd.	242–1197
Greeley	Weld County General Hospital
16th St. at 17th Ave.	352–4121
Longmont	Longmont Community Hospital
1950 W. Mt. View Ave.	776–1422
Pueblo	129 Colorado Ave.	542–8680

CONNECTICUT

State Coordinator	State Department of Health
Hartford	566–3456

CITY	ADDRESS	TELEPHONE
Bridgeport	Bridgeport Hospital 267 Grant St.	334–0131
	St. Vincent's Hospital 2820 Main St.	336–1081
Danbury	Danbury Hospital 95 Locust Ave.	744–2300
Hartford	St. Francis Hospital 114 Woodland St.	249–8281
	State Department of Health State Office Bldg.	566–3456
Middletown	Middlesex Memorial Hospital 28 Crescent St.	347–9471
New Britain	New Britain General Hospital 100 Grand St.	224–5672
New Haven	The Hospital of St. Raphael 1450 Chapel St.	772–3900
	Yale-New Haven Hospital 789 Howard Ave.	436–1960
Norwalk	Norwalk Hospital 24 Stevens St.	838–3611
Stamford	Stamford Hospital Shelburne Rd. at West Broad St.	327–1234
Waterbury	St. Mary's Hospital 56 Franklin St.	756–8351

DELAWARE

Wilmington	501 W. 14th St.	655–3389

DISTRICT OF COLUMBIA

Washington	Children's Hospital 13th & W Sts., N.W.	835–4080 or 4081

FLORIDA

State Coordinator	Department of Health and Rehabilitative Services Jacksonville	354–3961
Apalachicola	George E. Weems Memorial Hospital Franklin Square	653–3311
Bartow	Polk General Hospital 2010 E. Georgia St.	533–1111
Bradenton	Manatee Memorial Hospital 206 2nd St.	746–5111
Daytona Beach	Halifax District Hospital Clyde Morris Blvd.	255–4411
Fort Lauderdale	Broward General Hospital 1600 S. Andrews Ave.	525–5411
Fort Myers	Lee Memorial Hospital	334–5286
Fort Walton Beach	Ft. Walton Beach Hospital 207 Hospital Dr., N.E.	243–7611
Gainesville	Alachua General Hospital 315 S.W. 10th St.	372–4321
	J. Hillis Miller Health Center University of Florida	392–3591
Jacksonville	St. Vincent's Hospital Barrs St. & St. Johns Ave.	389–7751
Key West	Monroe General Hospital Stock Island	294–3741
Lakeland	Lakeland General Hospital Lakeland Hills Blvd.	686–1111
Leesburg	Leesburg General Hospital 600 E. Dixie	787–7222
Melbourne	Brevard Hospital 1350 S. Hickory St.	727–7000
Miami	Jackson Memorial Hospital 1700 N.W. 10th Ave.	371–9611

CITY	ADDRESS	TELEPHONE
Miami Beach	Mt. Sinai Hospital 4300 Alton Rd.	532–3611
Naples	Naples Community Hospital 350 7th St. N.	649–3131
Ocala	Munroe Memorial Hospital 1410 S. Orange St.	629–7911
Orlando	Orange Memorial Hospital 1416 S. Orange Ave.	241–2411
Panama City	Memorial Hospital of Bay County 600 N. MacArthur Ave.	785–7411
Pensacola	Baptist Hospital 1000 W. Moreno St.	434–4811
Plant City	South Florida Baptist Hospital	752–1188
Pompano Beach	North Brovard Hospital 201 Sample Rd.	941–8300
Punta Gorda	Medical Center Hospital 809 E. Marion Ave.	639–2191
Rockledge	Wuesthoff Memorial Hospital 110 Longwood Ave.	636–2211
St. Petersburg	Bayfront Medical Center, Inc. 701 6th St., S.	894–1161
Sarasota	Sarasota Memorial Hospital 1901 Arlington Ave.	955–1111
Tallahassee	Tallahassee Memorial Hospital N. Magnolia Dr. & Miccosukee Rd.	877–2181
Tampa	Tampa General Hospital Davis Islands	251–6995
Titusville	Jess Parrish Memorial Hospital 951 N. Washington Ave.	269–1100

West Palm Beach	Good Samaritan Hospital 1300 N. Dixie Hwy.	655–5511
Winter Haven	Winter Haven Hospital, Inc. 200 Ave. F, N.E.	293–1121

GEORGIA

State Coordinator	Department of Public Health Atlanta	656–4839
Albany	Phoebe Putney Memorial Hospital 417 3rd Ave.	436–5741
Athens	Athens General Hospital 797 Cobb St.	549–9977
Atlanta	Grady Memorial Hospital 80 Butler St., S.E.	523–4711
Augusta	University Hospital University Place	724–7171
Columbus	The Medical Center 19th St. & 18th Ave.	324–4711
Macon	Macon Hospital 777 Hemlock St.	746–4113
Rome	Floyd Hospital Turner & McCall Blvd.	235–0451
Savannah	Memorial Hospital Waters Ave. at 63rd St.	345–3200
Thomasville	John D. Archbold Memorial Hospital 900 Gordon Ave.	226–4121
Valdosta	Pineview General Hospital Pendleton Park	242–3450
Waycross	Memorial Hospital 410 Darling Ave.	283–3030

GUAM

State Coordinator	Department of Public Health and Social Services Agana	42–4158

CITY	ADDRESS	TELEPHONE
Agana	Guam Memorial Hospital	746–9171

HAWAII

State Coordinator	Department of Health Honolulu	531–7776
Honolulu	Kauikeolani Children's Hospital 226 North Kuakini St.	531–3511

IDAHO

State Coordinator	State Department of Health Boise	384–2494
Boise	St. Luke's Hospital Pharmacy 130 E. Bannock	342–7781

ILLINOIS

State Coordinator	Department of Public Health Springfield	525–7747
Aurora	Copley Memorial Hospital Lincoln & Weston Aves.	896–4611
	St. Charles Hospital 400 E. New York St.	897–8714
Belleville	Memorial Hospital 4501 N. Park Dr.	233–7750
Belvidere	Highland Hospital 1625 S. State St.	547–5441
Berwyn	MacNeal Memorial Hospital 3249 Oak Park Ave.	484–2211
Bloomington	Mennonite Hospital 807 N. Main	828–5241
	St. Joseph Hospital 2200 E. Washington	829–9481

Cairo	St. Mary's Hospital 2020 Cedar St.	734–2400
Canton	Graham Hospital Association 210 W. Walnut St.	647–5240
Carbondale	Doctors Memorial Hospital 404 W. Main St.	457–4101
Carthage	Memorial Hospital End S. Adams St.	357–3133
Centralia	St. Mary's Hospital 400 N. Pleasant Ave.	532–6731
Champaign	Burnham City Hospital 311 E. Stoughton St.	337–2533
Chanute AFB	USAF Hospital Chanute Air Force Base (Limited for treatment of military personnel and families, except for indicated civilian emergencies)	495–3133 495–3134
Chicago	Presbyterian-St. Lukes Hospital 1753 W. Congress Parkway	942–5969
Chester	Memorial Hospital 1900 State St.	826–2388
Danville	Lake View Memorial Hospital 812 N. Logan Ave.	443–5221
	St. Elizabeth Hospital 600 Sager Ave.	442–6300
Decatur	Decatur Memorial Hospital 2300 N. Edward St.	877–8121
	St. Mary's Hospital 1800 E. Lake Shore Dr.	429–2966
Des Plaines	Holy Family Hospital 100 N. River Rd.	299–2281
East St. Louis	Christian Welfare Hospital 1509 Illinois Ave.	874–7076
	St. Mary's Hospital 129 N. 8th St.	274–1900

CITY	ADDRESS	TELEPHONE
Effingham	St. Anthony's Memorial Hospital 503 N. Maple	342–2121
Elgin	St. Joseph's Hospital 277 Jefferson Ave.	741–5400
	Sherman Hospital 934 Center St.	742–9800
Elmhurst	Memorial Hospital of DuPage County 315 Schiller St.	833–1400
Evanston	Community Hospital 2040 Brown Ave.	869–5400
	Evanston Hospital 2650 Ridge Ave.	492–6460
	St. Francis Hospital 355 Ridge Ave.	492–2440
Evergreen Park	Little Company of Mary Hospital 2800 W. 95th St.	422–6200 HI 5–6000
Fairbury	Fairbury Hospital 519 S. 5th St.	692–2346
Freeport	Freeport Memorial Hospital 420 S. Harlem	233–4131
Galena	The Galena Hospital District Summit St.	777–1340
Galesburg	Galesburg Cottage Hospital 674 N. Seminary St.	343–4121
	St. Mary's Hospital 239 S. Cherry St.	343–3161
Granite City	St. Elizabeth Hospital 2100 Madison Ave.	876–2020
Harvey	Ingalls Memorial Hospital 15510 Page Ave.	333–2300

Highland	St. Joseph Hospital 1515 Main St.	654–2171
Highland Park	Highland Park Hospital Foundation 718 Glenview Ave.	432–8000
Hinsdale	Hinsdale Sanitarium & Hospital 120 N. Oak St.	323–2100
Hoopeston	Hoopeston Community Memorial Hospital 701 E. Orange	283–5531
Jacksonville	Passavant Memorial Area Hospital 1600 W. Walnut St.	245–9541
Joliet	St. Joseph's Hospital 333 N. Madison St.	725–7133
	Silver Cross Hospital 600 Walnut St.	727–1711
Kankakee	Riverside Hospital 350 N. Wall St.	933–1671
	St. Mary's Hospital 150 S. Fifth Ave.	939–4111
Kewanee	Kewanee Public Hospital 719 Elliott St.	853–3361
Lake Forest	Lake Forest Hospital 660 Northwestmoreland Rd.	234–5600
LaSalle	St. Mary's Hospital 1015 O'Conor Ave.	223–0607
Libertyville	Condell Memorial Hospital Cleveland & Stewart Aves.	362–2900
Lincoln	Abraham Lincoln Memorial Hospital 315 Eighth St.	732–2161
McHenry	McHenry Hospital 3516 W. Waukegan Rd.	385–2200
Macomb	McDonough District Hospital 525 E. Grant St.	833–4101

CITY	ADDRESS	TELEPHONE
Mattoon	Memorial Hospital District of Coles County 2101 Champaign Ave.	234–8881
Maywood	Loyola University Hospital 2160 S. 1st Ave.	531–3886
Melrose Park	Westlake Hospital 1225 Superior St.	681–3000
Mendota	Mendota Community Hospital Memorial Dr.	7461
Moline	Moline Public Hospital 635 10th Ave.	762–3651
Monmouth	Community Memorial Hospital West Harlem Ave.	734–3141
Mount Carmel	Wabash General Hospital 1418 College Dr.	262–4121
Mount Vernon	Good Samaritan Hospital 605 N. 12th St.	242–4600
Naperville	Edward Hospital S. Washington St.	355–0450
Normal	Brokaw Hospital Franklin & Virginia Ave.	829–7685
Oak Lawn	Christ Community Hospital 4440 W. 95th St.	423–7000
Oak Park	W. Suburban Hospital 518 N. Austin Blvd.	383–6200
Olney	Richland Memorial Hospital 800 E. Locust St.	395–2131
Ottawa	Ryburn Memorial Hospital 701 Clinton St.	433–3100
Park Ridge	Lutheran General Hospital 1775 Dempster St.	692–2210

Pekin	Pekin Memorial Hospital 14th & Court	347–1151
Peoria	Methodist Hospital 221 N.E. Glen Oak Ave.	685–6511
	Proctor Community Hospital 5409 N. Knoxville	691–4702
	St. Francis Hospital 530 N.E. Glen Oak Ave.	674–2943
Peru	Peoples Hospital 925 W St.	223–3300
Pittsfield	Illini Community Hospital 640 W. Washington St.	285–2115
Princeton	Perry Memorial Hospital 530 E. Park Ave.	875–2811
Quincy	Blessing Hospital 1005 Broadway	223–5811
	St. Mary's Hospital 1415 Vermont St.	223–1200
Rockford	Rockford Memorial Hospital 2400 N. Rockton Ave.	968–6861
	St. Anthony's Hospital 5666 E. State St.	226–2041
	Swedish-American Hospital 1316 Charles St.	968–6898
Rock Island	St. Anthony's Hospital 767 30th St.	788–7631
St. Charles	Delnor Hospital 975 N. Fifth Ave.	584–3300
Scott Air Force Base	USAF Medical Center	256–7595
Springfield	Memorial Hospital 1st & Miller Sts.	528–2041
	St. John's Hospital 701 E. Mason St.	544–6451

CITY	ADDRESS	TELEPHONE
Streator	St. Mary's Hospital 111 E. Spring St.	672–3189
Urbana	Carle Foundation Hospital 611 W. Park St.	337–3313
	Mercy Hospital 1400 W. Park Ave.	337–2131
Waukegan	St. Therese Hospital W. Waukegan St.	688–6470 688–6471
	Victory Memorial Hospital 1324 N. Sheridan Rd.	688–4181
Woodstock	Memorial Hospital for McHenry County 527 W. South St.	338–2500
Zion	Zion-Benton Hospital 2500 Emmaus Ave.	872–4561

INDIANA

State Coordinator	State Board of Health Indianapolis	633–5490
Anderson	St. John's Hickey Memorial Hospital 2015 Jackson St.	694–2511
Angola	Cameron Memorial Hospital, Inc. 416 E. Maumee St.	665–2141 665–2166
East Chicago	St. Catherine Hospital 4321 Fir St.	EX 7–3080
Elkhart	Elkhart General Hospital 600 E. Blvd.	523–5350
Evansville	Deaconess Hospital 600 Mary St.	426–3405
	St. Mary's Hospital 3700 Washington Ave.	477–6261

	Welborn Memorial Baptist Hospital 412 S.E. 4th St.	423–3103
Fort Wayne	Parkview Memorial Hospital 220 Randalia Dr.	484–6636
	St. Joseph's Hospital 700 Broadway	742–4121
Frankfort	Clinton County Hospital 1300 S. Jackson St.	654–4451
Gary	Methodist Hospital of Gary, Inc. 600 Grant St.	882–9461
Goshen	Goshen General Hospital 200 High Park Ave.	533–2141
Hammond	St. Margaret Hospital 25 Douglas St.	WE 2–2300
Indianapolis	Marion County General Hospital 960 Locke St.	630–7351
	Methodist Hospital of Indiana, Inc. 1604 N. Capitol Ave.	924–8355
Kokomo	Howard Community Hospital 3500 S. La Fountain St.	453–0702
Lafayette	Purdue University Student Health Center	749–2441
	St. Elizabeth Hospital 1501 Hartford St.	742–0221
La Grange	La Grange County Hospital Route 1	463–2144
Lebanon	Witham Memorial Hospital 1124 N. Lebanon St.	482–2700
Madison	King's Daughters' Hospital 112 Presbyterian Ave.	265–5211
Marion	Marion General Hospital Wabash & Euclid Ave.	662–1441
Mishawaka	St. Joseph Hospital 215 W. 4th St.	259–2431

CITY	ADDRESS	TELEPHONE
Muncie	Ball Memorial Hospital 2401 University Ave.	284–3371
Portland	Jay County Hospital 505 W. Arch St.	726–7131
Richmond	Reid Memorial Hospital 1401 Chester Blvd.	962–4545
Shelbyville	William S. Major Hospital 150 W. Washington St.	392–3211
South Bend	Memorial Hospital of South Bend 615 Michigan St.	234–9041
	St. Joseph's Hospital 811 E. Madison St.	234–2151
Terre Haute	Union Hospital, Inc. 1606 N. 7th St.	232–0361

IOWA

State Coordinator	Department of Health Des Moines	281–5785
Des Moines	Raymond Blank Memorial Hospital 1200 Pleasant St.	283–6254
Fort Dodge	Bethesda General Hospital Lutheran Park Rd.	573–3101
Iowa City	University Hospital Pharmacy Department	356–1616

KANSAS

State Coordinator	State Department of Health Topeka	296–3708
Atchison	Atchison Hospital 1301 N. 2nd St.	EM 7–2131

Dodge City	Trinity Hospital 1107 6th St.	227–8133
Emporia	Newman Memorial Hospital 12th & Chestnut Sts.	342–7120
Fort Scott	Mercy Hospital 821 Burke St.	BA 3–2200
Great Bend	Central Kansas Medical Center 3515 Broadway	792–2511
Hays	Hadley Memorial Hospital 201 E. 7th St.	625–3441
Kansas City	University of Kansas Medical Center Department of Pharmacology Rainbow Blvd. at 39th St.	AD 6–5252
Lawrence	Lawrence Memorial Hospital 325 Maine St.	843–3680
Parsons	Labette County Medical Center South 21st St.	421–4880
Salina	St. John's Hospital 139 N. Penn St.	TA 7–5591
Topeka	Stormont-Vail Hospital 10th & Washburn Sts.	234–9961
	State Department of Health State Office Bldg. Topeka Ave. at 10th	296–3708
Wichita	Wesley Hospital Medical Library 550 N. Hillside Ave.	685–2151

KENTUCKY

| State Coordinator | State Department of Health
Frankfort | 564–4830 |
| Ashland | King's Daughters' Hospital
2201 Lexington Ave. | 325–7755 |

CITY	ADDRESS	TELEPHONE
Fort Thomas	St. Luke Hospital 85 N. Grand Ave.	441–6100
Lexington	Central Baptist Hospital 1740 S. Limestone St.	278–3411
	University of Kentucky Medical Center	233–5833
Owensboro	Owensboro-Daviess County Hospital 811 Hospital Court	683–3513
Paducah	Western Baptist Hospital 2501 Kentucky Ave.	444–6361

LOUISIANA

State Coordinator	State Department of Health New Orleans	527–5822
Bogalusa	Washington-St. Tammany Charity Hospital 400 Memphis St.	735–1322
Monroe	St. Francis Hospital 309 Jackson St.	325–6454
New Orleans	U.S. Public Health Service Hospital 210 State St.	899–3409
Shreveport	T. E. Schumpert Memorial Hospital 915 Margaret Place	422–0709 424–6411

MAINE

State Coordinator	Department of Health & Welfare Augusta	623–1511
Togus	Veterans Administration Center Kennebec County	623–8411

MARYLAND

State Coordinator	State Department of Health Baltimore	382–2668
Annapolis	Anne Arundel General Hospital Franklin & Cathedral Sts.	268–4444
Baltimore	Baltimore City Hospital 4940 Eastern Ave.	DI 2–0800
	Johns Hopkins Hospital 601 N. Broadway	955–6371
	University of Maryland Hospital Redwood & Greene Sts.	955–7592 Night: 955–8761
Bethesda	Suburban Hospital Emergency Room 8600 Old Georgetown Rd.	530–3880
Cumberland	Sacred Heart Hospital 900 Seton Dr.	729–5200
Easton	Memorial Hospital S. Washington St.	822–5555
Hagerstown	Washington County Hospital King & Antietam Sts.	733–3000
Silver Spring	Holy Cross Hospital Forest Glen Rd.	495–1225

MASSACHUSETTS

State Coordinator	State Department of Public Health Boston	727–2700
Boston	Childrens Medical Center 300 Longwood Ave.	232–2120
Fall River	Union Hospital 300 Hanover St.	679–6405
New Bedford	St. Luke's Hospital 52 Brigham St.	997–1515

CITY	ADDRESS	TELEPHONE
Springfield	Mercy Hospital 233 Carew St.	788–7321
	Springfield Hospital Medical Center 759 Chestnut St.	787–3200
	Wesson Memorial Hospital 140 High St.	ST 5–1241
Worcester	Worcester City Hospital 26 Queen St.	799–7094

MICHIGAN

State Coordinator	Department of Public Health Lansing	373–1320
Adrian	Emma L. Bixby Hospital 818 Riverside Ave.	265–6161
Ann Arbor	University of Michigan Medical Center	764–5102
Battle Creek	Community Hospital 200 Tomkins St.	Woodward 3–5521
Bay City	Mercy Hospital 100 15th St.	Twinbrook 5–8511
Berrien Center	Berrien General Hospital Dean's Hill Rd.	471–7761
Coldwater	Community Health Center of Branch County 274 E. Chicago St.	279–9501
Detroit	Children's Hospital 5224 St. Antoine St.	833–1000
	City Health Department 1151 Taylor Ave.	TR 2–1540
	Mount Carmel Mercy Hospital 6071 W. Outer Dr.	864–5400

Eloise	Wayne County General Hospital 30712 Michigan Ave.	722–2500
Flint	Hurley Hospital 6th Ave. & Begole	Cedar 2–1161
Grand Rapids	Blodgett Memorial Hospital 1840 Wealthy, S.E.	456–5301
	Butterworth Hospital 100 Michigan, N.E.	451–3591
	Grand Rapids Osteopathic Hospital 1919 Boston Street, S.E.	452–5151
	St. Mary's Hospital 201 Lafayette, S.E.	459–3131
Hancock	St. Joseph's Hospital 200 Michigan Ave.	482–1122
Kalamazoo	Bronson Methodist Hospital 252 E. Lovell St.	342–9821
Lansing	St. Lawrence Hospital 1210 W. Saginaw St.	372–3610
Marquette	St. Luke's Hospital W. College Ave.	Canal 6–3551
Midland	Midland Hospital 4005 Orchard Dr.	TE 5–6711
Monroe	Memorial Hospital of Monroe 700 Stewart Rd.	CH 1–6500
Petoskey	Little Traverse Hospital 416 Connable	Diamond 7–2551
Pontiac	St. Joseph Mercy Hospital 900 Woodward Ave.	338–9111
Port Huron	Mercy Hospital 2601 Electric Ave.	Yukon 5–9531
Saginaw	Saginaw General Hospital 1447 N. Harrison Rd.	753–3411
Traverse City	Munson Medical Center	947–6140

CITY	ADDRESS	TELEPHONE

MINNESOTA

CITY	ADDRESS	TELEPHONE
State Coordinator	State Department of Health Minneapolis	378–1150
Bemidji	Bemidji Hospital	751–5430
Brainerd	St. Joseph's Hospital	829–2861
Crookston	Riverview Hospital	281–4682
Duluth	St. Luke's Hospital	727–6636
	St. Mary's Hospital 407 E. 3rd St.	727–4551
Fergus Falls	Lake Region Hospital	736–5475
Fridley	Unity Hospital 550 Osborne Rd.	786–2200
Mankato	Immanuel-St. Joseph's Hospital 325 Garden Blvd.	387–1851
Marshall	Louis Weiner Memorial Hospital	532–2263
Minneapolis	Fairview Hospital 2312 S. 6th St.	332–0282
	Hennepin County General Hospital 620 S. 6th St.	330–3930
	Minnesota Department of Health 717 Delaware St. S.E.	378–1150 Night: 929–6491 784–1869
	North Memorial Hospital 3220 Lowry Ave. N.	588–0616
	Northwestern Hospital 810 E. 27th St.	332–7266
Morris	Stevens County Memorial Hospital	589–1313
Rochester	Rochester Methodist Hospital	282–4461

St. Cloud	St. Cloud Hospital	251–2700
St. Paul	Bethesda Lutheran Hospital 559 Capitol Blvd.	227–8611
	Children's Hospital 311 Pleasant Ave.	227–6521
	St. John's Hospital 403 Maria Ave.	228–3132
	St. Joseph's Hospital 69 W. Exchange	222–2861
	St. Luke's Hospital 300 Pleasant Ave. c/o Emergency Room	228–8201
	St. Paul-Ramsey Hospital 640 Jackson St.	222–4260
Virginia	Virginia Municipal Hospital	741–3340
Willmar	Rice Memorial Hospital	235–4543
Worthington	Worthington Municipal Hospital	376–4141 Night: 376–6834

MISSISSIPPI

State Coordinator	State Board of Health Jackson	354–6650
Brandon	Rankin General Hospital 350 Grossgates Blvd.	825–2811
Columbia	Marion County General Hospital	736–6303
Greenwood	Greenwood-LeFlore Hospital River Rd.	453–9751
Hattiesburg	Forrest County General Hospital 400 S. 28th Ave.	582–8361
Jackson	Baptist Hospital 1190 N. State St.	948–5211

CITY	ADDRESS	TELEPHONE
Jackson	St. Dominic-Jackson Memorial Hospital 969 Lakeland Dr.	266–5281
	State Board of Health Division of Preventable Disease Control	354–6650
Keesler (Biloxi)	USAF Hospital Keesler Keesler Air Force Base	432–1521
Laurel	Jones County Community Hospital Jefferson St. at 13th Ave.	425–1441
Meridian	St. Joseph Hospital Highway 39, N.	483–6211
Pascagoula	Singing River Hospital Highway 90E	762–6121
University	School of Pharmacy University of Mississippi	234–1522
Vicksburg	Mercy Hospital-Street Memorial 100 McAuley Dr.	636–2121

MISSOURI

CITY	ADDRESS	TELEPHONE
State Coordinator	Missouri Division of Health Jefferson City	635–4111
Cape Girardeau	St. Francis Hospital 825 Good Hope St.	334–4461
Columbia	University of Missouri Medical Center 807 Stadium Blvd.	442–5111
Hannibal	St. Elizabeth Hospital 109 Virginia St.	221–0414
Joplin	St. John's Hospital 2727 McClelland Blvd.	781–2727
Kansas City	Children's Mercy Hospital 24th & Gillham Rd.	471–0626

	Kansas City General Hospital and Medical Center 23rd & Cherry St.	HA 1–8060
Kirksville	Kirksville Osteopathic Hospital 800 W. Jefferson St.	665–4611
Poplar Bluff	Lucy Lee Hospital 330 N. 2nd St.	785–7721
Rolla	Phelps County Memorial Hospital 1000 W. 10th St.	364–3100
St. Joseph	Methodist Hospital and Medical Center 8th & Faraon Sts.	232–8461
St. Louis	Cardinal Glennon Children's Memorial Hospital 1465 S. Grand Ave.	865–4000
	St. Louis Children's Hospital 500 S. Kingshighway	367–6800
Springfield	Lester E. Cox Medical Center 1423 N. Jefferson St.	865–9631
	St. John's Hospital 1235 E. Cherokee	881–8811
West Plains	West Plains Memorial Hospital 1103 Alaska Ave.	256–3141

MONTANA

State Coordinator	State Department of Health Helena	449–2544
Bozeman	Bozeman Deaconess Hospital 15 West Lamme	586–5431
Helena	St. Peter's Hospital	442–2480

NEBRASKA

State Coordinator	State Department of Health Lincoln	477–5211

CITY	ADDRESS	TELEPHONE
Lincoln	Bryan Memorial Hospital 4848 Sumner St.	473–3244
Omaha	Children's Memorial Hospital 44th & Dewey Sts.	553–5400

NEVADA

State Coordinator	Department of Health & Welfare Carson City	882–7458
Las Vegas	Southern Nevada Memorial Hospital 1800 West Charleston Blvd.	385–1277
Reno	Washoe Medical Center Kirman & Mills Sts.	785–4129

NEW HAMPSHIRE

State Coordinator	Department of Health & Welfare Concord	225–6611
Hanover	Mary Hitchcock Hospital 2 Maynard St.	643–4000

NEW JERSEY

State Coordinator	State Department of Health Trenton	292–5616
Atlantic City	Atlantic City Hospital 1925 Pacific Ave.	344–4081
Belleville	Clara Maass Hospital 1A Franklin Ave.	751 1000
Boonton	Riverside Hospital Powerville Rd.	334 5000
Bridgeton	Bridgeton Hospital Irving Ave.	451 6600

Camden	West Jersey Hospital Mt. Ephraim & Atlantic Aves.	963–8830
Denville	St. Clare's Hospital Pocono Rd.	627–3000
East Orange	East Orange General Hospital 300 Central Ave.	672–8400
Elizabeth	St. Elizabeth Hospital 225 Williamson St.	289–4000
Englewood	Englewood Hospital 350 Engle Ave.	568–3400
Flemington	Hunterdon Medical Center Route 31	782–2121
Hasbrouck Heights	Hasbrouck Heights Hospital 214 Terrace Ave.	288–0800
Livingston	St. Barnabas Medical Center Old Short Hills Rd.	992–5500
Long Branch	Monmouth Medical Center 255 2nd Ave.	222–2210
Montclair	Mountainside Hospital Bay & Highland Aves.	746–6000
Morristown	All Souls Hospital 95 Mount Kemble Ave.	538–0900
Mount Holly	Burlington County Memorial Hospital 175 Madison Ave.	267–0700
Neptune	Jersey Shore Medical Center-Fitkin 1945 Corlies Ave.	988–1818
Newark	Children's Hospital of Newark United Hospitals 15 S. 9th St.	484–8000
	Newark Beth Israel Hospital 201 Lyons Ave.	923–6000
New Brunswick	Middlesex General Hospital 180 Somerset St.	828–3000

CITY	ADDRESS	TELEPHONE
New Brunswick	St. Peter's General Hospital Easton Ave.	545–8000
Newton	Newton Memorial Hospital 175 High St.	383–2121
Orange	Hospital Center at Orange 188 S. Essex Ave.	678–1100
Passaic	St. Mary's Hospital 211 Pennington Ave.	473–1000
Paterson	Paterson General Hospital 528 Market St.	684–6900
Perth Amboy	Perth Amboy General Hospital 530 New Brunswick Ave.	442–3700
Phillipsburg	Warren Hospital 185 Roseberry St.	859–1500
Point Pleasant	Point Pleasant Hospital Osborn Ave. & River Front	892–1100
Princeton	Princeton Hospital 253 Witherspoon St.	921–7700
Saddle Brook	Saddle Brook Hospital 300 Market St.	843–6700
Somers Point	Shore Memorial Hospital New York & Sunny Aves.	927–3501
Somerville	Somerset Hospital Rehill Ave.	725–4000
Summit	Overlook Hospital 193 Morris Ave.	273–8100
Teaneck	Holy Name Hospital 718 Teaneck Rd.	837–3070
Trenton	Helene Fuld Hospital 750 Brunswick Ave.	396–6575

| Union | Memorial General Hospital
100 Galloping Hill Rd. | 687–1900 |

NEW MEXICO

State Coordinator	Department of Public Health Santa Fe	827–2663
Alamogordo	Gerald Champion Memorial Hospital 1209 9th St.	437–3770
Albuquerque	Bernalillo County Indian Hospital 2211 Lomas Blvd., N.E.	265–4411
Carlsbad	Carlsbad Regional Medical Center Northgate Unit	887–3521
Clovis	Clovis Memorial Hospital 1210 Thornton St.	763–4493
Las Cruces	Memorial General Hospital Alameda & Lohman	524–8641
Raton	Miners' Hospital of New Mexico S. 6th St.	445–2741
Roswell	Eastern New Mexico Medical Center 405 Country Club Rd.	622–8170

NEW YORK

State Coordinator	State Department of Health Albany	RG 4–2121
Albany	Albany Medical Center New Scotland Ave.	462–7521
Binghamton	Binghamton General Hospital Mitchell Ave.	772–1100
	Our Lady of Lourdes Memorial Hospital 169 Riverside Dr.	729–6521
Buffalo	Buffalo Children's Hospital 219 Bryant St.	878–7374 878–7503

CITY	ADDRESS	TELEPHONE
Dunkirk	Brooks Memorial Hospital 10 W. 6th St.	366–1111
East Meadow	Meadowbrook Hospital	542–2323 542–2324
Elmira	Arnot Ogden Memorial Hospital Roe Ave. & Grove St.	734–5221
	St. Joseph's Hospital 555 E. Market St.	733–6541
Endicott	Ideal Hospital of Endicott 600 High Ave.	754–7171
Ithaca	Tompkins County Hospital 1285 Trumansburg Rd.	272–7480
Jamestown	Jamestown General Hospital Hospital Park	484–1161
	W. C. A. Hospital 207 Foote Ave.	487–0141
Johnson City	Wilson Memorial Hospital 33–57 Harrison St.	797–1211
Kingston	Kingston Hospital 396 Broadway	331–3131
New York	New York City Department of Health 455 1st Ave.	340–4494
Niagara Falls	Niagara Falls Memorial Hospital 621 10th St.	285–2571
Nyack	Nyack Hospital N. Midland Ave.	EL 8-6200
Oswego	Oswego Hospital 110 W. 6th St.	FI 3-1920
Rochester	University of Rochester Medical Center and Strong Memorial Hospital 260 Crittenden Blvd.	275–3232

Syracuse	Upstate Medical Center 750 E. Adams St.	GR 6–3166
Warsaw	Wyoming County Community Hospital 400 N. Main St.	796–2233
Watertown	House of the Good Samaritan Hospital Washington & Pratt Sts.	782–8110

NORTH CAROLINA

State Coordinator	State Board of Health Raleigh	829–3446
Asheville	Memorial Mission Hospital 509 Biltmore Ave.	252–5331
Charlotte	Mercy Hospital 2000 E. 5th St.	334–6831
Durham	Duke University Hospital	684–8111
Hendersonville	Margaret R. Pardee Hospital Fleming St.	693–6522
Jacksonville	Onslow Memorial Hospital College St.	347–1241
Wilmington	New Hanover Memorial Hospital 2431 S. 17th St.	763–9021

NORTH DAKOTA

State Coordinator	State Department of Health Bismarck	224–2348
Bismarck	Quain and Ranstad Clinic Burleigh County	223–1420 Night: 223–5000 Night: 223–4700
Dickinson	St. Joseph's Hospital 7th St. W.	225–6771
Fargo	North Dakota State University Pharmacology Department	237–8115
Grand Forks	Grand Forks Deaconess Hospital 212 S. 4th St.	775–4241

CITY	ADDRESS	TELEPHONE
Jamestown	Jamestown Hospital 419 5th St. N.E.	252–1050
Minot	St. Joseph's Hospital 304 4th St.	838–0341
Williston	Mercy Hospital Washington Avenue & Broadway	572–2188

OHIO

State Coordinator	Department of Health Columbus	469–2544
Akron	Children's Hospital 182 Bowery St.	253–5531
Canton	Aultman Hospital 2600 6th Street, S.W.	452–9911 454–5222
Cincinnati	The Children's Hospital Elland & Bethesda Aves.	281–6161
Cleveland	Cleveland Academy of Medicine 10525 Carnegie Ave.	231–3500 231–4455
Columbus	The Children's Hospital 17th Street at Livingston Park	258–9783
Dayton	U. S. Air Force Hospital Wright-Patterson Air Force Base	257–2968
Mansfield	Mansfield General Hospital 335 Glessner Ave.	522–3411
Springfield	The Community Hospital of Springfield & Clark County 2615 East High St.	323–5531
Toledo	Maumee Valley Hospital 2025 Arlington Ave.	382–3435
Youngstown	St. Elizabeth Hospital 1044 Belmont Ave.	746 7231

OKLAHOMA

State Coordinator	State Department of Health Oklahoma City	427–6232
Lawton	Comanche County Memorial Hospital Gore Blvd.	355–8620
Oklahoma City	State Department of Health Laboratory Services and Communica- ble Disease Control 3400 N. Eastern	427–6232
Ponca City	Ponca City Hospital 14th & Virginia Ave.	765–3321
Tulsa	Hillcrest Medical Center 1120 S. Utica Ave.	584–1351

OREGON

Portland	Pediatrics Department University of Oregon Medical School 3181 S.W. Sam Jackson Park Rd.	228–9181

PENNSYLVANIA

State Coordinator	State Department of Health Harrisburg	787–6436
Allentown	Allentown Hospital Association 17th & Chew Sts.	434–7161
Chambersburg	The Chambersburg Hospital 7th & King Sts.	264–5171
Chester	Sacred Heart General Hospital 9th & Wilson Sts.	494–0721
Danville	George F. Giesinger Memorial Hospital Montour County	275–1000
Easton	Easton Hospital 21st & Lehigh Sts.	258–6221
East Stroudsburg	General Hospital of Monroe County 206 E. Brown St.	421–4000

CITY	ADDRESS	TELEPHONE
Erie	Erie Osteopathic Hospital 5515 Peach St.	864–4031
	Hamot Hospital Association Second & State Sts.	455–6711
	St. Vincent Hospital 232 W. 25th St.	453–6911
Hanover	Hanover General Hospital 300 Highland Ave.	637–3711
Harrisburg	Harrisburg Hospital Front & Mulberry Sts.	782–3639
	Polyclinic Hospital 3rd and Polyclinic Ave.	782–4141
Johnstown	Mercy Hospital 1020 Franklin St.	535–5353
Lancaster	St. Joseph's Hospital 250 College Ave.	397–2821
Latrobe	Latrobe Area Hospital Association 2nd Ave.	539–9711
Lewistown	Lewistown Hospital Highland Ave.	248–5411
Philadelphia	Department of Public Health University Ave. & Curie St.	WA 2–5523
Pittsburgh	Children's Hospital 125 Desoto St.	681–6669
	St. John's General Hospital 3339 McClure Ave.	766–8300
Scranton	Community Medical Center 316 Colfax Ave.	343–5566
Sharon	Sharon General Hospital 740 E. State St.	981–1700

Wilkes-Barre	The Mercy Hospital of Wilkes-Barre 196 Hanover St.	822–8101
	Wilkes-Barre General Hospital North River & Auburn Sts.	823–1121
York	Memorial Osteopathic Hospital 325 S. Belmont St.	843–8623
	York Hospital George St. & Rathon Rd.	854–1511

PUERTO RICO

State Coordinator	University of Puerto Rico Rio Piedras	765–4880 765–0615
Aguadilla	District Hospital of Aguadilla	891–0200
Arecibo	District Hospital of Arecibo	878–3535
Fajardo	District Hospital of Fajardo	863–0505
Mayaguez	Mayaguez Medical Center Department of Health	832–8686
Ponce	District Hospital of Ponce	842–8364 842–2080
San Juan	Medical Center of Puerto Rico	764–3515

RHODE ISLAND

State Coordinator	State Department of Health Providence	521–7100
Kingston	College of Pharmacy University of Rhode Island	792–2763
Pawtucket	Memorial Hospital Prospect St.	724–1230
Providence	Rhode Island Hospital 593 Eddy St.	277–4000
	Roger Williams General Hospital 825 Chalkstone Ave.	521–5055

CITY	ADDRESS	TELEPHONE

SOUTH CAROLINA

State Coordinator	State Board of Health Columbia	758–5664
Charleston	Medical College Hospital 80 Barre St.	792–0211
Columbia	Columbia Hospital 2020 Hampton St.	254–7382

SOUTH DAKOTA

State Coordinator	State Department of Health Pierre	224–5911
Sioux Falls	McKennan Hospital 800 East 21st St.	336–3894
Vermillion	University of South Dakota Department of Pharmacology	624–3432

TENNESSEE

State Coordinator	State Department of Public Health Nashville	741–3644
Chattanooga	T. C. Thompson Children's Hospital 1001 Glenwood Dr.	624–5020
Columbia	Maury County Hospital Mt. Pleasant Pike	388–2320
Jackson	Madison General Hospital 708 W. Forest	424–0424
Johnson City	Memorial Hospital Boone & Fairview Ave.	926–1131
Knoxville	University of Tennessee Memorial Research Center Alcoa Highway	971–3261

Memphis	Le Bonheur Children's Hospital Adams Ave. at Dunlap	525–6541
Nashville	Vanderbilt Hospital 1161 21st Ave. S.	322–2351

TEXAS

State Coordinator	State Department of Health Austin	GL 3–6631
Abilene	Hendrick Memorial Hospital 19th & Hickory Sts.	677–1011
Amarillo	Northwest Texas Hospital 2203 W. 6th St.	376–4431
Austin	Brackenridge Hospital 14th & Sabine Sts.	478–4490
Beaumont	Baptist Hospital of Southeast Texas College & 11th St.	833–7409
Corpus Christi	Memorial Hospital Medical Library 2606 Hospital Building	884–4511
El Paso	R. E. Thomason General Hospital 4815 Alameda Ave.	544–1200
Fort Worth	W. I. Cook Memorial Hospital 1212 W. Lancaster Ave.	ED 6–5521 Night: ED 6–5527
Galveston	Medical Branch Hospital University of Texas 8th & Mechanic Sts.	765–1420 765–2408
Grand Prairie	Mid-Cities Memorial Hospital 2733 Sherman Rd.	264–1651
Harlingen	Valley Baptist Hospital 2101 S. Commerce St.	423–1224
Laredo	Mercy Hospital 1515 Logan	722–2431
Lubbock	Methodist Hospital 3615 19th St.	SW 2–1011

CITY	ADDRESS	TELEPHONE
Midland	Midland Memorial Hospital 1908 W. Wall	682–7381
Odessa	Medical Center Hospital 600 W. 4th St.	337–7311
Plainview	Plainview Hospital 2404 Yonkers St.	296–9601
San Angelo	Shannon West Texas Memorial Hospital 9 S. Magdalen St.	653–6741
San Antonio	Bexar County Hospital District 7703 Floyd Curl Dr.	223–1481
Texarkana	Wadley Hospital 1000 Pine St.	793–4511
Tyler	Medical Center Hospital 1000 S. Beckham St.	594–9361
Waco	Hillcrest Hospital 3000 Herring Ave.	753–1412
Wharton	Caney Valley Memorial Hospital 503 N. Resident St.	523–2440 Night: LE 2–1440
Wichita Falls	Wichita General Hospital Emergency Room 1600 8th St.	322–6771

UTAH

State Coordinator	State Division of Health Salt Lake City	328–6191 328–6131
Salt Lake City	University Hospital University of Utah Medical Center	328–3711

VIRGIN ISLANDS

State Coordinator	Department of Health St. Thomas	774–1321

St. Croix	Charles Harwood Memorial Hospital Christiansted	773–1212 773–1311
	Ingeborg Nesbitt Clinic Fredericksted	772–0260 772–0212
St. John	Morris F. DeCastro Clinic Cruz Bay	776–1469
St. Thomas	Knud-Hansen Memorial Hospital	774–1321

VIRGINIA

State Coordinator	State Department of Health Richmond	644–4111
Alexandria	Alexandria Hospital 709 Duke St.	931–2000
Arlington	Arlington Hospital 5129 N. 16th St.	524–5900
Blacksburg	Montgomery County Community Hospital Route 460, S.	
Charlottesville	University of Virginia Hospital Pediatric Clinic	924–2231
Danville	Danville Memorial Hospital 142 S. Main St.	793–6311
Falls Church	Fairfax Hospital 3300 Gallows Rd.	698–3111
Hampton	Dixie Hospital Victoria Blvd.	722–7921
Harrisonburg	Rockingham Memorial Hospital 738 S. Mason St.	434–4421
Lexington	Stonewall Jackson Hospital	463–3131
Lynchburg	Lynchburg General Marshall Lodge Hospital, Inc. Tate Springs Rd.	VI 6–6511
Nassawadox	Northampton-Accomack Memorial Hospital	442–2011

CITY	ADDRESS	TELEPHONE
Norfolk	Office of Chief Medical Examiner 427 E. Charlotte St.	625–1306 627–3238
Petersburg	Petersburg General Hospital Mt. Erin & Adams Sts.	732–7220
Portsmouth	U. S. Naval Hospital	397–6581
Richmond	Medical College of Virginia 1200 E. Broad St.	770–5123
Roanoke	Roanoke Memorial Hospital Belleview & Lake Aves.	342–4541
Staunton	King's Daughters' Hospital 1410 N. Augusta St.	885–0361
Waynesboro	Waynesboro Community Hospital 501 Oak Ave.	942–8355
Williamsburg	Williamsburg Community Hospital Mt. Vernon Ave.	229–1120

WASHINGTON

State Coordinator	State Department of Health Olympia	753–5871
Aberdeen	St. Joseph's Hospital 1006 North H St.	533–0450
Olympia	St. Peter Hospital 420 S. Sherman St.	352–0301
Pasco	Our Lady of Lourdes Hospital 520 N. 4th Ave.	547–7704
Seattle	Children's Orthopedic Hospital 4800 Sandpoint Way, N.E.	LA 4–4341
Spokane	Deaconess Hospital 800 W. 5th Ave.	RI 7–4811
Tacoma	Mary Bridge Children's Hospital 311 S. L St.	BR 2–1281

| Vancouver | St. Joseph Community Hospital
500 E. 12th St. | 695-4461 |

WEST VIRGINIA

State Coordinator	State Department of Health Charleston	348-2971
Beckley	Beckley Hospital 1007 S. Oakwood Ave.	252-6431
Belle	E. I. DuPont de Nemours & Co.	949-4313
Charleston	Charleston General Hospital Elmwood Ave. & Brook St.	348-6286
	Memorial Hospital 3200 Noyes Ave., S.E.	348-4211
Clarksburg	St. Mary's Hospital Washington & Chestnut Sts.	623-3444
Huntington	Cabell-Huntington Hospital 1340 16th St.	696-6160 696-6161
	St. Mary's Hospital 2900 1st Ave.	696-3762
Martinsburg	King's Daughters Hospital	267-8981
Morgantown	West Virginia University Hospital	293-4451 Night: 293-5341
Parkersburg	Camden-Clark Hospital 717 Ann St.	428-8011
	St. Joseph's Hospital 19th St. & Murdoch Ave.	422-8535
Ronceverte	Greenbrier Valley Hospital 608 Greenbrier Ave.	647-4411 647-4412 647-4413
Weirton	Weirton General Hospital St. John Rd.	748-3232
Weston	Stonewall Jackson Hospital 504 Main	269-3000

CITY	ADDRESS	TELEPHONE
Wheeling	Wheeling Hospital 109 Main St.	233–4455

WISCONSIN

State Coordinator	Department of Health and Social Services Madison	266–1511
Eau Claire	Luther Hospital 310 Chestnut St.	832–6611
Green Bay	Bellin Memorial Hospital 744 S. Webster Ave.	437–9031
Kenosha	Kenosha Hospital 6308 8th Ave.	656–2201
Madison	University Hospital Department of Pharmacology 1300 University Ave.	262–3702
Milwaukee	Milwaukee Children's Hospital 1700 W. Wisconsin	344–7100

WYOMING

State Coordinator	State Department of Public Health Cheyenne	777–7275
Casper	Natrona County Hospital 1233 E. 2nd St.	235–1311
Cheyenne	Laramie County Memorial Hospital 23rd & House Sts.	634–3341

APPENDIX B:
Calorie Chart

Foods with 0–40 Calories

Asparagus
Bouillon
Cabbage
Carbonated beverages, sugarless
    sweeteners
Carbonated water
Carrots
Cauliflower
Celery
Chard
Clear soups (fat-free)
Coffee, black
Cottage cheese, 1 tbs.
Cucumber
Dill pickles
D-Zerta Gelatin
D-Zerta Pudding
Endive
Escarole
Fizzies
Flav-R-Straws
India relish
Jams, 1 tsp.
Jellied clear soups
Lemonade with artificial sweetener
    and 1 oz. lemon juice
Lemon juice or slices
Lettuce
Lime juice or slices
Mineral water
Mustard greens
Olives, 4 green
Parsley
Peppers, red or green
Pickled onions
Pimientos
Postum, black

Radishes
Sauces (Worcestershire, A-1,
    Tabasco)
Sauerkraut, 1 c.
Scallions
Shimmer Low Calorie Gelatin
    Dessert
Squash, summer
Tea, plain
Vinegar
Watercress
Wheat germ
Yeast, brewers', 2 tsps.
Yogurt, 2 tbs.

Beverages, Nondairy

	CALORIES
Apple juice, canned or frozen, 8 oz.	125
Apricot nectar, 8 oz.	170
Carbonated drinks (cola, ginger ale, etc.), 8 oz.	75–95
Cider, sweet, 8 oz.	125
Coconut milk, 8 oz.	60
Coffee, black	0
Coffee with 1 tsp. sugar, 2 tbs. light cream	75
Grapefruit juice, canned, sweetened, 8 oz.	135
Grapefruit juice, fresh, unsweetened canned, or frozen, 8 oz.	100
Grape juice, 8 oz.	160
Lemonade with artificial sweetener and 1 oz. lemon juice, 8 oz.	10
Lemonade with sugar, 8 oz.	105

Orange juice, fresh, unsweetened
canned, or frozen, 8 oz. 110
Pineapple juice, canned or
frozen, 8 oz. 120
Postum, black, 8 oz. 5
Prune juice, 4 oz. 85
Sugarless beverage concentrates,
8 oz. 10
Tea, plain 0
Tomato juice, 8 oz. 50
V-8 juice, 8 oz. 50

Breads and Cakes

	CALORIES
Angel food cake, 2-inch section of 8-inch cake	110
Bagel, 1 medium	125
Biscuit, baking powder, 1	140
Bread crumbs (dry), grated, 1 c.	340
Breads:	
Boston brown, 1 slice, ½ inch thick	70
French, Italian, 1 slice	55
Gluten, 1 slice	20
Raisin, 1 slice	65
Rye, 1 slice	55
White (enriched), 1 slice	65
Whole wheat, 1 slice	55
Brownie, 2-inch square	140
Chocolate layer cake, 2-inch section of 8-inch cake	420
Cinnamon bun with raisins, 1 average	200
Coffee cake with frosting, 1 cake, 4½-inch diameter	195
Corn bread, 2-inch square	140
Cracker meal, 1 tbs.	34
Cruller, sugared, 1 average	160
Cupcake, with frosting, 1 medium	230
Danish pastry, 1 small	140
Doughnuts:	
Jelly center, 1 average	225
Plain, 1 average	135
Spiced or sugared, 1 average	150
Fruitcake, dark, 1 piece, 2 by 2 by ½ inch	105
Gingerbread, 2-inch square	205

Ladyfingers, 1 large 50
Matzo, 6-inch diameter 80
Muffins:
   Bran, 1 average (2¾-inch
    diameter) 105
   Corn, 1 average 125
   English, 1 average 120
   Plain, 1 average 125
Pancake, plain, 4-inch diameter 65
Pancake with ½ tbs. butter, 1 tbs.
   syrup 165
Popover, 1 average 100
Pound cake, 2 by 2 by ½ inch 105
Rolls:
   Enriched, 1 small 40
   Frankfurter, 1 average 85–110
   Hamburger, 1 average 85–130
   Hard, 1 average 95
   Parker House, 1 average 80–85
   Whole wheat, 1 average 100
Sponge cake, 2 by 2 by ½ inch 100
Waffle, plain 5½-inch diameter 230
Waffle, Slim Jim, 1 40
Zwieback, sweetened, 1 piece 35

Cereals, Grains, and Flours

	CALORIES
All-Bran, 1 c.	195
Alpha-Bits, 1 c.	110
Apple Jacks, 1 c.	115
Barley, 2 tbs.	100
Bran Buds, 1 c.	200
Bran Flakes (40%), 1 c.	135
Bran & Prune Flakes, 1 c.	120
Carnation Instant Breakfast with 8 oz. skim milk, 1 envelope	210
Cheerios, 1 c.	100
Cocoa Krispies, 1 c.	115
Cocoa Puffs, 1 c.	110
Corn Bursts, 1 c.	110
Corn Crackos, 1 c.	90
Corn Flakes, 1 c.	80
Corn Flakes & Blueberries, 1 c.	110
Corn Flakes & Strawberries, 1 c.	110
Corn grits (hominy), cooked, 1 c.	125
Cornmeal, cooked, 1 c.	120
Cornstarch, 1 tbs.	30

Cream of Wheat, cooked, 1 c.	135
Farina, cooked, 1 c.	100
Flour:	
Arrowroot, ¼ c.	225
Buckwheat, 1 c. (sifted)	340
Corn, 1 c. (sifted)	405
Rice, 1 c. (sifted)	440
Rye, light, 1 c. (sifted)	285
Soy, low-fat, 1 c.	230
White, all-purpose, 1 c. (sifted)	400
White, all-purpose, 1 tbs.	30
White, cake, 1 c. (sifted)	325
Whole wheat, 1 c. (sifted)	400
Fortified Oat Flakes, 1 c.	165
FrostyO's, 1 c.	155
Fruit Loops, 1 c.	115
Grape-Nuts, 1 c.	400
Hominy, 1 c. (cooked)	125
Honeycomb, 1 c.	80
Kix, 1 c.	100
Krumbles, 1 c.	135
Lucky Charms, 1 c.	85
Muffets, 1 average	85
Oatmeal, cooked, 1 c.	150
Pablum, 1 c.	140
Pep, 1 c.	105
Pettijohns wheat, cooked, 1 c.	145
Product 19, 1 c.	105
Puffa Puffa Rice, 1 c.	120
Puffed Rice, 1 c.	105
Puffed Wheat, 1 c.	150
Quaker Diet Frosted Rice Puffs, 1 c.	55
Quaker Diet Frosted Wheat Puffs, 1 c.	40
Quaker Diet Puffed Rice, 1 c.	45
Quaker Diet Puffed Wheat, 1 c.	40
Quaker Life, 1 c.	150
Raisin Bran, 1 c.	150
Ralston, cooked, 1 c.	125
Rice Chex, 1 c.	100
Rice Krinkles, 1 c.	160
Rice Krispies, 1 c.	110
Shredded Ralston, 1 c.	200
Shredded Wheat, 1 large biscuit	100
Shredded Wheat, Spoon Size, 28 biscuits	108
Special K, 1 c.	75
Stax, 1 c.	115

Sugar Crisp, 1 c.	220
Sugar Frosted Flakes, 1 c.	145
Sugar Pops, 1 c.	110
Sugar Smacks, 1 c.	110
Super Sugar Crisps, 1 c.	150
Tapioca (granulated), 1 tbs. (raw)	35
Toast'em Pop-ups, 1 pop-up	175
Toasties, 1 c.	80
Total, 1 c.	105
Trix, 1 c.	200
Wheat Chex, 1 c.	100
Wheatena, cooked, 1 c.	150
Wheat germ, 1 tbs.	35
Wheaties 1 c.	105

Condiments

	CALORIES
Capers, 1 tbs.	10
Garlic, 1 clove	2
Herbs	0
Horseradish, prepared, 1 tbs.	10
Lemon juice, 1 tbs.	5
Olives, green, 6 small	60
Olives, ripe, 6 small	75
Pickle, dill, 4 inches	10
Salt	0
Spices	0
Tomato catsup, 2 tbs.	30
Vanilla extract, ½ tsp.	5
Vinegar, all types, 1 tbs.	5

Cookies and Crackers

	CALORIES
Animal crackers, 1	10
Arrowroot Biscuits, 1	20
Butter Thins, 1	20
Chocolate chip cookies, 1	55
Chocolate grahams, 1	60
Chocolate snaps, 1	20
Chocolate Wafers, 1	35
Coconut Bar, 1 small	20
Corn Thins, 1	10
Date-Nut Bar, 1	20
Devil's Food Squares, 1	60

Estee Dietetic:

Cheese Thins, 1	5
Chocolate and Vanilla Sandwich, 1	35
Dutch Assorted Cookies, 1	30
Raisinettes, 1	5
Vanilla-Filled Wafers, 1	20
Fig Newtons, 1	55
Fritos Corn Chips, 1 bag (small)	120
Gaiety Creme Sandwich, assorted, 1	110
Gaiety Creme Sandwich, chocolate, 1	110
Ginger cookies, 1	25
Ginger Snaps (Old-Fashion), 1	30
Ginger Snaps (Zu-Zu), 1	15
Graham crackers, 1	35
Graham crackers (Sugar Honey), 1	30
Holland Rusk, 1	55
Lemon Snaps, 1	15
Lorna Doone Shortbread, 1	40
Macaroons, 1	105
Mallomars Chocolate Cakes, 1	60
Malted Milk Wafers, 1	20
Mello Squares, 1	60
Mickey Mouse Cookies, 1	10
Oatmeal cookies, 1	115
Oreo Creme Sandwich, 1	60
Oyster Crackers, 1	5
Oysterettes, 5	20
Peanut Cheese Sandwich, 1	35
Potato chip, 1 (2-inch diameter)	10
Pretzel, 1 medium	75
Raisin Fruit Biscuit, 1	55
Ritz Cheese Crackers, 1	20
Ritz Crackers, 1	15
Ry-Krisp, 1 double square	20
Saltina Biscuit, 1	15
Saltines, 1	20
Saltines (Snow Flake), 1	15
Social Tea Biscuit, 1	20
Soda Cracker, 1, 2½-inch diameter	25
Sugar Wafers (vanilla), 1	30
Trentores, 1	25
Triangle Thins, 1	10
Triscuit, 1	25
Uneeda Biscuit, 1	25
Uneeda Lunch Biscuit, 1	15
Waverly Wafers, 1	20

Wheat Thins, 1	10
Whole Wheat Wafers, 1	20
Wuests Gluten-Nut Wafers, 1	75

Dairy Products

	CALORIES
Butter, 1 tsp.	30
Butter, whipped, 1 tsp.	20
Cheeses:	
Bacon processed spread (Kraft), 1 oz. (2 tbs.)	95
Bleu, 1 oz.	105
Camembert, 1 oz.	85
Cheddar (American), 1 oz.	110
Cheddar (American), grated, 1 tbs.	30
Cheez Whiz (Kraft), 1 tbs.	45
Cottage, all types, 1 oz.	30
Cream, 1 oz.	110
Edam, 1 oz.	90
Limburger, 1 oz.	95
Neufchâtel, 1 oz.	70
Old English processed spread (Kraft), 1 oz.	100
Olive Pimento spread (Kraft), 1 oz.	65
Parmesan, grated, 1 tbs.	25
Pimento spread (Kraft), 1 oz.	70
Pineapple spread (Kraft), 1 oz.	70
Provolone, 1 oz.	50
Relish spread (Kraft), 1 oz.	70
Roka Blue (Kraft), 1 oz.	100
Roquefort, 1 oz.	100
Swiss, 1 oz.	105
Velveeta, 1 oz.	92
Cream:	
Heavy (40%), 1 tbs.	50
Light (20%), sweet or sour, 1 tbs.	30
Eggs:	
Boiled, 1	75
Fried, with 1 tsp. margarine, 1	110
Poached, 1	75
White only, 1	15
Whole, raw, 1	75
Yolk only, 1	60
Margarine, 1 tsp.	30

Margarine, whipped, 1 tsp.	20
Milk:	
Buttermilk, 8 oz.	86
Condensed, 4 oz.	490
Evaporated, 4 oz.	175
Evaporated skim, 4 oz.	90
Goat's, 8 oz.	165
Nonfat dry, 1 tbs.	25
Nonfat liquid (fortified or modified), 8 oz.	100
Whole, 8 oz.	160
Milk and cream substitutes:	
Coffee-mate, 1 tsp.	11
Kreemit, 1 tsp.	7
Perx, 1 tsp.	8
Milk drinks:	
Cocomalt (all milk), 8 oz.	280
Cocoa (whole milk), 6 oz.	175
Cocoa (with 3 oz. skim milk and water), 6 oz.	115
Eggnog (all milk, without liquor), 8 oz.	235
Hot chocolate (whole milk), 6 oz.	210
Hot chocolate (skim milk), 6 oz.	145
Hot chocolate (all water, with 1 tbs. whipped cream), 6 oz.	135
Milk, chocolate, 8 oz.	185
Milk shake (fountain), 8 oz.	350
Ovaltine (whole milk), 8 oz.	220
Ovaltine, chocolate (whole milk), 8 oz.	250
Soda, ice-cream, 8 oz.	255
Yogurt, plain (whole milk), 8 oz.	160

Fats, Oils, and Dressings and Mayonnaise

	CALORIES
Bacon fat, 1 tbs.	125
Boiled dressing (homemade), 1 tbs.	30
Chef Style Dressing (Ann Page low calorie), 1 tbs.	18
Chicken fat, 1 tbs.	125
Chili sauce, 1 tbs.	17
French dressing (commercial), 1 tbs.	55

Lard, 1 tbs.	125
Low-calorie French dressings, 1 tbs.	9–15
Low-calorie mayonnaises, 1 tbs.	10–25
Mayonnaise (commercial), 1 tbs.	100
Oil (olive, corn, or peanut), 1 tbs.	100
Seven Seas Low Calorie Dressing, 1 tbs.	15
Suet, rendered, 1 tbs.	120
Vegetable shortenings, 1 tbs.	110

Fish

	CALORIES
Anchovies, 5 thin fillets	35
Bass, baked without butter or oil, 1 serving (4 oz.)	285
Bluefish, broiled with 1 tbs. butter or oil, 1 serving	270
Brook trout, broiled, 1 serving	175
Butterfish, fried, 1 serving	215
Caviar, 1 tbs.	100
Clams, raw, 1 serving	80
Codfish cakes, 2 balls or 1 large cake	200
Crab, soft-shell, raw, 1	75
Crab meat, canned, 1 serving	75
Eel, fresh, 1 serving	180
Fish sticks, homemade, breaded, 5 sticks	200
Flounder, baked, 1 serving	100
Haddock, fried, 1 serving	200
Halibut steak, 1 serving	125
Herring, fresh, 1 serving	165
Herring, pickled, 1 serving	360
Lake trout, broiled, 1 serving	225
Lobster meat, fresh, 1 serving	125
Mackerel, broiled, 1 serving	225
Oysters, raw, 6 to 10	80
Perch, fried, 1 serving	280
Porgy, baked, 1 serving	100
Porgy, fried, 1 serving	200
Salmon, canned, 1 serving	100
Salmon, smoked, 2 to 3 small slices	90
Salmon steak, baked, 1 serving	200
Sardines, 1	35

Scallops, raw, 5 to 6 medium	100
Shad, broiled, 1 serving	250
Shad, raw, 1 serving	190
Shad roe, baked, 1 serving	260
Shrimp, fresh or canned, 4 to 6	65
Shrimp cocktail, 1 tbs. sauce, 4 to 6 shrimp	90
Smelts, baked, 1 serving	200
Sole, baked, 1 serving	100
Swordfish, broiled, 1 serving	300
Tuna, canned in oil, drained, 1 serving	150
Tuna, Chicken-of-the-Sea chunk pack, 1 serving	150
Tuna, Chicken-of-the-Sea Dietetic Chunk White, 1 serving	90
Tuna, Star-Kist chunk pack, 1 serving	155
Whitefish, baked, 1 serving	155

Fruits (Canned, Frozen, and Raw)

	CALORIES
Apple, 1 medium	75
Apple, baked, with 2 tbs. sugar, 1 large	200
Applesauce, artificially sweetened, ½ c.	50
Applesauce, canned, with sugar, ½ c.	150
Apricots, canned, with 2 tbs. syrup, 4 halves	100
Apricots (Diet Delight), ½ c.	45
Apricots, dried, 4 to 6 halves	80
Apricots, raw, 2 medium	40
Avocado pear, ½ medium	245
Banana, 1 average	130
Blackberries, fresh, ½ c.	40
Blueberries, fresh, ½ c.	40
Cantaloupe, ½ melon, 5-inch diameter	50
Cherries, canned, with syrup, ½ c.	105
Cherries, fresh, 15 large	75
Cherries, Maraschino, 1	20
Cranberries, ½ c.	25
Cranberry sauce, 1 rounded tbs.	40
Cranberry Sauce (Ocean Spray Low Calorie), 1 rounded tbs.	25

Currants, red, raw, ½ c.	30
Dates, dried, pitted, 3 to 4	85
Figs, dried, 1 large	65
Figs, raw, 1 large	20
Fruit cocktail, canned, ½ c.	100
Fruit Cocktail (Diet Delight), ½ c.	40
Grapefruit, canned, ½ c.	90
Grapefruit (Diet Delight), ½ c.	35
Grapefruit, fresh, ½ medium	50
Grapes, seedless, 30 (¼ lb.)	35
Grapes, Tokay or black, 30	85
Honeydew melon, ½ melon, 5-inch diameter	65
Lemon, 1 medium	30
Lime, 1 medium	30
Loganberries, fresh, ½ c.	45
Nectarine, 1 medium	30
Orange, 1 medium	70
Orange segments, ½ c.	45
Peach, fresh, 1 medium	45
Peaches, canned, with 1 tbs. syrup, 2 halves	70
Peaches (Diet Delight), ½ c.	30
Peaches, frozen, ½ c.	106
Pear, fresh, 1 medium	60
Pears, canned, with 1 tbs. syrup, 2 halves	100
Pears (Diet Delight), ½ c.	35
Pineapple, canned, with 1 tbs. light syrup, 1 slice	80
Pineapple (Dole Low Calorie), ½ c.	60
Pineapple, fresh, sliced, ½ c.	60
Plums, canned, with 1 tbs. syrup, 2 medium	75
Plums, fresh, 2 medium	50
Prunes, cooked, no sugar, with own liquid, 4 to 5	75
Prunes, cooked, with sugar and lemon, 4 to 5	200
Prunes, dried, 1 large	25
Raisins, seeded, dried, ½ c.	215
Raisins, seedless, dried, 4 tbs.	215
Red raspberries, fresh, ½ c.	45
Red raspberries, frozen, ½ c.	120
Rhubarb, artificially sweetened, ½ c.	25
Rhubarb, sweetened with sugar, ½ c.	135
Strawberries, fresh, ½ c.	25

Strawberries, frozen, $\frac{1}{2}$ c.	115
Tangerine, 1 large	45
Watermelon, $\frac{3}{4}$ by 10 inches	100
Watermelon, cubed, $\frac{1}{2}$ c.	30

Ice Creams, Ices, and Sherbets

	CALORIES
Banana split, Royal, large	1150
Cone, unfilled	45
Frozen custard, 1 scoop or $\frac{1}{2}$ c.	150
Ice cream, all flavors, 1 scoop or $\frac{1}{2}$ c.	150
Ice cream, Dixie cup, 1	145
Ice cream sandwich, 1	255
Ice milk, all flavors, 1 scoop or $\frac{1}{2}$ c.	140
Ices, all flavors, 1 scoop or $\frac{1}{2}$ c.	115
Sherbet, all flavors, 1 scoop or $\frac{1}{2}$ c.	120
Sundaes, all flavors	330–350

Meats and Poultry

	CALORIES
Beef:	
Brisket, 1 slice	110
Chipped beef, creamed, $\frac{1}{2}$ c.	210
Chipped beef, dried, 6 slices (4 by 5 inches)	210
Chuck, pot-roasted, 1 slice (2 by $1\frac{1}{2}$ by $\frac{1}{2}$ inch)	95
Flank, 1 slice (4 by $2\frac{1}{2}$ by $\frac{1}{2}$ inch)	250
Ground beef, broiled, $\frac{1}{4}$ lb.	225
Hamburger (top round), no visible fat, $\frac{1}{4}$ lb.	195
Pie, frozen, 1 pie	430–530
Porterhouse steak, $\frac{1}{3}$ lb.	515
Roast beef, 1 slice (3 by $2\frac{1}{2}$ by $\frac{1}{4}$ inch)	95
Roast beef, trimmed, lean only, 2 slices (3 by $2\frac{1}{2}$ by $\frac{1}{4}$ inch)	70
Round of beef, 1 cube (4 by $2\frac{1}{2}$ by $\frac{3}{8}$ inch)	215
Rump, pot-roasted, 1 slice (5 by $3\frac{1}{2}$ by $\frac{1}{4}$ inch)	320
Shank (soup meat), 1 cube (3 by $2\frac{1}{2}$ by $\frac{3}{8}$ inch)	170
Sirloin steak, 1 cube (4 by $2\frac{1}{4}$ by 1 inch)	250
Stew, with carrots, onions, & tomatoes, 1 c.	260
Lamb:	
Chop, loin, 1	105
Chop, loin, lean only, 1	65
Chop, rib, 1	130
Chop, rib, lean only, 1	50
Chop, shoulder, 1	215
Leg, roasted, 3 slices (3 by 3 by $\frac{1}{4}$ inches)	250
Stew, with onions & potatoes, 1 c.	250
Pork:	
Bacon, 2 strips	100
Bacon, Canadian (lean), 2 slices	70
Chop, loin, fried, 1 medium	235
Ham, deviled, 1 rounded tbs.	95
Ham, fresh (cooked), 1 slice (2 by $1\frac{1}{2}$ by 1 inch)	125
Ham, smoked (cooked), 1 slice (3 by 2 by $\frac{1}{2}$ inch)	125
Ham, spiced, canned, 1 slice	125
Pork loin, roasted, 1 slice (3 by $2\frac{1}{2}$ by $\frac{1}{4}$ inch)	100
Pork roast, with fat, 4 oz.	300–600
Sausage, 3 inches	95
Spareribs, roasted, 6 average ribs	250
Poultry:	
Chicken, broiled or fried with 1 tbs. oil, 4 oz.	250
Chicken, creamed, 1 c.	415
Chicken, hen, stewed, 3 slices	245
Chicken, roasted, 3 slices ($3\frac{1}{2}$ by $2\frac{1}{2}$ by $\frac{1}{4}$ inch)	200
Chicken breast, fried with 1 tbs. oil, 4 oz.	290
Chicken leg, 5 oz.	160
Chicken pie with peas & potatoes, 2-inch square	230
Chicken salad with 1 tbs. mayonnaise, 4 oz.	225
Duck, roasted, 1 small slice	200
Turkey, roasted, 3 slices ($3\frac{1}{2}$ by $2\frac{1}{2}$ by $\frac{1}{4}$ inch)	200
TV dinners (complete):	
Beef, 1 dinner	350

Chicken, 1 dinner	540
Chopped sirloin, 1 dinner	485
Ham, 1 dinner	310
Meat loaf, 1 dinner	370
Turkey, 1 dinner	315
Variety meats:	
Brains, calves', 2 pieces (2½ by 1½ by ⅞ inch)	125
Kidneys, beef, 3 slices (3 by 2½ by ¼ inch)	140
Liver, beef, 2 slices (3 by 2¼ by ⅜ inch)	170
Liver, calves', 2 slices (3 by 2¼ by ⅜ inch)	150
Liver, chicken, 1 medium	75
Tongue, beef, 3 slices (3 by 2 by ⅛ inch)	160
Veal:	
Breast, stewed with gravy, 1 c.	255
Chop, lean, ½ lb. raw	150
Cutlet, breaded, 3½ by 2½ by ½ inch	215
Stew, with carrots & onions, 1 c.	240
Other:	
Bologna, 1 slice, 5-inch diameter, ⅛ inch thick	65
Chili con carne, 6 oz.	530
Chow Mein, 1 serving	300
Corned beef, boiled, 3 thin slices	100
Corned beef hash, ½ c.	230
Frankfurter, 5½-inch long	125
Liverwurst, 1 slice, 3-inch diameter, ¼ inch thick	80
Luncheon meat (Spam, etc.), 1 slice	80
Meat loaf, 1 slice (4 by 2 by ½ inch)	115
Salami, 1 slice, 4-inch diameter, ⅛-inch thick	70
Tamales with sauce, ¼ can	155

Almonds, salted, 12 to 15 medium	95
Brazil nuts, 1	50
Butternuts, 1	20
Cashew nuts, 1	10
Chestnuts, 1	10
Coconut, 1 by ½ by ½ inch	35
Filberts, 1	10
Hickory nuts, 1	5
Litchi nuts, 1	5
Mixed nuts, 8 to 12	95
Peanut butter, 1 tbs.	100
Peanuts, 1	5
Pecans, shelled, each half	10
Pine nuts (pignolias), 1	5
Pistachio nuts, 1	5
Walnuts, black, 2 tbs., chopped	95
Walnuts, English, 1	10
Walnuts, plain, 1	10
Water chestnuts, 1	5

Pasta, Pizza, and Rice

	CALORIES
Macaroni, 1 c.	210
Macaroni (Buitoni), 1 c.	190
Macaroni and Cheese (Stouffer's, frozen), 1 c.	370
Macaroni and cheese, decalorized, 1 c.	175
Noodles, 1 c.	120
Noodles and Chicken (Stouffer's, frozen), 1 c.	105
Pizza, cheese, ⅛-inch slice of 14-inch pie	185
Ravioli, cheese, with sauce, 8 squares	725
Rice, white, 1 c.	135
Spaghetti, 1 c.	160

Nuts

	CALORIES
Almonds, 1	5
Almonds, chocolate, 5 medium or 8 small	85

Pies

	CALORIES
Apple, ⅙ of medium pie (8-inch diameter)	375
Apple, Slim Jim, 1 pie	125

Apricot, ⅙ of medium pie	390
Banana cream, ⅙ of medium pie	400
Blackberry, ⅙ of medium pie	365
Blueberry, ⅙ of medium pie	370
Blueberry, Slim Jim, 1 pie	115
Cherry, ⅙ of medium pie	370
Chocolate, ⅙ of medium pie	295
Coconut custard, ⅙ of medium pie	310
Cream, ⅙ of medium pie	300
Custard, ⅙ of medium pie	265
Lemon chiffon, with crumb crust, ⅙ of medium pie	210
Lemon meringue, ⅙ of medium pie	280
Mince, ⅙ of medium pie	400
Peach, ⅙ of medium pie	405
Pecan, ⅙ of medium pie	570
Pineapple, ⅙ of medium pie	400
Pineapple cheese, ⅙ of medium pie	365
Pumpkin, ⅙ of medium pie	330
Raisin, ⅙ of medium pie	435
Shoofly, ⅙ of medium pie	440
Strawberry, 1 crust, ⅙ of medium pie	275
Strawberry cream, ⅙ of medium pie	405

Puddings

	CALORIES
Apple Brown Betty, ½ c.	255
Apple dumpling, 1 medium	345
Apple snow, ½ c.	75
Apricot whip, ½ c.	100
Banana custard, ½ c.	125
Banana whip, ½ c.	85
Bavarian cream, orange, ½ c.	290
Blancmange, ½ c.	150
Bread pudding with raisins, ½ c.	210
Butterscotch pudding, instant (Jell-O), 1 serving (4 in pkg.)	190
Chocolate pudding, ½ c.	220
Chocolate pudding, instant (Jell-O), 1 serving (4 in pkg.)	205
Custard, baked, 1 custard c.	205
Custard, boiled, ½ c.	165
D-Zerta:	
Chocolate (with skim milk), ½ c.	55
Chocolate (with coffee), ½ c.	15

Other pudding flavors, with water, ½ c.	15
Gelatins, fruit flavors, ½ c.	10
Floating island, ½ c.	150
Gelatin, dry, 1 tbs.	35
Jell-O, plain, ½ c.	65
Jell-O, with 1 tbs. whipped cream, ½ c.	120
Junket, ½ c.	105
Lemon sponge pudding, ½ c.	115
Rice pudding, baked, with raisins, ½ c.	170
Shimmer (low-calorie gelatin dessert), ½ c.	10
Tapioca, ½ c.	135

Soups

	CALORIES
Beef noodle (Campbell's), ¾ c.	50
Beef with vegetables (Heinz), ¾ c.	61–77
Bouillon, beef, canned, ¾ c.	25
Celery, cream of (Campbell's), ¾ c.	145
Chicken, cream of (Campbell's), ¾ c.	145
Chicken gumbo (Campbell's), ¾ c.	50
Chicken noodle (Campbell's), ¾ c.	140
Clam chowder (Heinz), ¾ c.	65
Consommé, chicken, canned, ¾ c.	25
Instant bouillon cubes:	
Beef (Herb-Ox), 1 cube	10
Chicken (Herb-Ox), 1 cube	15
Chicken (MBT), 1 cube	10
Onion (Herb-Ox), 1 cube	15
Vegetable (Herb-Ox), 1 cube	10
Madrilène, jellied, 1 serving	20
Mushroom, cream of (Heinz), ¾ c.	170
Onion (Campbell's), ¾ c.	65
Pea soup (Heinz), ¾ c.	75
Tomato, cream of (Campbell's), ¾ c.	120
Vegetable beef (Campbell's), ¾ c.	75

Sugar and Sweetening Agents

	CALORIES
Honey, 1 tbs.	60

Karo, 1 tbs.	60
Maple syrup, 1 tbs.	50
Molasses, 1 tbs.	45
Sorghum, 1 tbs.	50
Sugar, brown, 1 tbs.	50
Sugar, powdered white, 1 tbs.	40
Sugar, white granulated, 1 tbs.	50
Sugar replacements (non-cyclamate):	
Pillsbury's Sweet 10 liquid	0
Saccharin	0
Sucaryl (liquid)	0
Sucaryl, granulated, 1 packet	4
Sweet 'n Low, granulated, 1 packet	3.5
Sweet 'n Low sugar substitute, 1 tsp.	15
Sugar Twin, granulated, 1 packet	1.5

Sweets

	CALORIES
Almond Joy, 1 bar (2 pieces)	295
Apple butter, 1 tbs.	40
Baby Ruth, 1 bar	140
Bar candy (average, including nut and peanut bar), 1 bar	270
Butterscotch, 1 average piece	20
Caramels, 1 medium	50
Chewing gum, 1 stick	4–5
Chewing gum (artificially sweetened), 1 stick	0
Chocolate cream, 1 average	55
Chocolate kisses, 1 kiss	20
Chocolate marshmallow, 1 average	45
Clark, 1 bar	135
Fondant, 1 average	40
Forever Yours, 1 bar	120
Fruit drops (Estee Dietetic), 1 drop	5
Fudge, chocolate, 1¼-inch square	120
Good and Plenty, 1 piece	5
Gumdrops, 1 large or 8 small	35
Hard candy, 2 pieces	40
Jam or jelly, 1 tbs.	55
Jam (Louis Sherry Low Calorie), 1 tsp.	1
Jelly beans, 10 jelly beans	65

Jujubes, assorted flavors, 1 oz. box	60
Krackle (Hershey's), 1 bar	130
Life Savers, 1	6–10
Lollipop, 2¼-inch diameter	110
Maple sugar, 1 piece (small)	50
Mars, 1 bar	175
Marshmallows, 1 average	25
Mason, all types, 1 small box	100
Milk chocolate (Estee Dietetic), 1 section	15
Milk chocolate (Hershey's), 1 bar (small)	155
Milky Way, 1 bar	120
Mints, chocolate, 1 medium	85
M & M's, 1 oz. bag	140
Mounds, 1 bar (2 pieces)	320
Mr. Goodbar (Hershey's), 1 bar	160
Necco Wafers, 1 roll	200
Oh Henry, 1 bar	200
Orange peel, candied, 1 piece	30
Peanut brittle, 2½-inch square	110
Popcorn (popped), with 1 tsp. butter, 1 c.	55
Semi-Sweet Chocolate (Hershey's), 1 bar	160
Semi-Sweet Chocolate Bits (Nestlé's), 1 bit	3
Snickers, 1 bar	125

Toppings

	CALORIES
Betty Crocker Fluffy White frosting mix, 1 tbs.	10
Coconut, shredded, 1 tbs.	40
Dream Whip Dessert Topping, 1 tbs.	40
Lucky Whip, 1 tbs.	20
Qwip, 1 tbs.	30
Reddi Wip, 1 tbs.	30
Top Wip, 1 tbs.	15

Vegetables

	CALORIES
Artichokes, 1 large head	50

Asparagus, 6 spears	25	Okra, 8 pods	30
Baked beans, pork and molasses,		Onions, raw, 1 medium	45
½ c.	160	Onions, young green, no tops,	
Baked beans, pork and tomato		6 small	25
sauce, ½ c.	150	Parsley, raw, 2 sprigs	1
Bamboo shoots, ½ c.	15	Parsnips, ½ c.	45
Bean sprouts, ½ c.	15	Peas, dried, cooked, ½ c.	175
Beans, green, ½ c.	20	Peas, fresh, ½ c.	65
Beans, red kidney, ½ c.	115	Peppers, green, raw, seeded,	
Beans, wax, ½ c.	15	1 medium	20
Beets, diced, ½ c.	35	Pimientos, canned, 1 medium	10
Broccoli, 1 stalk (5½ inches long)		Pinto beans, ½ c.	120
or chopped, ½ c.	25	Potato chip, 1 (2-inch diameter)	10
Brussels sprouts, 9 medium	50	Potatoes, baked, 1 medium	100
Cabbage, ½ c.	20	Potatoes, French-fried, ½ c.	240
Cabbage, shredded, raw, ½ c.	10	Potatoes, mashed, with milk and	
Carrots, diced, ½ c.	25	butter, ½ c.	125
Carrots, raw, 1 average (5 inches)	20	Potatoes, sweet, baked, 1 medium	200
Cauliflower, ½ c.	15	Potatoes, sweet, candied, 2 halves	360
Celery, raw, 1 stalk (5 inches)	5	Potatoes, white, boiled, 1 small	120
Chard, ½ c.	15	Pumpkin, canned, ½ c.	35
Chicory or curly endive, 15 to 20		Radishes, raw, 2 small	5
medium leaves	10	Rice, cooked, 1 c.	200
Collards, ½ c.	40	Rutabagas, ½ c.	40
Corn, ½ c. or 1 ear (5 inches)	85	Sauerkraut, canned, ½ c.	15
Cucumber, ½ medium	5	Scallions, 5 average	20
Eggplant, 2 slices or ½ c.	25	Spinach, ½ c.	25
Endive, 1 oz.	5	Spinach soufflé, ½ c.	160
Escarole, 4 small leaves	5	Squash, summer, ½ c.	15
Garlic, 2 cloves	5	Squash, winter, ½ c.	50
Greens, beet or turnip, ½ c.	25	Succotash, frozen, ½ c.	135
Kale, ½ c.	20	Tomatoes, ½ c.	25
Kohlrabi, ½ c.	25	Tomatoes, cherry, 8 to 10	30
Leeks, 3 to 4	40	Tomatoes, raw, 1 medium	30
Lentils, ½ c.	100	Tomatoes, pureed, canned, ½ c.	45
Lettuce, 3 small leaves	5	Turnips, diced, ½ c.	20
Lima beans, ½ c.	75	Watercress, 10 sprigs	2
Mushrooms, no oil, 10 small or		Yams in skins, ½ c.	225
4 large	15		

APPENDIX C:
Genetic Counseling Services in the United States, Canada, England, and Australia*

UNITED STATES

Alabama

Laboratory of Medical Genetics
University of Alabama Medical Center
Birmingham 35233

Alaska

Public Health Service
Arctic Health Research Center
College 99701

Arizona

Genetic Counseling Center
St. Joseph's Hospital
P.O. Box 2071
Phoenix 85001

Department of Zoology
Arizona State University
Tempe 85281

Arkansas

Birth Defects Center
University of Arkansas
4301 Markham
Little Rock 72201

California

Kern County Health Department
Bakersfield 93305

Department of Zoology
University of California
Berkeley 94720

Department of Medical Genetics
City of Hope Medical Center
Duarte 91010

Fresno County Health Department
515 S. Cedar Ave.
Fresno 93702

Department of Pediatrics
University of California at Irvine
Irvine 92650

Medical Genetics Unit or Biochemical
   Genetics Laboratory
University of California School of Medicine
La Jolla 92037

Genetics Research & Chromosome Service
Department of Pediatrics
Loma Linda University Medical Center
Loma Linda 92354

Departments of Pediatrics and Biochemistry
Children's Hospital
Los Angeles 90054

---

* Derived from *The International Directory of Genetic Services*, 3rd ed., compiled by Henry T. Lynch, M.D., eds., Daniel Bergsma, M.D., and Henry T. Lynch, M.D. The National Foundation-March of Dimes, 1971.

L.A. County-USC Medical Center
Genetics Birth Defects Center
1200 N. State St.
Los Angeles 90033

Department of Medicine & Pediatrics
UCLA School of Medicine
760 Westwood Pl.
Los Angeles 90024

Department of Pediatrics
USC Medical School
1200 N. State St.
Los Angeles 90033

Departments of Pediatrics and Medicine
University of California
Center for Health Sciences
Los Angeles 90024

Department of Pediatrics & Genetics
Kaiser Foundation Hospital
280 W. MacArthur Blvd.
Oakland 94611

Department of Birth Defects
Children's Hospital Medical Center
Oakland 94609

Ross General Hospital
1150 Sir Francis Drake Blvd.
Ross 94957

Birth Defects Center
Sacramento Medical Center
2315 Stockton Blvd.
Sacramento 95817

Department of Pediatrics
St. Benardine's Hospital
San Bernardino 92404

Mercy Hospital-Medical Center Clinic
4077 Fifth Ave.
San Diego 92103

Birth Defects Center
Children's Health Center
San Diego 92123

University Hospital
San Diego County
P.O. Box 3548
San Diego 92103

Department of Pediatrics
University of California
San Francisco Medical Center
San Francisco 94122

Santa Barbara County Health
   Department
4440 Calle Real
Santa Barbara 93105

Kaiser Hospital Pediatric Clinic
900 Kiely Blvd.
Santa Clara 95051

St. John's Hospital
1328 22nd St.
Santa Monica 90404

Department of Pediatrics
Stanford University Medical Center
Birth Defects Clinic
Stanford 94305

Division of Medical Genetics
Harbor General Hospital
1000 W. Carson St.
Torrance 90509

Ventura County Health Department
Ventura 93001

Colorado

Department of Pediatrics
University of Colorado
4200 E. 9th Ave.
Denver 80220

Presbyterian Medical Center
Department of Pathology
Denver 80218

Connecticut

Department of Health
Connecticut Twin Registry
79 Elm St.
Hartford 06115

Department of Pediatrics and Medicine
Yale Medical School
New Haven 06520

Department of Cytogenetics
P.O. Box 308
New England Institute for Medical Research
Ridgefield 06877

District of Columbia

Department of Obstetrics & Gynecology
Columbia Hospital for Women
2324 L St. N.W.
Washington 20037

Medical Genetics Unit or Department of
    Pediatrics
Howard University
College of Medicine
Washington 20001

Departments of Pediatrics and Obstetrics
Georgetown University Hospital
3800 Reservoir Rd. N.W.
Washington 20007

Malcolm Grow USAF Medical Center
Human Genetics Service
Washington 20231

Reproductive Genetics Unit
George Washington University Clinic
2150 Pennsylvania Ave. N.W.
Washington 20037

Genetic Counseling & Research Center
George Washington University Hospital
Washington 20037

Department of Neurology
Children's Hospital
2125 13th St. N.W.
Washington 20009

Florida

Department of Medicine
University of Florida
Gainesville 32601

Birth Defects Center
J. Hillis Miller Health Center
Gainesville 32601

Department of Pediatrics
University of Miami Child Development
    Center
1150 N.W. 14th St.
Miami 33136

Georgia

Department of Psychiatry
Emory University
Georgia Mental Health Institute
Atlanta 30306

Division of Prenatal Pathology
Emory University School of Medicine
80 Butler St. S.E.
Atlanta 30303

St. Joseph's Hospital
Department of Pathology
265 Ivy St. N.E.
Atlanta 30303

Department of Endocrinology
Medical College of Georgia
Augusta 30902

Central State Hospital
Milledgeville 31062

Hawaii

Department of Birth Defects
Kauikeolani Children's Hospital
Honolulu 96817

Population Genetics Laboratory
University of Hawaii
2411 Dole St.
Honolulu 96822

Idaho

Idaho Mental Retardation Program
Boise 83701

Mental Retardation Program
Idaho State School & Hospital
Box 47
Nampa 83651

Illinois

Amniocentesis Service
Michael Reese Hospital & Medical Center
530 E. 31st St.
Chicago 60616

University of Chicago
Department of Obstetrics & Gynecology
5841 S. Maryland Ave.
Chicago 60637

Department of Pediatrics
University of Chicago
950 E. 59th St.
Chicago 60637

Presbyterian-St. Luke's Hospital
1753 W. Congress Parkway
Chicago 60091

Department of Experimental Pathology
Mount Sinai Hospital Medical Center
Chicago 60608

Department of Genetics
Children's Memorial Hospital
Chicago 60614

Department of Pediatrics
Cook County Hospital
700 S. Wood St.
Chicago 60612

Illinois State Pediatric Institute
1640 W. Roosevelt Rd.
Chicago 60608

Department of Research
Evanston Hospital
2650 Ridge Ave.
Evanston 60201

Department of Pediatrics
Loyola Medical Center
Hines 60141

Department of Zoology
University of Illinois
Urbana 61801

Indiana

Department of Medical Genetics
Indiana University Medical School
Indianapolis 46207

Iowa

Department of Pediatrics
University Hospital
Iowa City 52240

Kansas

Department of Medicine
Kansas University Medical Center
Kansas City University 66103

Department of Clinical Pathology
Wesley Medical Research Foundation
Wichita 67214

Kentucky

Department of Pediatrics
University of Kentucky Medical Center
Lexington 40506

Child Evaluation Center
University of Louisville Medical School
540 S. Preston St.
Louisville 40202

Louisiana

Birth Defects Center
Department of Pediatrics
LSU School of Medicine in Shreveport
Shreveport 71101

Department of Anatomy
Tulane University
New Orleans 70112

Pediatrics-Heritable Disease Center
LSU School of Medicine
1542 Tulane Ave.
New Orleans 70112

Maryland

Department of Pediatrics
Sinai Hospital
Baltimore 21215

The Moore Clinic
The Johns Hopkins Hospital
Baltimore 21205

Human Genetics Laboratory
John F. Kennedy Institute
707 N. Broadway
Baltimore 21205

Massachusetts

Birth Defects Center
20 Ash St.
Boston 02115

Clinical Genetics Division
Children's Hospital Medical Center
Boston 02115

Department of Pediatrics
Massachusetts General Hospital
Boston 02114

Department of Pediatrics
Massachusetts General Hospital
Fruit St.
Waltham 02114

Michigan

Department of Human Genetics
University of Michigan
Ann Arbor 48108

Department of Pediatrics
University of Michigan Medical Center
Ann Arbor 48104

Department of Biology
University of Detroit
Detroit 48221

Department of Pediatrics
Henry Ford Hospital
2799 W. Grand Blvd.
Detroit 48202

Blodgett Memorial Hospital
Pediatric Neuro-Muscular Disease Clinic
1810 Wealthy S.E.
Grand Rapids 49506

Department of Zoology
Michigan State University
Lansing 48901

Lapeer State Home & Training School
Medical Department
Lapeer 48466

Department of Mental Health
Plymouth St. Home & Training School
Northville 48167

Minnesota

Dight Institute for Human Genetics
University of Minnesota
Minneapolis 55455

Human Genetics Unit
Minnesota Department of Health
Minneapolis 55440

Medical Genetics Division
Department of Laboratory Medicine
University of Minnesota Hospital
Minneapolis 55415

Genetics Consulting Service
Mayo Clinic
Rochester 55901

Mississippi

Department of Preventive Medicine
University of Mississippi Medical Center
Jackson 39216

Missouri

Department of Pediatrics
University of Missouri Medical Center
Columbia 65201

Neurology Department
Children's Mercy Hospital
Kansas City 64108

Cardinal Glennon Hospital
1465 S. Grand Blvd.
St. Louis 63104

Division of Medical Genetics
Department of Pediatrics & Medicine
Washington University Medical School
St. Louis 63110

Montana

None

Nebraska

University of Nebraska Medical Center
42nd & Dewey Ave.
Omaha 68105

Department of Preventive Medicine
Creighton University School of Medicine
Omaha 68131

Birth Defects Clinic
Children's Memorial Hospital
Omaha 68105

New Hampshire

Departments of Pathology & Medicine
Dartmouth Medical School
Hanover 03755

New Jersey

Hackensack Hospital Association
Child Evaluation Center
243 Atlantic St.
Hackensack 07602

Department of Pediatrics
College of Medicine of New Jersey at Newark
100 Bergen St.
Newark 07103

New Mexico

Department of Pathology
University of New Mexico Medical School
Albuquerque 87106

New York

N.Y. State Department of Health
Birth Defects Institute
Albany Medical College
Department of Pediatrics, Room K116
Albany 12208

Downstate Medical Center
Department of Pediatrics
450 Clarkson Ave.
Brooklyn 11203

Pediatric Service
Coney Island Hospital
Ocean Parkway and Ave. Z
Brooklyn 11235

Department of Pediatrics
Jewish Hospital & Medical Center of
    Brooklyn
Brooklyn 11238

Department of Medicine
Buffalo General Hospital
100 High St.
Buffalo 14203

Department of Pediatrics
State University of New York
Children's Hospital
Buffalo 14222

Genetics Unit, Pediatrics Clinic
Meadowbrook Hospital
P.O. Box 175
East Meadow 11554

Medical Services Division
Creedmoor Institute, Station 60
Jamaica 11427

Genetics Laboratory
North Shore Hospital
Manhasset 11030

Human Genetics (Medicine)
New York-Cornell Medical Center
525 E. 68th St.
New York 10021

Department of Pathology
N.Y. Medical College-Metropolitan Hospital
97 St. & 1st Ave.
New York 10029

The New York Blood Center
310 E. 67th St.
New York 10021

Department of Pediatrics
Mount Sinai School of Medicine
New York 10029

Medical Genetics
Beth Israel Medical Center
10 Nathan D. Perlman Pl.
New York 10003

Genetic Counseling Program
Albert Einstein College of Medicine
Bronx Municipal Hospital Center
New York 10461

Department of Pediatrics & Genetics
Hospital for Joint Diseases
1919 Madison Ave.
New York 10035

Department of Medical Genetics
N.Y. State Psychiatric Institute
New York 10032

Cleft Palate Clinic
St. Luke's Hospital Center
New York 10025

Presbyterian Hospital
New York 10032

Department of Pathology or Department of
    Pediatrics
NYU Medical Center
550 First Ave.
New York 10016

Division of Genetics
Rochester University Medical School
Rochester 14620

St. John's Episcopal Hospital
Smithtown 11787

N.Y. State Institute for Mental Retardation
1050 Forest Hill Rd.
Staten Island 10314

Department of Pediatrics
Upstate Medical Center
Syracuse 13210

Department of Cytogenetics
Letchworth Village
Thiells 10984

North Carolina

Department of Pediatrics
Birth Defects Clinic
Chapel Hill 27515

Department of Obstetrics & Gynecology
Duke Medical Center
Box 3274
Durham 27706

Moses H. Cone Memorial Hospital
1200 N. Elm St.
P.O. Box 13227
Greensboro 27405

Birth Defects Evaluation Clinic
Western Carolina Center
Morganton 28655

Bowman Gray School of Medicine
Genetics Section, Department of Pediatrics
Wake Forest University
Winston-Salem 27103

North Dakota

None

Ohio

Department of Pediatrics
Children's Hospital Research Foundation
Cincinnati 45229

Department of Medical Genetics
Cleveland Psychiatric Institute
1708 Aiken Ave.
Cleveland 44109

Department of Pediatrics
Case Western University Medical School
Cleveland Metropolitan General Hospital
Cleveland 44109

Department of Biology
Case Western Reserve University
Cleveland 44106

Department of Medicine, University Hospital
Ohio State University
410 W. 10th Ave.
Columbus 43210

Department of Pediatrics
Children's Hospital
Columbus 43205

Birth Defects Evaluation Center
1735 Chapel St.
Barney Children's Medical Center
Dayton 45404

Oklahoma

Department of Pediatrics
University of Oklahoma
Children's Hospital
Oklahoma City 73104

Oregon

Department of Pediatrics
Sacred Heart Hospital
Eugene 97401

Crippled Children's Division, Genetics Clinic
Rogue Valley Memorial Hospital
2825 Barnett Rd.
Medford 97501

Genetics Clinic, Crippled Child Division
University of Oregon Medical School
Portland 97201

Pennsylvania

Department of Pathology
Geisinger Medical Center
Danville 17815

Lancaster Cleft Palate Clinic
24 N. Lime St.
Lancaster 17604

St. Christopher Hospital for Children
2600 N. Lawrence St.
Department of Pediatrics
Philadelphia 19133

Division of Genetics
Jefferson Medical College
1025 Walnut St.
Philadelphia 19107

Department of Anatomy
Section of Genetics
Hahnemann Medical College
Philadelphia 19102

Department of Pediatrics
Children's Hospital
Philadelphia 19146

Children's Hospital
Pittsburgh 15213

Department of Obstetrics & Gynecology
Magee-Women's Hospital
Pittsburgh 15213

Rhode Island

Department of Pediatrics
Rhode Island Hospital
Providence 02902

South Carolina

None

Tennessee

Birth Defects Evaluation Center
University of Tennessee
Knoxville 27916

Department of Pediatrics
University of Tennessee
860 Madison Ave.
Memphis 38103

Hubbard Hospital
Department of Pediatrics
1005-18th Ave. N.
Nashville 37208

Department of Medicine
Vanderbilt Hospital
Nashville 37203

Department of Pediatrics
Meharry Medical College
Nashville 37208

Texas

Baylor University Medical Center
3500 Gaston Ave.
Dallas 75246

Department of Pediatrics & Human Genetics
University of Texas Medical Branch
Galveston 77550

Department of Biology
M. D. Anderson Hospital
Houston 77025

Department of Pediatrics
University of Texas Medical School
Texas Medical Center
Houston 77025

Department of Pediatrics
Baylor University College of Medicine
Houston 77025

Birth Defects Center
Texas Children's Hospital
6621 Fannin St.
Houston 77025

Department of Medical Genetics
Pasadena General Hospital
Pasadena 77501

Department of Pediatrics or Department of
  Anatomy
University of Texas Medical School
7703 Floyd Curl Dr.
San Antonio 78229

Utah

Department of Zoology
Utah State University
Logan 84321

Birth Defects Clinic
320 12th Ave.
Primary Children's Hospital
Salt Lake City 84103

Vermont

Department of Pediatrics
Mary Fletcher Hospital
Burlington 05401

Department of Medicine & Anatomy
University of Vermont College of Medicine
Burlington 05401

Virginia

Department of Internal Medicine
University of Virginia Hospital
Charlottesville 22901

Chromosome Research Laboratory
University of Virginia Medical School
Charlottesville 22901

Department of Pathology
DePaul Hospital
Norfolk 23505

Departments of Pediatrics, Biology, or
  Genetics
Medical College of Virginia
Richmond 23219

Washington

Department of Medicine
University of Washington
Seattle 98105

Department of Pediatrics
Dysmorphology Unit
University of Washington Medical School
Seattle 98105

Pathology & Clinical Pathology
St. Luke's Memorial Hospital
711 S. Cowley
Spokane 99210

Department of Pediatrics
Madigan General Hospital
Tacoma 98431

Wisconsin

Department of Medical Genetics
University of Wisconsin
Madison 53706

Department of Medical Genetics
University of Wisconsin Medical School
Madison 53706

Central Wisconsin Colony and Training
  School
317 Knutson Dr.
Madison 53704

Cytogenics **Labor**atory and Genetics Clinic
Milwaukee Children's Hospital
1700 W. Wisconsin Ave.
Milwaukee 53233

CANADA

Department of Pediatrics
4-120 Clinical Sciences Building
Edmonton 7, Alberta

Department of Pediatrics
Dalhousie University
Halifax, Nova Scotia

Department of Pediatrics
Queen's University
Kingston, Ontario

Department of Cytogenetics
Children's Psychiatric Research Institute
London, Ontario

Department of Neuro-Biology
Clinical Research Institute of Montreal
110 W. Pine Ave.
Montreal, Quebec

Medical Genetics Section
Sainte Justine Hospital
3175 Chemin Ste.-Catherine
Montreal, Quebec

Department of Medical Genetics
Montreal Children's Hospital
Montreal, Quebec

Division of Medical Genetics
Jewish General Hospital
Montreal, Quebec

Department of Biochemical Genetics
Montreal Children's Hospital
Montreal, Quebec

Department of Pediatrics
University of Ottawa
Ottawa, Ontario

Department of Pediatrics
University Hospital
Saskatoon, Saskatchewan

Department of Zoology
University of Toronto
Toronto, Ontario

Research Department
Mental Retardation Center
Toronto, Ontario

Department of Genetics
Hospital for Sick Children
Toronto, Ontario

Division of Medical Genetics
Department of Pediatrics
University of British Columbia
Vancouver, British Columbia

Department of Medical Genetics
Children's Hospital of Winnipeg
Winnipeg, Manitoba

Western Cytogenetic Laboratory
P.O. Box 3687
Winnipeg 4, Manitoba

ENGLAND

Medical Research Council
40 University Department of Biochemistry
Cambridge

Kennedy-Galton Center
Harperbury Hospital
Hertfordshire

Department of Genetics, Stead House
University of Leeds
Leeds 2

Department of Medicine
University of Liverpool
Liverpool

Clinical Genetics Research Unit
Institute of Child Health
London

Department of Hematology
King's College Hospital Medical School
London W.E.5

The Galton Laboratory
University College London
Wolfson House, 4 Stephenson Way
London N.W.1

Genetic Clinic
Moorfields Eye Hospital
City Rd.
London E.C.1.

Pediatric Research Unit
Guy's Hospital Medical School
London S.E.1.

London School of Hygiene & Tropical
    Medicine
Keppel St.
London W.C.1.E7HT

Department of Genetics
St. John's Hospital
Lisle St., Leicester Sq.
London W.C.2

Department of Medical Genetics
Royal Infirmary
Manchester

Laboratory of Human Genetics
University of Newcastle upon Tyne
19 Claremont Pl.
Newcastle upon Tyne

Population Genetic Research Unit
Medical Research Council
Oxford

Center for Human Genetics
117 Manchester Rd.
Sheffield S.10 5DN

Department of Child Health
University of Sheffield
Sheffield

AUSTRALIA

Department of Genetics
University of Adelaide
Adelaide 5001

Human Genetics Unit
Queensland Institute for Medical Research
Brisbane

Department of Preventive
    Social Medicine
University of Sydney
Royal Alexandra Hospital for Children
Camperdown 2006

Department of Genetics
John Curtin School of Medical Research
Box 334, GPO
Canberra

School of Human Genetics
University of New South Wales
P.O. Box 1, Kensington
New South Wales, 2033

University of Melbourne & Royal Children's
    Hospital Research Foundation
Melbourne

Department of Pathology
Royal Women's Hospital
Melbourne

Oliver Latham Laboratory
Psychiatric Center
North Ryde
New South Wales, 2113

Department of Medicine
University of Tasmania
Royal Hobart Hospital
Tasmania

Department Mental Health Services of
    Western Australia
Irrabeena Diagnostic Center
84 Thomas St.
West Perth 6050

APPENDIX D:
Community Mental Health Centers in the United States*

Many more centers than listed here are in the planning stage. If there is no center listed in your locality and you want to discover if one has opened up, ask your doctor or local Department of Health, or inquire at one of the centers listed here.

The following abbreviations are used in this list: MH, Mental Health; MR, Mental Retardation; MHC, Mental Health Center; CMHC, Community Mental Health Center; CCMHC, Comprehensive Community Mental Health Center.

ALABAMA

Huntsville-Madison County MHC
218 Randolph Ave.
Huntsville 35801

Mobile MHC
555 Stanton Rd.
P.O. Box 1524
Mobile 36617

Muscle Shoals MHC
635 West College St.
Florence 35630

University of Alabama Hospitals and Clinics
619 South 19th St.
Birmingham 35233

ALASKA

Gateway MHC
628 Park Ave.
P.O. Box 291
Ketchikan 99901

Kodiak Island Borough MHC
P.O. Box 712
Kodiak 99615

ARIZONA

Arizona Foundation MHC
5055 North 34th St.
Phoenix 85018

St. Lukes–Jane Wayland CMHC
1937 West Jefferson St.
Phoenix 85009

Northern Arizona Comprehensive Guidance
   Center, Inc.
2725 East Lakin Dr.
Flagstaff 86001

Tucson South MHC
St. Mary's Hospital
P.O. Box 5481
Tucson 85703

ARKANSAS

East Arkansas Regional MHC
Helena Hospital Dr.
P.O. Box 673
Helena 72342

Greater Little Rock CCMHC
4313 West Markham St.
Little Rock 72201

* Derived from *Directory of Community Mental Health Centers*, U.S. Department of Health, Education, and Welfare, 1971.

Ouachita Regional Counseling & MHC
119 Convention Blvd.
Hot Springs 71901

South Arkansas MHC
490 West Faulkner St.
El Dorado 71730

Southeast Arkansas MHC
1110 West 11th Ave.
Pine Bluff 71601

Texarkana Regional MH-MR Center
416 Ninth St.
Texarkana 75501

CALIFORNIA

Central City CMHC
4272 South Broadway
Los Angeles 90037

Central County MHC, Region III
3700 Edison
San Mateo 94403

Central MHC
675 South Bascom Ave.
San Jose 95128

Community Hospital of the
  Monterey Peninsula
P.O. Box HH
Carmel 93921

County of Marin—
  Marin Hospital District CMHC
250 Bon Air Rd.
San Rafael 94904

El Camino CMHC
660 South Fair Oaks Ave.
Sunnyvale 94086

Emanuel Hospital CMHC
825 Delbon Ave.
Turlock 95300

Fred Finch Youth Center
3800 Coolidge Ave.
Oakland 94602

Gateways Hospital
1891 Effie St.
Los Angeles 90026

Golden State CMHC
11600 Eldridge Ave.
Lake View Terrace 91342

Hemet Valley Hospital District CMHC
1116 East Latham Ave.
Hemet 92343

Ingleside MHC
7500 East Hellman Ave.
Rosemead 91770

Kedren CMHC
7760 South Central Ave.
Los Angeles 90001

Kern View Hospital CMHC
3600 San Dimas St.
Bakersfield 93301

Kings View CMHC
42675 Rd. 44
P.O. Box 631
Reedley 93654

Mission MHC
995 Potrero Ave.
San Francisco 94110

North County CMHC
270 Grant Ave.
Palo Alto 94306

Northeast Community Health Services
511 Columbus Ave.
San Francisco 94133

Olive View Medical Center CMHC
14445 Olive View Dr.
Sylmar 91342

Oxnard Regional MHC
620 South D St.
Oxnard 93030

Peninsula Hospital CMHC
1783 El Camino Real
Burlingame 94010

Resthaven Psychiatric Hospital & CMHC
765 College St.
Los Angeles 90012

St. John's Hospital CMHC
1328 22nd St.
Santa Monica 90404

San Fernando Valley CMHC
7335 Van Nuys Blvd.
Van Nuys 91405

San Jose CMHC
77 North Fifteenth St.
San Jose 95112

San Luis Obispo CMHC
2180 Johnson Ave.
San Luis Obispo 93401

Santa Barbara County CMHC
4440 Calle Real
Santa Barbara 93105

Simi–Conejo Regional MHC
2060 Tapo St.
Santa Susana 93063

South County MHC
799 Willow Rd.
Menlo Park 94025

South County CMHC
80 Highland Ave.
San Martin 95046

Sutter Hospitals CMHC
52nd and F Sts.
Sacramento 95819   –

Ventura CMHC
300 Hillmont St.
Ventura 93001

West Valley CMHC
14195 Capri Dr.
Los Gatos 95030

Westside CMHC
2201 Sutter St.
San Francisco 94115

COLORADO

Adams County MHC
4371 East 72nd Ave.
Commerce City 80022

Arapahoe MHC, Inc.
4857 South Broadway
Englewood 80110

Bethesda CMHC
4400 East Iliff Ave.
Denver 80222

Denver General Hospital CCMHC
West 8th Ave. and Cherokee St.
Denver 80204

Jefferson County MHC, Inc.
260 South Kipling St.
Lakewood 80226

MHC of Weld County
1220 11th Ave.
Greeley 80631

Midwestern Colorado MHC, Inc.
428½ Main St.
P.O. Box 1208
Montrose 81401

Southern Colorado CMHC
1600 West 24th Ave.
Pueblo 81003

CONNECTICUT

Connecticut MHC
34 Park St.
P.O. Box 1842
New Haven 06508

Stamford-Darien-New Canaan MHC
190 West Broad St.
Stamford 06902

DELAWARE

Southern New Castle County CMHC
10 Central Ave.
New Castle 19720

Sussex County CMHC
Beebe Hospital
Lewes 19958

DISTRICT of COLUMBIA

Area B CMHC
1125 Spring Rd., N.W.
Washington 20010

Area C CMHC
1905 E St., S.E.
Washington 20003

Area D CMHC
2700 Martin Luther King, Jr. Ave., S.E.
Washington 20032

FLORIDA

Brevard County CMHC, Inc.
1770 Cedar St.
Rockledge 32955

CMHC of Escambia County, Inc.
1201 West Hernandez St.
Pensacola 32501

CMHC of Volusia County
P.O. Box 1990
Daytona Beach 32015

Lake-Sumter CMHC
P.O. Drawer B
Eustis 32726

Manatee Memorial Hospital MHC
206 Second St. East
Bradenton 33505

MHC of Bay County Guidance Clinic
615 North MacArthur Ave.
Panama City 32401

Orange Memorial Hospital CMHC
1416 South Orange Ave.
Orlando 32801

Palm Beach County CCMHC
1041 45th St.
West Palm Beach 33407

Winter Haven CMHC
200 Avenue 2, N.E.
Winter Haven 33880

GEORGIA

Atlanta South Central CMHC
1039 Ridge Ave., S.W.
Atlanta 30315

Chatham County MHC
Eisenhower Dr. at Meridian Rd.
Savannah 31405

Clayton General Hospital CMHC
Riverdale 30274

Dekalb General Hospital CMHC
2701 North Decatur Rd.
Decatur 30033

Hall County MH Clinic
P.O. Box 1295
Gainesville 30501

Northside Hospital CMHC
1000 Johnson Ferry Rd., N.E.
Atlanta 30342

Valdosta-Lowndes CCMHC
P.O. Box 1727
Valdosta 31601

HAWAII

Maui MH Service
Department of Health
P.O. Box H
Waliluku 96793

Windward CMHC
45–700 Keaahala Rd.
Kaneohe 96744

IDAHO

Community Institute for Human Resources
1477 North Orchard St.
Boise 83704

Eastern Idaho CMHC
140 E. 25th St.
Idaho Falls 83401

Gateway CMHC
1553 East Center St.
Pocatello 83201

White Pine MHC
412–6th St.
Lewiston 83501

ILLINOIS

CMH Program at the Medical Center
1601 West Taylor St.
Chicago 60612

CCMHC of Rock Island & Mercer Counties
767 30th St.
Rock Island 61201

Garfield Park CCMHC
2449 West Washington Blvd.
Chicago 60612

Mental Health Authority for West
   Central Illinois
1415 Vermont St.
Quincy 62301

INDIANA

CMHC-Marion County General Hospital
960 Locke St.
Indianapolis 46207

IOWA

CMHC of Scott County, Inc.
2322 Marquette St.
Davenport 52804

Mercy Medical Center
Mercy Dr.
Dubuque 52001

Pottawattamie MHC
401 Willow St.
Council Bluffs 51501

KANSAS

High Plains CCMHC
208 East 7th St.
Hays 67601

North Sedgwick County CCMHC
1045 North Minneapolis
Wichita 67214

Prairie View MHC
East 1st St.
P.O. Box 467
Newton 67114

Shawnee CMH Corp., Inc.
1615 West Eighth St.
Topeka 66606

Wyandotte County MH & Guidance
   Center, Inc.
250 North 17th St.
Kansas City 66102

KENTUCKY

Appalachian Comprehensive Care Center
1539 Central Ave.
P.O. Box 790
Ashland 41101

Cave Run Comprehensive Care Center
325 East Main St.
Morehead 40351

Comprehensive MH-MR Center-
Comprehend, Inc.
Hord Building, Second St.
P.O. Box 630
Maysville 41056

CMHC of Western Kentucky
308 Guthrie Building
Paducah 42001

Eastern Bluegrass Comprehensive
Care Center
201 Mechanic St.
Lexington 40507

Green River Comprehensive Care Center
403 West 3rd St., Suite 301
Owensboro 42301

Lake Cumberland Comprehensive
Care Center
129 South Main St.
Somerset 42501

Mammoth Cave Comprehensive
Care Center
1006 Glenview Dr.
P.O. Box 175
Glasgow 42141

Mountain MH Services
413 South Lake Dr.
Prestonsburg 41653

North Central Comprehensive Care Center
216 West Dixie Ave.
P.O. Box 219
Elizabethtown 42701

Northern Kentucky Comprehensive
Care Center
2nd and Greenup Sts.
Covington 41011

Northern Kentucky Comprehensive
Care Center
718 Columbia St.
Newport 41071

Pennyroyal Regional MHC
735 North Dr.
Hopkinsville 42240

Southeastern Kentucky Regional MH–MR
Board, Inc.
P.O. Box 568, Doctor's Park
Corbin 40701

Southern Bluegrass Comprehensive
Care Center
City Municipal Building
P.O. Box 112
Danville 40422

Southern Kentucky Comprehensive
Care Center
925 Woodway Dr.
Bowling Green 42101

Upper Cumberland Comprehensive
Care Center
P.O. Box 701
Pineville 40977

Upper Kentucky River Comprehensive
Care Center
P.O. Box 800
Hazard 41701

Waverly MHC
8101 Dixie Highway
P.O. Box 58–337
Louisville 40258

West Central Louisville MHC
1123 South Third St.
Louisville 40203

Western Bluegrass Comprehensive
Care Center
419 High St.
Frankfort 40601

LOUISIANA

DePaul Hospital CMHC
1038 Henry Clay Ave.
New Orleans 70118

Louisiana State University CMHC
1542 Tulane Ave.
New Orleans 70112

Monroe Regional Mental Health Center
4800 South Grand St.
P.O. Box 1843
Monroe 71201

Region II MHC-Ruston MH Clinic
P.O. Box 111
Ruston 71270

Tallulah Mental Health Clinic
P.O. Box 109
Tallulah 71282

Terrebonne MH Center & Lafourche
MH Clinic
Legion Ave.
P.O. Box 1414
Houma 70360

Touro Infirmary CMHC
1400 Delachaise St.
New Orleans 70115

MAINE

Aroostook MHC
Fort Fairfield 04742

Child and Family CMHC
106 Campus Ave.
Lewiston 04240

Counseling Center
43 Illinois Ave.
Bangor 04401

Maine Medical Center CMHC
22 Bramhall St.
Portland 04102

MARYLAND

Baltimore Inner City CMHC
25 South Calvert St.
Baltimore 21202

CMHC of Prince Georges County No. 1
Bureau of Mental Health
Hospital Rd.
Cheverly 20785

Provident CCMHC
1533 Division St.
Baltimore 21217

Upper Montgomery MHC
18101 Prince Phillip Dr.
Olney 20832

MASSACHUSETTS

Boston State Hospital MHC
591 Morton St.
Boston 02124

Cambridge-Somerville MH &
Retardation Center
9 Sacramento St.
Cambridge 02138

Concord Area CCMHC
Community Agencies Building
Concord 01742

Dr. John C. Corrigan MHC
49 Hillside St.
Fall River 02720

Dr. Harry C. Solomon MHC
391 Varnum Ave.
Lowell 01854

Franklin-Hampshire Area MHC
20 Sanderson St.
Greenfield 01301

Massachusetts MHC
74 Fenwood Rd.
Boston 02115

MH Treatment, Training, and
   Research Center
80 East Concord St.
Boston 02118

Tufts CMHC
260 Tremont St.
Boston 02116

MICHIGAN

Borgess Hospital MHC
1521 Gull Rd.
Kalamazoo 49001

Calhoun-Branch Community Health
   Services Board
50 West Manchester St.
Battle Creek 49017

Community Health Center Compact
Altamont and Fisher Sts.
Marquette 49855

Grand Valley CMHC
1330 Bradford St., N.E.
Grand Rapids 49503

Midland Area MHC
4005 Orchard Dr.
Midland 48640

Mid-Michigan CMHC
255 Warwick Dr.
Alma 48801

Muskegon County CCMHC
61 East Larch Ave.
Muskegon 49442

North Oakland CMHC
140 Elizabeth Lake Rd.
Pontiac 48053

Northeast Michigan MH Centers, Inc.
1521 West Chisholm St.
Alpena 49707

Riverwood CMHC
2611 Morton Ave.
St. Joseph 49805

St. Lawrence Hospital CMHC
1201 West Oakland St.
Lansing 48915

MINNESOTA

Central Minnesota MHC
1321 13th St. North
St. Cloud 56301

Metropolitan CMHC
900 South Eighth St.
Minneapolis 55404

Northwestern MHC
120 LaBree Ave. South
Thief River Falls 56701

Range MHC, Inc.
624 13th St.
Virginia 55792

West Central MHC, Inc.
323 West 6th St.
Willmar 56201

Zumbro Valley MHC
2100 East Center St.
Rochester 55901

MISSISSIPPI

Coastal Mental Health Program
P.O. Box 429
Gulfport 39501

Comprehensive Center for Mental Health
Coahoma County Hospital
P.O. Box 1046
Clarksdale 38614

Jackson MHC
969 Lakeland Dr.
Jackson 39216

North Mississippi Medical Center
  MH Complex
830 South Gloster St.
Tupelo 38801

North Mississippi Regional
  Commission on MH & R
426 South Lamar Blvd.
Oxford 38655

MISSOURI

East Central Missouri MHC
704 East Monroe
Mexico 65265

Malcolm Bliss MHC
1420 Grattan St.
St. Louis 63104

Mid-Missouri MHC
803 Stadium Rd.
Columbia 65201

Ozark CMHC
2808 Picher
Joplin 64801

Western Missouri MHC
600 East 22nd St.
Kansas City 64108

MONTANA

Comprehensive CMHC
1245 North 29th St.
Billings 59102

Eastern Montana Region 5 MHC
502 2nd Ave. South
Glasgow 59230

Western Montana Regional CMHC
2829 Fort Missoula Rd.
Missoula 59801

NEBRASKA

Mid-Nebraska CMHC
2901 Second Ave.
Grand Island 68801

Panhandle MHC & MR Facility
4110 Ave. D
Scottsbluff 69361

NEVADA

NEW HAMPSHIRE

Dartmouth-Hitchock MHC
Maynard St.
Hanover 03755

NEW JERSEY

Hackensack Hospital CMH Service
66 Hospital Pl.
Hackensack 07601

Martland CMHC
100 Bergen St., Room 1618
Newark 07103

Multi-Service Center-Mt. Carmel Guild
17 Mulberry St.
Newark 07102

Raritan Bay MHC
570 Lee St.
Perth Amboy 08861

NEW MEXICO

Bernalillo County MHC
2600 Marble Ave., N.E.
Albuquerque 87106

Southwest MHC
1501 North Solano
Las Cruces 88001

NEW YORK

Brookdale Hospital CMHC
Brookdale Plaza & Linden Blvd.
Brooklyn 11212

CMHC-University of Rochester
260 Crittenden Blvd.
Rochester 14620

Comprehensive MHC-Mercy Hospital of
   Watertown
218 Stone St.
Watertown 13601

Convalescent Hospital for Children
2075 Scottsville Rd.
Rochester 14623

Dutchess County CMHC
North Rd.
Poughkeepsie 12601

Lincoln Hospital MHC
333 Southern Blvd.
Bronx 10454

Maimonides Hospital CMHC
4802 10th Ave.
Brooklyn 11219

Metropolitan CMHC
New York Medical College
5 East 102nd St.
New York 10023

Nassau Center for Emotionally
   Disturbed Children
72 South Woods Rd.
Woodbury 11797

Nassau County Medical Center
2201 Hemstead Turnpike
East Meadow 11554

North Richmond CMHC
355 Bard Ave.
Staten Island 10310

Rochester MHC
1425 Portland Ave.
Rochester 14621

Rockland County CMHC
Sanatorium Rd.
Pomona 10970

Sound View-Throgs Neck CMHC
2527 Glebe Ave.
New York 10461

Warren-Washington CMHC of Glens Falls
   Hospital
97 Park St.
Glens Falls 12801

NORTH CAROLINA

Alamance County MHC
1946 Martin St.
Burlington 27215

Cumberland County MHC
Cape Fear Valley Hospital
P.O. Box 1406
Fayetteville 28302

Halifax County CMHC
P.O. Box 577
Roanoke Rapids 27870

Lee-Harnett MHC
P.O. Box Q
130 Carbonton Rd.
Sanford 27330

Mecklenburg County MHC
501 Billingsley Rd.
Charlotte 28211

Orange-Person County MHC
413 West Rosemary St.
Chapel Hill 27514

Sandhills MHC, Inc.
P.O. Box 24
Pinehurst 28374

Southeastern Regional MHC
209 West 28th St.
Lumberton 28358

W. H. Trentman MHC of Wake County
3008 New Bern Ave.
Raleigh 27610

Western Carolina University MHC
P.O. Box 2784
Cullowhee 28723

NORTH DAKOTA

Memorial MH & MR Center
1007 18th St., N.W.
Mandan 58554

North Central MH & Retardation Center
17 West Central Ave.
Minot 58701

Northeast Region MH & Retardation Center
509 South Third St.
Grand Forks 58201

South Central MH & Retardation Center
1521 Business Loop East
P.O. Box 334
Jamestown 58401

Southeast Region MH & Retardation
  Services Center
P.O. Box 2013
700 1st Ave. South
Fargo 58102

OHIO

Child and Adult MHC
1009 Realty Building
Youngstown 44503

Clark County Comprehensive MH Program
13435 North Fountain Blvd.
Springfield 45501

Fallsview MHC
330 Broadway East
Cuyahoga Falls 44221

Good Samaritan MHC
1425 West Fairview Ave.
Dayton 45406

Muskingum Comprehensive MHC
2845 Bell St.
Zanesville 43701

Northwest CMHC
718 West Market St.
Lima 45801

Union Hospital MHC
Dover 44622

OKLAHOMA

Bi-State MH Foundation
P.O. Box 951
Ponca City 74601

Central State MHC
Box 151
Norman 73069

Tulsa CMHC
1620 East 12th St.
Tulsa 74120

OREGON

Lane County CMHC
1065 High St.
Eugene 97401

PENNSYLVANIA

Albert Einstein CMH & MR Center
York and Tabor Rds.
Philadelphia 19141

Altoona Hospital CMHC
Howard Ave. and 7th St.
Altoona 16603

Centerville Clinic MHC
Route #1
Fredericktown 15333

CMHC of Beaver County
176 Virginia Ave.
Rochester 15074

CMHC
Philadelphia Psychiatric Center
Ford Road and Monument Ave.
Philadelphia 19131

CMHC-Western Psychiatric Institute
  and Clinic
3811 O'Hara St.
Pittsburgh 15213

Hahnemann CMHC
314 North Broad St.
Philadelphia 19102

Hall-Mercer CMH & R Center of the
  Pennsylvania Hospital
8th and Spruce Sts.
Philadelphia 19107

Harrisburg Hospital MH & MR Center
South Front St.
Harrisburg 17101

Homestead Hospital CMHC
1800 West St.
Homestead 15120

Jefferson CMHC
1127 Walnut St.
Philadelphia 19107

Latrobe Area MHC
West 2nd Ave.
Latrobe 15650

Luzerne-Wyoming County MHC #1
103 South Main St.
Wilkes-Barre 18701

MHC of Monroe, Carbon & Pike Counties
206 East Brown St.
East Stroudsburg 18301

Northeast CMHC
Roosevelt Blvd. & Adams Ave.
Philadelphia 19124

Northwest Center
27 East Mount Airy Ave.
Philadelphia 19119

Robert Packer Hospital CMHC
200 South Wilbur Ave.
Sayre 18840

St. Francis CMHC
45th and Penn Ave.
Pittsburgh 15201

Temple University CMHC
3437 North 15th St.
Philadelphia 19140

West Catchment Area Comprehensive
   MHC of Erie County
232 West 25th St.
Erie 16502

West Philadelphia CMHC Consortium
P.O. Box 8076
Philadelphia 19101

PUERTO RICO

Aguadilla CMHC
Yumet Ave.
P.O. Box 1006
Aguadilla 00603

Arecibo CMHC
Arecibo District Hospital
Arecibo 00612

Bayamon CMHC
Victory Shopping Center
Bayamon 00619

Caguas CMHC
Calle Intendente Ramirez #14
Caguas 00625

Carolina CMHC
Carolina 00630

Farjardo CMHC
Celis Aguilero St. at A R Barcelo St.
Farjardo 00648

Mayaguez Medical Center CMHC
Calle Mendez Vigo No. 78
Mayaguez 00708

Ponce CMHC
Ponce Psychiatric Hospital
Ponce 00731

RHODE ISLAND: None

SOUTH CAROLINA

Anderson-Oconee-Pickens MHC
200 McGee Rd.
Anderson 29621

Charleston Area MHC
30 Lockwood Dr.
Charleston 29401

Columbia Area MHC
2550 Colonial Dr.
Columbia 29203

Marshall I. Pickens Hospital
715 Grove Rd.
Greenville 29605

Spartanburg Area MHC
149 East Wood St.
Spartanburg 29303

SOUTH DAKOTA: None

TENNESSEE

Helen Ross McNabb Center
1520 Cherokee Trail
Knoxville 37920

Jackson CMHC
238 Summer Dr.
Jackson 38301

Meharry CMHC
1005 18th Ave. North
Nashville 37208

Multi-County Comprehensive MHC
P.O. Box 299
New Shelbyville Highway
Tullahoma 37388

Plateau CMHC
P.O. Box 655
Burgess Falls Rd.
Cookeville 38501

Regional MHC of Oak Ridge
240 West Tyrone Rd.
Oak Ridge 37830

TEXAS

Amarillo Hospital District CMHC
2103 West 6th St.
P.O. Box 1110
Amarillo 79105

Bayshore MH & MR Center
821 Chelsea
Baytown 77520

Bell County MH & MR Center, Inc.
P.O. Box 704
Belton 76513

Central Plains CCMH/MR Center
P.O. Box 578
Plainview 79072

District VI MHC
3804 South Central Expressway
Dallas 75215

El Paso Center for MH & MR Service
4815 Alameda Ave.
El Paso 79905

Kingsville CMHC
Box 336
Kingsville 78363

MH-MR Center-Austin-Travis County
1516 Red River
Austin 78701

MH-MR Center for Greater West Texas
244 North Magdalen St.
San Angelo 76901

Northwest San Antonio MHC
Bexar County Hospital
4502 Medical Dr.
San Antonio 78229

Presbyterian Hospital of Dallas CMHC
8200 Walnut Hill Lane
Dallas 75231

Rio Grande Area III MHC-Starr, Webb
   & Zapata Counties
P.O. Box 1835
Laredo 78040

St. Joseph-Mid-Houston CMHC
1919 LaBranch St.
Houston 77002

Waco-McLennan County MH-MR Center
110 South 12th St.
Waco 76701

Wichita Falls Community Center
   for MH & MR
402 East Scott St.
Wichita Falls 76301

UTAH

Granite CMHC
156 Westminster Ave.
Salt Lake City 84115

Timpanogas CMHC
300 North 1100 East
Provo 84601

Weber County MHC
350 Healy St.
Ogden 84401

VERMONT

Northeast Kingdom MH Service, Inc.
90 Main St.
Newport 05855

Southwest Regional MHC
728 South Main St.
Rutland 05701

VIRGINIA

Institute for MH & Psychiatry
P.O. Box 3303
Norfolk 23514

Riverside Hospital MHC
J. Clyde Morris Blvd.
Newport News 23601

WASHINGTON

Comprehensive MHC of Tacoma-
  Pierce County
1206 South 11th St.
Building #2
Tacoma 98405

Eastside CMHC, Inc.
2253 140th St., N.E.
Bellevue 98005

Harborview CMHC
925 Terrace St.
Seattle 98104

Seattle MH Institute, Inc.
1605 17th Ave.
Seattle 98122

WEST VIRGINIA

Appalachian CMHC
201 Henry Ave.
Elkins 26241

CMHC, Inc.-Region II
P.O. Box 8069
3375 U.S. Route 60 East
Huntington 25705

WISCONSIN

Brown County Hospital CMHC
1320 Mahon Ave.
Green Bay 54301

CMHC of Sauk, Juneau, Richland Counties
710 North Webb Ave.
Reedsburg 53959

Milwaukee County MHC's (6 centers)
9191 Watertown Plank Rd.
Milwaukee 53226

Walworth County MHC
Courthouse
P.O. Box 290
Elkhorn 53121

West Central CMHC
P.O. Box 15
Independence 54747

WYOMING

Northern Wyoming MHC
50 East Loucks St.
P.O. Box 4098
Sheridan 82801

APPENDIX E:
Agencies for Parents

BIRTH DEFECTS

The National Foundation, 330 Madison Avenue, New York, N. Y. 10016

An organization devoted to fighting birth defects that sponsors research programs, supports birth-defect centers, assists patients suffering from such defects, and spreads information on the subject. There are chapters in every large community.

BLINDNESS

American Foundation for the Blind, 15 West 16th Street, New York, N. Y. 10011

A national agency which is a source of information on education, care, rehabilitation, and welfare services for the blind. It also manufactures and sells special aids and appliances for use by blind persons.

National Society for the Prevention of Blindness, 79 Madison Avenue, New York, N. Y. 10016

An organization devoted to the prevention of blindness. It gives information on vision aids to preserve partial sight and clinics for the blind.

CEREBRAL PALSY

The National Society for Crippled Children and Adults, 2023 W. Ogden Avenue, Chicago, Ill. 60612

A source of information on care, education, rehabilitation, and welfare services. It publishes booklets for parents on the subject and sponsors parents' organizations in all parts of the country.

United Cerebral Palsy, 321 West 44th Street, New York, N. Y. 10036

An organization with branches in most large cities. It carries on many programs and workshops for those with cerebral palsy. It also organizes parents' groups and publishes bulletins.

CHILDBIRTH, NATURAL (LAMAZE)

American Society for Psychoprophylaxis, 7 West 96th Street, New York, N. Y. 10025

An organization with branches in all large cities that gives courses in preparation for natural childbirth.

DEAFNESS

American Hearing Society, 817 14th Street N.W., Washington, D.C. 20005

With branches throughout the United States this organization offers facilities for testing hearing, advising on proper hearing aids, and teaching lip reading as well as providing training in speech and hearing.

The Alexander Graham Bell Association for the Deaf, 1537 35th Street, N.W., Washington, D.C. 20007

An organization which furnishes parents information on deaf children. It is also a source for schools that teach children speech and lip reading.

DIABETES

American Diabetes Association, 18 East 48th Street, New York, N. Y. 10017

This association works to promote an understanding of diabetes by patients and their families; to provide educational materials for parents; to promote research; to cooperate with doctors; and to sponsor summer camps for diabetic children.

EMOTIONALLY DISTURBED CHILDREN

National Association for Mental Health, 10 Columbus Circle, New York, N. Y. 10019

This association organizes mental health organizations and parent groups and furnishes information on places where parents can find facilities for the care and treatment of children who are mentally ill.

EPILEPSY

Epilepsy Foundation of America, 1419 H Street N.W., Washington, D.C. 20005

An organization for comprehensive information on epilepsy. It also mobilizes programs for equal education and employment for those with epilepsy, as well as programs for treatment and rehabilitation.

National Epilepsy League, 203 N. Wabash Avenue, Chicago, Ill. 60601

A prescription service for epileptic patients where the necessary drugs may be obtained on a nonprofit basis.

HEART DISEASE

American Heart Association, 44 East 23rd Street, New York, N. Y. 10010

An organization that provides information to parents of children with cardiac abnormalities and rheumatic fever. It also sponsors research on the causes, prevention, and treatment of heart defects. It has local branches in all large cities, to which parents can turn for advice and direction in caring for their child with an abnormal heart condition.

MARRIAGE COUNSELING .

American Association of Marriage and Family Counsellors, 6211 W. Northwest Highway, Dallas, Texas 75225

An agency listing information on marriage and family counseling services and marriage counselors in all parts of the United States. It certifies counselors and approves training institutions for them.

MENTAL DEFICIENCY

National Association for Retarded Children, 420 Lexington Avenue, New York, N. Y. 10017

This organization publishes advice for parents of retarded children and presents reading lists. It also devotes itself to the formation of parent groups throughout the country in which fathers and mothers of retarded children can work with one another and exchange ideas for the betterment of their children.

Association for the Help of Retarded Children

An organization dedicated to working for and directing parents with retarded children. There are branches in most large cities. They either run their programs by themselves or work through state facilities. They provide training programs for retarded children as well as sheltered workshops to keep them happily occupied and possibly learning a trade. They also foster social groups and social affairs for retarded adolescents and in many states conduct camps for retarded children. The location of branches may be obtained by writing to the National Association for Retarded Children.

MUSCULAR DYSTROPHY

Muscular Dystrophy Association of America, 1790 Broadway, New York, N. Y. 10019

This association, which has branches in all large cities, provides information and literature for parents of children with muscular dystrophy and also sponsors research on the condition. Through its "Patient's Services" division the organization gives direct aid to children suffering from the disease.

SPEECH DIFFICULTIES

American Speech and Hearing Association, 1001 Connecticut Avenue N.W., Washington, D.C. 20036

An organization providing information on the treatment of speech difficulties by facilities and individuals throughout the United States.

Bibliography

General

Baby and Child Care, by Benjamin Spock, M.D. (rev. ed.). New York: Pocket Books, 1968.
  The classic and ever-popular handbook for parents of infants and young children. This book, when first published in 1945, was a great force in liberalizing attitudes toward child care.

Child Development: An Introduction to the Study of Human Growth, by Arnold Gesell, M.D., and Frances L. Ilg, M.D. New York: Harper & Brothers, 1949.
  This is still the best book on what to expect of a child's behavior patterns and activities during the first ten years of life. Parents should realize, however, that the patterns described are not absolute.

How to Raise a Human Being, by Lee Salk, Ph.D., and Rita Kramer. New York: Random House, 1969.
  A most valuable book discussing the intellectual and emotional needs of children from birth through their development. This book is unique in its emphasis on avoiding problems before they arise.

Infants and Mothers, by T. Berry Brazelton, M.D. New York: Delacorte Press, 1969.
  In this well-written book the emphasis is placed on the fact that each child is an individual and that variations in developmental standards of normal children are considerable. Comparisons are made of the average baby, the quiet baby, and the active baby during each of the first twelve months of life.

The Magic Years, by Selma H. Fraiberg (reprint, 1959 ed.). New York: Charles Scribner's Sons, 1968.
  A charming book that follows the child's development during the first six years of life. It discusses the various steps in the child's progress and the problems that might arise.

Natural Parenthood, by Eda J. LeShan. New York: New American Library, 1970.
  A group of discussions on the problems of parenthood. The author is a child psychologist with a deep understanding of children. She has a rare ability to clarify subjects so that parents can arrive at common-sense decisions.

Your Growing Child and Sex, by Helene S. Arnstein. New York: The Bobbs-Merrill Company, 1967.
  An excellent aid for parents in understanding the sexual attitudes and behavior of their children. Especially valuable in understanding the teenager.

Adolescence

Today's Teen-Agers, by Evelyn Millis

Duvall. New York: Association Press, 1966.

This book provides parents of today with an understanding of the attitudes and activities of their adolescent boys and girls. By an author who has written numerous books for teen-agers.

What Every Child Would Like His Parents to Know, by Lee Salk, Ph.D. New York: David McKay Company, 1972.

Clear and informative answers to a great many of the questions most frequently asked by parents. Dr. Salk has for years devoted himself to teaching the emotional care of children to doctors, nurses, and parents. He has developed an exceptional understanding of children, parents, and family life.

Adoption

The Adopted Family, by Florence Rondell and Ruth Michaels (rev. ed.). 2 vols. New York: Crown Publishers, 1965.

This is a book for adoptive parents on all areas of adoption, from preparation for adoption to legal aspects and relationship with the child. The second volume includes a book for the adopted child called *The Family That Grew.*

Art

Young Children and Their Drawings, by Joseph H. Di Leo, M.D. New York: Brunner/Mazel, 1970.

A fascinating book on the developmental stages of children's drawings as a reflection of their personality and intellectual growth.

Autism

Autistic Children, by Lorna Wing, M.D. New York: Brunner/Mazel, 1972.

This is a guide for parents of autistic children written by a doctor long associated with the National Society for Autistic Children in England. The condition of autism is fully described, as is the role of parents in helping these children to develop to their best potential.

Breast Feeding

Nursing a Baby, by Karen Pryor. New York: Harper & Row, 1963.

A well-written, warm, and reassuring book on the methods, advantages, and satisfactions of breast feeding.

The Womanly Art of Breast Feeding. Franklin Park, Ill.: La Leche League, 1963.

A volume which strongly stresses the advantages of breast feeding. It discusses not only the means of preparing for it during pregnancy, but the methods of gaining the best from it after the birth of the baby.

Diet

Cooking for Your Celiac Child, by C. B. Sheedy and Norman Kaifitz. New York: Dial Press, 1969.

Divorce and Remarriage

Parents Without Partners: A Guide for Divorced, Widowed or Separated Parents, by Jim Egleson and Janet French Egleson. New York: E. P. Dutton and

Company, 1961.

A practical, constructive, and helpful guide written from both parents' points of view. It is especially valuable in helping parents to avoid as much as possible the upset their children must of necessity suffer, and to ease their children's readjustment.

Stepchild in the Family: A View of Children in Remarriage, by Anne W. Simon. New York: Odyssey Press, 1964.

An important book which brings an understanding of how a stepchild feels about his stepparents, stepbrothers, and stepsisters, and vice versa.

Drugs and Drug Addiction

Overcoming Drugs, by Donald N. Louria, M.D. New York: McGraw-Hill Book Company, 1971.

A complete discussion of all aspects of the drug problem, especially valuable for parents. A large portion of the book is devoted to young people and drugs, as well as to numerous questions and answers concerning drugs. An excellent chapter is included on a program for parents.

You, Your Child and Drugs, by the staff of the Child Study Association of America. New York: The Child Study Press, 1971.

A very helpful booklet written for parents, discussing not only the various drugs used but, more important, why boys and girls use drugs and how parents can best cope with this problem.

Education and Learning

Crisis in the Classroom, by Charles E. Silberman. New York: Random House, 1970.

An important and interesting discussion of the problems of modern education and some of the newer approaches being used to educate each child as an individual.

Handbook of Private Schools, edited by D. R. Young (52nd ed.). Boston: Porter, Sargent, 1971.

I Learn from Children, by Caroline Pratt (rev. ed.). New York: Cornerstone Library, 1970.

An exciting book by one of the early explorers in new forms of education. Many of the modern methods of making education enjoyable and stimulating for children are described in this book.

Schools Where Children Learn, by Joseph Featherstone. New York: Liveright, 1971.

An excellent discussion of various types of modern schools, with special emphasis on the open classroom.

Revolution in Learning, by Maya Pines. New York: Harper & Row, 1967.

A comprehensive report on the modern theories of early learning during the years from birth to six, with descriptions of various experimental programs at Harvard and elsewhere.

Handicaps

Caring for Your Disabled Child, by Benjamin Spock, M.D., and Marion O. Lerrigo. New York: The Macmillan Company, 1965.

A book for the parents of physically

or mentally handicapped children, giving an understanding of their development and advising on their recreation, education, and vocations.

Blindness

Our Blind Children—Growing and Learning with Them, by Berthold Lowenfeld, Ph.D. (3rd ed.). Springfield, Ill.: Charles C Thomas, 1971.

A classic volume for parents of blind children. In it Dr. Lowenfeld discusses the development, education, and training of these children, and the steps involved in making them secure and competent human beings.

The Blind in School and Society, by Thomas D. Cutsforth. New York: American Foundation for the Blind, 1951.

A truly amazing book by a blind person describing the mental and emotional development of the blind child and the problems he encounters. This book revolutionized the care and education of blind children.

Crippled Children and Cerebral Palsy

You Are Not Alone, by Lawrence J. Linck. Chicago: National Easter Seal Society for Crippled Children and Adults.

A parent describing for parents the means of helping a crippled child. It lists the associations, societies, and agencies that aid parents in all areas of their child's care and development.

Deafness

Deaf Children at Home and at School, by Dr. D. M. C. Dale. Springfield, Ill.: Charles C Thomas, 1967.

Emphasizing that the deaf child has the same needs and interests as any other child, Dr. Dale gives parents advice on minimizing this handicap. A full and excellent discussion of language development and the school education of deaf children is included.

The Hearing-Impaired Preschool Child, by Jean E. Semple, M.A. Springfield, Ill.: Charles C Thomas, 1970.

Helpful and practical suggestions to aid parents of deaf children in meeting and overcoming many of the difficult problems in helping their children to acquire speech. A series of home lesson plans is presented to make the child aware of sound and help him to understand speech.

Mental Retardation

Educable and Trainable Mentally Retarded Children, by Elmer W. Weber, Ed.D. Springfield, Ill.: Charles C Thomas, 1962.

A book defining the different degrees of mental retardation and showing parents as well as teachers how each child may be trained and educated to the best of his capabilities.

You and Your Retarded Child, by Samuel A. Kirk, Merle B. Kirk, and Winifred D. Kirk. Palo Alto, Calif.: Pacific Books, 1968.

A parents' guide to the care, education, and upbringing of retarded children.

Speech

Speech and Language Delay: A Home

Training Program, by R. Ray Battin, Ph.D., and C. Olaf Haug, Ph.D. Springfield, Ill.: Charles C Thomas, 1964.

A simple and short book explaining for parents causes and means of treatment of speech and language delay. It deals with the discipline, motivation, stimulation, and auditory memory of children with this condition. The program is based on the experience of thirty years.

Heredity

Heredity in Humans, by Amram Scheinfeld (rev. ed.). Philadelphia: J. B. Lippincott Company, 1971.

A clear and up-to-date explanation of this fascinating subject. The author has made this difficult subject understandable and extremely interesting.

Twins

And Then There Were Two: A Handbook for Mothers and Fathers of Twins, by 100 mothers of twins. New York: The Child Study Press, 1959.

A very helpful pamphlet based on experience that should make the care of twins much easier.

Working Mother

A Complete Guide for the Working Mother, by Margaret Albrecht. Garden City, N.Y.: Doubleday & Company, 1967.

A very helpful and practical book. It discusses not only the pros and cons of working in relation to the care and development of the child, but the effect on the husband-wife relationship as well.

Some Recommended Reading for Children

Children's Books of the Year, compiled annually by the Children's Book Committee, Child Study Association of America/Wel-Met. New York: Child Study Press.

Helpful in selecting good books for children.

A Baby Is Born, by Milton I. Levine, M.D., and Jean H. Seligmann. New York: Golden Press, 1966.

The story of how life begins told in a warm and direct manner for children from ages 5 to 10. This book is now in its twenty-third printing.

The Wonder of Life, by Milton I. Levine, M.D., and Jean H. Seligmann. New York: Golden Press, 1968.

This book on sex and reproduction is written for boys and girls of preadolescent and adolescent years. Although it is for the child himself to read and place on his bookshelf, it has been used by many elementary schools and high schools in their courses on sex education.

The Wonderful Story of How You Were Born, by Sidonie Matsner Gruenberg (rev. ed.). New York: Doubleday & Company, 1970.

Birth and reproduction presented as a story being told by a grandmother to children aged 5 to 10.

Going to the Hospital, by Bettina Clark, with the technical guidance of Lester Coleman, M.D. New York: Random House, 1971.

An ingenious "pop-up" book with numerous moving parts, among which are the hospital door and elevator, the hospital bed, and the operating room—designed to prepare the young child for an operation by familiarizing him with the hospital and its procedures.

Tommy Visits the Doctor, by Milton I. Levine, M.D., and Jean H. Seligmann. New York: Golden Press, 1962.

A child's visit to the doctor, described so as to familiarize a youngster with routine physical examinations. It has been republished in many different countries and languages.

A Visit to the Dentist, by Dr. Bernard J. Garn. New York: Grosset & Dunlap, 1959.

A book to acquaint the young child with the white-coated dentist and the "strange" instruments he uses. It is very reassuring and presents the dentist as a friend.

IMMUNIZATION RECORD

DISEASE	DATE OF ORIGINAL IMMUNIZATION		
	1ST CHILD NAME	2ND CHILD NAME	3RD CHILD NAME
DIPHTHERIA			
TETANUS			
WHOOPING COUGH			
POLIOMYELITIS			
SMALLPOX			
MEASLES			
MUMPS			
GERMAN MEASLES			
TUBERCULIN TESTS			
OTHER IMMUNIZATIONS			
INFLUENZA			
TRIPLE TYPHOID			
ROCKY MOUNTAIN FEVER			
TYPHUS			

DATE OF BOOSTERS OR REVACCINATIONS			DOCTOR
1ST CHILD NAME	2ND CHILD NAME	3RD CHILD NAME	